Behind Spanish American Footlights

Behind Spanish American Footlights

by WILLIS KNAPP JONES

University of Texas Press . Austin . London

Library of Congress Catalog Card No. 65–11145
Copyright © 1966 by Willis Knapp Jones
All Rights Reserved

Published with the assistance of a grant
from the Ford Foundation
under its program for the support of publications
in the humanities and social sciences
and
with a grant from Miami University, Oxford, Ohio
Manufactured in the United States of America
by the Printing Division of the University of Texas, Austin
Bound by Universal Bookbindery, Inc., San Antonio

Dedicated to

JOHN D. MILLETT

President of Miami University 1953–1964

Not only did he give assistance by arranging
reduced teaching loads and by grants, but he
also evidenced a time-consuming personal
interest in this research project

FOREWORD

Since the body of this book is long, the Foreword should be short, a sort of Colley Cibber *Apologia pro vita mea* to explain why and how this study of the Spanish American stage came into being.

I don't know when I first became interested in the theatre. As a youngster I built miniature stages and wrote plays for cardboard actors. One of my first writings accepted for publication was an immature play appropriately named *Nothing Doing*. Then when I went to Chile in 1917 I found the theatre the best place to brush up on spoken Spanish; so I started writing about plays and translating them. I began accumulating plays and critical works into a collection that now fills thirty-five feet of shelf space and numbers a thousand volumes.

From that to an acquaintance with Latin American playwrights and actors was a short step. After I had written several series of articles about the South American stage, Pedro de Andrea of Mexico asked me to compile a *Breve historia del teatro latinoamericano* (1956), the first general work to cover the whole Latin American theatrical scene. *Behind Spanish American Footlights* is the pioneer attempt to survey in English the same ground, and over a period of nearly five centuries. It makes use of notes accumulated during forty years, in visits to almost all of the countries, the latest in 1958.

Too frequently a historian of the theatre, looking for a play known to have been written, comes upon the blank wall of *"inédita."* And almost as frequently, none of the few printed copies has survived. I searched Asunción for copies of three plays proclaimed the best of the early twentieth century. Neither libraries nor families of the authors could provide even one. All a critic can do to evaluate such work is to depend on contemporary accounts, always a dangerous procedure.

Biographical details also present problems in countries where bibliographical accuracy is not always practiced. Not only did the birth and death of early writers go unrecorded, but even the dates of contemporaries frequently present difficulties. Two different birth-dates of one writer, in histories of literature, were corrected by the author himself and by his son with two new dates. One authoress told me her real age but added that, as a friend, I ought not to object to postdating her birth three or four years. Even the dates of writing and producing plays may differ, according to sources. Authentic corrections, therefore, will be welcomed.

My findings could be presented in several ways. One would be a consideration of trends, which would merely retrace the progress of the theatres in Europe and in the United States that have served as inspiration to the playwrights in Latin America. Another would be the listing of only the outstanding dramatists. Following that procedure, the Chilean theatrical history, for instance, could be summed up on a page, listing Daniel Barros Grez and perhaps Daniel Caldera of the nineteenth century, and Antonio Acevedo Hernández, Armando Moock, and Germán Luco Cruchaga of the first half of the twentieth century. That procedure would provide a cursory survey, since most of Chile's other dramatists are antiquated and, for the most part, disregarded even by lecturers on the theatre in their native Chile. I have chosen to assemble the names of the earlier and the minor playwrights too and to tell something about their productions. So I have tried to provide a fairly complete picture and to offer guidance to those who may wish to explore further. And I have proceeded similarly with all the other countries, beginning in the far south and journeying northward geographically to the Río Grande. I hope the details provided will offer more pleasant reading than merely a catalog of writers and plays.

Miami University   W. K. J.
Oxford, Ohio

ACKNOWLEDGMENTS

Writing that heading brings images of many people to whom I have become indebted in the course of this study. To cover the theatrical efforts of nineteen nations over a period of 475 years is a big task. Only by borrowing from the results of previous groundbreaking by others can one person do it. John Milton described the process in his *Brief Historie of Moscovia*: "What was scattered in many volumes, with no cursory pains I have laine together to save the Reader a far longer travaile." Many who pioneered in the study of Spanish American drama are still alive. They have been most generous with their aid.

José Juan Arrom of Yale and Harvey L. Johnson of Indiana have sent me copies of their many writings and useful suggestions and criticisms.

I think of a rainy Saturday when with Mariano Latorre and Ricardo Latcham I combed the secondhand book stores of Santiago in search of out-of-print copies of Chilean plays and critical works; of the packages of books from Juan Bautista Devoto of Argentina containing plays he thought I ought to know, and of his guidance among actors and dramatists during my two weeks' stay in his country; of Raúl Castagnino of Buenos Aires and Guillermo Ugarte Chamorro of Lima, generously sharing with me the treasures of their drama collections.

Walter Rela was an invaluable cicerone during my stay in Uruguay, as were Juan Carlos Sabat Pebet and Fernán Silva Valdés; and Dr. Américo Abad cast his eyes on what I later wrote about Uruguayan theatrical activity. Dr. José Chioino made much easier my investigations in Peru.

The active new generation in Chile was no less hospitable. Nené Aguirre, instructor in a course on the Chilean Theatre, turned over to me her lecture notes, and read in early form my chapters on Chile, as did Orlando Rodríguez. Hugo Miller and Tito Heiremans spent a morning discussing the activities of their group, and Gabriela Roepke supplied me with a file of theatre programs. Enrique Gajardo Velásquez loaded me down with mimeograph versions of many of the best Chilean contemporary plays, and mailed a second instalment to me a year later.

In Asunción, Josefina Pla put at my disposal her unpublished study of the Paraguayan theatre and helped out my faulty Guaraní so that the chapter on Paraguay's Indian theatre might be completed. She assembled actors and dramatists at a picnic with me, and later did me the honor to translate part of what I wrote into Spanish, for local publication.

Franklin Domínguez shared with me his knowledge of theatrical activities in the Dominican Republic, provided me with copies of practically all the published drama of his country, and later took time to see that I remained close to the truth in what I wrote. René Marqués was a delightful host at a party of drama lovers at his home in San Juan after our day of visiting theatres and playwrights. Then he generously read what I wrote about the Puerto Rican theatre after my return to the United States.

The aid of Rafael Pineda was invaluable in assaying the position of drama in Venezuela. Armando Maria y Campos has for years shared with me his helpful volumes on phases of Mexico's theatrical history, and Demetrio Aguilera Malta has been my guide, philosopher, and friend for even longer in everything pertaining to the culture of Ecuador.

There have been many others, each contributing something. Even from Castro's Cuba have come magazines and books to bring the Cuban picture up to date. A number of Central American officials have generously briefed me upon their countries' theatrical progress.

Finally, Miami University, in providing me with typing assistance, occasional reductions in teaching load, and a grant to spend the summer of 1958 visiting the Latin American theatrical centers, has encouraged me to complete something begun forty years ago.

To all who helped in this concoction, my gratitude. For errors still remaining in it they are not responsible. The cook who combines the ingredients gets the blame as well as the credit. As I have benefited from the work of many who preceded me, I hope that others will build on this work, so that a definitive study worthy of the growing Spanish American theatre will eventually take form.

W. K. J.

CONTENTS

INTRODUCTION

"To have great poets there must be great audiences, too," wrote Walt Whitman. Even more is needed to produce great dramatists. Scratch a Latin American and you will find a poet. Poets need no long period of apprenticeship, no prolonged concentration to write an intuitive poem that can be reproduced by hand for general distribution, or published in a newspaper or magazine, frequently founded by the writer and lasting for a couple of issues. To write an acceptable play, however, requires some acquaintance with the technique of drama, as well as persistence during a relatively extended period of uninterrupted writing time. And that is only the beginning. Before he can get a public, the playwright must find either money to publish it or people to perform it.

Since all these essentials are so rarely present at the same time, it is easy to understand why Latin America has not yet produced a dramatist equal to the quartet of Spain's Golden Age. After all, the death of Calderón in 1681 left some four thousand other practicing dramatists in Spain. It is doubtful if in all the period of the Spanish American theatre that many people have been ambitious to become a second Calderón.

But that need not mean there is no drama south of the Río Grande. Certainly the head of an Argentine university was wrong sometime ago in answering the suggestion for a course on Latin American literature with the declaration that there was no such thing. The poetry of the New World, where modernism started, has long pleased and influenced writers abroad. Readers have even found an epic or two to compare with those of the rest of the world. More recent has been the discovery of excellent short stories and novels, beginning with the jungle tales, that are unmistakably Latin American. And so a number of studies of Latin American literature have already appeared, beginning in 1896 with Manuel Poncelis' *Literatura hispanoamericana.* In 1916 Alfred Coester pioneered with *Literary History of Spanish*

America in English, and by 1945 Julio A. Leguizamón needed two volumes and 1,417 pages to cover the field. To most scholars, however, the Spanish American theatre has been an orphan child. Literary historians have long been content with a nod at Uruguay's Florencio Sánchez and the comment that he exerted no influence abroad and very little at home.

True, no one seriously claims superiority in world drama for Latin America. It has the flaws of youth. Its playwrights are sometimes childish or pompous, and often excited by ideas already threadbare. Its theatre still struggles against handicaps. National poverty and a lack of concentrated populations and socially minded audiences to inspire dramatists help to explain why the writers so often turn out unfinished plays with undigested ideas. England and Spain, during their theatrical Golden Ages, had leisure and the impetus of excited patriotism. The United States, when its theatre began developing, did not have to meet the competition with the movies that faced Latin American playwrights when the theatre to the south first really tried to achieve maturity.

However these are no reasons to ignore drama in our neighboring continent. Signs of life do exist. The sporadic folk theatre, from the *carpas* of Mexico to the circus pantomimes of Argentina, gives evidence of development. An increasing number of pleasant comedies and powerful tragedies are also being produced. The rising curtain often signals the treatment of a timely social problem. Several comedies have had as many as a thousand performances; one gaucho play was produced three thousand times, and a Mexican musical comedy can boast ten thousand performances. Though this may not prove quality, at least it indicates activity.

There is no "typical Spanish American play" any more than there is an "average Latin American." Any uniformity is too often the result of the many aping one European or North American success. One could logically, perhaps, expect many plays about Indians or revolutions, themes that have inspired excellent Latin American novels. But the Indians' patient and unresisting acceptance for centuries of the white man's civilization has left them too stolid to make good subjects for drama. What an Indian feels may be studied in a psychological novel; what he does is to suffer in silence, and dramas are not composed of silences. Nor do revolutions, despite the common North American impression, provide subjects for comedies. Even in an Argentine farce like "Juan de Dios, Soldier and Countryman" by Pico and González Pacheco, a revolution is regarded merely as a change in yokes, and the attempt to synthesize a revolution in the life of a character or two has never been very successful.

The pages of this study will show that Spanish American drama grew from Spanish seed. Pre-Columbian Indian spectacles had little effect on early white dramatists. But New World drama did not long merely copy Spain. The Peninsular stage followed an evolutionary pattern; in America, however, the classical and romantic strata are not easily separated. Many literary movements existed at the same time. So the Spanish American theatre did lead an independent existence.

Why did no world-amazing dramatists emerge, such as those produced by tiny Norway? The answer might be found in Spanish history where after the advent of a quartet of great playwrights during the Golden Age two centuries went by before Spain had another renaissance of the theatre. When Lope and Calderón were evolving, the embryonic New World dramatists had neither the time nor the theatres to perfect their techniques. Then while Madrid's dramatists became inbred imitating Lope, and brought on the cultural decline of the eighteenth century, the *ingenios* of Lima and Mexico were imitating the imitators. Certainly the breaking of new ground in the theatre of Spain with the coming of romanticism in 1833 helped produce a new generation of noteworthy dramatists, and today increased independence is evident in South America, too. Not many playwrights yet may challenge O'Neill and Arthur Miller, but at least many are becoming national. Their quality is improving.

If the stage is a mirror of nature, one important way of learning about Latin American life and customs is to study its drama. A person need not shut his eyes to the attraction of a flower garden just because there are no breathtaking, prize-winning blooms in it. Much that is striking and interesting and even charming is to be found by those who roam among the variegated offerings of Spanish American dramatists. True, some of the earlier plays seem artificial to modern tastes. The grandiloquence, for instance, of Olmedo's characters is objectionable unless the reader has some knowledge of Spanish American history and cultural background. To the Ecuadorians of the 1830's Olmedo's flowery speeches were as much to be admired as is an operatic aria of today, and they were presented in much the same way. Plays and playwrights must be studied against their period and background.

And if some of the plays even today reveal dramatists unacquainted with the mechanics of the stage and the frailties of the actors, a reader must remember the difficulties they face in finding opportunities to watch their work in rehearsals and before audiences. Until given presentation, their plays are only something lying flat on a printed page, if indeed they have been lucky enough to get beyond the manuscript version. However, the quickening tempo of dramatic activity south of the Río Grande gives hopes that playwrights will be increasingly able to discover their shortcomings through actual performances. The curtain seems to be rising on the Spanish American theatre.

Behind Spanish American Footlights

CHAPTER 1

Pre-Columbian Drama in America

If no great dramas were produced in the New World before the arrival of Columbus, that is no surprise. Even in Spain, as will be seen in the next chapter, the popular theatre did not come into being until years after the caravels of Columbus had set sail. But the earliest white visitors to America saw and described evidences of Pre-Columbian drama there.[1] Cortés, in his Second Letter to Charles V, while describing the punishment of a thief, mentions *un como teatro* in the market place of Tenochtitlán (Mexico City) on which a crier stood while giving details of the crime. Aroused by his words, the crowd attacked the criminal and beat him to death.

In his Third Letter, Cortés describes the stage in more detail as being "fecho de cal y canto, cuadrado, de altura de dos estados y medio [about fourteen feet], y de esquina a esquina había treinta pasos." On it the *representadores* stood to be seen by all in the plaza.[2] While it no longer survives here, a primitive theatre is still visible near Cuzco, Peru. What took place on this platform? No records have been found of the steps in the development of an Indian drama, but from the evolution in ancient Greece one can surmise. First came religious dances that eventually turned into pantomimes. Then, as in the case of Argentina circus performances in the nineteenth century, dialog was provided. This is as far as the Indians had progressed, with dialogs about gods and tribal heroes, when the Spaniards arrived. The Aztecs called them *mitotes,* from

---

[1] For more details, see José Juan Arrom, "Raíces indígenas del teatro americano," *Proceedings of the Twenty-ninth Congress of Americanists,* II, 299–305. See also Harvey L. Johnson, "Noticias dadas por Tomás Gage," *Revista Iberoamericana,* VIII, No. 16 (November, 1944), 269–271, n.20; and Arrom, *El teatro de Hispanoamérica en la época colonial,* pp. 13–35.

[2] José J. Rojas Garcidueñas, *El teatro de Nueva España en el Siglo XVI,* p. 23. Arrom, "Raíces indígenas," *Proceedings of the Twenty-ninth Congress,* p. 15, has a picture of its restoration. He also, p. 28, pictures the theatre near Cuzco, Peru.

the Náhuatl *mitotl*, "a dance." The Caribbean Indians referred to them as *areitos*, from the Arahuaco *aririn*, "to recite." With justice, therefore, did the chronicler Fernández de Oviedo (1479–1557) refer to them as "singing dances."[3]

The mid-sixteenth-century *Códice Ramírez*,[4] supposedly written by Juan de Tovar (1543–1626), uses the phrase *gracioso entremés* in describing a performance in the Temple of Quetzalcoatl, in Cholula, that took place on a stage somewhat more elaborate than the one in Cortés' account, since it was decorated with arches and flowers. Padre José de Acosta (1539–1600), a chronicler of colonial times from Mexico to Peru, quoted part of the *Códice Ramírez* account, here translated:

This temple had a fair-sized patio where in festival days there were dances and pastimes and amusing short plays for which there existed in the midst of the patio a little theatre, thirty feet square and whitewashed, attractively decorated with branches and flowers . . . where the people gathered after banqueting. The players came out and presented short plays, pretending to be the deaf, the halt, and the blind, coming to beg the idol to cure them; the deaf answering stupidly, the sick coughing, and the lame limping and complaining about their miseries. All this would make anybody laugh. Some of the players represented reptiles, others beetles, others frogs or lizards, and . . . they played flutes, which pleased the audience greatly . . . and it all ended in a dance."[5]

Padre Diego Durán (?–1588) adds more details as he describes boys, dressed like butterflies, who climbed trees on the stage and were shot at by Indians with blowguns. Finally the Goddess of Roses arrived and disarmed the Indians to protect the birds.[6] Durán tells of other fiestas *de danzas y farsas y entremeses y cantares*, some with dancing humpbacks, others with drunkards, and servants who pretended deafness when their masters gave them orders. The appearance of the cripples apparently seemed hilarious to the spectators.

Certainly all these sound more like pageants than a European-

---

[3] Gonzalo Fernández de Oviedo y Valdés, *Historia general y natural de las Indias*, Part I, Book V. Chapter 1.

[4] Published in Mexico, 1944, pp. 159–161. See Arrom, "Raíces indígenas," *Proceedings of the Twenty-ninth Congress*, p. 16; and Luis Leal, "El Códice Ramírez," *Historia mexicana*, III, 11–33.

[5] José de Acosta, *Historia natural y moral de las Indias*, Book V, Chapter 30.

[6] Diego Durán, *Historia de las Indias de Nueva España*, II, 231. This dance is also discussed by Angel María Garibay in *La poesía indígena de la altiplanicie*.

style play, for they lack that clash of interest necessary for good drama. Another performance, *Tum teleche*, described by Rojas Garciudueñas, did provide drama and suspense, at least for the chief actor, though he never took a curtain call. One warrior, tied by his foot to the Temalacatl or sacrificial stone, fought against a half dozen better-armed opponents, till he was wounded. Then he was laid on the circular stone and his heart was ripped out. Needless to say, the first Catholic priests to witness it forbade any repeat performances.[7]

Yucatán too had its spectacles. Fray Diego de Landa (1524–1579) found at Chichén Itzá "two small, tiled platforms with four stairways, on which farces and comedies are said to have been performed for the entertainment of the people,"[8] and Padre Sánchez de Aguilar, also of Yucatán, wrote of the "farsantes que representaban fábulas e historias antiguas."[9]

Much more has been written about the pre-Columbian theatre of Mexico than of any other nation, but there was activity elsewhere. A Venezuelan, Gilberto Antolínez, recently found what he believes to be a modernization of another ancient Andean Indian ritual, changed, but not destroyed by the white man's religion.[10] Flagellation formed part of it, as well as enactment of the birth and death of vegetation. He considers the performance that he saw a degeneration of what was originally a dramatization of the legend of Yuruparí, including his birth, his education, his murder by the parents of those killed for eating the fruit of the tree Wakú, and his resurrection and ascent to the skies by means of a palm tree. The play preceded his ceremonial worship. In this aboriginal play Antolínez saw tragedy and comedy as it epitomized Indian life—lively, but serious as befitting a people that rarely smile, and serving as release for the group sense of fear. This last, if true, aligns it with the Greek idea of katharsis. In Uyumbichu, Ecuador, a rural school successfully presented some of these rituals in 1941, modernized and with the pagan religious elements omitted.

Farther south the Indians of the High Andes, according to the first explorers, were found to have constructed large *corrales* (as the

---

[7] Rojas Garciudueñas, *El teatro de Nueva España*, pp. 29–31.
[8] Diego de Landa, *Relación de las cosas de Yucatán*, p. 120.
[9] Arrom, "Raíces indígenas," *Proceedings of the Twenty-ninth Congress*, p. 26.
[10] Gilberto Antolínez, "El teatro, institución de los Muku y Jirajara," *Revista de Cultura*, No. 56 (May, 1946), 113–129.

Spaniard called their innyard theatres) with high walls, in which to worship (*mochar*) their "false trinity."[11] One of the Spanish priests, Cieza de León (1518–1560), writes of large theatres with *gradas* (bleachers) where the Inca and his princes went to worship in a five-day-long festival that included *taquis* (perhaps dramatic songs or sketches, from Quechua *taki*, "a song"). The Quechua-speaking mestizo Juan Santa Cruz Pachacuti, who knew Spanish well enough to understand the significance of what he wrote, told how the Inca Huascar ordered a hundred Indian *llamallamas* (which Arrom, in quoting him, translates as "grotesquely masked actors") to perform *sus comedias* in the plaza of Pomapampa.[12]

The Indian terms for some of the actors, as set down by the early-seventeenth-century Felipe Poma,[13] imply that they did more than sing religious chants. He wrote that both the civilized Indians of Huancavilca and the jungle Indians of the Yungas had their *farsas y fiestas*, and mentioned the *sanca-rimac* (one who says gay things) and the *sanca chicuy asichicuj* (clown who makes people laugh).[14] Juan Polo (?–1575), a trained lawyer, pointed out the parallel between performances in honor of the Inca Feast of Intiraymi, with its dances, dialogs, and songs, and the observance of the Christian Corpus Christi.[15] And scholars continue to debate the significance of details, set down by the sixteenth-century Peruvian mestizo Inca Garcilaso de la Vega (1558–1616), in his *Comentarios reales que tratan del origen de los Incas* (1609). Using information obtained from his Inca princess mother and his aunts, he reported (Book 2, Chapter 27), after he had lived in Spain and had seen comedies and tragedies in Madrid theatres:

> The *amautas*, who were the philosophers, were skilled at composing comedies and tragedies that on solemn feast days were performed before the rulers and their guests at court. The actors were not base-born, but

[11] *Colección de documentos inéditos del Archivo de Indias*, III, 14–15; Arrom, "Raíces indígenas," *Proceedings of the Twenty-ninth Congress*, p. 28.

[12] Juan Santa Cruz Pachacuti, *Relación de antigüedad deste regno del Perú*, p. 210; Arrom, "Raíces indígenas," *Proceedings of the Twenty-Ninth Congress*, p. 30.

[13] Felipe Huamán Poma de Ayala, *El primer nueva crónica y buen gobierno*, p. 331.

[14] Arrom, "Raíces indígenas," *Proceedings of the Twenty-ninth Congress*, p. 30 n.

[15] Juan Polo de Ondegardo, *Información acerca de la religión y gobierno de los Incas*, pp. 21–22.

Incas and noble lords and children of governors, and the governors themselves, and war leaders, even to the commanders, in order that the dramas
might be properly performed, since they dealt with military deeds, triumphs, and victories, with the deeds and grandeur of dead kings and of
other heroic men. The plots of comedies dealt with agriculture and homey
and familiar things . . . They never performed shameful, vile or low *entremeses*; all dealt with serious and honorable affairs. And those who
performed well received jewels and gifts.

Of course, all these accounts are colored by the prejudices of the
writers. For one thing, most of them were scornful of "those backward pagans." For another, they knew the nomenclature of the theatre in Spain and frequently used that vocabulary for things that
were not the same at all, because they knew no other term to use.
Arrom points out one chronicler's misleading description of llamas
as "sheep of the land," and guinea pigs as "Indian rabbits."[16] Cortés
described the Aztec temples as "mosques." So the dramatic forms of
the New World called "comedy," "tragedy," and "farce" were not
always the equivalent of the Peninsular drama. And "theatre," with
its connotations of stage, audience, actors, and written play with
clash of interests, could certainly not be used to cover all these Indian performances.

Some have been so classified, however. For years scholars believed
that the play *Ollanta*[17] (or *Ollantay*) in the Quechua language represented something authentically Incan, preserved by oral tradition
until the white man came to write it down. The Indian system of
quipu "writing" by means of knotted and interwoven threads of vari-

[16] Arrom, "Raíces indígenas," *Proceedings of the Twenty-ninth Congress*, p.
32.

[17] Original Quechua version in phonetic alphabet with Quechua-French vocabulary and notes on the drama edited by Gavino Pacheco Zegarra (Paris,
1878). Facsimile and Latin translation by Dr. Hippolytus Galante of the Institute of Philology, University of San Marcos, in *Sphinx*, I, No. 2 (November,
1937). Versions in Spanish by Pacheco in *Biblioteca Clásica Americana* (Madrid,
1886); and in J. Basadre, *Literatura inca*. Constantino Carrasco made a three-act
play in verse, which he read before the Literary Club of Lima; it was published,
with prolog by Ricardo Palma, in Lima, 1876. See also Adolfo F. Olivares,
Poesía dramática de los incas. Ricardo Rojas, *Un titán de los Andes*, makes a
study of the legend from its beginning to his own *Ollantay* of 1939. For summary
and discussion in English, see E. C. Hills, "The Quechua Drama 'Ollanta'," *Romanic Review*, V (1914), reprinted in Hills, *Hispanic Studies*, pp. 47–105. Jesús
Lara, *La poesía quechua*, pp. 58–60 and 95–111, arguing for a Quechua original
of *Ollantay*, mentions and summarizes three others that he calls "pre-Columbian
plays distorted by Spanish missionaries."

ous colors, while it could represent mathematical information, could not transmit literature. Some reference books still call *Ollantay* a "native play." The one known performance, directed by Padre Antonio Valdés, priest of Tinta and Sicuani—towns fifty miles southeast of Cuzco—can be roughly dated, because the guest of honor was José Gabriel Condorcanqui, who as Túpac Amarú II claimed the ancient throne of the Incas. The performance, therefore, shortly (Condorcanqui only rebelled in 1780) preceded 1781, when Túpac Amarú II was executed for rebellion against the rule of Spain.

Dr. Valdés made no assertion that he was reviving an older play. Others made that claim for him. Clements Markham, who published an English version,[18] states in his introduction that Dr. Pablo Justiniani, the Indian who helped translate it, assured him that Valdés had merely set down the dialog as dictated by Indians. In corroboration, a number of versions, apparently earlier, have been discovered since then, one in the Convent of Santo Domingo, another in Sahuaraura. One version bears the date "Nuestra Señora de La Paz, June 18, 1735," years before the birth of Valdés. In their *Antigüedades peruanas* (1851), Manuel Eduardo Rivero and Juan Diego de Tschudi reported discoveries of still other manuscripts from the seventeenth and even the sixteenth centuries.[19]

Historical antecedents have also turned up. Cieza de León described a rebellion of nobles suppressed by the Inca, who magnanimously spared the ringleader and gave him a princess for a wife. The names Ollanta and Ollantay also appear in early chronicles.

The inclusion of real people and places motivated the original conviction, expressed by von Tschudi in his 1853 Vienna edition, that *Ollanta* was an old Inca play recently set down. Some corroboration was provided by José Sebastián Barranca, in his transcription of the Santo Domingo manuscript (Lima, 1868). He labeled both the characters and their customs "pagan." He also declared its Quechua language archaic and free of Spanish neologisms, and said he found no traces of Christianity such as a Spanish priest would have inserted.

On the other side, the discoverer of the manuscript in 1816, Val-

---

[18] C. R. Markham, *Ollanta, an Ancient Inca Drama.* See also Frances C. Wenrich, *Ollanta, an Ancient Peruvian Drama.*

[19] Arrom, "Raíces indígenas," *Proceedings of the Twenty-ninth Congress,* pp. 192–201, gives a more detailed analysis. For the Cuzco version in Quechua and Spanish, see *Ediciones populares del primer Festival del Libro Cuzqueño.*

dés' nephew, Narciso Cuentas, a doctor who claimed descent from
Túpac Yupanqui, declared it an original composition by his uncle, a
statement repeated by José Palacios in his *Mundo erudito* (1836,
Nos. 5–9). Argument from the play itself proves Spanish influence, as
a summary will show. The play recounts the rise of Ollanta, an Indian of humble birth, to the command of the Inca armies. In spite of
the warnings of his servant Piqui-Chaqui ("Flea-Foot") that he will
be beheaded, Ollanta aspires to marry Cusi-Coyllur ("Happy Star"),
daughter of Emperor Pachacutec.

The Queen summons dancing girls to entertain the unhappy Princess, who is sure that Ollanta has deserted her. Their idea of comfort
is to sing a gloomy *yaraví*, most ancient of Peruvian poetic forms, describing two loving doves, separated by cruel fate. One finally "flut-
ters and sinks down dead." Daring to ask permission to marry the
Princess, Ollanta is so violently refused that in a monolog that is one
of the gems of the play, he vows to revolt, and with an army of
rebels he captures the city of Cuzco. The act concludes with praise
of the Princess by invisible singers. Two of the lines are:

> A red flower blooms on her face in the midst of snow . . .
> Her soft neck, smooth as crystal, is white as snow.

The beginning of the next act dates the action of the play as 1448
because Pachacutec has just been succeeded on the throne by his
son Túpac-Upanqui. The young ruler receives reports that Ollanta's
army has defeated his own new general, Rumiñahui, at Ollantatambo, a town still standing thirty-five miles from Cuzco. In the final
act, Star's betrayal of her vows as Virgin of the Sun, and the discovery
that she and Ollanta have a daughter, Ima-Sumac ("Beautiful
Maiden"), have brought her imprisonment in the Temple of the Sun.
By treachery, Rumiñahui has captured Ollanta. Now appears the
first of the many reconciliatory children found in Latin American
plays. Twelve-year-old Ima, so lovely that she softens her uncle's
heart, wins pardon for both her parents. They all go to the Temple of
the Sun to release the Emperor's sister, and after their marriage,
since the Inca must make his traditional visits to all parts of his
kingdom, he asks Ollanta to replace him temporarily on the throne.

In addition to the impossibility of preserving through memory
alone for more than two centuries a play of such length, its whole
form is that of a Spanish Golden Age product. Indian plays had no

division into acts. Its basic *redondilla* with its rhyme was a verse form unknown to them. In small details, too, its Spanish ancestry is revealed. Garcilaso boasted that the Inca theatre dealt with serious affairs and noble characters. But noble characters could never have included the cowardly, deceitful servant, Flea-Foot, who even in his name is a *gracioso* straight out of a Lope de Vega comedy. And the play is full of Spanish ideology. In a primitive culture that lacked edged weapons, strangling, not beheading, was the common punishment. It seems doubtful, too, that an Indian would compare the neck of his copper-colored sweetheart to snow, as in the verses quoted. On the other hand, Spanish Golden Age lovers often used the "fire and snow" compliment.

Even greater departure from Indian customs can be found. None but the Inca's blood kin could marry a princess or could rule, even temporarily; yet here was a commoner doing both. The final scene reveals the most flagrant disregard of Inca traditions. The Temple of the Virgins of the Sun was the holiest place in Cuzco. Prescott's *Conquest of Peru*, Chapter III, cites terrible punishment for any man entering its premises: he was to be strangled and the town from which he came utterly destroyed. Yet not only do the Inca and the Queen go into the sacred precincts to release Star, but many of the nobles and even the common soldiers tag along. Thoughtful reasoning from the play, therefore, indicates that Padre Valdés, or some other man well acquainted with the Quechua language, but only slightly familiar with Inca customs, employed the technique of Lope or Calderón to give new form to an old Indian legend.[20] The so-called earlier-dated manuscripts have never been thoroughly examined by competent scholars.

This Inca stepchild has had considerable influence on later playwrights. In Peru it inspired *Ollanta* (Lima, 1876) by Constantino Carrasco, with prolog by Ricardo Palma; *Hima Súmac* (1892) by Clorinda Matto de Turner; and a modern adaptation (Lima, 1953) by César Miró and Sebastián Salazar Bondy; as well as an operetta in 1920 by Federico Blume and Luis Fernán Cisneros, with music by J. H. Valle-Riestra. In 1932 Buenos Aires was treated to a novelized version by Carlos Monsave and to an opera, followed in 1939 by its finest descendant, the tragedy *Ollantay* by Ricardo Rojas.

[20] Augusto Tamayo Vargas, "Tema, drama, y problema de *Ollantay*," *El Comercio*, July 13, 1953.

With *Ollantay* disposed of as a pre-Columbian drama, there still remains a Central American claimant for the honor: *Rabinal Achí* ("The Rabinal Champion"), composed in the Quiché language. This is no play lost for centuries, as scholars once supposed *Ollantay* to be. In backwoods San Pablo de Rabinal, Guatemala, it had been frequently performed till finally forbidden by the Church about 1825. In 1855 a parish priest, Etienne Brasseur de Bourbourg heard about it and wrote it down as dictated by an Indian of exceptional memory, Bartolomé Zis. For its performance on Sunday, January 20, 1856, his parishioners supplied music with an orchestra that included a *tun*, or drum made of a hollow log, calabash rattles and scratchers, flutes, whistles, and trumpets.

Certainly no priest could be suspected as author of a tragedy ending with a human sacrifice upon a stone altar. Its unrimed speeches resemble neither the medieval Spanish religious plays nor the Golden Age *comedia*. Everything from simplicity of plot to repetition of speeches marks it as an authentic Indian composition. The setting is a Guatemala village with a long name, Cak-Yug-Zilic-Cakacaonic-Tepicanic, whose ruins still exist a few miles north of Rabinal. The time is the thirteenth century, when there were still small, independent tribes, not yet united in the Quiché Empire. Five speaking roles are for men, one for a woman, and twenty-six parts are nonspeaking. Women in the Indian plays are traditionally silent, as are the supernumeraries for dancing and background.[21]

Act I opens with a song by the Rabinal Achí, champion of his

[21] There is a French translation in *Collection de documents dans les langues indigènes*, Vol. II. A Spanish version by Luis Cardoza de Aragón, "El varón de Rabinal," appears in *Anales de la Sociedad de Geografía e Historia*, VI (Guatemala, 1929); also in *Revue de l'Institut Français d'Amerique Latine*, II (September, 1945), 115–140, with a prolog by F. Monterde. See also José Antonio Villacorta, "Rabinal Achí, tragedia danzada de los Quichés," *Anales de la Sociedad de Geografía e Historia*, XVII (1942), 352–371, reprinted in book form, with music (Buenos Aires, 1944); and José Cid Pérez, "El teatro de America de ayer y hoy: Guatemala," *Boletín de Estudios de Teatro* (hereafter referred to as *Boletín*), No. 16 (March, 1947), 2–13 (a summary with pictures). Rafael Girard; "Una obra maestra del teatro maya," *Cuadernos americanos*, VI (1947), 157–188, discusses the modernizations. See also T. B. Irving, "Three Mayan Classics," *Universidad de San Carlos*, XLIV (January, 1958), 127–136, and *University of Toronto Quarterly*, October, 1950. For a general discussion, see Rojas Garcidueñas, *El teatro de Nueva España*, pp. 34–37; Arrom, "Raíces indígenas," *Proceedings of the Twenty-ninth Congress*, pp. 20–22; and Arrom, "Drama of the Ancients," *Américas*, IV, No. 3 (March, 1952), 16–19.

army, a sort of Biblical David or Goliath. He and his soldiers are
making a sortie from their besieged city. The Achí of the Quiché
encircling army breaks into their circle, brandishing his spear. Quickly captured, he offers to ransom himself, naming the treasures he will
pay for his freedom. The Rabinal champion replies that for 260
nights and days, the army of Quiché has deprived them of sleep,
while killing warriors and destroying towns. He agrees, however, to
go back to town and carry the captive's proposal to Governor Hobtoh
("Five Showers").

In Act II the Governor is holding court inside the city of the long
name. Beside him sits his wife, an admirable woman who says not a
word during the whole act. The Governor agrees to spare their enemy's life only if he becomes one of the Council of Twelve Eagles and
Jaguars and agrees to fight for him. In the third act, upon hearing the
terms, the prisoner angrily refuses, with insulting words that almost
bring execution on the spot, but on the chance that the Governor can
persuade him, he is taken into the city.

In the final act the enemy champion is brought before the Governor and given his last chance to change allegiance or be sacrificed.
He chooses death, with a final request to be allowed to dance with
the Mother of the Green Bird, probably the sweetheart of Rabinal
Achí. After a banquet and a ceremonial dance and time to say farewell to his valleys and his mountains, the prisoner is led to the altar
where his chest is laid open and his heart snatched out to the final
melancholy strains of the weird music.

Padre Brasseur observed that the acting entailed a severe strain
on the actors, weighted down as they were by heavy wooden masks,
but he also reported the use of substitute actors who occasionally
donned the masks to give the stars a breathing spell. His preface also
mentions seeing another play in Quiché, "The Old Man," whose dialog he was unable to obtain.

In a modernized form by Carlos Girón Cerna, as *Quiché-Achí*,
Rabinal-Achí was successfully staged in 1950 with Carlos Alberto
Mencos of the San Carlos University Theatre and his wife in the
leading roles. The revised version, while departing somewhat from
the original, is still far from a European drama. In the first act the
Princess Tzam Cam Carchaj ("Precious Emerald"), though betrothed to Prince Rabinal Achí, falls in love with the Quiché cham-

pion, whom she knows only by reputation. In the second act, before
the palace of Job Toj of Rabinal, the tribal champion is condemning
to death some of his captives when the Lord of Cagüek breaks
through the crowd. First they duel with words and the Rabinal
champion is angered by his adversary's boast that he can win away
the heart of the Princess. In Act III the boastful enemy is put to the
test. When he finishes dancing with the Princess, she swoons! "Thirteen times twenty days and nights," he is allowed for saying farewell
to his home before the final duel. His return in the fourth act finds
the Princess dead of love, with the Lords of Death and the chorus
bemoaning her passing. Nothing is left in life for Quiché-Achí. He
dances the dance of resignation. As the play ends, the Rabinal warriors close upon him and take him to the sacrificial altar.

There may have been other pre-Columbian spectacles. The *Popol
Vuh*, the sacred book of the Quiché-Maya people, tells of one that
took place when two brothers descended to Xibalba, the underworld,
to avenge their father. To quote from the English version:

Transformed into old men, they performed the dance of the owl, the dance
of the weasel, and the dance of the armadillo . . . Furthermore, they
burned houses as though they were really burning and instantly they
were as they had been before.[22]

Obviously many of these examples do not conform with the modern idea of a play. However, the basic theatre was there whenever
Indians staged even a Rain Dance or went through a pantomime in
masks. Imitation is the genesis of the theatre; Shakespeare was not
the only one who conceived of it as a mirror of life. And admonition
is a source of drama, whether it be advice by precept or warning by
horrible example. The seed of the primitive drama was the expression of religious worship or the development of a martial spirit by
tales of heroes. And finally the primitive actors added comedy,
chiefly for entertainment.

That investigator of American culture, Pedro Henríquez Ureña,
has summed up the scholarly research into pre-Columbian drama. He
points out that while no plays in the New World were like those of
Spain, all the elements existed separately on the American continent:

[22] Delia Goetz and Silvanus G. Morley translation, Part II, Chapter 13, p. 156.

the stage and the scenery in Mexico, the Peruvian division into heroic and comic themes, the comic improvisation, and the pageants concerned with agriculture.[23] Each represents a type of dramatic entertainment enjoyed by Indians before the arrival of the white man. But among all their theatrical production that survived, no combination resembling European drama has been found. That had to await the arrival of the Spanish.

[23] Pedro Henríquez Ureña, "El teatro en la América durante la época colonial," *Cuaderno de Cultura Teatral* (hereafter referred to as *Cuaderno*), No. 3 (1936), 9–50 (includes ten pages of bibliographical material).

CHAPTER 2

New World Elements in Early American Drama

First of the European plays to be performed in the New World was probably seen in Hispaniola, the earliest center of Spanish administration. The unrecorded performances in seminaries, antedating Llerena, will be discussed in the section on the Dominican Republic.

Probably the earliest plays on the mainland were performed by puppeteers accompanying Cortés on his expedition to Hibueras. When he left Mexico City in October, 1524, according to the chronicler Bernal Díaz del Castillo he took with him to entertain his troops "otro que jugaba a manos y hacía títeres."[1] Mexico was one more stop in the pilgrimage of the little figures that, according to Raimundo Lull (1235–1315), reached Spain from India, by way of Italy, in 1211.[2]

These were not, however, the first puppets in America. Díaz del Castillo reported that the early Indians also "saben hacer títeres."[3] After their start, the puppets frequently provided the only local theatrical entertainment in places where there were no human actors. And they continued to thrive here and there. In 1625, when Mexico had three theatres, Lima two, and even inland Potosí, Bolivia, was supporting one, the only playhouse for the entertainment of Buenos Aires was a puppet theatre. Two hundred years later Pérez Rosales had to admit that in Chile plays were "almost unknown." Punch and Judy shows had to suffice.[4] Even after theatres were built in Mexico, puppets alternated with live actors throughout the year, and replaced them during Lent. In 1786 the capital had four permanent puppet theatres, with uncounted portable stages that roamed the streets and villages to let young and old enjoy the antics of Juan

[1] Paul McPharlin, *The Puppet Theatre in America, 1524–1949.*

[2] Professor J. E. Varey of Westfield College, University of London, in a lecture at the Institute of Spain, April, 1951. See his *Historia de los Títeres en España.*

[3] Franklin Domínguez, *Marionetas,* p. 27.

[4] Vicente Pérez Rosales, *Recuerdos del pasado,* Chapter I.

Panadero, El Negrito, Don Folias, Nana Cota, and Juan Juancillo.[5] Because actors of the legitimate theatre were wasting so many of their free hours with the puppets, they were warned that year against "staying up till all hours." French soldiers accompanying Emperor Maximilian to Mexico in 1862 brought Grand Guignol puppets,[6] and the novelist-soldier General Vicente Riva Palacio, who accepted Maximilian's sword in surrender in 1867, was part owner of a puppet show, for which he supplied plays.

Ever since then puppets have remained popular in Latin America, with a recent flurry of activity, judging by advertisements of puppets and cardboard theatres in Argentine and Chilean newspapers and children's magazines. Schools in many Latin American nations use them in their teaching programs. Under the sponsorship of Mexico's Ministry of Education, Roberto Lago and Lola V. Cueto deserted their permanent puppet theatre in the capital in 1934 to take into the remote villages of Mexico some of the cleverest hand puppets that ever appeared on any stage. Under United Nations auspices a puppet show toured Central America in 1952 to impress health habits on the illiterate Indians. Part of the celebration of the fourth centenary of Cervantes' birth was a puppet performance of *Don Quixote* in the Palace of Fine Arts, Mexico, using a script by the well-known author Salvador Novo. Mexicans also enjoyed at least one puppet play for adults, Bernardo Ortiz de Montellano's *El sombrerón* (Mexico, 1946), in which a mythical Quiché-Mayan servant, with a human face and a big straw hat, symbolized the struggle between friendly fire and evil.[7]

The New World's first plays with human actors, however, had other purposes than entertainment. They were performed to impress Christian doctrines upon the pagans, a purpose always supposed to be in the minds of the conquistadors. Columbus had priestly companions in his caravels, sent along to convert any heathens they might encounter, and immediately after the conquest of Mexico in 1521, Charles V sent three of his closest religious advisors to help Christianize the mainland. They reached Tenochtitlán (Mexico City) in

[5] Ada M. Coe, "Notes on Puppetry," *Hispania*, XXVIII (1945), 197–207, with bibliography of puppet plays written by famous authors.
[6] Armando de Maria y Campos, *Teatro mexicano de muñecas*.
[7] See José J. Arrom, "Perfil del teatro contemporáneo," *Hispania*, XXXVI (February, 1953), 29–30.

May, 1523. By the following May twelve Franciscans had followed them. A number of Dominicans got there in 1526, and an Augustinian contingent arrived in 1535.

Discovering the uselessness of proselyting through interpreters, the priests determined to learn the many languages spoken by the inhabitants of Middle America, where at least thirty separate linguistic stocks still exist.[8] Putting down unwritten languages into the Roman alphabet and devising native grammars were only part of their task. In 1539 Juan Cromberger moved part of his printing equipment from Seville to Mexico City to help in the linguistics efforts. A Nahuatl grammar was printed in 1547, and between then and 1569 Fray Bernardino de Sahagún (1499 ?–1590) wrote his *General History of the Affairs of New Spain* in that language. It was not translated into Spanish till later.

Looking for ways to impress Christian doctrines on their Indian parishioners, the priests were glad at first to use plays brought over from Spain. Even if not of high literary caliber, they lent vividness to the sermons. But, after all, even in Spain the drama was not very advanced. Ruins of the Sagunto amphitheatre near Valencia do go back, in the opinion of some archaeologists, to the time of the Greeks, while remains of Roman theatres at Bilbilis (now Calatayud), Mérida, and a half-dozen other sites prove that early inhabitants of the Iberian Peninsula knew the delight of dramatic performances, some of them elaborate. Enough still remains of the amphitheatre of Itálica, near Seville, to indicate that a mock naval battle could be fought there on real water. Too, Spain was the birthplace of the dramatist Seneca (4 B.C.–A.D. 65) and one may surmise that some of his nine tragedies had been performed in his home town of Córdoba.

But, as in Rome, the theatre of ancient Spain fell on evil days. Performances became so immoral that in the fifth century St. Chrysostom refused Holy Sacrament to theatregoers. In 425 Spanish civil authorities, to make sure that believers had no counterattractions to keep them from church, forbade performances on feast days. Sundays were later included in the prohibition and finally, in 633, the Council of Toledo abolished the theatre altogether. When the Moors, who possessed no theatrical traditions, overran the Peninsula a century later, even the memory of the stage disappeared.

[8] Cyrus Thomas and John H. Swanton, *Indian Languages of Mexico and Central America*.

Scholars date the slow rebirth of the theatre from the trope of Tútilo, a handsome monk in the Benedictine Abbey of St. Gall, Switzerland, in 860.[9] Originally given in Latin, these dramatizations of the Christmas and Easter stories, like the fragmentary *Auto de los reyes magos* written in the Cathedral of Toledo in the twelfth century, were eventually performed in Spanish, and they continued to be written and performed, sometimes by priests not as dedicated as Tútilo, till once more the theatre fell into disrepute. King Alfonso X (1226–1284) declared in his *Siete partidas,* Título VI, Libro 34, that priests who performed in plays were as bad as those vile persons the minstrels and troubadours, who danced and sang before the public for the sake of the money received.

Alfonso XI (1300 ?–1350) repeated the censure at Compluto (now Alcalá) in 1348 and a half century later the Council of Arana and Compluto threatened excommunication to all priest-actors. Still, religious pageants were being performed before the altar in Saragosa in 1399 and in Barcelona in 1424, and perhaps the New World priests thought themselves far enough away to perform them, especially since their purposes were godly.

The earliest drama in America was the nativity play *Los pastores* performed by friars with Cortés. It has had a long life, and will be discussed in the chapter on Mexico. *Los pastores* was transferred bodily to the New World and at first had no American elements. But as soon as the priests learned the Indian dialects they began writing plays in those languages, and almost immediately New World drama began taking on the color of its environment. The development occurred in three steps: first the use of local dialects, then the inclusion of New World characters, and finally the dramatization of New World events.

The first New World play in a native tongue was probably "The Last Judgment," in the Nahuatl language of Mexico, written by Fray Andrés de Olmos (c. 1491–1571), and performed in Mexico in 1533. It was a good old fire-and-brimstone affair but slanted to a local problem. The priests had been worried about the number of Spanish soldiers who had acquired Indian mistresses. So Olmos put onto the

---

[9] The first Easter Introit, from Folio 484, p. 110 of St. Gall, is reproduced in *Classical Outlook*, XXXIX, No. 7 (Oxford, Ohio, April 1952). See also Edmund K. Chambers, *The Medieval Stage*, II, 309.

stage the Indian Lucía, who was living with a man to whom she was not married. Two characters symbolizing Time and The Church visited her with the warning that the Day of Judgment was approaching. They urged her, under threat of terrible punishment, to repent and regularize her status. The frightened Indian woman hurried to her confessor, only to be told that there could be no mercy for a sinner like her. To us that statement may seem to be a contradiction of the Church's preaching about repentance and pardon, but the sixteenth-century dramatist probably figured that if Lucía was forgiven, other Indians might believe that they could sin for awhile and eventually repent and be pardoned. At any rate the play achieved its purpose. Father Juan de Torquemada writing about it later, testified: "It opened the eyes of many Indians and Spaniards to turn to virtue and abandon their evil ways, and many erring women, moved by terror, became converted."

Some of these religious plays carried political overtones, like one performed in Asunción, Paraguay, in 1544. Father Juan Gabriel Lezcano wrote an Epiphany play that he and others performed on the steps of the cathedral. In the course of it, one shepherd brought echoes of Spain's fifteenth-century *Mingo Revulgo* by using the epithet "scurvy wolf" to refer to their former governor, Cabeza de Vaca, who had been deposed the previous April in America's first revolution.

Throughout the colonial period the chief occasions for theatrical performances were Church holy days, especially Corpus Christi, Christmas, and Easter; welcoming ceremonies for visiting dignitaries; and festivals to demonstrate loyalty to Spain, such as royal birthdays and coronations. Because of the close connections of all these to the mother country, they would seem to offer few opportunities for the introduction of Hemisphere accents; yet those gradually crept in.

Old World and New mingled in what is believed to be America's first play by a native-born dramatist—"The Spiritual Marriage between Shepherd Pedro and the Mexican Church," by Juan Pérez Ramírez (1545–1580 ?). It was written in 1574 to welcome Archbishop Pedro Moya de Contreras, the Pedro of the play, to his new charge in the cathedral in Mexico. This brief religious play shows its Spanish ancestry by the use of such symbolic characters as Divine

Love and Theological Virtues as well as the typical *bobo,* or comic
character. The language, too, is that of any cultured Spaniard, but
the shepherds provide a local and American flavor.

Still more Mexican touches can be observed in *Coloquio III,* written for the same occasion by the Spanish-born Fernán González de
Eslava (1534–1601), perhaps with the help of Juan de la Cueva, the
sixteenth-century dramatist of Spain who started Don Juan Tenorio
on his theatrical career. Cueva is known to have been in Mexico between 1574 and 1577. The prose and poetry of the seven scenes in
this play are full of popular words and local slang. The characters
as well as the themes are Mexican, so much so in fact that Viceroy
Martín Henríquez, one of the spectators, took offense at the comic
character whose make-up included a beard such as distinguished
the Viceroy and who appealed for civil disobedience against the
Viceroy's recently established sales tax. Henríquez complained to
the archbishop, who claimed complete innocence. Their quarrel was
eventually carried to the emperor in Spain, but meantime poor Eslava
went to jail for seventeen days as punishment for his too successful
attempt to mingle local politics with religion.

For those looking for American touches, Eslava provides a fertile
territory. His sixteen surviving short plays, termed by him "Coloquios," combine Spanish forms with local customs and background.
In *Coloquio V,* for instance, this sixteenth-century dramatist sounded
a Mexican note by following the Soul on a sort of Pilgrim's Progress
along the fortified road recently built by Viceroy Henríquez between
Mexico City and the silver mines in Zacatecas, with each of the seven
forts symbolizing some test of faith. Even more completely Mexican
is the curtain raiser for Eslava's *Coloquio VII,* written about 1570.
Teresa, proud of her descent from a conquistador, begs her husband,
Diego Moreno, to take her away from Mexico with its edicts against
the wearing of silken finery. He gets them passage on a China-bound
galleon. On board, they find Jonah fleeing from Nineveh, and the
rest of the play is devoted to the Biblical story of Jonah and the
whale.

Across the Caribbean in Santo Domingo, Cristóbal de Llerena (c.
1545–1610), a musician and university professor, was writing a play
so full of local allusions that it roused the wrath of the city fathers.
For the Corpus Christi celebration of 1588 he introduced a typical
bobo of the Spanish *entremés,* but one who criticized the corrupt

government of the island, the freedom allowed women, and the surfeit of priests and lawyers in the city. Shortly afterward, its author was hauled out of bed early one morning and shipped away from Santo Domingo.

As time passed, drama broadened and became a recognized weapon to criticize local political and social abuse. It was therefore more realistic than religious. After it was cast out of the Church, it took refuge with the populace, both in the homes of the wealthy and in the public squares, where it was the delight of the common people. The nobles, perhaps because their interests were still deeply rooted in Spain, liked plays that came from Madrid's stages. The lower classes cared little for tradition, provided they were entertained. Between the two tastes, considerable dramatic activity seems to have been encouraged.

The examples so far have been Spanish in form with New World elements added. Now was to come the next step. Though still developed according to Madrid's dramatic technique, the plays told stories about the New World. The first ones were short. As the impresario Arias de Villalobos of Mexico was to declare in 1621: "Only plays from Castile are performed; those from around here turn out badly." And so the only chance for a local dramatist to see his play on the stage was to write something that could be sandwiched between the acts of a play from Madrid. Even established dramatists with powerful patrons, like the Peruvian Pedro de Peralta Barnuevo (1664–1743), friend of the viceroy, stuck to surefire European material and wrote of gods and royalty. The first time he ventured to use a local theme was in the *entremés* introduced between the acts of his translation of Corneille's *Rodogune,* about 1716. In it he introduced four masked beauties of Lima, who joined with their typical Peruvian suitors to avoid a father's vigilance. This delightful little skit has been characterized by José Arrom in his study of the American colonial theatre as the one ancient play best able to stand the test of a performance today. It is completely national and full of the American spirit.

Actually, during the seventeenth century Spaniards saw more plays based on New World themes than were performed in America. Most of Spain's Golden Age dramatists wrote plays based on overseas events and people because of their romantic appeal to stay-at-home Castilians. Lope de Vega finished *El Nuevo Mundo descubierto por Colón* about 1604. He put Cortés onto the stage in *El Marqués de Valle,* Hurtado de Mendoza in *Arauco domado,* and even composed a curious Corpus Christi play based on characters from Ercilla's great epic poem of Chile, *La araucana.* Tirso de Molina wrote a trilogy about the Pizarro family: *La lealtad contra la envidia, Las hazañas de los Pizarro,* and *Amazonas de las Indias.* Calderón put Pizarro, his rival Almagro, and a crowd of Indians into a hodgepodge Peruvian religious play, *La aurora en Copacabana* (1672), that reveals how badly a great dramatist can sometimes write. Lesser dramatists like Francisco González Bustos wrote the much-performed *Los españoles en Chile,* while others turned out *Santa Rosa de Lima* and *Algunas hazañas de las muchas de García Hurtado de Mendoza.*

Lesser-known Americans also figured in plays by Spaniards; Doña Mencia de Nidos was represented in *La belígera española* by "Ricardo de Turia," and the much-traveled Ordóñez de Ceballos of Jaen inspired the fertile mind of Fray Alonso Remón to write *Un español entre muchas naciones* (Jaen, 1629). But of all the New World subjects for drama, one of the most romantic was the nun Catalina de Erauso, truly a self-made man, because she sneaked out of her convent, converted her nun's habit into a uniform, and sailed to America as a soldier of fortune. Several dramatists in Spain, including González Bustos and Pérez de Montalván, friend of Lope, told her story. The curious fact is that no playwrights living in America saw the dramatic possibilities of such striking personalities or wrote plays about them.

Failing such subjects, the most obvious subject for a truly national theatre in America would seem to be the Indians. The dramatists were surrounded by them, but to most settlers they represented either a potential peril or a source of cheap labor, neither concept likely to turn the Indian into the hero of a play. One sixteenth-century Peruvian dramatist, however, Gabriel Centeno de Osma, wrote in the Quechua language a play about Indians called "The Richest Poor Man." His model was the German Faust legend. The poor Indian contracted to sell his soul to the Devil (Nina Quiru), but when the time came to pay five years later, upon advice of an angel he appealed to the Virgin of Copacabana at her shrine on Lake Titicaca. She redeemed him and gave him spiritual gifts to make him the richest of poor men. In the eighteenth century this play received a skillful reworking as *Usca Páucar,* in which dignity was given the man who reneged on his bargain, by making him an impoverished but noble descendant of the Incas. From then on, only chieftains were considered worthy of consideration by the dramatists.

They were called "kings" in a play supposed to have been written about 1619 by Cristóbal Gutiérrez de Luna of Mexico and entitled *Coloquio de la nueva conversión y bautismo de los cuatro últimos reyes de Tlaxcala en la Nueva España*. It was a pageant introducing Cortés and Doña Marina. A chief also figured in a Chilean play whose title alone has been preserved, but with that much we can reconstruct the plot, because "El Hércules chileno" (1693) must have dealt with that stalwart figure of Ercilla's epic, Caupolicán, who proved his right to be the war chief of the Araucanians by sustaining a heavy tree trunk on his shoulder longer than any other Indian could. This lost play, written by a couple of local amateurs, was part of the welcoming ceremonies of the frontier city of Concepción for Chile's Governor Marín Poveda. He had left Spain as a bachelor, met Juana de Urdanegui in Lima, and married her in Concepción, in 1693. But the manuscript of the play, which was intended to give him an idea of the military problems facing him and his subjects, probably burned during one of the many raids by those same Indians on Chile's frontier city.

A century later, as stated in Chapter 1, Padre Valdés of Peru dramatized a legend of the Inca, his general, and his daughter in *Ollantay* (c. 1780), long mistaken for a survivor of pre-Columbian Indian drama. Across the Andes about the same time, Manuel José de Lavardén (1754–1809 ?) wrote about Indians in *Siripo*, telling of a chief who fell in love with the wife of one of the first explorers of the River Plate and who killed the husband to get her. When Lucía Miranda understandably refused to marry the murderer of her husband, the Indian also killed her. This play, too, has been lost, probably destroyed when Buenos Aires' first theatre burned in 1792.

With the passing of years the attitude of the dramatists toward the Indian changed according to the literary fad in vogue at the time they were writing. Two plays by some unknown Mexican about 1790 found humor in the ignorance and stupidity of the lower-class Indian. Their plots are simple. Their interest lies in the use of the vernacular language. One of them, *El entremés de las Posadas*, its plot based on the custom of making visits at Christmas, introduces a picaresque Indian, Pascual, who jabbers amusing broken Spanish with a servant

girl and a couple of sweethearts. The play ends with the singing of a
Christmas carol. The other *entremés, El criado indio*, presents the
worries of a hungry lad who has stolen some cloth and then, remembering how his brother and his Uncle Pegro had been punished for a
similar theft, tries to get rid of his loot.

The nineteenth-century rise of neoclassicism in the continent
brought a number of plays presenting the Indian as a great but
tragic figure. In the first quarter of the century Luis Vargas Tejada
(1802–1829), founder of Colombia's theatre, dramatized in *Suga-
maxi* (1818) the practice of human sacrifice before the coming of the
white man, and followed with other tragedies of the aborigines:
Saquesazipa (1818) and *Witikindo* (1820). His countryman, José
Fernández Madrid (1788–1830), wrote a play, *Guatimocín* (1824),
about the Aztec noble who suffered death by fire rather than reveal
to Cortés the hiding place of the tribal treasure. He also put the
daughter of a North American Indian chief onto the stage in the
tragedy *Atala* (1825), developed in pseudoclassical style.

A few of the romanticists also introduced the noble redskin into
their plays, but most of them, when they could tear their attention
from Crusaders and Moors, turned to their own colonial history. The
coming of realism ought, perhaps, to have filled the stages with
downtrodden and exploited Indians, but Indian protagonists are
hard to find. The Mexican novelist Mariano Azuela (1873–1952)
made an unsuccessful dramatization in 1950 of his 1916 novel, *Los
de abajo*. Ecuador, which contains all the ingredients for a *Tobacco
Road* of underprivileged Indians, has produced only one realistic
play about them, *Flagelo*, by the country's outstanding Indianist
novelist, Jorge Icaza (1906–   ). Its history will serve to explain the
dearth of such plays there and elsewhere.

After his success with the novel *Huasipungo*, Icaza, originally a
dramatist, decided to write a play about Indians. The result was a
realistic yet symbolic mingling of drama and ballet, called *Flagelo*.
It was printed in 1936, but no one in Ecuador would stage it and he
had to go to Buenos Aires for a performance. His fellow countrymen,
who will cue up to see an American movie and will patronize a theatrical performance of O'Neill or *Arsenic and Old Lace* or even
Charley's Aunt, neither bought the published version nor attended
the performances; so Icaza returned to the novels that do bring him
glory and cash.

Though the drama of Brazil is not given a place in this history of the Spanish American theatre, it might be said to parallel the development of Spain's colonies, though with a cultural lag. Its first play, *Pregaçao universal e o mistério de Jesús* (by Padre José de Anchieta [1534–1597], produced in Nicteroi in 1566), was purely European. Succeeding dramatists also failed to treat of local people or themes. They were not inspired by either Indians or Negroes, both of whom lacked theatrical traditions. Both Manoel Botelho de Oliveira (1636–1711), whose native Bahia named its first theatre (1733) after him, and António José de Silva (1705–1739) based their dramas on European stories. Indeed, not till 1838 was any national drama achieved in Brazil. Then Domingo Gonçalves de Magalhães (1811–1882) returned from Europe with his romantic tragedy *António José ou o poeta e a Inquisição* about a trial in Lisbon in 1739 of the dramatist mentioned above, who was charged with being a Jew. Six months later in the same year, Luis Carlos Martins Pena (1815–1848), produced a thoroughly Brazilian comedy, *O juiz de paz na roça* ("A Rural Justice of the Peace"). After that, Brazilian themes and types frequently appeared on the stage.

Dramatists in other parts of the continent were also slow to attempt full-length plays based on local stories. Juan María Domínguez of Colombia learned the perils of dramatizing contemporary events when in 1826 he wrote a five-act tragedy about the Colombian revolutionary heroine Juana de Salabarrieta, who had been executed as a spy by the Spaniards nine years earlier. During the first performance of his play in Bogotá, while the condemned La Pola was being led from the chapel to execution, the audience screamed its protests and refused to let the actors be heard. Finally the author had to go before the curtain to announce that because of the demands of the "respected public," the sentence of La Pola had been changed by Viceroy Sámano to banishment. The public then cried for the death of the Viceroy.

The romantic movement, however, was responsible for many plays about local history. Ignacio Rodríguez Galván (1816–1842) delved into Mexico's past for his *Muñoz, visitador de México* (1838), an early example of romanticism in his country. Its title character was sent by Philip II to inspect conditions in Spain's colony, but he became more interested in the wife of one of Mexico's officials, a situation that precipitated a revolt. Even more indebted to Mexico's colonial period was the prolific romanticist José Peón y Contreras (1843–1907), who unfortunately began too late, when romanticism was already dying.

Writers in other countries looked about themselves and dramatized what they saw. In Lima, Felipe Pardo (1806–1868) and especially Manuel Ascensio Segura (1805–1871) dealt with the early days of Peru's independence. The Chileans Daniel Barros Grez (1834–1903), Juan Rafael Allende (1850–1909), and the satirist Román Vial (1833–1896), left a dramatic picture of the Santiago of their time. Paul Groussac (1848–1925) and Roberto Payró (1867–1928) dealt with the period of Dictator Rosas of Argentina, and a host of dramatists on both sides of the River Plate have given immortality to the gauchos.

These works formed the transition stage that culminated in the thoroughly national theatres that have today developed in the different countries, and in plays that cannot be confused with the output of other regions. Completely Mexican were the tent shows, that provided safety valves for political tension and trained many of the outstanding comedians of the current Mexican stage and movies. The series of topical plays written and performed by Ernesto Albán, in which the character Evaristo looks at contemporary problems, are likewise unmistakably Ecuadorian. The Cuban *bufo,* a modern *commedia dell' arte* built about an unscrupulous Negro, a comic mulatto girl, and a newly arrived and stupid Galician, are no less Cuban. The majority of the thoroughly national plays are comedies; it seems easier to hit a national note in humor than in seriousness. But one cannot overlook the serious plays about the *jíbaro,* the Puerto Rican farmer, by Ramón Méndez Quiñones (1847–1889), Manuel Méndez Ballester (1909–), and René Marqués (1919–). All of these plays have departed so far from the traditions of the Spanish theatre that notes and glossary would probably be needed for their complete comprehension by a Madrid audience. In short, the Americanization of the New World theatre is today complete. The rest of this volume will follow its slow development in the various countries.

Paraguayan Drama

Drama in Paraguay parallels the race of the hare with the tortoise. Though off to an early start with a play performed as early as 1544, it later lagged so badly that the Montevideo Theatre Congress of 1941 declared it one of two Latin American countries (Panama was the other) that lacked any national theatre activity.

The deficiency was not for want of lovers of literature in its early days. Captain Juan de Salazar, who founded Asunción in 1537, was one; his will of 1557 mentions several volumes in Spanish (*libros de romance*) left to his children. These lost volumes may have been accounts of his own adventures in the New World. Perhaps he even had something to do with the first recorded play of Paraguay, when, to celebrate Corpus Christi in 1544, Father Juan Gabriel Lezcano wrote a pastoral farce in which he and others performed on the steps of the cathedral. Lezcano was a native of Valladolid, Spain, who had accompanied the Mendoza expedition to settle Buenos Aires. Harassed by the hostile Indians, he had fled with the survivors to settle among the more hospitable Guaraní Indians of Paraguay. He had been made chaplain by Irala on June 10, 1540, and priest three years later by Alvar Núñez Cabeza de Vaca.

Lezcano's play was more political than religious. In April, 1543, the citizens of Asunción, in America's first political uprising, had deposed and jailed their *adelantado*, Cabeza de Vaca. In a manner reminiscent of Spain's satirical *Mingo Revulgo* (c. 1475), the priest-playwright-actor refers in his play to the ex-Governor as a "scurvy wolf" (*lobo rrebaço*).[1] Enough other local references and color are

[1] Julio Caillet Bois, "El teatro en la Asunción a mediados del siglo XVI," *Revista de Filología Hispánica*, IV (1942), 1; Walter Rela, "Fundamentos para una historia del teatro paraguayo," *Jornadas de Cultura* (November, 1955), p. 28. See also Juan Francisco de Aguirre, *El discurso histórico que comprende el descubrimiento, conquista, y nombre de Río de la Plata* (1793); W. K. Jones, *Breve historia del teatro latino-americano*, p. 22; J. Natalicio González, "La instrucción pública en el Paraguay de la colonia," *Revista de las Indias*, 2ª época, No. 20 (August, 1941), 34–57.

included to make this a national work and not merely a transplanted Spanish religious one-act play.

Ulrich Schmidl and Barco Centenera have discovered mention of other dramatic performances in 1545 and 1551, the latter to celebrate the wedding of Francisco Ortiz de Vergara to Irala's sister.[2] Then comes a gap in recorded drama. Two Jesuit priests, Ortega and Filds, reached Paraguay in 1609[3] to begin building up a theocratic empire in the heart of South America between the Paraná and the Uruguay Rivers. Thirty settlements, from San Ignacio Guazú in 1609 to the unfinished Misión de Jesús in 1764, housed 100,000 Indians. From the first, drama was part of their pedagogic equipment, provided by the priests in the language of their parishioners.[4] This theatre in Guaraní is discussed in the next chapter.

During the flurry of theatrical performances in the Indian language, drama in Spanish continued to languish. True, there were a few signs of life after the end of activity with the Guaraní black-out. Josefina Pla, in her unpublished "historia crítica del teatro paraguayo," mentions performances in the Plaza de Asunción between 1767 and 1817, among them *La vida es sueño* and several plays by Moreto. In 1812 there was even a showing by an unnamed local dramatist. But in general one can say that the drama of Paraguay went into a decline. The reasons are not hard to find. Fate and geography have treated this region shabbily. Not only is it far inland, with thick jungles on three sides, but it gave no promise of quick wealth to prospective colonists at the conclusion of their long river journey. Its climate is not pleasant; Paraguay offers only a brief period of agreeable weather and then nine months of burning summer. The banks open at seven and close at eleven and that concludes business for the day. At the end of the eighteenth century Asunción had less than twenty thousand inhabitants. Spain showed its low opinion of the value of its colony by making no attempt to reclaim it when, on May 24, 1811, the citizens declared their independence and told their Spanish governor to go home.

For a short time, a junta took over the government, but in 1814 Dr. José Gaspar Rodríguez Francia came into power to begin twenty-

[2] Rela, "Fundamentos," *Jornadas de Cultura* (November, 1955), p. 30.

[3] Juan Max Boettner, *Música y músicos del Paraguay*, p. 53. He also lists, pp. 117–133, the dramatic offerings in Asunción, by years.

[4] *Die missionem der Jesuiten in Paraguay* (Gütersloh, Germany, 1891), quoted in Boettner, *Música y músicos*, p. 53.

six years of dictatorship. Realizing that his neighboring countries were casting covetous eyes on the territory, Dr. Francia practically sealed his frontiers and turned Paraguay into a hermit nation, with himself as "El Supremo." Everything from marriages to the sale of cattle required his personal approval. He disapproved of education. He left open only one primary school in Asunción, and with the declaration that "Minerva can sleep while Mars watches," he closed the only Paraguayan college in order to have more money for his army. To him the theatre was a frivolity, and the only national play recorded during his period of power was *El rosario perseguido* (1817), by José del Rosario Ayala.

A few years after Francia's death, in 1840, a more paternal dictator, Carlos Antonio López, came into power. López was ambitious for the cultural advance of his country. He brought a railroad and a telegraph system to Paraguay and sent to Uruguay for an Italian architect, Alejandro Ravizza, to build him a palace and a theatre. In addition, in 1852 he sent his son to Europe in search of someone to establish an adequate school system and to inaugurate a theatrical movement. He also decreed establishment of the first newspaper, *El Semanario*, which appeared on May 21, 1853.

The man selected as educator of the nation was Ildefonso Antonio Bermejo (1820–1892), born in Cádiz but a fugitive in Paris since the Spanish insurrection of 1846. Bermejo had written a half-dozen plays, including *El poder de un falso amigo* (1849), before Francisco Solano López arrived in Paris in 1852 to persuade him to bring literacy and culture to Paraguay. Arriving in Asunción in February, 1855, Bermejo first founded the newspaper *Eco del Paraguay*, and then the normal school, but eventually directed his attention to Don Carlos' theatre. The building was already being used. *Flor de un día* and *Los hijos de Eduardo* are listed as having been performed there, probably by amateurs directed by Bermejo. According to an advertisement in *El Semanario*, a Compañía Dramática Española was visiting Asunción. For Sunday, April 18, 1858, the paper announced that Carmen Rodríguez and Enrique López would offer Dumas' *Los colegiales de Saint Cyr* and the one-act *Inesilla la de Pinto*. On May 23 they performed *El duende* by Ramón de la Cruz, and the musical *El rapto de doña Savina*. *Don Juan Tenorio* opened on August 7, and *Traidor, inconfeso, y martir*, also by Zorrilla, on October 8.

December 4, 1858, however, was the gala day for the Paraguayan theatre. The same *El Semanario* advertised the approaching presentation in Don Carlos' theatre by the Spanish Company of Dramas and Comedies of the first poetic play written in Paraguay, *Un paraguayo leal,*[5] by Bermejo (Asunción, 1898). The announcement failed to mention that it was a revision of his 1849 tragedy, with new names, places, and some minor incidents, and with local color and phrases in Guaraní provided by his student, the poet Natalicio Talavera (1839–1867).

The Dictator's son, Francisco, now back from Paris with his Irish mistress, Elisa Lynch,[6] occupied one of the boxes, and when López, who had kept his military hat on during the whole evening, expressed displeasure with the performance, the diamond-studded Madame Lynch explained to the Dictator that if the play had satisfied him, it would have been too sophisticated for the Paraguayans. Somewhat appeased, President López ordered Bermejo to try again, this time with the Dictator's tastes in mind. Apparently the Spaniard did not follow instructions. While he directed national actors in plays by García Gutiérrez, de la Cruz, Bretón de los Herreros, and other Spaniards, the only other known writings by him in Paraguay are some *costumbrista* dialogs (*La Aurora,* 1860). After seven years he and his disgruntled wife returned to Europe where he wrote a violent attack on the "uncouth" Paraguayans and turned out a total of thirty-one plays, none of which was important.[7] Dictator López died in 1862, with his desire for plays still unappeased.

He was succeeded by his son, former Vice-President Francisco Solano López. The father had built the best army in South America and the son decided to use it, first in an alliance with Brazil and Uruguay against Argentina to protect Uruguay. His successes encouraged a visiting Spanish company of actors, headed by Pelayo Ascona, to flatter him with *La divertida historia de la triple alianza* (1864), a three-act comedy originally written in English by the American consul, Peter Bliss.[8]

Before long the Paraguayan War began. Ascona tried to give benefit performances to raise money for the army, but with the nation's

[5] J. Worth Banner, "Ildefonso Bermejo, iniciador del teatro en el Paraguay," *Revista Iberoamericana,* XVIII (July, 1951), 79–107.

[6] H. F. Varela, *Elisa Lynch,* p. 330; W. E. Barrett, *Woman on Horseback.*

[7] Juan J. O'Leary, *Ildefonso A. Bermejo, falsario, impostor y plagario.*

[8] Published in *El Semanario,* No. 652 (December, 1866).

existence threatened, none had time for plays, so he and his company returned broke to Buenos Aires. The outbreak of war also ended Marshal López' efforts to give his people a replica of La Scala of Milan. It remained half finished. However, in the palace that he built for Madame Lynch he did construct a theatre, a spacious room at present serving as the dining room in the hotel into which the old building has now been converted.

Overwhelming superiority of manpower and geographic location of the three neighboring countries proved too much for Paraguay, though its citizens fought courageously from 1865 to 1870. During allied occupation of Asunción, some Argentine soldiers produced plays imported from Spain for the entertainment of their comrades.

Gradually the citizens of Paraguay began the struggle to restore their nation and its culture. From 1880 on, a few hardy companies of foreign actors sailed their slow way up the river to perform in the capital.[9] Francisco Rodríguez and Enriqueta Quintana headed a company from Spain that reached Asunción in December, 1881. They found the National Theatre in such disrepair that they had to restore it and paint its boxes before they could open. Because so few patronized the performances, a continuous change in offerings was necessary, making the prompter more essential than usual. The newspaper comment following Moratín's *Lo positivo* was: "Excellent, but the prompter should lower his voice." Among their other offerings were: Larra's *Flores y perlas*, Echegaray's *La esposa del vengador*, Navarrete y Zárate's *Más vale maña que fuerza*, and Gil y Zárate's *Guzmán el bueno*.

The Paraguayan public, however, preferred zarzuelas, a type requiring more rehearsals than did the spoken plays. One such performance was so ragged that the manager went before the curtain to apologize that the orchestra was not prepared. That brought a denial from the pianist, Billordo. A fight followed. Then someone shouted "Fire!" and the theatre was emptied. A new pianist arrived from Buenos Aires before the next performance.

To boost attendance, various schemes were attempted. Prizes were raffled during the performances. Tickets were sent to leading families of Asunción, with bills following later. Still the theatre remained half empty. Discouraged, the players gave their "final performance."

[9] Boettner, *Música y músicos*, pp. 117–133, lists their offerings by years.

The next day, December 16, 1882, a newspaper advertisement declared that the company had not collected enough money for their return fare to Buenos Aires and would have to stay on in the bedraggled theatre.

Eventually came a change. In 1887 Teatro Olimpo came into existence. In 1888 an Italian physician, Dr. Silvio Andreuzzi, for sixteen years a resident of Asunción, built El Teatro Andreuzzi, now the dining room of Hotel del Paraguay. And finally even the National Theatre was reconditioned. A society was formed to take it over, install acetylene gas lights, and repaint it. Each contributing member was repaid by being assigned a box for all performances. The building was ready for the Fernández Company of Zarzuelas and Comedies that arrived from Buenos Aires in August, 1898, bringing something new, the idea of matinees besides evening performances. And to entice Paraguayans the director added three plays by local dramatists to the repertory. On August 22 they revived Bermejo's two-act play in verse, *Un paraguayo leal*, which, according to the newspapers, was "short but fairly successful." On August 29 the company staged *El Dr. Francia* by Benigno Tejeiro Martínez. *El heroismo de una madre o la guerra del Paraguay* by Segundo San Martín followed on September 6. The critics approved the last, though noting the omission of some details necessary for an understanding of the action, and indicating such anachronisms as horsecars in Asunción in 1862.

The de la Vega players, in April, 1899, brought Calderón's *Vida es sueño* and works by Dicenta, Zorrilla, and others, and these were followed by a succession of foreign troupes. Around 1900 a zarzuela, *La rosa paraguaya*, was written by the Spanish poet Victorino Abente y Lago. It was published about 1910, but there is doubt that it was ever performed. The next Paraguayan play came on November 21, 1906, when the Enrique Sánchiz Company of Zarzuelas performed the three-act poetic drama *La cámara obscura*, by the poet Alejandro Guanes (1872–1925). Also in 1906 Asunción got its first look at movies, about which it had been reading since 1900, when the Teatro Nacional offered a program billed as "Bioscopio Lírico," apparently a film with accompanying phonograph music. The next year, twelve films were run, with interspersed orchestra music. The theatre used gas for lighting, and spectators had to help by turning the lights up and down; not till 1912 was electricity installed in the National Theatre. Since that entering wedge, it has been movies that have attracted the crowds and brought the profits. The country's dramatists complain that their National Theatre is open to them only between the runs of profitable films.

The end of romanticism and the beginnings of modernism came in 1910, and a few local playwrights were lucky enough to get a showing. A satirical *paso de comedia, Diálogo de los muertos,* was written in 1909 by Fulgencio R. Moreno and published in 1910. In it President Francia talks with his aides. Juan O'Leary wrote *Una danza* (1910) and a historical play, *La gasparina* (1920), named from a dance originated during the epoch of Dr. Gaspar Francia. It was published in one of the magazines through whose pages scholars search today for plays of the early period. In 1912 a group of theatre-loving friends of Luis Ruiz Gómez performed two of his plays: *Amemos a nuestros hijos* and *Mostrarse humano.* The manuscripts have disappeared. December, 1912, saw Paraguay's first revue, when Domínguez' *Tierra guaraní,* three scenes in one act of talking and singing, was performed.

In 1915 visiting players held a competition for plays by Paraguayan dramatists, but results are not recorded. Perhaps *La flor del valle,* the three-act offering by Rafael Rodríguez Rojas (1859–1918), published in *El Liberal* that year, was one of the winners. Rojas later wrote *María Victoria,* which was performed in Concepción. His other plays were neither performed nor published locally, so eventually he moved to Buenos Aires, where he acquired a reputation as a bohemian.

In May, 1915, the Chico de la Peña Dramatic Company, with the Paraguay-born Aurora Mendoza as leading lady, brought Asunción a repertory of plays by Ibsen, Benavente, and the Quinteros, as well as *Nuestros hijos* by Florencio Sánchez of Uruguay. The two-act comedy *La cena de los románticos* by Leopoldo Centurión (1893–1922), and his slow-moving but well-developed two-act drama *El huracán,* reminiscent of Spain's rural dramas, were performed the following year, after having previously been published in *Letras.*[10] *El huracán* was influenced by *El rento,* by the Spaniard Vicente Medina. It is about a rural family who cannot pay the landlord; so they force the daughter to marry him instead of the farmer she loves. While the Centurión version does not specify time or setting, it has a few local ex-

[10] *Letras,* II (Asunción, 1916), 75–98.

pressions and references. Centurión himself, tall, lean, and handsome, acted in it. Leo-Cen, as his friends called him, thus became the earliest contributor to the national Paraguayan theatre, whose activities were now beginning. He was one of an erratic group of drug-takers and suicides, though his own death came through tuberculosis. He founded the magazine *La Crónica* in 1913, in which he revealed himself as an ironic political commentator, but his last comedy of manners, *El final de un cuento*, performed in 1920, also reveals his caustic nature and his cynicism about human frailties. None of his plays is completely national.

Other names should be included in this first wave of national dramatists. From the pen of Ignacio Alberto Pane (1880–1920) came *La canción de las tijeras* (1917), one of the three best plays composed by the generation of 1900. The other two were *Una danza* by O'Leary and the ironic *Diálogo de los muertos* by Moreno. All are lost.

Another of this group is Eloy Fariña Nuñez (1885–1929). This poet and philosopher was called "The Guaraní with the Greek soul." He wrote a tragedy, *Entre naranjos y cocoteros*; a comedy *La ciudad silenciosa*; and two dramas, *El Santo* and *El sonador*. They still exist, because Fariña ended his career as a newspaper man in Buenos Aires, where the plays were performed and preserved.

Now appeared what might be called the 1916–1923 school of dramatists, who wrote without stages or actors or much hope of performance.[11] First was the dramatist who really put life into the Paraguayan theatre, Eusebio Aveiro Lugo (1890–   ), whose first play, the three-act drama *La chala*, was performed by a group of Paraguayan amateurs at the National Theatre, November 5, 1917. Lugo's group, *La Compañía Paraguaya de Dramas y Comedias*, also performed other plays by him, which include the one-act *Las ruinas del rosal* (published in *La Liberal,* as was the one-act *El camino de la fuente*); a dialog, *El hispano y la india*; and the three-act drama *La muerte de la quimera*, also published in *El Liberal*. His last plays were the one-act Biblical *María de Mágdala* and the historical *La epopeya del mariscal*, in three acts, about Dictator López, performed in 1926 by Carlos Brussa. Lugo was also the first president of the Sociedad Paraguaya de Autores Teatrales.

[11] An unsigned article in *La Democracia* (Asunción), August 14, 1938, p. 5, lists as "outstanding" the six dramatists mentioned here.

Another of this group was the poet and journalist Leopoldo Ramos Jiménez, (1896–) who pioneered in Paraguay's social drama with his *La inquisición del oro* (1917), a tragedy about labor problems in the selva where the herb maté is grown. It was performed by the author and his friends in the Teatro Nacional. Later he wrote *La herencia*. Most productive of all playwrights of this period was the busy Dr. Pedro Juan Caballero (1900–1946), who was congressman, journalist, and professor at the School of Medicine, as well as the founder of the Compañía Paraguaya de Comedias, and author of nine realistic plays performed by it. Though he wrote with no national theatrical tradition behind him, his works were serious and sincere, with no striving for the easy laugh. They were realistic pictures of everyday life and were therefore national in spirit and locale. They included the four-act comedy about divorce, *El pasado* (1917); the three-act, back-to-nature comedy *El imán* (1918); the three-act *El vencido* (1923), about a medical student; followed by the medical *El clínico* (1923); *Los buitres* (1925), a tragedy about a girl who gave up an honest rustic lover for the snares of the city; *El castigo*; *De pura cepa*; and *Cuestión de honor*. None of them survives. After his death, his family, to whom his medical reputation was more important than his playwrighting, burned all his papers.

In the years following, Carlos Frutos (1888–1926) wrote *Para el amor no hay barreras* (1918); and a priest, Arturo Tavarozz (1886–), wrote the patriotic three-act tragedy *El abanderado del Batallón 40* (1922), about the Paraguayan War of 1864–1870. Miguel Pecci Saavedra (1890–), critic and humanist, wrote some excellent plays under the pen name "Arnaldo Miriel," before he exiled himself to Buenos Aires—some say because of López Decoud's violent criticism of his *Mona Lisa y Leonardo*. His plays include the one-act *Los convidados a una cena* (1923); the three-act *María del Carmen* (1925), performed in Buenos Aires; *Mona Lisa y Leonardo* (1927); and the monolog *Manos blancas* (1924).

J. Demetrio Morínigo (1895–) was another dramatist of this period. Among his plays are *Martirios de una madre o La venganza del coronel* (1915), a three-act drama of the Paraguay War; *Sor Felisa* (1920), in three acts set in Venezuela and Paris; a two-act comedy, *Amor que redime*; *El castigo*, in three acts; and a three-act high comedy, *Flor de arroyo*. His most recent plays are *El testamento de don Torcuato* and *Reivindacación*.

Because he began writing dramas at an early age, Benigno Villa (1901–   ) must be included in this chapter. Practically all his plays are set in the country districts, with all or part of each written in the Guaraní language. In collaboration with Juan B. Otaño, Jr., he wrote a comedy, *Chifladuras del día* (1920), followed in 1926 by a bilingual, rural comedy, the *costumbrista Guavirami*. The brief *Kurusu Isabel* ("The Cross of Isabel," 1930), based on a legend about miraculous powers ascribed to a cross placed at the scene of a tragic accident, was followed by the comedies *Apayuai* ("Hodgepodge") and *Anichevene che yvro* ("No Longer a Fool"), both of 1936. *El amor rondaba cerca* (1937), and the three-act *Comedia de aficionados* mark the end of his first period. In 1958 Villa began again with *Casilda*, an Enoch Arden play of the Paraguayan War, published in the first number of the Juvi series of plays started by two young Asunción publishers, Juan Villa Cabañas, the playwright's son, and Manuel Argüello. The series was intended to include the outstanding plays of the Paraguayan repertory. Twelve were announced for 1958–1959, and the fact that *Casilda* had gone into a second edition augured well for the enterprise, but the public failed to support the venture, and it ended. Villa is now working on three new comedies.

Last of this generation was Manuel Ortiz Guerrero (1899–1933), a revolutionary spirit banished, at the age of thirteen, to Brazil, where he contracted an illness that caused his premature death. Though at his best as a poet, and very influential in Paraguayan literature, Ortiz also entered the field of drama with the one-act *Eireté*, performed in Villarica in 1921. It and his other plays are included in his *Obras completas*, published in 1952. They are the one-act tragedy, *El crimen de Tintalila* (Asunción, 1922), and a four-act drama, or historical pageant, *La conquista*, about Ayolas and a Guaraní Indian princess. The latter was performed and published in Asunción in 1926. Concepción Leyes de Chaves, head of the Paraguayan National Library, later dramatized this legend of the princess in *Urutaú*, a sort of Guaraní *Ollantay*, published in Río Lunado (1951).

Unfortunately the public of Asunción was not ready for local drama. They preferred the movies, though they would attend performances of foreign plays. Arsenio López Decoud's translation of *Lady Windermere's Fan* kept the box office busier than anything by Lugo, and traveling thespians from Buenos Aires could fill the theatre for several weeks.

The outstanding Uruguayan actor Carlos Brussa (1887–   )[12] came to Asunción in 1926 with a repertory of twenty River Plate works. He found so much Paraguayan drama available that he included four local plays in his offering. One was the work of Facundo Recalde (1896–   ), *El juguete roto* (1925), a weak play in three acts about an unfaithful wife in Montevideo and her husband's trip to Paraguay. Recalde went on to write *Mujer* (1927), a three-act comedy, first performed that year by the Spanish company of Mercedes Díaz–Arsenio Perdiguero, along with Alsina's *El derecho de nacer* and Josefina Pla's *Víctima propiciatoria. Mujer* was later revived by Báez and his Paraguayan actors. Recalde also wrote the one-act *El no de los niños* (1926), suggested by Moratín's masterpiece, and the three-act drama about conditions in rural Paraguay, *La estafa.*

Another choice of Brussa was a work by the dramatist Luis Ruffinelli (1889–   ), *Sorprendidos y desconocidos* (1924), which some critics consider the first important work of the Paraguayan theatre in Spanish. Its theme is the need to educate women for the problems of life and marriage. The play was first performed October 14, 1924, by the visiting Argentine company of Roberto Ribelli. Ruffinelli later wrote the two-act drama *Victoria* (1926), performed by the Spanish poet and playwright, Francisco Villaespesa, not only in Paraguay but during his South American tour. It justifies divorce. Later, while the Seventh Pan American Conference was meeting in Montevideo, in 1934, Ruffinelli wrote the three-act, satirical *La conciencia jurídica del barrio* about the Chaco War. He considers it his most important work. Certainly it is his most original in its satire of proponents of internationalism whose motives are essentially selfish. Its characters are allegorical and generalized, and the theme can easily be given a universal application. *El Cuarto Poder* ("The Fourth Power," i.e., the press) is a satire which was performed many times in Paraguay by the Karr-Prandi Company with Paraguayan extras, beginning August 2, 1934. In the midst of the Chaco struggle, Ruffinelli also wrote "War Time," first in a Guaraní version, *Guariní ro* (December 4, 1935), and then in Spanish, *Cuando la guerra.* Another war play was the work of Florinda Vargas, published in *El Liberal.* She wrote it, directed it, and acted in it at the Municipal Theatre in 1933.

[12] Angel Curotto, "Carlos Brussa," *Boletín,* No. 12 (March, 1946), 55–62.

But most important among the men whose plays were chosen for production by Brussa was Arturo Alsina (1897–   ), an Argentine-born citizen of Paraguay. His first drama, *La marca de fuego* (1926), shows the influence of Florencio Sánchez in recounting the downfall, through alcoholism, of an aristocratic family. Though melodramatic, it proved its lasting qualities in a successful revival in 1956. In 1926 also, Alsina's *Flor de Estero* was performed by the Argentine company of Defilippis Novoa. Scenes from this poetic comedy about Indians, with touches of Pirandello, were published in *Juventud.* Also in 1926 he directed his own short-lived Compañía de Comedias Paraguaya in his *Evangelista.* In it the actress Angélica Taranto portrayed the daughter willing to sell herself to save the lives of her father and her brother. Then came his Ibsenesque social drama, *El derecho de nacer* (1927), most enthusiastically received. It showed the growing skill of the author—a progress proved by *Intruso* (1934; published 1960), a three-act comedy about an illegitimate older son who is scorned as an intruder by the sisters he has helped to support. Leonor Karr and Victor Prandi performed it in the Teatro Municipal.

After that, lack of available actors discouraged Alsina till 1939 when the possibilities for radio presentation on PROAL (Pro Arte y Literatura), a program directed by Josefina Pla and Roque Centurión, induced him to complete his *La llama flota* and *Fuego en la cúpula.* Since then he has written *La sombra de la estatua* (1940) and, recently, *La ciudad soñada.* Alsina's name is one of the important ones in Paraguayan drama. He was active in establishing the Society of Authors in 1928 and the Autores Paraguayos Asociados in 1951, dissolved as "subversive" by Chief of Police Méndez Fleitas after he failed to get some of his friends included. Literature has long been a bond servant of politics in Paraguay. Alsina was also a member of the Directorial Commission of the Teatro Municipal, that disappointing organization that has done so little to encourage the production of Paraguayan plays. But one can understand the scarcity of dramatists in impoverished Paraguay by considering that this important figure in national drama had to turn to his original trade of pharmacist to earn a living.

Josefina Pla (1907–   ) is, like Alsina, an adopted Paraguayan, but more fiercely loyal than many a native-born citizen. Coming at the age of seventeen from the Canary Islands, she integrated herself into the literary life of Asunción. A poetess from an early age, she also wrote her first tragedy at the age of twelve. At that time, she had to conceal it from her scornful father, but later her husband encouraged her to write *Víctima propiciatoria* (1927), which was produced by a visiting troupe in Asunción.

Meantime, Roque Centurión Miranda (1900–1960) had become interested in the theatre. His *Cupido sudando* (1924), now lost, was a romantic one-act farce about a policeman who visited his sweetheart without the consent of her parents. To perform it and other national plays, he organized a troupe of actors with Alsina, Caballero, and Lugo; but discouraged by the meager audiences in Paraguay he went barnstorming in Europe. He returned just in time to take a group of musicians and entertainers to the troops in the Chaco War. Back in Asunción, he established an Academy of Declamation to improve the quality of Spanish spoken by the bilingual Paraguayans. Much later his Academy developed into the Escuela de Arte Escénico, one of whose modern offshoots is TEA (Teatro Experimental Asuceño), devoted to raising the standard of produced plays.

For the stage, Centurión wrote an unpublished play in Spanish, *La vida comienza mañana;* librettos in Guaraní for two musical plays, *Tapyi ocara* ("Country House")and *Ñandutí* ("Lace"), for which José Asunción provided music; and *Tuyú* ("Mud"). But a greater contribution than his playwriting was his founding and directing of several companies of actors and his long struggle to train actors, culminating in 1948 in the establishment of the Escuela de Arte Escénico, in which his silent, but hard-working, partner was Josefina Pla.

He had begun collaborating with her in 1932, in a four-scene revue in mixed Spanish and Guaraní, *Episodios chaqueños.* With her he did his best work. Their local-color comedy, *Desheredados* (1933), through its picture of three generations of the Rodas family attacked the rich people who let the poor Paraguayans fight the Chaco War for them. Then Doña Josefina went to Spain with her husband for a showing of their ceramics. The Spanish Civil War trapped them there and cost her husband his life. Back in Paraguay in 1938, Josefina Pla found the theatre dead because of the Chaco War. In protest against the senseless censorship, she and Centurión wrote *La hora de Caín* (1938). For eight months in 1939 she and Centurión collaborated in radio's PROAL, a daily newspaper of the air with two evenings a

week of plays, both Paraguayan and world drama. In expectation
that the theatre would eventually be revived, the collaborators completed *La huella* and their favorite, *Paterfamilias*, a tragedy of rugged old Martin Sorondo and Romualda, his common-law wife for
thirty-five years.

In 1941 appeared the first light of approaching dawn in the theatre. Shocked by the declaration of the River Plate Theatrical Congress that the theatre was dead in Paraguay, El Ateneo Paraguayo
was created by a merger of two cultural groups, Gimnasio Paraguayo and Instituto Paraguayo. It was dedicated to the development
of national art, music, and drama. It hired Fernando Oca del Valle,
exiled from Spain, to revive the moribund stage, and this small hurricane went to work. Under his enthusiasm the Elenco Teatral came
into being to perform national plays. Following a couple of plays
from Spain, it revived Ruffinelli's *Sorprendidos y desconocidos*. Then,
with the declaration that he found nothing else by local writers worth
performing, Oca del Valle ended the season with Casona and Linares
Rivas, of Spain.

To remedy this lack of local material, a play contest was held in
1942. In it the Pla-Centurión combination made a clean sweep. Their
Aquí no pasa nada[13] won the first prize. The second award went to
their *Sobre en blanco o Paréntesis*, published in *Revista Municipal*
(1960), while their *María Inmaculada*, about a virgin mother, got
honorable mention.

The prize winner was a universal play, taking place in any South
American capital, about a man who cherishes a child which his wife
has had by another man, a temporary lover. Such an un-Paraguayan
attitude is shared by only one other character in Spanish drama,
Orozco in Pérez Galdos' *Realidad* (a later play by George Neveux,
Demanda contra desconocido also deals with a similar situation),
and a major scandal developed when the *Aquí no pasa nada* was
first performed in 1942. Fruit was hurled by the spectators and insults by the critics. Only a few commented on its undoubted merits.

By herself, Josefina Pla wrote a number of children's plays: *El
final de Caperucita* (1944); *Azud, Mazud y Kazud; El rey que rabió;*
and *El príncipe de oro.* For adults she wrote *La humana impaciente*
(1939) about a woman's longing for maternity. Her series of dra-

---

[13] Performed December 17, 1942; published in Asunción, 1945.

matic sketches of eight women was called *Momentos estelares de la mujer* (1949). *Edipo en Nueva York* (1949), *La fiesta en el río* (1949), the dramatization of three episodes from *Don Quijote* (1950), *La tercera huella dactilar* (1952), *El pan del avaro* (1953), and the religious drama *El hombre en la cruz* (1956) in collaboration with "Marcelo Guitart" (José Carlés), are other experiments of this indefatigible woman who also teaches in the school for drama and has just built a little theatre, *El Galpón*, in her patio for the presentation of Paraguayan and other short plays, including her one-act comedy *Una novia para José Vai* ("Ugly Joe"), and *La casa de Pilar Sosa* (1959).

The last twenty years have seen a quickening tempo in the Paraguayan theatre.[14] One of the first of the new generation was Jaime Bestard (1892–   ), by profession an artist, who studied in France and Spain. Upon his return to Asunción in 1935 he taught painting at the Gimnasio Paraguayo and later at El Ateneo Paraguayo. In 1942, when El Ateneo was offering prizes for original national plays, he won with *Arévalo*, a powerful triangle about the orderly of a general. It has been revived several times. Between canvases, this artist has written six other dramas whose publication is promised: *Los gorriones de la loma* (1944), attacking materialism; *Los hilos invisibles*, of man as a puppet; *El día de la verdad*; *Expreso nocturno*; *Capilán Figueredo*; and *La hora H* (1957).

Another important contributor to the contemporary renaissance of the Paraguayan theatre is Juan Ezequiel González Alsina (1919–   ), newspaper editor, lawyer, politician, and Cabinet member. This disciple of Casona began with dramas which had universal themes. His first play, the three-act *La quijotesa rubia* (1945), was called the best Paraguayan comedy of its kind when the Ateneo players introduced it. *El gran rival* (1950), when performed by the same group, was also well received because of its theme, in spite of weaknesses of construction and dialog. Isabel's illegitimate baby is her rival for the affections of the doctor who runs a maternity home for unmarried mothers.

Since 1950 Alsina has turned to national themes in a half-dozen unpublished plays of increasing dramatic power. They include *Cirilo Timoteo*, a romantic play of customs; *Más allá de las casas altas* and

[14] D. M. S., "El teatro Paraguayo," *Paraguay*, I (September, 1957), 21–22, lists actors, directors, companies, and theatres.

La verdad está en nosotros, social dramas; *Bolí,* a war play; and *Ña Patricia,* a political satire like *La conciencia jurídica del barrio* (1956), but one which deals patriotically with the national spirit—a mixture of Indian and Spanish elements. In spite of its excellent humorous dialog it is not up to his first play.

As part of this theatrical renaissance, a new crop of Paraguayan actors also appeared. Products of El Ateneo were Ernesto Báez, Carlos Gómez, and César de Brix among the men, and Nelly Prono, Sara Giménez and Emigdia Reishofer among the women. The last-mentioned joined with Jacinto Herrera in Buenos Aires, and then combined with her brother-in-law, Ernesto Báez, to form their own company. Báez, a product of the Salesianitos group directed by Padre Casanello, was originally an excellent serious actor, but since he found how easily he could make people laugh he has concentrated on humorous roles. Besides acting, Báez has written two comedies: *La tierra es de todos,* and its revision, *A la sombra del yngá* (a tree, 1946), and *La familia Quintana,* rewritten as *La señora del ministro* (1947).

This last comedy turned out to be tragic. El Ateneo had persuaded the government to build it a fine new theatre that was taking form when Báez and the Ateneo troupe performed *La señora del ministro* ("The Minister's Wife"). One of the President's Cabinet, imagining in the play a slight to his wife, cut off the appropriations, and for sixteen years the unfinished theatre has remained a monument to the power of politics in Paraguay.

For Báez, Nestor Romero Valdovinos (1916–   ) wrote his popular farce *Hilario en Buenos Aires* (1948). His next venture, *Más allá del río* (1949), was a failure on the stage. The increasing popularity of the theatre in Asunción is attested by the literary people who began writing plays,[15] even if they were neither performed nor published, like the three social plays in verse by the great poet, Herib Campos Cervera (1905–1953): "El hachero," set in the selva; "Estrella roja"; and the historical "Insfrán."

Augusto Roa Bastos (1918–   ), a short-story writer and author of the fine novel *Las inocentes,* managed to see an Ateneo production of his *Mientras llega el día* (1945), written in collaboration with Oca

[15] Carlos R. Centurión, *Historia de las letras paraguayas.* See especially Vol. III, p. 134.

del Valle, before he went into political exile in Argentina, but his better "Miércoles de ceniza" and "El niño del rocío" remain unpublished and unperformed. Benigno Casaccio Bibolini (1907–   ), author of the novel *La babosa,* wrote one of the best of modern Paraguayan plays, *El bandolero* (1932), called by its author "voces dramáticas" and suggesting Valle Inclán.

By his few plays, José María Rivarola Matto (1917–   ) has also marked himself as a dramatist to be watched. His one-act *Un ataúd para un usurero* started to be humorous but turned out to be metaphysical. *El sectario,* about a human conflict growing out of political sectarianism, was surpassed by another of Paraguay's outstanding national plays, his *El fin de Chipí González* (1954), a modern miracle play concerned with a champion football player about whose fate the Devil and an angel debate.

Most productive of this generation of dramatists is Dr. Manuel Frutos Pane, a journalist and politician who knows how to appeal to the public taste. *Amor imposible* (1954), in four acts dealing with local themes, and the rural *El duelo de los pobres* (1955) were followed by two universal plays, *La lámpara encendida* and *El tesoro de los pobres.* Then he returned to the local scene with a four-act drama bearing the name of a flower, *Pacholí* (1957), but referring to a pretty girl. His *La tejedora de ñandutí* (1956), hailed by some as the first national musical comedy, was really a reworking of an earlier musical comedy dating from the beginning of the century. It, in turn, served as germ for the delightfully melodic *Raida Potí* ("Honorable Country Girl") (1958), performed by Báez and his sister-in-law with Kika da Silva, a student of the Escuela Municipal de Arte Escénico, in the title role. The composer of its melodies, Eladio Martínez, led the orchestra of three harps and three guitars. Its success led Dr. Frutos Pane to try again with the zarzuela *María Pacurí* (1959), which was the hit of the 1959 season, shattering all records with a run of sixty performances. For its thin plot (a foreigner lives with María and decides he wants to marry her), a number of tuneful songs and dances were provided, making an authentic folklore spectacle of rural Paraguay. A new zarzuela, *Reseda,* was prepared for the 1961 season.

Dr. Frutos Pane also wrote some straight dramas. *Pa-i* (Padre) *Ernesto,* won the 1957 Church prize for a religious play. Cynics noted that report of his award appeared in the newspapers two days before the judges' decisions were handed in.

More serious is the work of another young dramatist, Mario Halley Mora (1928–   ), a newspaper editor, whose first plays deal with the national scene. *En busca de María* (1956) never brings María onto the stage. *Mi asesino* was his second play. Carlos Gómez, director of the Gómez-de-Brix troupe, collaborated with him in *Mi grillo y yo* (1957), a comedy with a universal appeal. Halley Mora's *Un traje para Jesús* is a modern miracle play whose chief character is Jesus, disguised as an ordinary citizen trying to achieve civic union and peace and working a miracle with the help of an ignorant Paraguayan chauffeur. It was the favorite of the 1958 season. Originally a prolog explained its significance, but after the first performance it was omitted as unnecessary. The play made up Volume II of the short-lived JUVI publications. Halley's more recent "Setiembre 21" (1958) is still unproduced; however, 1959 saw three plays by him on the Asunción stage. One of the best of his works so far was *Se necesita un hombre para caso urgente*, with good construction and vivacious dialog. A girl advertises her urgent need to marry so she can inherit an estate, but after the legalities are settled he must divorce her. The complications are reminiscent of some Buenos Aires farces, but it was enthusiastically received. Another inheritance problem was the germ of Halley's *Tres nietos para la abuela*, where the heir turns up with three grown grandchildren. It is also fast moving, with amusing dialog, and is more dramatic than his earlier plays. *Cuando Ernesto se hace el loco* was too slapstick for either public or critics.

Now Paraguay is welcoming playwrights who started their careers in 1958. Rogelio Silvero, theatrical critic, produced *Cañón 105*. José Carlés (1927–   ) branched out for himself in the promising *Perdónanos nuestras deudas* (1958); a philosophic monolog, *El hombre y la vida* (1951); and three educational plays for children: *Juguemos al teatro, El censo,* and *Las partes de la oración,* all performed. Padre César Alonso wrote a modern *auto sacramental* in *San Blas* (1942); and Carlos Colombino (1937–   ) has brought surrealism to Paraguay's stage with his one-act *Momentos para los tres* (1958), followed by a two-act drama, *El payaso o la cárcel* (1959). Also Mercedes Jane (1914–   ) has appeared as director and star of her own play, *Nunca es tarde para el amor* (1959), which reveals her capability in all three fields of the theatre.

Perhaps the name of Isaac Rubin should also be mentioned. Between 1956 and 1959 he wrote four poor comedies. The fact that all were performed is a sad commentary on the lack of good plays and good critics in Asunción. In contrast is the work of a naturalized Paraguayan, Mariela de Adler, born in Moscow in 1917, but a resident of Asunción since she was twenty. Extensively acquainted with continental drama, she was successful from the start. Her first attempt, *Juvenilia*, won the 1953 Escuela de Arte Escénico prize. *Payé* was given honorable mention. Her three-act comedy, *El millón*, was performed by Báez, for whom she also wrote the farce *Consultorio astrológico*. *Felicidad para todos* won honorable mention in the Ateneo Paraguayo competition. Señora Adler has completed a total of ten plays, most of them dealing with the national scene, and has become a highly esteemed and active contributor to the Paraguayan stage.

All this has been the Paraguayan theatre in Spanish. But existing beside it in this bilingual nation, and competing with it for attention, is a cycle of drama in the Guaraní language. The Guaraní language appears on the stage nowadays chiefly for comic effects. It is the theatre in Spanish that is showing encouraging signs of activity. National plays are being published, and occasionally bought, but at least the demand by Asunción's reading public for world drama has resulted in a number of new bookstores.

The chief complaint now about the Paraguayan theatre is a lack of good critics. In the last decade of the nineteenth century Otto Pollitzer (1865–1913) came from Trieste, and by his critical articles in his newspaper taught the theatre-going public what to look for. Since then too much criticism has been based on friendship or enmity, providing no help to a practicing dramatist in his striving to improve. This lack of professional criticism is understandable when one learns that the salary of the drama critic on Asunción's leading newspaper is $8 a month. However, optimism returns with the thought that the national theatre in this out-of-the-way nation is actually only forty years old. It began with no traditions. It lived in spite of lack of public and private support, through the economic chaos of the war.[16] The dramatists who continued writing without theatres or actors, with only a nebulous dream of some day seeing their plays on the stage, deserve honor. Handicapped, because of distance and an

---

[16] Julio César Pompa Preda, "Éxito del teatro paraguayo," *El País* (August 15, 1958), pp. 7–8.

impoverished country, by inability to have first-hand contact with the living theatre of an outside world, they continue their struggle to keep Paraguayan culture alive. And while they may not yet have produced many outstanding plays, they have completely refuted the charge that the theatre is dead in the interior of South America.

CHAPTER 4

The Guaraní Theatre of Paraguay

More than any other Latin American country, Paraguay is bilingual. Spanish is the official language, but what many of the Paraguayans use and most of them understand is what they call the "confidential speech," Guaraní. Though its original vocabulary, created by the pre-Columbian agricultural Indians, has been expanded through borrowings from Spanish into a poetic language excellent, as they say, for lovemaking, suffering, and fighting, it is hardly a language for scientific expression or precise thinking. Yet in four hundred years the white man's language has been unable to replace it.

There are many reasons for this persistence. When the Jesuits reached Paraguay in 1588, they employed the Guaraní language to instruct the natives. Elsewhere the Indians were eventually forced to learn Spanish, but in the Jesuit empire between the Paraná and the Uruguay Rivers the aboriginal converts were sheltered for nearly two centuries from disturbing contacts with European culture. Their Bible and catechism were printed in Guaraní, and that was the only language to which they were exposed.[1]

Using the theatre for teaching, the priests wrote *loas, entremeses,* and even operas in Guaraní, to be performed by the Indians. Details of one season of drama have been provided by J. Pfutenhauer.[2]

In the *reducción,* or mission center, the Indian actors paraded in the afternoon, dressed in the comic costumes of their roles, whether animal or human. The performances began at eight o'clock in the plaza near the church, where one sheltered box was provided for the authorities. The rest of the spectators sat in a semicircle on the ground. On the first night the plays were *autos sacramentales,* the

[1] For a discussion of the process that resulted in an "ethnic mass of unusual uniformity," see Juan Natalicio González, *Proceso y formación de la cultura paraguaya;* Hipólito Sánchez Quell, *Estructura y función del Paraguay colonial;* and George Pendle, *Paraguay, A Riverside Nation.*

[2] *Die Missionem der Jesuitem in Paraguay* (Gütersloh, 1891), quoted in J. M. Boettner, *Música y músicos del Paraguay,* p. 53.

titles mentioned being *Saint Ignatius* and *San Justo and the Shepherd*. *Entremeses* provided the second night of entertainment, with *The Student* and *The Barber and the Drunkard* on the program.

Even in Asunción there were many performances by Indians. A troupe from the Guaicurúes' reservation performed there in 1611 in plays written by themselves. And the Jesuit chronicler mentions other plays, long and short, dealing with Biblical subjects, especially between 1623 and 1628. Such theatrical activity drew attention to the new converts.

Researchers in the Guaraní theatre can find other data and dates. In 1622, for instance, plays celebrating the canonization of Ignatius de Loyola were directed by Padre Roque González de Santa Cruz, who was later killed by Indians. In 1634 there were not only theatrical performances observing the centenary of the Jesuits, in which the mingling of sacred and profane brought censure from the chronicler Natalicio González, but when the new governor, Pedro de Luengo y de Navarra, arrived, the performance by Indian children to welcome him so amazed his attendants that they could not believe that "children descendants of savage beasts rather than man could have been so well trained in so short a time."[3]

On February 27, 1767, Charles III of Spain decreed the expulsion of the Jesuits. When the order reached Viceroy Buccarelli in Buenos Aires, he rounded up the five hundred unresisting Jesuit priests in his domain, loaded them onto the warship *Príncipe*, and sent them to Rome, leaving their 100,000 Indian parishioners without spiritual guidance. The theocratic empire decayed quickly. Never taught to make decisions for themselves, and with no knowledge of Spanish, the Indians could not fit into the colonial system and so slipped back into the jungle, and for the next half century there are no recorded evidences of Guaraní culture, though the Indians continued to use the language.

After Paraguay's independence in 1811, the governing junta tried to eliminate the Guaraní language and teach everybody Spanish, an attempt nullified by Dictator Francia three years later. In his belief that ignorance was bliss, especially among subjects of a dictator, Francia closed not only the schools but the frontiers against European culture. A different policy, adopted by his successor, Dictator

[3] J. L. Trenti Rocamora, *El teatro en la América colonial*, p. 226.

Carlos Antonio López, in 1842, brought teachers from Spain who might eventually have had the effect of spreading Spanish and displacing the language of the Indians except for the war that ensued. The Paraguayan War brought about a patriotic return to the original language of the country. Newspapers in Guaraní sprang up, poetry in the language flourished, and an anonymous folksong, *Campamento Cerro León*, largely in Guaraní, became the unofficial national anthem. Paraguay's first modern play in Spanish, *Un paraguayo leal* (1858),[4] by Ildefonso Antonio Bermejo (1820–1892), contained many Guaraní expressions in conformity with its avowed purpose "to show the excellent qualities of the rural population."

The war left Paraguay in economic and cultural ruin, with half its population wiped out in battle and with its women outnumbering the men ten to one. No wonder that Guaraní, the "mother tongue," continued its popularity. The impoverished city dwellers, with social barriers destroyed through the rise of the numerous agricultural inhabitants, saw the influx of Guaraní words into their speech, as Spanish terms were also infiltrating the vocabulary of the lower classes. This time it was President Caballero who tried to purify the Spanish. His Reglamento del Colegio Nacional (1886) prohibited all use of the Indian language. But it was one thing to issue edicts and another to enforce them. Even though the upperclass elements of the city were willing to obey, the country people, with limited ambitions and necessities, remained colonial and spoke Guaraní.

This was still the situation in Paraguay in 1910, when the world of the theatre showed signs of more activity than the previous occasional visits of troupes from Buenos Aires. The plays in Spanish, by dramatists who had their eyes on Europe and naturally followed foreign trends, have already been noted. But at the same time came the faint stirrings of a dramatic movement in the Guaraní language, with inspiration sought in the soil of Paraguay.

First representative of the Guaraní theatre was Francisco Martín Barrios (1893–1938). He commenced with short skits, curtain raisers for his longer plays in Spanish, in which he starred. Then in 1922 he wrote *Caacupé*, a sort of dramatic pageant dealing with the celebration of the Day of the Immaculate Conception as observed in the city of Caacupé, about thirty miles from Asunción. He tried to put

[4] Published by H. Kraus, Asunción, 1898.

onto the stage the mingled throngs of worshipers, beggars, and sight-seers from town and country. *Caacupé* has no problem and no strug-gle but, like the Ramón de la Cruz *sainetes* of two centuries earlier in Spain, it recreates the environment, with its humor and color.

Then followed Benigno Villa (1901–   ). After a first comedy in Spanish in 1920, in collaboration with Juan B. Otaño, Jr., he deter-mined to attempt something beyond the light, humorous skit. He wanted to reproduce realistically the life of the rural regions of Para-guay, an aim which meant using both Spanish and Guaraní. The re-sult was the bilingual comedy *Guavirami* (1926), dramatizing the peasant legend that the fruit of that tree was a love charm. The com-edy describes young people on a ranch who go looking for the magic fruit with completely satisfactory results. Following this first Para-guayan attempt at a bilingual play, Villa wrote in Guaraní the rural *Apayuai* (1936), and *Anichevene che yvro* (1936). After that he wrote a few plays in Spanish and then forsook the theatre till very recently. His contemporary drama *Casilda* (1958) has several scenes entirely in Guaraní.

Another dramatist of the Guaraní theatre, who also had other aims than a costumic reproduction of the colorful and quaint was Rigo-berto Fontao Meza (1900–1936), a bohemian who began in Spanish with the one-act social drama *Naufragio* (1924), then wrote a num-ber of sketches and serious short plays in Guaraní that he and his friends performed in the suburbs of Asunción. Among them were *Ye castigá yva* ("The Unpunished") and *Pytagua che retame* ("A Stran-ger in My Country"). Unfortunately the public had not been edu-cated to the serious thesis drama in Guaraní, and his efforts met with failure.

What can be considered the first full-length play in Guaraní was the comedy *Mboraijhú pajhá* ("The Height of Love"), by Felix Fer-nández (1898–   ). The author, a teacher of band music at the Insti-tuto Paraguayo, presented the three-act play so successfully on July 6, 1926, at the Municipal Theatre that it had to be repeated the fol-lowing night. Leads in the cast were Cirina Gómez and a fellow bandsman, Darío Gómez Serrato. Roque Centurión Miranda was the character actor.[5] It too is set in the country and gives a serious pic-ture of rural life. Though in showing dramatists the possibility of

---

[5] Carlos R. Centurión, *Historia de letras paraguayas*, III, 134.

dealing with serious subjects, Fernández made his greatest contribution to the theatre in Guaraní, he also wrote a number of lesser works, which he took on tour to practically every community in the nation that could furnish him a stage. Some, like *Jacinta* and *Mamerta*, bore the names of their chief characters; other titles indicate their theme, like *Jue ocara* ("The Rural Judge"), *Ocara gua pe ocara* ("The Country for the Country People"), and *Paraguay memby* ("A Son of Paraguay"). There was also the brief *Maynumby* ("Hummingbird," i.e., "The Flirt"), and several children's plays: *Perú-i* ("Little Peter"), and *Nda ya veí la escuelape* ("I Don't Like School"). Most of them were played for laughs.

The Chaco War, beginning in 1932, interrupted the development of the Spanish theatre in Paraguay. However, with the war came the revitalization of the Guaraní language. The nation that had been using Spanish in its official proclamations saw the necessity of also employing the language of the Indians to communicate with the country people, on whom the burden of the conflict first fell. The theatre in Guaraní also took on new life, and it might be said to have been purified. There was no longer demand for the frivolous or for the artificial. It had to face the ancient antagonisms: the country against the city, the sacrifices of the rural classes against political chicanery, the blood and sweat on the battlefield against the bureaucracy back of the lines.

Emphasizing this clash came *Episodios chaqueños*[6] by Josefina Pla (1907–   ) and Roque Centurión Miranda (1900–1960), in four bilingual scenes that portrayed life in the trenches as soldiers at the front and behind the lines united before the emotions of danger and sacrifice. Its purpose was to stimulate the citizens' confidence in their army. The performance on November 28, 1932, was so successful that it was repeated the next two nights, an unusual experience for any Paraguayan dramatist.

Josefina Pla is an adopted Paraguayan, who wrote largely in Spanish, but she did provide the libretto for Paraguay's only national opera, *Parasy*, with music by the Czech Otaker Platil, recently deceased. Her collaborator, Roque Centurión Miranda, wrote librettos in Guaraní for two musical plays, *Tapyi ocara* ("Country House") and *Ñandutí* ("Lace"), as well as the tragedy *Tuyú* ("Mud") (1933),

---

[6] Published in part in *El Liberal*, Asunción, 1933.

attacking those who profiteered at home while patriotic soldiers were dying at the front. With the melodramatic subtitle, *Angaipá rembiapó* ("The Work of Sin"), *Tuyú* tells of a widow whose son is sent to the front. The commissioner, that eternal villain of the Guaraní theatre, succeeds in ruining both widow and her daughter. When the son returns from the front with a bullet in his gun for the crooked commissioner, his mother gets between them and is the victim. The subtitle takes away the bite of social criticism by implying that hers was the blame. Some may find the psychology faulty and the dialog at times artificial, but the dramatic structure by an actor who went on to head Paraguay's National School of the Drama (1948) is excellent. In order to reach a wider audience, Juan José Pérez Camino translated this play into Spanish for performances that same year.

Another example of the desirability of two versions of a play in this bilingual nation was a three-act comedy, *Guarini-ro* (1933, produced December 4, 1935), by Luis Ruffinelli (1889–   ), put into Spanish as *Cuando la guerra*. María Pabla, engaged to Juan Andrés, a soldier at the front, finds herself in poverty and want. The commissioner takes advantage of her. The law tries to punish her attacker, ignoring Juan, who has returned with a paralyzed arm, but he determines to take his own revenge and not depend on others. So they are reunited. The author provided a symbolic interpretation of his play: María (the Paraguayan nation) was ravished by the commissioner (Bolivia), who took advantage of the paralysis of his victim's protector. But the imminence of danger restored the power of the people and made them victorious. Even disregarding this symbolism, *Guarini-ro* is the best-constructed piece of the Guaraní theatre.

All of these playwrights wrote sporadically. The outstanding dramatist of this theatre in the primitive language of Paraguay was Julio Correa (1890–1953). His father was the son of a Polish nobleman; his mother belonged to a wealthy Brazilian family. Julio was one of five children, reduced to poverty by the death of his father. He shared the life of the Guaraní-speaking laborers and eventually married a country-born schoolteacher.

Correa first timidly attempted to write poetry. Then in 1931 he produced what he called "Dialogs of the Streets," reminiscent of Ramón de la Cruz, but with social criticism and mordant satire added.

His first contact with the stage was in the role of an old woman in a play in Guaraní. Then his friend Facundo Recalde persuaded some clubwomen to sponsor the performance of a play by him about the exploited and dispossessed farmers. Early in 1933 came Correa's first serious play, *Sandía yvyguy* ("Melon under the Leaves," i.e., "Draft Dodger"), an attack on the injustice of letting the wealthy buy themselves free from the draft and sending the poor to the front. Correa tried to get permission to stage it in the Municipal Theatre, but although the director had rented the theatre for a month to a musical revue from Argentina for twenty-one thousand pesos, he now demanded twenty-five thousand from Correa for a single night. So Correa was forced to construct his own stage of planks on sawhorses in a suburban bar. And since he could not use that location for rehearsals during the daytime, his players, including his wife, Georgina, as the leading lady, practiced in a nearby barbershop during the siesta hour.

The public approved of his courageous protest against fraud and injustice. They recognized his sensitive ear for the dialog of the common people, and though he had no formal training in playwriting— he had read no plays and seen few performances before he started writing—his deep sympathy for the problems of the frustrated and tormented lower classes gave substance and appeal to what he wrote.

Encouraged by his first success, Correa went on with other plays; several more were produced during that same rich year of the Guaraní theatre, 1933: *Yuac-jhu-güi-reí* ("Whom the Lord Loveth He Chasteneth"), *Ña ne mbaera yn* ("For Us Alone"), and his masterpiece, *Carú-pecá* ("Undernourished"). Some critics see in *Carú-pecá* a resemblance to Florencio Sánchez' mighty *Barranca abajo* (1905), and point out that where the proud Zoilo of Sánchez' tragedy is driven to suicide by the injustice and cruelty of others, Caraí (Don) Martínez, in Correa's comedy, with the support of his family, has the will to fight back and triumph. Sánchez' work is superior, however, in that the spiritual course of each individual parallels the economic and social changes in the family. Besides, the Sánchez theme is timeless, dealing with a long-established situation and with universal emotions. Correa wrote well about an unusual situation brought about by external factors and dramatized it for the purpose of criticism and censure.

After belated recognition by the government, and with the Municipal Theatre now at his disposal, Correa went on to produce eleven plays in five years. He occasionally repeated. Characters reappear: the elderly person full of sage advice, the young couple in love, the landowner, the moneylender, and the evil commissioner. None was published, since Correa feared that someone might perform them without his permission. Their titles indicate their content: *Guerra aya* ("During the War"), dealing with the abuses of the families while their men are at the front; *Terejho yevy frente pe* ("Get Back to the Front"), about the temptations of the soldiers on leave; and *Peicha guarante* ("So Must It Be"), about the moral degradation of the city dweller. This last play was recently translated into Spanish by Josefina Pla. Less grim are *Yuac-jhu-güi-reí* ("Just from Being in Love"), *Poa ñanda ya yocoi* ("With a Little Bit of Luck"), and *Honorio Causa* ("On Account of Honorio"), with a jibe at President Morínigo's many honorary degrees. Still unproduced are "Pleito riré" ("After the Trial"), "Yvy yara," ("The Earth's Master"), and "Coa nda ya yocoi" ("This Can't Be Stopped").

In staging his plays, Correa was director, wardrobe manager (improvising because of his scanty funds), scene painter, and occasionally actor. He could always count on a first-night audience, curious about the current target of his indignation.

The events of the war and his reactions gave additional impact to his writing, and because of their social significance he so impressed critics that they proclaimed his the only really national theatre, scorning any possibility of cultural achievement of a theatre in Spanish. With the passage of time, however, Correa's popularity and significance faded. Problems growing out of the civil war of 1947 and subsequent political events made antiquated the rural problems he had treated. The increasing use of machinery and the immigration of other people modified the situations portrayed by him, and though occasionally some dramatist, like Narciso Colman, son of the poet "Rosincrán," writes plays in Guaraní, none possesses the "pathetic realism" and authoritative voice of Correa.

With Correa's retirement, the theatre in Guaraní collapsed. One cannot predict that nothing can revive it, since anything might happen in this idyllic country, but at least now the language is heard on the stage chiefly for comic effects. Even dramatists ambitious for a popular theatre no longer write plays in the language of the Indians. The popular musical comedy of 1958 by Frutos Pane and Eladio Martínez bears the Guaraní title of *Raida potí* ("The Pure Country Girl"), but the lyrics and dialog are in Spanish, and so is the Frutos

Pane-Moreno Gonzales musical play with the title *María Pacurí*, that opened in September, 1959, for a record-breaking run.

How can a bilingual Paraguay truly express itself then? Will it be through one theatre in Spanish and another in the language of the aborigines; or perhaps in bilingual performances like the early *Guavirami* and the more recent *Episodios chaqueños?* Two modern dramatists are attempting to find a solution by offering Guaraní culture in Spanish attire. The war play *Bolí* ("Bolivians") by Juan Ezequiel González Alsina (1919–   ) and the recent amusing comedy of a star football player fought over by an angel and a devil, *El fin de Chipí González* by José María Rivarola Matto (1917–   ), use neither the Castilian of Spain nor the Guaraní of Paraguay but a sort of Guaraní-ized Spanish, intelligible to their fellow-countrymen today while full of the authentic color of the old Paraguay. Perhaps this will be the ultimate course of the theatre in Guaraní as it faces the changes of a modern world.

CHAPTER 5

Uruguayan Drama

The theatres of Uruguay and Argentina are, for practical purposes, usually considered together. The River Plate unites, rather than divides, the region. Luis Ordaz explains the appropriateness of speaking of "el drama rioplatense." After all, dramatists journey back and forth across the river, and those from Montevideo have in the past found it easier to get their plays tried out in the more numerous and active theatres of Buenos Aires.[1] Roberto F. Giusti declared: "Our theatre is one, rioplatense; it is impossible especially today to make a division between Uruguayan and Argentine dramatists." The Argentine Vicente Rossi in 1910 wrote the book *Teatro nacional rioplatense*, while Walter Rela, himself Uruguayan, made no attempt to separate the two dramatic outputs in his meaty *Literatura dramática suramericana contemporánea*.

A few literary historians, however, are more nationalistic. José A. Dibarboure holds out for a separate Uruguayan movement "even before independence, and formalized by an unmistakable manifestation of intellectual processes, taking form in the '90's."[2] He points out that from 1808 on, Uruguay had a sequence of dramatists, decade after decade, and offers to list half a hundred. He follows Alberto Zum Felde[3] in dividing the progress of Uruguay's drama history into three cycles: 1808–1856, 1856–1890, 1890 to the present.

Actually Montevideo had a theatre before it had playwrights. J. C. Sabat Pebet, collector of *realia* concerned with Uruguay's drama, ran upon the story of Manuel Cipriano Melo y Meneses (1740–1813), who built the country's first playhouse.[4] This Lisbon-born adventurer left an unhappy homelife in Brazil to run away to Argentina. At fif-

[1] Luis Ordaz, *El teatro en el Río de la Plata*, p. 37.
[2] José Alberto Dibarboure, *Proceso del teatro uruguayo: 1808–1938*, p. 7.
[3] Alberto Zum Felde, *La literatura del Uruguay*, pp. 70–94.
[4] Juan Carlos Sabat Pebet, *Las bibliotecas de D. Manuel Cipriano de Melo y Doña María Clara Zabala.* See also his "Sobre los orígenes teatrales Montevideanos," *Boletín*, No. 11 (December, 1945), 242–243.

teen he was fighting in the Spanish army. Then by smuggling and slave trading he became wealthy, but Buenos Aires proved perilous, so in 1790 he settled in Montevideo. Having been charmed by the drama while studying navigation in Cádiz as a boy, Melo decided to build a theatre in his new homeland. He sent to his friend Olaguer y Feliu for actors out of a job because of the burning of Buenos Aires' Teatro de la Ranchería the previous year. Melo opened his theatre in 1793 with a performance of Lavardén's *Siripo*. Apparently he continued to operate it, because when he died during the siege of Montevideo, Figueroa referred to him as "rico propietario, fundador y dueño del teatro."[5]

Plays for its repertory could also apparently be found. Sabat Pebet uncovered a list of volumes in the private library of Hermano José Boulet, an Andalusian priest from Santa María. Among his other books were six volumes of Calderón's *Autos sacramentales*.

Once built, Montevideo's Casa de Comedias was a constant problem for Melo, as both governor and the *cabildo* struggled for its control. For one performance the governor refused admittance to the councilmen. They were finally allowed to return to their free boxes, but then the governor insisted that each actor, on his first appearance, must bow to him. The council demanded equal recognition and took the matter to the *audiencia*, or court, in Buenos Aires, which sided with the governor. One dissatisfied councilman journeyed to Spain and persuaded the Consejo Supremo to declare that the theatre belonged to the people and to their representatives, and that the governor had no jurisdiction over it.

At first the Montevideo *coliseo* staged only imported plays. There were no local playwrights. Uruguay's first known dramatist was forced into his craft by circumstances. Juan Francisco Martínez, chaplain of the troops sent by Montevideo in 1806 to drive the invading British out of Buenos Aires, was so proud of the part played by his countrymen that to celebrate the victory he wrote a lyric piece in two acts, *La lealtad más acendrada y Buenos Aires vengada.*[6]

This work by Padre Martínez, performed immediately after the

[5] Francisco Acuña de Figueroa, *Diario histórico del sitio de Montevideo*, I, 243.

[6] First printed in *Parnaso oriental* (Montevideo, 1837), III; reprinted in *Primera Serie, textos dramáticos* (Buenos Aires: Facultad de Filosofía), I, No. II. See also Gustavo Gallinal, "Documentos relativos al padre Martínez," *Revista del Instituto Histórico y Geográfico del Uruguay*, III (1924), 663–691.

withdrawal of the British fleet, before the two hundred spectators who could crowd into Olaguer y Feliu's Coliseo Chico, is more a series of historical reports in various meters than a play. In a setting of a virgin forest, Mars, representing the Argentine army, is congratulated by the nymphs Argentina and Uruguay for his defeat of the British Neptune. Martínez' original idea was to dress the women in military uniforms, but the Coliseo censor, Dr. Domingo Belgrano, refused to allow on his stage any women masquerading in men's clothes. The priestly author also arranged for the performance of his work in Montevideo's coliseum the same year, and suggested that it be made an annual memorial event.

At first, as evidenced by this play, patriotism and politics were more prevalent than literary quality in Uruguay's early plays. Zum Felde looked in vain among the productions of this first period of dramatic history for perspective, comprehension of history, and ability to combine actuality with fiction.

However, a few productions with these qualities did exist: a mysterious "L.A.M." [perhaps Luis Ambrosio Morante (1775–1837)] was the author of a five-act drama in verse, *Idamía o La reunión inesperada*. And Bartolomé Hidalgo in 1816 wrote the first of what he called "unipersonales," *Sentimientos de un patriota*, a sort of monolog about America's struggle for independence, set to music and accompanied by living tableaux.

Ventura de la Vega (1807–1865), who in Spain provided the transition between neoclassicism and modernism with *Hombre de mundo* (1845) and eighty other plays, is sometimes claimed by Uruguay, since he was born in Montevideo. His plays continue to be performed on both banks of the River Plate. Actually he left Montevideo for Madrid at the age of eleven.

The chief figures of Uruguay's first period, among those who remained and wrote in Uruguay, were Acha and Magariños Cervantes. Francisco Xavier de Acha (1828–1888) made his debut with the romantic *Una víctima de Rosas* (1845), while the Argentine Dictator Rosas was still in power. It was followed by his four-act drama *La fusión* (1851), which symbolized the peace of October 8, 1851, between the Uruguayan Blanco and Colorado political parties through the marriage of children of two families that had long been quarreling. The spectacle ended with the playing of the national anthem. Though it was not much of a drama, if Uruguayans had been moved by this playwright's presentation of the sufferings and horrors of fratricidal strife, the nation would not have had to endure another half century of it.

Alejando Magariños Cervantes (1825–1893), best known as a novelist, wrote the comedy *Los percances matrimoniales,* followed by the historical *Amor y patria* (1856), five acts in verse which recounted the episode of the thirty-three patriots who crossed the River Plate in 1825 to free Montevideo from the power of Brazil.

During his exile Pedro P. Bermúdez started a five-act historical drama in verse, *El Charrúa* (1842), about some unrealistic Indians who fought the Spaniards in 1573. Somehow the manuscript got lost, but in 1853 the dramatist rewrote it from memory for performance and publication, with the enthusiastic approval of the censor, Acuña de Figueroa, who wrote:

> Apruebo como censor
> y aplaudo como oriental
> a *El Charrúa* y a su autor;
> y ambos logren prez y honor
> en el teatro nacional.

Unfortunately, in spite of his knowledge of dramatic structure and his ability to write fluent verse, this member of the Bermúdez family did not continue as a playwright.

Washingtón P. Bermúdez (1845–1913) came at the end of Uruguay's first period with his historical, *costumbrista Artigas;* and Heraclio C. Fajardo put onto the stage *Camila O'Gorman* (1856), dramatizing his belief that the woman shot by Rosas' orders in 1848, supposedly for spying and for having a love affair with a priest, was really executed for denying her favors to Rosas and to the priest who was the chief witness against her. The play has more thesis than drama.

Romanticism was the chief characteristic of Uruguay's second period. Earliest of its figures was the poet Eduardo Gordon, who used verse for all his plays with their complicated plots. *Desengaños de la vida* (1858), *La fe del alma* (1866), and *El lujo de la miseria* (1876), *costumbrista* comedies with their criticism of society, are among his best, but his work is practically forgotten today.

The first play written by Orosmán Moratorio, Sr. (1852–1898), was the romantic *Cora* (1877), though his *juguete, Una mujer con pantalones,* was first to be performed. He would have been forgotten, too, as one more minor dramatist and facile versifier in spite of his historical *Patria y amor,* the romantic *Luisa o Las campanas de la aldea* (1878), *Culpa y castigo* (1879), *María* (1880), and the fantastic *En el año 2,000,* if he had not decided to write about gauchos in *Juan Soldao* (1893). His son Orosmán, Jr. (1883–) was a theatre critic under the name "Fox," and author of a half-dozen plays.

The beginnings of the gaucho theatre will be discussed in the chapter on early Argentine drama, but in it Uruguay also played an important and independent part. Even as early as 1790 Uruguay was infamous for its wild outlaws. That year a proclamation in Montevideo called for the raising of a troop to capture these evil people "de todas las costas que llaman guachos o gauderios."[7]

The actor chosen to play the first gaucho in the Carlo Brothers' Circus was an Uruguayan, José J. Podestá (1858–1937), who was born and learned to become a clown and acrobat on Uruguay's southern shores.[8] It was he who added the words to the original pantomime of the gaucho act and afterward carried the script to another Uruguayan dramatist, Dr. Elías Regules (1860–1929), who smoothed it out and later collaborated with Podestá on another gaucho play, *Juan Cuello.* For Podestá, Regules went on to make a dramatic adaptation of the epic poem *Martín Fierro,* and wrote *El entenao* (1890) and the one-act *Los dos guachitos* (1894), in six scenes. Though not well received, they were part of the current gaucho theatre.

Also it was for a Montevideo audience in 1890 that the fiesta scene of *Juan Moreira* was expanded and the *pericón* dance substituted for the original *gato.* Uruguayans were the first to appreciate the national spirit of *Juan Moreira* and to recognize its dramatic values. And, finally, a Uruguayan was the first to attempt an imitation, and so initiate the gaucho theatre. Abdón Arózteguy (1853–1926), a political refugee living in Buenos Aires, became so homesick after attending a performance of *Juan Moreira* that he returned to his room and in three days completed *Julián Jiménez,* about another gaucho

---

[7] Emilio A. Coni, *El gaucho,* III.

[8] Raul H. Castignino, *El circo criollo,* pp. 76–92; and *Centurias del circo criollo,* pp. 27–48.

persecuted by the "authorities," which rivaled the Podestá play and had at least a thousand performances.[9]

Following such models, Moratorio, an experienced dramatist, set down the blood-and-thunder story of *Juan Soldao*, one of the most artistic of the gaucho dramas, or as its author called it, a "Creole-satirical-political drama." It was first performed in Montevideo, November 14, 1893, by Podestá-Scotti Company. This "best of the gaucho plays"[10] has a prolog, two acts of three scenes each, and an epilog. In the prolog, a newspaperman queries a government official concerning mistreatment of the gaucho by authorities, and disguised as a Negro, is permitted to investigate.

His experiences fill the two acts. He sees the commissioner mistreat Juan Soldao and make love to his wife, renege on a bet about a horse race, rig the district elections, and condemn Juan to serve in the army. Juan gets killed seeking his freedom, but first kills the commissioner.

This play put into circulation the saying that the *campo* is habitable only for people with a saber (i.e., authority). It was printed in Moratorio's *Obras dramáticas* (1896), and in the *Revista de la Comisión de Teatros Municipales* (1960), a review published for a while to make available the out-of-print masterpieces of the Uruguayan theatre.

Best representative playwright of the romantic period of Uruguay's drama and the author perhaps most likely to please today's audiences was Samuel Blixen (1868–1911), poet and critic who brought to the theatre in prose the viewpoint of a man of culture with good technique and an optimistic philosophy, though he displayed few national traits. His inspiration was Ibsen. His flaw is lack of action, except in *Ajena* (1898). His first attempt, *Un cuento del tío Marcelo* (1891), had its première presentation in an Italian version. He was more successful with his comedies *Ajena* and *Jauja* (1895). His best work is a *Suite de las cuatro estaciones*, which began with *Primavera* (1896) and *Verano* (1899); the last two, *Otoño* and *Invierno*, were not written till the next century.

Other Uruguayan dramatists who linked the romantic period to

---

[9] Dora Corti, *Abdón Aróztegui*.

[10] Fernán Silva Valdés, "Los primitivos en el teatro uruguayo," *La Prensa*, December 21, 1958.

the realistic period that came next include José Cándido Bustamante, with *La mujer abandonada* (1876); and Estanislao Pérez Netto, with *Apariencias y realidades.*[11]

One other important Uruguayan dramatist appeared before the end of the century. Victor Pérez Petit (1871–1947) did most of his writing in Buenos Aires, where he produced dramas and thesis comedies with both rural and urban settings. Moderation and sentimental psychology characterize most of the plays in his eleven-volume *Obras completas* (Montevideo, 1942–1944), and many of them have an air of the library, where he spent so many years. Of his plays beginning with *Yorick* and ending with *Claro de luna,* the best is probably *La rondalla,* but Pérez Petit takes his place among gaucho dramatists with *¡Cobarde!,*[12] set in 1852 in the *estancia* of Cerro Largo in his native Uruguay. Podestá-Scotti introduced it in Montevideo in 1894.

In *¡Cobarde!,* the old revolutionist has taught his son Pedro that a gaucho's chief possession is his honor. Natividad gets Pedro's promise not to harm her father, a promise kept even when the father threatens Pedro with a whip at the fiesta. Pedro's own father, misunderstanding, calls the boy a coward and kills Natividad's father.

In the original version, Pedro, scorned by everybody and learning that the police have killed his gaucho father, commits suicide, an act the critics called illogical and counter to gaucho psychology (*Barranca abajo* was later criticized for the same flaw). In 1912 Pérez Petit revised the ending, to make Pedro sacrifice his life to save his father from the authorities.

¡Cobarde! was a forerunner of plays in the third cycle of the Uruguayan theatre, plays of the common people, told in the vernacular. Society had changed. No longer did the Banda Oriental contain gauchos in rebellion against society. Its rural sections were now populated by farmers, superstitious perhaps, and uninterested in progress, but at least law-abiding. Realistic drama about them started with Florencio Sánchez, who put an end to the artificial, romantic imitations of European models.

Patriotic Uruguayans, like Dibarboure, point out that Sánchez was born in Montevideo and passed twenty-five of his thirty-five years on Uruguayan soil. He chose it as the setting for *La gringa, Ba-*

[11] Agustín del Saz, *Teatro hispanoamericano,* I, 297–304.
[12] Published in *Máscara,* No. 50 (November, 1944); and in *Revista de la Comisión de Teatro,* No. 5 (1960).

rranca abajo, En familia, and *Marta Gruni.* And if most of Sánchez'
plays were first performed in Argentina, it was only because there
was a more thriving theatre there. Sánchez' work, however, is discussed separately, in Chapter 8. The Uruguayan theatre owes him
neither ideas nor technique. Another Sánchez would be an anachronism, a step backward, and the search for one has delayed the
development of dramatists in his country. They could imitate better
models.

Among the half-dozen River Plate plays that stem from him is the
first work of the schoolteacher José Pedro Bellán (?–1930), *¡Dios te
salve!* (1920), a three-act, dated tragedy about Petrona, who sacrifices herself for the drunken husband who deserts her, and about her
two children. *Amor,* a drama; *Vasito de agua,* a comedy; *La ronda
del hijo; Interferencias;* and what some consider his masterpiece, *El
centinela muerto,* are also by Bellán. He also wrote less realistic plays,
like *Blanca Nieve,* for children.

Of all the Latin American dramatists, however, the one who might
best be termed Sánchez' successor was a fellow Uruguayan, Ernesto
Herrera (1886–1917), who paralleled Don Florencio in many ways,
and whose first play was performed the year of Sánchez' death. Both
writers were brought up in poverty and misery. Both were self-educated and both had newspaper training. Their bohemian customs
were similar. They were the only two dramatists ever sent abroad for
training at government expense, and even in the premature deaths
that ended their careers they were alike.

An illegitimate child, Ernesto Herrera got what schooling he could
in the office of the anarchistic newspaper *El pueblo,* where he was
especially influenced by Gorki, whom he tried to resemble. Initially
a poet, he then wrote a collection of stories, *Su majestad el hambre*
(1910), which he appropriately labeled "cuentos brutales." To better treat the problems of the social outcasts of his time, he finally
turned to drama.

Herrera's first attempt, *El estanque,* in 1910, the year of Sánchez'
death, is a "truculent drama" about two young people falling, through
ignorance, into incest. It is the most romantic of his output, in addition to its symbolic use of crows, willows, and the pool in which
Belisario's mistress and mother of his unclaimed son commits suicide.
Herrera's first play, with its opening act synthesizing life in rural
Uruguay and with its dramatic final scenes, provides a foretaste of

the rest of his plays, even to the flaw of unrealistic portrayal of educated people and their conversation—a trait which again links him with Sánchez.

Mala laya (1910), written in one day to earn an advance of fifty pesos (Sánchez, too, dashed off plays under pressure), is the melodrama of Samuel, whose land is stolen and daughter dishonored by the wealthy *patrón*, José María. The violent gaucho, knife in hand and illegitimate grandson beside him, confronts the rich man and demands justice for both wrongs.

Next came *El león ciego* (1911), a high point in Uruguayan drama, written when Herrera was twenty-two. It has been reprinted, appropriately, in Año I, No. 1 of the *Revista de la Comisión de Teatros Municipales* (1958). For the old *caudillo* Gumersindo, product of the gaucho code of courage, there is no place in times of peace and civilization. He resembles Zoilo of Sánchez' *Barranca abajo*, except that Herrera was interested in psychology and Sánchez in portraying the ambient. The dramatist, while revealing his repugnance at the situation, fails to give sufficient power and artistic expression to his feelings. However, the dialog, in spite of many localisms now interesting chiefly to a philologist, is vigorous. Many historians believe that the decrease in the number of bloody political clashes between Blancos and Colorados in Uruguay after 1911 was due to this play's dramatic argument against the senselessness of violence. Herrera was more convincing with his message than Acha had been in *La fusión* half a century earlier.

La moral de misia Paca (1911) maintains that conventional morality often glosses over misery. Its basic idea is not original—a young girl married to an elderly invalid—but the self-centered mother is one of the author's best-developed characters, with a psychological verity that makes readers regret that Herrera did not develop this vein. It is true that in handling the idea as a surgeon handles a case, he does weaken the drama, but it follows the Sánchez manner, with good dialog and an advance in technique over some of Herrera's earlier efforts.

After writing it he was sent to Europe by the Uruguayan government, and in Madrid he attempted a drama about a seduced woman of a middle-class family. *El estanque* had pictured the results, *El pan nuestro* (1912) dealt with the causes. For the sake of her family, the woman gives up happiness, and even honor. As she receives in return only uncomprehending hatred, Herrera follows the steps that lead her to suicide. Some critics believe *El pan nuestro* to be Herrera's best play, with a second act that demonstrates his maturing technique, but Madrid theatre managers turned it down as too bitterly realistic, and even when later performed in Montevideo it never achieved the popularity of *El león ciego*.

During much of his life, Herrerita, as his friends called him, had been sickly. Lack of food and irregular hours had weakened him. His hacking cough had been practically a trademark, and when, upon his return from Europe, he went to a Montevideo clinic for what he thought a sore throat, it was diagnosed as advanced tuberculosis. He died not long afterward. Before the year ended, a volume, *El teatro uruguayo de Ernesto Herrera,* was published in Montevideo (1917) through the contributions of his friends.[13]

Since Herrera's death, according to Hugo Pedemonte, "Uruguayan drama is a frustrating compilation of ambitions."[14] Some dramatists have had more ambition than others and are represented by a larger number of titles than are those who became discouraged after a few attempts. Listed in some sort of chronological order, one of the first names of the twentieth century is a cosmopolitan. Otto Miguel Cione[15] (1875–1945) was born in Paraguay, became an Uruguayan citizen, and lived most of his life in Buenos Aires. He treated themes as diverse as gauchos and philosophy in well-constructed plays, mostly performed in Buenos Aires, though his earliest play, *El gringo* (1904), had its genesis in Montevideo. Cione became more realistic in *Partenza, Paja brava,* and *Gallo ciego.* In the three-act tragedy *El arlequín* (1908), he reveals his acquaintance with Ibsen's *Ghosts.* It is more carefully constructed than some, with keen observation but not much dramatic movement, even though through the inherited

---

[13] See also Carmelo M. Boner, *El teatro de Ernesto Herrera*; Samuel Eichelbaum, "Ernesto Herrera," *Cuaderno,* No. 4 (1936), 31–48; George O. Schanzer, "Vida y obras de Ernesto Herrera," unpublished thesis, University of Iowa; Schanzer, "A Great National Drama of Uruguay," *Modern Language Journal,* XXXVIII (1954), 220–223. For a comparison between Herrera and Sánchez, see Arturo Berenguer Carisomo, *Las ideas estéticas en el teatro argentino,* p. 374.

[14] Hugo Pedemonte, "Panorama de la actual literatura uruguaya," *Panorama das Literaturas das Américas,* II, 817.

[15] For Cione's biography and list of plays, see *Boletín,* No. 18 (October, 1945), 35–36.

results of alchoholism the father goes crazy and the son turns out to be an idiot. Pablo Podestá produced it in 1908.

Among Cione's long list of twenty-six plays, the reader will find most rewarding: *La barca errante, Clavel del aire, Casa de vidrio,* and *La rosa de Jericó.* One of his contacts with Sánchez was in the one-act-play contest of 1906, for which Florencio Sánchez wrote *Moneda falsa,* Cione's *Presente griego* won the judges' votes, though many letters to the newspapers later expressed preference for Sánchez' entry. This type of contest had become popular since 1887 when Vital Aza began pulling titles out of a hat in Madrid for competing dramatists to develop into one-act plays. Clara della Guardia introduced the idea to Buenos Aires in 1899. In 1903, in the José de Podestá competition, Coronado won with *Culpas ajenas,* while among the twenty-seven River Plate dramatists for whom Gregorio de Laferrère provided titles in Buenos Aires in 1906, plays by Uruguayan dramatists Cione and Sánchez won the official and the popular decision.

Another Uruguayan who found the Argentine theatrical scene more attractive was Carlos Mauricio Pacheco (1881–1924),[16] author of seventy lively and colorful *sainetes criollos* completely national in spirit and detail. Following Trejo and Soria, he started in 1900 with a pantomime, *Blancos y colorados,* written for a circus in Montevideo. Later, with Pedro Pico he wrote the *sainete Música criolla* (1906) and himself sang the leading role. From that same year came his most representative *Los disfrazados,*[17] with music by Antonio Reynoso, set in a Buenos Aires carnival and introducing the kindly Don Pietro, who never made fun of others but was deceived by his pal, Machín. The title comes from the observation by one character that everybody wears a mask. Pietro's exclamation: "Eh! Miro l'humo" became a slang phrase to cover one's unhappiness.

Pacheco used to tramp the streets of Buenos Aires at night to learn "the moral and spiritual aspects of the anonymous soul of our country." He set them down in such plays as *Don Quijote en la pampa* (1907). Among his best plays are *La ribera* (1910); *La Mazorca* (1915), about Rosas' secret police; *Vida inútil* (1918), *Pájaros de presa,* and *Los equilibristas,* which reveal the influence of Ibsen and

---

[16] Martín Lemos, "Tres figuras del viejo sainete criollo," *Boletín,* No. 28 (January, 1950), 18–21.

[17] Reprinted in *Bambalinas,* No. 49 (March 15, 1919).

Sánchez. While his characters are more human than those of Sán-chez, Payró, and Sánchez Gardel, his attempts to please his audience sometimes resulted in cheap comedy, melodrama, or falsification of the Argentine scene.

Sánchez was also the model for Vicente Martínez Cuitiño (1887–) especially in the dull plays of his early period where he followed the technique of a dramatist whose technique was his weakest point. Under morbid surroundings weaklings succumbed to the pressure of society. *Mate dulce* (1911) presents a villain born to be hissed, as Fernando and his chum get the mother drunk so they can take the daughters out for some fun.

Malón blanco, winner of the 1922 Buenos Aires Municipal Prize, presents more morbid people in Giuseppe's inn. The Italian is trying to sell his daughter to a wealthy patron, in spite of her determina-tion to marry a jailbird. However she finally turns out to be a gold digger. More sprightly is *El espectador o La cuarta realidid* (1928), considered the first vanguard play of the River Plate. It is largely a discussion of the facts of life by artists and authors in a nightclub, with the Spectator frequently interrupting them. The title implies that a fact has one social reality, the drama gives it a second, the in-terpreting actors a third, and the Spectator feels it as a fourth reality.

Born in Uruguay, Martínez Cuitiño went to Buenos Aires as a child and turned to the stage. He directed the Camila Quiroga company during its tour in Spain. Many famous actors have appeared in his plays. Benavente directed his *El segundo amor,* to star María Melato in Lola Membrives' company. *El amigo Raquel* gave Paula Singer-man a chance to play a "flapper" in Argentina before that type hit the North American stage. Pablo Podestá starred in *La fuerza ciega*, in which a seduced girl marries the son of her seducer and tries to per-suade the young man to kill his father.

The American critic Mildred Adams considers this the best play by Martínez Cuitiño, though she also admires *El derrumbe* and *Rayito de sol*. Perhaps the best of his social plays is *Diamantes que-brados* (1934), with brave Rosina trying to redeem an unpleasant and decadent family. The poetic *Horizontes* (1934) presents Zaida, who can look into the future for happiness for others but who finds only sorrow for herself. Most of Martínez Cuitiño's characters, how-ever, are unsympathetic, so that his comedies are as gloomy as his tragedies. A major part of his plays have been published. They neither rise to a dramatic pitch nor provide a sense of resolution. While his dialog flows smoothly, it contains little humor or revelation of character. He has made his greatest contribution to River Plate drama by his untiring work as director of theatres and encourager of actors and dramatists during his long years as president of Argentores, Argentina's organization of dramatists.

Edmundo Bianchi (1888–   ), careful writer and excellent observer, has spent most of his life away from Uruguay as a diplomatic representative. Yet he has had time for sixty original plays and at least a hundred translations from four languages. His version of *Tartuffe* was especially admired. He began with the two-act, social *La quiebra* (1910), a great success in Montevideo. His *Perdidos en la luz* (1913), in four acts, introduced first in Buenos Aires, denies that a man has a right so to lose himself in science as to forget life and its obligations.

Many of Bianchi's plays have received Uruguayan awards, beginning with *El hombre absurdo* (1932) that reverses the *O locura o santidad* theme. *Los sobrevivientes*, a *misterio*, was declared the best Uruguayan play of 1939, and had a long Buenos Aires run. In six scenes, it presents the annual banquets of aging people till the last survivor dies toasting the past. But even at that moment, Lila, sweetheart of the law student Miguel, feels the birthpangs of a new generation.

During the World War II Bianchi's plays *Sinfonías de los héroes* (1940) and *El oro de los mártires* (1941) won Uruguayan National Theatre prizes. The motto on Bianchi's bookplate, "Pienso alto; siento hondo," might well serve as the description of his drama.

The first work of Uruguayan-born Carlos María Princivalle (1887–) after *El desertor*, performed 1908 in his native Salto, was a robust story of Spanish conquest in Peru, *El último hijo del sol* (1915). An Uruguayan company took it on tour to Lima. Later Princivalle turned to rural drama like *El toro* (1922) and its superior sequel, *El higuerón* (1924), in which a thieving farmer engulfs his neighbor's land. In the lawsuit, the commissioner sides with wealth, but drought and locusts provide fitting punishment and drive the thief's son to suicide. For the wronged landowner, science, pest control, and irrigation, provided by the brother-in-law Timoteo, promise an optimistic outcome to the problem of land for everybody.

Witty comedies like *El despertar del nene, Antropos o El animal hombre, El hombre natural,* performed by the National company, and *Juan* (1948) in which three old maids talk about a long-dead sweetheart, Juan, as if he were still alive, showed one side of Princivalle, in contrast to his vigorous *El blasón* and *Caín y Abel* and the delicate and moral farcical version of the old Spanish play, *Los títeres de Maese Pedro.* And in addition, as president of Uruguay's Society of Authors and professor of the History of the Theatre in the Municipal School of Dramatic Art, he contributed to the success of both new and arrived dramatists.

Francisco Imhoff (1880–1937) cultivated high comedy and wrote static, drawing-room plays. He began with a play of civil war and gauchos, *Sangre de hermano* (1917). The hero of the comedy *Cantos rodados* (1918), his best play, is an aging man wasted morally, spiritually, and physically; yet he takes a young wife. The dialog is good, but it sidesteps the obligatory clash of passions, and so it reads better than it plays. Imhoff also wrote the feminist *Las dos llamas* (1924), *El himno de la vida,* and the controversial *Eutanasia* (1927), which deals with both mercy killing and the subconscious.

Carlos Salvagno Campos (–1956) while a minor dramatist, reveals literary qualities in such plays as *La salamandra* (1925), about a woman who wants a son; *Don Juan derrotado* (1927), who was restored by his loving wife; and *La mujer solitaria* (1928), about Claudia and her search for love.

With the name of Ismael Cortinas (1884–1940) is associated a long list of plays, beginning with his greatest Argentine success, the one-act *El credo,* written at the age of nineteen, and including *René Mason, Fuego sagrado, La rosa natural, Oro muerto,* and *Una farsa cruel.* He wrote *Cosas de América* for Roberto Casaux.

Yamandú Rodríguez (1889–1957), most Creole of the poets, made a name with his poetic drama *1810,* performed in Teatro Solís in 1917. In *Frayle Aldao* (1933) he sacrificed poetry and improved drama in its story of the love of Luciano and Joaquina, with complications provided by General Félix Aldao, governor of Mendoza during the period of Rosas. The certainty of death provides breathtaking suspense. Its sequel, *El matrero,* with music by the Argentine Felipe Bueno, has several times been performed at Teatro Colón.

Justino Zavala Muniz (1898–   ), author of several excellent *costumbrista* novels, and senator or exile depending on the political party in power, turned to *La cruz de los caminos* (1933) to express his beliefs about *latifundia*. Its four acts and twenty scenes show the government's unwillingness to take land from the wealthy for the poor. So Telemaco, the gaucho, victim of the villainous Victoria, leaves with his wife, Jesusa, in search of a region without poverty and with a new song for gaucho singers.

When the government refused to allow young people to attend Zavala Muniz' *En un rincón del Tacuari* (1938), because of its theme of incest in the pampas, the indignant author rang down the curtain and published the play, with comments in articles and letters, one of which saw in the attempt of Candido against his daughter, as Deshecho and Paula look helplessly on, a fable about the League of Nations.

Hopelessness is the theme of *Alto alegre* (1940), concerned with the daily life of a miserable pampa settlement, some of whose citizens seek solutions in the stars, others in suicide. In *Fausto Garay—un caudillo* (1942) Zavala Muniz tells the tragic story of a gaucho and his Indian, Mansilla. Deserted by his promised supporters, Garay goes down in defeat in his efforts to uphold justice on the pampas.

In all his plays, Zavala's prose, while beautifully expressed and breathing life into his characters, does not move them to the dramatic clash that is required for drama, and though realistic, they are not moving. But Uruguayan drama owes much to this champion of the theatre who has always been eager to help the beginning dramatist and to fight for an uncensored stage.

Realism carried to its utmost appears in the works of two collaborators signing their plays "Borges, médico rural," and "Elsa Fernández, maestra rural," from Tacuarembó in the north, where their plays are set. After a beginning with two tragic novels, they invaded the theatre with *Loj infelice* (1940) and *Tierra ajena* (1942), which was awarded the Ministry of Education prize. In dialect, of which its title is a sample, and which is spoken by all except the rural schoolteacher, *los infelices* recount their unhappy lives. The play is aptly subtitled "Tres angustias en siete cuadros." The other play with "dos angustias y una esperanza" discusses the lies of political candidates, and cruel Nature that drives the peasants from their small farms. The *esperanza* comes through the efforts of the young "doctor" to get the government to confiscate and distribute the acres of the big landowner, an effort that brings death to the fighter for the farmers. These

plays are gloomy and the number of scenes makes the action disconnected, but they were written for a purpose.

More productive has been Juan León Bengoa, born in Montevideo
in 1895, who began in 1921 with a prizewinning comedy, *Los sacri-
ficados*, performed in Teatro Solís. Then he went to Madrid to study
law and to Buenos Aires in a diplomatic capacity, where he attended
the production of a number of his plays: *Las vestales, La grieta*
(1924), *Una mujer en la casa*, (with Pedro Pico in 1924), *La inmaculada,* and others. He returned to Spain in 1928 where *Labios
pintados, La danza de la osa mayor,* and *Nadie sabe quien era* were
performed by his own company. Too busy as a lawyer for the next
six years to write more, he eventually returned to Montevideo and
the theatre with *Tu vida y la mía* (1934) and other successes, including *La espada desnuda* (1949) about civil war between 1876 and
1880, and *La patria en armas* about Artigas, called the best play of
1950, and *Golillas rojas,* performed in Teatro Artigas.

After directing the radio theatre SODRE, Bengoa founded a "little
theatre," San Antonio, in 1957, which opened with another of his
many historical plays, *La sandalia de madera*, set between 1818 and
1832, with its chief character the Franciscan monk Castañeda. In another vein, Jorge Luis Borges (1899–) collaborated with Dr.
Adolfo Bioy Casares (1914–), better known as a novelist, in what
they called "dos films," really movie scripts, published in 1955, both
of them satires: *Los orilleros*, like the scenario for a gaucho movie,
and *El paraíso de los creyentes*, a script for a gangster melodrama
that takes its name from the phrase which means to designate ("fin-
ger") somebody to be killed. Both are experimental plays intended
to be read rather than performed.

Also along experimental lines is *Farsa* (1938), by the diplomat and
fiction writer Adolfo Montiel Ballesteros (1888–), first performed
in Buenos Aires' Teatro del Pueblo in 1935. He sought realism
through puppets, with seven "fantoches," including a poet, reporter,
merchant, etc., and seven "notables," and with the first two acts taking place A.D. 5,000. The outstanding farces of the Uruguayan theatre,
however, are the work of Eduardo Blanco-Amor, published in 1953.
They include *Amor y crímenes de Juan el Pantera*, a sort of Punch
and Judy story, and *La verdad vestida* (1942), about Society and the
State at odds, and containing the observation that if Truth ever took

off her clothes, she would be arrested. In *Angélica en el umbral del cielo* (1943), the author debates human imperfection versus divine perfection as Angélica yearns to return from eternity to the anguish and sorrow of human love.

The decline of the theatre of Argentina has also brought soul searching among the writers across the Río de la Plata. In July, 1958, some candid opinions were voiced during a round-table discussion by actors and authors seeking reasons for the lapse of the Uruguayan national theatre as a popular spectacle. The common opinion was that the country was a consumer, not a creator of culture. According to some speakers, one difficulty was the eternal search for someone to fill the gap left by Florencio Sánchez. The critics judge each new local dramatist by the norms applied to experienced playwrights from abroad. Dramatists at the conference pleaded for tolerance and a lower level of expectation, especially since experience is hard to acquire in a country where playwriting is not profitable enough as a profession to allow a person to dedicate himself to it alone.

Discussing choice of themes, some complained of the lack of atmosphere in Montevideo. Jacobo Langsner (1924–   ) set his *Los elegidos* on the top floor of the Empire State Building, not in Montevideo's Palacio Salvo. But, by contrast, Otermin used Montevideo powerfully in his *Ruina en la casa Ocampo*. One playwright, citing Shakespeare's international appeal, insisted that it is the Uruguayan spirit, not the theme or scene, that makes for its strictly national drama. Another suggested that narrow regionalism is avoidable when a writer selects a theme interesting to everybody. These are thoughts applicable to dramatists throughout the Hemisphere.

But the discussion underscored the undeniable present activity in Uruguay's theatrical life. One reason is the large number of theatres now available and seeking local plays. Stirrings could be first seen when the Teatro Solís, deteriorated and closed during the Second World War, was repaired and reopened in 1947. At the same time the government began sponsoring a national company of actors, La Comedia Nacional, that not only performs in Montevideo but takes national plays on tour to Buenos Aires and even to Chile and Peru. In eight years the company introduced seventy plays, classical and modern, with at least one Uruguayan play to balance every foreign title, as required by law. To discover plays, it has sponsored con-

tests in which as many as a hundred manuscripts have been submitted. To the "half hundred Uruguayan dramatists" from 1805 on,
as suggested by Dibarboure, Alberto Ruscone adds an equal number
in his "Resumen de la literatura Uruguaya en el siglo actual."[18] To
copy the list would mean little. Many on it will be content with the
plays they have already written. Only a few will continue to write,
and from them will come the names that some future historian of
Uruguay's theatre will be proud to set down.

The Municipal Theatre also established a theatrical school to provide new blood. Some graduates have joined the national company.
Others work with the dozen or more experimental theatres at which
Argentines look enviously when they admit that there is more theatrical activity on the east bank of the River Plate than in Buenos Aires.

Most famous, perhaps, of these playhouses is El Galpón (1951),
that has been offering three performances a week. Another is El Teatro Circular, in which the painter Hugo Mazza began as stage de-
signer and ended as unpaid director. After an auspicious start, internal
dissent, the enemy of these unpaid amateur groups, brought about a
split-off of part of the company to establish El Nuevo Teatro Circular.
The division of talent explains the uneven quality of acting in a 1959
translation of *Vestido da noiva* (1943) by the Brazilian Nelson Ro-
drigues. I joined two hundred people for the première that started a
half-hour late at ten o'clock and continued till twelve–forty-five.

Most Uruguayan experimental theatres use translated foreign hits
and avoid plays by local writers, who are on hand to demand a percentage from the box office. However, dramatists still persist and
some of them get a hearing from the amateur groups. Four recent
playwrights include Judge Juan Carlos Patrón (1906–   ), whose
Procesado 1040 (1957) deals with legal injustice; Angel Curotto
(1902–   ), experimenter along many lines with at least a hundred
plays, including *Gato con botas* for children; and Ernesto Pinto
(1908–   ), whose poetic religious plays, *El bosque librado* (1948)
and *La última puerta* (1951), were accepted for performance by
Comedia Nacional. The 1962 winner of the Teatro Municipal prize
was Novas Terra, author of *El jasmín azul*. Earlier plays by him include *M M Q H*, *Pan y circo*, and the hit *Todos en París conocen*.

[18] Alberto Ruscone, "Resumen de la literatura uruguaya en el siglo actual,"
Panorama das Literaturas das Américas, II, 779–806.

The names of two other dramatists ought to be added to complete the picture of Uruguay's drama. Hector Plaza Noblía (1924–   ), associated with the Experimental Teatro de Cámara as an actor, is also a dramatist with a long line of titles. His first, *El cono de luz,* was successfully performed in Teatro Solís in 1951. Then came *El puente, La clave perdida, Ensayo No. 4, Odiseo, La casa quinta* (1953), and the one-act *Cajita de música,* with three characters, chiefly Roberto who refuses to let his sister Berta play the music box since it brings back the unhappy memories of his youth.

Latest of Plaza's theatre of ideas, with few characters and little action, is *Alcestes o la risa de Apolo* (1955), dealing with another character who refuses to face reality. He makes an imaginary statue of Apollo, ignoring the real one.

The most recent literary figure to emerge as an important Uruguayan dramatist is Fernán Silva Valdés (1887–   ), who gained fame as a nativist poet back in 1921.[19] Deciding, at the age of sixty, to use his thorough acquaintance with the gauchos to put them onto the stage, he wrote *Santos Vega,* which was performed by Comedia Nacional in Teatro Solís in 1952, and in summer theatre, 1953–1955, along with Calderón and Lope. Most critics consider it his best work.

The traditional Santos Vega was a gaucho minstrel so successful in poetry competitions that when he was finally defeated, it was believed to be by the Devil in disguise. A dramatized version by Juan Nosiglia, from the novelized story by Eduardo Gutiérrez, was performed in 1890 amid the stream of gaucho plays. Silva Valdés made his Vega a Creole Faust, sinning through pride in his singing and losing his soul through treachery to the Devil. The plot is expanded by the inclusion of two daughters of a Galician country storekeeper, both of whom strive for the love of the gaucho singer, while the wealthy landholder, Don Pedrito, schemes to get Flor. Vega is interested only in arranging a singing contest with Juan Sin Ropa, which occupies the final act. Unbeaten by the Devil's representative, Vega is finally slain by the Devil and whisked away so that he may become a legend. When the two girls kneel beside the dead gaucho, they discover that his body has disappeared, along with that of Juan Sin Ropa. In this mystery play, with its kinship to the moralities of the Middle Ages,

[19] Agustín del Saz, *El teatro del poeta nativista del Uruguay.*

Silva Valdés intended to represent Vega as another fantasy formed by popular imagination.[20]

Other plays by Silva Valdés have a similar link with the past. His *Los hombres verdes* (1956) is called "misterio de la selva misionera." *El burlador de la pampa* is a "misterio del medioevo platense," and *Por la gracia de Dios* (1954) has a subtitle: *Comedia mágica*. *Los hombres verdes,* based on a Guaraní Indian legend, presents the conflict between carnal and spiritual love in the jungles of Misiones. The action happens offstage as harvesters of the maté (tea) leaves decide to make some spare money by collecting heron feathers, but instead they capture an angel, and for awhile their adoration of her makes them forget earthly women.

Silva Valdés was one who, like the Argentine Laferrère, began writing excellent plays with only a short apprenticeship. True, he did first produce *Una limosna por Dios* which he termed "un simple ensayo primitivo." Like his *Pulgarcito,* it was never printed. *Por la gracia de Dios* (1957) reveals at times a lack of sureness, and *Los hombres verdes* fails to get all the possible dramatic suspense out of the situation.

His attempt at a modern drama, *Barrio Palermo* (1953), was greeted by critical opinions that so much local color and carnival atmosphere had been introduced into the last two acts as to make them slow and undignified; even so, the whole play is so short that a ballad had to be written as prolog. It was first presented as a short radio drama. As a document of a decadent Don Juan of 1900, it is an interesting *costumbrista* work, for which the author thought it necessary to include eight pages of glossary in the printed edition.

Another interesting experiment is Silva Valdés' four-act dramatic poem *Vida de dos cuchillos* (1957), about two gaucho knives in a store window and their adventures. Here the poet and the playwright combine felicitously. And while he is still experimenting with his craft, the Spanish drama critic Agustín del Saz has declared, "The dramaturgy of magic realism of Silva Valdés is a brilliant truth that is triumphing in the River Plate theatres."[21]

---

[20] Walter Rela, *El mito Santos Vega en el teatro del Río de la Plata;* Julio Imbert, "El teatro rioplatense y Fernán Silva Valdés," *Revista Nacional,* No. 199 (1959), 1–15.

[21] Saz, *El teatro del poeta nativista del Uruguay.*

CHAPTER 6

Springs of Drama in the River Plate Region

More articles and books have been devoted to Argentine drama than to any, and perhaps all, other Latin American countries. This concentration is logical, because while regions like Mexico, Peru, and Chile had a few theatres where plays held the boards between operas and concerts, Buenos Aires for centuries has had a large play-loving population, in addition to societies and scholars that investigated theatrical history. Very few other Latin American nations have ever established a theatrical museum.

In comparison with some, this region of the New World drained by the Paraná-Paraguay River was slow to begin, though after the start furnished by Padre Lezcano in Asunción, occasional clergymen along the tributaries of the Río de la Plata produced religious plays.[1] Two were performed on a temporary stage in the plaza of Cajamarca in 1596. A letter by the Jesuit Diego de Torres, for instance, reported local performances in 1610 in Mendoza, Córdoba, and Tucumán, while *La vida de San Ignacio,* by an unnamed dramatist, was such a smash hit in Santiago del Estero that popular demand brought repeat performances first in patios, then in the Cathedral of Buenos Aires to a capacity audience including the bishop and other Church and society personages, who gave presents to the best actors.

In its constitution the University of Córdoba, established in 1664, called for *un teatro* in the main building. While the *actos* were doubtless chiefly official functions, examinations, and graduation exercises, the Jesuits did stress the educational value of properly supervised dramatic performances.[2] A sample of such a play is *Drama de Adán,* found and published by the Jesuit priest Padre Dreidemie, whose

[1] José Torre Revello, "El teatro en la colonia," in *Humanidades,* XXIII (1933), 147–150.

[2] Jaime Potenze, "Breve história crítica del teatro argentino," *Cuadernos Hispano-Americanos,* 13 (January, 1950), 99–111, refers, without giving titles, to theatrical performances in the middle of the seventeenth century in the college in Buenos Aires founded by the Jesuits.

unknown author sought realism by having God and St. Michael talk Latin, while the other characters used the more worldly Spanish and Guaraní.[3]

Plays from Spain were also early brought to the New World. Padre Tomás Gage broke the monotony of the sea voyage from Cádiz to Veracruz in 1625 by taking part in a "comedy out of Lope de Vega, acted by soldiers, and young friars."[4] By the next century Argentina was seeing so many plays that the Father Superior of the Jesuit college in 1713 prohibited performances by students on account of the time they lost from their studies. One can only guess at whether they were Golden Age plays from Spain or the original work of these students for priesthood.

The first native-born Argentine writer of dialog to be recorded by name was Antonio Fuentes del Arco, who in 1717 wrote and performed in his native Santa Fe a *loa* in gratitude to Philip V who had just eliminated the *sisa*, or shipping tax, on Paraguay tea between Asunción and Buenos Aires, to the profit of Santa Fe, the port that handled the *yerba mate*. So, preceding a performance of Moreto's *No puede ser guardada una mujer*, three gentlemen conversed about the many benefits bestowed by King Philip on his colony. Though certainly "Argentine," it was far from "drama."[5]

Discovered by Padre Furlong in 1946, the *loa* is reprinted in *Estudios* with a few details of the author's life. While the tax was reimposed in 1730 and not finally permanently abolished until 1743, the date of the first royal remission seems the more likely to have inspired the dialog. So it precedes the celebration in 1740 on the occasion of the canonization of St. Francis Regis, as well as that other play, *Las glorias del mejor siglo*, by the Jesuit Valentín de Céspedes, copied in Córdoba in 1748, and long considered the earliest locally written work.[6]

By declaring that the 1747 festivities in Buenos Aires to celebrate

[3] Oscar J. Dreidemie, "Los orígenes del teatro en las regiones del Río de la Plata," *Estudios*, LVII (1937), 61–80

[4] Thomas Gage, *The English-American, His Travail by Sea and Land*. See also Harvey L. Johnson, "Noticias dadas por Tomás Gage a propósito del teatro en España, México, y Guatemala, 1624–1637," *Revista Iberoamericana*, VIII, No. 16 (November 1944), 257–273.

[5] José Luis Trenti Rocamora, "La primera pieza teatral argentina." *Boletín*, IV, No. 15 (December, 1946), 224–234.

[6] *Ibid.*, "El teatro en la época colonial dentro de los límites del Virreynato de Río de la Plata," *Lyra*, IV (1946), 35.

the coronation of Ferdinand VI eclipsed all previous occasions, the chronicler implied there had been earlier moments of drama. Perhaps he had a dim memory of a performance of *Judith* by Juan de Vera Tassis y Villarroel (c. 1636–1707) in 1721, so well done that the audience demanded its repetition the following day,[7] or the celebration two years later of the wedding of the Prince of Asturias to Luisa Isabel de Orleans on December 11, 1723, for which the *cabildo* paid José de Arellano "los gastos de las comedias." Their titles are omitted in the administrator's records.

Certainly the ten days of celebration, beginning November 14, 1747, must have been a gala occasion for Buenos Aires' 10,223 inhabitants. On the first day, Governor Andonegui, Mayor Rodríguez de Vida, and representatives of the religious and trades organization saw Calderón's *Las armas de la hermosura* performed by soldiers from the fortress of San Baltasar de Austria (in construction from 1595 to 1720). The next day, besides Calderón's *Afectos de odio y amor*, Jesuit-trained Indians from Paraguay performed an opera. The third day saw a double feature, Calderón's *La vida es sueño* and Moreto's *Primera es la honra*. Then came a spell of bad weather to break into the program of dramas, masses, and fireworks. The rains lasted so long that citizens who had lent lumber and curtains for the stage began demanding their return, so the remainder of the celebration was canceled, except for the plays that were performed in the fortress later.

Possibly the difficulty of borrowing material from private citizens motivated the building of a small theatre that same year by Eusebio Maciel. In 1755 Governor Andonegui tried to persuade the *cabildo* to underwrite another, but was refused.[8] In 1757, however, a shoemaker, Pedro Aguiar, built one for the actor Domingo Sacomano, recently arrived after a tour of Peru and Chile. Aguiar was shipped back to Spain by the Church fathers for matrimonial irregularities, so José Antonio de Prada took over the tiny theatre for a year, presenting chiefly puppet shows, but then it closed. The trouble was that if any large number of spectators wanted to witness a play, the only feasible system was a temporary stage in one of the plazas.[9]

[7] *Ibid.*, "Gente de teatro del Buenos Aires colonial," *Boletín*, No. 17 (June, 1947), 69–83.

[8] J. A. Pillado, *Buenos Aires colonial, edificios y costumbres*, I, 25.

[9] Trenti Rocamora, "El primer teatro porteño," *Boletín*, No. 16 (March, 1947), 22–23, studies and declares unverified the statements by A. Taullard,

While Jerónimo Matorras, one of Buenos Aires' richest citizens, paid for several dramatic performances in his own gaily decorated patio in celebration of the coronation of Charles III in 1760, the colony's main jubilation for the event took place around a stage on what is now the Plaza de Mayo. Two plays by Calderón, *El cisma de Inglaterra* and *El segundo Scipión,* were supposed to figure in the three weeks of festivities, but the second drama was rained out.

In 1776 the River Plate region was raised to the status of a viceregency. With the arrival of the Mexican-born Viceroy Juan José de Vértiz y Salcedo, on June 12, 1778, the drama in Argentina found an enthusiastic patron. It took him a long time, however, to convince the city fathers of the desirability of a permanent center for plays, like the Coliseo built in Cuba in 1776 by Governor Marqués de la Torre. To overcome the objections of the Church, Francisco Velarde, who had been performing on temporary stages, had promised that if the *cabildo* would give him a twenty-year lease, he would build a theatre equal to any in Spain.[10] When the lawmakers suggested a delay till the matter could be referred to Spain for settlement, Velarde offered to build a temporary shed with wooden walls and thatched roof at the corner of Peru and Alsina Streets near the fruit market, then called Ranchería, now Mercado Viejo. He pointed out that its nearness to the Artillery Barracks would provide a clientele, as well as volunteer firemen if his nine-thousand-peso investment ever caught fire.

Viceroy Vértiz backed him, recognizing in the theatre another cultural advance for his capital, along with his new printing press and the College of San Carlos, already planned. But there were citizens strenuously opposed to an "anteroom of Hell" in their city. Fray Josef de Costa, the Franciscan preacher to the Congregation of San Juan, already established in La Ranchería district, threatened with

---

Historia de nuestros antiguos teatros, and Enrique García Velloso, *El arte del comediante,* and sets the date as November, 1783, for the construction of La Ranchería. For details of the 1757 theatre, see Jorge Escalada Yriondo, "Alquiler de terreno con destino a teatro," *Revista del Notariado,* No. 516 (July, 1944); and José Torre Revello, "Los teatros en el Buenos Aires del siglo XVIII," *Boletín,* No. 10 (September, 1945). The 1771 date derived from reference to this suburb as a place devoted to dances and sports at least twelve years before the building of the theatre there.

[10] "Documentos del teatro la Ranchería," *Máscara,* No. 49 (October, 1944), 10–11.

eternal damnation anyone witnessing even a masked ball in the theatre that was gradually winning supporters. The Viceroy's answer was to have this fiery relic of ancient strife between church and stage exiled to a distant parish. The priest who replaced him took the hint and assured his parishioners that "El señor Baile" could very "honestamente" marry "Señora Devoción."

When the impresario agreed to a reduced ten-year monopoly, and the Viceroy promised that all plays would be submitted before performance to a Church censorship, lest they bring a blush to the cheeks of maidens, and ordered that twenty-five precautions ordered by Ferdinand VI for Madrid theatres be followed in Buenos Aires, the *cabildo* granted permission with one final stipulation: "Si es posible que en la concurrencia para la dibención se ebite la mescla de los sexos." The theatre was built in 1783.

Velarde's Casa de Comedias, popularly called Teatro de la Ranchería, was not very large. The floor space was filled with hard, pine benches, providing seats for about a hundred *blancos* at two *reales* apiece. Fenced off by a railing at the rear was standing room for one-*real* customers—"los que no lo sean blancos," according to the prospectus. The spectators, squeezed and nearly decapitated within this pit, christened it "degolladero."

Runways along both sides of the main floor provided space for more standees, beneath the red-and-yellow-decorated box for the high government official (who did not have to pay admission) and beneath bleachers set up on the right for men and on the left for women, according to the *cabildo's* stipulation. Three hundred in all could attend a performance. Later several other boxes were built, practically on the stage.

The stage was provided with a pull-curtain bearing the motto "Ridendo consigo mores." On the grand drape could be read: "Es la comedia espejo de la vida." Lighting was provided by candles, since tallow was cheap and oil scarce. Backstage were stored 10 curtains, 75 flats, and 376 pieces of costume, in addition to a library numbering more than 1,000 playscripts, including 2 volumes of Calderón, 8 volumes of other Spanish Golden Age dramatists, 380 separate scripts of long plays, 123 *sainetes*, and many monologs, dialogs, and musical plays.[11]

[11] Trenti Rocamora, "Gente de teatro del Buenos Aires colonial," *Boletín*, No. 17 (June, 1947), 69–83.

Performances began at 7:00 P.M. in summer and 6:00 P.M. in winter. When some of the wealthy refused to attend, saying that the streets were too dark and dangerous when they went home, Viceroy Vértiz inaugurated street lighting in Buenos Aires by setting up candles in lanterns at streetcorners. Then he announced that from the profits the theatre manager would contribute two thousand pesos a year for the support of the Foundling Hospital, for which the rich *porteños* had previously been taxed. The citizens could have their choice of supporting the theatre or paying their money directly as taxes. Unfortunately Vértiz did not remain long enough to see the outcome of his planning. His term expired in 1784 and he was succeeded as viceroy by the Marqués de Loreto.

When Velarde asked in 1786 for a renewal of his contract, he pleaded for reduction in his contribution to the foundling home because of small profits. Not only had puppet shows, acrobats, bullfights, and cockfights taken his audience, but the law closing the theatre during Lent had made possible only about thirty performances a year.

Velarde failed to mention two other handicaps to the popularity and progress of River Plate drama: poor actors and poor plays. Martin Paulet, a French actor who had joined Velarde's company four years after the opening of La Ranchería, was the only professional actor among them. And their repertory was a monotonous repetition of Golden Age plays, frequently a revised version by some local *injenio* on the theory that four eyes see more than two. Around 1787 a box of the current plays from Madrid accompanied another immigrant actor, but all students of eighteenth-century Spanish drama know its low quality.

One good result of this dearth of Spanish material was the incentive it provided to local authors to write for the stage. So it was that 1789 brought the first important original work by a Buenos Aires-born playwright. While studying law at Chuquisaca about 1774, José Lavardén (or Labardén, 1754–1810)[12] wove passages of the Chilean epic *La araucana* into a practice play and completed *La*

---

[12] Ricardo Rojas, "Ensayo filosófico sobre la evolución de la cultura," in *Obras*, Vol. XI; Mariano G. Bosch, *Manuel de Lavardén, Poeta y filósofo*; José Juan Arrom, *El teatro de Hispano-américa en la época colonial*, pp. 206–207 (with an explanatory letter by Lavardén about his purposes and technique); Alberto Ghiraldo, "Un precursor del teatro en América," *Atenea*, XXXVIII (1937), 88–97.

muerte de Felipe de Macedonia and *La pérdida de Jerusalem*. Now on Carnival Sunday, 1789, at La Ranchería he saw a production of his tragedy, *Siripo*, the first Spanish-Indian conflict on the stage, which made Lavardén a forerunner of the Indianistic movement. His source was an Argentine story first set down by the grandson of an Indian woman, Ruy Díaz de Guzmán, in Chapter III of his history, *Argentina* (1612). Henríquez Ureña believed *Siripo* was inspired by a play in Italian, *Lucia Miranda* (Bologna, 1784) by the Valencian Jesuit, Manuel Lassela.[13] Others suspect that Lavardén dramatized the thousand lines of Díaz' history as he had previously used Ercilla's epic. At any rate he treated it in the classic form approved by Aristotle rather than in the baroque style then in vogue in Europe.

The plot concerns the love of Mangora, and later of Siripo, chiefs of the Timbú Indians, for Lucía Miranda, the wife of Sebastián Hurtado, one of that little company left in 1529 by the explorer Cabot in the fort of Sancti Spiritu, where the Carcarañá River joins the Paraná. In the story, used in several novels and poems by other writers,[14] Lucía spurns the love of the Indian, though its alternative was the torture of her husband and her own death by fire. Those of Buenos Aires' 24,754 inhabitants who attended opening night must have felt unsettled to see conquistadors and Indians on a stage usually filled by Romans or Golden Age Spaniards.

Since Buenos Aires had no theatrical critics till *El Telégrafo* began publication in 1801, and the play itself has been lost, there is no way of judging the impact of Lavardén's lines. What is purported to be Act II, in fifteen scenes, still exists, but either it is a different version or Lavardén's status as the most popular poet of the River Plate is undeserved. What has come down to us follows the eighteenth-century, French-influenced Spanish dramatists rather than Golden Age geniuses. One wonders what could have been left for the last three acts, since Act II ends within thirty lines of the conclusion of Díaz' account.[15]

[13] Pedro Henríquez Ureña, "El teatro de la América española en la época colonial," in *Cuaderno*, III, 1936).

[14] Hugo Wast, Luis Bayón Herrera, Manuel Ortega, Echeverría in his play *Mangora*, and even Thomas More, *Mangora, King of the Timbussians or The Faithful Couple* (London, 1718).

[15] Those interested in the matter of other versions, plagiarism, and the involved history of *Siripo* should consult Ricardo Rojas, *Historia de la literatura*

Lavardén's drama was repeated in Montevideo, where a theatre had been built in 1792, also in Buenos Aires during the Indian festivities of 1813, and again in 1832, when the manuscript was probably destroyed in the fire that destroyed the "New Theatre." La Ranchería was already gone. What Velarde had feared, had happened. After two brilliant seasons, during which it helped celebrate the oath of allegiance to Charles IV in 1789 and Charles' second anniversary in 1790, the "temporary theatre" ended in a blaze of glory on August 16, 1792, when a skyrocket ignited its thatched roof. Malicious *porteños*, remembering the Church's continual criticism of the stage, suspected that during the Festival of San Roque one of the rockets had been carefully aimed from the Church of San Juan. But La Ranchería had accomplished its purpose. Though the clergy managed to delay the building of a successor for twelve years, La Ranchería had fostered a love of the theatre and had brought street lighting to Buenos Aires decades ahead of any other New World capital.

Even without a home, Argentine drama did not die. Plays were written and presented in private homes. Bosch reprints what is probably the oldest Creole play, *El amor de la estanciera*, dating from around 1787 and performed in 1793.[16] Rojas ascribes it to Dr. Juan Baltasar Maciel.[17]

Set at a *choza*, or ranch house, under an *ombú* tree, with authentic *paisanos* who use cattle skulls for chairs and employ colloquial language, this brief play in crude verse tells of the arrival of Marcos Figueira, a Brazilian salesman, to marry the Creole Pepa. When the Brazilian blusters and pulls a gun, all turn against him, and he surrenders and has to cook the wedding supper.

Though the play contains no actual mention of gauchos, everything is thoroughly Argentine. Besides talk of barbecues and cheese-

---

argentina: Los coloniales, p. 723 n. "Jean Paul" Echagüe, *Teatro argentino*, pp. 129–139, discusses *Siripo*. See also Arturo Berenguer Carisomo, "Siripo," *Boletín*, No. 8 (January, 1945), 1–22, with a reprint of the spurious, according to Bosch, second act; see Mariano G. Bosch, "De quien es el Siripo," *Boletín*, No. 12 (March, 1946), 5–18.

[16] Published in *Publicaciones del Instituto de la Literatura Argentina*, ed. Ricardo Rojas, Vol. IV, No. 1. See also Mariano G. Bosch, *Teatro antiguo de Buenos Aires*, p. 95.

[17] Ricardo Rojas, *Historia de la literatura argentina: Los gauchescos*, pp. 337–341, 565–566.

making, it includes the first Creole dance on the Argentine stage. Scorn of city dwellers and foreigners is also foreshadowed:

> Más vale un paisano nuestro
> Aunque tenga cuatro trapos,

says the parent, and Pepa agrees:

> Por fin es hombre de campo
> y sabe bien enlazar.
> El me cogerá las vacas
> y me ayudará a ordeñar.

Perhaps because it records an Argentine's victory over his Brazilian rival, *El amor de la estanciera* was frequently revived whenever political difficulties arose with Brazil.

Apparently the Church did not object to privately produced plays like this, but it put pressure on the *cabildo* against any proposal to build a new theatre. Finally, in 1804, the new viceroy, Marqués de Sobremonte, talked the *cabildo* into advancing three thousand pesos toward the expense of an adequate *coliseo*, though its construction was delayed by worry about a British army of invasion.

In the midst of the long discussion of an "adequate" theatre, the coffee merchant Ramón Aignase and the actor José Speciali got permission to set up a *coliseo provisional* at what is now Reconquista and Cangallo Streets. The Mercedarians across the street protested "the Idol Dagon resting beside the Ark of the Covenant." But Sobremonte assured them it would be a temporary makeshift. And so El Coliseo Chico was built in nineteen days, to serve fifty years until the city fathers appropriated enough to finish El Coliseo a half century later, in 1857.

Zafira, a Spanish version of Voltaire's *Zaïre*, marked the opening of El Coliseo Chico on May 1, 1804, with Josefa Ocampo, formerly of La Ranchería, and José Speciali in the chief roles. Prices were low: admission, two *reales*; seats, one *real* in the gallery, three in the orchestra, and twenty in a box.

The city's only theatre became the center of social life. It was here on June 24, 1806, that Viceroy Sobremonte, giving a party for the suitor of his daughter, Mariquita, and planning to witness *La vida es sueño*, received warning of the British invasion. The frightened official shot out of the theatre, as a later couplet declared:

> Al primer cañonazo de los valientes
> disparó Sobremonte con sus parientes.

That was almost the end of this theatre. A band of patriots tried to bomb it when it became barracks for some of the 1,560 British who had captured a city of 55,000 inhabitants. But the powder failed to explode, and El Coliseo Chico remained to house the celebration of the Reconquista in 1808.

Highlight of the festivities on that occasion was a two-act poetic melodrama, *La lealtad más acendrada y Buenos Aires vengada*,[18] by Juan Francisco Martínez, the chaplain of the Uruguayan forces that had crossed the Plata to help drive out the British. In a variety of poetic meters, *silvas* and *octavas reales*, as well as the ballad form, Mars, representing Argentina, defeated the British Neptune, cheered on by Liniers and by Uruguayan nymphs.

For awhile Córdoba, too, enjoyed dramas, due chiefly to a Spaniard, Cristóbal de Aguilar (1742–1828), who spent seventy-four years as a resident of Argentina before his death. He was a Calderonian disciple; his reflective dramas bore such titles as *La industria contra la fuerza*, *El premio de la codicia*, *Venció el desprecio al desdén*, and *El triunfo de la prudencia y oficios de la amistad*.[19]

Buenos Aires began living its own drama. Having beaten the soldiers of Britain's king on their own soil, the *porteños* thought they could defy a French-born king in Spain; so on May 25, 1810, they forced the resignation of the viceroy and set up a junta to rule in the name of the deposed Spaniard, Ferdinand VII. But when Ferdinand regained the throne and revealed himself a tyrant, they broke bonds with Spain at the Congress of Tucumán, July 9, 1816. Whether they would become a monarchy or a federation of states was not decided, but their colonial days were over.

On May 25, 1812, the second anniversary of their first step toward freedom, the temporary Coliseo was repaired and reopened with a play, *El 25 de Mayo*, by a Peruvian mestizo, Luis Ambrosio Morante (1775–1837), librarian, prompter, and general factotum of the theatre.[20] In spite of being written by a Peruvian who drew inspira-

[18] Published by Instituto de Literatura Argentina (1925), Vol. I, No. 11.

[19] José Luis Trenti Rocamora, "Cristóbal de Aguilar," *Boletín*, No. 20 (March, 1948), 7–18 (with a summary of *Venció el desprecio al desdén*).

[20] For a detailed and footnoted history of the Buenos Aires theatre, 1757–1817, see Luis Ordaz, *El teatro en el Río de la Plata*, 2d. ed., pp. 17–37. For Morante, see Raúl Castagnino, *Milicia literaria de mayo*, pp. 48–57.

tion from an original in French about the French Revolution of 1792, the play can properly be called Argentine in its re-creation of the original May 25, as the patriots wait in the plaza in the rain, hoping the *cabildo* will accept the resignation of the viceroy and itself become the first patriotic junta of their free government.

Under the inspiration of this new urge for liberty, the Spanish red and yellow was ripped from the official box and replaced by the Argentine blue and white—colors chosen because a ship in the harbor had a cargo of cloth of those particular colors.

At last Argentina had a national theatre and a locally written play about and for Argentines to act. From a few planks on sawhorses to a thing of bricks, glass, and roofing, the stage had been gradually evolving. Now it was on its way to becoming what Marsili calls "el ingenio nativo, con los caracteres, ambientes, y motivos peculiares, la idiosincracia de esa entidad formidable y distincta,"[21] which is the soul of what has been the most vital of all Hispanic-American theatre.

[21] Ernesto Marsili, *El verdadero origen del teatro argentino*, p. 40.

CHAPTER 7

Beginnings of Argentine National Drama

No sudden change in the Argentine drama came with independence. Luis Ambrosio Morante, having pleased the colonists with his musical *25 de mayo*, continued to delight the citizens of the new republic with the plays he went on writing. He may have been the author of *Triunfo de la naturaleza* (1814), set in Quito ("Departamento del Perú") in which the Inca princess Cora achieves freedom and marries the conquistador Molina, instead of being sacrificed as a Virgin of the Sun. Others ascribe this play to the Portuguese Vicente Pedro de Acuña. Manuel Belgrano later rewrote it as *Molina* (1823).

Morante's production of *Siripo* for the 1813 season revealed his hatred of the Spaniards. The original "evil redskins" of Lavardén's play are converted into "noble savages," driven to deeds of violence by Spanish deceit and betrayal. He probably also wrote the powerful *Túpac-Amarú*, performed on May 25, 1821, another patriotic occasion. While the Argentines did not object to Morante's hymn of hate against the mother country in this celebration, protests followed his *Cornelia Bororquía*, set in Córdoba and directed against the Inquisition. He was criticized for attacking religion.

To raise the standards of literary taste in the new nation, Governor Puyrredón in 1817 called together twenty-eight leading writers to form the Society of Good Taste in the Theatre. Included were the poet López y Planes, author of Argentina's national anthem; Santiago Wilde, who owned a circus arena and adapted plays; and Olaguer y Feliu, who had built El Coliseo Chico. At their first meeting, July 28, 1817, Esteban Luca was elected president, Juan Ramón Rojas outlined a program, and Padre Camilo Henríquez, one of those who fled from Chile following the collapse of the 1817 rebellion, promised to give it publicity in the pages of his newly founded *Censor*.

Among their projects were the abolition of bullfights and cockfights and a break with Spanish dramatic traditions by reviving the best of the colonial repertory and encouraging local dramatists, as

well as translating the best foreign plays. Also they would take steps
to prevent their best actors and actresses from being "seduced" to
the Montevideo stage.[1]

The future looked bright. They started with performances, which
were social events, of *Le Bourgeois Gentilhomme* and Voltaire's
Orestes. Then they looked for local plays. One of those considered
was the sentimental *La Camila o La patriota de Sudamérica*, just
completed by Padre Camilo Henríquez (1769–1825).

The good Father, unfortunately, had no idea how to write a play.
It was he who later convinced the Chileans that the stage ought to be
a school, and in *Camila* and his later *La inocencia es el asilo de las
virtudes* he practiced his theory. More important to him than the
story of the woman who had lost her fiancé in Ecuador and was living in an Indian tribe with a college-trained chief, were the play's
preachments for religious tolerance and education. Those in the Society with "good taste" rightly decided against performing a drama
that had no drama, but its author, hurt and indignant at the criticism
of his brain child, resigned and by his talk and writing killed the
Society.

President Rivadavia then tried to start a literary society whose
members would hear and discuss plays by their fellows. In the Rivadavia Salon the classicist Juan Cruz Varela (1794–1839) read his
tragedy *Dido* (1821), taken from Virgil, and defended his distortion
of history by insisting that the classical unities were more important.
His associates did not care for the play. They were better pleased
with his other tragedy, *Argia* (1822), set in Thebes and modeled on
Antigone by way of Alfieri, but neither of them dealt with the American scene. Manuel Belgrano, nephew of the famous general, also read
his New World tragedy, *Molina* (1823), with a story of the Inca Cora
and her Spanish conquistador.

More typical of Argentina, however, was a three-act farce by some
unremembered author, *Las bodas de Chivico y Pancha* (1823),[2] actually a series of episodes. In the 1823 original Chingolo tells his
friends Chivico and Juancho of the drive to get recruits for the federal army and of his adventures in a theatre, but later comedians sub-

---

[1] *Boletín*, No. 17 (June, 1947), 108; Raúl H. Castagnino, *Milicia literaria de
mayo*, pp. 59–78.
[2] Mariano G. Bosch, "Orígenes del teatro nacional argentino," *Boletín*, Nos.
18–19 (September, 1947), 177–179.

stituted their own humorous monologs.[3] The famous comic actor Felipe David established the tradition of reciting in gaucho dialect the *Oda del Bagre Sapo*, about the defeat of the Brazilians, the "mud catfish" of the title, at the Battle of Pozos.

Act II deals with the wedding. Pancha's parents suggest that she and Chivico pull together like a yoke of oxen. Papa warns her to have the maté hot when her husband gets home. The groom also gets advice before the priest blesses them.

The final act, after a free-for-all when two gauchos want the same dance partner, ends, like the *Amor de la estanciera* and so many other skits, with the wedding banquet and dance, possibly to whet the appetite of the audience for their own dinner after the show.

In 1829 Juan Manuel Rosas (1793–1877) came onto the scene as governor, and except for one brief period ruled as dictator till 1852, when he was defeated at the Battle of Montecaseros. Since he had little interest in drama, the theatre had a hard time.[4] However this period marked the arrival of romanticism in Argentina. The time was ripe. For twenty years the Argentines had endured the tenseness of a struggle for independence, followed by ten more of civil convulsion. Most of the plays, the dull neoclassic products of the literary societies, never reached the stage, partly because of their limited appeal. But now Rosas, newcomer on the scene, was a typical romantic type, an unknown from the south brought up among raiding gauchos and Indian fights. And at the appropriate time Esteban Echeverría sowed the seeds of romanticism. Ricardo Rojas once remarked that if Echeverría had not appeared, someone else would have expressed the feelings of these new times.

The first stirrings in the drama came from such European plays as the adaptation in 1825 by the Venezuelan Fernández Madrid of Chateaubriand's *Atala*, full of the passions of a white man for a North American Indian girl, a tragedy romantic in spirit, though cast in the neoclassic mold. Then followed a half-dozen French plays by Victor Ducange (1783–1830). The first one, *Trente ans ou la vie d'un jouer* was performed, in Magnolio Juárez' translation, in Buenos Aires on July 28, 1831. Though a second-rate dramatist, Ducange was popular

---

[3] Several interpolations are reprinted in Mariano G. Bosch, *Historia del teatro en Buenos Aires*, pp. 502–509; see also Tito Livio Foppa, *Diccionario teatral del Río de la Plata*, pp. 707–711, 1003–1006.

[4] Raúl H. Castagnino, *El teatro en Buenos Aires durante la época de Rosas.*

in Europe and in Argentina till 1852. The first production brought floods of letters from "Románticos" and "Antirrománticos" to *Gaceta mercantil, Diario de la tarde,* and other newspapers.[5]

Then followed translations from Alexander Dumas, and to a lesser degree from Hugo, Scribe, and Delavigne. Finally Rosas exercised his dictatorial powers to check the Francophiles and restore admiration for Spain, and on June 9, 1838, came the first performance of *El trovador,* by García Gutiérrez, to inaugurate the new Teatro de la Victoria. For fifteen years it was Buenos Aires' favorite play, though the other Spanish romantic dramatists were quickly introduced, ending with Zorrilla and his *El zapatero y el rey* in 1841.[6]

Local dramatists, too, admiring liberty and hating tyranny—especially in distant periods and countries—began writing plays about noble women and mysterious and courtly heroes amid tempestuous nature and entangled in completely unreal webs of passion. In spite of their religious beliefs, the dramatists let their characters be pushed around by fate. Though Rosas rarely attended the theatre, his counselor Medrano, his associate Vicente López and son Vicente Fidel and others tried their hand; Castagnino mentions many others, though with the comment that the Argentine theatre gained little by the efforts of these romanticists.[7] However, the seeds sown were to produce such social romanticists as Alberto Ghiraldo and Rodolfo González Pacheco in the twentieth century.

Luis Méndez wrote *Carlos o El infortunio*; Rafael Corvalán, *El renegado o El triunfo de la fe*; Carlos Zee, *Manfredo de Zuavia*; and Jaime Roldos, *El hermitaño de Burriach* and *El pordiosero del valle de Santa María.* Colonel Nicasio Biedma produced the drama *Hernando o El doncel de Bañares,* and even that sailor of fortune Admiral Brown left a couple of unfinished tragedies among his papers. The Frenchman Albert Larroque (?–1881), passing through South America, took time to write the tragedy *Juan de Borgoña o Un traidor*

---

[5] Raúl H. Castagnino, "El Romanticismo en el teatro porteño (1830–1852)," *Lyra,* Nos. 174–176.

[6] Mariano G. Bosch, "1700–1810: Panorama del teatro," *Cuaderno,* No. 13 (1940), 13–32; Julio A. Leguizamón, *Historia de la literatura hispanomericana,* II, 200–202; Castagnino, *El teatro en Buenos Aires,* pp. 535–544; Castagnino, "Teatro del Río de la Plata," *Boletín,* No. 1 (January, 1943), 6–12.

[7] Castagnino, "El Romanticism en el teatro porteño, *Lyra,* Nos. 174–176.

a la patria (1845), which proved his culture if not his skill as a dramatist.[8]

However, along with this dull and formula-ridden European drama came a livelier side, the local *sainetes*. Many who turned out serious dramas also occasionally let themselves go in lighter local-color plays. Zee was author of *Un primo o Miñoné Fan Fan*. Biedma wrote *Si algo valgo, el público lo dirá* and *Todo por la patria*, and Larroque wrote *El artículo 6º o Un marido de dieciseis años*, set in the period of Richelieu.

Taking time from his duties as surgeon with Rosas' army, Dr. Claudio Mamerto Cuenca (1812–1852) produced a five-act satirical comedy in verse, *Don Tadeo*, with its well-characterized hero, his bad-humored wife, Rufina, enemy of youth and progress, and the amusing old Don Diego. Had he lived, Dr. Cuenca would doubtless have concluded his tragedy *Muza o La cristiana Jimena*, set in Spain amid Visigoths and Arabs and influenced by Quintana's *Pelayo* and Moratín's *Hormesinda*. But he was killed at the Battle of Montecaseros, where the power of Rosas came to an end. In the Doctor's pocket was a half-finished anti-Rosas poem!

One reason for the lack of good drama during the twenty years of Rosas' power, was, in the opinion of Castagnino, that the various factors necessary for an active stage never got together. The public was fed on circuses and cockfights, the players were unwilling to remain in Buenos Aires, and the critics and literary lights had fled into exile all over South America.

Most active of the exiles, and characterized by Leguizamón as "honrado artista dentro de su tiempo y su medio," was Pedro Echagüe (1821–1889).[9] A fugitive in Bolivia, he wrote *Primera es la patria* and the brief *De mal en peor*. Upon his return to Buenos Aires, he completed *Rosas* (1860), covering the closing moments of the Dictator's power; it reworked his earlier *Rosas y Urquiza en Palermo*. Plot, setting, characters, and sentiment are all Argentine. What Echagüe lacked was a feeling for "good theatre." At its first performance, part of a May 25 celebration, Mitre and Sarmiento were among the spectators.

Echagüe's verse was uneven and his multiple activities in journal-

---

[8] Bosch, "1700–1810: Panorama del teatro," *Cuaderno*, No. 13 (1940), 6–12.
[9] *Ibid.*

ism, politics, and soldiering prevented his concentrating on drama, but he revised the patriotic one-act *Primera es la patria* (1861) and wrote a three-act prose comedy *Padre hermano y tío padre* (1862) about Buenos Aires; the two-act, poetic *Un beso*; the three-act *Amor y virtud* (San Juan, 1868), with a Chilean setting; *Memorias de un coronel*; and *Las niñas.*

From Montevideo, Bartolomé Mitre (1821–1906), later President of the Republic, attacked Rosas en *Cuatro épocas* (1840), five acts of prose and verse detailing the life of the chief characters between 1825 and 1839. It survived only one performance. His translation of Hugo's *Ruy Blas* (1841) was more successful, but his *Policarpa Salavarrieta* never got to the stage and has been lost.[10]

José Marmol (1817–1871) while writing the anti-Rosas novel *Amalia* (1853), dramatized his own unhappy exile in *El poeta* for a run of three performances. His romantic *El cruzado* held the stage for one night.

Though all these early plays show that the false impression of the cultural sterility during Rosas' administration was largely fostered by his enemies,[11] only one has lasted. *El gigante Amapolas y sus formidables enemigos* (1842), the work of the author, philosopher, and statesman Juan Bautista Alberdi (1810–1884), classified by him as a "peti-pieza,"[12] was revived in the Teatro Libre Tinglado of Buenos Aires in 1945 by Aurelio Ferretti. Its satirical purpose is obvious in its title, where "Giant Poppies" replaces "Dictator Rosas."

After the overthrow of Rosas, progress toward a good theatre came slowly. Colonel Lucio Victorio Mansilla (1831–1913), besides his humorous *Una tía*, wrote a racial play in a few hours on a bet. The plot, based on a story by Eugene Sue, *Atar-Gull o Una venganza africana* (1855), is set in Pernambuco and tells of the passion of a black slave for his white mistress. Also, in collaboration with Nicolás Granada (1840–1915), Mansilla completed the comic *Lluvia de sobrinas.*

By himself Nicolás Granada served as a link between the romantic period and the realistic era, with his *Las flores del muerto* (1892). He had been interested in the theatre long before *Juan Moreira*, but fol-

---

[10] César Tiempo, "Mitre en el teatro," *Máscara*, No. 93 (June, 1948), 2–4.
[11] Castagnino, *El teatro en Buenos Aires.*
[12] Reprinted in Bosch, *Historia de los orígenes del teatro nacional.* See also *Boletín Argentores*, No. 51 (May, 1946), 11–12.

lowed that trend with three of his own gaucho plays. Along other lines
are his historical *Atahualpa* (1897), dealing with a character popular
in many countries; a Paraguay War play, *Juca Tigre;* a Creole drama,
Bajo el parral (1911); and a four-act anti-Rosas play, *El minué federal*
(1912). The personal favorite of this dramatist who was sometimes
called "the Latin American Gil Vicente" was *La gaviota* (1903).[13]

The realistic *América libre* (1860) by Bernabé Demaría was never
performed, because the children of General Belgrano succeeded in
having it declared derogatory to the revolutionary hero.[14]

Luis V. Varela (1845–1911) blended Zorrilla and Echegaray in
Amor filial, El ciego (1869), and *Capital por capital.* Casimiro Prieto
Valdés produced *Don Quijote en Buenos Aires.*

The first work by an Argentine woman reached the stage on November 28, 1877, when the curtains opened on *Contra soberbia
humildad,* by Matilde Cuyas (1859–1909), performed as a benefit
for the leading lady, Matilde de Macías de Cortés, wife of the company's director. Those who received it warmly did not realize its relationship to Moreto's *Desdén con el desdén.*[15]

Some of the Argentines by now were beginning to believe that it
was time to break away from the influence of Spanish dramatists.
One of the first to do so was Nemisio Trejo (1862–1916), who has
therefore sometimes been called Argentina's first national playwright.[16] Actually he fused national themes and Spanish technique.

In 1875 Salesian priests, recently arrived in Buenos Aires, founded
the Colegio (really high school) de San Carlos. One of the beliefs of
the order was the value of plays as teaching devices; so in 1878 they
built Los Galpones Theatre. To provide scripts for their amateur
actors, while some of the fathers were translating and adapting from
French and Italian sources, Trejo looked about for local scenes and
themes to dramatize. For form he took the one-act *sainete* of Ramón
de la Cruz, as modified by Carlos Arniches and Pedro Múñoz Seca in

[13] Augusto Raúl Cortazar, *Nicolás Granada y su importancia en la revolución
teatral;* Arturo Jimenez Pastor, "Nicolás Granada," *Cuaderno,* No. 14 (1940),
105–130. His collaboration with Mansilla is reprinted in Bosch, *Historia de los
orígenes del teatro nacional.*

[14] It was, however, finally published in Bernabé Demaría's *Obras literarias*
(1906) and in Bosch, *Historia de los orígenes del teatro nacional.*

[15] Anon. in *Hogar* (Buenos Aires, December 10, 1937); recently published
with notes by Facultad de Filosofía y Letras.

[16] Martín Lemos, "Tres figuras del viejo sainete," *Boletín,* No. 28 (January,
1950), 13–18; Tulio Carella, *El sainete criollo.*

Spain. Counting his last *Mujeres lindas* (1916), he wrote fifty-two short plays, many of which received a hundred or more performances each. Their national flavor is apparent in their titles: *Libertad de sufragio*; *El hijo del gaucho en el colegio*; *La visita de los gauchos*, in which a cowboy *milonga* is sung; and even a musical *¡Brr, qué frío!*

Since the Salesian Order had fifty-four houses throughout Argentina, all of them performing plays at some time or other, the contribution of Trejo and his associates in developing a playgoing public cannot be minimized, though of course there were other factors.

Later, Trejo's works were performed in the regular theatres. In 1890 he wrote a local-color spectacle, *Un día en la capital*. That same year his *Fiesta de don Marcos* was presented 150 times, a record surpassed by the 500 performances of his topical *Los políticos* (1897). One of his last and best was *Los inquilinos* (1907). The story goes that the manager of the Comedia Theatre ran a contest for local *sainetes* and from the nearly ninety anonymous manuscripts selected four, rating *Los inquilinos* first. When the envelopes were opened, all four turned out to be the work of Trejo. Between 1890 and 1930 more than two hundred Argentine authors turned out *sainetes*.

The creator of Argentina's historical dramas, David Peña (1862–1930),[17] began with a poetic play written, as he confessed, on a bet. *¿Qué dirán la sociedad?* (1883) takes place in the home of an aristocratic Buenos Aires family. Zorrilla and Echegaray were Peña's models, but this play also foreshadowed his interest in the psychological development of character. The only popular plays in vogue when he commenced writing were zarzuelas, performed by actors from Spain; so his next attempt was the musical *La lucha por la vida* (1885), whose failure discouraged him for twenty years. He became a professor of history.

In 1903, following Podestá's success with national plays, Peña organized a club, Fomento del Teatro Nacional, that was short-lived and ineffective. But again it turned him to the theatre with *Próspera* (1903), a propaganda play for his political party, and *Inútil* (1904), a pathological experiment written while Peña was under the influence of French writers.

As a professor of history, Peña then initiated a series of national plays with *Facundo* (1906) about the gaucho *caudillo*, made famous

[17] Aida Cometta Manzoni, *David Peña, Noticias para la historia del teatro nacional*.

(or infamous) by Sarmiento. It was followed by *Dorrego* (1909), *Liniers* (1917), and *Alvear* (1924). In their analysis rather than portrayal of character, and in their lack of gripping drama, these plays belong rather to the study of a professor than to the stage. However, Peña did indicate the path. The philosophic *El loco* and a thesis play, *Un cuerpo*, were departures from it, but he returned to the national theme in *El tigre del Chaco* (1926) and in a dramatization of Carlos Reyles' novel, *El embrujo de Sevilla* (1926).

There were gaucho plays before the famous *Juan Moreira* of 1884–1886. In fact the first local dramatist to publish his plays, Francisco F. Fernández (1841–1922), an ex-student of medicine, wrote a psychosociological four-act tragedy, *Solané*, whose dreamer hero was the first stage gaucho persecuted by the politicians. Before the hero could carry out his plans for the betterment of his people he was assassinated. Fernández' *Obras dramáticas* were published in 1871 and 1881 and contain *El borracho*, performed in Madrid; a Peruvian historical drama in three acts, *Monteagudo* (1871), whose secondary characters are more realistic than is the hero; *Clorinda*, set in Venice; and a couple of allegories.[18] Fernández was an important forerunner of the Argentina national theatre.

Manuel F. Langara wrote *Los gauchos argentinos* (1878),[19] involving Federalists and Unitarians. And there was also a one-act *Gauchos y gringos* (1884), written in Rosario by a Spanish newspaperman, Justo S. López de Gómara (1859–1923), who had brought with him to Argentina a wide acquaintance with Spain's theatrical practices. He wrote a total of twenty-four plays, among them *Del paseo en Buenos Aires*, a musical play of customs that, when performed in 1890 in Teatro Onrubia, was the first to receive the author's 20-per-cent royalty. Among his other famous plays were *Amor y patria, Curupayti*, about the Paraguayan War, and *Valor*

[18] Published in Francisco Fernández, *Obras dramáticas,* and in *Instituto de Literatura Argentina,* ed. Ricardo Rojas, III, 5. See also Ricardo Rojas, *Un dramaturgo olvidado, Don Francisco Fernández y sus obras dramáticas;* B. Hernández Gwynne, *Francisco Fernández: notas biográficas;* Raúl H. Castagnino, *El circo criollo,* pp. 60–76; Leguizamón, *Historia,* pp. 210–211; *Solané* in *Colección de textos dramáticos,* III, ed. Jorge M. Furth.

[19] Published with prolog and notes by Ismael Moya. In the 6-volume *Origenes del teatro nacional* of the Instituto de Literatura Argentina, Ricardo Rojas cites more than forty earlier examples of primitive drama. See especially Part II, "Noticias para la historia de nuestro teatro nacional." Many were published by the Instituto de Literatura Argentina, which Rojas founded.

cívico, describing the 1890 revolution, but he wrote no other plays about the gauchos.

The rest of Buenos Aires' theatrical fare, apart from the early works of Martín Coronado and David Peña, were musical comedies and circuses. Castagnino indicates that the seed of the circus was an acrobat, Arganda, performing in the theatre of Aguiar and Sacomano, in 1757.[20] From then on, came a sequence of acrobats, tightrope walkers, and animal trainers who provided practically the only form of entertainment for the *porteños* from the burning of La Ranchería, in 1792, till 1804. Finally in the Circo Chearini that arrived from Uruguay in 1829 various acts had been organized into a real circus. It and almost all of its successors concluded with some thrilling pantomime of racing horses and shouting men.

The Politeama Argentino, built in 1874, was the arena for many later circuses. And it was here in 1884 that the Carlo Brothers' North American Circus was closing its Buenos Aires season with the dramatic *The Italian Bandits of Calabria*. For its final week, in appreciation of its warm reception by the citizens, the manager, the famous English clown Frank Brown (1858–1943), sought something typically Argentine. Earlier, for six weeks between November 28, 1879, and January 8, 1880, the newspaper *Patria Argentina* had published serially a novel, *Juan Moreira*, by the popular author Eduardo Gutiérrez (1853–1890). The real Juan Moreira had been a dirty, ugly, cruel, and treacherous criminal, captured and executed in Mercedes in 1874.[21] Gutiérrez had idealized him into a romantic victim of official and military oppression, as liars and scoundrels like Wyatt Earp, Wild Bill Hickok, and Bat Masterson have been romanticized on the TV screen in the United States. The Gutiérrez combination of melodrama and local color suggested it as subject for a pantomime, so Brown took his idea to the author but found him dubious.

"Which of your gringos could portray a local gaucho?" asked Gutiérrez.

Brown suggested José J. Podestá (1856–1937), known as "Pepino

[20] Bosch, *Historia del teatro en Buenos Aires*, pp. 132–134; Castagnino, *El circo criollo*, and *Centenarias del circo criollo*, p. 15.

[21] Enrique García Velloso, "Eduardo Gutiérrez y la verdad sobre Juan Moreira," *Memorias de un hombre de teatro*, refers to articles by Juan Alvarez in *La Prensa* (Buenos Aires) on May 18 and June 6, 1927. See also Foppa, *Diccionario teatral*, pp. 937–941; Domingo F. Casadevall, *El tema de la mala vida en el teatro nacional*, pp. 28–30; and Castagnino, *El circo criollo*, pp. 60–75.

el 88," a clown in a rival circus whose singing to his own guitar playing and whose wisecracking with the ringmaster had amused all
Buenos Aires. Though still dubious, Gutiérrez agreed, and the opening night was set for July 2, 1884. Eager to see their circus idol, this
Italian acrobat from Uruguay, performing as an Argentine gaucho,
the citizens of Buenos Aires bought out the 3,500 seats in the Politeama amphitheatre. Police had to be called to keep out the ones who
couldn't get tickets.

After the regular circus acts the gaucho pantomime began. The
first scene presented Juan Moreira trying to recover the money he
had lost to the storekeeper Sardetti. The Italian denied the loan, and
the judge, whose advances had been scorned by the gaucho's wife,
Vicenta, declared for Sardetti. In the rest of the play the furious
Moreira killed the gringo shopkeeper and had to flee, with soldiers in
pursuit. After several narrow escapes, Moreira was overtaken and
stabbed in the back as he tried to leap over a fence.

For eleven evening performances and a matinee the Politeama
never had an empty seat. The pantomime might have continued in-
definitely except that the circus was under contract to open in Rio. So
the brief run of *Juan Moreira* ended, and Podestá went along to Brazil as one more clown and acrobat.

The next season, the Carlo Circus returned to Argentina and with
its profits and its new partner, Alejandro Scotti, bought a theatre in
the fashionable seaside resort of La Plata. Proof that they had missed
the significance of *Juan Moreira* lies in the fact that their performances closed with something called *José the Spanish Bandit*, till one
day Podestá suggested reviving the Argentine pantomime. It proved
as much of a hit as ever to all the audience except the Frenchman
Leon Beaupuy, who owned the boardinghouse where the circus performers lived and who had attended on a pass.

"Not bad," he conceded, "but it would be better with talking. Why
don't you get Gutiérrez to write some dialog?"

The novelist refused. He had written so many other stories in the
meantime that he was not interested. So it was Podestá who got a
copy of the novel and blocked out dialog. On April 10, 1886, at Chi-
vilcoy, one hundred miles southwest of Buenos Aires, a play that was
to have an enormous effect on Argentina's theatre had its première
under a corrugated iron roof in a portable wooden shed. There was
lots of action, with horses racing down the aisles and into the ring

between the stage and the bleachers, and a gaucho fiesta with singing and dancing. But it was the dialog that stirred the emotions of the spectators.

The play was not yet in its final form. It was taken to Montevideo in 1890, where its national quality was recognized. There it was reinforced by extending the fiesta scene and substituting the typical *gato* dance for the original *pericón*, with the advantage of presenting more dancers. Then back to the Politeama for its final elaboration.

Most enthusiastic of the fans in Buenos Aires was a young medical student, DeNegri, who hung around the Politeama more than the medical school. One night, in the spontaneous ad-libbing that often works into an established success, some of the actors poked fun at an Italian member of the cast, Antonio Cocoliche, but he could think of no reply. The next night DeNegri played his part. Wearing a ridiculous costume and speaking barbarous Italianized Spanish, he made the replies that should have been made on the previous occasion. His performance stopped the show, and from then on till his death DeNegri played "Cocoliche," the part he had created, and made him a stock character who popped up in other plays. Now *Juan Moreira* had everything, crime, punishment, pity for the downtrodden, music, and humor. What could be more typically Argentine? The gaucho could dance, strum the guitar, and sing. He was quick with knife and lasso. He combined the qualities of Daniel Boone, Buffalo Bill, and Robin Hood. And the success of *Juan Moreira* was followed by a flurry of "noble outlaw" plays that fell into a pattern[22] like that of the North American Western fiction. The heroic and wronged gaucho was pitted against the soldier villains. Often there was a minor villain, an Argentine-born Italian, so that even if the hero was finally vanquished by the law, the audience could have the thrill of watching one character win a victory over the oppressors.

Some critics minimize the effect of this play in the long run of Argentine drama. A number of dramatists since 1880, when President Avellaneda averted civil war and began the national period by making Buenos Aires into a federal district, achieved prominence without perhaps ever having heard of *Juan Moreira*. But, in contrast to writers like Soria, Granada, and Laferrère, there were just as many

---

[22] Castagnino, *El circo criollo,* pp. 70–71, lists a dozen.

who helped to rub the crudeness from the gaucho play and give it a literary polish. Its successors were many.

Besides Granada, already mentioned, who because of *Juan Moreira* became interested in the dramatic possibilities of the gauchos, Dr. Martiniano Leguizamón (1858–1935) was the author of one play, *Calandria* (1896, *Argentores*, No. 8, 1919), the first gaucho play with literary style and the most frequently performed of the early Argentine plays. While a student, he wrote one *entremés*, *Los apuros de un sábado* (1879), which has been lost, and later the one-act *Del tiempo viejo* (1916), which has been forgotten, as well as the four-act "La muerta," which he himself decided was not worth publishing.

This dramatist confessed his indebtedness to the Spaniard Juan del Encina for the play that has been called an eclog.[23] It is a break with the earlier cowboy plays. There is no blood and thunder. The hero has a sense of humor that leads him to play tricks on his pursuers instead of shooting them down, a trait that makes him, as Ordaz declares, a blood brother of that shrewd and mischievous Creole in Payro's *Casamiento de Laucha*, brought to the stage a half century later in a dramatization by Raúl Larra.[24] So Leguizamón's creation was a forerunner of the more matured characters of Payró and Sánchez.

In *Calandria* the minstrel gaucho, Servando Cardoso, like the mockingbird from which he got his nickname, loves the selva too much to be caged up in the army, so he flees, with the law in pursuit as usual, but he turns on his pursuers in the dark and ties them beside their campfire. However, while he visits his sweetheart Lucia, they capture his horse and so he is helpless. But Captain Saldaña has an understanding heart and assigns him to the cavalry, with permission to marry his *flor del pago*.

Such a happy ending, instead of a rain of bullets and death, brought criticism, which Leguizamón answered with a declaration that he was seeking a solution of the gaucho problem by turning him into a useful citizen.

The author directed the first performance, bringing together five

---

[23] Julia Grifone, *Leguizamón y su égloga, II*, 77–227. See also Delio Panizza, "Martiniano Leguizamón," *Cuaderno*, No. 15 (1940); and Juan Cantes, "Bibliografía de *Calandria*" (with 460 entries), *Boletín del Instituto de Investigaciones Históricas*, Año XX, Tomo XXVI (1941).

[24] Ordaz, *El teatro*, p. 45.

members of the Podestá family and overseeing every detail from costume to gesture. After this theatrical family decided to split into independent companies they selected *Calandria* for their final performance together, March 17, 1901. It was again revived in 1935 by the National Company as "the most modern of the old plays."

In 1902 came a different sort of gaucho play, *Jesús Nazareno*, whose protagonist argues for peace but resorts to violence. Its author, Enrique García Velloso, continued the Biblical parallel by having the gaucho Jesús chained in public stocks between two cattle thieves.

Older than Leguizamón and García Velloso, but making his contributions to the gaucho theatre in a later period was Martín Coronado (1850–1919). A present of a volume by Bretón de los Herreros induced Coronado to begin writing plays that would deal with Argentine customs as Bretón's had described life in Spain. Coronado was always a leader in the drive for a national theatre, especially when he was president of the Argentine Academy of Letters.[25]

His first play, however, *Rosa blanca* (1877), had nothing national about it; it was a romantic story of Irene who went mad on her sister's wedding day. There is little differentiation of character through speeches; and it has a melodramatic ending in which Dr. Gaspar, who loves Irene, discovers the reason for her melancholia.

Between this and his final *La chacra de don Lorenzo* in 1918 (*Escena* No. 546, 1928) Coronado wrote twenty-four plays, half of them in verse. Castagnino sees three periods in Coronado's production: twenty years as a romanticist, ending with *Justicia de antaño* (1897); nine years of concentration on national themes, from his 1899 masterpiece *Piedra de escándalo* (*Escena* No. 541, 1928), with the first of its five hundred performances in Buenos Aires in 1902, to *Hombre de la casa* (1911); succeeded by a discouraging period after his popularity waned because of the realism introduced by Sánchez.[26] After vainly trying to cultivate the new type of comedia, Coronado finally returned, at the urging of Podestá, to his second manner to write the sequel to his greatest success.

[25] Arturo Berenguer Carisomo, "Martín Coronado, su tiempo y su obra," *Cuaderno*, No. 15 (1940), 9–40. See also *Boletín*, Nos. 29–30 (April–September, 1950) commemorating the centenary of Coronado's birth; and Raúl H. Castagnino "La iniciación teatral de Martín Coronado," in the same issues of *Boletín*.

[26] Raúl H. Castagnino, "Integración del repertorio de Coronado," *Boletín*, No. 20 (1948) 2–6; Ordaz, *El teatro*, pp. 48–50.

During the nine years of his second period Coronado made his greatest contribution to the Argentine national theatre. Sometimes, in spite of the accuracy of Echagüe's astute characterization of him as a literary anachronism always looking to the past, Coronado dealt with contemporary problems. *Los parásitos* (1904) blames the bureaucrats for the ills of the middle class. *La tormenta de verano* (1905) about middle-class marital conflicts, and *Parientes pobres* (1907) about class snobbery, along with *Salvador* and *Cortar por lo más delgado*, are also modern.

However, Coronado also found inspiration in the days of Indian fighting. His 1906 *El sargento Palma* (Comisión de Cultura, 1942) tells of the fruitless sacrifice of the Federalist soldier for a girl already engaged to somebody else. Historical, too, were: *Luz de luna y luz del incendio* (1883) about Rosas; *La vanguardia* (1907); and *1810*, written for the centenary of Argentine independence.

However it is for *Piedra de escándalo* (1899), a riotous success whose run of twenty-eight performances broke records in the history of the Argentine theatre,[27] and its sequel, *La charca de don Lorenzo* (1918), that this lyric-poet-turned-dramatist will be chiefly remembered.

Piedra de escándalo, containing stanzas still recited for their lyric beauty, has an involved plot. The only real character is the old gringo grandfather Lorenzo, likable, providing a touch of humor, and a far step from the earlier *cocoliche* in *Juan Moreira*. Coronado realized Lorenzo's importance and revived him in the sequel. Though it was as much inferior to the first as most sequels are, the two plays are the most popular of the gaucho cycle because their characters are realistic, hard-working gauchos rather than the romanticized adventure-loving escapists of so many other dramatists. It was with these characters, described with dramatic force and in rustic poetry, that Coronado laid the foundations for Granada, Payró, and Sánchez.

By now the Argentine pampas had been changing with the coming of civilization. Railroads crossed it. The frontier had disappeared. The Indian was pushed out. Following the invention of barbed wire, the wide expanses were fenced, and with the development of a settled society the nomadic life of the gaucho came to an end. Plays about him also changed and lost their Wild West character. Instead

[27] Enrique García Velloso, *Memorias de un hombre de teatro*, pp. 1–13; Ordaz, *El teatro*, pp. 48–50.

of fleeing a posse, he had to face problems arising from these new conditions.[28]

Typical of this phase is *Sobre las ruinas* by Roberto Payró (1867–1928), written in 1902, performed in 1904. Its author, a journalist and author of the amusing gaucho fiction *El casamiento de Laucha* (1906) and *Cuentos de Pago Chico* (1908) wrote drama only occasionally. A total of eight plays represents the output of this burly writer, unmistakable under his broad-brimmed black hat, but they epitomize his country's history. Not till he was thirty-three did he find actors for his first one-act *Canción trágica* (1900), set in the time of Rosas. He wrote two earlier unproduced plays, "Renata," from a novel by Zola, and *Triunfador* (published 1897). His poetic *La cartera de justica*, published serially in a Bahía Blanca newspaper in 1888, then dropped out of sight till 1940.

In 1902 he completed his drama *Sobre las ruinas*, the first of his "theatre of ideas."[29] Because José Podestá did not consider it worth staging, it was not performed, however, till 1904, ten months before the opening of *La gringa*,[30] and "after many vicissitudes," as the book version declared. There was an earlier publication in the magazine *Ideas*. In Sánchez' play, it is the foreigner who stands for progress; in Payró's, the Argentine engineer and the son of the unadaptable gaucho combine efforts to build a new house on the old ruins—old-style customs and heart, but new ideas. Payró's play of a gaucho destroyed by his unwillingness to conform to progress ended the original gaucho cycle in the Argentine theatre.

Payró was also first to stage a legal problem. In 1905, in another "theatre of ideas," feeling the influence of Isben through performances of the Italian Zaconi, he gave *Marco Severi* (*Escena*, No. 88, 1920), timeliness because of the discussions then current about the decisions of Judge Magnaud and the "law of residence" being debated in the national legislature.[31] The story related that an Italian had been a thief in Italy in a moment of great need. Should he be extradited by the Italian government years later, after he has established himself

---

[28] Jorge Max Rohde, *Las ideas estéticas en la literatura argentina*, Vol. II, from Lavardén to Sánchez.

[29] Castagnino, *Esquema*, p. 76. See also J. C. Picone, "El teatro de Roberto Payró," *Claridad*, No. 18 (1929).

[30] Ordaz, *El teatro*, pp. 78–81, 89–92, discusses the similarities and differences between these two plays. See also A. M. Oteiza, *Payró y la Argentina*, pp. 29 ff.

[31] Castagnino, *Esquema*, p. 76.

as an honest and successful Argentine citizen? Melodrama and co-incidence flaw the logic, but its emotional appeal cannot be denied. Payró's other plays and translations, spaced far apart with a period between of life in Europe, are not of much importance in the development of the theatre. *Alegría*, written in six weeks during his final illness, as a vehicle for Florencio Parravicini to mark his transition from comic to serious actor, deals with a circus clown turned cattleman in Santa Cruz. It was performed April 18, 1928, two weeks after the author's death. Noted as a novelist, Payró allowed his actors to talk too much. Even though their dialog is lively and colorful, it often takes the place of character development. He wrote too fast, and theme is sometimes more important than action. Payró's *Teatro completo* (Buenos Aires, 1956) contains honest and sincere expressions of the Argentine spirit of his times. His plays teach good manners and morality, and stamp him as one of the most Argentine of dramatists, but while he elevated the stage and gave it social intensity, his plays are rarely revived today.

Various types of gaucho plays have continued popular on the Argentine stage down to the present, as Western novels still have their appeal in this country. Alberto Ghiraldo (1875–1946), in a melodrama *Alma gaucha* (1906) appealed for sympathy for the conscript gaucho Cruz, who escaped from jail, killed an officer and was executed, still unreconciled. This tragedy offers a gallery of minor figures, most of them better portrayed than Cruz and his *china*, Alma.

The José Hernández epic poem *Martín Fierro* was dramatized in 1915 by José González Castillo (1885–1937), though with more pageant than drama, in three acts and eleven scenes. Rodolfo González Pacheco (1881–1949) presented a heroine named Pampa in *La inundación* (1920) along with a liberty-loving gaucho whose talk is more fanciful than authentic as he declares: "Don't fence me in!"

Even Enrique Larreta (1875–1961), best known for his novel of Spain, *La gloria de don Ramiro*, put the wandering gaucho Ladislao, of the kind they call a *linyera*, into a play of that name in 1932. After fighting injustice and insuring the marriage of his unrecognized daughter, Pastora, to the gaucho Evaristo, Ladislao again starts his wanderings.

Most productive of modern gaucho dramatists is Alberto Vacarezza (1896–1959), whose sentimental *Lo que pasó a Reynoso* (1936) played six hundred performances, and whose *Allá va el resero*

Luna (1942) also had a long run. It was appropriate, therefore, that on April 10, 1936, the fiftieth anniversary of the first night of *Juan Moreira*, Vacarezza should write a special piece to honor old José Podestá, the original Juan. It was a nostalgic occasion, like looking at old pictures of pony-express riders and stagecoaches.

The gauchos have gone. The hard-working immigrants from Italy began tilling the land that the gauchos only rode across. And the resulting economic problems challenged a new school of dramatists. All this prepared the way for Florencio Sánchez.

CHAPTER 8

Florencio Sánchez

The serious Argentine theatre at the beginning of the twentieth century looked toward Europe for inspiration. In Buenos Aires four companies from the continent were producing plays by Hauptmann, Hervieu, Ibsen, and dramatists from Spain and Italy.[1] Only in *sainetes*, brief and usually humorous, could be found national themes and types, and those generally from the lower class of the port and city.

At this moment the dramatist Florencio Antonio Sánchez appeared on the dramatic scene. Sánchez was born in Montevideo, Uruguay, January 17, 1875, the first of eleven children. His parents were of the middle class, his mother a sixteen-year-old girl with little formal education and his father a militant member of the Blanco (conservative) political party. Their frequent change of residence while Florencio was young prevented much formal schooling and discouraged the boy from his ambition to become a lawyer. His admirers, mentioning his lack of education, quoted Anatole France: "Since I studied nothing, I learned much," and called Florencio "an instinct with many eyes and ears."[2]

His school attendance ended completely at the age of fifteen, when his uncle got him a job as secretary of a political commission, work that lasted till his pompous boss discovered Florencio writing humorous articles about him for a newspaper under the pen name "Jack the Ripper." Florencio decided to become a newspaper man. He shifted back and forth between Uruguay and Argentina, a spendthrift with such poor salaries that he became well acquainted with the meaning of that word *miseria* that appears so often in his pages.

He associated with a group of political protesters who organized themselves into "The International Center of Social Studies." The vague urge to cure social and economic troubles and achieve liberty and justice filled the River Plate region with social revolutionists who

[1] Ruth Richardson, *Florencio Sánchez and the Argentine Theatre.*
[2] Fernando García Esteban, *Vida de Florencio Sánchez.*

argued that laws were responsible for injustice and should therefore be abolished. It was for this group that Sánchez composed his first play, which he called *Ladrones*.

In 1896 the Blanco leader Aparicio Saravia tried to oust President Idiarte Borda, a Colorado, in a civil war. Florencio took part in the fighting, but the sight of Uruguayans shooting each other so sickened him that he became disillusioned about people who advocated change through force, and determined to use his pen to make citizens aware of what need improving.[3]

Sánchez' next dramatic effort was a political play called *La gente honesta*, written while he was a reporter in Rosario, Argentina. The night it was supposed to open, June 26, 1902, a city official, a former editor of his paper who knew his employee's biting pen, heard that he was being lampooned in the skit and got Mayor Lamas of Rosario to call out the police to prevent the performance. When Sánchez protested he was beaten and barely escaped arrest; but, determined to get his work before the public, he set type all that night at the newspaper office and had the play ready for distribution next morning. In 1907 he revised it as *Los curdas*, but it folded in a week and added nothing to his literary reputation.

Still determined to put a play of his onto the stage, Sánchez rewrote the old *Ladrones* as a zarzuela, under the new title *Canillita*, a nickname the reporters had given one of the skinny Rosario urchins who sold their newspaper. It was performed in October, 1902, with a soprano taking the role of the newsboy. Rumor assigned the authorship of its songs to a friend, Cayetano Alberto Silva, but even if original they would never have established Sánchez as a lyric poet. Its authentic dialog, full of slang, and the sentimental plot gave it popularity, and it ran for twelve performances. Fifteen months later when it opened in Buenos Aires it supplied a new word to Argentine slang, and newsboys today are still called *canillitas*. Every November 7, the anniversary of Sanchez' death, the Buenos Aires *canillitas* congregate at his monument to honor him.

Earlier, in 1899, at his aunt's house in Montevideo, Sánchez had met Catalina Raventós, seven years younger than he. When her mother asked him about his assets, Florencio replied proudly: "I have my pen."[4] Toward the end of 1902 he learned that another suitor

[3] Julio Imbert, *Florencio Sánchez, vida y creación.*
[4] Roberto F. Giusti, *Florencio Sánchez.*

was courting Catalina. The thought of losing her at first filled the
mercurial author with thoughts of suicide. But he had no money to
buy a revolver, and poison seemed a dismal prospect. While he la-
mented his fate the success of *Canillita* suggested a way of proving
himself something more than the easygoing bohemian that Catalina's
parents considered him. With a plot in mind but with neither manuscript paper nor money to buy any, he stopped one night at the post
office where he made off with a pad of telegraph forms, blank on one
side, and by morning he had completed his first act.

There are many versions of what happened next, since everyone
who ever knew Sánchez has anecdotes to relate. Because of his previous failure with managers of theatres, he took the first act to a
friendly dramatic critic, Joaquín de Vedia, hoping through him to get
the ear of a director. Neither the title, *Los hijos de hoy*, nor the theme
impressed Vedia, but Sánchez finished the play anyway and left it
with Vedia for his opinion. With nothing to do one evening, the
critic began leafing through the first act, then with mounting interest
read on. By Vedia's own account, he grabbed the fistful of telegraph
blanks and dashed with them to Director Soria of the Teatro de la
Comedia.

"Here is the best play written so far in Buenos Aires!"

The manager offered the young playwright a contract and a royalty
of ten pesos an act a night. On Friday, August 11, 1903, the curtain
rose on Sánchez' first important play, retitled by Vedia *M' hijo el
dotor*. The tall, stoop-shouldered Florencio Sánchez, with a face that
hinted of Indian blood, attended opening night in a new suit, bought
with advance royalties. He had been driven to purchase it because
the doorkeeper had thought him a tramp when he tried to attend a
rehearsal in his old suit, whose rumpled appearance indicated his
pressing needs.

The first performance of *M' hijo el dotor* brought immediate fame
to Florencio Sánchez. True, many of the audience were bewildered
by the psychology of the city-educated Julio. Whether he was a rascal or an egotistical creature suffering from too much Nietzsche is not
made clear. One critic called the play an abortion from Ibsen and
Sudermann, but the realism of the first act and the authentic conversation, so different from the ranting in most of the plays of the period,
were very appealing. Even in competition with four foreign companies offering theatre-goers a different drama from abroad every

night, Sánchez' play ran for thirty-eight nights, a record that compared favorably with other popular plays that year, as for instance
the twenty-nine performances of García Velloso's *Jesús Nazareno*
and the twenty-five of Coronado's *Piedra de escándalo*. Only the
seventy-five showings of the farce *Jettatore*, by Laferrère, bettered its
record. Sánchez' friends began calling him "M' hijo el dotor." Following its run in Buenos Aires Podestá took it for two performances
to the Teatro Solís in Montevideo, and Sánchez' fellow countrymen
jammed the theatre. President José Batlle led the applause from his
box, and the play had to be held over for two additional showings.

Much has been written about Sánchez' borrowing of material. Some
believe *My Son the Lawyer* was inspired by Sudermann and by an
Italian play by Rovetta.[5] But much of the author's inspiration was
more personal. He himself had had ambitions to become a *dotor*, and
his advanced ideas must have annoyed his father, Olegario, namesake
of the old man of this play.

In other plays, too, he depicted relatives, as for instance the characters of *Midsummer-Day Partners*. His friend Luis Doello Jurado
writes that the name of the protagonist of *Barranca abajo*, Zoilo Gutiérrez, and many of the characteristics of its gaucho King Lear were
derived from what he had told the dramatist about a relative.

Even the scene involving the escape of Jesusa's thrush, for which
investigators have tried to give credit to Palacio Valdés' *Marta y
María*, was based, according to Sánchez' widow, on an incident in
her own home while Florencio was courting her.[6] So the dramatist
should be given some credit for setting down, realistically, the sort of
life he had observed and known.

He did not introduce realism to the River Plate.[7] It had appeared
in fiction as early as 1880, in accurate local-color sketches and slice-of-
life stories. Even some realistic novels with touches of naturalism had
already been written. On the stage, too, Payró and Laferrère had displayed realism as well as an awareness of contemporary social problems. What Sánchez did, beginning with *M' hijo el dotor*, was to give
the culminating touches to realism. By his efforts he ended imitation

---

[5] Roy Temple House, "Florencio Sánchez, A Great Uruguayan Dramatist,"
Poet Lore, XXXIV (Summer, 1923).

[6] Imbert, *Florencio Sánchez, vida y creación*.

[7] Robert F. Giusti, "Florencio Sánchez y el teatro rioplatense," *Inter-American
Review of Bibliography*, Nos. 17–18, pp. 73–88.

of European theatre and gave a nudge to the nationalistic movement on the Argentine stage.

Those who call him a naturalist, however, err. Dardo Cúneo may be right in terming him, on account of his pessimism and fatalism, "America's representative of Naturalism."[8] But his naturalism is not of the Zola-esque variety. In wanting to make over the social structure he follows Ibsen. But Julio's final cry of "Oh, Life! Life!" is a shout of hope and optimism and not the kind of pessimistic despair at the folly of it all that Ibsen's Brand uttered in 1866 or that Gorki expressed in *The Lower Depths* (1903). Sánchez describes the seamy and the unhappy side, but implies that something can be done about it.

Looking back at *M' hijo el dotor,* critics now see in it the seeds of all the rest of Sánchez' dramas. It had both rural and city background. It mingled the theatre of ideas and social protest with one of action. But beyond that, it established Sánchez as a realist with a gift for what Giusti called "the pure and simple representation of truth."[9] It also revealed some of the faults that run through his later dramas. Echagüe declared Sánchez "lacks equilibrium in his ideas and impartiality in his views of the world," and therefore "fails to present pictures serene, ample, and impregnated by diverse and multiform human truths."[10] Or, as Ricardo Rojas phrased it, Sánchez lacked the "gift of philosophic generalizations to broaden his material and an intense inspiration of poetic evocation to embellish the life of their souls." He was unable to transfigure mentally and spiritually the details he observed so well.

His first long play foreshadowed, too, his habit of attacking on too broad a front the injustice and social conditions against which he protests in his major works. So many targets are set up that the clearness of their delineation is often blurred. His logic can sometimes be questioned, and his psychology is occasionally unconvincing.

In such an unnatural speech as when city-bred Julio declares his love for Jesusa, one realizes the dramatist's lack of opportunity to observe the educated and wealthy among his countrymen. Technically, too, while the exits are usually motivated, Sánchez ignores the time element of the entrances. For instance, someone calls Jesusa and, as

[8] Dardo Cúneo (ed.), *Obras de Florencio Sánchez.*
[9] Giusti, *Florencio Sánchez*; Tabaré J. Freire, *Florencio Sánchez, Sainetero.*
[10] Juan Pablo Echagüe, *Seis figuras del Plata,* pp. 123–157.

though poised in the wings, she appears instantly. Collisions between newcomer and departing actor could be frequent.

But the total result of *My Son the Lawyer* was to win the admiration of most critics, increase the demand by managers for further plays by Sánchez, and gain the consent of Catalina's parents to her marriage, which took place five weeks after opening night. Before the ceremony, one of "Catita's" friends tried to dissuade her with the warning that Florencio was displaying signs of tuberculosis, but she refused to believe it.

Following *My Son the Lawyer* came a total of twenty plays, eight long and twelve short ones, product of the six years that comprised Sánchez' life as a dramatist. Someone has calculated that his total writing time for all of them was not more than thirty-five working days.[11] The implication is that the rest of Sánchez' life was wasted in drunken brawls and in quarrels with actors and managers. It is quite true that when in need of money Sánchez wrote rapidly, sometimes finishing a play in twenty-four hours. But those who consider the rest of his hours unproductive are unaware of how little of a writer's creation is done while he is actually holding a pen. Many anecdotes prove how true this was with Sánchez. Report has it that *Los muertos* (1905), acclaimed at its first performance as his masterpiece, was written in one night in a rented hotel room while the author, surrounded by friends, consumed cigarets and cups of maté. But the truth is that years before, Sánchez had been struck by the idea that a man without will power is a walking dead man. From then on he had been mentally composing the play, and had even announced its title several months earlier. Most of the dialog was already in his mind, waiting to be written down. So, in the name of justice, the conception of Sánchez as a lazy bohemian should be corrected. At least part of his listlessness can probably be ascribed to the onset of the tuberculosis that was to end his life so soon.

On August 1, 1904, Buenos Aires attended Sánchez' very nationalistic *sainete*, *Cédulas de San Juan*, which proved again his ability to create atmosphere and to report with almost stenographic accuracy the conversation of the uneducated classes. The same year came the two-act *La pobre gente*, a gloomy picture of life in a city slum.

The story ran that the composition of his next masterpiece, *La gringa*, took him only a day. Actually it would take that long merely

[11] Dora Corti, *Florencio Sánchez*, Tomo I, No. 9, pp. 195–330.

to copy the manuscript. As for its composition, toward the end of 1902 Sánchez spent a month on a ranch near Santa Fe. At that period in Buenos Aires' theatrical history the Italian immigrant appeared on the stage chiefly as the villain or the comic character in the melodramatic gaucho plays. But on the ranch Sánchez saw at first hand the competition which these industrious foreigners provided to the easygoing Creoles. Even the title was provided at this time, because the daughter of his host was nicknamed "La Gringa." One wonders whether he had ever heard of the short play *Gauchos y gringos,* written in 1884 by a newspaperman, Justo López de Gómara (1859–1922), also a resident of Rosario. At any rate Sánchez had two years to mull his story over, so that when a manager required a play in a hurry to keep his theatre open, Sánchez might well have echoed an earlier dramatist: "I have it all finished except putting it on paper."

This play, considered by many critics as his masterpiece, and called by Rojas "the tragedy of the Argentine race," had a mixed reception when it opened on November 21, 1904. There was no applause at the dramatic climax of the third act. At this point the dramatist had really solved its dramatic problem whether Creole inefficiency and tradition could stand against the gringo industry, but the program announced another act to come. Perhaps the Argentine custom of paying royalties according to the number of acts had tempted Sánchez to provide a sort of epilog, restating and re-solving the problem to provide a happy ending. The run of only ten performances lay more in difficulties among the actors than lack of public support. Gradually the play gained popularity in spite of criticism that the symbolism of the *ombú* tree was far-fetched and that Sánchez carried to extremes the struggle between old and new. The emotion, the realistic picture of the pampas, the lifelike characters, and the patriotic appeal at the end, with the promise of a new Argentina built on the fusion of the two races, have made it the most performed of all of Sánchez' plays. It inspired, among other plays, *El gringo* by Otto Miguel Cione and *La gringada* by Enrique Queirolo. *Sánchez* believed it was his best play and the one most likely to endure.

Better technically, and more enthusiastically received by first-nighters was his next play, *Barranca abajo,* performed April 26, 1905. One wonders whether the title came from the subtitle of Part II of *Calandria* or from a popular expression. Certainly the dramatist's own observation of life on the pampas was the source of the characters. Two of them are outstanding as the best rounded of all his creations. Triumphal revivals of *Barranca abajo* in Buenos Aires in 1956 and in Montevideo in 1960 show how well it lasts.

In general Sánchez' plays lie on the surface, without very profound psychology. The story, the customs, the picturesque language, and the atmosphere were his chief interest. He shows himself a master in portraying typical people in representative environment, and manifests little desire to plumb the souls of the individuals. Most of his women are hardly more than puppets provided to develop the action. What they look like or why they act as they do is only fleetingly revealed. Even the sickly Robustiana, so ironically named, has little personality, and there is no explanation why she is so snubbed by the other women. Jesusa, too, in *M' hijo el dotor* never comes entirely to life. Perhaps the author was better acquainted with less admirable women. Certainly Martiniana, though only a minor character in *Barranca abajo*, is the most real of all his women.

The dramatist is somewhat more successful with his men, but only one of them assumes a rounded personality: Zoilo, that good gaucho driven to despair and suicide by the women around him. Some critics even objected that the author was psychologically unsound in making a tough old gaucho commit suicide. In the original version, Zoilo, having once been prevented from hanging himself, persuades Aniceto into letting him try again. For the second night's performance, however, Sánchez was persuaded to let him hang without arguments, which dulls the thesis but improves the play. Both endings have been reprinted in *Medio siglo de farándula* (Córdoba, 1930), the memoirs of the actor who interpreted Zoilo, José J. Podestá.

Barranca abajo ends one cycle of Sánchez' plays, those with a rural setting. Cúneo makes a threefold division of his productions, including a preliminary grouping of "first plays" that includes two of slight importance; then the four "rural plays"; and from 1905 on, "city plays," subdivided into those concerned with the middle and upper class and those dealing with the poor people.[12] The last classification contains nine, the other group five, all spiritual tragedies belonging to the realm of the sociologist, if not the psychopath. Giusti sees two kinds: those that mirror life and those that analyze it and uphold a thesis.

[12] Cúneo (ed.), *Obras de Florencio Sánchez*; Vicente Salaverri (ed.), *El teatro del uruguayo Florencio Sánchez*.

En familia (October 6, 1905) was declared by *La Nación* "the most complete of Sánchez' plays." Certainly it demonstrates complete hopelessness. The drama showed its author abandoning completely his interest in local color and picturesque rural language. He had turned to the consideration of an unhappy social condition, with carefully developed action, and the critics applauded the result. The audience, on the other hand, offered a mixed reaction. One reason probably was that the father, Jorge, was played by Pablo Podestá, who had a reputation for his portrayal of low comics. The audience kept expecting him to be amusing, and were disappointed. So, in spite of praise by critics, *En familia* lasted only seventeen days. It might have closed sooner, but the manager had paid seven hundred pesos for it and kept the play running until Sánchez could complete *Los muertos,* also about middle-class people. This play had a different reception. The critics treated it coldly, but the public flocked to see it. On its opening night excited spectators rushed to the stage to prevent Lisandro from cutting the throat of his wife's sweetheart. In its heyday it was considered Sánchez' masterpiece, but for present-day tastes the melodrama is not convincing. *Los muertos,* too, was written on telegraph blanks, not because Sánchez could not then afford other paper, but because he was convinced that that kind of stationery brought him luck.

Nuestros hijos (May 2, 1907), another play about the middle class, is sometimes considered a thesis play, stressing the idea that motherhood is never a crime, but critics complained there was no need to rant for three acts to put over a belief already generally accepted. Sr. Díaz is the dramatist's spokesman concerning the ills of society. In fact, Imbert declares that Díaz was intended actually to be the dramatist, endowed with Sánchez' own vehemence and vocabulary.[13] The play appealed to audiences, and a version in Italian was performed in Buenos Aires the year after its première in Spanish.

Among Sánchez' other plays with upperclass characters is the three-act *El pasado de una vida,* preliminary statement of marital unfaithfulness, later expanded in *Nuestros hijos.* Its first two acts develop the whole story and leave nothing for the final act.

Los derechos de la salud (December 4, 1907), the last of the middle-class plays, is the story of Luisa, dying of consumption and

[13] Imbert, *Florencio Sánchez, vida y creación.*

watching her sister Renata replace her in the affection of her children and her husband. This was Sánchez' only play performed in Montevideo before being presented in Buenos Aires. Whether it is a thesis play stating Sánchez' conviction that health has its rights—the subject of the essay that Luisa's husband is writing—or whether it was something inspired by Sánchez' worry over his own health has been debated. Its inevitability and simplicity made one critic declare it his greatest play, but the public never patronized it and thought the dialog extremely unreal. Still, Unamuno admired it enough to try to persuade a Madrid company to present it. The fact that it came from unknown Uruguay and was the work of a writer with the commonplace name of Sánchez was too great a handicap for success in Spain. In 1942 it was made into the movie *Pasión imposible*, highly praised by the Argentine press.

In the other subgroup, plays dealing with the lower class, no one can criticize the authenticity of the dialog. First came *Canillita*, performed in Buenos Aires two months after *M' hijo el dotor*. Its accuracy of observation was proved by a Sunday-afternoon performance in January, 1904, given free to the newsboys whose life it depicts. They participated with all the zeal of a showboat audience and almost mobbed the villain. After that, Sánchez received a new nickname, "Canillita."

La gente pobre (1904), in two acts, followed, portraying the degradation of a poor family whose father is too weak to assume responsibilities and who uses his children to earn more money for his vices. It shows the dramatist's naturalism, though it has a romantic ending. Sánchez used this theme again in his last play, *Un buen negocio* (1909), the poorest of his writings, in which at the conclusion the villain has an unmotivated change of heart. Perhaps the author's illness and pressing need for money can excuse its mediocrity. Imbert has another explanation of its shortcomings and complete falsity: he suggests that Sánchez was taking the first uncertain steps in the direction of another style of playwriting.

Mano santa (June 2, 1905) was a brief respite in his list of grim plays. It has no plot, but as a slice of life it reveals the dramatist's power to observe and reproduce. It is a farce about a fake healer. Poverty, which in Sánchez' opinion was the cause of most woe and suffering, motivated his dramatic *sainete*, *El desalojo* (July 16,

1906), in which the author attacks the "wrong kind" of charity and argues that society should provide money so that a mother can bring up her own children. The critics ignored it. His most theatrical short play, *La tigra* (January 2, 1907), provides a tense conclusion: only as a prostitute could the mother earn enough to bring up her daughter.

Late in 1906 a competition for short plays was organized by the Labardén Conservatory, named for that dramatist who in 1789 wrote Argentina's first historic play, *Siripo*. Each of the twenty-seven competitors was assigned a title to be built into a play. "Moneda falsa" fell to Sánchez, and for it he developed another of his lifelike characters. It also marked the last time he included a gringo in the cast. In spite of its enthusiastic reception by the audience and laudatory articles about it in the papers, when the final awards were made, *Moneda falsa* was passed over with an honorable mention. The indignant audience demonstrated in the street, then marched to one of the newspaper offices to register a protest. After second looks, the critics agreed that, though not perfect, it was better than any of the three prize winners. This play about a rascal, unjustly treated by the law but too weak to go straight, is still a favorite with amateur dramatic groups.

Having dominated the Argentine theatre, Sánchez was ambitious for a wider stage. Several of his plays had already been translated into Italian and performed, so he hoped that a voyage to Europe would stimulate a world appreciation of his drama. A benefit performance that he had counted on to buy his ticket left him actually owing money to the performers, but, by playing the Uruguayan government against groups of his admirers in Argentina, the invalid got himself a political appointment to Italy.

Exhausted by the voyage, he reached Genoa in October, 1909, then made Milan his home. But he got no hearing for his plays. Labor troubles in all of Italy and family difficulties for the manager most interested in mounting his dramas ruined Sánchez' hopes of triumph. In his disappointment over the coolness with which he was received, his tuberculosis became worse. Long years of irregular habits were demanding a reckoning. His money gave out. Ill and with his usual aversion to steady work, he lived in poverty. On November 7, 1910, the writer who had helped introduce realism into the theatre of the

River Plate died and was buried in the cemetery of Milan. In 1921, with appropriate ceremonies, the Uruguayan government brought home the ashes of its most illustrious literary personage.

His plays continue to live as theatre, if not as literature. There is a volume in English of his plays.[14] Cúneo mentions a Japanese version of *My Son the Lawyer*. It is ironical that the dramatist who set himself up to improve the morals and social conditions of his time was banned as immoral in Argentina when the "colonels" came into power in 1943, but elsewhere he is honored and performed, and many printed editions testify to his popularity with the reading public. Because of his efforts, the Argentine theatre received new life, new technique, and an inclination toward local themes and problems as well as local color. After a long line of trite and sentimentalized gauchos, Sánchez offered audiences a feeling of spontaneity, with vivid and authentic characters presented on the stage with truth and sincerity. He appeared at just the right time, when the Argentine stage was tired of its farces and imported plays.

Perhaps Florencio Sánchez is not a great dramatist in comparison with masters of literary style who have influenced writers outside their countries. His writing is unequal, with some of his plots and situations trite and weak. But his good qualities made his theatre an artistic inheritance and an important phase of the Argentine national theatre. Even "Jean Paul," who scorned him as an "Ibsencito criollo," agreed that in the handling of local color, as an observer of certain aspects of life, and in his scenic construction none equaled him.

The comment made about him by Carlos Roxlo may best sum him up:

He does not found the national theatre, but he creates a type of play; he imposes it and makes it popular. He . . . makes it a theatre of modern thesis and national customs. . . . With action? Yes, with action. One idiomatic phrase is enough, a gesture occasionally, a whistle sometimes. In certain cases, a man dressed in a *chiripa* [gaucho blanket], or a woman wearing a *rebozo* [shawl] crosses the stage. That is Florencio Sánchez.

[14] Willis Knapp Jones (trans.), *Representative Plays of Florencio Sánchez*.

CHAPTER 9

The "Gringa" Theme in River Plate Drama

No other nation of Hispanic America owes more than Argentina does to immigration from Europe, which began by 1513. Most of the other areas had large Indian populations to supply laborers and wives to the Spaniards. Argentine Indians, however, never became peacefully inclined toward the white man, so the population increased only as new colonists arrived from across the Atlantic. As late as 1716, when Peru was mourning the death of 80,000 citizens from earthquake, fever, and starvation, the whole of Argentina contained hardly 16,000 people and even at the time of its independence it numbered only 40,000.

The 638,000 inhabitants of Argentina in 1890 were there chiefly because of the insistence of the statesman Juan Bautista Alberdi (1810–1884) that "To govern is to populate." He encouraged the immigration of foreigners, "gringos" as they were called by the native-born "criollo." Some believe the term originated because their chatter was "all Greek" (*griego*) to the Spanish-speaking inhabitants of the River Plate region. Certainly it did not arise—as some have tried to explain the Mexican use of it for North American cowboys—because their favorite song was "Green grow the rushes, O!"

Once in their new homeland, the gringos found their place not only in national life but in Argentine literature. To most Creoles the gringo with his incomprehensible talk and queer customs was amusing. As a comic fellow is how the Spanish-born dramatist Justo López de Gómara drew him in *Gauchos y gringos*, which was produced in Rosario in 1884. And comedy was his role when one night in April, 1890, the character "Cocoliche" was introduced into the play *Juan Moreira*, as already described.

Though by now Italy had supplied nearly 65 per cent of Argentina's population, the ignorant Italian with his barbarous Spanish was a stock comic character. The epic poem *Martín Fierro* describes one Italian. In the Owens' translation:

He spoke so thick that no one there
    Could understand his lingo . . .
A Napolitano he said he was,
    Which I take is a kind of gringo.

Subsequent plays in which a *cocoliche* appears include *Julián
Jiménez* (1889) by Abdón Arózteguy (1853–1926) of Uruguay, *Amor
y lucha* by Ezequiel Soria (1870–1936), and that popular play *Los
políticos,* by Trejo. The *sainete Los disfrazados* by Carlos Pacheco
lists in the cast of characters: "un guachito, un cocoliche, una vecina,
etc.," and Sánchez uses the term in his *Canillita.* So widespread did
cocoliche become in prose and poetry that in 1902 Ernesto Quesada
was moved to discuss the characteristics of this type in an article in
the review *Estudios.*

For a score of years the gaucho continued to be the hero of plays;
the gringo remained the clown. Eventually thinkers began to realize
that the gaucho had become an anachronism in the progress of Argentina. Inhabitants of the rural regions needed less encouragement to
struggle with the police to prove valor, and more to struggle with
nature to prove energy. Serious dramatists pondered the caricature
of the hard-working gringos, and, seeing them taking over the old
homes and old fortunes of the Creoles, wondered about their upset-
ting the homogeneity of the nation. The immigrants were threaten-
ing the fortune of the conservative Creoles, who were too blind to
see that Argentina was entering a new phase of social revolution.
Instead of being a jabbering clown, the gringo was now no laughing
matter. At all levels, from newcomer to citizen, these foreigners deserved serious sociological study.

One of the earliest serious gringo parts is the grandfather Lorenzo
in Coronado's *Piedra de escándalo* (written 1899). Coronado also introduced non-Italian gringos, like the Basque in his *Flor del aire* and
the Englishman in his patriotic *1810,* written for the centenary of
Argentine independence. The gringo engineer in Payró's *Sobre las
ruinas* has been discussed: to the old gaucho Pedro it would be an
insult to his ancestors to adopt the foreigners' practices. But the best-
known play on this theme is, of course, *La gringa* (1904) by the man
generally considered the greatest playwright of Ibero-America, Florencio Sánchez. Here is the plot:

Nicola, a gringo, obtains, by industry, from the gaucho Cantalicio the *estancia* that the Argentine's ancestors won by blood. The Italian considers his daughter, the gringa Victoria, too good to marry the son of the shiftless Cantalicio, but eventually the young suitor redeems himself by his industry. "Won't they make a fine pair!" Nicola boasts at the end. "Daughter of pure gringo stock . . . son of pure Creole stock. From them will come the strong race of tomorrow." The play ends with the stirring challenge: "To work!"

La gringa is full of symbolism. Cantalicio, returning to his farm to see what the gringos are doing with it, finds them chopping down an *ombú* tree which, though useless for timber or firewood, was the symbol of the gaucho. The injuring of the old cowboy by an automobile brought a protest from the critic Echagüe, who protested that was carrying too far the feud between tradition and progress. In his article in *La Nación* after the first performance, Echagüe really found little about the play to arouse his enthusiasm.

To most dramatists, however, *La gringa* suggested a new source of dramatic material. Otto Miguel Cione followed it with *El gringo*, and Enrique Queirolo (1880–1942) wrote *La gringada*. Not only its name but its theme have been worked over by River Plate dramatists ever since. Both before and after the performance in New York in 1910 of Israel Zangwill's play *The Melting Pot*, Argentines saw their own country in that role and have so proclaimed it dramatically in many guises.

In *Mustafá* (1921), by Armando Discépolo and de Rosa, Argentina the melting-pot-nation is praised by the Turkish peddler-hero and by the Italian Gaetano, whose son is to wed the Turk's daughter. "This is the hospitable land," says the Italian in barbarous Spanish. "It accepts all sorts of immigrants . . . And the fine thing is that, in spite of the mixture, all get along with one another, French with Germans, Italians with Africans. This is a paradise! (*Este é no paraíso*)." The babel of tongues is further reproduced in a one-act play *Babilonia* (1925) by Discépolo, where the servants' quarters of a Buenos Aires house echoes to a hodgepodge of German, Galician, French, and Italian.

With his first glimpse of Argentina the immigrant is impressed by the need for hard work, and this necessity is the theme of a three-act *sainete*, *Ganarse la vida* (1907) by Pedro Pico, which picks up the immigrant as he steps onto the mainland at the old Boca, or waterfront. Stage directions indicate: "An immigrant ship has just tied up at the wharf, and the confused newcomers sort out their possessions amid venders of Paraguayan oranges and Argentine peanuts and newspapers." Setting and characters will be longer remembered than the plot.

Work is stressed in several plays by Carlos Pacheco, including *Los fuertes* (printed in 1922). Its setting is the ivy-covered, many-windowed Immigrant Hotel, Buenos Aires' Ellis Island, within a stone's throw of fashionable Paseo Colón. Its building about an open patio could house six thousand newcomers till they could be distributed to their destinations. "You've got to work hard," declares one of the immigrants in this play."You need strength," adds another.

For those with strength and industry, Argentina is pictured as a land of opportunity. That is the theme of *Mamá Clara* (1920) by Federico Mertens. Clara, once an immigrant, has risen to wealth by operating a vegetable stand. "What is our class," she asks, "if it isn't immigrants who by their industry are making their fortunes or have made them?"

Of course not all immigrants are wholly admirable, and realistic dramatists have not overlooked the rascals. Alberto Vacarezza is one of their chief critics. His play *Tu cuna fué un conventillo* (1920) is full of gringo crooks. The villain of his *Minas de Caminiaga* (1935) is an Italian usurer, foiled by the Creole hero. The first of these, "Your Cradle Was a Tenement House," is a comedy of customs in three scenes, which had a record run of three thousand performances in Buenos Aires in the first twenty-five years of its existence. "El Gallo," big shot in the underworld, is giving a party in the tenement where once he took Rosalia away from her fiancé, Maldonado. But now Maldonado, back from a term in the penitentiary, recklessly bluffs both El Gallo and the girl and walks off with her before the big shot's assembled guests. Within ten minutes he brings her back, explaining that he did not want her but merely wanted to put El Gallo in his place.

The play has several other complications. The action is rapid, with drama and farce alternating amid vivid and kaleidoscopic scenes. Much of the humor comes from attempts by the immigrants to imitate the exploits and even the language of their favorite "badmen."

In another play, *Los contagios* (1915) by Dr. Belisario Roldán, the gringo, Dr. Cagliari, is the contagion-carrier. He infects others with the virus of immorality. *Morriña, Morriña mía* (1921) by Enrique García Velloso, turns the spotlight on gringo rascals involved in Argentina's white slave ring, but the dramatist did not mean it as a general stigma on all gringos, because it is another foreigner, the Galician Santiago, who saves the victim, Inesiña, while the Creoles do nothing.

At least one group of plays takes the Creole point of view in hating all gringos, good and bad. They picture the old settler pushed out of his possessions by some upstart foreigner. This was the angle of Martín Coronado's *Sebastián* as early as 1907. This, too, accounts for the hatred of the newcomers expressed by the "Old Creole" Clemencia of Pedro Benjamín Aquino's *Criolla vieja* (1922). She does not condemn her servant Adela for getting drunk at a carnival and giving herself to a man. It is only when she learns that the father-to-be is a gringo that she explodes: "Aren't you ashamed? The least you could have done was to pick a Creole!"

One play, *La tapera* (printed in 1919) by Alberto Novión, shows the actual uprooting of one of the old-timers, driven by progress from the lands of his ancestors. The railroad has obtained a right-of-way across Indalecio's farm, and Italian laborers arrive to build a station on the site of the mud cabin where he had hoped to die. This intrusion adds one more cause for his hatred against the foreigners. So he refuses even a drink of water to a track layer, taking him for a symbol of "cevelización."

The symbolism of the *ombú* tree, found in *La gringa*, also occurs here as the old gaucho Indalecio declares: "There's our old *ombú*, always the same. Only dead will they be able to take it away. And that's what ought to happen to all *crioyos*: to die in the soil where they were born, like the *ombú*." The same symbolism is repeated in Carlos Pacheco's *La vida inútil* (1918). The overseer Escudero could not bring himself to accompany his daughter and her husband to their new home. There they will be like a new tree and a new kind of people. Escudero intends to stay where he is, "like the *ombú* forever bound to this piece of land." Like most of the conservative old gauchos, however, he admires their determination to get ahead.

This attachment to the land is not, of course, unique among the Creoles of Argentina, but it is certainly much discussed in their plays. One such example is the conversation among the young people in Roberto Cayol's *Ciudad incrédula* (1919) after the Creole Lisandro has lost his farm through crooked politics.

"We ought to think in the Argentine way (*argentinamente*) about land," says one character. "Why?" demands the grandson. "So that foreigners may triumph tomorrow on Argentine land?" And the answer comes back: "Land has no nationality. That's what we give it by our thinking."

There must have been something about their thinking, then, that brought the gringo plentiful harvests from farms where the Creoles had almost starved. And the dramatists who reported those successes did it without any signs of envy. While it is true that audiences even today laugh at the gringos' uncouth Spanish, they see them as sympathetic characters and applaud their spirit of progress. Most of them, at least in the stage versions, were successes. It is true that Giácomo, the sixty-year-old gringo in the play of the same name (1924) by Discépolo and de Rosa, loses his fortune and his store in Rosario, supposedly through bad management, but it is eventually disclosed that the real cause of his poverty was that he sold out and splurged on a trip through Europe with a girl he saw at the theatre.

Even in *Mateo* (1923), by Discépolo, when the old horse that gave its name to the play can no longer draw the cab that provides a living for Miguel, the spirit of progress lessens the old man's tragedy because Miguel's son, Carlos, has learned to operate a taxicab.

As gringo immigrants worked, prospered, and became Argentines, a conviction developed, best expressed in *Marco Severi* (1905) by Roberto Payró, that they became new people whose previous life was unimportant. In the Payró play, one who had been a thief in Italy is now a respectable printer in Argentina. When papers arrive for his extradition, the Argentine Minister of Foreign Affairs is the one who launches a movement to save him and finally gets a pardon by cable from the King of Italy.

With such traditions of success and respectability built up for the gringos, it is no wonder that not only Próspero in *La gringa*, but Creoles in many other plays saw a distinct advantage in marriages with the gringos. In Vacarezza's *Minas de Caminiaga* (1935), the domineering mother wants her two daughters to marry foreigners, even though they may be only a pseudo count from France and a blusterer from Genoa. In the three-act *¡Cobarde!* (1894), written in one day by Victor Pérez Petit, old Gil wants his daughter Natividad to forget the gaucho Pedro in favor of the Italian Rampli. Mamá Clara, in the Mertens play of that name, picks for her older daughter

the gringo Bonifacio, "a stupid fellow, but honest and hard-working."
In *Un rincón del pasado* (n.d.) by André Demarchi, María's father
tries to arrange a marriage for her with the gringo Nicolás Brandi.

Nicolás Granada's *Al campo* (1902) shows Indalecio, though an
enemy of the gringos, forced by his wife's nagging to move to Buenos
Aires in search of a gringo husband for his daughter Gilberta. Even
the gringo-hating heroine of Alberto Novión's *Misia Pancha la Brava*
(1915), a prickly-pear sort of character with spines outside but sweet-
ness within, ends by marrying an Italian widower, for whose two
gringa daughters she engineers successful marriages.

And so it goes. Each of these plays makes concrete the idea that
gringos are better matrimonial timber (even those whose heads seem
to be wooden) than would be any shiftless gaucho or Creole and
that gaucho blood needs to be vitalized by gringo corpuscles.

Of course some matches were obviously doomed to disappointment. Such failures are deserved. In the amusing one-act *sainete* by
Carlos Pacheco, *La quinta de los Reyes* (1916), Patricio, friend of
the decadent Reyes family, schemes for a marriage to get back the
family estate that had been taken over by the Italian Santelmo and
his gringa wife, Juana. Through trickery to both, he gets their daughter married to Luis Reyes. But the old Reyes home has been turned
into a babel of tongues, a boarding house for gringos. Instead of
being proud of the estate, Luis only figures how quickly he can turn
it into money and escape.

Other cases where marriage to a gringo turns out wrong are found
in *El gringo* (1904) by Otto Miguel Cione, and *El zapato de cristal*
(1915) by Enrique García Velloso. In the first, an aristocratic señorita
marries the rich gringo Nicolotti to restore the splendor of her ruined
family, but she has nothing in common with the once humble immigrant and continues to see her former sweetheart. Nicolotti's ultimate solution is his own suicide.

A close parallel is García Velloso's "Glass Slipper" in which once-
rich parents of Mariana arrange a loveless marriage to Pietro Rovetta
for the sake of the family fortune. Again it is a former sweetheart
who complicates the plot, but it gives García Velloso an exciting
final act full of blackmail, stolen letters, and hush money, and some
of the best "theatre" in Argentine drama.

However, unhappy marriages were the exception. The happiness
of the majority of matches with gringos is reflected in the pronounce-

ment of the proud Creole ranch owner in Alberto Novión's *La gaucha*
(1906). She is listing the benefits brought to her country by foreigners as she backs her son's choice of the gringo Elena rather than some
Argentine girl. Elena's father, Luigi, has been reminiscing to his wife
in Italianized Spanish: "Remember, Old Lady, when we arrived here
practically empty-handed? Now we have this farm, thanks to our
hard work."

The Gaucha, hearing them, is moved to add: "And an Argentine
to defend the country."

Fermín, young son of the immigrants, asks a question which shows
what the Gaucha means: "Father, when do I start taking my military
training?"

Gringo children who forget their foreign ancestry are usually taken
to task, as was the daughter in *Mamá Clara*, or the son in *En un burro
tres baturros* (1923), by Novión. By telling Alfredo of his early struggles as an immigrant, the father persuades him to marry the gringa
Pilara.

Of all the River Plate plays treating the gringa theme, perhaps the
one most worthy to receive the mantle of Florencio Sánchez' *La
gringa* is *El bronce* (1920), by Dr. Belisario Roldán (1873–1923).
It parallels *La gringa* in many ways. Representative of the Creoles
are Doña Dolores and her three children, Emilio, Carola, and the
anarchistic Carlos. Typifying the gringos are Giacomo Robinetti and
his son Juan, a medical student of whom even the Creoles declare:
"That gringo will go places."

It is the Creole mother, not the father as in *La gringa*, who wastes
the family patrimony and has to mortgage the estate. Dolores' philosophy has been simple: "If money is plentiful, spend it; if it is
scarce, look for it; if it comes, accept it; and if it doesn't come . . .
forget it!" Still, this philosophy does not solve her pressing problem
of finding cash to meet the payments. When the need grows too great,
the mother conquers her antagonism to gringos and finds one of them
who will advance the money, just as Nicola did in Sánchez' play.
Dolores' lawyer voices the theme of the play: "As this family is being
reconstructed, so is Argentina's race of tomorrow being formed by
the fusing of several metals which end by producing the most noble
of all, the most resonant and firm, that glorious metal, bronze." The
play ends as the Creole mother, Dolores, begins to suspect she is

falling in love with the gringo Giacomo, a widower of fifteen-years' standing.

Whether the melting-pot days of Argentina are over is too early to say. In 1931 the Argentine Immigration Department reported that for the first time Argentina had "exported" more people than she had "imported." But the gringo is still there, including foreigners from all nations. And the Italians still predominate. Argentina's roster of artists include names like Ballerini, Sívori, Fiorini, and Pellegrini. Vacarezza and Discépolo figure among her dramatists, and many foreign names appear in the casts that play them. In a recent Argentine Cabinet, four ministers bore Italian names. And so long as the influence of sons and second-generation sons of Italy continue to be strongly felt, so long will the theme of *La gringa* continue to provide inspiration for dramatists of the River Plate.

CHAPTER 10

Well-Known Twentieth-Century Argentine Dramatists

In the nineteenth century Argentina had known moments of plentiful dramatists, and other moments with an abundance of actors, frequently from Spain. But the active period of its drama really began toward the end of the century, when both conditions were occurring at the same time. The variety of offerings, with the melodramas of gauchos and the *sainetes* about the rest of Argentina's population, was developing a playgoing public, especially among the middle and lower classes. The large Podestá family, making its entry into the spoken theatre with *Juan Moreira,* provided actors who could pronounce the language of the ordinary Argentine, where previously the lisp of the Madrid-trained actors had made them unconvincing in that role.

And so the twentieth century produced a tremendous number of Argentine dramatists, too many even to try to catalog. For the ordinary student, a discussion of Florencio Sánchez and a half dozen other outstanding purveyors of drama will be enough to show the activity of drama in Buenos Aires. Another chapter will be devoted to the second line of writers, important in their way and superior to the best of many other Latin American countries. Specialists can turn to other sources[1] for a listing of the many other writers whose one or two plays may have had merit, but who for some reason or other wrote no more and cannot be classified as active or outstanding. In 1946, according to *Argentores,* Buenos Aires had twenty-three theatres performing plays to a monthly attendance of 420,000 Ar-

---

[1] Some are listed in two unpublished Ph.D. dissertations: Maurice Elstun, "The Origin of the National Theatre of Argentina, 1900–1920" (University of North Carolina); and Theodore Apstein, "Contemporary Argentine Theatre, 1920–1942" (The University of Texas). These studies have been augmented by the excellent work of Luis Ordaz, *El Teatro en el Río de la Plata,* 2d ed. See also Thora Sorenson, "Recent Developments in the Argentine Theatre," *Hispania,* XXXIX (December, 1956), 445–449; and Tito Livio Foppa, *Diccionario teatral del Río de la Plata.*

gentines, who paid sixteen million pesos a year admission. In 1961 there were twenty-eight commercial theatres and fifteen independent ones. Of the plays offered their audiences, an enormous number have found their way into print, though the small editions, cheap paper, and fragile format make acquiring and preserving them difficult.

Beginning in 1917, *La Escena, revista teatral* began appearing every Thursday with a full-length play, usually by an Argentine dramatist, priced at fifteen centavos a copy. The series went at least to No. 778. The next year *Bambalinas* took up the idea, followed by *Argentores*, the publication by the society of that name, which came into being in 1934. They were priced at thirty centavos each, and appeared every two weeks. By 1949 they had issued No. 289. In 1937, *Talía* began with a new play every two weeks, while *Teatro moderno* entered the competition in 1939. Many others, like *Teatro del Público* made a brief appearance. Certainly several thousand of these paperback plays became available for play readers, though they are hard to find today. Some of these sources are given for plays mentioned here.

Here are nine of the outstanding dramatists, in chronological order of their birth.

Gregorio de Laferrère
(March 8, 1867–November 30, 1913)

If Florencio Sánchez founded the tragic theatre of the River Plate, Laferrère was the father of its cosmopolitan comedy. Born in Buenos Aires, he returned for awhile to the France of his father, and then devoted the rest of his life to politics and aristocratic clubs in Buenos Aires. He was representative of this cosmopolitan capital because his six long plays and score of lesser dialogs could take place almost as well in Paris or London.[2]

Laferrère began playwriting after betting his friend Francisco Beazley that he could turn out a better play than the one they had just seen together. He confessed that he had no urgent message, no feeling of social consciousness; he wanted only to entertain. Thinking of Gautier's *Jettatura*, about a man who killed his sweetheart by merely looking at her, Laferrère wrote the comedy *Jettatore* (1904), and sent it to Podestá, who returned it with the comment that it was not theatrical. However Vedia, a friend of the socialite,

[2] Gregorio Laferrère, *Obras escogidas*, ed. Monner Sans; and Laferrère, *Teatro completo*.

had a different opinion, and it was put onto the stage with Podestá in the leading role of Carlos, in love with Lucía.

Carlos spreads the rumor that Lucas, the parents' choice, is a *jettatore* who with his evil eye jinxes all who come near him. Carlos' friends combine to convince even the skeptical father so that he accepts Carlos as son-in-law. It was a hit.

Podestá, convinced now that Laferrère could write good theatre, accepted his *Locos de verano* in 1905. This hilarious "You Can't Take It With You" introduces a mad household and amusing episodes. One of the twenty-nine characters comments: "We are neither imbeciles nor fools. Simply human beings. That is what the world is, and that is life."

Laferrère revealed his serious side first in *Bajo la garra* in 1906 (*Argentores*, No. 100, 1936), a tragedy about the effect of gossip on the erring wife and the deceived husband. But even here, he is the ironical humorist who does nothing to punish the villain whose slander started the trouble.

Better in its character analysis is his 1908 masterpiece, *Las de Barranco* (*Argentores*, No. 165, 1939). While it resembles *Las de Caín* by the Quinteros, which appeared the same year, Laferrère had completed it several years earlier. Doña María, the widow of Captain Barranco, (played by Orfilia Rico), schemes to find husbands for her three daughters among those who rent rooms in her rural home. Carmen, one daughter, retains some idea of ethics, and the powerful scene between her and Linares disproves the charge that this author presents only puppets. The fourth-act conversation between mother and daughter, with its pathetic curtain, is as good dialog as any to be found in Argentina drama. This realistic ending, instead of the happy ending of the commercial theatre, places Laferrère among the modern playwrights with whom logic weighs heavier than audience appeal. Originally moving the audiences to laughter, it now arouses pity and sympathy. Perhaps the scorn of Laferrère which some of his contemporaries revealed, arose from his pose of being able to toss off successful plays at will. He once gave an airy description of his method of writing plays, which Beltrán quotes in his abbreviated form of *Las de Barranco*:

My opening scene is written by chance, according to the whim of the moment, with any number and any type characters that happen to come to my mind. Then I let my imagination go to work, and there they are, each with individuality. I know all about them: how they are dressed, how tall they are, how they think and feel on any given occasion. Their future actions then develop logically so that my whole problem is reduced to finding the theme that will bring to life the final scene.[3]

Pedro E. Pico
(July 13, 1882–November 12, 1945)

Master of dialog, painter of people and customs, Pedro Pico was the outstanding dramatist of the early twentieth century for his sympathetic and poetic short plays, though his desire to entertain was sometimes stronger than his feeling for veracity and logic. His activities extended from his first *sainete, La polka del espiante* (1901) to *Novelera,* performed in 1945 after his death. His collaborations with at least eight other dramatists add a score of titles to his list, which runs above a hundred. Some are lively, with amusing conversation; some are gloomy. Though most contain a challenge to the spectators to do something about the social problems of their country, "good theatre" was his chief aim. And he is one of Argentina's few dramatists who could make a living from his plays. Incidentally, it was his demand for a payment for each performance of his *Del mismo barro,* instead of selling it outright for a few pesos an act, that began the royalty system in Argentina.

He wrote in many categories. Among his farces are *No hay burlas con el amor* (1921), *¡Caray, lo que sabe esta chica!* (1932), and *Yo no sé decir que no* (1934).

Especially remembered for his dramatizations of the social problems of the immigrants, Dr. Pico used the form of the Spanish *sainete* for his *La polka del espiante,* which is about the arrival of an immigrant ship, also the theme of his three-act *sainete, Ganarse la vida* (1907). The penniless foreigners crowding into Buenos Aires inspired *Un robo* (1905), with its appeal for the adoption of orphans. The attempt to bring up a family, even if it means raiding the city dump, is the theme of his realistic yet sentimental *Del mismo barro* (1918). Its lifelike conversation and vivid and varied characters put it among his best. Sometimes the immigrants escape to the country, as in *Pasa el tren* (1919), a triangle about Laura who marries the

---

[3] Oscar Beltrán, *Antología de poetas y prosistas americanos,* pp. 348–396.

track boss Pietro to provide a home for her mother and sister, although she loves the locomotive engineer Antonio.

Having himself lived long in the pampas, Dr. Pico followed Sánchez' realistic lead in two of his best plays, *Tierra virgen* (1910) and *La seca* (1917), the latter depicting the grimness of drought. He even tried melodrama in *La verdad en los ojos;* and politics, in collaboration with González Pacheco, in the three-act *Juan de Dios, milicio y paisano* (1935), which stresses the futility of change by revolution. But Dr. Pico is most esteemed as an interpreter of women. The three-act *La solterona* (1914), perhaps his best, deals with the psychology of thirty-five year old María Luz, working in a fashion shop while the man she loves runs away with her younger sister, Rafaela. *La novia de los forasteros* (1926) and *Pueblerina* (1928) are excellent examples of Pico's dramatic treatment of women, as is his serious *Las rayas de una cruz* (1940), the most nearly perfect of his plays, where two lives cross briefly and a politician sacrifices everything for a temporary success.

His three-act *Querer y cerrar los ojos* (1941) brings a happy ending to the story of an old man's falling for a pretty servant; and the last play performed before his death, *La historia se repite* (1945), shows a daughter learning that love means "comprehension, tolerance, and tenderness." Lighter is *No hay novedad* (1905), titled from the report of the watchman when the lover outbids the jealous husband who has hired him to keep an eye on his wife.

Set among the people of the theatre are two plays: *Las pequeñas causas* (1919), showing the actors' keen desire for love and a home; and *La luz de un fósforo* (1926), in which Rodrigo refuses to let anyone who is clever visit his mistress, Cholita—but the stupid, nearsighted Golito does not seem dangerous. Complications come when Golito boasts of his friendship with the actress and attempts to make good his boasts.

Pico's death was a great loss to the Argentina stage, and his plays are still being revived.

Armando Discépolo
(September 18, 1887–1952)

Discépolo, creator of the *grotesco criollo,* showed both of his interests when, in collaboration with Rafael José de Rosa (1884–1956), he wrote and directed *Entre el hierro* (1910), which was performed by Pablo Podestá. In 1916 Roberto Casaux found starring vehicles in Discépolo's *El movimiento continuo* (*Bambalinas*, No. 7, 1924; *Teatro Argentino*, No. 35, 1932) about a swindler and a perpetual-motion machine, as well as in another of the collaborations of Discépolo and de Rosa, *Conservatorio "La Armonía"* (1917). *La espada de Dámocles* (1918) another farce, added to Discépolo's reputation as a regionalist. *El chueco Pintos* (1913) amused theatregoers with its story of a man who hoped to be made chief of police by the politician for whom he was fomenting a revolution.

Even in his plays that are not regionalistic, like *¡Levántate y anda!* (1929), set, according to Discépolo, in "any Catholic country," the author's pessimistic attitude is revealed, along with its thesis that not the Church but the people in it are the weak and evil ones.

It was, however, as an independent dramatist that Discépolo earned his high place in the Argentine theatre. An admirer of Pirandello, he also wrote about nonconformists, who in his context are people whose tragic flaw is an inability to change with changing conditions. Sympathy and contempt mingle, with the protagonist often laughing at himself and his sufferings. First, in 1923, came *Mateo* (*Bambalinas*, No. 275, 1923; *Argentores*, No. 32, 1934), centering around an old cab driver who sees the end of his era with the arrival of the automobile. Like many of Discépolo's characters, Mateo fights more with himself than with the outside world, and his tragic disintegration results from his surrender to the blows of fate.

Stéfano (1928), in *Tres grotescos de Armando Discépolo* (Buenos Aires, 1958), about a musician at odds with those about him, is one of his masterpieces and is the play generally mentioned as a sample of this dramatist's *grotesco criollo*. Eventually Stéfano has to confess that his failure is caused by his own inability and not, as he had believed, by the intrigues of his associates who, in reality, had been trying to cover up his inadequacies.

In his 1934 *El relojero* (*Argentores*, No. 13, 1934), this dramatist reveals his fascination with maladjustment and spiritual deformity. But it is not only as the profoundly sad writer of tragedies who presents the anguish of static people in a developing Argentina that Discépolo the dramatist will be remembered. He was also one of the greatest directors of the Argentine stage, translator of many foreign plays, and collaborator in all the movements to renovate and improve the national theatre.

Francisco Defilippis Novoa
(February 21, 1892–December 27, 1930)

Defilippis, like Discépolo, dealt in sentiment and the problems that motivate mankind. But Discépolo depicted their individual application, while Defilippis tended to stress their general significance and give them a symbolic treatment.[4]

This journalist and rural schoolteacher in Entrerríos made no stir with his first brief *La pequeña felicidad,* when it was performed by some of his drama-loving students. The performance by visiting actors of his one-act *El día sábado* (1913) and the production by Pablo Podestá of his *La casa de los viejos* (1914) were also failures.

Not till Vedia accepted for the actor Casaux his three-act political satire *El diputado de mi pueblo* (1918) were the abilities of this provincial *costumbrista* recognized, but from then on to his death Defilippis placed an average of three plays a year. He became a student of the European theatre, especially of Ibsen, Andreiev, and Toller.

In his first period, politics and abnormal psychology were his chief themes, and situation and action of most importance. An idiot, Pascualín, who says nothing through the long one-act *Los inmigrantes* of 1921 (*Teatro Argentino*, No. 42, 1921), brings about a happy ending by killing the villain who was trying to break up a contented home.

The mystical side of this romantic-realist writer became apparent early for a human rather than a Biblical interpretation, though he did complete a series of plays in which the heroine was named Mary and the male characters had aspects of Christ in accepting suffering without complaint and in maturing through their troubles.

Defilippis once tried, in a trilogy, to sum up his social ideas about women, showing that affection and forgiveness are not confined to any one social class. In the first play, the three-act *La loba* (1920), he conceives of the bestial lower class as a swamp; yet even in its muddy surface a star, María Magdelena, may be reflected. In the second, *Una vida,* a man's salvation results from the faith of a middle-class woman. Best of the three is *La madrecita* (1920), about the noble aristocrat Sara. Deserted by her husband, Jorge, for another woman,

[4] Ordaz, *El teatro,* 2d ed., p. 157.

she still continues to love him, and when he returns repentant, she considers him a sort of prodigal son and forgives him. Clear dialog and mounting action characterize all three plays.

Craftsmanship was expected of Defilippis. A critic attending the first performance of *Turbión* (1922) wrote:

If Defilippis had not been the author, I would have been uneasy when the second-act curtain fell, because after the tempest between Sofía and her daughter Celia, both in love with the same man, anything else would have been anticlimactic.[5]

But suspense, growing from a violent internal conflict, continued to mount in the final act, and in spite of weak dialog *Turbión* became one of the season's most dramatic hits. Because of its poetry, symbolism, and universality its literary quality was better than that of most of the other plays.

The Biblical overtones of the very successful *La samaritana* (1923) are evident. In it a sculptor's mistress kills herself rather than destroy the artist's marriage when his wife and son appear. The long speeches in *María la tonta* (1927) again demonstrate the poetic side of the dramatist. The play itself put him among the vanguardists. The mission of María, as she explains, is that of all women: "to love her child, her brother, and her husband, and never chide them." And the katharsis achieved through her tragedy is almost Grecian. The theme is repeated in the final shout of a chorus of women: "Love, Love, Love!"

Nearer to the spirit of the modern theatre are two more vanguardist plays with symbolic touches, in which honor is involved. *Tu honra y la mía* (1925) presents the situation of a man admired by his family under one name and laughed at and patronized by the aristocratic gamblers under another. Not till the final curtain does the audience learn whether the boy, determined to kill his father, can be convinced that the dual personality was adopted for the good of the family.

Even more mordant is Defilippis' cynical indictment of society in his excellent *El alma de un hombre honrado* (1926). Ramón Cáceres during his lifetime could not put up with the selfishness and falseness about him, but in the abode of suicides he learns that his supposed honesty on earth was achieved by closing his eyes to what he knew to be evil.

Tú, yo, y el mundo después (1929), combining reality—the strug-

---

[5] Anonymous reviewer in *La Nación* (Buenos Aires).

gle between Laucha and Clarisa for Clarisa's husband—with fantasy
—dwarfs striking a huge bell and Time declaring he is only mortal—
is Defilippis' artistic success. Clarisa, spurning her faithless husband,
directs the words of the title to her unborn child.

The last brief play, performed in 1930, before Defilippis' death,
He visto a Dios (*Apuntador*, No. 6, 1931), was, in its technique as
well as its implications, his masterpiece. The interest in action which
marked his first period had been replaced by philosophy. When the
watchmaker Carmelo, a fence for Buenos Aires thieves, is protected
against a trickster who promised to return his dead son, he turns
on his protector.

Luis Ordaz calls Francisco Defilippis Novoa a poet who expressed
himself in drama but never lost himself in pretty words.[6] He was a
dramatist with something to say. He had a love for his fellow man
and a hope for the future. Though his dialog was at times unreal, the
ideas he expressed were always challenging.

Samuel Eichelbaum
(November 14, 1894–)

Such characterization as "the only true playwright in Argentina"
and "the most important living playwright whose language is Spanish,"[7] have been applied to this son of Russian Jewish immigrants,
who wrote a three-scene *sainete*, *El lobo manso*, at the age of seven.
However, not till 1919 did Eichelbaum really begin his playwriting
career, when the Muiño-Alippi troupe performed his one-act *En la
quietud del pueblo* (1918). Moving after that to Buenos Aires with
his family, Eichelbaum collaborated in several short plays with the
already established Pedro Pico.

The first of what critics consider his plays of the conscious and the
subconscious was the three-act Ibsenian tragedy, *La mala sed* (1920),
in which the father's *mala sed*, a dominant sex urge, was transmitted
to the son Atilio and to the daughter Esther. The play was said to reflect the personality of its author.

In the preface to its printed version, José León Pagano remarks

---

[6] Ordaz, *El teatro*, 2d ed., pp. 148–156. See also Alejandro Berruti's article on
Defilippis in the memorial number of *El Apuntador*, I, No. 6 (February 8, 1931).

[7] Roy Temple House, in *Books Abroad*, 18 (1944), 68; Theodore Apstein,
"Samuel Eichelbaum, Argentine Playwright," *Books Abroad*, 19 (1945), 237–
241. See also Alfredo de la Guardia "Raíz y espíritu de Eichelbaum," *Nosotros*,
III (April 1, 1938), 2.

that the success of the tragedy depended on a few melodramatic scenes rather than a well-rounded dramatic development. Besides, it shifts interest in the final acts and ends in a suicide that solves nothing, but *La mala sed* did give promise of what Eichelbaum might write, with practice and maturity.

For fifteen years that was the sort of thing he produced—plays about tormented characters and illegitimate children. Critics thought Freud was responsible for the three-act *Un hogar* (1922) till Eichelbaum assured them that he had never heard of Freud when he wrote about the arrival of an admirable cousin at the house of a disagreeable family.

Between 1923 and 1926, Eichelbaum, in partnership with Pico and Rodolfo González Pacheco, managed a stock company, Los Tres, that toured Argentina and its neighboring countries. Their one-act plays were published in 1928: Pico's *Trigo gaucho*, González Pacheco's *El hombre de la plaza pública*, and Eichelbaum's *N.N. Homicida*. In the last, the murderer of the man who killed his mother and turned his wife into a prostitute, philosophizes with a railroad-crossing guard about his crimes before he commits sucide. It was greatly admired by critics.

Most of the product of Eichelbaum's next period, both one-act and longer plays, seemed like experiments along many lines. One was his racial protest *Nadie la conoció nunca* (1926), with two powerful scenes: one of action in which Ivonne, Jewish mistress of a wealthy *porteño*, rages against his drunken friends for staging a mock Jewish pogrom, and the other of dialog as she reveals herself as a Jewess who had seen her father killed under similar circumstances.

After the violent and melodramatic *Nadie*, he wrote a quiet and tender *Cuando tengas un hijo* (1929), showing the author's growing interest in psychological melodrama, and characterized by Apstein as "one of the most moving, heartbreaking, simple, unassuming, real plays ever written."[8] One of the best constructed of his early plays, it concerns a father and his lonely son, groping for understanding, and a woman, lonely, too, and seeking a home. They are typical of the lonely people in subsequent plays by Eichelbaum. Two great Argentine actresses got their start in this play: Elsie Singerman as the boy Horacio and Luisa Vehil as Rosa, the lonely woman.

[8] Apstein, "Samuel Eichelbaum," *Books Abroad*, 19 (1945), 239.

Eichelbaum's mature period opened with *El gato y su selva* (1936), which has an unusual amount of action and credible characters who talk like real people. Eleuterio, living with two devoted aunts, considers himself an independent feline creature of the jungle. The wife of a friend gets a divorce to marry him, but he assures her that a cat cannot be domesticated.

The play reveals the dramatist's ability to depict character, as in the weak and pitiful Aunt Eufrasia. Here, as in *Tejido de madre* (1938), the "big moment" occurs offstage. This dramatist's interest lay not in the external action but in the spirit and the soul; his three models were: Dostoevski for his treatment of the dregs of the soul psychologically considered, Ibsen for the theatre of ideas, and Strindberg for the bitter human depth of his characters.

However, 1940 saw a change. *Un guapo del 900*, Eichelbaum's first drama of manners, marked his beginning steps along a nationalistic road toward a universal drama. Incidentally it was also his first financial success. Eichelbaum did not invent a new theme. As the aunts in their way looked after Eleuterio, so the bullies, Ecuménico and Ladislao, look after the politician, Don Alejo. But in no earlier play does Eichelbaum present so richly human a character as the wine-swizzling Trinidad López, their mother.

To protect Alejo's reputation from an unfaithful wife, Ecuménico kills her lover Clemente, a political rival of the husband. Then in order to bring peace to his soul he thinks he must confess. In what is one of the finest third acts of the River Plate theatre, in a drama that won both the Municipal and the National Drama Prizes for 1940, the gangster listens to his mother's pleas to keep silent and stay out of jail so he can cross her arms when she is laid in her casket.

The author does not indicate exactly what happened. As was his custom in earlier plays, Eichelbaum states the problem, leaving it for the spectators to surmise that Ecuménico will confess his crime and hang for it, that Natividad will applaud his decision though it breaks her heart, and will soak up more liquor to make endurable the few lonely days of life left to her. Few authors could so skilfully combine the tender and the grotesque without caricaturing both.

Another work, perhaps the finest from Eichelbaum's pen, was his second play of 1940, *Pájaro de barro*. Like most of his dramas it is more comprehensible when read than when seen. It deals with the

Creole Felipa, another lonely creature, who gives herself to a sculptor, but finds him more interested in his clay than in her.

Critics may declare that Act I is merely an interlude between the prolog and Act II, and that the "big moment," in which she determines to be a bird that can dominate its clay and fly by itself, comes after the curtain falls for Act II, but it is one of Argentina's finest poetic plays.

After several lesser attempts came another excellent drama of manners, *Un tal Servando Gómez* (1942), whose title indicates the universality, the synthesis of the title character. In many ways, this is the most pleasing of Eichelbaum's plays, for there is no psychological abyss for its characters. The idealistic teamster Servando gives asylum to a former sweetheart of his, and her son. When her husband, whose mistreatment caused her to flee, comes after them, Eichelbaum as usual, avoids any scene of violence. The boy so shames his father that the man begs forgiveness, and the three go off together for a drink. An unnecessary lapse of time that disrupts the unity and clouds the motivation is a technical flaw in this otherwise excellent drama of a man's love for a woman and her son.

Eichelbaum has written later plays. His *Dos brazos* (1952), showing the dramatist's low opinion of North Americans, received adverse criticism; yet when produced by an independent theatre it was one of the successes of the 1955 season and won the National Literature prize. In 1959 he published *Las aguas del mundo. Rostro perdido* (1961) depicts a *petite bourgeoisie* closely resembling that of Marcel Pognol. Set in a boardinghouse, it has a "Grand Hotel" theme. Though weakly plotted and reaching an impossible climax, it provides an excellent cross section of contemporary Buenos Aires life.

Eichelbaum has also contributed to the national theatre in other ways. He organized and directed several groups of players. He has been an officer in several of the Writers' Clubs, and was one of the judges of the 1945 Argentores Play Contest, winnowing through the 314 submissions to choose the 113 selected and the 20 best for production. (However, something went wrong and none of them got onto the stage till long afterward).

There is no doubt that Samuel Eichelbaum is one of the Argentine dramatists who will achieve permanence, and one of the leading playwrights of Latin America.

Alberto Vacarezza
(April 1, 1888–August 6, 1959)

If popularity and record-breaking runs indicate important dramatists, Vacarezza deserves a place in this group. Then, too, he ends the
cycle of writers of *sainetes criollos* that ran from Trejo through
Carlos M. Pacheco, Soria, García Velloso, and Sánchez to him.[9] Developing the earlier techniques, Vacarezza himself wrote so many
that when the curtain rose on the national-prizewinner *San Antonio
de los Cobres* in 1938, he celebrated it as his hundredth play. The
Creole *sainete* form really had to come to an end then, because with
so few available type characters and situations, there was nothing left
for newcomers except to ring the changes again—which many did to
a boresome degree—or to spice them with sex or crime. Vacarezza
can boast, like Cervantes, that his work is thoroughly moral. The rascals have had their moments of nobility. The evil ones come to a bad
end.

One interesting example is *El arroyo Maldonado* (1922) representing the collaboration of the two greatest of Argentine *saineteros*,
Pacheco and Vacarezza. Observant students may be able to spot the
two styles and identify the contributions made by each author.

A good example of the plotting and technique of Vacarezza is provided by his much-performed *El conventillo de la paloma* (1929).
The heroine is a gun moll who gives up her criminal companions and
moves into a tenement house among poor but relatively honest people. All the men except one fall in love with her, to the consternation
of their wives. In such slices of life, Vacarezza tries to make his social commentary. Most of them turn out happily. That is part of his
formula.

Asked one day by José González Castillo to define the Creole
sainete, of which he wrote about two hundred, Vacarezza composed
an impromptu sonnet:

> Un soneto me manda hacer Castillo
> y pa' poder zafarme de este brete
> en lugar de un soneto haré un sainete
> que para mí es trabajo más sencillo.

[9] José González Castillo lists a score of dramatists who experimented with the
form before Vacarezza perfected it. See "El sainete criollo," *Cuaderno*, No. 5
(1936), 50; Ordaz, *El teatro*, pp. 112–119.

> La escena representa un conventillo.
> Personajes: un "grébano" amarrete,
> Un gallego que en todo se entremete,
> Una "grela," dos "taitas," y un "vivillo."
> Se levanta el telón; una disputa
> se entabla entre el "yoyega" y el "goruta"
> de la que saca el "rana" "pa'l completo . . ."
> El guapo despreciado por la "garaba"
> se arremanga al final . . . Viene la biaba
> y se acaba el sainete y el soneto.

Later, in his *Villa Crespo* Vacarezza inserted a song on the "nuevo arte de componer sainetes." The *sainete*, he believes, must possess:

> La humanidad, la emoción,
> la alegría, los donaires,
> y el color de Buenos Aires
> metido en el corazón.[10]

And "the color of Buenos Aires" is what Vacarezza achieved. When he turned Carlos Arniches' *La locura de don Juan* into his own *Don Juan Almacenero*, it became typically Argentine, with its pícaro of Spain tranformed into a Buenos Aires chauffeur.

But this second-generation Italian author had no need to borrow themes from Spain. The slums of Buenos Aires provided him abundant material, after he had begun his career with a gaucho play in 1909. His first public recognition was a prize in the National Theatre Zarzuela Contest of 1911—though one judge wanted to throw out his entry, *Los scruchantes*,[11] because he could not understand its slang. Throughout his career Vacarezza used the dialect of the lower class, plus some of his own invention for humor, such as punning on proper names. From his 1929 *El conventillo de la paloma* (*Escena*, No. 282, 5th ed., 1930), comes this bit of punning dialog:

> CONEJO—¡Qué se Llorca! Hace como tres Mezzadri que la anda Buscandiotti y no la puede Trovesky.
> MIGUEL—Entonces es Segura que se Azcondosky.
> CONEJO—¡Vaya a Saavedra!

---

[10] Raúl H. Castagnino, *Esquema de la literatura dramática argentina, 1717–1949*, p. 93.
[11] Reprinted in Luis Ordaz, *Siete sainetes porteños*.

Among the best of his plays of *mala vida*, might be mentioned *El conventillo nacional*; *El conventillo de Gavilán*; his most popular *Tu cuna fue un conventillo* (*Escena*, No. 114, 1920; *Argentores*, No. 32, 1920), which broke all Argentine theatrical records with a run of three thousand performances; *La otra noche en los corrales* (1918); *Va . . . cayendo gente al baile* (1919); *La vida es un sainete* (1925); and *La fiesta de Santa Rosa* (1926).

But Vacarezza was also a dramatist of the gauchos. *El último gaucho* (1916), a *sainete* in three acts, dealt with conditions in the pampas in 1879. *El cabo Rivero* (1928) and *La china Dominga* (1932) were others, but his best-known plays of this type are *Lo que pasó a Reynoso* (*Argentores*, No. 115, 1936), and *Allá va el resero Luna* (*Argentores*, 1942). The first, with six hundred performances the first two years, tells of a gaucho who kills a bully in self-defense, only to discover that the dead man was the brother of his sweetheart. The second, with two hundred performances the first year, follows the career of a cowpuncher who, even after becoming a police sergeant, retained his gaucho sense of justice. The local color is provided by a scene where the *pericón* is danced and maté is drunk.

The day of the Argentine gauchos is over. Perhaps, as critics claim, interest in plays about them has died out, too, and writers of *sainetes* are "back numbers"; but for the centenary of San Martín in 1950 the dramatist especially selected to write an appropriate play was Alberto Vacarezza and the title of his play was *El cantar del gaucho*.

Conrado Nalé Roxlo
(February 15, 1898–   )

Nalé Roxlo was born in Buenos Aires after his family had fled from the political tyranny of President Santos of Uruguay. Led into a literary life by his famous uncle Carlos Roxlo, Conrado began as a poet, and won the unanimous decision in the 1923 Babel competition with his volume of verse.

Then the humorist in him came to light in a series of magazine articles signed "Chamico." Finally, the fantasy of the poet provided the theme and protagonists, and the humorist worked out plot and supporting characters for his first drama, *La cola de la sirena*, performed in 1941. It received the National Theatre prize for the year. In it Patricio so charms the mermaid Alga that she allows herself to be netted and submits to a surgical operation to remove the scales that imprison her legs. But as she becomes like other women, she loses her attractiveness for Patricio, so she goes back into the sea. "Dreams can live among us," one character declares, "only at the cost of horrible mutilation."

Nalé Roxlo's next play abandoned completely the ingredients of his first success. For one thing, the setting of *Una viuda difícil* (1944) goes back to the colonial period of Argentina. Fantasy was forgotten. The first-night audience saw Paulina Singerman, Argentina's original flapper, now more mature but hardly more serious, romp through a farce unpoetic and unsymbolic. The Viceroy, in honor of his wedding anniversary, offers to pardon Mariano, a seven-times murderer, if some kind-hearted woman will take him as her husband. The widow Isabel, resenting her sweetheart's coldness, is ripe to sacrifice herself. Once married, she discovers her husband is a timid soul, who had claimed one unsolved murder to win status in his rough community and then had all the rest saddled on him. Humor and drama combine as he acquires toughness and takes revenge upon the man who jilted Isabel.

José Juan Arrom finds a slight resemblance between *La viuda difícil* and García Lorca's "The Shoemaker's Prodigious Wife,"[12] but the dissimilarities outnumber the parallels. The Argentine play has a definiteness about location and even about date. It is Buenos Aires around 1808. The conversation sounds real when compared to Lorca's.

Its successor, *El pacto de Cristina* (1945), first performed in Madrid and Lisbon in 1948, is more than a reworking of *Faust*. The girl Cristina is the one in love, protected by her purity from both Crusader Gerardo and the Devil. However, what she has considered a harmless pact turns out to be a promise to give up her son to be the Anti-Christ. She might have escaped her pact with "Old Jamey" by trickery, as in *Merchant of Venice* or in Casona's *Barca sin pescador*, or the dramatist might have provided a come-to-realize ending. But Nalé wanted to use a personal *diabolus ex machina*, rather than the symbolic devil of Faust or the sophisticated devil of today's theatre, so he let Christina die as pure as she had lived, with the sound of her unborn child's voice in her ears. With three other plays, this was published in his *Teatro*.

---

[12] José Juan Arrom, "Perfil del teatro contemporáneo," *Hispania*, XXXVI (February, 1953), 30–31.

After three hits, Nalé Roxlo could be forgiven one failure. At least his Biblical *Judith y las rosas* (1956) had its good points and it won the Argentores award in 1957, but the poet and the humorist clashed in its composition, and it was disappointing. As in all his work, however, one finds human dialog with touches of both humor and poetry, sentiment sincere and unforced. Perhaps its failure with the public resulted from its departure from the Biblical version, because Judith kills Holofernes through passion, not hate, with the intervention of a gardener whom the king uses as a double.

Camilo Darthés (November 12, 1889–   )
Carlos S. Damel (May 11, 1890–July 15, 1959)

Critics are as unable to separate the contributions by each of these collaborators, *binomios* the Argentines call them, as to divide the Alvarez Quintero brothers. But "Darthés y Damel," without first names, are the most popular of the recent writers for the Buenos Aires stage, and, since the death of Pico, the most successful.

Whether a play like their *Los chicos crecen* was great art or not, never worried them as they counted up its more than four thousand performances all over the Spanish-speaking world. They knew it had given pleasure and entertainment, and it was their favorite.

These two men lived separate existences. Juan Fernando Camilo Darthés is a retired businessman, and Dr. Carlos S. Damel was a practicing eye surgeon. Back in 1911, when both were students in Buenos Aires, they gravitated toward the theatre. The protagonist of their first collaboration, the brief, juvenile *La última escena*, killed his sweetheart with a hatpin! Yet the play ran four nights in a little theatre in Calle Pueyrredón and made them partners in half a hundred later plays. Nine of them have been printed in the *Argentores* series of the Sociedad de Autores de Argentina, of which Dr. Damel was several times president. The first play ever to be reprinted with a new number in this fortnightly publication was No. 162 in 1938, Darthés y Damel's favorite *Los chicos crecen*, originally produced the preceding year and winner of the Primer Premio Nacional.

Its chief character is the failure Cazanave, who comes to Buenos Aires, where he is befriended by Dr. Zapiola. To save his benefactor, he has to claim the doctor's mistress as his own, then learns she is already his common-law wife, because Zapiola, at a time when Cazanave was supposedly mortally ill, had borrowed his name to register the children. The comedy is full of complications before it reaches a satisfying final curtain.

This play explains some of the popularity of these authors. The plot is logical yet full of suspense. The conversation of both upper and lower class is authentically *porteño*. The characters are psychologically convincing, and there is humor, both of situation and dialog. But it also provides sincere and simple sentiment, for the predicament of Cazanave gives him audience appeal, and there are also some of those "winsome children" that so often are only a blemish in Latin American comedies.

The many unfaithful wives and husbands in the works of Darthés and Damel make one wonder how accurately these playwrights portray the life of Buenos Aires. Abandoned children also figure in some of their dramas. But, at least, the audiences seem never to object. *Amparo,* national prize winner for 1943–1944, and one of their finest comedies, had a record of more than a thousand performances. Amparo is the wife of an aimless but brilliant writer who abandons her and their five children. She sacrifices herself to bring them up. Later, after winning the Nobel Prize for Literature, he comes back, but only to bring her three more children from a love affair he had abroad and to ask her to be their *amparo* while he continues his aimless existence. This play is one of their many that were also filmed.

Marital relationship provides the conflict in *Ni la quiero ni me importa* (1940), where a wife leaves her husband and he brags that he doesn't care. *Mi felicidad y tus amigas* (1942) features a gin rummy game that almost breaks up a marriage, and an argument about the best way to brown *fideos* causes another family row.

One of their tours de force changes its title according to the actor who plays the lead. Written as *Manuel García* (1946), it tells of wealthy Claudia, resentful of parental supervision, and of her offer of 80,000 pesos to the actor García to play the part of her husband for three months. He hesitates because Darthés and Damel are working on a starring vehicle for him, but eventually is persuaded by the money. The humorous experiences of the pseudo lovers in trying to avoid discovery finally force them to announce the death of the husband. But the adventure has been so delightful that they decide to ask the dramatists to write it into a play for both to perform. Though the original premise is hard to believe, once accepted, the rest is logical. The gift of the collaborators was that they could make even an antiquated plot delightful to see, as proved by *Un pucho en el suelo* (1940), about a girl who claims to be with child in order to force her parents to consent to her marriage to the man she loves.

Practically the entire output of this team is set in Buenos Aires. However one of their most delightful comedies portrays life in a small town south of the capital. The Quinteros might have written *La hermana Josefina* (1938), the story of Josefina, a quack doctor who does a thriving business with charms to cure diseases and with seances with dead relatives. Even the regular doctor reluctantly appeals to Josefina's hocus-pocus to cure one of his hypochondriac patients. Her success so disgusts him that he announces he is giving up his practice and returning to Buenos Aires. At the end, however, Josefina is revealed as a thoroughly trained physician, unaccepted in the capital's medical circles because of her sex, but successfully meeting the small-town patients on their own superstitious level. A complete partnership between the doctors precedes the final curtain.

It is a genial play, revealing a minute observation of the world; it enjoyed an original run of 114 nights and has had frequent revivals. While not entirely typical, since it is not set in the sophisticated capital, it does show the technical skill of the collaborators, a skill frequently employed later, though at the end showing perhaps signs of carelessness. Luisa Vehil opened her 1954 season with their *¡Qué pequeño era mi mundo!* and a group of young actors made their debut in Teatro Smart with *¡Mentira, mentira!* These collaborators did not deny that they had a few failures, but among the fifty plays they wrote together, the failures were so few that even critics have forgotten them in remembering the many smash hits by these two authentic voices of contemporary Buenos Aires life, Darthés and Damel. Their final collaboration was a comedy, *Envidia*, which was celebrating its hundredth performance the night that Dr. Damel died.

CHAPTER 11

Some Contemporary Argentine Dramatists

For ease in consulting, the following Argentine dramatists are listed alphabetically. To name all of the playwrights active during this century and to list their plays would fill this volume. But the best of them are here discussed.[1]

Roberto Arlt
(1900–1942)

Arlt, really Godofredo Christophersen, son of a Prussian father and an Italian mother and born in Buenos Aires, was a product of the Teatro del Pueblo, who eventually became leader of the independent movement.[2] Director Leónidas Barletta (1902–   ) dramatized as *El humillado* (1931) a chapter of Arlt's excellent novel *Los siete locos* (1930). Then Arlt went on to write his own plays, first *300 millones* (1932), a combination of reality and fantasy that included such characters as El Hombre Cúbico and Rocambole. In this bitter farce, a servant girl, in reality tempted by the son of her employer, lives in a dream world till her adventure ends. Then, confronted by reality, she commits suicide.

One of Arlt's best is the one-act *Prueba de fuego* (1932), in which Guinter, to prove his love for Frida, offers to burn all his money. Having convinced her, he confesses that his wealth is really in the bank; he loved money too much to burn it. The clash between real and artificial values gives this play its appeal. The reverse of Pirandello, Arlt began with the actual, and ended with the abstract in creating his conflict.

After that, he began experimenting in the Teatro del Pueblo, and

[1] For the most complete coverage published, see Tito Livio Foppa, *Diccionario teatral del Río de la Plata*.

[2] Alvaro Yunque, "Roberto Arlt," *Nos*, Series II, XVIII (1942), 113–114; Luis Ordaz, *El teatro en el Río de la Plata*, pp. 228–235. Pascual Nacarrati, who acted in all Arlt's plays, wrote "El teatro de Roberto Arlt," *Trompo*, 2ª epoca, I (September, 1945), 2.

the result was not impressive. Arlt's strength lay in the ideas rather than in the effectiveness of their dramatic expression, but he earned a place in Argentine theatrical history as the only avant-garde dramatist who persisted and turned out a quantity of plays. *El fabricante de fantasmas* (1936) was Arlt's only experience with the commercial theatre. In this play a dramatist murders his wife and is driven by remorse to kill himself by the same method with which he killed her.

Arlt's next play, *Saverio el cruel* (1936), was his first to attract serious attention, and many consider it his best play. It concerns the joke played by Susana and her frivolous friends on the butter seller, Saverio. He hears her story that she is a queen unthroned by a rebellious colonel, and enters into the imaginary situation, during which the cruelty of a dictator is exposed. Finally Saverio reveals his knowledge that it is all a farce. Begging his forgiveness, the girl confesses her love for him, but, still uncertain whether the fantasy has ended, Saverio refuses her and Susana, now the demented one, shoots him. This tragedy is a social commentary comparing the frivolity of wealth with the misery of poverty; both groups are upset when their situations are interchanged.

With *La fiesta de hierro* (1940), in which an arms manufacturer celebrates his commercial success, Arlt returned to Teatro del Pueblo. The play tells of a pageant concocted by a public-relations man, and involves a complicated plot of a photograph used for blackmail, unholy mysteries, and participants killed by idols. It reveals Arlt as a master of suspense and the dramatic, though some critics objected to his overlaying a farce with social criticism and classic tragedy.

At the time of his death Arlt was completing *El desierto entra a la ciudad* (1942), written along new and mystic lines. The courtiers of Caesar, to entertain their ruler, decide to play a joke on the first man who passes the palace. He turns out to be a beggar carrying a dead baby in a bag. The shock to the monarch makes him a madman, or a saint, and the rest of the play tries to decide which.

Eight plays, all except two performed during Arlt's lifetime, comprised his entire output. His successful experimentation along so many lines makes more lamentable his untimely death. His theatre is full of unbelievable themes and people with peculiar psychology. Farce and tragedy continually mingle. Bad luck is the villain of most of the plays; this dramatist, whom his first biographer, Raúl Larra, called *Roberto Arlt, el torturado,* attacked a society that condemns human creatures to exile or desolation. Readers, and probably spectators, are bewildered at the brusque development in many of his plays, but Arlt was acknowledged as the leader of the New Drama, and a street in Buenos Aires bears his name.

Drawing on the still-unpublished material in possession of his daughter, Mirta Arlt, and on the memoirs in the magazine *Trompo* of the actor Pascual Naccarate, who introduced most of Arlt's plays, Raúl H. Castagnino has just completed *El teatro de Roberto Arlt* (1964), a critical study of a dramatist who, had he lived longer, might have been one of the great names in River Plate drama.

Emilio Berisso
(1878–1922)

Author of only a few plays, Berisso was critic enough to destroy his *Los cimientos de la dicha* (1915) because he regarded it as weak. *La amarra invisible* (1915) was also rather weak and confused in its account of an unhappy marriage. But *Con las alas rotas* (1917), in which Camila Quiroga first achieved prominence, was successfully performed by her all over the world, then made into a movie. Its theme of a woman's virtue was handled again by Berisso in *El germen disperso* (1919), the last, and in the opinion of many, the best play by this dramatist. It was published in Buenos Aires the year of its première.

Alejandro E. Berruti
(1888–1964)

Author of at least eighty plays, Berruti will also be remembered for his other contributions to the Argentine stage. He was one of the founders of the organization Argentores in 1934, and as its librarian has labored ever since to build up its library of national plays, Buenos Aires' chief source of material for a study of Argentina's drama. However, Berruti also wrote *Madre tierra,* which he brought out in 1920 (*Escena*, No. 127; *Argentores*, No. 249, 1945), a realistic play with naturalistic overtones. In this tragedy, farmers of Santa Fe struggle against the drought and the grasping desire of rich landowners. Its modernization in 1955 by Osvaldo Dragún, proved its timelessness. It is full of simple humanity, and the audience sympathizes with the hard-working gringo Pietro who tries to defend the land he has made productive (the heartless owner has acquired possession by legal trickery). Unnecessary was the political preachment put into the mouth of the generous rural schoolteacher, Don Alfredo. The audience understands why Pietro kills the landowner. In addition, in 1934 came Berruti's story of a practical joke, *Les llegó su San Martín* (*Argentores*, No. 9, 1934), and other comedies like *Quién tuviera 20 años, Papá Bonini, ¡Cuidado con las bonitas! Milonga, Tres personajes en busca de un autor*, and a four-way collaboration, *Los conquistadores del desierto*, with García Velloso, Folco Testena, and González Castillo.

José Jacinto Berrutti
(1871–1951)

While still a student in the normal school, the man who was to become director general of Buenos Aires schools showed several plays to the actor Rogelio Juárez. His encouragement resulted in Camila Quiroga's appearance in 1919 as the unselfish rural schoolteacher in Berrutti's *La maestrita del pueblo* (*Bambalinas*, No. 93, 1920). In its debate of environment versus heredity, Margot, the teacher, sends her sweetheart back to his former orphan fiancée. The teacher can solve all problems except her own. Following *La maestrita's* approval by the critics, Berrutti went on to write the fifteen plays that appeared in his two-volume *Teatro* in 1926. Blanca Podestá produced his one-act *Idilio de la sierra* and the long *Alma doliente* together in 1922.

Mr. Brown (1926) tells of the efforts of a British-born banker to find a Christmas tree for his unappreciative family. However, Berrutti's best play (1929) is another comedy about school teaching, *El señor maestro* (*Argentores*, No. 187, 1940). Juan de Dios, after years of teaching young and old in his rural community, has a run-in with Brizuela, the political boss, and loses his job to a former pupil, Delfina. At first she refuses to supplant him, but he persuades her to educate the young while he teaches the old to revolt against selfish politicians. Like most of the plays of Berrutti, it is stronger in matter than in manner, for the speeches are often commonplace, though relieved by touches of humor.

Bernardo Canal Feijoo
(1893–   )

A tragedy by Canal Feijoo, *Pasión y muerte de Silverio Leguizamón* (1937), is one of the outstanding plays of the modern theatre. Performed first in the Teatro del Pueblo, it was later used to open the Teatro Municipal San Martín and won the Municipal drama prize. First published the year of its première, it was considerably revised in the Buenos Aires 1944 edition, though without any change in the basic anachronism, which was related to the fact that in the seventeenth century, land grants by the king lasted during the lifetime of the recipient and his successor, then lapsed. Canal imagines that this condition is in force a century later and that Silverio is occupying land that no longer belongs to him. When a legal claimant appears, Silverio refuses to be evicted and he and his followers fight the alcalde, kill the new owner, burn the farm, and then have to flee. The rest of this powerful play, in many scenes, describes Silverio's life among the Indians, and his flight from pursuers—in traditional manner, but with literary and dramatic superiority. Eventually he is captured and condemned to die. After a flogging he is left on the ground, covered with a cape. In the morning, the dead body of a stranger has mysteriously replaced the body of Silverio, who becomes a legendary figure.

Later, and less successfully, the poet and essayist Canal Feijoo turned to rural legends, in *Los casos de Juan el zorro,* a tragedy; *Tungasuca;* and *Vuestra América.* He has also been very active as a judge of play contests and in associations of playwrights.

Arturo Capdevila
(March 14, 1889–)

Educated for the law in Córdoba, Capdevila became a judge and a professor of philosophy and sociology before surrendering to literature. Five volumes of poetry preceded his romantic first plays, *La sulamita* (1916) and *El amor de Scheherazada* (1919). Moving to Buenos Aires after winning a literature prize in 1920, he wrote the rest of his poetic and historical plays: *La casa de los fantasmas* (1926); *Zincalí* (1927); *Cuando el vals y los lanceros* (1937), about colonial Buenos Aires; *El divino marqués; Blanca d'Oria;* and *Joan, Gorín e Satanás.* In 1936 the Barcelona Cámara Oficial del Libro published the last-named play in recognition of Capdevila's interest in Catalán culture. After that his increasing duties as professor of Argentine and Latin American Literature at the University of La Plata ended further dramatic writing.

Carlos Carlino
(March 14, 1910–   )

One of the important contemporaries is the poet Carlos Carlino, author of dramas of the earth. As a student, he began his rural plays with the one-act *Cuando trabaje* (1946), in dialect, about an impoverished father who promised shoes to his boy when he got work, meanwhile spending the little he had at the saloon. It was performed by a university group and published with Carlino's other plays in 1958. His next rural drama, *Tierra del destino* (1951), was one of the Teatro del Pueblo's outstanding successes. It is the story of two country boys attracted to city factories by shorter hours, better pay, and more chances for fun, although the parents can't keep the farm going. As they are about to lose the results of thirty years of hard work, one son, disliking the city, comes back to the farm, to provide a happy ending.

More mature, while still revealing his interest in the problems of the soil, was *La biunda* (1953), whose performance in one of Buenos Aires' Independent theatres won Carlino the Argentores gold medal for 1956 and the Ministry of Education award. The heroine is a pure country girl working for wealthy Chaco. *Esa vieja serpiente engañadora* (1956), also in rural dialect, shows a husband who preserves his honor by killing a peon. In different veins are Carlino's play for children, *Las andanzas de Juan Tordo* (1956), and the humorous *Un cabello sobre la almohada* (1958). In its sprightly dialog an innocent husband gets the better of a jealous wife.

Roberto Lino Cayol
(1887–1927)

Cayol first appeared as a dramatist in 1909 with *El anzuelo,* winner of first prize in a newspaper competition. As he developed, critics likened him in his dialog to Benavente, and Jean Paul characterized his *La muerte de aquella noche* as "not poetry but in the style of poetry." He dealt in images. Among the chief works of his large production are: *Una broma de Arlequín* (1914), suppressed after six performances; *La nube* (1910); *El festín de los lobos* (1918); *Los espantojos;* the popular *Jaulas de oro; La ciudad incrédula* (1919); *La perra vida* (1910); and *La mala estrella* (1924). There is little that is new or striking in his plots, but he was a careful writer and his language added charm to his plays. Critics lament the fact that so many of his fifty-six plays dealt with trivialities when he possessed such great potentiality as a serious dramatist, as revealed by *Una hora de locura* (1926).

Arturo Cerretani
(1907–   )

A novelist who turned to the theatre after completing *Muerte del hijo* (1933), Cerretani's 1935 *A la salud del viajero* (*Argentores*, No. 45, 1935) was a success, but his rural tragedy, *La mujer de un hombre* (1936), though it won a prize and marked him as a skilful craftsman, was withdrawn, as immoral, on the eve of production. In it Gerardo lives in the pampas with two concubines till discovered by his wife, Estela. His murder of the husband of one concubine lands him in jail. When he returns there is a "Stranger" in the house and Estela is not sure which she loves, but the author tried to restore morality by re-uniting the original couple. The climax might have come from O'Neill.

To insure a production next time, Cerretani used the Bible story of Abraham and the Egyptian Hagar, in *La casa sin dueño* (1940).[3] He wrote six plays and a dozen novels.

Agustín Cuzzani
(1924–   )

One of the contemporary dramatists of talent is Cuzzani, whose experimental *Una libra de carne* (1954), a modern social satire, introduces a main character who has only one word to say in the whole play. It was produced by Los Independientes. Its merits may have resulted in the over-appreciation of Cuzzani's immensely popular *El centro forward murió al amanecer* the following year. His *Los indios estaban cabreros,* about frontier days, was the hit of the 1957 season, though critics raised their eyebrows at its brashness. *Sempronio,* in which love is more powerful than atomic bombs, appeared recently in two versions, while "Para que se cumplan las escrituras" is still in manuscript. All Cuzzani's plays exhibit expressionism, and are both ironic and bitter.

[3] For more details see an unpublished Ph.D. dissertation by Theodore Apstein, "Contemporary Argentine Theatre, 1920–1942" (The University of Texas), pp. 138–140.

Osvaldo Dragún
(1929–)

Dragún, a master of dialog and of rapier-like satire, was a product of the Little Theatres. His first attempt, *La peste viene de Melos* (1956), was an unimportant tragedy, but the following year his trio of one-act plays, *Historias para ser contadas,* revealed his mastery of theatrical technique. The situations are uncomplicated: a man suffering from a toothache he cannot relieve, a man believing himself responsible for an epidemic of bubonic plague in South Africa, and a man converted into a dog, but all these "tragi-comedies of daily life" are criticisms of mechanized and dehumanized existence.

His *Los de la mesa diez* (published 1962), about the problems of a middle-class family, and *Y nos dijeron que éramos inmortales*, about youth caught between problems of war and peace, continue to augment Dragún's reputation. His most important work is a historical tragedy, *Túpac Amarú* (1957), involving human dignity and telling of the Indian revolt of 1780 from the viewpoint of its captured leader, who was tortured, blinded, and eventually burned. However the Indian's chief oppressor, Areche, also dies a victim of conscience and the clash of revolt against Spanish oppression. Dragún is one of the best of Argentina's contemporary dramatists in the vividness and power of his writing.

Julio Filiberti Escobar
(1892–1957)

In the *Teatro Popular* edition of Escobar's *La cabra tira al monte* (1919) appears a list of his productions to that date—twenty-four original plays and twenty-four "translation and adaptations," though his knowledge of foreign languages was limited. Since then he has tripled those figures with his light comedies. Manrique, the 1926 dramatist hero of *La última copa* (*Bambalinas,* No. 471, 1927), may have been speaking for his creator in remarking that he would have starved if he had concentrated on philosophic plays. In other prologs Escobar complains that the poor taste of managers and public discourages the artistic plays of which he is capable. He also explains the accusation that his characters are unpleasant, as are the evil woman in his greatest success *La víbora de la cruz,* the false friends of *Trago amargo* (1920), the faithless people in *Palabras de casamiento,* and the fake doctor in *Charlatanes*. He is not to be blamed that life is unpleasant, he says; he merely has set down what he sees, in the belief that when people are most miserable they are most human.

"Muérete y verás" is one of Escobar's favorite themes. An early farce, *La muerte de un vivo* (1915), tells of Socrates pretending to die and watching from his coffin the reaction of his friends. His wife can hardly wait to get him to his grave before joining her lover. In *El trago amargo* (*Bambalinas*, No. 124, 1920), all goes wrong with Luciano as his secretary, Williams, schemes to warn him against his fair-weather friends. In 1933 this play had a sequel, *Gente alegre* (*Nuestro Teatro*, No. 11, 1933). In 1928 *Lágrimas de cocodrilo* (*Bambalinas*, No. 608, 1929) offered another pretended death, this time of an unsuccessful dramatist. Upon seeing his posthumous fame, he decides he had better stay dead. One looks to Escobar for brief entertainment rather than for a tug at the heart or an appeal to reason.

Juan Carlos Ferrari
(1917–   )

Nuevo Teatro, founded in 1949, gave Ferrari his start as dramatist of the problems of young people. First came his monodrama *Cuando empieza el luto* (1951), then *Ese camino difícil* (1952). A kind of *Diablo cojuelo* story in forty-eight scenes, it looks down on problems of Buenos Aires life, which are given continuity by Marta and Alberto, who were chosen by El Viejo to appear in a television show. It is charming to read as published in *Talía*, and its performance in Nuevo Teatro was one of the greatest successes of the Independent Theatres. One or another of them has first introduced all the rest of Ferrari's comedies except *Por arte de magia* and *Las campanas de Verona*, which were presented first on TV. Ferrari's vigorous and realistic sketch, *La ñata*, was introduced in Córdoba, and *El mazorquero*, *Historia de verano*, and *Canasta* were also performed by amateurs. Nuevo Teatro in 1958 performed *Las nueve tías de Apolo* (*Talía*, 1958), a modernization of mythology set in a Buenos Aires suburb where Aunt Melpómene and her sisters educate Apolo physically but with no thought for his life as a citizen. The voting scandal of 1931 provides substance for one act, and putting the end of the play eighteen years later gives opportunities to the dramatist to discuss Argentina and the Second World War. Ferrari is a skilled dramatist who is steadily improving.

Aurelio Ferretti
(1907–   )

Ferretti is an active voice of the modern Argentine theatre whose many farces have brought respect for his ability to criticize morals and customs with a laugh. To hold up for criticism the problems of today he uses a classical style of which Molière would have approved.

Long interested in the formation of an independent theatre, Ferretti joined with César Tiempo, Eichelbaum, and others back in 1929 in organizing *La mosca blanca,* out of which eventually came the Teatro del Pueblo. Then he became organizer and director of the Teatro Libre Tinglado and was responsible for the revival of Alberdi's *El gigante amapolas* in 1945. Appropriately he was on the national committee to celebrate twenty-five years of the Independent Theatres in 1955.

Ferretti's first play, *La multitud,* won honorable mention in *Cultura* 1937 and the 1945 Premio Municipal for beginning dramatists. But he soon forsook the theatre of the masses, for the series of farces at which he excels. His *Fidela* was one of twenty selected for Argentores performances in 1945 from more than three hundred entries. Pilluelo cuts the strings of three puppets, Fidelia, Marido, and Galancete, so that for a time they became human in a triangle situation that causes Fidelia to remark on the similarity between life and the stage.

In his excellent *Farsa del héroe y del villano* (1946) Pedrín pays the villain, Gabino, to let him win, so as to impress Bolera, the girl at the inn; but her reaction is to pity the loser, with the comment that women like men who suffer for them. *Bonome, La farsa del hombre y el queso* (1946) won the Argentores and the Municipal prizes for the same year; the protagonist tries to get the object of his wife's pity arrested as a robber. *Bodas del diablo,* a four-act farce of 1947 (*Argentores,* No. 281, 1949), continues Ferretti's satire of society; *Farsa de farsas,* set in a gambling casino, debates a possible formula for good and evil as the police and the women of the morality committee come to raid it.

In *La farsa del consorte* (1950), the marriage records in the town hall have burned and the wives consider themselves free. More recently, Ferretti's *El cajero que fue hasta la esquina* (1958), prize winner by audience vote in the Ministry of Education drama contest and a commercial hit in Buenos Aires, was also performed by an amateur group in Bolivia. The characters are the embodiment of the general concept of man in his relationship to society, although due to their farcical treatment they sometimes seem to reverse reality.[4]

Enrique García Velloso
(September 2, 1880–January 27, 1938)

In the published *Los conquistadores del desierto* (1927), the listings of García Velloso's plays covers six pages. This most picturesque of dramatists must have felt compelled to make up for shortness of stature by length of bibliography. *Chin Yonk* (1895), a musical done in collaboration while he was still a student, and suggested by the stir about Jack the Ripper, heads the list, and the posthumously performed *El copetín* (1939) ends it. And in between came more than 150 plays of practically every genre and interpreted by practically every actor and actress who performed in Buenos Aires during García Velloso's lifetime. Definitely he was a forerunner of the modern theatre.

But this was only one phase of his activity. He was a founder and first president of Argentores. He lectured on many subjects in many places. He wrote the comprehensive *Arte del comediante* (1926), and his *Memorias de un hombre de teatro* (1942) is a history of the Argentine drama and the dramatists of his lifetime. He also directed dozens of performances and helped many young dramatists get a reading for their manuscripts.

When he began writing, most of the actors in Argentina were from Spain. Their pronunciation did not matter in García Velloso's successful musical comedies *Gabino el mayoral* (1898) and *Chiripá rojo* (1900),[5] but he blamed the Castilian pronunciation of the supposedly patriotic Argentines in *Corneta de Belgrano* for its failure. Therefore, to the Podestá family, whose speech was authentically River Plate, he entrusted the performance of his gaucho play *Jesús nazareno* in 1902 (*Escena*, No. 52, 1919). Its première antedated by four months Coronado's *Piedra de escándalo*, which had been written two years earlier. Though today *Jesús nazareno* seems an immature and unconvincing melodrama of adultery and death, its protest of the "loco

---

[4] See Aurelio Ferretti, *Farsas* (with three plays) and *Farsa del Cajero que fue hasta la esquina*.

[5] Pictures and details of their first nights are in *Memorias*, pp. 285–290.

dios" against political vices of its time gave it a riotously successful
first night and a run of a month.

The next year the Podestás split into several companies, but Jerónimo Podestá was sought out when Velloso finished his *Caín*
(1903). The playwright was then only twenty-three and might have
continued learning and maturing, but unfortunately for any lasting
fame, he was always in a hurry to finish a play, and he had plenty of
material. Like Lope de Vega, he dramatized fads. So he wrote *Tango
en París* (1913). The craze for mineral baths provided the idea for
Las termas de Colo-colo (1918), in which the hot baths are visited by
a Russian princess, a couple of nuns, a ruined nobleman, and a thief.

Typical of his products was *El campo alegre* (1909), for he brought
happiness onto the stage. Many of his best plays are comedies, like
Fruta picada (1907), which introduced him to Madrid theatregoers.
It has a theme—that an easygoing sinful life does not pay—but the
succession of amusing episodes gives little time for seeking a moral
lesson. García Velloso did once, however, voice a social protest: *Morriña mía* (1921) attacked white slavery.

His dramas with historical background reveal one of his greatest
gifts, the ability to handle crowds on a stage. In *Amores de la virreina*
(1914), about Buenos Aires in 1795, no fewer than twenty-five characters occupy the stage, but García Velloso was a director and knew
how to manipulate them to avoid mere spectacles. *Mamá Culepina*
(1916) has twenty-two speaking parts besides the crowds of soldiers,
Indians, captives, and frontier villagers, but they do not mask the
striking figure of the title character, the honorable companion of a
soldier in the pampas. The struggle of this powerful comedy centers
around a rescued captive whose soldier husband is accused of the
murder of the company captain, who also loved the captive. Mamá
Culepina, posing as a fortune teller, gets the real murderer into the
firing squad, where he confesses rather than kill an innocent man.
The power of this play, called the first really local-color play of Argentina, lies in its re-creation of a period of history so dramatic that
it lends verisimilitude to actions and emotions that elsewhere might
be branded as melodrama. The threads of humor are an integral part
of the story and are not inserted merely for laughs. It was revived in
1941.

For his experimenting along many lines and for his 132 performed
plays, García Velloso was an important pioneer. Among his other

plays worth reading even today are *El zapato de cristal* (1915), *La victoria de Samotracia* (1917), *Una bala perdida* (1921), *Un hombre solo* (1925), and *La sombra del pasado* (1928). His collection, *Comedias escogidas* (Buenos Aires, 1939), contains some of his best works.

Alberto Ghiraldo
(1874–1946)

Ghiraldo was a rebel. He fought against society in behalf of those he considered oppressed, and his nine original plays, collected in his two-volume *Teatro argentino* (Buenos Aires, 1946) present oppressed tenant farmers, exploited laborers, and other mistreated people. The gaucho Cruz in *Alma gaucha* (1906) was the first, a figure subjected to military discipline in the barracks, who brought more tragedy on himself and his companion Alma by his every attempt to resist.

Los salvajes, written during Ghiraldo's long stay in Spain, was a *tríptico*, intended to show the Spaniards that some of the "civilized" people of Argentina were more savage than the "savage gaucho." In three scenes, where the *pericón* was danced, where the drunks quarreled at a *pulpería*, and where Facundo was slain at a rancho, Ghiraldo tried to show that when passions conquer will power, a man is a savage.

Columna de fuego (1913), dealing with quarrels between the jobholders and the jobless in the Port of Buenos Aires, was for a while in 1919 denied permission to be performed in Valencia, in spite of Benavente's high praise of it, on the ground that it overstressed the clash of capital and labor.

Rebelling at the ordinary attitude toward Facundo Quiroga as portrayed by Sarmiento and others, Ghiraldo wrote *Copa de sangre* from the point of view of the assassin Santos Pérez, and brought out the tragic grandeur of the tyrannical *caudillo*. He also made dramatizations of *David Copperfield, Ramona,* and other novels and in them Ghiraldo's poetic ability was not concealed by his rancor against most of mankind.

José González Castillo
(February 25, 1885–October 22, 1937)

Besides his contributions to Argentores and other organizations, González wrote three kinds of plays which make him remembered.

Beginning in 1909 with *Luiggi,* inspired by Sánchez, he showed himself a rebel against society with a series of dramatizations of social
questions. Religion, illegitimate children, the right of divorce, and
homosexuality all figured in the controversial series: *Los invertidos*
(1914), *El hijo de Agar* (1915), *La mujer de Ulises* (1918) (*Bambalinas,* No. 59, 1919). *La mujer* argued for absolute divorce, with its
plot of a woman married to an unworthy husband and abandoned. At
the moment when love of another man promises happiness for herself
and their daughter, the husband returns to demand her fidelity.
Among González' other plays are *La santa madre* (1920) with Martínez Cuitiño; *La zarza ardiendo* (1922); and, after a break, *Hermana
mía* (1935). He also wrote a number of amusing comedies, like *La
purpurina* (1915), *El hombre que se volvió cuerdo* (1921), and
Vidalita (1922). Another product was his dramatization in three acts
of the gaucho poem, *Martín Fierro,* performed in 1915 (*Argentores,*
No. 199, 1941; Buenos Aires, 1942). This latter Comisión de Cultura
edition filled four pages with a listing of Gonzalez' plays.

But principally, González Castillo earned the name of "Argentina's
Ramón de la Cruz"[6] with brilliant and amusing short *sainetes,* like
Del fango (1907), *El retrato del pibe* (1908), *Entre bueyes no hay
cornados* (1909), *La serenata* (1911), *El salto mortal* (1915), and
Los dientes del perro (1918), which with Alberto Weisbach (1883–
1929) had a run of 1,000 performances.

Rodolfo González Pacheco
(1881–1949)

The plays of González Pacheco are usually more literary than dramatic. His over-rhetorical dialog offers striking figures of speech, not
development of action. But the beauty of language in his sublimated
gaucho theatre gained him popularity, along with his love of nature
and liberty and his scorn of "la lay" (*sic*) as being representative of
true justice. For that the dramatist was several times imprisoned and
exiled.

His first play, *Las víboras* (1916), in one act, about Diego's seduc-
tion of the daughter of his boss, also marked the first appearance together of those great actors Enrique Muiño (1881–1956) and Elías
Alippi (1883–1942). Through old Evangelisto, González Pacheco

---

[6] Raúl H. Castagnino, *Esquema de la literatura dramática argentina, 1717–
1949,* p. 70.

voices his hatred of the barbed-wire fences that restrict freedom on the pampas. It was considered the best play of the year. Then came *La inundación* (1917), about the farm girl Pampa and the engineer who blows up the dam on the Colorado River. It was revised in 1942. *Hermano Lobo* of 1924 (*Teatro del Pueblo*, No. 10, 1936) contains a poetic apostrophe to nature, as the old gaucho Martín looks over the friendly pampas at twilight, while sipping maté with Jiménez. Others, less important, followed: *A contramano* (1927), *El grillo* (1929), and *Juana y Juan* (1932). By himself González wrote fourteen staged plays.

With Pedro Pico, he wrote two plays: *Nace un pueblo* and *Juan de Dios, milicio y paisano* (1935), both technically excellent. His final play, *Cuando aquí había reyes*, about Negro rites in the time of Rosas, was written by himself alone. Chosen in the Argentores 1945 competition, it received its first performance in Yiddish, in 1947 under Discépolo. Máscara performed it in Spanish, and the Comedia Nacional del Uruguay put it into their reportory in 1956. So, though florid, the plays of González Pacheco are fresh and have been popular. Fifteen plays make up his *Teatro completo* (Buenos Aires, 1953).

Carlos Gorostiza
(1920–)

A dramatist of promise who has not kept his promises is Carlos Gorostiza. The independent Máscara Theatre witnessed the première of his *El puente* (1950), a clash-of-classes play with good local color, which he directed himself. It was later transferred to the professional stage, with Armando Discépolo as director. *El fabricante de piolín* (1950) was Carlos Gorostiza's next offering, a much weaker play, but in 1954 he showed his real talents in his dramatization of Guillermo House's novel *El último perro*, the most discussed play of the season, not only because Nicasio was a gaucho of the crude and primitive bygone days, but because of its excellent local color and because the production used a turntable stage with one exterior and two interior sets.

After the Nuevo Teatro group was forced out of the Patagonia Theatre, the Comisión Nacional de Cultura selected Gorostiza's *El juicio* for performance there. It added little to his reputation. *El caso del hombre de la valija negra* was amusing but not important, and the critics scorned *El reloj de Baltasar* (1955). In 1957, in the Cervantes

Theatre, nationally subsidized, *El pan de la locura* gave a better idea of Gorostiza's ability. It is a tense dramatization of an actual happening in Europe, when bread from poison flour sold by an avaricious miller brought an epidemic to a small town.

Paul Groussac
(1848–1929)

Groussac, born in France and knowing hardly a word of Spanish when he reached Buenos Aires as an immigrant at the age of eighteen, became a dramatist remembered for one play, *La divisa punzó* (published in 1939), that took its name from the red badge used by the followers of Dictator Rosas.[7] This leading figure in Argentine literary circles got the idea in 1921, and delved for background in the newspapers of 1839 and 1840. He wrote the play in 1922, and it was accepted by Camila Quiroga who wanted to play the role of Manuela, the Dictator's daughter. Joaquín de Vedia, tutor of so many other playwrights of this period, helped get it ready for the stage, where it was the hit of the 1923 season. In 1948 it was revived for a run of one hundred performances. Except for a one-act *La monja*, it was his only play.

The tragedy concerns the trickery of the supremely egotistical Dictator who does not spare even his own daughter to maintain his power. It follows history closely except that, for the love interest, Groussac invented an Englishman, Jaime Thompson, whom Manuela gives up when her father makes her feel his need for her.

Though he worked on two other plays, *El escollo* and *Las dos patrias*, Groussac's duties as national librarian and professor of history and his blindness prevented their completion.

César Iglesias Paz
(October 1, 1881–August 18, 1922)

Dr. Iglesias Paz, a lawyer, gravitated toward the theatre beginning in 1907 with his *Más que la ciencia* (1913), followed by one or two more plays a year until his death. His plays of distinction and taste show Benavente's influence. He was essentially a portrayer of women.

---

[7] Domingo A. Arizaga, "La divisa punzó," *Nos*, LXV (July, 1929), 151–156; Manuel A. Orozco, "La divisa punzó vista por un provinciano," *Nos*, L (June, 1925), 230–266.

In *La conquista* (1913) his theme was that woman's conquest of man should start after, not before, the marriage ceremony. In *La enemiga* (1913), perhaps his best work, a woman will not fight to keep her husband from another charmer, for fear of appearing vain. True love, however, is on her side.

La dama de coeur (1914) pictures women as more fond of cards than of their families. But to show he was not entirely disdainful of women, Iglesias followed it with *La mujer fuerte* (1915) about one who will not be daunted by life's blows. Then he reversed himself in 1916 in *El vuelo nupcial* (*Bambalinas*, No. 41, 1919), a three-act comedy in which a woman gives up her real love to marry a man she hardly knows, after which she shuns people and things likely to reveal the weakness of their bonds. *El complot del silencio* (1917) is Iglesias' attack on false shame that keeps girls ignorant of the opposite sex till after marriage.

However, this dramatist with the brown mustache and clothes that looked as though they had been slept in was not always a social censor or reformer. He could write a meticulous gem like his 1916 *Diplomacia conyugal* (*Argentores*, No. 213, 1942) and also that farce of lively and amusing dialog *A liquidar tocan* (1919), in which a bachelor tries to clear his quarters of earlier souvenirs before the arrival of his fiancée and her mother. *El pecado original* (1918) is also excellent. Iglesias Paz' complete output of eighteen plays was published in the three-volume *Teatro* (Buenos Aires, 1925).

Julio Imbert
(1918–)

Besides having written the best biography of Florencio Sánchez (1954), and founding Las Cuatro Tablas theatre (1951) in Rosario to produce foreign and national plays, with his wife Graciela Ensinck as the star, the poet Julio Imbert has written some excellent plays, performed not only in his own theatre but at the capital.

After publishing poetry volumes, he wrote *La lombriz* (1950), which was presented to inaugurate the Cuatro Tablas before being produced at the Teatro del Pueblo. His three-act *El diablo despide luz* (1954) was a hit at Teatro del Pueblo in 1954, as was *Este lugar tiene cien fuegos* (1952), about a tormented existentialist poet excited by the monotonous music of a flute played by a monstrous young man. His three-act *Comedia de naranja* (1953) was performed on the radio, and his long tragedy *Los navegantes del Genesis* (1960) had a successful public reading.

Imbert is also the author of several one-act plays: *La mano* (1951, performed 1952), *El diente* (1951, performed 1956), and *La noche más larga del año* (1958) winner of first prize in the 1957 University of La Plata contest. Recently this experimenting writer completed some *obras en medio acto: Un angel en la mantequería* (1956), *Ursula duerme* (1957), a dramatic jewel with three characters; *El perfume* (1959), and *Electra* (1961).

El diente (1951, performed 1954) is Imbert's plea for solidarity among mankind, which he imagines as a big incisor tooth. Antonio and Antonia are human, the other characters are symbolic of man's suffering and oppression: "Hombre-flor," "Hombre-caña," etc. Antonio, caressing his pregnant wife, sees blood on her neck (but green where Hombre-flor has spilled his inkwell), and since he has noticed the same color on Hombre-flor, Antonio kills him.

Puyutá (1955) was the first play performed by the Amigos del Arte in Rosario. Imbert's plays are lively and so are his characters, especially those of the feminine roles written for his wife.

José de Maturana
(1884–1917)

Rural dramatist of the first decade of the twentieth century, Maturana is remembered for the lyrical qualities of his plays, even in the rebellious *Canción de primavera* of 1912 (*Escena*, No. 75, 1919) about María Rosa, daughter of the *estanciera* and the peon Jacinto, and in *Canción de invierno*. He also wrote *La flor silvestre* and *La flor de trigo*, but his best play was *El campo alegre* of 1909 (*Escena*, No. 20, 1918). Romanticism, concentrated in feeling and local color, characterized him from his first short *A las doce* (1906) and the very popular *¡Qué calor con tanto viento!* to his later *sainetes* and eclogs.

Federico Mertens
(April 27, 1886–1960)

A director of several important companies of actors, and during the last years of his life stage director of Teatro Municipal, Mertens made his original transition from humorous essays to the stage, with *Gente bien* (1908), inspired by Laferrère. His *Las d'enfrente* of 1909 (*Talía*, No. 8, 1936) brought cries of plagiarism from the superior *Los de Barranca* performed shortly before it. Mertens' friends knew his inspiration had come from seeing the performance of the genial Orfilia Rico in Alberto Novión's *La gaucha* (1906) long before Laferrère thought of his play. Eventually its director answered the accusations with the announcement that he had been holding the manuscript for at least a year.

Mertens' originality was frequently displayed later, especially in his 1920 *Mamá Clara* (*Escena*, No. 133, 1921), in which his favorite actress, Orfilia, played the domineering Catalan servant who prettied herself to make the son of her rich employer fall in love with her, and then showed her shrewdness by building a vegetable-stand business into a fortune to use when her father-in-law's wealth was gone.

Once Mertens tried unsuccessfully to be "arty," with *Amor del sendero* (1946): in the romantic setting of 1800 a woman shows jealousy at her younger sister's success with men. Its author introduced his characters as puppets, and they stayed that way throughout the play, but his earlier comedies, *El tren de las 10:30* of 1918 (*Bambalinas*, No. 17, 1919), *La familia de mi sastre* (1918), and *La zarza en llamas* (*Argentores*, 1941) won him an enthusiastic following among theatregoers.

Alberto Novión
(1881–1937)

Born in France but emigrating to Buenos Aires at the age of fifteen, Novión began as a writer of gaucho plays. *Doña Rosario* and *La tía Brígida* (1905) show his warm sympathy with rural life. *La gaucha* of 1906 (*Escena*, No. 74, 1919), in one act, opened at the Teatro Nacional and presented Italians as the hope of modern Argentina. Simona, the gaucha servant, defending Elena, the daughter of Italians, against a rich Argentine who had dazzled her, gave Orfilia Rico one of her greatest roles, and inspired Federico Mertens to become a playwright.

La cantina (1908) marked Novión's shift in interest that eventually made him Argentina's dramatist of the immigrants, as well as one of her best writers of short plays. Sometimes they were comedies, like *La madriguera* (1911), where an ignorant Italian gets the better of confidence men who try to cheat him and get paid off in a counterfeit ten-peso bill. Sometimes they were tragic, like *La chusma* (1913), set in a saloon where the immigrants seek happiness in forgetfulness. Always they won their audience. With Pacheco he popularized the *sainete* in Buenos Aires.

Natural action, sparkling dialog, and well-defined characters appear in *El patio de los amores* and especially in *Misia Pancha la brava* (1915), fifth of his full-length productions in a total of twenty-eight. In some ways it is the reverse of *La gringa*, but it was Pancha, the real gaucha who marries a gringo, as interpreted by La Orfilia, that made it a success.

Facha tosta is another character study, but the delightful *Tan chiquita y quiere casarse* (1936) shows Novión's ability in plotting. For *La muchacha del circo* he went to the circus. Most popular among readers, if its four printed editions are an indication, is Novión's only attempt at high comedy, the three-act gaucho *¡Bendita seas!* (1921; *Escena*, No. 20, 1921, and No. 161, 1929; *Proscenio*, No. 2, 1948), originally introduced by Camila Quiroga and revived by Lola Membrives in 1926, and Novión's most successful play outside of Argentina. It is a simple but emotional story of motherhood and sacrifice: María, once the mistress of Pancho, wants to run away for fear Pancho's legitimate son Enrique may guess he is the half brother of her Javier. But the young man learns of her nobility and begs her to remain on the *estancia*.

In his long career Novión portrayed many nationalities among the immigrants, especially the Basques in *El vasco de Olavarría* (1920; *Argentores*, No. 114, 1936) and *Airiños de miña terra*, and the Aragonese in *En un burro tres baturros* (1923; *Argentores*, No. 76, 1935). In the latter a boy is ashamed to let Pilara, his sophisticated fiancée, meet his parents until he discovers that her wealthy father was another of the uncouth peasants who had come with his own Papa to the New World, with no wealth among them except one donkey.

Another side to Novión was his experimenting with the type of comedy called grotesque. *Don Chicho* (1933) is an excellent example. Though sometimes showing a tendency toward caricature, Novión's people are usually well individualized. One of the best examples is his *El corazón en la mano* (1937), which was posthumously performed.

Alberto Marcelino Oteiza
(March 27, 1919–   )

Professor Oteiza, of La Plata, produced his *Luz en los ojos* (1939) at the age of twenty. Then little was heard of him till he brought out his three-act comedy *La doctora Dosset* (1952). His three-act *Remordimiento* (1955) has to do with the changes produced in Laura by the so-called maternal instinct. The dramatist's skill in character drawing is demonstrated in Julián, especially in his scene with Montero. The one-act *Ciudad universitaria* (1957) is a fantasy in which professor Godoy is fired from the University for possessing seditious books, planted in his library as part of a plot to bring in another teacher more likely to graduate Carlos. The Professor dies on learning of Carlos' complicity, just as the repentant student has got him reinstated. *¡Y yo soy el héroe!* (1959, published 1962), in three acts demonstrating the uselessness of revolutions, represents Oteiza's most recent work, besides studies of Lope de Vega and a volume about Payró. *La loca del puerto* was read to the public in 1962. It reveals life in the author's seaport home.

José León Pagano
(1875–   )

Noted for his technical excellence, his ingenious plots, and his high spiritual values, the long-lived critic Pagano turned dramatist to produce *Más allá de la vida* (1902), a study of genius in infirmity, about a writer; *El dormidor* (1903), concerning a philosopher; and his best work, *Almas que luchan* (1906), in which a newspaperman crusades in the world of finance. A score of his plays have been performed on stage and radio. He was vice president of Argentores, 1958–1961.

Antonio Pagés Larraya
(1918–   )

Among the younger generation, Pagés Larraya used with excellent effect a mythical gaucho in his *Santos Vega el payador*, performed in Buenos Aires in 1953; then went on to succeed again with *La tierra no pregunta* (1955). A brilliant scholar, he has written a dozen books and taught in many foreign universities. His play writing has suffered.

"Ivo Pelay"
(1893–1959)

Under the pen name of "Pelay," Guillermo Juan Robustiano Pichot wrote a dozen diverting comedies, several of which enjoyed long runs, beginning with *Mala vida* (1911). *Judío* (1926) was a three-act *folletín escénico*. *Llegan parientes de España* (1939; *Argentores*, No. 167, 1939), a three-act comedy, had three hundred performances the first year. *El viudo alegre* (1940; *Argentores*, No. 183, 1940) is a hilarious attack on the divorce laws. In *Jesús, María y el otro* (1940; *Argentores*, No. 177, 1940), the old family servant María looks after the gaucho and his family. *Burro de cargo* (*Argentores*, No. 209, 1942) won the national culture prize of 1941. *Gran colmao el tronao* (1943), had a run of four hundred performances, but Pelay's most popular comedy was the 1944 *Rodríguez, víctima del presupuesto* (*Argentores*, No. 240, 1944), with five hundred performances in its first two years. While the purpose of the play is obviously amusement, Pelay does satirize the vices of bureaucracy. Through seventeen years of government employment, Rodríguez never shared the graft of his assistants. Then in a budget cut he loses his job, but with the help of an inspector and the use of his knowledge of all the previous departmental crookedness, he wins reinstatement. It is very amusing to witness. *Semilla de Mirasol* (1942) and *Don Fernández* (1947) were also successes. In his last plays Pelay collaborated with his sons, Guillermo and Horacio, also dramatists.

Juan Oscar Ponferrada
(1907–   )

Ponferrada, a postmodernist poet, deserves a place in Argentine theatrical history. Not only has he filled every position around the theatre from actor and manager to stage technician, but he is also author of two important plays. One is a poetic tragedy of sex and superstition, *El carnaval del diablo* (1943), based on folklore and the fear of the supernatural, and set in northern Argentina during La Chaya, a pagan festival. It has a prolog to establish its atmosphere of violence and death, and its poetic dialog shows the influence of Lorca. The other play, *El trigo de Dios* (1948), expressing the soul of his country, shows Ponferrada as an exponent of Argentine nationalism.

María Luz Regás
(August 5, 1914–   )

One of the women on the Argentine scene is María Luz Regás Velasco, daughter of the Spanish zarzuela actress La Velasco. After beginning with plays for children, like *Corazoncito* (1937), Miss Regás unsuccessfully assailed the regular stage with *Julia Conde, secretaria general* (1939) and *Llegaré a tus brazos* (1941). With Juan Albornoz, son of the actress Lola Membrives, she wrote the morbid *Vacaciones* (1943; *Argentores*, No. 236, 1944), a modern and realistic comedy successfully introduced by Mecha Ortiz. It was the 1943 municipal prize winner. The widow Estela invites two married relatives of her dead husband to spend the spring vacation with her, and a rearrangement of affections almost brings tragedy.

Finally, in 1944, by herself and along different lines, Miss Regás arrived, with the comedy *Papá es un gran muchacho* (*Argentores*, No. 247, 1945). Its plot is simple. Augustín, the playwright, has difficulty avoiding entanglements with an actress for whom he is writing a play and with the fiancée of his son. But with estrangement and even divorce in sight, the children decide that Papa is a great boy and should be forgiven.

Ricardo Rojas
(1882–1957)

Dr. Rojas, best known for his monumental history of Argentine letters, also wrote several historical plays. *Elelín* (1929) concerns conquistadores and Indians. *La casa colonial* (1932) is a Moratín-type play about Alzaga's conspiracy. Rojas' only permanent contribution, however, is *Ollantay* (1939),[8] inspired by the Inca legend but reworked into a lyric drama about individual freedom.

The struggle between the Inca Yupanqui, son of the sun, and Ollantay, son of the earth, is handled like a Greek tragedy, with a Wagner-like theme in each act.

Act I—The Rift (between Ollantay and Yupanqui)
Act II—The Abduction
Act III—The Capture (in Ollantatambo, through treachery)
Act IV—The Punishment

[8] Fernando Lizarralde, *El Ollantay argentino*; Raúl H. Castagnino, "El teatro en la obra de Rojas," *Revista Iberoamericana*, No. 46 (July, 1958), 227–238.

In this dramatic conclusion, Ollantay goes to his death, sure that the sun is not omnipotent. In the final speech, Coyllur declares that the son of Ollantay's that she will bear will be the founder of the coming race of free men, the ancestor of the liberator of earth's children from the tyranny of the sun.

Tempted again by legends, this time of Spain, Dr. Rojas produced *La Salamanca* (1943), about an old nobleman in love with his young ward but thwarted by a stranger who reveals himself as Christ. The play lacked the scope of the magnificent and national *Ollantay* and had only a short run.

Belisario Roldán
(1873–August 17, 1922)

When *La Escena* inaugurated its weekly series of plays, it began with *Mr. Frank* by Dr. Roldán, and during its existence, he appeared more frequently than any other dramatist. He wrote a total of twenty-nine plays.

Los contagios (1915; *Escena*, No. 65, 1919), his first play, criticizes those contaminated by a thirst for money. Magallanes, faced with loss of his fortune, wants to meet conditions honestly, but his son and his wife try to conceal their poverty. His wife even compromises her honor to get money. Another way of facing poverty is shown in *Mr. Frank* (1917). The whiskey-drinking but faithful English valet, once saved by his wealthy employer, takes the impoverished family to live at his small farm after the death of his benefactor.

El rosal de las ruinas (1916; *Escena*, No. 73, 1919, thirteen editions) a three-act poetic tragedy, also based on family pride, was Roldán's greatest success. Like his popular three-act drama in verse, *Puñal de los troveros* (1921; *Escena*, No. 369, 1925, six editions), it shows him a follower of the romanticist Coronado. *El señor Corregidor* (1917; *Escena*, No. 55, 1919) also in verse, deals with family honor in colonial Buenos Aires where Carlos, an adopted son, takes the blame for the real son's theft. The Corregidor accepts the sacrifice, but Elena, previously unable to choose between the two as suitors, now accepts Carlos, ennobled by his actions.

The present also attracted Dr. Roldán. He attacked Yankee ideas of education in *La niña a la moda* (1915; *Escena*, No. 15, 1918), whose heroine turns from home and marriage to athletics, smoking, and gambling. But the role she plays in a comedy written by the bishop, causes a change in her outlook and she becomes a good girl. Obviously the dramatist was not at his best when trying to preach.

Bronce (1920; *Escena*, No. 94, 1920), the work that shows Roldán's affinity to Sánchez, has already been discussed. Roldán's popularity is attested by the fact that in 1915 six of his plays ran in the Buenos Aires theatres: *Los contagios, Luz de hoguera, Hacia las cumbres, La viuda influyente, El mago de la suerte,* and *La niña a la moda.*

In 1922 Dr. Roldán voiced his opinion of women in two plays: *El burlador de mujeres* and *La virgen de la purezas;* then, in ill health, he committed suicide.

José Antonio Saldías
(December 31, 1891–March 14, 1946)

What would *Argentores* have done if Saldías had continued the career he started at the age of fifteen when he entered the Naval Academy? After he turned to the theatre he wrote sixty plays that were performed, half of them full length; in January, 1943, founded the *Boletín de Estudios de Teatro;* and between 1942 and his death, directed the Instituto Nacional de Estudios de Teatro, publisher of the invaluable *Cuadernos de Cultura Teatral.*

Of Saldías' dozen unforgettable dramas, his earliest (following his debut in a brief *costumbrista* play in 1913) was *El distinguido ciudadano* (1915), in collaboration with Raúl Casariego. It was one of Roberto Casaux's two greatest personal successes. In it, Gregorio and his friends celebrate May 25 in Paris, where Simón Bellagamba offers to pay Gregorio's passage back to Buenos Aires if he will use his gift of gab to get Simón elected to Congress. Employing his talents for his own aggrandizement, Gregorio gets himself elected and proclaimed distinguished citizen.

Caballos de bastos (1917), an excellent comedy with a punning title, follows the fortunes of Teodoro Bastos, a gambler who plans to buy a race horse, turns honest, and marries a rich girl. "Love!" he exclaims. "It's made an honest man of even me." Despite its picaro out of Spain's Golden Age, it is thoroughly national, with Argentine slang and characters of the upper and lower classes. *Delirio de grandeza* of 1918 (*Argentores*, No. 21, 1934) is another outstanding comedy.

Saldías entered the gaucho field with one of his best, *La gringa Federika,* who taught German to the children of Lisardo Subillaga and finally married the old gaucho. Its original version appears in

Bambalinas, No. 630, 1930; in its final revision it was printed in *Argentores,* No. 184, 1940.

Those who wonder why Saldías concentrated on gay farces and gayer musical comedies should read his *Casa de barro* (1924) in which the main character, the successful playwright Pancho, explains to his brother that he writes plays of customs, and leaves the high-brow and psychological stuff to the universities. This was when Manager Pascual Caicavallo was eagerly welcoming *sainetes* in his "Catedral del género chico," while serious dramatists could not find theatres for their plays. But the sympathetic and human comedies of Saldías never had that trouble.⁹ His final play was his sixtieth, *Mire que es chico el mundo* (1946). He left two others incomplete.

Julio Sánchez Gardel
(December 15, 1879–March 18, 1937)

Sánchez Gardel, leaving Catamarca in 1897 to study law, could not forget his native region. In Buenos Aires he wrote several undistinguished plays, beginning in 1900 with *La otra,* and was about to go home discouraged when he distilled his nostalgic memories of Catamarca into *Noche de luna* (1907). It became a smash hit; so he remained at the capital writing.

Después de misa (1910), a little gem in the Alvarez Quintero tradition, concerns another student about to leave Catamarca for Buenos Aires. Sánchez Gardel's best play, however, is *Los mirasoles* of 1911 (*Argentores,* No. 166, 1939; Buenos Aires, 1942). Again like something by the Quinteros, Azucena, the daughter, though loved by Dr. Centero, turns her gaze like the sunflower toward far-off Buenos Aires, from which she expects a fairy-tale prince to come to marry her. Finally the doctor gets his chance to go to the capital. That he remained in the village for love of Azucena was criticized as a concession to those who wanted happy endings.¹⁰

Such criticism may have decided Sánchez Gardel to change his technique. In 1913, in his next play, *La montaña de las brujas* (Teatro Argentino, No. 58, 1921), he tried to revive Greek tragedy, and to

⁹ For critical articles on Sandías, with list of his plays, see *Boletín Argentores,* No. 50 (January, 1946), 3–7, and No. 56 (October, 1946), 13–14. See also Castagnino, *Esquema,* p. 102.

¹⁰ Juan Oscar Ponferrada, "La sugestión telúrica en el teatro de Sánchez Gardel," *Cuaderno,* No. 22 (1947), 95–133.

provide the violence and tears missing in his earlier plays. Mystery, superstition, and barbaric passion fill it and make it a forerunner of Argentina's later and more authentic folklore theatre like *Los afincaos* (1940) by Bernardo González Arrili (1892–) and Enzo Aloisi (1886–). The jealous husband Tadeo, not sure that León is his son, throws his wife's supposed lover off the cliff and lets her die, too —of pneumonia. His other son, Daniel, uses hypnotism on Inda, the daughter of an overseer. The play takes its name from the location of the witchcraft scene in which Zoilo tries to make Inda love a wandering gaucho, Juan de Dios. Complications involving dead bodies, spells, and ghost stories fill the last two acts till León, revenging his mother's death, proves the power of heredity by beating his father's head on the stones. Daniel runs off with Inda.

The performance of *Witches' Mountain*, Argentina's first long play translated into English, started an argument, as some critics proclaimed it one of modern Argentina's most powerful plays, but others considered it artificial melodrama saved only by its excellent local color. Its sequel *El zonda* (1915) brought more heat to the discussion. Named for the hot Andean winds, it is based on a legend about feuds between aboriginal tribes.

The quantity of adverse criticism discouraged Sánchez Gardel, and though he did write a few other *costumbrista* and regional plays, and was five times president of Argentores, the last seven years of his life saw no more productions.

Noche de luna, Las campanas, Los mirasoles, and *La montaña de las brujas,* picked as his best plays, were collected in *Teatro* (Buenos Aires, 1955).[11]

"Malena Sandor"
(December 31, 1913–)

Not many women in Argentina have written for the theatre. First, perhaps, was Juana Paula Manso de Noronha, who published her *Revolución de mayo* (1864), though there is no record of its performance. Priority in the field of production goes to *Contra soberbia, humilidad,* by eighteen-year-old Matilde Cuyas (1859–1909), performed one night, November 28, 1877, in Teatro Alegría, Buenos Aires.

---

[11] See Ismael Moya, *Costumbrismo en el teatro de Sánchez Gardel;* Vicente Martínez Cuitiño, "Elogio de Sánchez Gardel," *La Nación,* August 17, 1941.

Other *comediógrafas* include Eduarda Mansilla de García, (1838–1892), and others more modern: Salvadora Medina Onrubia, *La solución* (1921); Angela G. Moreno, *La otra* (1921); María Laura Segré, *La vida se construye* (1922); Lola Pita Martínez, *Marcela* (1922); Alcira Obligada, *Cantares y lágrimas* (1924); Amelia Monti, *La canalla* (1925); Carolina Alío, *Pobres almas* (1927); and finally the great poetess Alfonsina Storni (1892–1938), *El amo del mundo* (1927) and *Farsas pirotécnicas*.[12]

Of the contemporary dramatists, first and most likely to endure is "Malena Sandor" (pen name of María Elena James de Terza), a writer of Jewish extraction who began with the one-act *Yo me divorcio, papá* (1937) and triumphed in 1938 with the prize-winning *Una mujer libre* (*Argentores*, No. 221, 1942), which was presented at the Teatro Nacional and awarded the Cultura prize. Rio enjoyed it in Portuguese the following year.

Una mujer libre is the sort only a woman could write. Liana Menéndez emancipates herself through divorce for a career as a sculptor. But as a divorced woman, she attracts too many men, especially the husband of her friend Ana María. How she sends César back to his wife with the impression that nothing has happened is the exterior action. But deep within the play lies a woman's fear of going through life alone.

Miss Sandor's *Yo soy la más fuerte* of 1943 (*Argentores*, No. 231, 1943) is a melodrama in which, without motivation, a woman tries to prevent her stepson from marrying his sweetheart. Her *Tu vida es la mía* of 1945 (*Argentores*, No. 252, 1945) has a woman forcing her sister into a marriage she does not want by claiming the other woman's lover as her own. That also complicates her own life, but Marcela is clever and gets away with it. The second act's interweaving of several furious conversations shows the technical skill of Miss Sandor.

Unfortunately the cool reception of her plays and her mounting debts from trying to get them performed persuaded her to leave Argentina for Spain, where, with others, she wrote the good musical comedy *Penélope ya no teje* (1946) and the less successful *La respuesta fue dada* (1957), a confused story of the effect upon an aristocratic Roman family when a prisoner of World War II finally returns, wondering why he had sacrificed himself. A couple of coincidences convince him there is a God.

[12] Castagnino, *Esquema*, p. 113.

Carlos Schaefer Gallo
(1889–   )

One of the group that also included Beltrán, García Velloso, and González Castillo was Schaefer Gallo, a playwright of German-Creole parentage, from Santiago del Estero. His first play, *La novia de Zupay*, was accepted and performed in Buenos Aires in 1913. It and his *La leyenda de Kakuy* (1915) were based on legends of northern Argentina, anticipating Juan Oscar Ponferrada's *El carnaval del diablo* (1943), but Schaefer did not continue this line.

Editing the humorous *Caras y caretas* and the serious medical *Cruz Verde*, writing radio sketches and movies, and collaborating with many of the best-known dramatists kept Dr. Schaefer busy. With the actor Elías Alippi, he wrote *La borrachera del tango* (1921). He also collaborated with García Velloso, José León Pagano, and the Spaniard Villaespesa. His *La ley gaucha* (1933), in verse about Güemes, won a first prize in an Argentores competition. His *La raíz de la piedra* won another in 1945. Several of his plays, like *La mazorquera de Monserrat*, treated of the Rosas era. He also tried high comedy and comic *sainetes*. One of the most discussed was *El gaucho judío*, a psychological study of the Jewish cowboy Esau, separated by his religion from the other gauchos, who killed a rival in a quarrel over a Christian girl and thereby faced double persecution. Its authentic gaucho language added to its deep emotion and "good theatre" gave it importance.

Schaefer was also a facile writer of *sainetes*, like the amusing yet disturbing *Los dueños de Buenos Aires* (*Escena*, No. 775, 1933). Recently published was *La leyenda de Kacuy* (*Argentores*, No. 18, 1957).

Ezequiel Soria
(February 23, 1873–1936)

Directing the famous Florencio Parravicini Company was the last act in the career of Soria in the Argentine theatre—a career that started as an escape from the legal profession. Had he passed his final examinations, Soria would have been expected to return to his small home town to practice. So he flunked them and wrote *El año 92*. It was in the style of the current zarzuelas, and Andrés Abad y Antón supplied the music. Supposedly dealing with Argentina's contingent for the Columbus celebration, it was a satire on the political scene.

Still using contemporary material, Soria then wrote *Amor y lucha* (1895), about a possible war with Chile, and then the zarzuela *Sargento Martín* (1896), which concerned the earlier Paraguayan War, though with humor substituted for historical accuracy.

In 1897 he tried something new on the Argentine stage, a serious *sainete*. *Justicia criolla* is set in the patio of a tenement house where black Benito, a janitor in the Congress Building, argues with a Galician, caretaker of the Supreme Court. With music by Antonio Reynoso, it ranks high among Argentine zarzuelas. *La ley suprema* set in northern Argentina also dates from this year. After writing the excellent *El deber* (1898), whose action takes place in Buenos Aires, and after publishing six examples in *Zarzuelas criollas* (Buenos Aires, 1899), Soria left for a two years' stay in Europe, where he saw great plays and became acquainted with Spain's *género chico*.

Returning to Argentina in 1902, he was asked to select and direct plays for a proposed season of national drama. The season included works by Granada, Coronado, and a few of his own, like *Política casera* and *Entre el fuego*, in which he directed Podestá. It was Soria also who directed Sánchez's first attempt, *M' hijo el dotor*.

Soria then wrote some serious plays: *Cristián, El escudo*, and *Amor*. In the first, Cristián, the illegitimate son of wealthy Ordóñez, is brought up by his mother and her husband, ignorant of the injustices of the world. In a complicated plot, Cristián tries to get Ordóñez convicted for murder but is himself killed. The wealthy man, looking down at his dead son, wonders whether he has triumphed or lost. *Amor* also deals seriously with injustice in another of the plays that make Soria almost as memorable as his creation of the Creole musical comedy, or his directing of several famous actors. He played an important role in Argentine drama between 1899 and 1919.[13]

Roberto A. Tálice
(1902–   )

Dr. Tálice, born in Uruguay, came to Buenos Aires at the age of twenty-one and has been part of the Argentine theatrical scene ever since. His more than a hundred plays, written alone and with col-

---

[13] Ismael Moya, *Ezequel Soria, zarzuelista criollo.*

laborators, and his presidency of Argentores make him Argentine in spirit, though Montevideo has frequently honored its absent son with drama prizes.

Tálice began with *¿Cuándo?*, and at the age of seventeen his *Los infieles* was produced at Montevideo's Teatro Solís. After reaching Buenos Aires, except for *Sábado del pecado* (*Argentores*, No. 291), a Uruguayan Casa de Teatro prize winner which he wrote in collaboration with the Italian Alejandro de Stefania, he has turned out, by himself or in collaboration with Eliseo Montaine, a constant stream of technically excellent long plays that have been performed and forgotten. *Noche en los ojos, La llama eterna* (1947; *Argentores*, No. 272, 1947), winner of both the Cultura and the Municipal drama prizes for the year, *Oculta verdad* (*Proscenio*, No. 3, 1948), and *El amor comienza mañana* were some of the early ones.

The first half-dozen issues of *Repertorio* (1952–1953) reprinted his plays, ranging from pirate adventure to a study of sterility. This last, *Machorra*, about a woman who will not become a mother through adultery with her brother-in-law, moved all the reviewers to insist it had nothing to do with García Lorca's *Yerma*. Tálice is more realistic than Lorca, and more hopeful, and the heroine's virtue is rewarded by the return of her repentant husband.

Tálice's *La mujer incompleta o Don Juan vencido* a three-act monodrama, also suggests Lorca in its frustrated and childless woman whose dream of love ends in the murder of her lover and her suicide. *El hombre prohibido*, with its touches of *La casa de Bernarda Alba*, is part of Tálice's Lorca phase. Its five women and one man are tangled in jealousy and hate and sex, and an innocent woman becomes the victim of her own folly. All these plays were originally performed by Maruja Gil Quesada.

Ciudadano del mundo of 1941 (*Argentores*, No. 213, 1942) was selected for inclusion in the Aguilar *Diccionario* as representative of Tálice's style. His 1944 *John, Jean y Juan* (*Argentores*, No. 238, 1944) is a hilarious farce which also manages to contain both poetry and drama.

Besides all this writing, Dr. Tálice has also directed some of the best plays of the last twenty years. He put onto the stage, for instance, Moock's experimental *Del brazo y por la calle*. His talents are varied and all contribute to the Buenos Aires stage.

"César Tiempo"
(1906–   )

Israel Zeitlin, who signs his plays César Tiempo, was born in Russia, but reached Buenos Aires before he could talk. He got interested in the stage while still a student at the Colegio Nacional, where he played Crispín in a performance of *Los intereses creados*. He was also one of the *Mosca blanca* group to produce national plays in 1929.

In 1933 he made his appearance as a dramatist with *El teatro soy yo,* published that same year. It satirizes intolerance of race and creed. Plans are made for performing a play by Myriam; she protests the director's interest in a play by the Negro Gaspar Liberión, of "an inferior race." But when critics are harsh about both (successful) plays, because of the races of their authors, and the Negro shoots himself, Myriam sides with him as an outcast of society also. She wonders whether Heaven will also separate blacks and whites, Jews and Christians.

More powerful is Tiempo's *Pan criollo* of 1937 (published 1938), one of the important modern Argentine plays. Awarded the 1937 Premio Nacional de Teatro, it went, in spite of its huge cast, on tour through Argentina, Uruguay, and Paraguay. It is set in the ghetto of Buenos Aires, and in the original production the great actor Muiño plays Don Salomón Lefonejo, whose daughter Lía elopes with a Christian. Cast out by her father, Lía and her husband and child finally come back and are forgiven. The Creole soul, declares the old man, is like *pan criollo,* a product of many hands and many races. The newspaper reviews, collected in the illustrated printed version, testify to the enthusiastic reception of this philosophic yet deeply human comedy, which presents love as a link between Russian Jews and the inhabitants of the pampas.

An epilog, omitted in performance, was separately played as the one-act *Alfarada* (1935), with its prolog spoken by Myriam, from Tiempo's first play. From its title, the name of the special tax paid by Jews and Moors in Christian Spain, comes the charge that Jews today are subject to discrimination. Its author later wrote *Clara Beter vive* (1941), played by Camila Quiroga, which did not come up to the *Pan criollo*. Its title comes from the pen name Tiempo used for several of his early volumes of verse. Since then, as theatre critic, writer of movie scenarios, and feature writer under the pen name of

"Full Time," he has contributed few plays to the stage. However he did collaborate with Arturo Cerretani in a musical comedy (1945), and in the 1951 prize-winning *La dama de las camelias*. His 1957 *El lustrador de manzanas* (*Argentores*, No. 20, 1958), with Luis Arata in the role of the stepfather who holds the family of spend-thrift children together, ran for two years in Buenos Aires. It is a sentimental comedy showing none of the author's earlier racial bitterness.

"Alvaro Yunque"
(1889–1957)

Arístides Gandolfi Herrero, under the pen name of "Alvaro Yunque," was a critic and stage director and also author of such works as the semiserious study of psychological and character development *Un diamante en el apéndice*, in which a man swallows a diamond worth 100,000 pesos. Besides being the portrayal of a mother's selfless love for her son, it satirizes human frailty, greed, envy, and jealousy.

The play *13313*, subtitled "Absurdo," is a reminder that life's lottery contains losing tickets. It is a one-act study of a couple who attempt to understand each other in their futile old age, contrasted with flashback scenes of youth, optimism, and love; it is not a happy play. Neither is *La muerte es blanca y hermosa*. But in a lighter vein are Yunque's *Comedieta burguesa*, *El hígado y los riñones*, and *Dos humoristas y ella*, and his comedy *Somos hermanos* (1938) is a model of its kind. *Violín y violón* concerns Rosas. Yunque assisted several experimental groups, especially Teatro Libre (1925) and Máscara.

Others

New blood is now creating a revival in the River Plate theatre. Though not much has appeared in print about them, a few names should be mentioned that will undoubtedly achieve more space in later histories of drama: Mauricio Rosencof, Roberto Fabregat Cúneo and his brother, as well as three of the 1964 vintage; all are about thirty years old. Sergio de Cecco puts today's Argentine life into the mould of classical tragedy; Roberto M. Cossa writes realistically about the drifting middle-class society; and Germán Rosenmacher follows César Tiempo in his tragedies of the spiritual problems of Jews in Buenos Aires.

Collaborators

Besides those dramatists who wrote individually, the Buenos Aires stage in the last half-century has seen the collaboration of many dramatists.[14] One playwright who appeared to join up with many other dramatists was Tito Insausti (1894–1951). With his brother Rafael he wrote *Dinero* (1939); with Arnaldo Malfatti (1893–   ) he wrote *Esta chica es un demonio* (1940; *Argentores,* No. 195, 1940) and *Tiburón* (1946; *Argentores,* No. 260, 1946). Their *Una cándida paloma* of 1945, (*Argentores,* No. 266, 1946) won the National prize for that year.

Best known among collaborators for their dramatic hits of literary quality are Darthés and Damel, already discussed. Most productive among collaborators were probably Carlos Goicoechea (1892–   ) and Rogelio Cordone (1898–1951), authors of nearly a hundred plays distinguished by good plotting and humor.[15] Among them are *Se casa el vasco Chapara* (1939; *Argentores,* No. 175, 1940) whose protagonist marries a widow, and *¡Odioso de mi alma!* (1942; *Argentores,* No. 232, 1943). Others worth knowing are: *La boína blanca, Me alegro de haber nacido, Papá de mi corazón, ¡Qué gran hombre es mi papá!, Noches de carnaval,* and *Cayó una piedra en el Charco* (1926; *Bambalinas,* No. 433, 1926).

One of the outstanding results of collaboration was *Así es la vida* (1934) by Arnaldo Malfatti (1893–   ) and the Spaniard Nicolás de las Llanderas (?–1938). Though the era of the *sainete* ended about 1930 in Argentina, these collaborators used the *sainete* technique in a three-act picture of thirty years of Argentine middle-class family life, narrating what happens to Ernesto Salazar in 1905, 1916, and 1934. The play is simple and realistic, and critics explained its popularity and success by the fact that its many spectators sensed their own participation in the events.

Carlos Olivari (1902–1956) combined once with Cordone, in 1946, in *La barra de la esquina* (*Argentores,* No. 263, 1946) but it was with Sixto Pondal Ríos (1907–   ) that he was most successful. After their weak *Arrempujen Fóbal Club* (1935), they struck their stride in *La tercera invasión inglesa* (1936), *Amor al contado* (1937) and their excellent *La estancia de papá* (1938). From then on, with at least

[14] *Máscara,* No. 56 (October, 1946) p. 23, publishes the portraits of a number of these *binomios.*

[15] Castagnino, *Esquema,* p. 112, lists about twenty of their greatest successes.

one a year, they have produced light but amusing plays whose success seems to have made Pondal Ríos forget that once he was a sensitive poet. They even collaborated in a musical comedy, *El otro yo de Marcela*. Marital difficulties have provided themes for some of what have now become their machine-made hits, among them *Ya es hora de que te cases, papá, No salgas este noche* (1942), *Los maridos engañan de 7 a 9* (1943; *Argentores,* No. 235, 1943), *Si Eva se hubiese vestido* (1944), and *El viejo verde* (1945; *Argentores,* No. 256, 1946). There is no doubt about the popularity of their productions.

The lawyer and university professor Román Gómez Masía (1902–1944) wrote *La mujer que ellos sueñan* (1931) with Francisco Collado for a performance by Eva Franco. Then by himself in 1932 Gómez Masía dramatized a short story by Andreyev for the poetic *Ausencia* (*Argentores,* No. 31, 1934) and with it won the 1933 Círculo de Autores prize. It was finally performed in 1945 at the Florencio Sánchez Theatre. It was followed by the irreligious *El señor Dios no está en casa* (1932; *Biblioteca Racionalista,* No. 20, 1937) about business in Heaven being carried on by the saints in the absence of the boss. Though acclaimed as the best political satire by an Argentine author, it had to wait till 1937 for performance in the Teatro Libre, and then only after considerable rewriting. Another excellent but brief political farce by Gómez Masía was his *Temístocles en Salamina* of 1933 (published 1942). With a colleague, José María Monner Sans (1896–   ), he then wrote a trio of successful plays: *El tren 48, Yo me llamo Juan García* (1933), and in 1942, just before his death, *Islas Orcadas* (*Argentores,* No. 215, 1942), a psychological study of six members of an exploring expedition to the Orkney Islands. Another play, *La isla de gente hermosa*, might have been improved by rewriting had Gómez Mosía lived.

Tito Santoro Bonazzy, born in Italy in 1909, and his Argentine wife Elena Crouzel (1912–   ) entered eight plays in an international contest by *Teatro Moderno* in 1954, in which, according to the details in the magazine, plays by 125 authors from twenty-nine countries were submitted. Their entries, in Italian and Spanish, got the prize. The winning plays have been published in several languages, but there is no indication of productions, though they have had much publicity.

Among the present-day collaborators, a critic-poet-dramatist and an actor-director have been doing the most serious work. Professor

Juan Bautista Devoto (1916–   ) and Alberto Sabato (1911–   ) started with the three-act *Fuego en la nieve* (1949) and the one-act *Peregrino del mundo* the same year. After *Luz en las sombras* (1950) came their outstanding *Estatua de sal* (1952), introducing the powerful character Adelina, performed also in Madrid and warmly praised by Benavente and other dramatists and critics in many lands. Sabato directed and took the lead in this surrealist tragedy about flowers that betray the twenty-year-old, retarded Lucas and a mysterious *hombre de negro* who tempts Adriana.

To prove the success was no accident came *Los cínicos* (1952), deeply philosophic, and rising above existentialism even while showing man at the whim of good and evil. Daniel is symbolic of the goodly life, Laura is the evil influence, Claudio represents ambition; also in the cast are "El gran cínico" and four lesser cynics.

Following the one-act *Estampa de un anochecer* (1953) came another experiment, *Un responso para Lázaro* (1955), quickly translated into Portuguese for a production in Rio, to silence those who considered it a closet drama. It also received the gold medal for the 1954 Ministry of Education competition. With a Greek chorus whose members are individualized, a single set, and modern use of lights, it tells of the efforts of the passionate Raquel to separate the weak-willed Lázaro from his domineering wife, Javiera. But Lázaro confesses: "Mi voluntad no alcanza para nada." Only death can free him from her spell.

With developing technique and seriousness of concept, these collaborating dramatists followed this delicate though powerful play with another experiment, *Tres damas en la noche* (1958), a "narración dramática en tres actos," as its authors termed it. Under its earlier title, *Tres señoras aburridas*, it was unanimously awarded first prize in the 1955 Ministry of Education Drama Contest; Ferretti's *Farsa del cajero que fue hasta la esquina* was second choice. Then without explanation, the whole contest was called off and new judges appointed who, probably for lack of any classical background, reversed the order. However, the real value of the Devoto-Sabato work was recognized by its choice for the 1958 Sociedad de Escritores contest. In 1961 it enjoyed a radio broadcast.

The trio of women symbolize the Fates under English names: Señoras Spinner, Read, and Cutter. An absconding banker, with his current mistress, stops at their abode in his flight across the mountain pass, accompanied by a sculptor guide and a girl picked up along the way. The situation gives the authors opportunity to make observations about life and art, then the banker's fate overtakes him, and he falls to his death from a window, with his stolen gold.

In 1962 the Municipality of La Plata awarded its prize, and publication, to the Devoto-Sabato *Tejido de sombras*, a tragedy in which Fabio's mother stabs the homosexual Gerardo, who has tried to break up her son's marriage.

Neither of these thoughtful dramatists has ever produced what is known through the rest of the continent as the "Buenos Aires comedy," but their stature is greater than many who have been content with the facile and popular laugh-getters.

The Theatre of the Masses has played an important part in Argentine theatrical development, as elsewhere in the Hemisphere. While the subject does not deserve separate treatment, it should be mentioned somewhere. As early as 1928 Alberto Ballerini (1892–1931), himself a theatrical director, suggested that if the common people were to be expected to acquire a love for drama, steps must be taken to attract them into the theatre. He proposed the establishment of a Teatro del Pueblo, offering the best of world and national drama at low prices.[16]

Not till 1930 did anyone do anything about it. Then Leónidas Barletta (1902–   ) found a small place, christened it Teatro del Pueblo, and started an educational theatre. One hundred and twenty spectators could be seated, at a cost of fifteen cents a ticket. Five hundred performances of fifty different plays took place the first year. Finally the government offered financial backing, and in 1935 the Teatro del Pueblo moved to larger quarters with three hundred seats, and eventually into its own beautifully equipped theatre with 1,500 comfortable seats at prices cheaper than the movies. Experimenters were welcomed, and a number of dramatists, like Arlt, got their chance here.

However, its purpose as a *teatro polémico* brought it into conflict

---

[16] "Buenos Aires; Teatro del Pueblo," *Panorama*, No. 17 (1941), 1; John Erskine, "The People's Theatre," *Tomorrow* (March, 1943), 17–19; Enzo Aloisi, "Tras de las candilejas," *Américas*, IV, No. 3, 21–23, 44–45; Theodore Apstein, "New Aspects of the Theatre in Latin America," *Conference of Latin American Fine Arts* (Latin American Studies, No. 13, The University of Texas, pp. 27–41); Willis K. Jones, *Breve historia del teatro latinoamericano*, pp. 193–205; Ordaz, *El teatro*, pp. 207–224.

with Perón, and his hoodlums burned it along with other buildings that had been used as centers of resistance to his dictatorship. A number of other sites of drama experiment, like Teatro Juan B. Justo and La Máscara, are discussed by Ordaz.[17] Argentina also began developing independent theatres, many run by trade unions, syndicates, and part-time drama enthusiasts. They became so numerous that in November, 1960, they cooperated to launch *Revista de Teatro*, each issue to contain a complete play, reports of the achievements of the affiliated theatres, and general articles about world theatre.

These "people's theatres" are not confined to Argentina. The chapters on Mexico and Venezuela, for instance, will mention some. In Uruguay, clubs which produced propaganda plays and theatres which espoused political slants launched Florencio Sánchez and Ernesto Herrera. In northern Chile, too, there was a theatrical movement for a dozen years before 1925, inspired by Recabarren, leader of the Communist movement in the country. He wrote plays himself for the instruction of workers in the nitrate fields and encouraged others, and they were performed in the *filarmónicas*, or clubs, of workers. Most of these works deserve to be lost; their importance rests in their anticipation of a theatre of the masses a quarter century later, now visible in the provincial groups of amateurs mentioned in the chapter on modern Chile. The whole problem of a proletariat theatre would deserve a volume to itself.

[17] Ordaz, *El teatro*.

CHAPTER 12

Early Actors and Actresses of Latin America

The success of a country's theatre rests fundamentally on its actors. A hungry drama lover may be content to see a play even poorly acted because his imagination can transform the performance, but the person who has to be wooed into the theatre needs the impression of reality, provided by skilled actors, to make him overlook the artificiality of a play world full of conventions, where rooms have three walls and their occupants must be directed before they walk and talk. No wonder the world of the movies, where everything is made to look real, seems more convincing and enjoyable.

From the beginning, actors have always been the problem of the Latin American theatre. At first priests or members of their congregations trained by them took the parts. The Jesuits in Paraguay even performed operas with casts from their Guaraní parishioners. A play in Peru as early as 1563 got its actors from the members of the trade guild that sponsored it. Seminary students acted in a Corpus Christi play in Santo Domingo on June 23, 1588, that brought exile to its author, Cristóbal de Llerena. In the first plays in Argentina, soldiers filled the roles, both masculine and feminine, and aristocrats joined with soldiers in the first play in Santiago de Chile in 1633. In southern Chile, the welcoming drama, "A Chilean Hercules," for the governor who came to Concepción in 1693, used men and women of that frontier town. Even as late as the nineteenth century, Spanish Governor Marcó del Pont drafted his soldiers for minor roles, and Chile's first President, Bernardo O'Higgins, got the actors for the first national theatrical company from among the Spanish prisoners he had captured. Captain Francisco Cáceres, from Seville, captured at Valparaíso by Admiral Cochrane, was the leading man.

Of course long before this period professional actors had reached America. At the end of the sixteenth century eight members of a barnstorming troupe whose activities in Madrid had been ended by King Philip's decree of May 2, 1598, prohibiting stage productions in his realm, turned up in Callao, Peru, on June 28, 1599, where they signed an agreement to perform plays by Lope de Vega in Lima.[1] The profits were to be divided into eight-and-a-half parts, of which the leading man, Francisco Pérez de Robles, was to receive one part for his acting, another part as rental for his 668-pesos worth of costumes and stage property, and a quarter part as director and treasurer. To his illiterate wife, Isabel de los Angeles, who had to sign with an X, went one-and-a-half parts as leading lady. The other six performers divided the rest. Thanks to Pérez de Robles, Lope's work reached the New World a century and a half before Thomas Kean introduced Shakespeare to America in 1750 at a theatre on Nassau Street, New York City.

Spaniards, unlike other nationalities, had no prejudice against seeing women on the stage, though for lack of women willing to appear before the public, boys frequently played the feminine parts, as in the England of Shakespeare. The first woman to appear on an English stage was a visiting Italian actress, who played before Queen Elizabeth in 1608, but no English woman showed herself before an audience till the wife of the actor Coleman appeared with him in *The Siege of Rhodes* in 1656. In France as late as 1629 the populace was showing its displeasure with actresses by pelting them.[2]

In Spain, on the other hand, Lope de Rueda's wife was one of his strolling players in the middle of the sixteenth century. A contract dated March 15, 1583, assured Juana Vázquez of nine and a half *reales* a performance with Juan Luna's company in Madrid, for the season lasting till Shrovetide.

In the New World, however, no names of locally born actresses can be found that early. Not till the seventeenth century is there mention of a Mexican actress, and she a murderess, pardoned by the viceroy because she was needed for a current performance. Another actress, who killed her sweetheart, for motives of love mingled with Ecuador-Peru rivalry, had her crime dramatized into a vehicle for her dramatic success. In the seventeenth century an actress in Lima's Coliseo became popular as "La Empedradora," because her husband

---

[1] A. S. W. Rosenbach, "The First Theatrical Company in America," *Proceedings of the American Antiquarian Society*, October, 1938, pp. 1–13.

[2] Rosamond Gilder, *Enter the Actress*; Karl Mantzius, *History of Theatrical Art*, II, 284; H. B. Baker, *The London Stage*.

had a street-paving contract; and two stars of eighteenth-century Colombia were known as "La Jerezana" (because of her Spanish birthplace) and "La Cebollino" (from her husband's name).

But the reputation of all of them was fleeting compared to a trio of unforgettable later actresses. The earliest was Perricholi, about whom Offenbach composed an opera, Merimée spun his *Carrosse du Saint Sacrament*, and Thornton Wilder wrote *The Bridge of San Luis Rey*. Micaela Villegas was a Peruvian *chola*, that is, part Indian, born in Lima, September 28, 1748. Eventually her parents had three girls and three boys, too many for the father to support, so "Miquita," possessor of a beautiful singing voice and skilled on the harp and the guitar, went into show business.

The year she was thirteen Peru got a new viceroy, a sixty-year-old bachelor, Manuel de Amat, a Catalan who had previously governed Chile. He was inaugurated October 12, 1761. Lima's theatre, along with hundreds of its citizens, had been destroyed by the earthquake of 1746, but in 1762 the New Coliseum was ready, built by Pablo de Olavide at a cost of 43,000 pesos, and from his box close to the stage Viceroy Amat could look at the popular Micaela. Apparently it took nearly four years, however, before either really saw the other.

When the Viceroy developed an interest in an actress it was a blow to the aristocratic ladies of Lima, and the birth of Micaela's son, Manuel, in 1769, acknowledged as his own by the Viceroy, caused even more criticism. But most aristocrats, along with the common people, flocked to see "Miquita" perform, and she managed to persuade Marza, the theatre manager, to pay her the enormous wages of 150 pesos a month.

She must have been beautiful. Though some biographers mention a pug nose, and one speaks of smallpox marks, the only portrait of her, a contemporary miniature in the Museum of La Quinta de Presa, does not bear out her detractors. Poems were written to her tiny feet and hands. She was graceful, her voice was musical, and only once was her ability as an actress questioned. During one afternoon performance, as she was interpreting the heroine of Calderón's *Fuego de Dios en el querer bien*, the actor-manager Maza muttered that another actress could act "a hundred times better." In sudden rage Micaela raised the riding whip she was carrying and slashed Maza across the face. By Spain's Honor Code, violence before a representative of the king was an insult to the king himself. Amat quickly left the theatre, with most of the audience trailing him.

That night Amat's royal coach visited her home and the Viceroy ordered her never to appear again on the stage. Someone overheard their parting and reported that he had ended with: "Adios, perra chola (Farewell, you half-breed dog)." Through his missing teeth, his Catalan accent made the epithet sound like "Perricholi," and her enemies seized on the name as an insult. It is more believable, however, that, still fond of her, the Viceroy had really used his pet Catalan name for her, "Pretixol" (jewel), but a Peruvian would not know that word.

Both box office and Viceroy missed Micaela, and friends finally arranged an apology and reconciliation. On November 4, 1775, the curtain rose on "Perricholi" as she now proudly called herself. Viceroy Amat, there in his finery, set the tone of the occasion by shouting from the royal box: "Have courage and perform well, Perricholi!"

She did. Lima had never seen such an ovation. For a year Perricholi was Lima's leading lady on the stage and in the Viceroy's palace. Then a new viceroy was appointed, and with the end of Amat's influence the enemies of both of them grew bolder. The insults took literary form in the anonymous *Drama de los palanganas Veterano y Bisoño*,[3] a hundred pages of vitriol that Amat escaped by leaving for Spain, December 4, 1776. Perricholi remained behind, fighting to maintain her popularity. She succeeded. She married a fellow actor and they leased Lima's best theatre. She continued to perform till the death of her husband, in the next century. Then she made her will, bestowing much of her accumulated wealth on her daughter and on her son, Manuel de Amat, who went to Spain for his education. The remainder, after reserving enough to pay for her burial and for four candles for her funeral, she gave to the poor.

To find a substitute for her, *El Diario*, a Lima newspaper, advertised (July 23, 1792) for "a good-looking girl trained in singing and acting," to whom the management offered an excellent salary of ninety pesos a month, "for working only holidays and not all holidays," and two hundred pesos bonus ("glove money" they called it). But Peru

---

[3] *Drama de los Palanganas, Veterano y Bisoño*, ed. Luis Alberto Sánchez, in *Revista Chilena de Historia y Geografía*, Vols. 84–86. See also Antenor del Pozo, *El de Junient en el drama de los Palanganas.*

never produced another actress like the fiery *chola* Micaela Villegas, "La Perricholi," from Lima.[4]

The other two great actresses of the early Latin American theatre were Uruguayans. Trinidad Guevara (1798–1873) was the first Creole actress of the River Plate.[5] Though not as beautiful as her predecessors on the Buenos Aires stage (López, Montes de Oca, and Ugier), her charming speaking voice and wonderful stage presence made her outstanding. Also she contributed to the New World stage the idea that the creation or interpretation of characters was more important than the melodious reading of lines. Though the public still favored a bombastic and grand-opera way of delivering speeches, Trinidad's artistic fire, the expression of her eyes, and her ability, without overplaying, to suggest pathos or horror, eventually won the admiration of critics and public. Even Francisca Ugier, reigning favorite, had to agree that this girl who had started in a servant-girl part at the age of sixteen, was her superior.

For a time, when Buenos Aires succumbed to the craze for the opera, Trinidad, who could not sing, lived and performed in Uruguay and Chile. Then in 1832 she joined the great Casacuberta, and acted in comedies and tragedies till her death at the age of seventy-five, the year before the birth of her great successor and fellow Uruguayan, Orfilia Rico (1874–1922).

Orfilia, the child of two Spanish musical-comedy stars, was born in Montevideo, where her mother had to interrupt a performance of *Los hijos del capitán Grant* to produce her own *hija*. At the age of five Orfilia performed in Eusebio Blanco's *El pañuelo blanco*. A few years later, at the head of a group of child actors, she offered a repertory from Benavente, Echegaray, and other Spanish dramatists.

Married at the age of seventeen to a Spanish actor-manager, she had four children before he ran off to Mexico and to another actress. Orfilia then had to return to the stage. In 1900 Jerónimo Podestá and the rest of his family were appearing for a season in Montevideo.

---

[4] Augusto Tamayo Vargas, "La Perricholi fue limeña," *Turismo*, IX, No. 98, and in *Estudios de Teatro Peruano*, Series VI, No. 18. See also Antonio Garland, "Miquita la Perricholi," *Estudios de Teatro Peruano*, No. 20.

[5] Mariano Bosch, *Historia del teatro en Buenos Aires*, pp. 106–116; Arturo Capdevila, "Noticias del teatro argentino en los años gloriosos de Trinidad Guevara," *Cuaderno*, No. 1 (1936), 19–29; Capdevila, "Las varias muertes y la verdadera defunción de Trinidad Guevara," *Cuaderno*, No. 19 (1944), 9–22.

On the eve of one performance Anita Podestá became ill. Somebody thought of Orfilia. Without a rehearsal, indeed without even having read the play, she went onto the stage that night. Years of previous practice in following a prompter who read lines just ahead of the actors gave her ability to achieve such a triumph that a contract was signed at once. When the company returned to Buenos Aires and the Teatro Apolo, which the Podestás opened April 6, 1901, Orfilia was introduced to Argentine audiences in *Bohemia criolla*. No one could call her pretty. She was big-boned and built like an Italian peasant woman, but she had no trouble getting engagements. With Florencio Parravicini, with Pablo Podestá, and with her own company, she became the most popular national actress. One has only to look at the titles of plays appearing after 1906 to know which were written for her: *La gaucha, Criolla vieja, Abuela Graciana, Misia Pancha la brava, Mamá Clara, Mamá Culepina, Doña Remedios*, all built around a dynamic, middle-aged woman, to be interpreted by an actress whose stage career ended before she was forty-eight.

She introduced Sánchez' *M' hijo el dotor* (1903), *Barranca abajo* (1905), and *Los muertos* (1907). For a whole season, she played Saldías' *Delirio de grandeza*, and one of her greatest successes was a record-breaking run of 146 performances of *Las de Barranco* (1908), by Laferrère, deliberately underplayed. She was a static actress. She did not believe violent movement was necessary to express strong emotion, but Federico Mertens, several of whose plays she brought to life, tells of watching her rehearse a play written and directed by Dr. Roldán.[6] The leading man, continually criticized by the director, finally protested and asked why he never made suggestions to Orfilia.

"She's bringing out things in her role that I didn't realize were there," Roldán replied, "while you're not expressing even what I put into your part."

In the midst of her pyramiding success, Orfilia Rico was taken ill in October, 1922, and died shortly afterward, one of the great stars of the Latin American stage.

Other great actresses of Latin America of a more recent vintage come to mind, Singerman, Membrives, Quiroga, Xirgú, Virginia Fábregas, and Luisa Martínez of Cuba, but some note must be taken of the early actors too. One of the best was an adopted son of Mexico,

---

[6] Federico Mertens, "Orfilia Rico," *Cuaderno*, No. 21 (1945), 69–87.

Eusebio Vela (1689–1736).[7] Born in Toledo, Spain, and possibly having had some acting experience in Madrid, he was first heard of in
Mexico in 1713, performing in El Coliseo with his brother. In 1718 he
took over the management, but that started his troubles. Careless
about money, he ran into debt and could not pay the actors. At a
time when the popularity of cockfights and the terror of a smallpox
epidemic kept theatre audiences small, Vela was glad to go back on
salary. As a final blow, the theatre burned.

Another was built in which he, his brother, and two actresses that
they had married, all performed. Besides acting, Eusebio wrote more
than a dozen plays, thus collecting money from all phases of the
theatre, but while he was the outstanding theatrical figure in Mexico
for a quarter century, his life ended in poverty.

A predecessor of Roberto Casaux of Argentina and Fernando Soler
of Mexico, great names of the twentieth century, was the greatest
masculine figure of the early Latin American stage, Juan Casacuberta
(1799–1849).[8] The son of an Uruguayan father and Argentine
mother, he first apeared on the stage in a servant's role at the age of
seventeen. His first important part was the ghost in a one-act farce,
El valiente y la fantasma. Then he went on to become the dominating
figure on the South American stage. His handsome figure, his singing
voice, and his grace in dancing were important factors, though his
pride and vanity proved a handicap, especially when he found himself in competition with the popular Chilean actor Francisco Cáceres
(1780–1836), who had first appeared in the Coliseum in Buenos Aires
in 1825. The public in general admired Cáceres' shouting and violent
gestures, in spite of the objections of one critic who wrote in the
British Packet:

The acting of Señor Cáceres would be more appreciated if it were more
natural; the agitation and panting which he applies with such success in
some characters gets tiresome and unbelievable when constantly practiced.[9]

---

[7] Armando de Maria y Campos, *Andanzas y picardías de Eusebio Vela*; J. R.
Spell and Francisco Monterde, *Tres comedias de Eusebio Vela.*

[8] Juan Carlos Sabat Pebet, *Juan Casacuberta*; Raúl H. Castagnino, *El teatro
en Buenos Aires durante la época de Rosas*, pp. 140 ff.; Bosch, *Historia*, pp. 173
ff.; Elsa Martínez, *Casacuberta*; Arturo Berenguer Carisomo, "Casacuberta,"
Boletín, No. 26 (July, 1949), 50–54.

[9] Quoted in Castagnino, *El teatro en Buenos Aires*, p. 88.

However the ordinary theatregoer preferred Cáceres' style to the restrained one that Casacuberta had learned when he made a special visit to Rio to observe the technique of the European stars Talma and Maiquez.[10] So the public remained faithful even though Cáceres was getting too fat and too old to be convincing as a romantic hero. Even Trinidad Guevara at first preferred to work with Cáceres; but in 1832 the egotistical Casacuberta refused a subordinate role in the company of his older rival. After that, Casacuberta performed in Buenos Aires only when Cáceres went touring to Uruguay or Chile.

Between engagements Casacuberta enlisted in the army of Lamadrid against Rosas, and had to flee to Chile when it was defeated at Arroyo del Medio in 1841. From then on even his great ability played a second role to his bad luck. His compatriot Sarmiento, also a refugee in Chile, got him a chance to perform in Valparaíso in *Mancha de sangre*, but when the nearby customs house caught fire on opening night, many of the lukewarm audience, more accustomed to actors who tore passions to tatters, thought the firemen would provide more drama and forsook the theatre.

Casacuberta had better success during his year and a half in Peru, but when he returned to Santiago his opening performance conflicted with a violin concert by Camilo Sivori and his audience was so small that he called off the show and took them all to hear the Italian artist. Later he developed an admiring Chilean following, but news of Rosas' defeat and of Cáceres' retirement decided him to return to Argentina. To get passage money across the Andes he gave a farewell benefit performance of Ducange's *Las siete gradas del crimen*. On his way back to his boardinghouse, with his pockets full of money, Casacuberta died of a heart attack.

Most famous of River Plate players of that century was not one man, but a whole family: the Podestá tribe. José Podestá, who started the family's theatrical tradition, was born in Montevideo in 1858, of Italian immigrants. As a young man he practiced acrobatics on the sandy beaches, until he received an offer to join the Felix Henault circus.

He did not know, the day he joined the company in Durango, that the star acrobat, Caballé, had just been killed and that he was the new attraction. Though frightened, he successfully concluded his per-

[10] Pablo Acchiardi, "Casacuberta y el arte del actor," *Cuaderno*, No. 14 (1940), 61–100.

formance and stayed with the company for six months before re-turning to Montevideo for the safer job of a gymnastics instructor.[11]

Seeking more money, Podestá organized his five brothers into an equestrian team and joined another circus. One day its leading clown walked away, and José was asked to replace him. His mother made his costume from a sheet and decorated it with cloth cut from his father's old black coat. The patches on the seat looked like figures, so he Italianized his name and became "Pepino el 88," one of the most famous of Argentine clowns.

His fame, his horseback-riding ability, and his routine of singing gaucho songs to his own guitar accompaniment made him the logical choice to portray the downtrodden gaucho Juan Moreira in a panto-mime written to conclude a circus performance. With his long black hair and curly beard, and wearing silver-decorated clothes and broad-brimmed hat, he introduced this landmark in River Plate dramatic history in 1884. Two years later he added dialog to make it a regular play.[12] He went on to star in many other plays, and his chil-dren and grandchildren, many "born in the wings" as the expression has it, continued the tradition, even after his death in 1937. A photo-graph of a cast of one play at the Apolo in 1907 shows seven of the Podestá family. Five of them had roles in *Piedra de escándalo* (1902), another landmark in Argentine drama. Blanca Podestá, who got her start as Jesusa in Sánchez' first, *M' hijo el dotor*, became the most famous actress of the family; but the youngest son, Pablo (1877–1923), who introduced many of Sánchez' plays, was the greatest of them all, especially in *Barranca abajo*. A third generation continues to win honors in the adopted land of their grandfather.[13]

The history of child actors in the Latin American theatre is a story apart. There must have been juvenile performers before the group headed by Gemma Cuniberti delighted the court of Pedro II of Bra-zil in 1847.[14] Orfilia Rico and her small companions antedated the

---

[11] Enrique García Velloso, *El arte del comediante*, I, 177.

[12] Oscar Beltrán, *Los orígenes del teatro argentino* pp. 146–148, José Podestá, *Medio siglo de farándula*.

[13] Vicente Martínez Cuitiño, "Elogio de Pablo Podestá," *Boletín*, No. 11 (April, 1944), 43–47; Orestes Cosentino, "Pablo Podestá," *Máscara*, VII (No-vember, 1947), 8; Alberto P. Cortazzo, "Don Gerónimo Podestá," *Cuaderno*, No. 23 (1949), 41–97; Mariano G. Bosch, *Historia de los orígenes del teatro nacional y la época de Pablo Podestá*.

[14] Lafayette Silva, *Historia do teatro brasileiro*, p. 417.

Compañía Infantil in Guayaquil (1927–1930), which was directed by Eduardo Beltrán, with five of his own offspring as a nucleus, and which gave basic training to so many later leaders in Ecuador's theatrical world.[15]

This is not a complete list of excellent actors on the Latin American stages. With so many governments and universities founding schools of the theatre, and so many amateur experimental groups providing practical experience, other good actors are sure to be developed, to provide material for some future historian. To paraphrase Whitman, "To have great drama, there must be great actors, too." The Latin American actors are on their way.

[15] Willis K. Jones, "El Drama en el Ecuador," *Anales de la Universidad de Guayaquil*, II, No. 2, 221.

CHAPTER 13

Beginnings of Drama in Chile

In comparison with other Latin American regions, the theatre in colonial Chile had a slow start, for a number of reasons.

One was the poverty of the country, which even delayed its colonization when Almagro took back to Peru a pessimistic report of its resources, following his visit of exploration in 1535. A century later, Chile's capital had only two hundred houses. The fact that its two thousand inhabitants supported 240 monks in four monasteries and 104 nuns in two convents, revealed a religious fervor that also worked against drama. At prospect of any public performance, the Church voiced its disapproval, and the faithful upheld that stand.

Another cause for the slow development of the theatre was the lack of education among Chile's population. Most of them were unschooled adventurers, whose battle in one New World region after another before eventually reaching Chile had caused them to forget even the little they might have once learned. And in Chile they faced still more fighting and few leisure hours. Having had little previous acquaintance with stage plays, they found bullfights and cockfights more to their taste. It is not hard, therefore, to understand how Europeans could exist in this region for a century or more before performing any play worthy of recording.

Indeed, more drama was produced in Spain about Chile than in Chile itself. Nine dramatists, including Ruiz de Alarcón, Guillén de Castro, and Vélez de Guevara, collaborated in 1622 to write *Algunas hazañas de las muchas de don García Hurtado de Mendoza, Marqués de Cañete.* Lope de Vega set *El arauco domado* in Chile; somebody, probably Ricardo de Turia, brought Araucanian Indians into his *La belígera española,* and González Bustos penned *Los españoles en Chile.* All these plays were eventually performed in the Chile of their setting, but not till many years after their première in Madrid.

The earliest mention of any dramatic activity in Chile has been

discovered by Zlatko Brncic Juricic.[1] In the records of the Assembly
for May 2, 1556, appears an order to the various guilds to perform
during the Corpus Christi celebrations, under a penalty of a fine of
six gold pieces, something called "invenciones," a word later used to
describe dramatic spectacles based on Biblical incidents. Any works
of the imagination, whether drama or fiction, were forbidden by law
in the Spanish colonies. Possibly a parade of masked and dancing
figures could have satisfied the law. Certainly they could not have
been very artistic because even in succeeding years the Church authorities criticized their crudity as well as their immorality. Further
decrees by Philip III in 1616 caused Santiago and the provincial
towns to commemorate the Immaculate Conception with *loas*, recitations, and theatrical performances.

The first definite mention of plays in Chile, however, occurs in the
description of a celebration sponsored by Governor Francisco Laso
de la Vega in gratitude for his recovery from illness. It spread over
four weeks. On his saint's day, September 11, 1633, on a stage four-
and-a-half-feet high, plays were presented by "military men, lawyers,
and notables of the realm." The preliminary speeches and music took
so much time, however, that part of the proposed program had to be
postponed to a later date.

At first most of the clergy approved of such performances, perhaps
because they were based on religious themes and had been previously censored by the Church. When a few dissenters tried to prevent
performances, Fray Gaspar de Villarroel even wrote a defense of the
theatre.[2]

Of these early plays all details have been lost except the plot of one
sainete, tentatively dated by José Toribio Medina as 1616, which
deals with a schoolteacher, Tremendo, who orders his pupils to bring
him donations of bread and who hires a boy, Silverio, to beat anyone
who disobeyed. The hungry Silverio eats the food, then to conceal his
theft, beats the children. But when the bully thrashes the son of a
doctor, the father storms into the school and starts a free-for-all with
which the play ends.

Certainly this plot is a simple one, but in that respect it resembles
primitive drama everywhere. One of the first products of Spain's

[1] Zlatko Brncic Juricic, "El teatro chileno através de cincuenta años," *Anales
de la Universidad de Chile*, CXI (1951), Nos. 85–86, 113–168, especially p. 146.
[2] Transcribed in Benjamín Vicuña Mackenna, *Historia de Santiago*, I, 508 ff.

stage, Encina's *Auto del Repelón* (c. 1500), also concerns a struggle over food, between shepherds and University of Salamanca students.

Scholars have also found mention of religious plays produced for their own amusement by students at the Jesuit College of Convictorio Carolino, and by nuns in the convents. Vicente Grez published details of some religious plays performed publicly in 1654 at the Compañía Church, the center of Santiago's social life.[3]

However, the first play in Chile that followed the formula of Spain's Golden Age is believed to have been "El Hércules chileno," written early in 1693 according to the chronicler Pedro Pascual de Córdova y Figueroa.[4] In 1553, when the independent Araucanian Indians wanted to discourage Pedro de Valdiva and his gold-hunting Spaniards, they had poured the melted metal down the white men's throats, and, to be sure their point got across, they declared the Biobío River an impassable boundary, thus making Concepción Chile's frontier city. When Tomás Marín de Poveda of Granada came to Chile in 1693 as captain general, he traveled first to the southern frontier to examine Chilean defenses, and was joined there by Juana Urdánegui, to whom he had become engaged in Lima. To celebrate their wedding, the social lights of Concepción arranged a program of fourteen plays, of which the only one mentioned by name was "El Hércules chileno." It was obviously based on the life of Chief Caupolicán, the principal figure in South America's greatest epic poem, Ercilla's *La araucana*, which was published in installments from 1569 to 1589. The play manuscript was probably destroyed in some raid on Concepción, after it had served its purpose to welcome Chile's new governor. Few of the citizens could have read it anyway. And so the seventeenth century closed in Chile with few plays, no permanent theatre, and no theatrical tradition.

In 1702 someone in the port city of Valparaíso constructed a shed for a few performances, but it was too small for any large crowd. In 1712 the French visitor Frezier wrote of witnessing an open-air performance of farces and dances in Valparaíso on the porch of San Francisco Church.[5] Not till 1791, however, was there an actual theatre in the port city. Then one was built by an impresario, Loreto Inojosa. It had an octagonal-shaped auditorium with raised seats

---

[3] Vicente Grez, *La vida santiaguina*, pp. 75–102.
[4] Manuel Gamir Aparicio, *Compendio histórico del teatro*, p. 115.
[5] Amedée F. Frézier, *Relation du voyage de la Mer du Sud aux côtes du Chili.*

and a thatched roof. But Vicuña Mackenna declares it was used more for cockfights than for plays.[6]

Up the coast, in La Serena, Chile's first evening performances took place when the citizens held a belated celebration on April 23, 1748, of the coronation in Spain of Ferdinand VI. The offerings were *El alcázar del secreto*, by Solís, whose leading actor had a pleasing voice, and *Resucitar en agua o San Pedro de Masnara*, by Lanini, Ruiz, and Jacinto Hurtado de Mendoza.[7]

Santiago itself had no regular theatre till the next century. In 1709 Governor Juan de Ustáriz, who had seen the Little Theatre built by Philip II in his Escorial Palace, constructed a *salón de comedias* in his Santiago official home, but no record of its activities remains. Bishop Alday's later comments about the "ungodly practices" of the theatre where boys took female parts may refer to performances here.[8]

Lack of details of this and other theatrical activity can probably be attributed to the difficulty of printing and to the rigors of censorship. The only proof that the Chilean theatre was not completely dead lies in a few brief *loas*, preserved perhaps by the people praised in them. The earliest one, in 1746, welcomes the new bishop, Juan González de Marmolejo, come to Santiago from Paraguay.[9] It contains no dramatic clash of interests. Six abstract characters, including Understanding, Memory, and The Future, join in greeting him. The last two lines may contain a subconscious resentment of the Church's domination, as the author declares:

> He who writes this is not free
> To ignore your mighty qualities.[10]

Perhaps these theatrical Dark Ages benefited the colony. At least that was the contention of one historian, Carvallo Goyeneche, who

[6] Benjamín Vicuña Mackenna, *Historia de Valparaíso.* (Vols. III and IV of *Obras.*) See also Brncic, "El teatro chileno," *Anales de la Universidad de Chile*, p. 148.

[7] Brncic, "El teatro chileno," *Anales de la Universidad de Chile*, p. 161.

[8] Vicuña Mackenna, *Historia de Santiago*, I, 584–593.

[9] Reprinted in J. T. Medina, *Historia de la literatura colonial de Chile*, Appendix; and in Eugenio Pereira Salas, *El teatro en Santiago del Nuevo Extremo, 1709–1809*, Appendix.

[10] Brncic, "El teatro chileno," *Anales de la Universidad de Chile*, p. 152.

insisted that the high moral tone of Chilean society was due to lack of contact with the bad examples that filled most of the dramas.[11] Certainly Spain tried to protect the minds of its New World subjects. Article 23 of the Ordinance of 1776 by Tadeo de la Croix is full of prohibitions. Plays about kings murdered or driven from their thrones were forbidden lest they give ideas to discontented colonists; and plots dealing with conquest were frowned on to prevent bad feeling among the conquered. How many ambitious dramatists were discouraged by these prohibitions will never be known. They cut off New World writers from the themes about which they knew most. Conquest was the subject of one lost play, a drama written by a Peruvian about the daughter of the chief who held him captive. Núñez de Pineda (1607–1680), who spent eight months of 1629 as a captive of the Araucanian Indians, mentioned it in his chronicle, *El cautiverio feliz.*

Even so, the theatre in Chile was slowly developing. The public had begun to demand entertainment, and to provide it appeared Chile's first theatrical producer, José Rubio. He obtained permission from Governor Agustín de Jáuregui for a series of twenty performances between Christmas 1777 and Lent 1778. Local talent was hired at a peso a performance and the plays came from Spain: *Desdén con el desdén* by Moreto; others by Lope de Vega and Calderón; a cheap but popular comedy, *El dómine Lucas* by José de Cañizares; and a drama that violated De la Croix's injunctions, *Los españoles en Chile,* by González Bustos. Though not very professional, the performances so delighted Santiago audiences that they clamored for an extension of the season. Now, however, the Church stepped in. When Rubio had submitted his original request, the bishop of Santiago, Manuel de Alday y Aspe, was away, visiting distant parishes. Now back in Santiago, he raised instant objections by sending Governor Jáuregui a long treatise about the immorality of the theatre.[12] He pointed out that in many places actors, and especially actresses, were forbidden the rites of the Church because of their loose morals. He quoted one parishioner whose pleasures at the theatre were destroyed by

[11] Quoted by M. L. Amunátegui, "Establecimiento del teatro en Chile después de la independencia," *Revista de Santiago,* I (1888), 481.

[12] Benjamín Vicuña Mackenna, "Teatro en Chile," *Revista de Santiago,* V, pp. 584–593.

thoughts that those who entertained her were damned on account of their profession.

Theatre-loving Judge Juan Rodríguez Ballesteros answered the objections in a reply directed to the Governor. Unable to decide between the two briefs, Jáuregui sent both to the viceroy in Peru, who sided with the Church, thus temporarily ending Santiago's hope for a permanent theatre. And, as Jáuregui was transferred to Lima as viceroy, and the governor who succeeded him, Brigadier Ambrosio de Benavides, had no interest in the stage, Santiago's theatrical famine continued for ten years.

Following the death of Benavides came a governor who liked plays. He was the Irishman Ambrose O'Higgins. Bishop Alday was dead. No other priest dared oppose the governor, and so the drama was revived. Seizing on the coronation of Charles IV as an excuse, O'Higgins proclaimed three days of festivities in 1789, and asked Rubio to perform plays near the Mapocho River, the site of the present market, on a stage constructed from materials left after the building of La Moneda, the new residence for Chile's governors. The titles were *Los españoles en Chile, El dómine Lucas, El Mayor monstruo, los celos,* by Calderón, and *El Genízaro de Ungría* (1786) by Matos Fragoso. There was also a locally translated version of Rousseau's *Hypochondriac.*

Though the Chilean historian Barros Arana mentions the appearance of women on the stage, "chosen from among the most talkative in Santiago"[13] to take part in some Christmas plays around 1780, actors must generally have been men, judging by the excitement in Santiago in 1793 when a woman performed in public. Her beauty and social prominence created a scandal. Mariano Latorre names her as "Josefa Morales, a lovely Creole."[14]

That same year Governor O'Higgins received a petition from Antonio Aranaz not only to perform plays, but to build a theatre to house them. He had brought a company of actors from Cádiz to Argentina, where the troupe broke up, so he came on to Chile. Bishop Sobrino presented himself before O'Higgins with horrified objec-

[13] Diego Barros Arana, "El teatro en Santiago," in *El Correo del Domingo,* No. 11 (June 29, 1862); Pereira Salas, *El teatro en Santiago,* p. 8.

[14] Mariano Latorre, "El teatro chileno en la colonia," *Atenea,* XCIII, No. 288, (June, 1949) 472.

tions. "If the man has money to spend, let him build a reform school or an orphanage." When it was pointed out that theatrical performances elsewhere had provided money for charities, the Bishop agreed to let Aranaz have a brief season. Two years later, with one of the socialites of Santiago, Ignacio Torres, Aranaz tried again with better success, in a season that ran from Christmas to Lent.

O'Higgins' departure to become viceroy of Peru was observed on April 10 and 11, 1796, with a *loa* in which characters representing Chilean cities reported their progress under the Irish adventurer. It served as a prelude to the Spanish play *El más justo rey de Grecia* (1715), by Gerardo Lobo. O'Higgins' successor, President Pino, was welcomed to Santiago by two other dramatic performances in 1798.

Aranaz and Torres tried that same year to give Valparaíso's three thousand citizens a place to witness plays other than the mayor's house, but again the Church blocked them, though it could not halt the reading and discussion of plays in literary salons. The wife of Governor Muñoz de Guzmán, Doña Luisa Esterripa, who had lived at the Court of Charles IV, was hostess of one weekly group, attended by Juan Egaña, Manuel de Salas, Torres, and others.

Finally the persistent efforts in Santiago of José de Cos Irriberi, begun in 1799, won from the town council permission for a "temporary theatre."[15] They granted it with nine provisos, among them: that from his profits he contribute a hundred pesos a year to some charity; that his proposed plays be first submitted to a supervisor; that he keep the sexes separated in the audience; and that at the end of ten years he donate the building to the government. Thus in 1802, in the Plazuela de las Ramadas, the citizens of Santiago finally watched the erection of their first theatre.[16] Oláez of Argentina went into partnership with Judas Tadeo Morales for its construction, and together they built the first two-story theatre in all of South America.

One of those most interested in the new building was Juan Egaña (1761–1836), born in Lima and a protégé of the Governor's wife. And one of the first performances in the new theatre (1803) was his adaptation of the melodrama *Cenobia* (1729) by Metastasio (1698–1782). Dedicated to "Marfisa," as the Governor's wife was called, it is

---

[15] For his long and detailed brief, see Pereira Salas, *El teatro en Santiago*.
[16] For complete details of the cost and repertory of El Coliseo, see *ibid.*, pp. 18–31; also Raúl H. Castagnino, *El circo criollo*, p. 16.

the earliest long dramatic work written in Chile that is still preserved. For the adaptation, titled *Al amor vence el deber*, Egaña provided the ever-present *loa* (all published, London 1829), a dialog between Love and Latona, mother of Apollo, about the virtues and charitable acts of Marfisa. According to Egaña's own account, a violent spring rain drove the spectators from the cheap, unroofed seats and made so much noise that no one could hear. The second performance went off better. The next year Egaña wrote a *loa* for the birthday of Charles IV, *El cuadro magnífico de Pitágoras*. Of his other plays and *loas*, only the titles have been preserved.

Although the Church, especially Padre Urrutia, fought against theatrical performances, they continued until the death of Governor Muñoz de Guzmán in 1808. Indeed, from vague references it is believed that a company of French actors visited Chile during Muñoz' term of office and under the patronage of his wife.

The colonial period of Chile really ended with Muñoz, though there was still one more Spanish governor, Marcó del Pont. He got to Chile after the first Chilean attempt at independence had failed with the patriots' defeat at Rancagua. Wrestling with the problem of dissuading them from further struggle, the Governor restored the theatre at the corner of Merced and Mosqueto Streets, the first one in Chile with a roof, in the hope that the unreal world of the stage would make the hot-blooded Chileans forget their political aspirations. The program of plays performed by Nicolás Brito and Josefa Morales was chosen for that purpose. On December 21, 1815, the first Chilean newspaper advertisement of a dramatic performance appeared in the *Gaceta del Rey* to announce the opening of the theatre at 8:30 P.M., Christmas Eve, with *El sitio de Calahorra o La constancia española* by Padre Raimundo Diodado Caballero. For two *reales*, spectators who were willing to sit in the *cazuela*, or gallery, could witness a display of Spanish loyalty. For an extra *real*, there were seats in the *patio*, or orchestra. Plutocrats willing to spend two pesos could occupy one of the eighteen boxes on the first floor. Later offerings were by Calderón, Moreto, and others.

For supporting players the Governor used soldiers from the garrison. Perhaps they were not actors, but Marcó del Pont would not let them be criticized. One disgusted spectator who shouted that a certain soldier-actor would do better at his regular labor, fortifying the Santa Lucía Hill, found himself there the next day, breaking stone.[17]

Finally, in 1818, came the liberating Battle of Maipú that brought independence to Chile under O'Higgins, the son of the old Governor. The country entered into the second period of its national, as well as its theatrical, history. Even before that date, Camilo Henríquez (1769–1825) was already campaigning (1812) in *Aurora de Chile,* a very early Chilean newspaper, for plays of political significance, and in 1818 the newspaper *Argos de Chile* proposed a *teatro decente.* One of the first acts of Supreme Director Bernardo O'Higgins, who realized the educational value of drama, was to direct Colonel Domingo Arteaga to rush construction of a temporary playhouse on Calle Ramadas, now Esmeralda. Buenos Aires already boasted several theatres, and it was O'Higgins' ambition to make Santiago a second Buenos Aires, despite the objections of those who looked on plays as a licentious diversion and a grave danger to the spiritual health of the new nation.

It may be symbolic that the first theatre of the republic was built behind a church where the present Central Market starts, on land called "El basural de Santo Domingo." On a scorned dump heap, this much abused contribution to cultural life in independent Chile had its beginning. If its progress was slow, one must remember the number of intelligent Chileans in exile at the time the country became a nation. In their new freedom from everything connected with Spain, those intellectuals still living in the country turned to France, and so the way was opened for romanticism.

The new theatre was officially opened in December, 1818, with all but two of the actors Spanish prisoners of war. The director was Colonel Latorre, who had surrendered in Valparaíso to Admiral Cochrane. The actresses were Chileans. The newspapers were solidly behind the endeavor. *Argos de Chile* suggested the forming of a Society of Good Taste, like the one that censored the stage in Buenos Aires, and *El Telégrafo* called upon Chilean dramatists to forget the customs of the Greeks and the problems of the Romans, and to write about the noble Araucanian Indians and the glorious heroes of

[17] For a list of the Brito performances from December, 1815, to November, 1816, see Margaret V. Campbell, *The Development of the National Theatre in Chile to 1842,* p. 12.

Chile's struggle for independence. It also commented shrewdly that only when the public stopped scorning the art of declamation and looking down on actors would the quality of the performances rise.

Valdivian-born Padre Camilo Henríquez (1769–1825), one of the most active of Chilean patriots, published a series of articles on the theatre in *El Mercurio de Chile* in 1822, declaring that the theatre was not only a place for entertainment, but a school as well, and therefore it should be subsidized by the government. While a fugitive in Buenos Aires in 1817, he had written two dramas, *La inocencia en el asilo de las virtudes*, in three acts, once thought lost, and *La Camila o La patriota de Sudamérica* in four acts. *La Camila* anticipated the advice of *El Telégrafo* in being American, but Henríquez was a better critic than a dramatist. The play is set in Ecuador after the Spaniards have killed most of the patriots, but one family has taken refuge with the chief of an Indian tribe who had been educated in a Quaker college in the United States. Henríquez' idea for one dramatic scene was a lengthy conversation between the cacique and his wife about two plays he wants to perform for their educational value. Fortunately it was never played in Chile.

Meanwhile, in 1819, the government-sponsored players moved to a corner of the Instituto Nacional on Calle Catedral. Here was presented the only surviving play by the Argentine-born poet Bernardo de Vera y Pintado (1780–1827), nephew of a captain general, Chilean by adoption, and author of the first Chilean national anthem.[18] It was a *loa* to introduce the tragedy *Guillermo Tell* on February 12, 1820.

The Institute, however, needed extra space, so Colonel Arteaga had to lease a private home and remodel it. It became Chile's first permanent theatre, not demolished till 1836. It opened on August 20, 1820, the saint's day of O'Higgins, with a version of Addison's *Cato of Utica* (1713), an extremely popular play in Latin American theatrical history after it was translated into Spanish by Bernardo Calzada in 1787. The leading man was Sergeant Francisco Cáceres, recently captured by Admiral Cochrane.

Contemporary newspaper accounts give details of the building, in what is now Plaza Montt-Varas. It seated 1,500 spectators, who paid

---

[18] Domingo Amunátegui, *La alborada poética en Chile después del 18 de Septiembre de 1810.*

the same prices as in the earlier playhouse. Its company included three leading men, four character actors, three comics, and seven actresses (women had definitely won a place on the stage by now). The chief actor, Francisco Cáceres of Seville, received ten pesos a performance. Singers, who were in the lowest pay scale, received 10 per cent of that amount—three *reales* a night. The eight-piece orchestra divided twenty pesos a performance.

Six or eight earthenware jars of grease with wicks floating on them provided the illumination, but their smoke and stench were so great that, according to a newspaper man's account, women fainted.[19] The reporter was also amused at the Spanish army uniforms used by the supposedly Roman soldiers. But realism in costuming continued to be unknown in Chilean theatres till the Uruguayan actor Luis Ambrosio Morante arrived in 1822, the first professional actor seen in Chile. He was no matinee idol, being dark-skinned, big-bellied, and not tall, but when he spoke, audiences forgot his ugliness. Acting with him was Lucía Rodríguez, reputedly the loveliest and greatest Chilean actress of all time. In his company, too, were Toribia Miranda and the Peruvian Máximo Jiménez.

In competition, Juan Casacuberta (1799–1849),[20] the greatest masculine figure on the Latin America stage, came from Argentina to perform in Santiago, with a repertory including romantic plays from Spain. The Chilean theatre may be said to have been created by the performances of Morante and Casacuberta. From them the citizens of Santiago learned about the finer points of acting. So hotly were the relative abilities of these two leading men debated that it was arranged to have each appear in performances of *Hijo de Edipo* on successive nights. This formal comparison of their techniques only strengthened the convictions of the partisans of each.

A sidelight on the status of acting during this period was furnished by the diary of the English artist Maria Graham. In her entry for Friday, August 30, 1822, she wrote:

[19] For an idea of theatrical performances of the period, see the novel *Ideal de un calavera* (1863) by Alberto Blest Gana, pp. 280–307 in the Zigzag 1942 edition. Apparently the theatre was uncomfortable, the costumes inappropriate, the acting terrible, and the audiences unruly.

[20] Juan Carlos Sabat Pebet, *Juan Casacuberta.* See also Mariano Bosch, *Historia del teatro en Buenos Aires,* pp. 173 ff.; Raúl H. Castagnino, *El teatro en Buenos Aires durante la época de Rosas,* pp. 140 ff.; Renée Pereyra Olazábel, *Casacuberta, un actor bajo la tiranía.*

I determined to take a box at the theatre tonight, and went with my friends to the play in Santiago. . . . [The] building reminded me of a provincial temporary theatre; but the earthquakes of Chile apologize for any external meanness of building but too satisfactorily: the interior is far from contemptible; I have seen worse in Paris. The stage is deep, the scenery very good, the proscenium mean. On the green curtain there is wrought in letters of gold:

"He aquí el espejo de virtud y de vicio,
Mirad en él y pronunciad el juicio."

The Supreme Director's box is on the right hand of the stage. It is handsomely fitted up with silk of the national colours, blue, red, and white, bordered with gold fringe. Opposite is the box of the Cabildo, a little less handsome, but decorated with the same colours. The theatre is a very favorite amusement here, and most of the boxes are taken by the year, so it was by favour only that I obtained one tonight. The theatre was quite full and the general beauty of the women was particularly conspicuous on the occasion.

[After the arrival of Supreme Director O'Higgins, the national hymn was sung, though some in the audience sat and turned their backs.]

The farce was *The Madmen of Seville*. The *graciosa* [sic] of the piece, a beggar, has by some accident got into the bedlam [insane asylum] of the city and the amusement consists in the different tricks played to him by the patients of the hospital, who each insist on taking him as a companion. I was half sorry not to be able to join in the excessive mirth apparently cause by the piece, but I was rather glad when it was over. We all enjoyed some ices very much, which were brought into the box; and we were not the only persons who regaled themselves in the same manner, though I think sweetmeats and wine seemed to be the favourite refreshments. The gallery is appropriated to the soldiers, who enter gratis.[21]

A permanent playhouse and available actors inspired dramatists. However, there is some doubt about the date of one of their plays. The patriotic *La hija del sur o La independencia de Chile,* by Manuel Magallanes, bears a subtitle declaring it was performed in the Teatro de la Nación, April 5, 1823. If true, this makes it the first play with a Chilean theme by a Chilean author performed by a Chilean troupe. However, Arteaga's theatre of this name, built by subscription, was not completed till 1827. Perhaps the date is a misprint for

[21] Maria Graham, *Journal of a Resident in Chile during the year 1822,* pp. 217–219.

1828, in which case, Magallanes' ill-fated *La Chilena* came first, in 1827. At any rate, "The Daughter of the South" deals with the Chilean defeat at Cancha Rayada, March 19, 1818, when O'Higgins had been wounded and Santiago heard that San Martín was dead. Elisea, the daughter of the South, heard, too, that her husband, Lisandro, was dead, so she seized a saber to seek revenge against the oncoming Spaniards. But everything turned out happily, and the audience gave Magallanes an ovation.

This was a time of political turmoil for Chile. O'Higgins, eager to make Chile quickly into a nation, thought that a dictatorship was the only method. He sent to Rome to get help from the Pope. But the citizens had not fought the power of Spain to succumb to new intervention. They rebelled. Wise enough to see his error, O'Higgins resigned in 1823 and was replaced by Ramón Freire, head of the opposition. Freire in turn became Dictator and attacked the Church that had supported his predecessor. The theatre took an anticlerical attitude. Morante, from Buenos Aires, appeared in *Aristedomo* by Voltaire, July 28, 1824, and in the anticlerical and anonymous *El Abate seductor*. Morante also played the lead in Cañizares' *El falso nuncio de Portugal* (1824), with make-up to resemble one of the hated local priests.

Meanwhile Arteaga's theatre had been condemned, and a room in a Santiago café was used for five months in 1827. In it Teresa Samaniego, recently arrived from Spain, reversed theatrical traditions by making an appearance as a man, Philip II, in Alfieri's play of that name. Previously it had been boys who played women's roles.

And it was here that Magallanes offered his second play, *La chilena*, whose speedy composition in six hours, to help celebrate the election of Federalist President Pinto, was evident. The actors fumbled their lines, and while the public applauded every Federal reference, they hissed everything else, including the author, who, at the final curtain destroyed the prompter's copy and vowed never to write another play. Anyway, jealousies between the actors of the Teatro Nacional split the company.

Chilean drama was having a hard time. The government wanted patriotic plays and used them for political purposes. Critics wanted more attention paid to local customs and the Indians. The Church fought all kinds of dramatic performances with equal zeal.

Arteaga, still laboring to develop Chile's drama, tried a new plan

and sold stock in a private playhouse that was completed in 1827. To
provide plays, President Pinto invited the Spaniard José Joaquín Mora
(1783–1864) to Chile. His first official act was to write the poetic
three-act *Marido ambicioso* for Chile's Independence Day, September 18, 1828. Though it somewhat paralleled a play of the same name
by Picard, no one accused Mora of plagiarism. In those days, a writer
was not a plagiarist if he improved on his sources, as Mora did. Indeed, his play has been called the best dramatic piece written in
Chile up to that time.[22] This humanist and theatre critic was also
author of the one-act *El embrollón*, performed in Valparaíso, December 2, 1829. Another successful play which received critical acclaim was the comedy *Los aspirantes* by Gabriel Real de Azúa, an
Argentine living in Santiago. Andrés Bello, while applauding the
play, did, however, criticize its excessive classicism.[23]

Again political unrest swept Chile as two political groups tried to
replace the weakening Federalists. The Conservatives, called "pelu-
cones" (for their powdered wigs), and the Liberals, scorned as "pipio-
los" (for the sound made by little chickens when hungry), quarreled
over a constitution and fought in civil war that ended with the defeat of the Liberals in the Battle of Lircay, April 17, 1830. The new
Prime Minister, Diego Portales, was a lover of the theatre. He did
much to restore order, till he was assassinated in 1837 and the regu-
larly elected President Prieto assumed power.

With all this drama in life, the theatre was having a hard time. To
attract the public, "urban drama" under such titles as *Adulación y
fingimiento o El intrigante* was advertised with songs by the actors,
or "comedies of flight," in which Calderón's *La vida es sueño* was
decked out with a flight by Clarín from the back of the stage, and a
soldier flew out of the window.[24]

As a more legitimate means of developing a theatre-going public,
Andrés Bello, (1781–1865), a Venezuelan who arrived in Santiago in
1829 by way of London and entered into many phases of Chile's na-

---

[22] M. L. Amunátegui, "Establecimiento del teatro en Chile después de la
independencia," *Revista de Santiago*, I (1888), 481.

[23] Quoted with his other theatrical opinions by Mariano Latorre, in "Anotaciones sobre el teatro chileno," *Atenea*, XXVI (September, 1949), 252. See also
Andrés Bello, *Obras Completas de Andrés Bello*, pp. 714–715, in which appears
an article written by Bello for *El Araucano*, No. 173 (January, 1834), a newspaper which he founded and to which he contributed.

[24] Latorre, "Anotaciones," *Atenea*, No. 291 (September, 1949), 252.

tional life, not only as editor of its civil code, creator of its normal school, and rector of its university, but also as encourager of its cultural life, began writing critically about plays that were being performed locally. By this means he founded Chilean dramatic criticism. He began with Chile's first opera season, June, 1830, to February, 1831, sung by a traveling company from Italy. Through Bello's writing new interest in the theatre developed. Chile learned about works on the European stage, especially French and Italian drama, and for a decade, not only in Santiago but in Valparaíso,[25] as romanticism took possession of the Chilean stage, translations alternated with plays by Larra, Hartzenbusch, and García Gutiérrez.[26]

In 1839, Andrés Bello, who up to now had been most productive in educational fields, made his own contributions to the stage. Earlier he had written an *auto*, *La infancia de Jesús*, and a drama in verse, *España restaurada o El certamen de los patriotas*, both lost, as are most of his *juvenilia*.[27] His brief *Vacuna*, performed in Caracas in 1804, to welcome European experimenters with vaccination, has been preserved. But now, in 1839, he made a translation of *Thérese*, by Dumas, followed the next year by *Una posada en Valencia*, a version of Sheridan's *The Rivals*, already put into Spanish as *Amores de novela* by Trueba y Cossio in 1824. The Bello translation was long regarded in the Spanish-speaking world as his own original work and was so published in Amunátegui's *Primeras representaciones dramáticas en Chile* (1888).

In 1840 Victorino Lastarria (1817–1888) adapted *El proscrito* of Frederic Soulié. Santiago Urzúa translated Dumas' *Paul Jones*. The first work by Hugo to be performed in Santiago appeared as *Anjelo, tirano de Padua* in 1841. Rafael Minvielle (1800–1887) provided Spanish versions of *Hernani* by Hugo, *Anthony* by Dumas, and *Les Filles de Marbre* by Barrière. The sons of Andrés Bello also translated romantic plays.

Another Chilean, a politician and Supreme Court judge who earned the title of "The First Romanticist," was Salvador Sanfuentes y Torres (1817–1860). He translated Molière and Racine and still

[25] Roberto Hernández, *Los primeros teatros de Valparaíso*.

[26] For a list and criticism of the plays in both cities and in Concepción, see Campbell, *Development of the National Theatre*, pp. 40–62.

[27] See P. Grases, "Andrés Bello, el primer humanista de América," in Bello, *Obras completas*, I, cxxxiv ff.

had time to write original plays with fantastic plots and exaggerated characters: *Carolina, Cora o La virgen del sol, Caupolicán, Juana de Nápoles* (1850), *El castillo de Mazini,* and *Don Francisco de Meneses,* all printed in 1863, after his death.

All this time Andrés Bello had been laboring to create a public eager to attend the theatre and able to appreciate the good and bad in the plays they saw. He wanted writers to handle national themes. Finally, after years of unsettled politics, came peace and time to pursue culture. Exiles from Argentina, escaping the tyranny of Rosas, fled to Chile, and one of them, Domingo Faustino Sarmiento, became editor of *El Mercurio de Valparaíso.* In July, 1841, while criticizing a poem by Bello, Sarmiento remarked on the lack of literary men in Chile and on the spiritual laziness of its poets. That marked the turning point. Eager to disprove their foreign critic, Chilean writers formed societies, published magazines, wrote plays, and made 1842 a significant year in all forms of Chilean literature. At that moment the Chilean stage began paying less attention to foreign models and turned more to local themes. It became national.

CHAPTER 14

Chile's National Theatre

A fateful year in the history of Chile's national theatre was 1842. The country's economic situation had been improved by the discovery of the nitrate fields as well as by the mineral wealth in Chañarcillo. Chile's successful war against Peru and Bolivia had advanced its prestige as a military nation. And the cultural contribution by exiles from Colombia and Argentina, including the founding of the University of Chile, had created new interest in all fields of literature.

One bad result was a rash of romantic plays with such titles as: "His Father's Murder To Save His Mother"; "Three Famous Bandits or The Jailer's Sentimental Wife"; "The Secret Tribunal or The Invisible Judges"; and one with the intriguing title, "A Sweetheart Borrowed for Two Hours." But there were also theatrical productions of a higher caliber, largely brought about by the writings of Andrés Bello and by Sarmiento's polemic with him that got people talking about the stage and debating the new romanticist movement.

The company of Casacuberta started the year in Valparaíso with a repertory of nearly a score of different plays.[1] Amateur groups were also performing. And in Santiago romantic foreign plays in translation were popular, even though Sarmiento saw in romanticism a kind of literary Protestantism, with Dumas and Hugo in opposition against the established classic rules as Calvin and Luther had been against the Roman Catholic Church.

In Santiago, Bello's youngest son, Juan Bello (1825–1860) decided to write a drama in verse about a historical event, in collaboration with his friend Hermógenes de Irisarri (1819–1886). The father of one was Venezuelan, of the other Guatemalan. They outlined a play about Caupolicán, but as they began writing, questions about realism in the costuming of naked Indians rose to bother them, and the play was never finished. And so it was the older brother, Carlos Bello

[1] Margaret V. Campbell, *The Development of the National Theatre in Chile to 1842*, p. 67.

(1815–1854), who had the honor of writing the first national play of Chile, if a work about Frenchmen written by the son of a Venezuelan and an Englishwoman and performed by Argentine and Peruvian players can be termed national. It was called *Los amores del poeta.*

The Santiago public, attending its performance on August 28, 1842, did consider it truly national and received it enthusiastically, though Sarmiento censured the poet for setting it in Europe and hoped he would "pluck his next nosegay from the soil of America." Other critics believed its first act was so long and slowly developed that it was forced to rush to its denouement. In its performance, in what was called El Teatro de la Universidad—since it was near the Jesuit National University of San Felipe, now the site of the Teatro Municipal—the Argentine Máximo Jiménez appeared in the role of Eugenio de Gressey, a poet in love with a nineteen-year-old widow, Matilde de Monville, who was portrayed by the Peruvian Toribia Miranda.

Some of the success of the performance was undoubtedly due to the rumor spread by the dramatist that he was portraying local people. Those who read the play today, with its unmotivated action, consider it better as the libretto of an opera than as a drama. But it was revived in 1888 and had several successful performances before a public that hardly knew that Gressey was supposed to be Bello, Matilde a leading social light, and the colonel a well-known officer in the Chilean army.

On October 9, that same year of 1842, Santiago theatre-lovers attended another national drama, inspired by the success of the earlier tragedy. *Ernesto*, by Rafael Minvielle (1800–1887), was the work of a man born in Spain and educated in France, a teacher of commercial subjects in Argentina and translator of French plays. He came to Chile in 1837 and remained until his death. *Ernesto* was his first original composition, a thesis play discussing whether a soldier should blindly obey unjust orders. Ernesto Guzmán, a one-time official in the Spanish army, has been won over to the cause of Chilean independence and decides to remain in Chile after the Battle of Ayacucho. The Spanish father of his sweetheart, Camila, looks upon him as a traitor and forbids Camila to marry him. In despair, Ernesto poisons himself, dying with the expressed conviction that hatred ends at the grave and with the final words: "Ay! Camila, Patria. Chile!" Such patriotism won the critics' approval, though some of them did declare that the play contained more discussion than passion. Sarmiento wrote that the suicide was a confession of wrongdoing.

There was still trouble ahead for Chile's drama. In the tragic year of 1836 both Morante and Cáceres had died, and the theatre on the Plazuela de la Compañía where they had performed, the only one in the capital, had been condemned as dangerous and had been demolished. The smaller Teatro de la Universidad that replaced it in 1842 was the result of stock selling by Hilarión Moreno, an Argentine, and the Spaniard Juan Peso. Its first year of existence found it the center of a scandal.

The year 1842 had begun theatrically with a proposed national play, which was, however, never completed because of the impropriety of putting naked Indians onto the stage. Then came a produced play with nothing national about it, and another whose patriotism tried to redeem its wordiness. Then came a *petipieza*, sponsored by friends of a couple of Chilean actresses who decided to arrange a benefit performance in the new theatre. As curtain raiser for their regular play, some unknown dramatist wove a plot about the Chilean *zamacueca* which the prettier of the two dancers was to perform. Regular patrons of the theatre received invitations, accompanied by a rather revealing picture. The women of Santiago's society, incensed by such forward conduct, attended the performance chiefly to hiss; the men applauded the dance and judged the play most entertaining. It provided a lively evening and started off Chile's national drama with variety.

Meanwhile Valparaíso could boast a theatre that eclipsed anything in the capital. In 1842 two businessmen, Pablo del Río and Pedro Alessandri, had sought permission to build a new theatre in the port. Since Valparaíso already had one, rarely used except by amateurs and by companies en route from Santiago, the two were refused. On March 15, 1843, however, a youngster teasing a mouse with a match started a fire that destroyed two-million-pesos' worth of property in the port, and when rebuilding started, there was a place for the Victoria Theatre, with a seating capacity of 2,000.

When President Bulnes returned to the capital after dedicating the theatre, December 14, 1844, he added a paragraph to his presidential message to Congress requesting appropriations for a Santiago playhouse "as good as the Victoria in Valparaíso." He got it. Its cornerstone was laid in the midst of an exodus from the country. News of the discovery of gold near Yerba Buena, later San Francisco, had been brought by the brigantine *J.P.S.*, which reached Valparaíso harbor on August 19, 1848; and optimistic Chileans started heading northward for California in search of the gold they had never been able to find in their own country.

The government did everything possible to stop them, even to using the opening of the Teatro Repúblico, December 28, 1848, as an occasion for propaganda. For it Minvielle was commissioned to write a play, *Ya no voy a California.* A packed but unsympathetic audience attended the inauguration, in which everything went wrong. One actor became violently ill and had to be replaced. The lights proved troublesome. The prompter misplaced a page of the manuscript. But when a gallery patron threw a live turkey with streamers onto the stage like the dove of symbolic plays, the harassed manager rang down the curtain. Let them go to California if they wanted to! And they did in such numbers that a "Chile Town" sprang up at the foot of Telegraph Hill in San Francisco.

A week after the opening, the Minvielle play was again presented and this time it went through to its final curtain, but it never proved popular. Its failure may explain why Minvielle destroyed, unperformed, the dramatization he was finishing of Arthur Dudley's novel *The Red Star,* and went back to writing textbooks and teaching school.

Even while not unqualified successes, these plays showed the possibilities of using Chilean national themes on the stage. The publication in 1844 of Mariano José de Larra's articles on the theatre and *costumbrismo,* edited by Manuel Rivadeneyra, provided further encouragement, and for the next sixty years the best plays of Chile were to be found in the brief comedies of custom. Juan Uribe has listed more than forty dramatists who produced them.[2] José Victorino Lastarria (1817–1888), who told the newly founded Sociedad Literaria in 1842 that Chilean society contained all the elements necessary to convert Chile's literature into an expression of its nationality, was one of the first to produce them; his one-act *¿Cuál de los dos?* was published in *El Siglo* in 1844. Manuel de Santiago Concha introduced Sargento Candelaria in his excellent *La acción de Yungay* (1849).

[2] Pedro Ruiz Aldea, *Tipos y costumbres en Chile,* especially pp. xlvii–lii.

Eusebio Lillo (1839–1910) wrote *San Bruno* (1949), and José Antonio Torres (1828–1864) offered *La independencia de Chile* (published 1856).

Further impetus was given by the arrival in Chile of the Spanish zarzuela, or musical play of customs, first introduced in Copiapó in 1857. It taught Chilean playwrights how to draw on their own national customs, as Blest Gana and Barros Grez were doing in the field of the novel. Even these two novelists turned to drama long enough to provide important works for the stage.

Alberto Blest Gana (1830–1920) did not persist very far in this genre. However, his one attempt, *El jefe de la familia* in three acts, shows what he might have done had he not been more interested in becoming the Balzac of his country through the novel. Published serially in *El Correo Literario* in 1858, *El jefe* was not performed till a century later, when Miguel Frank's company produced it in Teatro Talía, Santiago, June, 1959. This ironic comedy of a paterfamilias dominated by his wife has been called the first theatrical expression of the Chilean national spirit. The play satirizes the aping of French customs. While it lacks dramatic tenseness, as might be expected in the work of a novelist, it did serve to inspire the greatest of Chile's *costumbristas*, Daniel Barros Grez (1834–1904).

Even in Barros Grez' first short play, the amusing *La beata o Los dos matrimonios* (1859), which he called "cuento drami-tragi-có-mico," this Chilean Bretón de los Herreros established his position as a national dramatist. Set in the church sacristy, it is a satire about women forgetting home duties for unimportant chatter. In his *El tutor y su pupila*, with its plot of an old man's desire to win his lovely ward from her younger admirer, an amusing old housekeeper provides the chief interest. Classical technique and lively local types made it a delightful comedy.

One of the best of Barros Grez' score of comedies of custom is *Como en Santiago* (1874)[3] about a provincial maiden deceived by a city slicker in an impoverished small town whose inhabitants try to do everything as they do it in Santiago. Its satire and witty dialogue with that popular theme—the clash of city and village—raise it above the ordinary *sainete*. After its first performance in Chillán in 1875 it was published in *La Revista Chilena*, then forgotten till its revival in

[3] Reprinted in *Teatro*, No. 4 (Santiago, 1955).

1947 by Domingo Tessier and the Teatro Experimental, which has several times repeated it to prove the timelessness of the story of hen-pecked Don Victoriano and his wife Ruperta and the upright *huaso* Manuel. It ranks high among Chilean comedies.

Besides his *El ensayo de la comedia,* a prize winner in a Lima competition of 1886, in which the actors, director, and author work on a play that parallels their own personal problems (like Tamayo y Baus' *Un drama nuevo*), Barros Grez dramatized a number of proverbs, with further success. Best is probably *Cada oveja con su pareja* (1879) where two mismated couples are eventually reshuffled. Amateur groups have recently revived *Ir por lana* (1880), in three acts, dealing with his favorite theme, December and May love. So, in reverse, does *El casi casamiento o Mientras más vieja más verde,* a rewriting of a chapter from his novel *El huérfano* (1881). Teatro Experimental revived it in 1952. *La colegialada* (1873) deals with young love in a hot-bath resort. Barros Grez also delved into his country's history in the three-act *El tejedor o La batalla de Maipú* (1873).

By his vivacity and local color, Barros Grez contributed along many lines to the development of Chile's national theatre. Nobody devised better dialogue and dramatic action, till Allende and Moock came along.

While Barros Grez was developing his technique Santiago enjoyed several historical dramas. Guillermo Blest Gana (1829–1904), brother of the novelist, achieved momentary popularity with *La conjuración de Almagro* (1858), which followed *Lorenzo García* (1847), and with a zarzuela, *El pasaporte* (1865).

Another popular dramatist of the time was José Antonio Torres Arce (1828–1864). His younger brother Victor Torres Arce (1846–1883) wrote sentimental plays like *El falso honor, Los dos amores* (1897), and *El sacrificio inútil* to wring the hearts of romantic women. Victor's *Honor de una mujer,* when performed by Matilde Garay in 1872, was declared by one critic to be "the first dramatic work worthy of this name ever written in Chile." A girl gives up her sweetheart to restore the family economic position, then goes mad when everybody misunderstands her.

The brother José Antonio is remembered largely for his historical play *La independencia de Chile* (1856), the first to bring onto the stage the guerrilla hero Manuel Rodríguez. Its popularity continued till it was replaced by the four-act play in verse *Manuel Rodríguez*

(1865), by the Chilean-Englishman Carlos Walker Martínez (1842–1905). This latter had better dramatic handling and not only was it a stage success from its opening scene (in which the disguised Chilean patriot is reading the posted announcement of a reward for his capture), but it went through five printings in book form. Walker showed his ability to humanize the villain San Bruno, but the dramatist's greatest flaw was his indecision whether to write a historical play or a romantic drama. So its impact was weakened.

The Chilean stage also was enjoying the services of three important members of the *costumbrista* movement. Román Vial y Ureta (1833–1896)[4] began writing ten years after Barros Grez. Though uneducated, this typesetter of Valparaíso became a successful dramatist because of a keen ear for dialog and a sense of the theatrical. His plays provide a vocabulary of seaport slang. He achieved popularity with his first attempt, the *juguete Una votación popular* (1869), which described election day in Valparaíso but was universal in its picture of crooked politics. It was followed by his best play, *Choche y Bachicha* (1870), in which the Englishman George (Choche) and Giusepe present the problems of Italian immigrants (called "bachichas") forty years before Discépolo and Vacarezza worked the same vein in the River Plate. Part of the humor lies in the way the Italian, by his mutilation of Spanish, makes himself a suspect in an arson investigation. *Gente alegre* (1895) was another successful *sainete*.

Vial also wrote the humorous sketch *Alo, alo, o El teléfono* (1892) after the Philadelphia World Fair had made that instrument known. More serious in purpose but poorer as dramas were his *Gratitud y amor, Dignidad y orgullo* (published 1872), *Los extremos se tocan* (1872), and *La mujer-hombre* (1875).

Few dramatists have been honored by having fans establish clubs to produce their plays, but that was what happened to Luis Rodríguez Velasco (1838–1919) after the Valparaíso performance of his gem, the three-act comedy *Por amor y por dinero* (1869). While everybody applauded its poetic lines which subtly criticized Santiago high society, some, especially after its Santiago première in 1872, attacked the *beata* Celestina Ramona, and the unethical forging of a telegram by the hero Lindor to help him win wealthy María.

[4] See Román Vial, *Costumbres chilenas*, which contains some of his surviving plays.

However, a group of admiring Valparaíso amateurs founded El Club Velasco to perform Rodríguez' plays about their city. Unfortunately, he never again equaled his first success, so El Club was compelled to perform Vial and Allende also.

Juan Rafael Allende (1850–1909), that "poet of the people," won immediate popularity with his first play, *¿Qué dirán?* performed in that famous year of 1872 as a benefit for victims of a smallpox epidemic. He went on to write seventeen poetic plays of varying merit, displaying an ability to invent dramatic situations and develop them with lively and amusing dialog. He adopted the technique of the zarzuela or the Spanish *género chico*, substituting the *rotos* of Chile for the lower class *chulos* of Spain in such plays as *Moro viejo* (1881) with its unforgettable drunken *roto*, and *José Romero alias Peluca* (1882), about another tough *roto*. Chilean courting practices provide the theme of *Para quien pelé la pava* (1891), that introduces a memorable bill collector. Allende's anticlerical tendencies, reflecting his belief that the clergy was largely responsible for Chile's slow progress toward democracy, can be seen in his short satirical *El padre Cobos*. *Víctima de su propia lengua* (1888) should also be mentioned.

Allende's patriotic plays, written to whip up war spirit during the War of the Pacific, are of less literary merit. He attacks Chile's enemies in the satirical *El general Daza* (1879) and *La generala Buendía*. When war threatened again in 1898, Allende once more lent his pen to propaganda in *El cabo Ponce* (1898) whose shoemaker protagonist, a wounded veteran of '79, is refused as a volunteer, but who shames his oldest son, Caupolicán, out of his frivolity so that he starts away to enlist. Allende's earlier plays were better. However, his four-act sentimental melodrama in verse *De la taberna al cadalso* (1901) also deserves to be remembered as deeply Chilean.

Better educated than his *costumbrista* predecessors was the university graduate Antonio Espiñeira (1855–1907). There was nothing outstanding about his first play, *Más discurre un hambriento que cien letrados* (1875). His first success, *Como pasarán las cosas*, performed in Santiago's Teatro Municipal in 1877, was alien to Chile, as were his two plays about Cervantes: the five-act cape-and-sword poetic drama *Martirios de amor* (1877) and *Cervantes en Argel* (1886), which might pass as the work of one of the best of Madrid's playwrights. His excellent *Pena de la vida* (1889), is set in fourteenth-century Flanders. However, his two-act masterpiece, a *sainete* with the punning title, *Chincol en sartén*, published in *La Estrella de Chile* in 1876, is pure Chilean, though he betrayed *costumbrismo* by trying to purify the folk language. In it, Chincol, a rural *huaso* and owner of the dog Mustafa, a chip off-the-old block, is challenged to a poetry match by Sartén, a *roto diablo* from the city. The self-assurance of Sartén brings about his own defeat. *Lo que no tiene sanción* is another comedy but it reveals keen psychology.

A December-May marriage provided the complications for Espiñeira's excellent one-act *En la puerta del horno* (1887). He also wrote one of Chile's few all-women plays, the amusing *Fuera de su centro* (1887), about the country-born Carmela and her attempts to adapt herself to the customs of a big city.

This was the golden age of Chilean *costumbrismo*, generally expressed in *sainetes*, or light comedies, and between 1890 and 1930 hundreds of them were written by at least two hundred playwrights. But nationalism in the theatre was also expressed in more serious plays. One of them, *El tribunal del honor*, by the twenty-five year old Daniel Caldera y de Villar (1852–1891), performed on August 10, 1877, has often been called the first national Chilean play. An announced revival in 1957 by the Teatro Ensayo never took place, though two amateur companies performed it.

Four years earlier this young journalist of San Felipe, just north of Santiago, had entered a play, *Arbaces o El último Ramsés*, in a fine-arts competition. Though judged the best, it got no prize because it was declared un-Chilean, since it was based on Bulwer-Lytton's *Last Days of Pompeii*. For his next attempt, therefore, the ambitious dramatist chose an incident he had heard discussed as a boy. It could hardly have been more Chilean: one participant was Mayor Sepulveda of Aconcagua, the other, General Arteaga, who was then in command of all of Chile's armed forces. The whole town knew how Sepulveda had caught Arteaga in an affair with his wife.

Changing only the names, Caldera built his play on the way in which Sepulveda (Juan on the stage) tries to solve his marital problem. In the final melodramatic act, in speeches that seem like the Calderonian Honor Code set to the music of romanticism, and with references that show the playwright's familiarity with *Othello*, Juan announces his decision. He has lost the case, he knows; therefore, as executioner, and in spite of his wife's pleas that she is about to become a mother, Juan stabs her.

While the play was very successful, the many criticisms it evoked against the author discouraged him from any further attempts. He got himself a newspaper job in Iquique for the rest of his short life and never tried drama again. But his one play always wins him mention among Chilean national dramatists, and *El tribunal del honor* (1877) has been called the best Chilean play of the nineteenth century.

From then on to 1900 only occasional locally written comedies and operas and musical plays performed by visiting companies of actors from Europe kept the dust off Chilean stages. A competition in 1883 sponsored by the Council of Public Instruction turned up two good plays, *Luis Carrera o La conspiración de 1817*, in three acts by Pedro Urzúa Cruzat (1853–1894), and the poetic *La Quintrala*, in three acts by Domingo A. Izquierdo (1859–1886), about the colonial Catalina de los Ríos, whose legend of villainy was made known in *Los Lisperguer y la Quintrala*, published in 1877 by Benjamín Vicuña MacKenna. Catalina has since appeared in a dozen other Chilean plays and novels.

Light and humorous sketches continued to be written, and investigators will run across the names of such minor playwrights as Julio Chaigneau (1848–1925), who dramatized life in Valparaíso in *Un dependiente de aduana,* and *Astucia quieren las cosas* (1872), and Carlos Segundo Lathrop (1853–1889), a Santiago publisher and author, in 1879, of patriotic plays inspired by the War of the Pacific: *La comedia en Lima, La toma de Calama,* and *Glorias peruanas.* He also was a *costumbrista* in *La pascua en Santiago* (1895), *El mojón de San Francisco* (1895), *Santiaguinos y porteños o El amor y el interés* (1884), and especially in the satirical *El roto en las elecciones* (1897), about a candidate who buys votes from the lower-class Chileans.

Most popular of all the plays of the period, however, was *Don Lucas Gómez* by Mateo Martínez Quevedo (1848–1923).[5] On July 14, 1885, this Copiapó lawyer and founder of the local fire department produced *Don Lucas* to help celebrate Bastille Day. While reading

[5] Willis K. Jones, "The Chilean Huaso Everybody Knows," *Pan American Magazine*, March, 1945, pp. 34–36.

Un huaso en Santiago, a short story by Daniel Barros Grez, Martínez Quevedo had been struck by its dramatic possibilities in its clash of city and country. He had seen ill-at-ease cowboys in the city. He had also been amused by the pseudo aristocrats and snobbish metropolitans he had known. So he combined both elements into Chile's most popular comedy, if sale of copies and number of performances is proof. In twenty years the dramatist collected royalties on 58,000 copies in six editions, and 673 performances, which in a country the size and population of Chile compares favorably with America's most performed rural play, *Aaron Slick from Punkin Crick* by Beale Cormack, whose record is some 25,000 performances.

Lucas is a typical *huaso* in poncho, big hat, and spurs with six-inch rowels. He has just come to Santiago from Curepto (where the author practiced law) to visit his brother Genaro and his two nieces. His ignorance of their customs and his misuse of big words provide part of the humor. Lucas proposes marriage to the romantic fifteen-year-old servant, Josefa, whom he hears singing a folk song. While awaiting her answer, he attends a horse race, meets a language-murdering Englishman, and returns with a family from his home town to dance a *cueca* for the finale.

This play contains all the elements of a sure hit. It permitted everybody to leave the theatre with a sense of superiority. Country people saw it as a jibe at the city snobs; those in the metropolis laughed at the antics of the hayseeds; and all Chile enjoyed the humor, the patriotism, and the stirring national dance that ended it.

Some have hinted that Santiago Miretti, who starred in the first performance, was really the author, but, although some of his contributions to the production eventually found place in the published version, the play itself was from the pen of Martínez Quevedo. His attempt at a sequel, *La mujer de Lucas Gómez,* was a failure. After the author's death, his son wrote an extra act for the seventh published edition, sandwiched between the two original acts—a fitting place for it because it is pure ham. No later Chilean play can boast an equal number of performances.

By now, the influence of Spain's one-act local-color *género chico* was beginning to be felt, though it did not really reach its height till about 1917. Adapters superimposed the life and customs of Chile upon the characters and problems of Madrid, and actors like Pepe Vila, Joaquín Montero, and Zapater were supplied with such plays as

Emilio Rodríguez Mendoza's (1873–1960) *Noches de lluvia* (1900) and Alarcón Lobos' (1872–1917) *Las esterlinas* (1900). Another excellent later play using the Spanish zarzuela form to express Chilean *costumbrismo* was *El te de doña Petrona y don Facundo* (1904) by Alberto MacKenna Subercaseaux (1875–1952). By 1908 this fusion of foreign model and local material had been completed. Chile had been an independent nation for a century and at last was able to speak for itself in the theatre as it had already been doing in fiction.

There were many reasons for this transformation which had started a quarter of a century earlier. Political and economic changes followed the conclusion of the War of the Pacific, especially as the developing nitrate fields created new wealth and a new social class, the laborers. The Revolution of 1891, shifting power from the President to Congress, opened the way to local autonomy. Political changes were reflected in the work of some of the dramatists, like Adolfo Urzúa Rozas (1863–1937), author of the gloomy *Un juez campesino* (1908) in one act, and *Puñalada que da la vida* (1903). The characters are veterans of the War of the Pacific, released from the army following the government's overthrow in the Revolution. They have retained their weapons and now, with depression facing them, are turning to banditry.

In 1911 the first of two incidents took place to give impetus to the theatre in Chile. The poets Carlos Mondaca (1881–1928) and Max Jara (1886–) had a success with their dramatization of Blest Gana's historical novel *Durante la reconquista* (1897). The following year a Spanish actor, Manuel Díaz de la Haza, built the Palace Theatre only a few blocks from the Plaza de Armas in Santiago and appealed to Chilean writers for short plays with few characters for himself and his lovely leading lady, Pepita Díaz.

A second company of actors was also organized, dedicated to national drama, and including Urzúa Rozas, Domingo Gómez Rojas, Juan Tenorio Quezada, and José Santos González Vera (1896–). They invited local plays.

Under such inspiration many authors were filled with ambition to turn playwright. One was Eduardo Barrios (1884–1963), who had already published a collection of short stories in Iquique.[6] His first short play, the romantic "Mercaderes en el templo" (1910), was

[6] Agustín del Saz, "El teatro hispanoamericano del siglo XX," *Historia general de las literaturas hispánicas*, IV, 2, 442–444.

never made public because its perfectionist author was displeased with it. Then he produced *Por el decoro* (1912), satirizing government bureaucracy. Then, employing a new technique, he wrote the serious *Lo que niega la vida* (1913) in which life denies the right to happiness to a middle-class family that has lost fortune and status. As in most of Barrios' plays, the action takes place rather in the soul than in any definite locality.

His best play, *Vivir* (1916), is psychological and filled with frustrated women. Its chief character is Olga, a cigaret girl of Valparaíso who follows her sweetheart Romero to the capital, only to discover that he is already married. In a dramatic conclusion, the grandmother demands that he take Olga as his mistress if he cannot make her happy as his wife. The small financial returns to the playwright discouraged Barrios about the theatre and he turned to novel writing, where he earned renown. Years later he collected some of his plays in *Teatro escogido* (1947).

Among other minor playwrights attracted to the theatre around 1912 was the actor-author Nicanor de la Sotta (1893–1927), who attempted to vitalize the theatre by performing his own plays, like *La golondrina* (1921), *Sueño de un vaquero* (1930), and that masterpiece of life in a small town, *Pueblo chico, infierno grande* (1920). Also, to reveal his serious side, he composed the rural drama *Sanción* (1922), in which he played the fifty-year-old Laureano. It won the Society of Theatrical Authors prize in 1927, on the eve of his death, which was brought about because he had left his own sickbed to attend the funeral of another actor, Arturo Bührle.

Also venturing into the theatre was the socialist poet, Victor Domingo Silva (1882–1960), who by then had on hand at least five plays: *El pago de una deuda* (1908), *Como la ráfaga* (1910), *Los cuervos* (1911), *El derrotero* (1912), and the drama *Nuestras víctimas* (1912). During the next ten years Silva was to complete *La vorágine* (1916) and half a dozen more. Another poet, Daniel de la Vega (1892–   ), offered de la Haza *El bordado incluso* (1915). De la Haza also accepted for his repertory *La silla vacía* (1912) by Juan Manuel Rodríguez (1884–1917), and *La Señorita Risa* (1916) and *Mal hombre* (1918) by René Hurtado Borne (1887–1960).

Hurtado Borne was the most active member of the Chilean Association of Dramatists, founded in 1915. One of its chief aims was to offer the capital a season of national plays, performed by two Chilean

actors, the comic Arturo Bührle[7] and the character actor Enrique Báguena. Chile's President Sanfuentes provided the funds. Aurelio Díaz
Mesa's one-act *Tío Ramiro* (1917), in addition to *Huelga* (1912) by
Santiago Ramos, were their first offerings in 1917. By 1918 they had a
fully organized company performing in the Teatro Comedia. Again
Rodríguez' rural comedy *La silla vacía* was a favorite along with *Los
payasos se van* by Hugo Donoso (1900–1918). Donoso was a respected drama critic at sixteen, a successful playwright at seventeen,
and dead in an auto accident at eighteen.

His *Los payasos se van* tells of the artist Rafael who visits his
aunt and falls in love with his cousin. But everything around the
house is so melancholy that he decides to become a clown as the
circus moves on. Homely philosophy, charming and amusing characters, and an easy movement make this play outstanding, though it
lacks any local color. It ran for a month and a half, unusual for Chile,
at that time.

Later Báguena replaced Bührle with Evaristo Lillo. Another member of the troupe was the golden-voiced Alejandro Flores (1896–
1962), whose long Spanish cape and romantic slouch hat were later to
make him a national figure.[8] During that season they used plays by
two of the three playwrights who were to become the most important
playwrights of the period: *Almas perdidas*, by Acevedo Hernández,
and *Pueblecito*, by Armando Moock.

In 1919 the troupe started a tour of the provinces. This time Moock
formed part of the company, and six of his plays figured in its repertory, including the tragic *Los perros*, *Un negocio*, and *El querer vivir*.
They also performed the completely Chilean farce *Entre gallos y
media noche* (1919) by Carlos Cariola (1895–1960). This play,
which Cariola called a *sainete criollo*, and which was later popularized by Rafael Frontaura (1896–   ) is, next to *Don Lucas Gómez*,
Chile's most popular comedy.[9] Between 1919 and 1930 Cariola wrote
Hermanitos, *Ay, qué vergüenza para la familia* and *Estos muchachos
de cincuenta años*, but none equaled his earlier farce about the stern
Chilean colonel who plans to marry off his niece Magdalena to a rich,
elderly widower. Following an amusing scene in a henhouse at mid-

[7] Pedro Sienna, *La vida pintoresca de Arturo Bührle*; Julio Durán Cerda,
Panorama del teatro chileno, 1842–1959, pp. 52 ff.

[8] Juan Cristóbal, *La vida romántica de Alejandro Flores*.

[9] Reprinted in *Finis Terrae*, No. 13 (Santiago, January, 1957), 35–61.

night, everything gets settled. The colonel even palms off his grouchy wife on the disappointed widower. A special epilog, also completely Chilean, was added for its two-hundredth performance. With the actor Frontaura, Cariola wrote the social drama *Abajo las castas*, and a series of amusing *sainetes*, including *El tuerto es rey* and *Doña Dorotea Dueñas dueña*.

With such successes on the stage and with a visiting troupe of Argentines featuring such local variety as the classic *Vidas inútiles* (1920) by Juan Ibarra Rojas and the amusing *Alo, alo, número equivacado* by Julio Asmussen (1897–), it is no wonder that Victor Domingo Silva (1882–1960) was moved to write in 1920 that the golden moment of the Chilean stage had arrived.

Unfortunately the Chilean public preferred less serious offerings by such dramatists as Pedro J. Malbrán (1895–1955) and his frequent collaborator Pepe Martínez (1897–), who were content to use their undoubted dramatic gifts merely to make the public laugh. Among Malbrán's comedies is *Día de los inocentes*, a play about Chile's April Fool Day, in which a newspaper article published by students makes the father of a mad family believe he has finally been elected mayor, and his fiction-reading wife is sure that life has turned out just as in her romantic novels. A good example of the Malbrán-Martínez collaboration is the hilarious *Casados en Marte* (1928), in which earthlings take a journey to Mars. Before a theatre-going public could be developed for the more serious playwrights and before these new plays caught hold, depression struck. The peso dropped to a quarter of its value when nitrate, Chile's chief export, was replaced by a cheaper synthetic. In spite of prizes offered and government help promised, the national theatre became inactive, except for the work of a few persistent people like Aurelio Díaz Meza (1879–1933), who had written the drama *Rucacahuín* (1913) and some *sainetes* and comedies: *Flores de campo* (1914), *Con su destino, Amorcillos*, and *Martes, jueves y sábado*, this last about a young man who meets his sweetheart on "Tuesdays, Thursdays, and Saturdays." It was successfully revived in 1956 by Teatro Experimental.

Foreign troupes and movies provided most of Chile's entertainment, though in 1927 the matinee idol Alejandro Flores (1898–1962) returned from his triumphs in Buenos Aires to perform a half dozen of his earlier plays, like *El derrumbe* (1919) and *Malhaya tu corazón* (1921). Joining with Rafael Frontaura (1900–), he played four successful seasons, with government help through President Carlos Ibáñez, and gave some of his country's playwrights an opportunity to see performances of their plays. Frontaura's own *La oveja negra* (1930) figured on the bills. For Flores and Frontaura, the diplomat Eugenio Orrego Vicuña (1900–1959), whose *Tragedia interior* had already been performed in Japanese in 1926, wrote his satirical drama of high society, *Vírgenes modernas* (1929). He drew from his experiences in Paris and contrasted the old-fashioned, honorable, and self-sacrificing Elena with the modern and flighty Elisa. Santiago's society declared him disloyal to his social class, but Orrego's reply was that the action could happen anywhere. His *Carrera* (1933), however, dealing with a figure of Chile's independence, was completely national.

Rafael Maluenda (1885–1963) a skilled novelist, wrote *La suerte* (1919), *El triángulo* (1930), and *La madeja del pecado* (1920). Even the critic and short-story writer Mariano Latorre (1886–1955) tried his hand at drama and produced *La sombra del caserón* (1920). The two leading men of the company, Flores and Frontaura, collaborated on *La compañerita* (1928) but they were not so amiable in their other relationships, and in 1931 their partnership ended and each established his own company. So terminated this period that first gave the Chilean public a concept of the theatre. From it three playwrights stand out: Acevedo Hernández, Moock, and Luco Cruchaga.

The first play of Antonio Acevedo Hernández (1886–1962) was performed December 24, 1913 by Urzúa Rozas and his group. *El inquilino* was written by a man born and brought up among the impoverished people of South Chile, who figure prominently in much of his writing. Having himself worked as a *campesino* on a tenant farm, Acevedo had seen the exploitation of these *inquilinos* by the big landowners. In defense of the downtrodden laborers, he took up his pen in behalf of social justice. He claimed to be a folklorist, with his ears open for phrases and legends. He had earlier (1910) written an idyllic play, *Camino de flores* (published 1916 and 1929), reminiscent of Martínez Sierra, showing the effect of a suicide upon two impressionable young girls. It remained unknown to most Chileans till in its revival it won the 1934 Santiago Municipal prize. *El milagro de la montaña* (1932) was another dramatized legend.

However, Acevedo Hernández was no *costumbrista* of the quaint and glamorous. He declared as his purpose "to reform through revolution," and a large share of his fifty plays deal with Chile's social problems. None has portrayed better than he the widows who mourn their husbands slain in cantina stabbings or the death of a baby through parental ignorance. But his lack of formal education and his ignorance of the modern theatre and of modern technique have prevented his making the most of his material. Even his bitter and crude *Cardo negro* (1913; published 1933), though sometimes called one of Chile's three best plays and an important step in the interpretation of Chilean life through drama, deteriorates after its superb first act. The conception is excellent, the drawing of characters good, but the second and third acts are weak. This psychological drama takes place in the plaza of a provincial town and introduces such characters as a blind poet, the town belle, and the village idiot. It has been called the first play to present the Chilean scene realistically without falsification either for humor or for tragedy. *La peste blanca* (1914), *Almas perdidas* (1917), and *Carcoma* (1919) that followed confirmed the impression that their author was a leftist. It is true that Acevedo began writing in answer to the call by the labor leader Luis Emilio Recabarren, in his newspaper *El despertar de los trabajadores,* for plays suitable to be presented for and by labor unions, but Acevedo denied any anarchistic motives. He was only revealing the plight of the lower classes.

This same tendency was observed in his *Caín* (1928), which appealed for sympathy for Adam's mistreated son. Without ever having heard of Byron's closet drama of the same name, Acevedo Hernández took the position that God had unjustly favored Abel, whose offering of a lamb had cost him no trouble. Cain, in contrast, had labored hard and long for the wheat that he put on the altar.

Part of Acevedo's output was set in Santiago, to which he had come as a poor lad in 1903, eager for any sort of job that would provide him food. In 1914 he wrote *La peste blanca,* about the capital's slums, and in *En el suburbio* he turned the spotlight on another of Chile's social problems. The language and psychology of both were faithful to the grimy, starving lower classes whose only pleasures were "vino, cantos y bailes."

Almas perdidas (1917) is another realistic play about the "lost souls" in a Santiago tenement house, one of whom is jailed for killing his unfaithful sweetheart and the other for killing a policeman to whom his girl had been sold by her rascal of a father.

It is in Acevedo's full-length plays, like the four-act *Por el atajo* of 1920 (published 1922) that he makes his most valuable contribution to Chile's theatre and shows his close affinity to the Uruguayan Florencio Sánchez. The dramatist's own favorite is his 1928 *El árbol viejo* (published 1934) that reveals his sentimental side, as the old patriarch Juan sees in himself a sturdy oak protecting the family. Actually, this drama, along with *La canción rota* (1921) and *Chañarcillo* (1933), are Acevedo's plays most likely to survive. The first, presented by Báguena-Bührle, deals with the feudal position of Chilean farm hands under Abdón, the cruel administrator. When he cuts off the irrigating water, the laborers revolt, and with his death they regain their rights. Plays like this raised more accusations of nihilism against their author.

The second play, *Chañarcillo* (1933), an epic like his *Joaquín Murieta* (1933), which was built about a bandit of California's gold rush, tells of the search for a Chilean silver mine. The action develops through movies and organ storm music. Having earlier heard the legend in Copiapó, Acevedo Hernández turned it into a four-act play when an impresario needed a play quickly. Revised by Pedro de la Barra, it was successfully revived in 1953 by the Teatro Experimental.

In complete contrast are his *costumbrista* farces, which reveal a humor lacking in his longer works. Examples are *Un 18 típico* (1928) about a rural celebration of Chile's Independence Day, or *De pura cepa* (published 1929) about a father and his son. These further substantiate Acevedo Hernández' claim to the title of Chile's outstanding *costumbrista*. Although he has never mastered the technique of drama, his substance and force are undeniable. Perhaps he should be classified as a folklorist, who turned to the stage in order to make Chileans better acquainted with themselves. Through his pictures he also succeeded in winning the world's sympathy for the lower classes among his countrymen. The enthusiastic reception of his *Los caminos de Dios* in Warsaw in 1955 confirmed his leftist sympathies, supposedly revealed again in another argumentative play, "El triángulo tiene cuatro lados" (1945), in defense of the masses; it was published in 1963. In his last years Acevedo Hernández lived in

Santiago, too ill to do much creative writing, though before his death he did complete the unproduced "El torrente" (1952) and "Cuando la muerte habló" (1953).

If Antonio Acevedo Hernández was the voice of the masses, his contemporary Armando Moock (1894–1942) spoke for the middle class.[10] The applause for his first endeavor, the brief *Crisis económica* (1914) and its twenty-eight pesos in royalty lured him from his studies as an architect, a decision that estranged him from his family. *Isabel Sandoval, Modas* (1915) was his first commercial play.

His first attempts to make a living by his plays were unrewarding. His novels and stories did earn him a few pesos and at times he received money as an actor, but he never stopped writing plays. During 1918 he formed part of the barnstorming troupe of Báguena and Bührle. He acted in his own *Mundial pantomim* (published 1919) and in his *Pueblecito* (1918), in which fat Bührle was the mayor and Báguena the priest. *Los siúticos, Un negocio,* and *Los perros,* all by Moock, also formed part of their repertory, till Bührle got involved with the leading actress and had to flee. Then the company was dissolved.

In 1920, at the request of the visiting Camila Quiroga, Moock crossed the Andes to Buenos Aires, where he received the appreciation that his countrymen had never accorded him. In Chile he had not only been known for his violent tongue, but he was resented for not having come into the theatre through the newspapers, as had most of the dominating clique. In Buenos Aires, however, the next year he had four plays in performance simultaneously. At that time the short skit was the fad on the Argentine stage. Moock's first attempt, *Cuando venga el amor* (1920), caught hold and started on a record-breaking run of 2,500 performances. Its plot is simple. Margot gets no thrill from kissing Rafael, so she willingly allows another girl to take him away while she waits for her real love to come along. Its sprightly conversation, however, gave it charm and popularity.

This was the first of about fifty-five plays, long and short, many never published, that earned Moock the phenomenal income of fif-

[10] Willis K. Jones, "Armando Moock, Forgotten Chilean Dramatist," *Hispania,* XXII (February, 1939), 41–50; Raúl H. Castagnino, "El sentido de la universalidad en el teatro de Armando Moock," *Boletín,* No. 14 (September, 1945), 134–136; Roberto A. Tálice, "La comedia de Moock que rechazaron todas las actrices," *Argentores,* No. 56 (October, 1946), 29–30. Tálice was referring to *Del brazo y por la calle.*

teen thousand pesos a year. Some are hardly more than ethical debates that gave him the reputation as a dramatist of ideas. Most are
humorous. Among them are the sentimental plays for which he will
be remembered, like *Mocosita o La luna en el pozo* (1929) and *Rigo-
berto* (1935).

The dialog of *Mocosita* offers interesting clues about its setting.
Most of its references associate it with Argentina. Baltasar, stuck in
a small town with a wife and nine daughters, longs for Buenos Aires.
There are also references to maté drinking. However Chilolo Vallejos
is a typical Chilean name, and autobiographical details show that
the author originally conceived of it as Chilean. For that reason it
could be performed by Alejandro Flores in 1929 as a Chilean play
and receive the prize as the best of the year, while it was also winning an award in Buenos Aires as a typically Argentine comedy.

Rigoberto, basically Argentine, was also awarded a Chilean prize
in 1935. Many consider it the best constructed of all Moock's plays.
Its title and inception came from a popular song of the time about
a henpecked husband and son-in-law. Other plays by Moock include
the satire of customs, *La señorita Charleston* (1927), performed in
Chile that year with Ventura López Piris and Frontaura; his most
popular play of ideas, *La serpiente* (1920), originally introduced by
Anita Novella; his prize-winning tribute to motherhood, *Alzame en
tus brazos* (published 1927); and the excellent tragedy *Monsieur
Ferdinand Pontac* (1922), full of autobiographical elements.

Following Moock's successes across the Andes, Chile made a belated attempt to recognize his ability by appointing him consul in
Vigo, Spain, in 1930. Upon his arrival he discovered that not only had
his *Serpiente* been produced in Spain more than three hundred times
without a peseta of royalty to him, but that Rudolph Valentino and
Nita Naldi had made a movie, *Cobra,* suspiciously reminiscent of it.
Eventually Paramount of Paris paid Moock several thousand dollars
for rights to exhibit the movie in a Spanish version. Since then *La
serpiente* has had nearly three thousand performances by emotional
actresses who coveted the role of Luciana, the lascivious woman who
preyed on her artist-husband. The first two acts show the dramatist's
mastery of his medium. Then the tragedy gets twisted to force the
analogy to the serpent that destroyed the tiger. But despite its poor
psychology it provides good theatre.

In his later years Moock experimented with *Del brazo y por la calle* (1939) which maintains the unity of time and uses only two actors. Both Madrid and Rio de Janeiro saw performances. His final play, *Algo triste que llaman amor* (1941), brought enthusiastic reviews calling him the most honest and industrious playwright of South America.

In all, Armando Moock wrote more than half a hundred plays of many categories. He once said that all but two or three of his full-length plays had enjoyed at least a hundred royalty performances apiece, not counting the unknown number of pirated performances. *Pueblecito* remains the best as a *costumbrista* play of Chile. Among his serious plays showing European influence, *Natacha, Canción de amor,* and *La serpiente* should be mentioned. The nearest to a modern *commedia dell' arte* is his *Mundial pantomim* (1919). One looking for a vehicle written to fit the personality of a specific actor should examine *Estoy solo y la quiero* (1929) or *Monsieur Ferdinand Pontac;* and finally, close to the Alvarez Quintero brand of popular and sentimental plays is *Alzame en tus brazos.*

Many of Moock's plays were never published. Some appeared in fugitive series that soon disappeared. A publishing concern in Santiago once proposed reprinting the best of his works in twelve volumes, but after two volumes had appeared, the Society of Chilean Dramatists, with which Moock had quarreled all his life squabbled about royalties and the venture ended. And so Moock continues to be the neglected Chilean dramatist. His blending of humor and pathos, his skill in dialog, his humanizing touches to his characters have caused his name to appear on billboards all over the world more frequently than the name of any other Latin American dramatist. The popularity of his plays proves that not all Latin Americans prefer gloomy tragedies when they attend the theatre. Though he was a prophet without honor in Chile, his profit elsewhere, when he managed to collect the royalties due him, was considerable.

The third important Chilean *costumbrista* of this era, coming a little later, was Germán Luco Cruchaga (1894–1936), whose *Viuda de Apablaza* (1928) has been rated along with *Tribunal del honor* and *Cardo Negro* as one of the three greatest Chilean dramas of the period. In 1926 Evaristo Lillo performed Luco Cruchaga's *Amo y señor,* about the impoverished widow of a famous soldier who marries her aristocratic daughter to "On Sepúlveda" a well-to-do grocer of Santiago "por interés," although the girl already loves a man of her social class. Luco Cruchaga's *No va más* deals with gamblers in the casino of Viña del Mar. His two-act *sainete Bailabuén* was performed in 1960 as a tent show by Pedro de la Barra. Luco Cruchaga's masterpiece, *La viuda de Apablaza* (1927), concerns life in Temuco, the southern frontier of Chile, about 1925; in it, for the first time, the attention of the theatregoing public was directed to the inhabitants of the Cordilleras and to the *arrieros* who take freight over the mountain passes to Argentina. The widow is a tough old character running her farm in a region whose original Araucanian Indian inhabitants also have a matriarchal system of government. She falls in love with Nico, the natural son of her husband, but when she realizes that he loves her niece, Florita, a city schoolteacher come to the country to convalesce, she takes herself out of the triangle by a gunshot.

Its author, an aristocrat of wealth with a training in the classics, decided on a career of fiction writing and traveled through Chile in search of material. A performance of Sánchez' *Barranca abajo* inspired him to imitate it with Chilean setting and characters, and he chose his grandfather's farm in southern Chile and the laborers he had known there. Their convincing portrayal, handled with sound technique, made *La viuda de Apablaza* a play that, following its original performance in 1928 by Elsa Alarcón and Evaristo Lillo, has several times been successfully revived, once by the Teatro Experimental in 1956, for a long Chilean tour. Luco surpasses his predecessors in his thorough study of his characters and the development of basic passions in a rural atmosphere. Though author of only a few plays, his careful writing, his expression of the soul of rural Chile, and his excellent technique give him a high place in the rapidly accelerating Chilean theatre of the first third of this century.

CHAPTER 15

The Contemporary Chilean Theatre

The creation of a living and lively contemporary Chilean theatre, following a decade of dullness, is largely due to the activity of two groups of university students who departed from the old traditions and attempted to find in the life around them a reality and a national spirit that had been overlooked by their predecessors. By founding two university theatre groups, they gave form and impetus to the movement.

Perhaps young Pedro de la Barra (1912–) was inspired by the successes of Recabarren's Laborers' Theatre and the efforts of Laferte and actors from the labor unions, around 1912, in their performance of plays of social significance. Their purpose had been to dramatize their communistic ideas for presentation before laborers starved for any sort of entertainment. But de la Barra, a student at the University of Chile, and some associates from Santiago, were following the itinerant mummers of sixteenth-century Spain who sought only the diversions of the common people. Traveling to southern Chile with a repertory of plays by Lope de Rueda and Cervantes, de la Barra's group proved the universal appeal of drama, regardless of the social or economic status of the audiences.[1]

Other manifestations of the theatre had been occurring in Chile. The creationist poet Vicente Huidobro (1893–1948), under French influence had written *Gilles de Raiz* (in French) and Chile's first guignol comedy, *En la luna* (1934). Margarita Xirgú had brought to Santiago's Municipal Theatre a repertory of plays by García Lorca, following his unnecessary death in Spain in 1936. Benjamín Morgado (1900–), organizer of the Unión de Escritores Americanos, had begun writing comedies for children: *Trasgolisto* and *El rey Midas*

---

[1] Fernando Alegría, "Chile's Experimental Theatre," *Interamerican*, IV, No. 10 (October, 1945), 24; Ricardo A. Latcham, "Curtain Time in Chile," *Las Américas*, IV, No. 9 (September, 1952), 16–19; Willis K. Jones, *Breve historia del teatro latinoamericano*, pp. 197–199; Willis K. Jones, "New Life in Chile's Theatre," *Modern Drama* (May, 1959), pp. 57–62.

(1935); but his plays for grownups eventually numbered a dozen, some performed by his company, some by professional groups. Deserving of mention are *La sombra viene del mar* (1943), the farce *X X saluda atte. a Vd.* (1961), and *Tempestad sin sollozos* (1959), which had a hundred performances.

Chile's political shake-up of 1938 was making its influence felt on the theatre in the formation of the Dirección del Teatro Nacional under Luis Valenzuela Arís (1879–1946), himself a writer of musical skits. When La Sociedad de Autores Teatrales de Chile (SATCH) of which Valenzuela was secretary, failed to encourage the many new writers eying the stage, he took his own steps and has been given credit by Morgado[2] for starting the renascence of Chile's theatre. The first wave of dramatists includes Morgado, Mayorga, Cariola, Hurtado Borne, Santiago del Campo, and two women, Magdalena Petit and "Gloria Moreno."

Women dramatists were for the first time beginning to assume importance in Chile. Of course there had been great actresses, like Elena Puelma and Pilar Matta, but now women started writing plays. Among the pioneers, now almost forgotten, were "Delie Rouge" (Delia Rojas de White, 1883–1943), Gaby von Bussenius, and Luisa Zanelli López (1894–), author of some thirty manuscripts. Ana Neves (1895–) had written one memorable drama, *Más fuerte que la sangre* (1926). But now in 1935 Magdalena Petit (1900–), though essentially a novelist, dramatized her own historical novel *La Quintrala* to bring onto the stage Doña Catalina, "The Passion Flower," a seventeenth-century Chilean murderess. A fantasy *Kimeraland* (1936) about an expedition to the moon in search of liberty; a children's play, *Pulgarcito* (1937); and at least eight other plays by her, including several historical dramas, followed.

Better suited to the stage were the works of the other woman dramatist, Ester (Chichi) Larraín de Irarrázaval (1906–), daughter and wife of Chilean diplomats. Under the pen name of "Gloria Moreno" she won the 1935 Society of Chilean Authors' contest with *Nina*, about a dressmaker who tries to get the most out of life, despite her futile husband. The actress, Antonia Herrero, who introduced it in 1937, also starred in Gloria Moreno's *Aguas abajo* (1940), about the

---

[2] Benjamín Morgado, *Eclipse parcial del teatro chileno.*

sentimental miller's wife, Anita, who is finally content to drift "downstream." A comedy, *Instituto de la felicidad* (1938; published 1943), and the three-act historical drama *La última victoria* (1942) about the abdication of Bernardo O'Higgins, with an English translation by the author, were other plays by Gloria Moreno. But the short *costumbrista La breva pelá* (1945) about rural courtship became her best-known play, and a favorite with amateur groups.

The men of this generation, however, were more productive. Cariola and Hurtado Borne, already mentioned, continued to write during this period, and Wilfredo Mayorga (1912–) began a series of plays, well received, that included *La Marea* (1939), *La bruja* (1941), and *El corazón limita con el mar* (1950).

Another productive dramatist was the critic Santiago del Campo (1916–1961). Tempted into playwrighting by Chile's developing interest in the theatre, and influenced by his friend García Lorca, del Campo wrote the first of a number of poetic plays, *California*, that won the 1939 Premio Municipal and was also performed in Argentina and Mexico. His realistic *Paisaje en destierro* (1937) was followed by a historical comedy, *Que vienen los piratas* (1942), showing the influence of Valle Inclán. Suggested by the sacking of the Chilean city of La Serena, it deals with the mistake of the Infanta in claiming for herself the love of Captain Night which is really directed toward her lady-in-waiting Viviana. Margarita Xirgú liked it well enough to add it to her repertory.

Much later del Campo's *Comedias de guerra* (1946) was performed by Teatro de Ensayo, that also produced his greatest success, the dramatization of the Blest Gana novel *Martín Rivas* (1954). His *El hombre que regresó* (1947) won a Teatro Experimental prize and he also wrote *Morir por Catalina* (1948) and *El depravado Acuña* (1953). In spite of his successes, however, del Campo preferred to be considered a journalist and critic.

All this activity was only beginning when de la Barra and his strolling players took to the road. Upon their return most of them scattered about their business, but some continued acting and a Teatro Experimental was formed to introduce European and North American dramatists to Chilean audiences. Official recognition by the National University of Chile came with the request that they prepare some appropriate play as part of the celebration of the University's centenary. *El caballero de Olmedo* by Lope de Vega was selected. The performance was so successful that the group was adopted by the University and encouraged to further efforts.

So a group that produced its first plays on a budget of 50 pesos collected from the patrons of a café, now found itself with a grant of 300,000 pesos from the Ministry of Education to establish what amounted to a professional company of actors, for that is what Teatro Experimental became. Some of its members also taught courses in what eventually became a school of drama to train not only actors, directors, and playwrights, but scene designers as well. In 1949 Agustín Siré, who had studied the organization of drama schools abroad, was selected as its head. Ballet, too, became a part of its curriculum.

In 1943 the Theatre offered Santiago audiences two original plays discovered through a competition: *Elsa Margarita* by Zlatko Brncic (1920–   ), a newly arrived refugee professor of music, and *Un velero sale del puerto* by Enrique Bunster (1912–   ).

Bunster, descendant of an English sailor who had been captured when he came ashore in Chile two centuries before to steal pigs, based his play on a Chilean legend of the skeleton mariner of Caleuche. With this encouragement to his efforts, Bunster went on, in 1940, with *La isla de los bucaneros* (published 1946), about a British butterfly hunter on Juan Fernández Island who found a pirate treasure. It won the Teatro Experimental prize for 1945 and the Municipal prize for 1946. J. G. Underhill, who translated it into English, declared it the equal of any contemporary European drama. Other plays by Bunster include the sketches *Nadie puede saberlo, Tren de carga* (1938), *El hombre y sus recuerdos* (1938), as well as the drama *El ministro salteador* (1962). But Bunster is still better known as a writer of humorous and exotic fiction.

After directing Teatro Experimental for a couple of years, de la Barra also tried his hand at several plays embodying his belief that a truly national theatre must have plays with national themes that interpret the national spirit. First came *La Feria* (1939). Another was *Viento de proa* (1948), about the adventurous Cecilia and the conservative Andrés aboard the collier *Chipana*, traveling from Lota to Iquique. It was first performed in England in 1951 as *Headwind*. More recently de la Barra wrote *La piojera* (1958), named after a low-class Santiago cafe. Few of them have been published, because they do not satisfy their perfectionist author. In 1957 he ceased directing at the University of Chile, expecting to have time for writing, but in 1960 he was asked to develop a similar drama school in Arica, and the plays remain unpublished.

The success of de la Barra's efforts motivated students of the Catholic University of Santiago to turn to drama, too. In 1943, under the encouragement of a student of architecture, Pedro Mortheiru, Teatro de Ensayo was founded. Its actors received enough pay to permit them to devote their entire time to the stage. Eventually both these professional groups became the nuclei of university schools of the theatre, offering work in playwriting, directing, acting, and scene designing. Upon graduation the members may be incorporated into the university troupes, or may go on to success on commercial stages in Chile and abroad.

Here is the explanation of the amazing activity in Chile's drama during the last twenty years. The existence of groups of actors willing to experiment with untried local plays gave tremendous impetus to all ambitious dramatists, who were further encouraged by almost yearly contests. Seminars in playwriting were inaugurated, followed by a congress in October, 1958, attended by 179 practicing playwrights. Amateur groups sprang up in the provinces and were stimulated by mimeographed plays available from TEUC and ITUCH. Competitions were arranged among these amateurs, first one in Santiago, and then, as their numbers increased, in regional elimination contests. ITUCH sponsors such a festival every two years.

With such activity the generation of 1950 came into being, to provide plays for all these groups. Here women played an important role. Two of them rate especially high, with two others not far behind.

María Asunción Requena (1915–   ) is one of the best. She writes plays as a relaxation from her profession of dentistry,[3] and her ability is attested by the number of prizes she has won. Her first effort, *Mister Jones llega a las ocho,* set in the pampas of southern Chile where she was born, won the 1952 Teatro Nacional Competition. The next year her *Fuerte Bulnes,* a historical play about a Chilean frontier town, marked her first association with Teatro Experimental,

---

[3] Jones, "New Life in Chile's Theatre," *Modern Drama* (May, 1959), pp. 60–61; Jones, "Chile's Dramatic Renaissance," *Hispania,* XLIV (March, 1961), 89–94.

and received a prize and a superlative performance in 1955. Four years later it had a showing in Hungary.

For her third attempt, *Cuento de invierno,* later renamed *El criadero de zorros de Magallanes* (1957), Dr. Requena introduced a woman administrator of a large estate in Tierra del Fuego who cannot decide whether her love for the land and its laborers is greater than her love for a man who courts her. *Pan caliente,* a tragedy of the desolation of southern Chile, was judged the best play in the 1958 competition of ITUCH, as the University of Chile's Teatro Experimental has been renamed. The following year she again competed successfully with *El camino más largo,* dramatizing the struggles of Dr. Ernestina Pérez, Chile's first woman physician, to get an education in a men's world. It has been performed in both Santiago and Buenos Aires. When the DuVauchelle broke with ITUCH and founded their own company in 1960, they performed *Piel de tigre* (1961), a play by Dr. Requena. But her attempt in the unfamiliar field of farce was not well received by the critics.

The other outstanding woman in this generation of 1950 is Isidora Aguirre (1919–   ). Beginning as author and illustrator of children's books, following her study of motion-picture making in France, she prepared for play writing in classes taught by Professor Hugo Miller in the Chilean Academy of the Ministry of Education.

In 1953 "Nene" Aguirre began writing poetic yet realistic short plays, like the one act comedy, *Pacto de medianoche* (1956) and the brief comedy *Carolina* (1955), based on the dramatist's own worries one time when she left Santiago without making sure she had turned off the gas stove. Of all modern Chilean plays, these two have probably been the most frequently performed by amateur groups in the provinces. An English translation, *Express for Santiago,* appears in the 1959–1960 *Best Short Plays* collection.

Dos y dos son cinco (1956), another comedy by Mrs. Aguirre, deals with laboring and middle-class people; but most important so far is her tragedy *Las Pascualas* (1957), in three acts, in which the dramatist provides a realistic explanation of three Chilean women of legend who committed suicide over the same man. With the main characters transformed by the dramatist into upperclass people, and provided with a chorus of lower-class servants to develop the theme, it became a play full of the poetry of life, and was performed by Teatro Experimental. Next came a serious tragedy, in collaboration with Manuel Rojas (1895–   ), author of the excellent novel *Hijo de ladrón*. *Población Esperanza* (1959), set in a desolate suburb of Santiago, deals with lower-class problems. The play was enthusiastically greeted at its première in the Theatre of the University of Concepción, where the authors received laurel wreaths.

Following its successful performances in Santiago and Buenos Aires, Nene Aguirre turned to another kind of drama, musical comedy. The musical play in Chile, based on Spanish models, has been discussed. Between 1900 and 1914 the stage had been dominated by musicals, most of them trivial. On account of the advances in staging and designing, especially by Bernardo Trumper, in the 1950's, Luis Heiremans was able to make theatrical history in 1958 with his musical comedy *Esta señorita Trini*. In 1959 Mrs. Aguirre provided the libretto for a charming musical comedy about the plight of flower sellers along the Mapocho River when Avenida O'Higgins was being widened, in 1929. She titled it *La pérgola de las flores*. After wild acclaim in Santiago it went on tour in 1962, not only to the provinces but to Argentina and Europe. It was especially successful in Spain. In 1963 her *Los papeleros*, a drama of social problems, showing the influence of Brecht, won second prize among thirty-seven entries in an ITUCH competition.

Despite her successes and eleven plays written and performed within six years, Mrs. Aguirre still considers herself an experimenting dramatist, employing realism and expressionism, but providing only such social criticism as the audience can gather from her characters. In *Las Pascualas*, for instance, the upper class lived a legend while the servants were the realists.[4] But whatever her beliefs, Mrs. Aguirre is one of the truest voices of the Chilean stage.

As María Asunción Requena is considered the author of historical plays, and Isidora Aguirre provides "Teatro Chileno," a third woman, Gabriela Roepke (1920–   ), only slightly less important, is classified as the psychological dramatist of her country. She is the only woman of the group who has studied in the United States.

Associated from its beginnings with Teatro de Ensayo, Miss Roepke provided its only national play when it toured Peru in 1955. This was *Los culpables* (1955), showing how an old maid's longing for happiness and wealth led to her attempt to murder her rich cousin. Under

---

[4] Enrique Bello, "Isidora Aguirre define los moviles de su teatro," *Ultramar*, No. 4 (April, 1960), 1–9.

the title *Juegos silenciosos* it was revived in 1959 for Santiago audiences. Among other plays by this energetic dramatist, who directs acting groups in several Santiago schools, are *La invitación* (1954), awarded both the Caupolicán and the Municipal prizes; *Las santas mujeres*, produced by Teatro de Ensayo; and her most recent, *La telaraña*. An earlier play, *Mariposa blanca* (1957), written while she studied in the United States, was published in translation in the 1959–1960 *Best Short Plays* volume as *The White Butterfly*, a sample of an excellent national drama.

Hardly known in the capital is the fourth woman dramatist, Dinka Villarroel (1909–   ), of Lota, whose first attempt, *Campamentos* (1945), dealing with labor problems in Chile's nitrate regions, was published in 1955 with a foreword by Acevedo Hernández. Its villain is a foreign engineer willing to sacrifice everything, including his daughter, to secure his own advancement. Her amusing one-act *La carta*, revised as *The Birthmark*, deals with the scandal caused by a published poem about the mole on Lucia's thigh; the poet's knowledge of the blemish is explained only when Lucia appears in a Bikini bathing suit. But most of Mrs. Villarroel's plays concern an older and more conservative Chile. The clash of white landowners and their ignorant Indian *inquilinos* in the Araucanian region, where she lived, provides the theme for her violent and melodramatic *La última trampa* (1956). *La cita en la cabaña* (1958) has gone through several revisions without satisfying its critical author[5]; among her latest plays are *Mañana a las seis* (1960) and *La casa en el cieno* (1961), both in three acts.

Many men too have taken advantage of Chile's interest in the theatre and the availability of actors created by the universities' activities. Six outstanding figures will be considered in chronological order.

Oldest of this new generation engaged in giving expression to the realities of their time is Fernando Debesa Marín (1921–   ), one of the founders of Teatro de Ensayo. It was Teatro Experimental, however, that produced his best play, the thoroughly Chilean *costumbrista* tragedy *Mamá Rosa* (1955), a present-day document about the decay of a rich middle-class household and the sacrifices of its faithful nurse, Rosenda. Though his profession of architect occupies most

[5] Jones, "New Life in Chile's Theatre," *Modern Drama* (May, 1959), pp. 61–62.

of his time, Debesa does assist ITUCH occasionally as an instructor, and returned to the stage as author of *Bernardo O'Higgins,* produced by ITUCH late in 1961. However, in spite of its historical and patriotic theme, it was not very successful.

Sergio Vodánovic (1926–   ) had his first dramatic success when his *El senador no es honorable,* written at the age of twenty-five, became the hit of Chile's first festival of plays. His next plays were light and amused the audiences, if not the critics. *Mi mujer necesita marido* (1953) was a starring vehicle for Flores and Frontaura in Chile and was made into a movie in Mexico. *La cigüeña también espera* (1955) is another comedy. After studying drama in the United States, Vodánovic wrote *Deja que los perros ladren* in 1958 (published 1960), about a father willing to do anything to become rich until he discovers that his son, tired of vain struggles for his ideals, is following the father's example. Though somewhat obvious, it is a powerful play with popular appeal not only in Chile, where it won the Municípalidad Prize in 1960, but in Argentina, Spain, and the United States. It also appeared as a successful movie. This drama, considered with his first play, marks Vodánovic as another hope of Chile's theatre in a universal, if not a national, vein.

Egon Raúl Wolff (1926–   ), an English-trained chemical engineer by profession, plans his plays in English before writing them. He was inclined toward the theatre by a Teatro Experimental competition and offered two powerfully realistic psychological plays: *Discípulos del miedo* (1957) and *Mansión de lechuzas,* performed in 1958 by the University of Concepción players as part of their program of six national works. Wolff matured quickly into one of the best of Chile's contemporary dramatists. His *Parejas de trapo,* a satire on Santiago's satisfied upper class, won the ITUCH 1960 competition, and much admiration was expressed for its dramatic characters and excellent construction. Critics in general consider *La niña madre* (1960), also known as *La Polla,* his masterpiece and one of the best Chilean plays of modern times. Its protagonist, "La Polla" is a prostitute who craves motherhood and respectability. Also in 1961, the Yale drama group performed an English translation under the title "A Touch of Blue."

Most active of the modern Chilean dramatists is Luis Alberto Heiremans (1928–1964), one of Teatro de Ensayo's talented products, who studied medicine but gravitated to the theatre. As an actor he starred in the dramatization of *Martín Rivas* in 1954. As an author of imaginative plays, well versed in the literature of Europe from having studied abroad on several scholarships, he has been averaging a play a year since his *Noche de equinoccio* (1951). *Los güenos versos,* an attempt at an *auto sacramental* with Chilean atmosphere, is a tender play about the funeral of a baby. *La hora robada* won the Municipal Prize in 1952. Teatro de Ensayo produced his *Navidad en el circo* (1954) in which he localized Henri Gheon's original idea. Heiremans' three-act *La jaula en el árbol* not only won the 1957 critics' prize but was produced in Bristol, England, and Chicago, as well as in Santiago.

In 1958 Heiremans was author of Chile's first musical comedy, *Esta señorita Trini,* which, with the colorful costumes of 1912, was so much a smash hit that it completely disrupted Teatro de Ensayo's timetable of other productions. *Moscas sobre el mármol* came the same year, with *Es de contarlo y no creerlo* in 1959, neither of which was very well received by critics. *Versos de ciego* (1961), a fantasy about wandering musicians who follow the Christmas star, also got bad reviews in Chile, but when a troupe from Teatro de Ensayo took it to Europe in 1960, along with Aguirre's *La pérgola de las flores* and Vodánovic's *Deja que los perros ladren,* it was enthusiastically received, especially in Spain. It also won the 1961 Santiago Municipalidad Prize. His *El abanderado* (1961) also won ITUCH prize and production and *El palomar a oscuras* (1962) has also appeared in a German version.

Two of the most recent crop of Chilean dramatists are Jorge Díaz Gutiérrez (1930–) and Alejandro Sieveking (1934–). The only available work by Díaz is a one-act comedy, *El cepillo de dientes,* issued in the mimeographed *Apuntes* of TEUC, as the group of the Catholic University has been renamed. Some consider Díaz the most interesting dramatist of Chile today. His plays are performed chiefly by the new and independent organizations. His *Manuel Rodríguez,* about a Chilean revolutionary figure, was produced by the Teatro Independiente group in the Santa Lucía Theatre in 1957. The others were introduced by Teatro ICTUS, a well appointed and active experimental theatrical group in Chile today. They include a three-part monolog, *Un hombre llamado Isla* (1961), the two-act *Réquiem para un girasol* (1961), and *El velero en la botella* (1962), in three scenes.

Their titles show the surrealistic tendencies of a dramatist who is bound to make his mark on the Chilean scene.

Someone has remarked that the Chilean generation of 1950, prematurely old and sad because of world unrest, has produced a "fulminating literature." In this "beat generation" of "angry young men," the sixth of Chile's masculine dramatists, Alejandro Sieveking, is typical. While a student in the School of Acting of the University of Chile, he wrote the tragedy, *El fin de febrero* (1957), about two girls who failed in school, and the suicide of Roberto, unsuccessful in everything, who was to be twenty in February. The next year his two-act *Mi hermano Cristián* (1958) was performed by ITUCH; his *El paraíso semi-perdido* (published 1962) was the hit of Chile's 1958 season. In 1959 he completed a one-act psychological play of soul-searching, *Donde no está la pared*. Then he extended himself to full-length plays, like *La madre de los conejos* (published 1961) and *Parecido a la felicidad* (1959), warmly received in Chile and taken on a tour of ten Latin American countries by a group of Teatro Experimental graduates. It concerns the romantic problems of a middle-class girl who abandons her family to live with her sweetheart, only to discover she really loves his friend. Without being derived from Tennessee Williams, it has something of his flavor and shows that the Chilean playwright profited from his study of United States plays. As a psychological dramatist he must be watched. In 1962 ITUCH performed his two-act *Ánimas de día claro* and TEUC staged *Dionisio*, scenes in a young boy's life.

Because of Chile's increasing theatrical activity, several successful novelists tried to follow the example of the nineteenth-century romantic novelist Valentín Murillo (1841–1896), who won new laurels on the stage. His plays, published in Valparaíso in 1882, included *El patio de los tribunales* (1872), a crime play. Camilo Pérez de Arce (1912–   ), who turns out detective stories under the name of "James Ernhard," began with *Bajo el signo de la muerte* (1951) and *Ser o no ser*. His surrealistic *El Cid*, produced by Teatro de Ensayo in 1950, was an interlude, to be followed by melodramas of crime, *Raza de bronce* (1954) and *Comedia para asesinos* (1957), the latter not only a Teatro de Ensayo prize winner but a success in Madrid. Other plays by him include *El correo del rey* and an unproduced "Sesenta Seis Tres" about a lottery ticket. Except for Gerardo Larraín, a dramatist with actual police experience who turns out thrillers like *Los críme-*

nes de M. Dubois (1959) and the superior *La razón final* (1956), Pérez de Arce is one of the few Latin American authors of crime drama.

A few other Chilean dramatists of today deserve an honorable mention. One important figure is Fernando Cuadra Pinto (1926–   ), who employs popular types and popular themes, especially in his recent works. After experimenting with *Cinco lagartos* (1943), he successfully entered the Teatro Experimental competition with *Encrucijada* (1945) and the classical *La Medea* (1948). The biblical *Murallas de Jericó*, which uses the sixth day of the siege of Jericho as a symbol of the search for truth, won the ITUCH first prize in 1950. Cuadra returned to the Chilean rural scene with *Elisa* (1953) and *Doña Tierra* (1957). His naturalistic *El diablo está en Machalí* (1958) was coldly received by audience and critics because of its prostitutes, its crude language, and its anti–North American bias, but Cuadra regained popularity in 1960 with the historical *Rancagua 1814* and the melodrama *El Mandamás*.

Enrique Gajardo Velásquez (1923–   ), who directed *El Mandamás* in 1960, is himself an occasional playwright when not teaching drama at the University of Chile and its extension centers or organizing amateur groups. The amusing *El zapatero de enfrente* (1953) is popular in drama contests, as is his well-developed *El secreto* (1954), suggested by an Italian story about a man who dies as he is trying to tell his wife a secret. Gajardo's three-act *Pool*, about the problems of young people in a provincial town, was an entry in the 1961 Festival of amateur actors organized by ITUCH.

Another of Chile's many part-time dramatists is Dr. Roberto Sarah (1918–   ). While a university student, he won second prize in the 1939 Dirección General de Teatro Competition with the three-act *Las idólatras*. Lent to a visiting Argentine actor, the manuscript was supposedly lost, though there are reports of nonroyalty performances across the Andes. It was followed by *Por encima de los dioses* (1941). The 1949 Teatro Experimental Competition lured Dr. Sarah back to his typewriter. His *Algún día*, submitted under the pen name of "Andrés Terbay," won the Competition and opened on Christmas night that same year, with Pepe Rojas and Elvira Travesi in the leading roles and with Alejandro Flores also in the cast. After fifty performances it was taken on tour, then returned to Santiago for two more honors, the Caupolicán Award of Theatre and Movie Critics and the Municipal Prize. An English translation was performed in London in 1951, and Margarita Xirgú's company revived it in 1955 for performances in Chile and Uruguay. *Algún día* covers three periods, ten years apart, beginning in 1930, and deals with the hopes of an Italian immigrant family that "some day" something fine will happen to them. It never does.

Dr. Sarah followed this play with *Mi vida para ti* (1950) and *El collar rojo*. The performance by Flores in *El viajero parte al alba* (1952) was applauded by the public but scorned by critics. The next year the dramatist visited his family home in the Middle East. On his return his *Una luz en la lluvia* (1959), originally called both *Providencia* and *Humo hacia el sur*, about melancholic southern Chile, was performed by Teatro de Ensayo, to a chilly audience.

Chile is now in the midst of great theatrical activity.[6] To list all the writers would be impossible, but a few others certainly deserve mention. Popular among the amateurs is Luis Cornejo Gamboa, whose *Lluvia de octubre* (1952) was revived for the 1955 festival of Teatro Experimental. Among his many other plays, the three-act psychological drama *El altillo* should be mentioned but his combined royalties have never permitted him to give up his profession as a plasterer.

Fernando Lamberg (1928–   ), author of *El que construyó su propio infierno* (1954) and the impressive one-act *El periodista* (1954), won second place in the 1958 National Contest with the unimpressive *Una antigua belleza* about an impossible Chilean heroine. His three-act comedy *Una madeja para trepar* (1959), however, was a success at several amateur competitions. His most recent is *Aprendices de la vida*, a competitor in the 1960 Gabriela Mistral Competition.

Dr. Alberto Daiber (1926–   ), who lives near Osorno, gathered his own troupe to perform his one-act farce *Inundación en Misipulli* (1956). *Ilusión de fotógrafo* (1956), *El living*, and *Maldita elección* (1957) have not yet been performed in Santiago. Renán Rojas (1937–   ) began at the age of thirteen to write plays in his provincial town and completed seven before he ever saw a theatrical performance. Finally ITUCH accepted his *Con el hombre en el cristal* (1960) and scheduled two more, *El círculo* (1959) and *El triángulo* (1961).

Some humor is finding its way onto Chilean stages. José Antonio

---

[6] Julio Durán Cerda, *Repertorio del teatro chileno.*

Garrido, a lazy but talented follower of Jardiel Poncela, is author of witty dialog in *Una noche distinta* (1952), *Papá no tiene vergüenza* (1955), and *Una camelia para Margarita* (1962). Felipe Ravinet (1925–   ) combines farce with realism in his one-act *Sí señora, aquí penan*, popular with amateurs, the longer *Arcadio* (1957), about a drunken angel on earth, and *A la diestra de Dios Padre*, which makes use of folklore.

For most of the humor, however, one must look to Chile's commercial theatre, which is also sharing some of the country's drama activity. The wealthy Miguel Frank (1920–   ) founded a company in 1948, originally to perform sophisticated foreign drama. When he could find no audience for it, he began writing his own plays. *Tiempo de vals* (1952) hit the public fancy. Then came the drama *Punto muerto* (1954), inspired, the author said, by *Blithe Spirit*. His farce *Matrimonio para tres* (1955) presents a woman who needs a baby in order to claim an estate of fifty thousand pesos. Since her husband was supposedly killed in an airplane accident, she takes another man. The return of the husband poses a problem in paternity. In Frank's amusing *El hombre del siglo* (1958), an angel descends on Chile to collect data for the Last Judgment and takes a job as butler in a Santiago home. Along serious lines he wrote *La primera piedra* and a psychological melodrama, *Punto muerto*.

The longest-running recent play in a Chilean commercial theatre was *El prestamista* in 1956 (published 1957), by the critic Fernando Josseau (1924–   ). Following the existentialist *El César* (1955) about a fatalistic dictator waiting to be killed, *Las goteras*, about a hunted man and a prostitute, and *Esperar el amanecer*, another hopeless play, Josseau clicked with a novelty, a three-act crime play with only one actor. Raúl Montenegro, a Teatro de Ensayo graduate, plays all three murder suspects in *El prestamista*, questioned by a detective represented by an offstage voice. Following a six months' run in Santiago, Montenegro and his tape recorder toured Buenos Aires and Montevideo, then returned for a long run in a small Santiago theatre. Meantime, Josseau completed *La torre de marfil* (1957) to follow *El prestamista*, when it should ever close, which it finally did.

Amateurs and independents provide a hearing for other dramatists. Juan Guzmán Améstica (1931–   ), a student at ITUCH, began by directing his own short *El caracol* in the 1959 Festival, then finished half a dozen other manuscripts, including *Wurlitzer*, Chile's entry in the first Latin American Play Competition in March, 1962. Jaime Silva (1934–   ), whose *El otro avaro* (1954) imposed the technique of Giraudoux on the classical style of Plautus or Molière, went on to write a much praised comedy with music, *La princesa Panchita* (1958), followed by five other plays, including *Las beatas de Talca* (1959) and *Arturo y el angel* (1962).

In 1961 Santiago was the scene of a drama festival with many groups from the provinces, producing short plays by their own local writers. One group of miners acted a tragedy by Mrs. Aguirre. So there is no sign of letdown, theatrically. Though the theatre in Chile may have been slow in starting, it has now assumed a leading position in the drama of the continent.

Peruvian Drama

The date of the first theatrical performance that took place in Peru depends on definitions. Obviously if one refers to European plays, performances did not start till after the arrival of the white man in 1532. If dramatic monologs, dialogs, and historical pageants are considered "theatre," then the Incas had entertainment in pre-Columbian times, and Arrom has compiled many references by explorers and missionaries to Indian performances witnessed when they first visited Peru.[1] Pedro Pizarro, cousin of Francisco, implied in his *Relación de la conquista del Perú* that women as well as men performed in the Inca plays.

Pedro Cieza de León (1518–1560) described a theatre with richly decorated seats where the Inca emperor came with his nobles and subjects to worship the figure of a god on a pedestal. Padre José de Acosta (1539–1600) witnessed dancers, some masked, representing different professions, in ceremonies of worship. He wrote of *taquis*, or ballads, sung to music, sometimes historical, sometimes full of superstition. Like the embryonic plays of the time of Aeschylus, they at least sought to increase religious feeling, correct vices, and remind the audiences of great moments in their past.

Pedro Sarmiento (1532–1608) reported *representaciones* of the life of the Inca, along with battles and victories. The paragraph by Inca Garcilaso de la Vega, son of an Incan princess and a Spanish conquistador, about the ability of the Indian *amautas* to compose comedies and tragedies has already been quoted.

European newcomers to Peru therefore might well have combined the best of the dramatic traditions found in the New World with the best of Spain's drama, then in its infancy. They had reached the country with the most advanced civilization of New World. The Incas were the only Indians to have domesticated animals; their farmers had developed at least thirty plants important to us today; their doc-

---

[1] José Juan Arrom, *El teatro de Hispanoamérica en la época colonial*, pp. 14 ff.

tors knew the values of cocaine and quinine. Their surgeons, despite knives of bronze, were doing successful trepanning. Their literary leaders composed lyric poetry and music.

Some of the Spanish dramatists did indeed for a time use Indian legends and legendary figures. But as the years passed, in their desire to "purify the drama" and remove from it any "earthiness disturbing to their parishioners," the priestly dramatists turned from native elements. Only in some historical plays did the names of the native inhabitants appear, and then endowed with European psychology. So, when the Indians took part in a play, as many of them did, it was commonly in such roles as Adam and Eve, or Cupid, or Alexander the Great, rather than as an Incan hero.

A Spanish friar had three possible reasons for writing a play in America: entertainment, either private or official; mental discipline; or provision of material for converting the Indians. *El auto del nacimiento del Hijo de Dios* is a sample of the last-named,[2] performed to make Christian doctrines comprehensible and vivid to the Indians.

Only one of these early dramatists is known by name: Florestán de Lasarte, a Latin teacher from Extremadura, reached Lima about 1551. Some identify him with an actor listed in the cast of Torres Naharro's *Comedia serafina*. But whether because of his stage experience or his knowledge of Latin and the plays of Plautus and Terence, the guilds of Lima entrusted to him the writing of their annual *autos* for Corpus Christi celebrations of 1557 and 1558. The plays have been lost, so nothing is known of their quality. Lasarte died before he could write any more.

The play for 1563, however, *El auto de la gula*, telling the story of Jacob and Esau, still exists, though nothing is known about Alonso Hurtado who wrote it and acted in it. In 1565 the *ayuntamiento* of Lima offered cloth for costumes as prizes for the best plays. Alonso González, born in Talavera, Spain, who had lived in Lima with his wife since 1551, won ten yards of velvet and ten of satin with his *Auto de Abraham*. Because he had come from Spain, scholars wonder whether this religious play was inspired by an earlier one of the same title, either that of Valladolid (1522) or one of Seville (1560) written by Alonso de la Vega. Lohmann gives a year-by-year listing of Lima's dramatic fare.[3] Some of the offerings had moments of humor,

---

[2] In Rubén Vargas Ugarte, *De nuestro antiguo teatro*, pp. 132–216.

[3] Guillermo Lohmann Villena, *El arte dramático en Lima durante el Virreinato*.

as in the English moralities, frequently provided by the player representing the Devil.

In 1568 the Jesuits reached Lima and became enthusiastic sponsors of didactic drama. The year of their arrival they publicly performed an *auto sacramental* in the Plazuela de San Pedro. Others of the order were to invite the viceroy and officials of Mexico to attend a *tragicomedia* in the Seminary of St. Peter and St. Paul in 1574, two years after they arrived in Nueva España.

The Jesuits were quick to learn the two Indian languages of Peru, the courtly Quechua and the popular Aymará. As Inca Garcilaso reported:

A Jesuit father wrote a play about the Virgin Mary in the Aymará language, which was staged by Indian boys and young men. . . . In Cuzco they staged another dialog about the Infant Jesus. . . . Another one in Lima, about the Holy Sacrament with part in Spanish and part in Aymará, was performed before the nobility and Indians.[4]

Much later, in 1712, a French visitor to Pisco saw Moreto's *San Alejo y Segismundo* performed by mulattos, amateur actors directed by a Jesuit priest, and this critic reported that they performed very well.

The inhabitants, however, wanted still more plays. In 1571, to enliven Cuzco's Corpus Christi, Viceroy Toledo ordered the guilds to perform appropriate plays or pay a fine of two hundred pesos. For Lima the city fathers used another plan. In 1574 they hired a professional actor, Sebastián de Arcos from Seville, to provide the plays. He formed a company of eight players, one of them a shipbuilder named Juan Bautista Durán, who thus discovered his ability in comic parts and from then on frequently appeared in plays until 1582, when Francisco de Morales supplanted him in popularity. Morales then remained the popular favorite till his death in 1600.[5]

In 1597, when Viceroy Luis de Velasco wanted an elaborate Corpus Christi program, he hired a young actor-manager, Jerónimo de Pineda, whose stage in the Plaza Mayor was a raised platform beside a curtained cart in which his actors dressed. Drama had come a long way from the simple dialog before the altar in a church.

[4] Garcilaso de la Vega, *Comentarios reales*, Book II, Chapter 28.
[5] José Alfredo Hernández, "Aspectos del teatro peruano," *Boletín*, Nos. 18–19 (June–December, 1947), 157.

The Jesuits had a second use for drama. To train their student preachers in elocution, they used *decurias*, or dramatic dialogs. Vargas includes two of them: *Santa María Egipciaca*, possibly by P. Vicente Palomino, and *Efectos que causa en el alma el que recibe el Santísimo* by P. Salvador de Vega.[6]

The third use was political, to show allegiance to their sovereigns in Spain or to welcome visiting dignitaries of church or state. Since no professional troupe was available, the Jesuit priests and the students at the University of San Marcos were usually the actors. Garcilaso describes the welcoming play for Francisco de Mendoza when he came to Cuzco in 1532. Lima, too, after its founding in 1534 by Francisco Pizarro, became another drama center. When Henry VIII was reigning in England and the Pilgrim Fathers were not yet even children, Lima was the cultural center of South America. Here the University of San Marcos was founded, three quarters of a century before the earliest English-speaking university in North America.

Lohmann tells the "ynvenciones" that greeted Gonzalo Pizarro when he entered Lima in 1546. The historian of Peru's theatre calls them "medieval plays of the type of Plautus and Terence,"[7] but they were certainly more crude, being at first simply dialogs between low-class people, the *bobos* of the early plays in Spain. On January 6, 1548, Pizarro was reported delighted with plays appropriate to Twelfth Night that he saw in the Cathedral of Cuzco. To appeal to a man without culture, they were probably broad farces of the sort that eventually became too broad: in 1552 the First Council, to prevent scandals in the Church, levied a fine of twenty pesos for performances without permission by Council. Later, in 1582, to avoid irreverence, another Council prohibited all comedies based on religious themes.

When La Gasca, after defeating Pizarro, reached Lima on July 17, 1548, part of his welcoming ceremony was a play, of unknown authorship. Later, on July 25, 1557, Lima offered its oath of loyalty to Philip II with other dramatic spectacles. Since news traveled slowly, it was not till December that Philip's subjects in Cuzco observed its *jura* to him with more plays.

---

[6] Vargas, *De nuestro antiguo teatro*, pp. 27–38, 218–227. See J. L. Trenti Rocamora, *El repertorio de la dramática colonial hispanoamericana*, pp. 58–60, for titles of other *decurias*.

[7] Lohmann, *El arte dramático*, pp. 6 ff.

Similarly, viceroys were welcomed to Peru by theatrical programs. Vargas lists the titles of all performances, from those for Martín Enríquez in 1584 to Salvatierra in 1630.[8] For the first-named, Padre José de Acosta wrote *Lázaro y el rico Epulón*, performed by the students of San Marcos. For Count Villar Don Pardo, the *auto*, *San Paulino de Nola* was the attraction, the leading role being taken by Jerónimo de Montesinos, later to become the Indian Demosthenes, the most eloquent preacher of Peru. For the Marqués de Cañete, García Hurtado de Mendoza, the viceroy's brother Hernando, then rector of the College of San Andrés, wrote the very timely *Mary Stuart*, and the handsome boy who portrayed the Scotch queen, killed by Elizabeth a few years previously, was royally rewarded by the Viceroy.

The *auto*, *Historia alegórica del anticristo y el juicio final*, performed to welcome Luis de Velasco in 1596 had a realism that would have delighted a later Belasco. The stage was filled with mummies and bones from the cemetery next door.

Arequipa, astride the main road between Lima and wealthy Potosí (which early had a theatre), must also have had considerable theatrical activity. Lohmann Villena mentions a Corpus Christi celebration there in 1564 which offered a comedy and three *entremeses*.[9] Dr. Harvey L. Johnson gives an account of activities during the years 1621 and 1636. He even found contracts made by Manuel de Ribera with thirteen professional actors for a season in the capital and a tour of the provinces. Articles signed in Arequipa fifteen years later by seven actors for a three years' partnership provide more information about the availability of actors and their pay in seventeenth-century Peru.[10] Their plays, like most of those performed in Lima, were imported from Spain. Beginning about 1554 the Peninsular booksellers ventured to print contemporary hits from the Spanish stages, and it was not long before these volumes found their way overseas. Not only did they make up part of the cargo of galleons, but many a priest, sailing for the New World, tucked a *parte* of a dozen plays into his baggage along with his volumes of sermons.

By 1593 Lope de Vega's plays were known in Lima. Professor

[8] Vargas, *De nuestro antiguo teatro*, pp. xxxiii–xxxiv.

[9] Lohmann, *El arte dramático*, pp. 19–20.

[10] Harvey L. Johnson, "Compañías teatrales en Arequipa," *Nueva Revista de Filología Hispánica*, VII (1953), 449–460.

Leonard discovered cargo manifests of some of the Silver Fleet, listing the books.[11] One vessel, *Nuestra Señora del Rosario*, that left Seville in 1605 carried sixty-one cases of 163 different titles belonging to Juan de Sarria, a bookseller of Alcalá de Henares, where *Don Quijote* had been published. They were consigned to his son in Porto Bello, Panama, and to his partner Miguel Méndez, a bookseller in Lima. Shipments like this explain how in 1607 in the backwoods town of Pauca in the District of Parinacocha, a fiesta in honor of Francisco de Toledo, the Marqués de Montes Claros, could include as one of the "ynvenciones" a scene in which Don Quijote and Sancho Panza discuss Dulcinea.[12] To pay freight charges across the Isthmus of Panama, young Sarria had to sell eight cases of books. Lack of space on the southbound vessel compelled him to leave eight more boxes on the docks in Panama, but forty-five cases containing 2,895 volumes reached Callao and Lima, and this was only one of many shipments that must have arrived from Spain through the years.

Naturally a large part of the titles were ecclesiastical books for the priests who had money to buy them and time and ability to read them, but on this list of the *Rosario* were the names of sixty-three plays, including nine by Lope published the previous year.

Of the other Golden Age playwrights, the first Lima performance of a Moreto play took place in 1659. Calderón's plays were first seen there in 1670, when the viceroy ordered a Calderón play substituted for the locally written Corpus Christi play planned. After that, two a year by Calderón were performed till the end of the century. Students used a quartet of Calderón plays to welcome the new viceroy in 1674. It has been calculated that during the colonial period Lima saw 194 performances from Calderón compared to 59 from Moreto, the second choice of Lima theatregoers.

Lima had still another source of dramatic entertainment. Imitating the 1538 statutes of the University of Salamanca, that called for a play a year by Plautus, Seneca, or Terence, Viceroy Toledo decreed in Lima in 1581 that the San Marcos University professor of Latin

[11] Irving A. Leonard, "A Shipment of *comedias* to the Indies," *Revue Hispanique*, II (January, 1934), 39–50.
[12] Luis Curie Gallegos, "La primera representación de *Quijote*," *Escena*, I, No. 3, 14–15; also Trenti Rocamora, *El repertorio*, p. 54. The original 1607 document was published in Madrid in 1913, and in Vargas, *De nuestro antiguo teatro*, pp. ix–xix.

must have his students perform one play in Latin and one in Spanish each year.[13] Somebody even wrote an original play in Latin that same year as part of the welcoming ceremonies for Viceroy Enríquez de Almansa.

Lima had no permanent stage on which to perform these plays. However, on October 13, 1594, according to Lohmann, the preaching friars opened a Patio de las Comedias near the Palo Bridge and put it in charge of Francisco de Morales and his wife, María Rodríguez.[14] This stage was not very elaborate, being hardly more than a few boards on sawhorses, with draperies behind them. Wealthy patrons could rent benches with backs, close to the stage. The others stood. Each entrance fee went to the friars. This theatre was soon followed by another. The *ayuntamiento*, at its meeting on February 14, 1596, gave permission to Morales to build another theatre, near the center of town, but it took so long to clear and pave the site that Mexico beat it into production with its elaborate theatre in the Calle de Arco.

Francisco de León got permission in 1597 to build a Casa de Comedias beside the Hospital de Nuestra Señora, which was to receive a share of the profits. These theatres were all without roofs; that improvement did not come till 1612, long after the arrival of the first professional touring actors, exiled from Spain by the edict of May 2, 1598, prohibiting all stage shows. These barnstormers included Francisco Pérez de Robles and his wife and leading lady, Isabel de los Angeles, who courageously started for Peru before there was a permanent settlement in the United States. This was 150 years before Shakespeare's mighty lines re-echoed in America when Thomas Kean performed in *Richard III* at the Nassau Street Theatre, New York, in 1750. The contact of these Spanish actors about wages, drawn up in Callao Harbor before they disembarked, is still preserved.[15]

Early Peru also had its puppet theatres: accounts mention a "Casa de Maravillas," built by a physician named Julio in 1597, thus antedating by nearly a century the marionettes of Leonor de Goromán,

---

[13] Arrom, *El teatro de Hispanoamérica*, p. 52.

[14] Lohmann, *El arte dramático*, p. 67; Julio A. Leguizamón, *Historia de la literatura hispanoamericana*, I, 281; Manuel Moncloa y Covarrubias, *El teatro en Lima*; Hernández, "Aspectos del teatro peruano," *Boletín*, Nos. 18–19, (June–December, 1947), 151–159.

[15] A. S. W. Rosenbach, "The First Theatrical Company in America," *Proceedings of American Antiquarian Society*, XLVIII (1938), 300–310.

who was once considered the first puppeteer in Lima.[16] Chroniclers also refer to a puppet show of 1630 in the cloisters of San Francisco.[17] Dr. Temple sees a relationship between the puppet activity of 1695 and 1795 and the inactivity during that period in the Peruvian theatre.

From 1604 on, Lima always had a theatre or two.[18] The Corral de las Comedias on Calle St. Bartolomé was favored by Viceroy Velasco to the extent of forbidding all other theatrical performances within a radius of five leagues of Lima, except in the coliseum on the property of the Hospital of San Andrés. The Corral was put in charge of Alonso de Avila. Could he have been related to the Juan de Avila, manager of the Corral del Príncipe that opened in Madrid in 1583?

Without available stage lights, that cause of so many later conflagrations, Lima's performances began at 2:00 P.M. in the winter, and 3:00 P.M. in the summer. They were confined to Sundays and occasional Thursdays. Night performances, traced back to a beginning in Aranjuez, Spain, in 1622, did not come to Peru till 1672.

To judge from the abundance of decrees against *huanchacos*, there were more gate crashers expecting free boxes than just the high officials of church and state. The latter never paid. One viceroy even requested an allowance of eight pesos a performance to buy himself *aloja*, the water sweetened with honey and spices that was sold between acts.

In 1606 the Lima theatre was moved to the home of Doña Ana de Rivera near Santo Domingo Church.[19] Three years later it occupied the bakery of the Hospital; then in 1612 a larger theatre was opened in the home of Miguel de Berrio Manrique on Calle San Agustín, later to be renamed Calle de las Comedias Viejas. There it remained for fifty years.

Another player from Spain, the beautiful María del Castillo, born

---

[16] Moncloa, *El teatro en Lima*, quotes Mendiburie, *Diccionario histórico*.

[17] Ella Dunbar Temple, "Letras en la Lima a fines del siglo XVIII," in *3*, No. 8 (March, 1941).

[18] Moncloa, *El teatro en Lima*; Irving Leonard, "El teatro en Lima," *Revue Hispanique*, VIII (April, 1940), 96; José Torre Revello, "El teatro en la colonia," *Humanidades*, XXII (1933), 145–165. See José de la Riva Aguero, *Por la verdad, la tradición y la patria*, II, 229–255 ("Lima Española"), for dating of early theatres and arrival of cultural material from Spain.

[19] Ismael Portal y Espinosa, *Del pasado limeño*, p. 138.

in Jerez about 1568, reached Lima in 1601, where she married Alonso de Avila, the manager of the Coliseum. The couple had to turn back to the Hospital of San Andres a *real* for each spectator. Since the Coliseum could hold four hundred people and the season included seventy-five performances, full houses might net the Hospitalers an annual income of around 3,750 pesos.

But Avila had no monopoly. Competing for audiences were Francisco de Morales and his new wife, María Isabel Rodríguez. They even introduced a local play called *Varios sucesos de Lima* (1622) by a Lima friend, Cristóbal Palomeque, who advanced four hundred pesos for expenses of production.

Other local plays find mention in the records. Between 1608 and 1621 the Andalusian immigrant from Seville, Diego Mexía de Fernagil, wrote a poetic eclog, *El Dios Pan.*[20] It was religious in tone: Pan symbolized the Holy Sacrament. The author was a member of the Academia Antártica of Lima, with the pen name of "Delio," but because of its dedication to Diego de Portugal, president of the Audiencia de Charcos, Vargas thinks this play was written in Potosí. A later eclog by Mexía, *El buen pastor,* was dedicated to Inés de Rivera of Medillín, Spain, at that time a nun in Chuquisaca (now Sucre). Actor Morales' son Antonio was also a dramatist, who provided *El blasón de los Alvarados* (1621) for his father's company. And Perú had other ambitious playwrights.

On November 28, 1632, Ana Morillo, described as an *autora de comedias,* which could mean either dramatist or impresario, died in Lima, leaving an estate of twenty thousand pesos. Surely she could not have made all that from the theatre, but nothing else is known about her, except that she may have been the "Amarilis" who wrote the celebrated letter to Lope de Vega.[21]

In 1622 a third troupe was formed in Lima by the dramatist Julián de Iraola, which he planned to take on tour. In a lawsuit, we find mention of still another company. In 1644 a merchant of Cuzco sued Jerónimo Ximénez y Duarte, described as an actor, and his son-in-law Alonso de Haro, for seventy-five pesos due on cloth for costumes.

---

[20] Vargas, *De nuestro antiguo teatro,* pp. 1, 26; see also Trenti Rocamora, *El repertorio,* pp. 54–55.

[21] Irving A. Leonard, "More conjectures concerning 'Amarilis Indiana'," *Hispania,* XX (1937), 113 ff. Del Saz (*Teatro Hispanoamericano,* I, 46) identifies her as the wife of the actor Gabriel del Río.

Haro was mentioned as having fled from the capital and joined another group performing in Pisco, leaving the settlement of the debt to his father.

Like the actors, theatres in Peru came and went. Finally on Sunday, November 12, 1662 the new Coliseum Imponente, taking its name from Madrid's showplace of 1640 and built by the Hospital of San Andrés, opened in Lima. *Santa Rosa de Lima* was an early offering. But drama in Peru was falling into a decline. Few professionals were arriving from Spain and local actors could not make a living. Since the Golden Age in Spain had come to its end with the death of Calderón in 1681, few new plays crossed the Atlantic. Two effects can be noted during the next seventy-five years: new life in the puppet theatres, and an increase in locally written plays.

At first they were short, as for instance, the *loas* or *entremeses* of Juan del Valle y Caviedes (1652–1694). Though an Andalusian, his plays were full of the spirit of Peru. Three of them are preserved: *El amor alcalde, El amor médico,* and *Baile del amor tahur.*[22] These plays in verse deal with phases of Cupid as related to captives of his power, to invalids, and to gamblers.

Another dramatist, this one born in Camaná, Peru, was Lorenzo de las Llamosas (1665 ?–1705 ?). The birth of a son to the Viceroy Mendoza in 1689 inspired his musical play *También se vengan los dioses.* But the dramatist must have indulged in sidelines. To escape accusations of crooked dealings he decided to flee to Spain, where he wrote a comedy, *Amor, industria y poder* (1695), and another musical play about Dido and Aeneas, *Destinos vencen finezas* (1698), for the birthday of King Charles III. Madrid's two theatres performed them. Then he dropped out of sight. In general, Llamosas' plays are more spectacles than dramas.[23]

One play written in the Quechua language by an unidentified dramatist, Gabriel Centeno de Osma, may belong in this period: *Yauri tito Inca.* A manuscript found in Cuzco in 1922 by Humberto Suárez Alvaro is assigned by some to the sixteenth century. In its Spanish translations it is called *El Pobre más rico.*[24] It deals with

[22] First edited by Luis Fabio Xammar and printed in *Fénix*, then reprinted by Escuela Nacional de Arte Escénico, Lima, 1950.

[23] See R. Vargas Ugarte (ed.), *Obras de Llamosas*, which contains a *comedia-zarzuela*.

[24] Gabriel Centeno de Osma, *El pobre más rico*, summarized in Jorge Basadre, *Literatura inca*, Vol. I of *Biblioteca de Cultura Peruana*, 135–146.

Yauri, an Indian Dr. Faustus, who sells his soul to the Devil in return for riches and the love of the Indian heroine, Cori Umiña. When the Devil tries to collect, five years later, an angel advises Yauri to pray to Mary, and so he is saved—to eat his cake and have it too.[25] This theme of the poor sinner now wealthy is repeated in the more famous *Usca Páucar*,[26] written to enhance the worship of the Virgin of Copacabana, on the shores of Titicaca. Though Centeno rouses little emotion in the spectator, the unknown author of the later version makes the audience feel the tragedy of this descendant of Incas, proud of his past, but now humiliated by begging and by the domination of others. No wonder he is willing to surrender his soul to recapture his former dignity.

Other plays in Quechua were written by the mestizo prodigy Juan de Espinosa Medrano (1632–1688), nicknamed "El Lunarejo" because of the mole on his face. His first work for the stage was written at the age of fourteen, and at eighteen this humanist was a professor of theology at the University of Cuzco. His *Auto sacramental del hijo pródigo* and his (probably) *Auto sacramental del robo de Proserpina y sueño de Endimión* are both in Quechua.[27] In the Spanish language, he dramatized the Biblical story of Jael and Sisara (augmented by four *graciosos*), using the technique of Lope de Vega; his title, *Amar su propia muerte*,[28] suggests his master's *Amar su propia desdicha*. It is well plotted and the verse is excellent, as one would expect from a critic made famous by his study of Góngora. In none of his work, however, does Espinosa reflect his Peruvian environment.

Shortly after the beginning of the eighteenth century Peru got a viceroy who loved the theatre. The Marqués de Castell dos Rius represented Philip V in Lima between 1707 and 1710. One of his first acts was to remodel a salon of the palace into a theatre, just in time to celebrate the birth of the future short-lived Luis I of Spain with a

---

[25] Teodoro L. Meneses, "El monólogo de Yauri Tito," *Sphinx*, Año 4, Nos. 10–12 (June–December, 1941), 119–123.

[26] Basadre, *Literatura inca*, pp. 334–402; Arrom, *El teatro de Hispanoamérica*, pp. 202–204. For other religious plays by priests, see Trenti Ricamora, *El repertorio*, pp. 57–62.

[27] Paul Rivet and Georges de Crequi-Montfort, *Bibliographie des langues aymara et kicua*, I, 129. For a translation of *Hijo pródigo*, see Basadre, *Literatura inca*, pp. 256–334; and Clorinda Matto de Turner, *Don Juan de Espinosa*.

[28] Vargas, *De nuestro antiguo teatro*, pp. 39–131.

comedia harmónica, i.e., with music. The presentation was *El mejor escudo de Perseo* (1708), based on Greek mythology. Its use of French-Italian technique foreshadowed the attempt to substitute neoclassical tragedies for Spanish *comedias,* a move that all but emptied the theatres of Spain as well as of America. One courtier who did not have to be courteous declared it a "scenic monstrosity in detestable poetry." The chief importance of this musical comedy lies in the high position of its author rather than in the high quality of his production.

Greater art is found in the works of several of his friends whose plays were also performed in the royal theatre. A soldier from Aragón, Jerónimo de Monforte y Vera[29] wrote a number of plays, whose loss is unfortunate if they were as good as his surviving *sainete, El amor duende* (1725),[30] in honor of the coronation of Luis I of Spain. While it has the artificial elements of many plays, as for instance introducing Amor as a character, the veiled ladies and practical joke played on a *caballero* of Lima are both local and amusing.

Among the Viceroy's other author friends was Miguel Sáenz Cascante (1640–1717), remembered by a play, *La Sagaritida,* about a hamadryad condemned to death when her sweetheart breaks his oath.

Another member of the Viceroy's Academia Antártica was the Conde de la Granja, General Luis Antonio de Oviedo Herrero, who must have died at a ripe old age since he made his will in 1714 at the age of eighty. He was the author of two plays: *Los sucesos de tres horas* and *De un gran yerro, un gran acierto.*

Even the rector of San Marcos, Padre José Bermúdez de la Torre (1662–1746) was inspired by his association with the Viceroy to turn dramatist. He penned a couple of *loas,* including one for December 27, 1709, to celebrate the Viceroy's birthday. Added interest is the description it contains of the royal theatre.[31]

Greatest of all the playwrights in this active period of Peru's theatrical history was Pedro de Peralta Barnuevo (1654–1743). This

---

[29] Antonio Pasquariello, "Two Eighteenth-Century Peruvian Interludes," *Symposium,* VI (1952), 385–390.

[30] Fernández de Castro, *Elisio peruano;* Lohmann, *El arte dramático,* pp. 540–553.

[31] Lohmann, *El arte dramático,* 343–344.

professor of mathematics and rector of San Marcos wrote a number of plays presented on the palace stage.[32]

When Diego Ladrón de Guevara left the bishopric of Quito to succeed Castell-dos-Rius, he had to be welcomed by a play, and Peralta also helped him celebrate Philip V's victory in the Battle of Villaviciosa in 1710 by writing *Triunfos de amor* (1711). It clearly resembles an earlier play by Llamosas, *También se vengan los dioses*. And when the archbishop of La Paz, Diego Morcillo Rubio de Auñón, became viceroy in 1720, he also demanded entertainment; so Peralta obliged with *Afectos vencen finezas* (1720), which in title and Greek environment echoes Llamosas' *Destinos vencen finezas* (1698).

Somewhere in between, perhaps in 1719, Peralta showed his knowledge of French drama by rewriting Corneille's *Rodogune* as *La Rodoguna*, about a mother and a daughter whose mutual hatred make them plan the murder of each other. Except for the dramatic last act, it is as dreary in Spanish as in French, but it does deserve preservation because of the authentically Peruvian *entremés* that came with it. Four ladies and their sweethearts and an indulgent father provide a delightful tale of Lima.

Another amusing play of local color by Peralta is *Baile del Mercurio galante*, in which he again mixes fable and reality, making Mercury a professor of mathematics of San Marcos who offers his satirical judgment on five pairs of sweethearts. Peralta's short skits represent his own originality, but for the finales of his plays he borrows from Molière, unsuccessfully, as Arrom feels. He missed the satire of Molière or he would have seen his own sins of bad taste and would have destroyed the plays. Still, they were intended only for an evening's diversion, and were then tucked away in a private library in Spain for two centuries.

Unconnected with the viceroy's court were several other dramatists of Peru. A Capuchin nun, Sor Juana María (1698–1748), whose real name was Josefa Francisca de Azaña y Llano and whose wealthy parents lived in Abancay, wrote *El coloquio de la navidad del Señor* (1747) the year she was made Abbess of the Franciscan Convent in Cajamarca. Only the titles of her other plays are preserved.

[32] Irving A. Leonard, *Pedro de Peralta y Barnuevo, obras dramáticas*; José de Riva Aguero, "Algunos datos sobre la biografía de don Pedro de Peralta y Barnuevo," *Revista de la Universidad Católica del Perú*, VI (1938), 241–285; Arrom, *El teatro de Hispanoamérica*, pp. 142–151.

From the Church also came Félix de Alarcón, a priest of Lima who composed *loas* for various plays and occasions. One was written in 1744, and another served in the February, 1748, celebrations of the coronation of Ferdinand VI to introduce a performance of Calderón's *Ni Amor se libra de Amor.*[33] Some of its characters are Fame, Homer, Diana, and Aeneas. More realistic and foreshadowing the national theatre is a short play by Padre Alarcón introducing a couple of Indians talking their usual bad Spanish. After it was published in Lima in 1759 the Inquisition ordered it destroyed.

The dramatist Fray Francisco del Castillo (1716–1770) figures in the *tradición*, *El Ciego de la Merced* by Ricardo Palma. Born in Lima, and nearly blind from childhood, he took holy orders in 1743 and for the rest of his life taught Latin and philosophy to the Mercedarian friars. Some of his plays still survive in manuscript. While *Mitridates, rey de Ponto* is dull and loquacious, *El entremés del justica y litigantes* is a short, amusing slice of life such as Quiñones de Benavente or Ramón de la Cruz of Spain might have produced.[34] In it a judge, trying to save the life of a man unjustly condemned to hanging, is interrupted by complaining clients. The dialog is natural and sprightly and the characters are more real than in some of Castillo's longer plays, like *La conquista del Perú*, in which the people in spite of their Indian names act like characters from Golden Age plays.

After 1750 life in Peru, as elsewhere in the New World, increased in tempo. Economically things were better. The Spanish Crown had begun to treat its rich colony more like a partner and less like something to be exploited. The colonists, however, were taking advantage of this new attitude. Rebellion was on the increase in America. The Indians rose in protest in 1750, and later, in Cuzco in 1780, Túpac Amarú II led a nationalistic movement.

With money more plentiful, sons of wealthy families could go for their education to Europe, while Europeans came more frequently to America's shores. And with developing culture, the drama benefited. Lima's theatre, the Royal Coliseum, had been destroyed by the earthquake of October, 1746, that practically wiped out the city, including

---

[33] Reprinted in Lohmann, *El arte dramático*, pp. 560–590. See also Vargas, *Nuestro antiguo teatro*, pp. 256–261.

[34] Vargas, *Nuestro antiguo teatro*, pp. 262–275. See also Vargas, *Vida y obras de Fray Francisco del Castillo Andraca y Tamayo*; and Trenti Rocamora, *El repertorio*, pp. 60–61.

nearly ten thousand citizens. But Pablo de Olavide was given the job of rebuilding the theatre with unclaimed material from the catastrophe, and when it opened in 1749 it was the first real theatre Lima had ever had. And this was the setting for La Perricholi, Peru's most romantic actress, Micaela Villegas (1748–1819), whose story is told in Chapter 12 with those of other great Latin American stage figures.

After her protector returned to Spain, she married a fellow actor and they leased the Royal Coliseum, where they performed chiefly works from Spain.[35] However, in 1791, according to *El Diario de Lima*, which rarely bothered to mention the names of authors, La Perricholi did appear in locally written plays: on June 23 in *La perla del sacramento y preciosa Margarita*, attributed by Barrera to *un anómino ingenio americano*; on June 24 in *Trajes y gastos de Lima*; and on July 10 in *El pardo de mejor amo y donado más dichoso, el beato Martín de Porras*.

While the transplanted plays of Spain were entertaining the populace of Lima, another play, already discussed, was being performed about 1780 in the small town of Sicuani, near Cuzco. This was *Ollantay* generally supposed to be the work of Padre Antonio Valdés, priest of Tinta. On the charge that it and other plays in the Indian languages were stirring the Indians to revolt, Visitador Areche forbade any further performances in native languages. This order largely ended the native Peruvian theatre for a long time, though occasionally in the next century dramatists used Indian themes past and present.

Some authors who might be mentioned include Manuel H. del Río (1805–1883), an Ancash writer of *auto sacramentales*; José Ramírez Jacome, also of Ancash, whose *El indio presidario* is a tragedy; Carlos Augusto Salaverry, with nearly thirty plays, from *Atahualpa* to *Ladrones*; Manuel E. Vega with *Huarac Coyllur*; Carlos H. Valenzuela Guardia with the opera *Yahuar-Yahuar* (1933) and the drama *Inti-Yahuar*; and "Gabriel Delande" (Octavio Hinostroza Figueroa), who besides movies and radio plays wrote *Los caballeros de poncho de vicuña*. One of the most active Indian dramatists of recent times is José Salvador Cavero (1914–   ), author of a number of plays in Quechua, such as *Yana payup* (1938). Juan Ríos has also won national prizes for Indian plays.

[35] Leonard, "El teatro en Lima, 1790–1793," *Revue Hispanique*, VIII (1940), 93–112.

Spanish plays continued popular. Professor Leonard, searching the pages of *Diario* . . . *de Lima,* found mention of many plays between 1790 and 1793, especially by Moreto and Calderón, and some from the contemporary Madrid stages. In their struggle for independence Peruvians then cut themselves off from anything Spanish, without having time to write any serious dramas of their own. However, some patriotic effusions have been preserved, like *Los patriotas de Lima en la noche feliz,* by the anonymous "M. C.," identified as Miguel del Carpio. Its description of the triumphant entry of San Martín into the capital and the fact that there is no mention in it of Bolívar, dates it as around 1821–1823.

This is only one of many plays in existence to refute the common statement that *Frutos de la educación* (1830) by Felipe Pardo y Aliaga was the first theatrical work written in an independent Peru.[36] Dr. Ugarte has found half a dozen—most of them without great merit. They include a performance on October 11, 1827, of the five-act, classical *La Antígona* by José Faustino Sánchez Carrión and a one-act dramatization of the jealousy murder of an Ecuadorian actress by her sweetheart in 1813, *La muerte de la Moreno por zelos de Cebada* (performed November 13, 1827). Ugarte attributes it to Manuel de Santiago Concha. Just before Christmas of 1829 the comic actor José María Rodríquez had a benefit performance of a three-act comedy, *La caridad siempre triunfa aunque el odio se la oponga* "por un hijo del País." After its resounding failure Felipe Pardo's enemies attributed it to him, but he took in the newspapers to declare that he "did not have the misfortune of having written such a monstrosity." He did, however, translate anonymously a five-act Portuguese play, *Inés de Castro,* performed in June, 1830; the presentation was eulogized by a newspaper critic as "the first time we have seen in our theatres a play well performed by all its actors."

There were a number of other European successes translated. Finally, on July 10, 1830, the curtain rose on *Cora o La Virgen del Sol,* whose American scene was emphasized in the advertising, and then on August 6, 1830, came what was certainly the best play of the ten years since Peru had become independent, *Frutos de la educación* by Pardo. In the next seventy-five years, Moncloa estimates, four hun-

[36] See Guillermo Ugarte Chamorro, "Piezas teatrales del Perú que procedieron a *Frutos de la educación," Estudios de Teatro Peruano,* Serie VI, No. 38 (1958).

dred plays by 120 Peruvian authors were performed in the capital.[37]

Felipe Pardo y Aliaga (1806–1868) was born in Peru, but when the patriots drove his father out of Cuzco, where he had been regent of the Royal Audience, young Felipe was taken at the age of eight to Spain for his education. There he studied with the teacher who also instructed Espronceda and Ventura de la Vega. After the feeling against Spaniards had died down, Felipe came back to Peru in 1828, with an ambition to become a literary man. In Spain he had seen the theatre used as a school for manners, and so he wrote *Frutos de la educación* (1830) that ridicules Bernardito who tries to impose a husband upon his daughter. The high point of the satire is a *zama-cueca*, danced with such abandon that the girl discourages her suitor.

Next this monarchist and campaigner against bad taste attacked people who scorned Spanish customs, in *Huérfana en Chorrillos* (1833). Don Quintín, a dandy who apes French customs, intends by any means to make an heiress his wife. At the seaside resort he would have kidnaped her, except for the opportune arrival of her two aunts, bulwarks of morality, and so the dramatist warns against the consequences of a dissipated life.

Don Leocadio o El aniversario de Ayacucho (1834) is Pardo's last play. It blends the severity of the European classicist with the grace and wit better revealed by his essays and poetry, to which he turned in disgust with the difficulties of a playwright's life. Still, his three plays do serve to recall the customs of his period and, at least in his psychology, he was greater than the more popular national dramatist who succeeded him.[38]

Manuel Ascensio Segura (1805–1871) was the great *costumbrista* of the early days of Peru as a republic. He had had experience in soldiering: as a boy he fought under his father's command at the Battle of Ayacucho (1824), and after Peru became independent he joined the national army during the troubled days when Chileans overran Peru trying to keep the Bolivian Santa Cruz from reviving the Inca empire. Disgruntled, like the rest of his countrymen, about 1833 he wrote the three-act "La Pepa," containing such violent attacks against soldiers that it was never published or performed. Less bitter and more humorous was Segura's first success, the one-act *Sargento Ca-*

---

[37] Moncloa, *El teatro en Lima.*

[38] For a comparison between the two, see Luis F. Xammar, "El teatro: la voz," *Boletín*, No. 11 (December, 1945), 201–204.

nuto (1839), also in verse, poking fun at the many boasting soldiers spawned by the wars in Peru and not forgetting the bullfight fans, who were equally uncontrolled. For good measure he warned against the futility of parents who try to arrange their daughters' marriages.

Next among the seventeen plays by this "grandfather of the Peruvian drama," whose name is immortalized in the Teatro Segura of Lima, was a three-act comedy of customs, *La saya y manto* (1842), which took its title from the billowy skirt and the shawl worn by such veiled Lima ladies as the Widow Rosa. With none of Pardo's straining for morals, it tells of fickle Mariano who courts the widow.

In this play, through the mouth of Don Juan, and also in a letter to the newspaper *El Comercio*, October 23, 1855, Segura expresses his purpose in writing, "The dramatist," he says, "ama a su patria y procura su ilustración y recreo," and also "se dedica . . . a corregir las costumbres, los abusos, los excesos," and, again, his plays have "el exclusivo objeto de corregir nuestros vicios y ensalzar nuestros talentos." Segura was too much the artist to overstress the censure and forget the drama, but in *La saya y manto* he does criticize faults in government administrations. And in *La moza mala* (1855), in which the chief crime of the *moza* is flirting through the grating in defiance of her father's orders, he holds up to scorn older people who don't act their age.

In *Ña Catita* (1856), originally three acts but revised into four and subtitled "A Peruvian Celestina," he shows the harm done when outsiders interfere with family life. Juliana wants to marry Manuel and has her father's backing, but the mother favors Alejo because he talks French. The old shrew Catita will side with the one from whom she can expect the most money, and it is her active conniving that complicates the action. *Ña Catita* is considered so typically Peruvian that for a century it has been the most performed and most applauded of all Peruvian drama.

Another, less known, but well developed and a storehouse of proverbs, is Segura's *Un juguete* (1858). Then came his final play, *Las tres viudas* (1862), technically better than *Ña Catita*, but was not published till 1924. Its versification is the most polished, and its psychology shows a new side to a developing artist. While Segura has mild censure for the immoral suitor, Pablo, he shows himself a more genial observer of the Peruvian scene than was the more critical Pardo, and although careless in his versification, his fresh imagination helped him to dominate the stage of Peru for thirty years. His death plunged his country into theatrical doldrums.

The way back was indicated by another *costumbrista*, the romanticist Pedro Paz Soldán y Unanue (1839–1895)[39] whose pen name was "Juan de Arona," but who was called "El Caballero de la Inteligencia." He traveled in Europe, translated Plautus, and wrote the first of his three plays, *El intransigente castigado* (published 1867) when he was only eighteen. It is a two-act comedy in verse.

Shorter but livelier was his one-act *Más, menos, y ni más ni menos* (1871). Taking place in a Lima boardinghouse, this *juguete* follows the courtship of Aurora by fat Pancho and skinny Canuto. She turns them both down and chooses her cousin, who is neither "more nor less."

Though set in Spain, Paz Soldán's final one-act play *Pasada pesada en posada* (1883) presents the Peruvian Ernesto as he falls in love with a married servant, Pilarica. This dramatist's final attempt, the allegory *Los hombres inmortales de la patria* (1890), had best be forgotten. In it, Glory gets Bolívar and San Martín out of their graves to discuss tyranny and peace!

In these Dark Ages of the Peruvian theatre, several women tried playwriting. Carolina Freyre de Jaimes (1844–1916), wife of the Bolivian dramatist Julio Lucas Jaimes ("Brocha gorda"), and mother of the outstanding modernist poet Ricardo Jaimes Freyre, dipped into the history of her native country for a couple of poetic tragedies about women: *María de Vellido* (Tacna, 1878) and *Blanca de Silva* (1879). Clorinda Matto de Turner (1854–1909), best known as author of the sociological Indian novel *Aves sin nido* (1889), wrote a three-act, prose, Inca drama, *Hima Súmac* (published 1892); performed in Arequipa in 1884) and *Pizarro*.

Among other minor dramatists, Manuel Moncloa y Covarrubias (1859–1911), better known as the historian of Peru's theatres, turned out a half-dozen comedies and a drama, *El Nudo* (1883). Even the poet José Santos Chocano (1876–1919) wrote prose dramas: *Vendimiario* (1900) and *El hombre sin mundo* (1903), as well as *Los Conquistadores* (1906) in verse.

In the latter half of the nineteenth century came the works of the more important Acisclo Villarán (1841–1927): *El cura de Locumba*

(1884), *El guerrero del siglo* (1884), *La caja fiscal* (1886), and *Moral, virtud y urbanidad.* In *Cora* he treated of a popular Inca theme. At the turn of the century came a few desultory plays like the shocking *Ronda de los Muertos* (1901), frank and grandiloquent with overtones of Ibsen and Echegaray, by the novelist and newspaperman Manuel Bedoya (1855–1921). His *Los conspiradores* was written later.

The Escuela Nacional de Arte Escénico thought the works of one author of this period worthy of preserving and has reissued two plays by Carlos Germán Amezaga (1862–1906).[40] From his eight plays it has rescued two dramas: *El juez del crimen* (1900) and *Sofía Perowskaia* (1901). Most of his pieces are short. The one-act *Vamos a Lima* deals with the War of the Pacific. The popular *Esquina de mercaderes* and *El practicante Colirio,* written for performance in the house of the novelist Matto de Turner, are his attempts at zarzuela. The one-act *Juez del crimen,* with its melodramatic final curtain, tells of a man's discovery of his mother's adultery. Sofía, in the three-act drama, *Sofía Perowskaia,* was an actress in St. Petersburg involved in spying and conspiracy. Antonio Vico, who first performed it in Lima, also played it fourteen times in Havana. Spanish critics like Fastenrath and Unamuno were enthusiastic over Amezaga's work. Some harsh newspaper criticism of his final play, *El suplicio de Antequera* (1902), a four-act historical tragedy in verse about Peru's colonial period, so roused the public that a flood of letters came to the defense of the man who had worked so industriously for the advance of Peru's theatre.

Carlos J. Barandarian courted both readers and playgoers in 1905 with his three-act drama in prose, *El doctor Jesús,* but without success. The dramatist who would probably have occupied the highest position among Peruvian dramatists of his time, if he had stayed at home and written about national themes, was Felipe Sassone (1884–   ), of Italian parentage. Discouraged by the theatrical situation in his country, he went to Spain as an operatic tenor and bullfighter. Returning in Madrid to the theatre, he set practically all his plays there and most of their premières there, with María Palay as interpreter. Besides being indebted for technique to D'Annunzio, they

---

[40] Guillermo Ugarte Chamorro, "Amezaga, autor teatral peruano," *Estudios de Teatro Peruano,* Serie VI, No. 35 (1957).

are marked by Benavente-like plots along with the melodramatic solutions of an Echegaray.

Sassone's masterpiece, *Lo que se llevan las horas* (1916), set in Madrid, deals with an Argentine couple, about to return home. The wife is in love with the husband's friend. *El miedo de los infelices* (1913), was first performed in Argentina, a year before its Madrid showing. It did not reach Lima till 1923. *La muñeca de amor* (1914) came next. Sorrow is the protagonist of his *¡Calle, corazón!* (1923), a five-act comedy in prose that shows his control over characters and action, as does his otherwise unimportant *Campo travieso.*

The arrival in Lima of the Spanish troupe of Paco Arias and Consuelo Abad in 1916, with their offer to present a few plays by local writers, gave new impetus to drama. "Julio de la Paz" (1888–1925— his full name was Julio de la Paz Baudouin but he never used the last part) had a chance to see his *El condor pasa* written in 1912, with music by Daniel Alomía Robles. Its colloquial language and authentic Inca tunes made it Peru's most frequently performed national play for a generation. He also collaborated with José Carlos Mariátegui (1891–1930) in a zarzuela, *Las tapadas* (1916), set in the time of the viceroys. Its first performance, in Teatro Colón, Lima, was a great disappointment. Equally unsuccessful was another musical, the brief *Los niños faites* (1918), involving police, garbage collectors, and sevrant girls. Discouraged, this newspaper reporter moved to Buenos Aires.

Later Mariátegui also collaborated with the novelist Abraham Valdelomar (1888–1919) in the poetic *La mariscala,* about that legendary figure of 1830, Francisca Subiaga de Gomarra, who was also the inspiration of an opera by that same title in 1942, the work of César A. Miró Quesada.

There was also a revival in 1921 of *La voz del corazón* (1897) by Juan de Dios Benavides, to celebrate the centenary of Peruvian independence. José Gálvez (1885–1957) produced *Cuento de antaño.* Antonio Garland (1891–1958) and Sebastián Bondy (1924–   ) collaborated to put *La Perricholi* onto the stage. A college professor of Cuzco, Alfredo Yépez Miranda, using the pen name "Angel Carreño," dramatized a 1674 legend as *El rapto de Olavita* (1937), in which the Marqués de Vista Florida seeks a husband for his daughter Magdalena. The message is that talent, not blood, is the mark of real nobility.

Wars, too, have served as inspiration for Peruvian plays. Enrique L. Vega started his dramatic career with the two-act tragedy, *El héroe de Huamachuco* (1914), about Chilean atrocities in 1883. "El Tunante" (Abelardo M. Gamarra, 1850–1924), wrote *Ya vienen los chilenos* (1886) and then the more serious and poetic *Ña Codeo* (1887), in three acts. Even the 1941 War with Ecuador inspired *José Quiñones* (Chiclayo, 1941) by Sergio Bermejo.

As the twentieth century continued, the quality of the drama improved. Ladislao F. Meza (1892–1925), called "The Last Romanticist," experimented with a number of styles. *El demonio llega* (1923), set in the interior of Peru, had a run of several weeks at Teatro Colón. Then, under the influence of Ibsen, Meza turned naturalist, and his treatment of social themes makes him the Peruvian most like Florencio Sánchez. *La ciudad misteriosa* shows the problems of Lima's slums through the eyes of a man from the country, while *El tablado de los miserables* portrays more slum life. The manuscript of Meza's *La feria de los arlequinos*, about Lima newspaper life, no longer exists. When some of the first-night audience walked out of the theatre, the author tore up the prompt copy. *La miseria del triunfador* and *La isla de los perros* are other naturalistic plays by this dramatist, whose turbulent life was as dramatic as his writings.

Humberto del Aguila (1898–), newspaper editor, economist, politician, and diplomat won the Ayacucho Centennial prize with his *Camino de luz* (1924), his best play (called *Sendero de luz* when performed by Villaespesa's Spanish company), and won La Cultura Peruana prize with *La irrompible cadena*. He began playwriting with *La dama blanca* (1923), about love and crime in the jungle. Also by him are *Las abandonadas, El gran cardenal,* and the cynical *Triunfadores* (1924).

José Chioino (1898–), one of the important names in the Peruvian theatre, and a leader in the esthetic rebellion of 1915, made his first bid for recognition with *Retorno* (1923), about the rights of a genius in a society, which showed he had read Bernard Shaw. His first success was the three-act comedy *La divina canción* (1923; published 1935), sometimes called *El provinciano*. Every man has in his heart a sad memory, his "Divine Song," is its theme. Since then he has written twelve plays. *Una vez en la vida* (1927) has, perhaps, been the play most frequently performed. He is a *costumbrista* of the whole of Peru. The three-act high comedy *Novio de emergencia* (1928) which has had performances in Lima and Chile, takes place in a small town, while one-act *Relato de medianoche* (1940) is set in the Amazonian jungles. The management of Teatro Segura brought two Argentine actors to help Elvira Flores introduce his three-act high comedy *La propia comedia* (1947). María Guerrero was contracted for *Tabú,* the winner of the 1950 Municipality of Lima award. Chioino is president of the Círculo Peruano de Autores, which is to publish his *La propia comedia,* along with *La dama blanca* by Del Aguila.

To this period also belongs "el genio insuperable," Leónidas Yerovi (1881–1917).[41] His first one-act play in verse, *La de cuatro mil* (1903) was a huge success. Its plot deals with the result of an error in listing the winning lottery tickets. It also shows the author's sympathy with the poor. Two years later, Yerovi's *Tarjetas postales* (1905) was another smash hit, but it earned him no money; so not till 1913 did he finish his third play, *Salsa roja.* He took it to the more active theatrical center of Buenos Aires. There Orfilia Rico performed both it and his best comedy of manners, *La gente loca* (1914), in two acts.

Now that he had the advantage of comments by drama critics, he reduced the number of characters in his next play, *Domingo 7*—about superstitions—and went on to write *Album Lima* and *La pícara suerte.* Changing his technique, he had just completed his masterpiece, *La casa de tantos* (1917), more serious and with a sympathy for human frailties and an understanding of the essential anarchy of the Spanish spirit, when he was assassinated. The play was not performed till after his death. It now seems to be lost. One manuscript copy burned in the Lima library conflagration of 1943, and even his son has none. His death left few practicing dramatists in Peru, and for several decades the theatre was lethargic. A few unimportant plays were printed, but neither professional nor amateur groups existed in the nation.

Through the efforts of Corina Garland and the sisters of Alejandro Miró Quesada and Percy Gibson Parra in 1938, there came into being a group called Asociación de Artistas Aficionados, which gave im-

[41] Luis Fabio Xammar, *Valores humanos en la obra de Leónidas Yerovi*; Xammar, "El teatro: el eco," *Boletín,* No. 11 (December, 1945), 198–204; Federico More, *Gregorio Reynolds y Leónidas Yerovi.*

petus to all phases of Peruvian culture. Guests at their Tuesday meetings included artists, musicians, and actors. It was a start. The A.A.A. performed a play a year. Finally it founded a school for actors and later a school of the ballet. Their performances, at first small functions, expanded till they finally occupied the Municipal Theatre. They chose at first from foreign plays and then from locally written manuscripts, beginning with a dramatization of Ricardo Palma's *tradición*, "The Viceroy's Ear," made by Bernardo Roca Rey (1918–), who was later to receive the first National Theatre award with his *Loys*, and then go on to another success, *La muerte de Atahualpa*. Incidentally, D. A. Centurión Cueva used the same title for his drama, published in Cajamarca in 1960. In spite of all their efforts, a visiting critic in 1944 found little trace of a national theatre in Peru.

It was to come, however. A National Theatrical Company with Edmundo Barbero and Santiago Ontañón was established. The government was moved to found La Escuela de Arte Escénico under the able direction of Peru's most active present-day student of the theatre, Dr. Guillermo Ugarte Chamorro. It began at once to produce plays and distribute mimeographed dramas and articles on national movements and figures.

The A.A.A. also continued active. It still is: in 1961, it performed Ionesco. Additional experimental groups took form: Harpegio, Histrión, La Farsa under Konrad Fischer, and even the Harlequinos at the YMCA. The University of San Marcos had its players, and later, through that splintering process so common among temperamental actors, a second University group emerged. Of all the new groups, the most important was El Club de Teatro, founded by Salazar Bondy in 1953, with the Argentine Reynaldo D'Amore (1923–) as director. Its theatre is only a small place in the cellar of a moviehouse, but it has been producing a half-dozen plays a year, foreign and local, and has started printing some of its successes. Less socially prominent, perhaps, than A.A.A., it is much more active.

This was the time that Peru seemed headed for a theatrical renaissance. In 1951 the fourth centenary of the University of San Marcos was celebrated by an open-air performance of Calderón's *El gran teatro de mundo* in the Plaza de Armas.

Manuscript competitions were established by the government and the winning plays were performed. El Círculo de Autores Peruanos, under its president José Chioino, turned its efforts toward encouraging the theatre. An open-air performance of Segura's *Lances de Amancaes* was successful. In 1954 the Escuela Nacional was responsible for 156 performances of nineteen plays, some written by Peruvians, before more than fifty thousand spectators.

With such encouragement came a new group of dramatists. Antonio Garland (1891–1958), whose one-act comedy *El regalo* had been well received in 1911, adapted a French work to bring *La Perricholi* onto the stage. Ciro Alegría (1909–), better known as a novelist, dramatized the tragedy of the rubber collectors in *La selva*, produced in 1953 by the Talía group.

Juan Ríos (1914–) won a prize in 1946 with *Don Quijote*, a rearrangement of some episodes of the novel to provide unity around the knight's search for Dulcinea, i.e., an ideal. Ríos has been one of the most active and promising of the new generation, having won four drama prizes. His classical *Medea* (1950) was well received. His tragedy *Ayar Manko*, a prize winner of 1952, was the success of the 1954 season, as *The Brothers Ayar*. *Argos* (1954) was also well received.

In 1961 Ríos gathered them into a single volume, including *Los mirmidones*; the grotesque puppet play *Los bufones* inspired by Velásquez; *La selva*, authentically New World; and the escapist *El reino sobre las tumbas* (1949), in poetry, about magic and the Priest Nemi and set in ancient times, as is most of Ríos' drama. Prometheus and Christ mingle in *El fuego*, as a prostitute, the new Magdalene, brings to the idealist revolutionary the presents obtained by his betrayal. There is a song-like quality, as Augusto Tamayo Vargas declares, about these plays that use human myths to sum up human emotions and ideals.[42] Ríos has become an outstanding figure in Peruvian drama.

Another prize-winning play of 1946, published with Ríos' *Don Quijote* in Miró Quesada's *Teatro Peruano Contemporáneo* (Lima, 1948), was *Esa luna que empieza* by Percy Gibson Parra. In its fantasy it combines prose and poetry with two plots involving birth, love, and death, though nothing is resolved, since Alba's husband goes to sea and Aura's Dionisio goes to the city to learn to improve the condition of people. Nor is it Peruvian. Its setting is *una playa cualquiera*.

---

[42] Augusto Tamayo Vargas, "Peruvian Literature in 1961," *Books Abroad*, 36 (1962), 269.

Judith (1948), a prize winner by Raúl Deustua (1920–   ) is another example of a universal rather than national theatre, but *Collacocha*, the success of the 1956 season, the work of Enrique Solari Swayne, deals with a domineering engineer in the Andes and his struggle against the Selva. It marked an important point in Peru's theatrical progress.

Of the current writers, the most successful is the newspaper writer and drama critic Sebastián Salazar Bondy (1924–   ), author of eleven plays already produced. After publishing three volumes of verse, he won a national prize with his first drama manuscript, the classical comedy, *Amor gran laberinto* (1947), whose very title is reminiscent of Sor Juana's *Amor es más laberinto*. After *Como vienen se van* (1949) he had a hit in *Rodil* (1952), an existentialist drama about the general who defended Callao in 1824–1826, and his mistress. The same year he wrote the one-act *El de la valija*. *No hay isla feliz* (1954), in three acts, is the tragedy of a man and a town that hope for a highway to Lima. It is an appeal for "togetherness" and a criticism of Peruvian society in beautiful literary language such as Arthur Miller might have employed. Indeed Salazar Bondy has a certain affinity with the North American social theatre. And yet he has another and pessimistic side, revealed in *Rodil*. The two phases combine in his *Algo quiere morir* (1956), an interpretation of Peruvian reality that goes beyond mere regionalism. Universality is apparent in its story of modern children and the unhappiness they cause. The first performance was by the Club de Teatro de Lima, which Salazar Bondy founded in 1953. *Algo quiere morir* shows him a master of dramatic technique. In his later *Flora Tristán*, we find more anguish and doubts, set in a historical framework. In 1961, as though marking the end of an epoch, Salazar Bondy had them all published in Buenos Aires in his *Teatro*. However he is still young and enthusiastic, and Peru's theatre can expect much of him.

The theatre in Peru has its ups and downs. Following recent political changes in the nation, cultural activity stopped till a new bureaucracy could be set up. La Escuela Nacional de Arte Escénico became El Instituto Nacional de Arte Escénico. Dr. Ugarte was replaced by Mario Rivera, who had to start afresh to generate enthusiasm. An old nightclub, La Cabaña, was remodeled as the new center, with a new theatre that began operation in 1960. In 1961 Ugarte was returned to control. At once all was activity. The Teatro Universitario de San Marcos came into being, with a program of foreign plays presented and read. Play contests were inaugurated. Groups of amateurs from the University took plays for performance before factory audiences, schools, and clubs. A stream of mimeographed studies and plays again began coming from the University for theatre lovers.

One of the groups, Histrión, planned a performance for 1961 of Osvaldo Dragún's *Túpac Amarú,* and invited its Argentine author to head a discussion on the use of modern methods of dramatic composition for ancient themes. The Compañía Nacional de Comedia also made 1961 noteworthy by a series of performances of not only European works but local productions, like the prize-winning national melodrama *La casa de los Siles* by Humberto Napurí (which left much to be desired in both subject and treatment) and Felipe Buendía's superior *Las nuevas galas del emperador.* Sarina Helfgott, a newcomer, was introduced through her *Entrar y salir por el espejo.*

Certainly Peru has all the ingredients for great drama, but the handicap of the lack of any real theatre—the ancient Segura was condemned and only recently restored, the Municipal is suited only for opera, and the theatres of the A.A.A. and the Club de Teatro hold less than two hundred people—challenges the enthusiasm of even the young playwrights who are doing their best for the advance of drama in Peru.

CHAPTER 17

Bolivian Drama

Obviously the Spanish province of Charcas could not have had a national theatre till it became the República Bolívar, as it did in 1825, after sixteen years of fighting (the Republic was renamed Bolivia on August 18, 1825). Nor could there have been dramatic activity in its capital, Sucre, until the three hundred-year-old town of Chuquisaca had been renamed Sucre to honor the victorious general of the battle of Ayacucho. Though there had long been centers of learning in the Andes (a university was founded in La Paz in 1583 and the University of Chuquisaca opened its doors in Sucre in 1624), the records indicate practically no theatrical performances spilling into them from Lima, from where the whole region had been distantly governed.

An exception in theatrical activity was the silver city of Potosí. After its founding in 1540, seven thousand mines tapped the *cerro* of silver, and 150,000 people flocked in to share its riches. Accounts tell of Doña Clara, the reigning belle, paying $15,000 for a jeweled dress and $500 for embroidered slippers. When the thirty gambling houses could not provide sufficient entertainment for the wealthy miners, theatres opened, with tickets going at $50 apiece. Nothing is known about the actors or their plays. Probably neither were of high caliber. After all, this was seventeen years before the birth of Lope de Vega, and even Spain's drama was meager. If the unknown playwrights of Potosí provided the type of lusty plays popular in later mining communities, it is easy to understand why the Viceroy Antonio de Mendoza agreed with the Council of 1552 and for the preservation of morality put an end to all except religious plays.

However, some theatrical activity persisted. There is a lone and indefinite reference to four companies of actors existing in Bolivia at some time in the seventeenth century, presenting plays on Sundays and holidays. The sale of tickets "brought $3,000 to $4,000, not count-

ing the rich income for the Royal Hospital from the more comfortable seats, since a box for a family cost $4 to $5."[1]

Details about one such Sunday performance were discovered by
Raúl Moglia in an 1899 edition by E. Rasco in Sevilla of *Relación de
la grandiosa fiesta que el señor gobernador D. Luis de Andrade y
Sotomayor, alcalde ordinario de la imperial villa de Potosí, hizo a la
renovación del Santísimo Sacramento a 4 de Marzo de 1663.*[2] It describes in verse a garden set up in the Potosí plaza, "with as many
wild animals as Noah had," including lions, tigers, monkeys, birds,
etc. In addition there were puppets "en el Muro de un castillo, muy
embanderado, y cañas que manaban vino, chicha, y agua a un tiempo." The beautifully decorated church is described, and after the
Solemn Mass and the sermon, according to the anonymous poet:

> Tres niños bizarros
> una loa echaron luego
> con mil donaires y gracias,
> quedando el pueblo suspenso.

Early in the next century there was a temporary theatre in the
Calle de Mercado, La Paz. Perhaps that was the scene of the performance of a *loa* discovered by Arrom which bore the date "1786"
and the signature of Pedro Nolasco Crespo.[3]

Ten years later another theatre was built with the sanction of the
cabildo, "to point vice, correct corrupt customs and abuses, and end
nocturnal crimes, through the good example of the entertainment."[4]

In 1837 Marshal Santa Cruz ordered the construction of another
playhouse better suited to a new country, and donated for that purpose his own house beside the presidential mansion. Work was delayed for seven years, but the theatre was finally completed and was
inaugurated on November 18, 1845.

In Chuquisaca, the only theatre found by General Sucre when he
visited there in 1827 was an improvised stage in a large room belonging to the Convent of San Francisco. It was made to serve till 1841,
when the unused Convent of San Agustín was taken over. The Con-

[1] Vicente de Ballivián y Rojas, *Archivo boliviano, colección de documentos
relativos a la historia de Bolivia.*

[2] See Raúl Moglia, "Relación de la grandiosa fiesta y representación escénica
en Potosí en 1663," *Revista de Filología Hispánica*, V (1943), 166–167.

[3] José Juan Arrom, *El teatro de Hispanoamérica en la época colonial*, p. 205 n.

[4] *Ibid.*, p. 189.

vent was the scene of the celebration of the Victory of Ingavi that year and remained in use till 1896, when the Third of February Coliseum was built and the Convent restored to its original purpose.

Any complete study of the Bolivian theatre, even since it became a nation, is difficult. The investigator finds little preserved material. The National Library in La Paz has such a small collection of national drama that during a rearrangement of shelving, its volumes were misplaced and all were lost. The list of plays in the collection in the University of La Paz covers only one page in its copy-book catalog. From private collections and other sources[5] some information can be assembled and a list of dramatists compiled, but the result can be hardly more than a catalog. Díaz de Medina says that Bolivia has no real dramatist with technical skill and an impressive number of plays. This is not, of course, literally true.

Says José Macedonio Urquidi: "In Bolivia the development of the theatre preceded that of the novel."[6] The first play performed in independent Bolivia seems to have been the work of a professor in Cochabamba, Mariano Méndez, whose students at the Colegio de Huérfanos performed his four-act satirical comedy *Aviso a las solteras* in 1834. It was published that same year by the College of Arts in La Paz de Ayacucho. There is little noteworthy about its thirty-one pages except its priority.

Blanco Encalada Ventura (1782–1857) added an entry to early Bolivian drama with *La Marquesa de Senneterre*, though it hardly classifies as a completely national comedy, since it was published in the *Galería dramática nacional* in Santiago de Chile, in 1846.

And so the first real Bolivian dialog is generally considered to be *El plan de una representación* (1857), a satirical discussion by students arranging for a play about politicians, office seekers, misers, cowards, etc. It was written by Professor Félix Reyes Ortiz (1828–1882), under the pen name of "Fray Tirso." It served as prolog to an evening of dramatic entertainment by the students for Dictator José

[5] Santiago Vaca Guzmán, *La literatura boliviana*; Joaquín Gantier, *El teatro en sucre*; Angel Salas, "La literatura dramática en Bolivia," *Bolivia en el primer centenario de su independencia*; Enrique Finot, *Historia de la literatura boliviana*, Part II, Chapter III, and Part III, Chapter IV; Fernando Díaz de Medina, *La literatura boliviana*; Willis K. Jones, *Breve historia del teatro latinoamericano*, pp. 111–114.

[6] José Macedonio Urquidi, "Panorama de Bolivia," *Panorama das Literaturas das Américas*, I, 43–101.

María Linares, who was so pleased with it that he had it printed by the Tipografía de Vapor that same year.

Afterward Reyes, inspired by Dumas, went on to write longer romantic plays, like his 1859 five-act drama *Odio y Amor* (published 1875). The passionate characters of Zuela and Violante conceal real citizens of Sucre. Reyes also wrote *Los Lanza* (1875; published 1885), a historical drama in three scenes, generally considered his best, about the twin guerrilla fighters for independence, Victorio and Gregorio García Lanza. Reyes was also author of a couple of comedies in verse: *Chismografía* (1876), a *sainete* of intrigue in one act, and *¡Qué progreso de muchachos!* (1877), which is critical of the audacity of youth. He wrote excellent satirical and elegiac poetry besides, and a minor novel, *El Templo y la Zafra* (1864). After a lifetime as journalist, lawyer, and politician, he died insane, in La Paz.

A contemporary of his was Benjamín Lenz (1836–1878), author of a half-dozen plays. Reyes had signed his first attempt "Fray Tirso." Lenz used the pen name "Lego de Fray Tirso" for his *Ensayo que sirvió de prólogo a la representación del drama "El templario"* (1858).

When *Don Manuel*, an "ópera bufo-seria en dos actos" by "Manuel Carrasco" was announced in June, 1859, the knowing ones ascribed it to Lenz. But immediately after its cold reception by critics and public, Lenz was quick to deny its authorship, and it was published anonymously in 1861. It is a plotless attack on the politician Manuel Hermenegildo Guerra for his crooked dealings, and was called "ópera" because of the choruses, which sometimes criticize and sometimes mockingly praise the protagonist.

However, after an interval Lenz did write and produce *El guante negro* (1872) about the Rosas period in Argentina, *La mejicana* (1876), *El hijo natural, Borrascas del Corazón,* and the drama *Amor, celos y venganza.*

These historical plays of Reyes Ortiz and Lenz started the flood of historical plays of the rest of the century. First to come was the important *Iturbide o Ambición y amor* (1862) by the lawyer-poet José Rosendo Gutiérrez (1840–1883). Then others appeared in print. The published ones numbered more than sixty in the next forty years, three times the quantity of the Bolivian novels that achieved print.[7]

Commenting on the overhelming number of imitations of Spanish

---

[7] Finot, *Historia de la literatura boliviana*, p. 178.

romantic plays based on local history, Enrique Finot quotes the opinion of José Eduardo Guerra that the Bolivian dramatists would have done better to attempt comedies of customs. No nation has an overabundance of dramatic historical episodes, but local color and social problems, of which it has plenty, would have interested and developed a public that might have put new life into the theatre.

One such was *Genaro* by Luis Pablo Rosquellos, Jr., with its duel between rivals, performed at the Teatro Nacional in Sucre, July 15, 1874; at least it has terse dialog. He later wrote *Lo que puede una carta.*

The sort of play advocated by Guerra was *La herencia de un loco* (1887) by Manuel María Gómez, in three acts and prose, dealing with the deceiving of lower-class women. Another Finot, Emilio, coming later, began with history and changed to *costumbrista* comedies. But that was in the twentieth century, after the decline of the theatre and the increase in the number of published Bolivian novels.

Among those who sought in early history for themes was José Pol Terrazas, whose five-act tragedy in prose, *Athawalpa* was performed only once, in the Achá Theatre in his home town of Cochabamba in 1869, and was published in 1887. In it the influences of Dumas, Hugo, and Zorrilla are evident. Even today critics find its technique excellent, the development full of suspense, and the secondary Indian and Spanish characters, in their rivalry for the love of Queen Cora, evidence of the dramatist's acquaintance with psychology.

Not as much can be said of a series of Inca and conquistador plays that it inspired. José David Berrios (1849–?) of Potosí was full of patriotism, but short in dramatic power, inept in character portrayal, and monotonous in the poetry of his *Huáscar y Atahuallpa* (1875) and *Atahuallpa y Pizarro* (1879). But he persisted in the use of verse as the only form befitting drama. Neither of these two plays by Berrios is as moving as Pol's drama in prose. Berrios also sought inspiration in later periods of his country's history for his 1871 *Alonso de Ibáñez o La primera centella de libertad* (published 1881); an allegory, *Apoteosis de Bolívar* (published 1894); and a one-act fantasy in verse, *Calama o La flor del desierto* (1881), whose action takes place during the War of the Pacific.

In the jungles of Santa Cruz, José Mariano Durán Canelas published dramatizations of local phases of the war for independence in *Warnes y Aguilera o La batalla del Pari* (1890) and *La cabeza de*

Warnes. While slightly falsifying history, he did reproduce the essential Bolivian spirit.

The greatest figure of Bolivian romanticism, however, was Ricardo José Bustamante (1821–1886). He was the first Bolivian honored by being made a corresponding member of the Royal Spanish Academy. After long residence in France, as well as in Argentina and Brazil, he expressed himself in novels, poetry, and drama in verse. Best known is his American three-act comedy in verse, *Más pudo el suelo que la sangre* (Sucre, 1869), in favor of environment over heredity. If the prefatory note: "Escrito en París en 1845" is true, it antedates the 1857 dialog by Reyes Ortiz.

Nataniel Aguirre (1843–1888), best known as the "father of the Bolivian novel," wrote good enough dramas to have one critic term him "the best—or the least bad—of his period." This native of Cochabamba began his drama career in Lima in 1865 with the three-act *Visionarios y mártires,* about Ubalde and Aguilar and Peru's war for independence. In 1869 came *Represalia de héroes,* written and published in Cochabamba but dealing with Nicolás Bravo and an episode in Mexico's struggle for independence. Though to modern tastes it seems heavy and oversentimental, it has been considered one of the five or six greatest works of the Bolivian theatre, and its author is classified as a romanticist of the Echegaray school of violence, with touches of Byron and Hugo. He went on to write *Condehuillo o La calle del pecado,* made into a movie in 1952, and the volume *La bellísima Floriana, Don Ego y otros* published in Paris, in 1911. More famous than any of his plays, however, was his excellent novel, *Juana de la Rosa* (Cochabamba, 1885), which inspired Bolivian novelists to tackle national themes. His son, José Aguirre Acha (1877–   ), wrote, among his other romantic products, the patriotic monolog *El deber patrio* (1905) about the immolation of Paredes, the hero of the Acre campaign of 1899–1902 against Brazil. His *La capital disputada* classifies as another of the half-dozen outstanding plays of Bolivia. It deals with the rivalry of La Paz and Sucre as capitals of Bolivia.

Among other historical dramatists is Claudio Pinilla (1859–   ), whose one-act *Murillo,* about the martyr of La Paz's revolt of 1809, had a number of successful performances. Emilio Finot (1886–1915) handled the same period in *La revolución de 1809 en Chuquisaca,* prize winner in a drama contest in Sucre during the Centenary of

Independence. Unfortunately he found nothing dramatic in the struggle for freedom, and the actors, members of a Spanish musical-comedy company, fitted their parts badly, so the performance was a failure. Better are some of Finot's other plays. *Ana Barba*, his first attempt, was a one-act drama published in Santa Cruz in 1911 and
dealing with the war for independence. The one-act *El falso brillo*
was a comedy, printed in Sucre in 1914. Finot wrote the three-act
drama "El cobarde" and the one-act "Las apariencias engañan" just
before his untimely death, and they were never published.

The most famous name among Bolivian dramatists is Ricardo
Jaimes Freyre (1868–1933), companion of Rubén Darío in the modernist movement. His father, Julio Lucas Jaimes (1843–1914), the
famous "Brocha gorda," had previously written a patriotic drama,
Morir por la patria (1882), and the comedy *Un hombre en apuros*
(1885). His mother, Carolina Freyre de Jaimes (1844–1916), is classified as a Peruvian dramatist because of her several excellent plays
about women: *María de Vellido, Blanca de Silva,* and *María de
Padilla,* published in 1879.

Their son, Ricardo, a medieval soul with a huge moustache, wrote
an elaborately plotted three-act colonial drama in verse, *Los Conquistadores* (Buenos Aires, 1928), about plots and villainy among
Spaniards surrounded by Indians. María Guerrero starred in it as
Catalina del Enciso. While the poetry weakens its dramatic appeal,
it is superior to his two-act prose treatment of a Bible theme in *La
hija de Jefthé* (La Paz, 1889), which tells of Jephtha's sacrifice of
his daughter to Jehovah.

If Ricardo Mujía (1861–1934) is remembered as a dramatist as
well as a poet and diplomat, it will be because of his lyrical drama
Bolívar en Junín, whose stirring portrayal of the founder of Bolivia
made it very popular at the end of the century. Mujía also published a two-volume *colección de ensayos dramáticos* (Sucre, 1880–
1882). His *El mundo que juzga* (1886), in three acts, is a drama of
some importance, and his two comedies, *El orden superior* and
Pepetes, were performed in Sucre at the beginning of the twentieth
century.

At the end of the century came Isaac G. Eduardo (1868–1910),
who wrote romantic novels and two plays. *Arbol que crece torcido*
(1892; published 1897) is a poetic comedy in two acts. *Contra el
destino* (1892; published 1900), in three acts, won a Municipal

Drama prize with its plot of a soldier supposed to have perished in the Battle of Tarapacá during the War of the Pacific. When the soldier, inevitably, turns up, his brother commits suicide so the soldier can marry his former sweetheart. Angel Salas ranks this play high among Bolivian dramas in prose.

Later, José Agustín Morales used the same battle situation in *El 79* (1917), but in 1924 tempers flared when the plot appeared again in the very successful *La hoguera*, and its author Antonio Díaz Villamil was accused of having plagiarized Eduardo. He was declared innocent in a jury trial.

Other patriotic plays include Francisco Molina's melodrama *Sangre boliviana* (1904) and the one-act *Patria libre* (1909) by Romualdo Romero, a Spanish actor living in Santa Cruz.

History of other countries also inspired some of Bolivia's dramatists. José Rosendo Gutiérrez (1840–1883), essayist, historian, and bibliographer, pictured the downfall of Mexico's emperor in 1809 as the result of liberal republican currents in the New World, and also wrote a three-act melodramatic tragedy, *Iturbide o Ambición y amor* (1862), which provides unusually good character portrayal. Its versification, too, is superior to that of most of its contemporaries, but Gutiérrez apparently quickly lost interest in the theatre, or was discouraged by the delay in the performance of his play, which did not take place till 1868, in La Paz; he spent the rest of his life compiling a bibliography of 2,200 works about his native land, and forgot the stage.

Later came Hermógenes Jofré (1841–1890) of Oruro, perhaps the best of Bolivia's nineteenth-century dramatists. His first work, a four-act tragedy, dealt with the Argentine Dictator: *Las víctimas o Los favoritos de Rosas* (1864). Also in four acts was *Los mártires*, published in Oruro in 1868, and called Bolivia's best play of the century. Though ostensibly set in Haiti, actually it dramatized the massacre of Bolivian political prisoners, among them ex-President Jorge Córdoba, in La Paz in 1861 by Colonel Plácido Yáñez. Beginning in the main plaza of Santo Domingo, it introduces the commander of the army, Mauro Tuerca (really Yáñez of Bolivia) who orders the execution of the spy Murcia, despite his mother's dramatic appeal, and of General Hernán (i.e., Cordoba), following a prearranged "uprising" to provide an excuse.

Jofré's mastery of technique can be seen by comparing his play with another using the same episode, written by Gabriel René Moreno (1836–1908). Though he spent the last fifty years of his life in Chile turning out history, bibliography, and criticism of poetry, Bolivia considers René Moreno one of its greatest writers. Jofré's version is superior in vividness, sentiment, and a dramatic sweep of progress.

Except for a half-dozen plays, Díaz de Medina's criticism[8] was just when he wrote in 1954 that most of the two hundred or more Bolivian plays of the nineteenth century, written in a patriotic attempt to restore the theatre, are weak and unfinished. Even those with good dramatic situations are faulty in resolution and in character development. Whether this was due to the romanticist tendency to rush into writing without mature thought, or to the playwrights' lack of opportunity to study their plays in production, the result was the same: a lack of outstanding Bolivian plays and playwrights. Unfortunately José Guerra was right: the list of playwrights tempted by history is far longer than those who were challenged by the dramatic possibilities of Bolivia's everyday life and social problems.

But there were a few social dramatists. Even before the twentieth century *El Wolfram* (1918), with which Alberto Saavedra first attracted attention, Pedro B. Calderón published his *Antonio de Montes*, three acts in verse. It was produced January, 1889, at the Potosí Teatro Municipal. Also, Jenaro Sanjinés (1844–1891) wrote *Progresos de Sucre, Una mujer mártir, Bruno el hilador, El príncipe desterrado,* and *Berruecos y el cadalso,* and turned a couple of plays by Ferrari into Spanish.

In spite of these efforts, the nineteenth century ended without the development in Bolivia of any dramatist with the quantity of plays and the technical skill to win recognition in the rest of the continent. The theatre in Europe, so influential in shaping the nation's early dramatists, had long before been transformed into a critic of customs and an exponent of ideas, but the change was not perceived by Bolivians until brought to their attention by Spain's modernist dramatists. The cult of beauty brought new life to Bolivia, as the writers realized that not only must they have something to say, but must

---

[8] Díaz de Medina, *La literatura boliviana*, pp. 224–243; Agustín del Saz, "El teatro hispanoamericano del siglo XIX," *Historia general de las literaturas hispánicas*, IV, II, 436–437.

labor to express it well. The example of Villaespesa inspired a number of poetic plays.

Gregorio Reynolds (1882–1948) for instance, who had status as an excellent poet, produced *Quimeras, poema escénico* (Oruro, 1915), in addition to a translation and adaptation in verse of Sophocles' *Oedipus Rex* (published 1924). A gift for self-criticism would have improved it, but the discouraging struggle to get a performance even when he himself played one of the roles, drove him back to philosophy and epic poetry.

The theatre of ideas proved tempting to some dramatists, but they saw it chiefly as a vehicle for preachment and propaganda, so that one critic complained that Bolivian literature is more *against* something than *for* anything. The public is attracted to a theatre for entertainment, not sermons; so in Bolivia they stayed away. Perhaps homilectitis was the trouble of Octavio Salamanca of Cochabamba. In 1941 he optimistically published *Dramas y comedias, tomo primero*, containing two temperance preachments, *Borrachín-Borrachona* and *Prisioneros*; a farce set in Tontonia; along with the three-act *Ahombradas*, a "drama de un traidor," against the vices of the younger generation. No *Tomo segundo* has ever appeared.

Perhaps, too, as some critics claim, Bolivia's dramatists did wrong in following Dicenta instead of Benavente, and Martínez Sierra instead of the Quinteros. A few Bolivians of the twentieth century were nudged into naturalism by Ibsen and Sudermann. Especially was this influence true with Enrique Baldivieso, whose *Lo que traemos al mundo* reflects Ibsen's *Ghosts*, and whose *Derecho de matar* is another social play that roused much controversy at its first performance. However in *Dios de la conquista* (1922) and *Hurpillay* he goes back to romanticism and Atahualpa.

Finally, a few dramatists in the twentieth century were tempted into symbolic drama by Rostand, Bernstein, and Bataille. One effort, by the poet Federico More (1889–   ), was *Interludio*, the only Bolivian play with an English translation.

However, some of the old currents persist. Most productive of all recent Bolivian dramatists is Alberto Saavedra Pérez (1895–   ), author of at least forty plays. He began his career with the patriotic three-act drama *Sangre y gloria* (1918), followed by *¡Santalla, nada!* (1919). A big year for him was 1922, when six of his plays were on the stage in La Paz, but he surpassed himself in 1923 when eight plays by him were performed in Buenos Aires in one week. His early social drama, *El Wolfram* (1918), has already been mentioned. Best of the rest of his output are *Por querer volar* (1920); the comedies *Los platos rotos* (1922), *La gloriosa* (1922), and *Las cholitas del amigo Uria* (1922), an excellent example of the *costumbrista* theatre that should be more often cultivated in this picturesque nation.

Costumbrismo has been attempted in Bolivia by only a few dramatists. Alfredo Santalla Estrella produced a mixed-up and dragged-out one-act farce, vaguely Bolivian, about a May-and-December love, *Los celos de D. Ubaldo o Militares . . . ni en pintura* (1929). It enjoyed a run of 104 performances in La Paz and 62 in Chile its first year. Then Santalla turned to contemporary history and dramatized the 1930 popular revolt against President Siles in his tragedy *Palabra de cadete*, which reached the stage four months after its military cadet hero had died among the rioting students. Its local vocabulary, especially in the speeches of the Indian servants, makes it incomprehensible to the average reader.

Some *costumbristas* have written whole plays in the Indian languages. Nestor Lizarazu wrote *Mañacu* in Quechua, the language of the Inca nobles. The essayist Zacarías Monje Ortiz was the author of two plays in the Aymará language of the common Indians of Bolivia. One was *Zupay Marca* ("City of Monsters"), as the Indians termed a big city of whites and mestizos among whom they were forced to live. Some critics term it Bolivia's first indigenous play. The other, *Natacha*, has white people as its chief characters. Monje Ortiz also wrote two comedies in Spanish: *Los nuevos pobres* and *Los hijos del viento.*

Other dramatists dealt with the Indians in plays in Spanish; *Tupaj Katari*, by the novelist Raul Botelho Gonzálvez (1917–), takes place in the jungle. As a result of this interest the Tiahuanaco Dramatic Company was organized in La Paz in November, 1929, dedicated to the "Creole and indigenous drama." Angel Salas (1895–), Bolivia's director of public health, and a historian of the theatre, wrote the 1926 *El último Huayño* (published 1928). He was also author of the three-act comedy *La mejor escuela*, and of *El otro amor*, *El invasor, La raza,* and the three-act drama in verse *La huerta* (1924).

Antonio Díaz Villamil (1897–1948), normal school teacher and director of education in several governments, in 1920 dramatized the amusing 1909 novel *La candidatura de Rojas* by Armando Chirveches (1881–1926), which was also put onto the stage in a version by A. Montellano of Oruro. But after that, Díaz Villamil devised his own plots. His 1922 three-act drama *La voz de la quena* (published 1927) was named from the Indian flute, and the title of his four-act *El nieto de Tupaj Catari* (1923) indicates its Indianist slant. The high point in Bolivian *costumbrismo*, his three-act *La Rosita* (1924), has what a critic called "salpicaduras indígenas" as do *La herencia de Caín* (1921) and *La renta. El precio de un muñeco* (1921) is a light comedy in one act.

The best drama by Díaz Villamil, performed August 13, 1924, was the three-act *La hoguera*, whose title suggests that the nation is a fire. For fuel this fire requires heart's blood. The theme is foreshadowed in the first act as Leopoldo, son of Bolivian Elena and a Chilean colonel, argues with his fiancée cousin, Irma, about the relative beauty of the Chilean *copihue* flower and the Bolivian *khatutas*. Loyalty to Chile and Bolivia clash as Leopoldo, having heroically led the Bolivians to victory at Tarapacá, is forced to decide the fate of his father who has been captured as a Chilean spy. An Indianist touch is provided in a letter written by Elena in the native Aymará. The reported run of five hundred performances for this play[9] is incredible for a nation as theatrically backward as Bolivia. Augusto Guzmán attributes it to the subject—Bolivia's ultimate loss of its Pacific shoreline—and to the hokum of the final act which brought tears to the audiences, even if jeers to the critics.

Díaz Villamil never equaled this success with any of his other plays, among which are a collection: *Teatro escolar* (1939); *¿Quiere ser Vd. candidato?* (1942); *Cuando vuelva mi hijo* (1942); *El hoyo* (1942); *El traje del señor diputado* (1946); *La niña de mis ojos* (1948); and three plays published together in 1947, *Plácido Yáñez, Gualaychos,* and the sentimental *Vals del recuerdo*. Díaz Villamil also contributed to the progress of the theatre in Bolivia by founding La Sociedad Boliviana de Autores Teatrales in 1923 and El Ateneo de la Juventud (1924). All members of the Sociedad had to have their plays approved by the group before performance or publication.

The 1920's was a most active decade in Bolivian drama. Two dramatists whose first works appeared in time to make them eligible

---

[9] Armando Correia Pacheco (ed.), *Diccionario de la literatura latinoamericana: Bolivia*, p. 30.

were Diego Madrazo, with his prize-winning *Don Juan Tenorio en el altiplano* (1922), and Julio N. Burgoa, with a one-act *sainete, En la tierra que estuvieres* (1922). Two other brief plays by Burgoa followed: *Por un santo* (1923) and *El Vatiri* (1924).

Los lobos del altiplano by Federico Avila y Avila, performed in Tarija in 1930, sounds like an Indianist play, and certainly *Las bocas hambrientas* (1956) by Fernando Medina Ferrera, though perhaps not a sociological study of the Indians, deals with their economic status. Definitely Indian in theme is the three-act *Charcas* (1938), a pageant written by Joaquín Gantier to celebrate the four hundredth anniversary of the founding of his native Sucre. Part I, dealing with the Inca period just before the arrival of the conquistadores, is written in the Quechua language. Part II describes a chess game in 1766, during the colonial period, and Part III is set in the era of the Republic, 1825, with Bolívar and Sucre, the victor at Ayacucho, among the characters.

Other local-color plays of the twentieth century with no Indian slant include a comedy *Lo que pasa en la redacción de un diario*, by Julián Céspedes Rivero, and *Carmen Rosa* (1912) by Fabián Vaca Chávez (1881–). In the latter the author shows the futility of attempting to introduce "the delicious carelessness of Europe" into conservative Bolivia. He claims that the characters represent characteristic types of Bolivian society.

With Potosí as background, Valentín Meriales wrote the comedy *El alma provinciana*, the drama *La mala senda* (published in Sucre), and a well-plotted play of Creole customs, *El cristal de marfil*. Critics compare him for his irony and his interest in the lower classes with Charles Louis Philippe.

One of Bolivia's outstanding plays, the three-act *Aniversario de boda* (1915), by the poet Nicolás Ortiz Pacheco (1893–1953), reveals the dangers of trying to be a *costumbrista* in Bolivia. At its opening in Sucre some of the capital's society, suspecting themselves to be the inspiration of its lurid pictures of manners, hissed and tried to stop its performance. The young author, mounting the stage, threatened to name the originals of all the characters if they did not keep quiet. Then he moved to La Paz, where the next year he presented *Pliegues del honor* (published 1916). Again the object of a hostile demonstration, he gave up the genre at which he had proved himself proficient, and spent the next twenty years in Chile. Returning, he became editor of an important La Paz newspaper. Before his death, he tried drama again, with *Paraíso espiritual.*

Humberto S. Palza, essayist and director of foreign relations, was another to devote his attention to the foibles of his countrymen, in comedies like the ironical two-act *sainete* of social customs, *Mi novio el extranjero* (1920), revived in 1957 by a group of amateurs in Tupiza for local consumption and for a trip to Chile. Palza also wrote the dramas *El viajero, Tinieblas,* and the three-act *La felicidad desconcierta* (1922); the high comedy *Ciénaga florida;* and the three-act *Las pobres vidas,* performed in La Paz in 1926.

Only some future study concentrated on the Bolivian stage can find space for all who have written a play or two before turning to some surer way of earning a living. But the important contemporary dramatist Raúl Salmón must not be overlooked. He began his experimenting with *Condehuyo,* the theme used by Aguirre, but turned out what Salmón termed a "suburban play." He also wrote *La escuela de los pillos,* then struck his stride with the historical play *Viva Belzú,* and *Siembra* (1955), which discussed Bolivia's social and revolutionary foment.

The poet Franz Tamayo (1880–1956) was temporarily a playwright of lyric tragedies, like *La Prometheida o Las Oceanidas* (La Paz, 1917) and *Scopas* (1939). Walter Dalence (1898–) of Potosí, son of the author of Bolivia's first novel, *Los misterios* (Sucre, 1861), wrote two dramas: *La revancha* and *El honor,* and two comedies, *Cuesta arriba* and *La bohemia.* Adolfo Costa du Rels (1891–), son of a French engineer, and with French and Spanish training, wrote the sentimental comedy of passion and moral decision, *Hacia el atardecer,* about a woman who is growing old, and offered it in a 1919 Chilean Club de Señoras competition. Then he took up the more lucrative writing of short stories in French.

In the 1920's, under the influence of European and North American dramatists, there was a flurry of activity in Bolivia's theatres as the few practicing playwrights of Bolivia turned away from their own social problems and traditions to consider universal themes. But the output ceased with the outbreak of the Chaco War. Few plays were inspired by it; it was the best depicted by fiction writers and poets. An exception, Joaquín Gantier mentions this struggle between Bolivia and Paraguay in several of his plays. In *Con el alma de cristal* (1933) he presents two characters who conceal a crime so that the thief can go to war with a clean slate. In *Ansiada paz* (1937) wounded and exchanged prisoners are returning from the battlefield, and the soldier Julio, who calls himself "harapo de la guerra," declares that only in death can he find his "longed-for peace."

Ernesto Vaca Guzmán is the only other dramatist who has writtten of that war—in a three-act comedy, *13 de Artillería*, performed in Oruro in 1936. It has a scene at the front, but also deals with the problems presented in marrying a gringo. "Let's be proud of being Bolivians" is its patriotic final speech.

Vaca Guzmán improved in his craft as he went on. In 1937 students in La Paz performed his so-called "puppet show," *Mirando atrás*, that begins with a "bull session" and ends with the arrival of policemen to arrest troublemakers. In an epilog, the students return and declare that only by the efforts of university people can honest government come to the nation. More recently Vaca Guzmán wrote *Berenice* (1951) and something with the intriguing title of "Canción de cuna para un elefantito" ("Cradle Song for a Baby Elephant"), not yet in print.

Technically the best of all Bolivia's dramatists is Mario Flores (1901–   ), who started his dramatic career in Bolivia with the successful two-act comedy *Cruz Diablo* (1920) and *La agonía de don Juan*. Unappreciated, he moved to Buenos Aires, where he has been part of a theatrical group that did not know he was Bolivian. In Argentina he wrote the three-act comedy *Santa Ludovica* (1921) for the great character actress Orfilia Rico, in which she was performing when she died. A string of successful comedies followed: *¡A París, muchachas!* (1921), *Una conquista* (1922), *Una aventura galante* (1923). More frivolous are *Boîte Russe* and *Una noche en Viena*, with clever plots and at least one thousand performances each.

With his brother, Alfredo, Flores wrote the popular *Luces de Buenos Aires* (1930). He is best known as an Argentine *costumbrista*, whose comedies *Fray Milonga* (1928) and *El padre Liborio* (1928) made these characters household words in Buenos Aires. The first had two thousand performances in Buenos Aires. The second, a *sainete* introducing a charitable but gay small-town curate and an inquisitorial priest, was finally closed by Church authorities after its five hundredth performance—because the curate played a guitar!

But for all his successes in Argentina, Mario Flores must still be classified as a Bolivian, if only for his political satire *Veneno para ratones,* performed in La Paz in 1950, possibly the finest work of the Bolivian theatre, though it is impossible to obtain a copy in either La Paz or Buenos Aires. Díaz de Medina[10] compares it to something by O'Neill or Sartre as a dramatic psychological and sociological play, an X ray of the human soul that leaves to the audience the decision about who is to blame for the ills of society. Other critics classify Flores' *La gringa Federica* (1935) among the ten best plays of Bolivia. A recently listed work performed in Buenos Aires is *Fuente de oro* (1959).

With Flores out of the country and most other writers quitting the theatre after vainly seeking actors and productions, the only Bolivian writer faithful to the stage was a Normal School professor of Sucre, Joaquín Gantier (1903–   ), now retired, whose persistence may be explained in part by the fact that he has always had potential actors among his pupils and his friends. He has also been able, fortunately, to give his plays permanence in printed form.[11]

In 1933 Gantier took the role of the father in one of his best plays, *Con el alma de cristal,* about the Chaco War, in a benefit for the wounded soldiers. *Los hermanos Méndez Goba* (1936) warns against selfishness in brother-and-sister relationship. *Hermano* (1951) is somewhat similar. The clash between a stepfather and his wife's favorite daughter is the subject of *Ídolos* (1937). The war play *Ansiada paz* came that same year, as did a one-act *El hijo pródigo,* a eulogy of schoolteachers. His collected *Teatro Infantil-Adolescente* (1940) contains plays with a moral, including *El San Juan de Pérez Holguín,* in which a painter seeks a model for the expressive eyes of his saint.

Gantier's excellent rural comedy, *El molino,* partly written in the Quechua language, appeared in 1943 in the magazine *Kollasuyo, No. 45,* and his brief *Hacia una vida superior* was performed on the Día de Maestros, June 4, 1943, to recruit teachers and show Bolivian youths how to live better. *Divorcio* (1946) portrays a father who is punished for getting a divorce. Like others among Gantier's plays, it is more thesis than theatre; but his tragedy in verse, *Angélica,* has been highly praised. In the last fifteen years Gantier has apparently

[10] Díaz de Medina, *La literatura boliviana,* p. 321.

[11] Willis K. Jones, "Bolivia Hails a Dramatist," *Poet Lore,* Vol. 49 (Autumn, 1943), 279–282.

not published anything, but for more than two decades he was an active figure.

Perhaps he finally encountered the usual difficulty of Bolivian dramatists: inability to find actors. But in recent years there have been at least a few sporadic attempts to bring new life to the theatre. After the Chaco War a number of literary people in various parts of the republic tried to revive drama, which accounts for a new flurry of plays about 1950. Many represent the first and only play by some young Bolivian now better known in another field of literature. Among the plays was a three-act comedy, *Campeonas de Rummy-Canasta* (published 1954), by "Hugo Blym," as the humorist and critic Hugo Vilela de Villar (1910–   ) signs much of his writing. *Manos de Luz* by the fiction writer Rodolfo González, *Doña Simona*, a historical play by Luis Felipe Vilela, and the domestic comedy *Máscara* by Victor Hugo Villegas, were others.

Guillermo Francovich (1901–   ), after a career as lawyer, diplomat, and philosopher, also chose this period to indulge a new interest, and wrote two historical dramas (each in three acts), both published: *El monje de Potosí* (1952) and *Un puñal en la noche* (1954). The latter explores a psychological conflict: though it glorifies Marshal Sucre, the traitor Matos is practically the hero.

At present Bolivia reports several troupes of actors, varying in their activity. Carlos S. Cervantes directs the Teatro Municipal of La Paz, which brought a visiting group from Spain for a two-weeks run in 1958 but called it off after three performances. Pepe Arellano, an excellent actor and considered by some to be one of the world's great directors, had better success with three plays—*The Fox and the Grapes, View from the Bridge,* and *Waiting for Godot*—the next year in the Paraninfo of the University. Raúl Salmón, besides directing broadcasts over Radio Altiplano, manages the Compañía de Teatro Social. A number of *grupos libres* are federated under Director Jorge Gallardo Calderón. There is a Teatro Infantil under Rosa Fernández de Carrasco and an English-speaking community theatre in La Paz. Both Fernando Irazoque Camacho of the University of San Andrés in La Paz and Luis Carranza Siles of the University of San Francisco Xavier de Chuquisaca in Sucre have their experimental theatres.

In the provinces the Talía group of Oruro performs occasionally, but the most active dramatic organization in Bolivia is the Nuevos

Horizontes group in the small city of Tupiza. With a population of less than five thousand to support them, these actors under Director Liber Forti and his wife, Gladys, have been producing four or five plays a year since 1945, besides issuing a theatrical bulletin and publishing a series of national and translated foreign plays. Each year they tour the nearby towns. In 1959 a troupe of six actors and two actresses barnstormed for two weeks as far as the Argentine frontier. They even made a tour of Chile, where several actors remained to enroll in a school of drama.

The embers of drama are not entirely cold. The Biblioteca Paceña was recently established to publish national drama. Its first two books were an ancient religious play, *Comedia de nuestra señora de Guadalupe* (published 1957), by Fray Diego Ocaña, and *La casa de Mariana,* by the contemporary Eduardo Olmedo López. The most recent historian of Bolivia's theatre, Díaz de Medina, has even classified a "centennial generation of dramatists," headed by the poet Victor M. Ruiz with his *sainete Five O'Clock Tea* (1922) and *Los que pagan,* about the uncertain life of a government employee.[12] Others include Luis Sánchez Rossel, author of *El precio del Triunfo,* and Alberto Saavedra Nogales, who wrote *El triunfo del prejuicio.* Antonio Barrenechea, author of *Víctima,* should be added to his list of promising playwrights, along with Jorge Gallardo, who wrote the psychological *Corazón adentro,* and the critic Luis Azarduy, author of *Los millones de Arlequín,* a scenic poem, and of the comedies *Así lo quiere S.S.* and *Constitución.* Antonio Hartmann of Cochabamba is author of several *costumbrista* plays.

One hopeful oasis in Bolivia's cultural desert was the celebration on March 14–20, 1961, of its first Festival del Teatro, put together too quickly, but opening the way for others. Only Bolivian plays were produced, though for 1962, international plays were promised. The most popular of the six offerings was *La casa sobre la roca* by Mario Flores, produced by the Teatro Nacional company. Mother Isabel, played by the great Elena Ortiz de Zarate, tells her two children, Jack and Lucy, that their father is dead. Actually he is in jail as an embezzling bank cashier. His return creates the problem of the play.

Another offering was *El sable de Melgarejo,* by Juan Atanasio Lara, a historical play in verse by a nineteenth-century dramatist,

[12] Díaz de Medina, *La literatura boliviana,* p. 349.

modernized and lengthened by his grandson. It was performed by the Magisterio Experimental group. The Teatro Popular group performed two: *La guerra del Chaco*, poorly constructed and in bad taste, and *Vidas destruidas*, by a beginning dramatist, Jorge Bustillo B. It had humor and tragedy but no unity.

The actor Hugo Roncal and his Sierra-Roncal group worked too fast to get ready their antialcoholic play, *La Candelaria*, while Monroy Atada performed a tragedy with a tear-jerking ending, involving a number of young people in a pension. It was called *Los chicos de la calle*, by Humberto Roda.

Only two of the six plays had real literary and theatrical merit, but the venture was valuable in letting the dramatists see what their work looked like back of the footlights. A number of other young playwrights are hoping for a similar experience. Díaz de Medina lists some of them who with experience may lend luster to the future Bolivian theatre.[13] They include the poetess María Teresa Solari, and Francisco Alvarez García, Carlos Oropeza, Octavio Díaz de Oropeza, Carlos Aramayo Ruiz, José Rúa, Abel Reyes Ortiz, Adán Sardón, Francisco Villarejos, and Humberto Viscarra.

[13] *Ibid.*

CHAPTER 18

Drama in New Granada

New Granada was the name given to a region of colonial South America as extensive as all of the United States east of the Mississippi, but so divided by mountains and blocked by jungles that intercommunication between the various sections was almost impossible. Yet its inhabitants managed to achieve a certain homogeneity that remained even after the viceregency split into the republics of Ecuador, Colombia, and Venezuela. Because culture, of which drama is a part, reflects the history of a region, a brief review of the history of this northern part of the South American continent will be useful.

Exploration of its Caribbean shoreline began with Ojeda in 1499. Venturing beyond Hispaniola and Trinidad, he came upon an Indian village on poles in the shallow water of Lake Maracaibo. It was a sight reminiscent of Venice, and so he called the region Venezuela (Little Venice). The next year Balboa sailed still farther west, and honored Christopher Colombus by naming that region Colombia.

Jungles and mountains made settlement slower and more difficult than in other parts of the New World. The savage and independent Indian tribes also added to the problems. Following the defeats of Montezuma in Mexico and Atahualpa in Peru, the victorious Spaniard won the allegiance of the subjects of their empires, but the inhabitants of New Granada, to get the Indian servants so necessary for their mining and agricultural projects, had to conquer innumerable small tribes, many of whom rebelled later and wiped out the settlements of their white conquerors. Not until 1527 did colonization really begin in northern South America, and then chiefly at the instigation of some German moneylenders who had heard the legend of El Dorado, and hoped to recover from the gilded chieftain the cash they had advanced to Charles I. This desire accounted for the founding of Cartagena, Colombia, in 1533 as one of the three New World ports of trade with Spain, the other two being Vera Cruz in Mexico, and Nombre de Dios in Panama, later replaced by Portobelo. Cartagena was especially alluring to the gold-thirsty pirates of the Spanish Main, and became the most frequently attacked and sacked city of the New World.

Even though united, each of the three parts of what was to be New Granada insisted on a certain amount of individuality and political independence. Of their present-day capitals, Quito was founded first, in 1534, on a site that had been the chief city of Indian tribes for centuries. Four years later Gonzalo Jiménez de Quesada, considered by some the inspiration for Don Quijote, gave the name of New Granada to the territory of the conquered Chibcha Indians and founded Santa Fe de Bogotá. It became the *audiencia*, or court, of the whole region in 1550. Not till 1567 did Santiago de León de Caracas come into being, and for a while its very existence was jeopardized by its savage Indian neighbors.

Disillusionment over the lack of gold discouraged development. Indeed what little treasure was discovered in the interior had to be spent on arms to defend the coast, and the end of the seventeenth century found New Granada an impoverished and unattractive region, governed from faraway Peru by a viceroy who had no interest in it.

After the Bourbons came to the throne and the War of Spanish Succession ended, King Philip V made New Granada a viceroyalty in 1717. But the reluctant Viceroy Villalonga, sent over as its first ruler, protested so strongly at the useless expense of maintaining a government in Santa Fe, that in 1723, the viceroyalty was abolished, and the region reduced to the ranks of a captaincy general. Only the fear of its loss to England during a war caused its re-establishment as a separate viceroyalty in 1739. Santa Fe de Bogotá again became the center of control to oversee the captaincy general of Venezuela and the presidency of Quito.

During the colonial history of New Granada, Bogotá, as the home of the viceroy, was the center of culture for the whole territory. Such a development had also been true in Mexico and Lima, the residences of the other New World viceroys. Here lived the poets and the scholars, and here were the universities. Bogotá could boast two: the University of San Francisco Javier, founded in 1622, seventy-one years after those in Lima and Mexico, and the Dominican University, founded in 1624. Not till a century later, in 1721, did Venezuela's University of Santa Rosa open its doors. The University of Quito dates from 1787.

One of the evidences of a nation's culture is its theatre. Quite probably there were early unrecorded theatrical performances in Cartagena, though its establishment as a center of defense may imply that its inhabitants were too busy fighting to develop a taste for the drama. Nor were there any large groups of natives, like those in Brazil or Mexico, for whom the priests might want to dramatize Bible stories as a means of evangelization. Whatever the early activities elsewhere, the first documented theatrical performance in this whole region took place in Guayaquil, the port for Quito on the Pacific.

Unlike so many Pacific cities that are located far enough inland to be safe from pirates, Ecuador's largest city is only a few miles from the ocean, up a winding river. Twice founded—in 1535 by Belalcázar and in 1537 by Orellano—not only did its enemies often lay it waste, but the frequent fires, that still occasionally rage through its buildings of bamboo and mud, consumed most of its early documents. Chávez Franco, however, found and reproduced several that declare that in 1550 "los ciudadviejeños hacían su teatro al aire libre en la Plaza de la Matriz . . . bajo la dirección de los corregidores y los jefes militares."[1] Plays, perhaps locally written pantomimes, about the siege of Granada or episodes in the life of the Cid or chapters of *Amadís de Gaula* may have served to fan their martial enthusiasm.

The next documentary evidence, from the record of the council, reveals that on July 25, 1568, the year of the construction of Madrid's first theatre, Guayaquil enjoyed what may have been its first Spanish-style comedy. Nine years after Peru's first dramatic dialog and forty years after the Mexicans had seen their first play, a fiesta in honor of Santiago, Guayaquil's patron saint, opened with a bullfight in the Plaza de Santo Domingo, followed by a *comedia* in the Plaza Concepción. The primitive stage was erected where the Proveedora stands today. The city's first real theatre, however, did not come till the time of Governor García de León de Pizarro (1770–1790).[2] It was built in the same Plaza Concepción.

What plays were performed on these temporary platforms will

---

[1] Modesto Chávez Franco, *Crónicas del Ecuador antiguo*, p. 470; Armando de Maria y Campos. *Entre cómicos de ayer*, p. 175.

[2] Chávez Franco, *Crónicas*.

never be known; perhaps some of the printed collections of dramas that began issuing from the presses in Spain by 1565 had, by now, reached Ecuador.

Much more is known about the next recorded play in this region, that was performed in Bogotá in 1580. The occasion was a visit by the bishops of Santa Marta and Cartagena to Archbishop Zapata. Tomás Ramírez writes about it as having begun at five o'clock in a house owned by Juan de Moscoso, near the Chapel of Humilladero, on what is now the corner of La Tercera.[3] The play was *Los Alarcos,* and though the name of the author was not mentioned and the manuscript has been lost, its tragic story is well known from many later versions also based on the ballad of the Infanta Solisa who orders Count Alarcos to kill his wife so he may be free to marry her.[4]

According to Professor Arrom, several plays were presented for the Corpus Christi celebrations "twenty years after the settlement of Santiago de León de Caracas."[5] That would make 1589 the earliest recorded date in Venezuelan theatrical history. After that, the citizens of all three capitals had frequent opportunities to enjoy plays. Performances whose descriptions have fallen under the eyes of historians were surely only a part of the total number, but they indicate the kinds and demonstrate how similar was the theatrical development in all parts of Spain's American possessions.

The great majority of locally written plays were *loas,* in the form of monologs or short plays with mythological characters, and they usually preceded a play imported from Spain, which was the feature of most patriotic or religious celebrations. In Caracas, the *ayuntamiento* gave permission for a play on the Day of St. James, June 28, 1600. *Loas* crop up in the theatrical history of all three parts of New Granada. The preservation of those still extant can probably be explained by the vanity of those honored by them. When they disappeared, it was doubtless due to a feeling that they were ephemeral and not worth preserving anyway.

One that disappeared is remembered because of its mention in Padre Diego Molina's *Ramillete compuesto de varias y diversas flores*

---

[3] J. V. Ortega Ricaurte, *Historia crítica del teatro en Bogotá,* 1st ed., pp. 4–5.

[4] Vernon A. Chamberlain, "Dramatic treatment of the Conde Alarcos theme," *Hispania,* XLII (December, 1959), 517–523.

[5] José Juan Arrom, "Actos del cabildo de Caracas, 1573–1600," *Universidad de la Habana,* XXI (1946), 6–24.

del discurso, describing the welcome at Riobamba, Ecuador, in 1732, to the Marqués de Maenza. Molina's manuscript, in the Quito Library, tells of locally written *loas* to accompany a performance of Moreto's *Guardar una mujer no puede ser*.

Fifteen years later, in 1747, another *loa*, more interesting as an antique than as dramatic literature, was the work of an Ecuadorian who signed himself "El D. D. J. C. D. C. de Q." The work was published in Madrid the same year under the title: *Loa que representó el Colegio Mayor y Seminario de S. Luis de la ciudad de Quito celebrando la elección del obispo de Santa Marta, hecha en el Doctor D. Juan, nieto Poto de Aguila, natural de Popayán y colegial que fue de dicho colegio, y hoy obispo dignísimo de la Sta. Iglesia de Quito.*[6] Both these plays are allegorical, with nothing national about them except the occasion for their performances.

In Colombia several *coloquios*, or dialogs, for fiestas in Cartagena, Colombia, were written by the local druggist, Juan de Cueto y Mena (1604–1672?), preserved because they were published in 1662.[7] One in honor of the Archbishop of Valencia, was *Paraphrasis Panegírica*. The other bore the title *La competencia en los nobles*.

Equally alien were plays in a similar welcoming ceremony for Ruiz de Castilla, when he came to Ecuador as president of the *audiencia* early in the nineteenth century. The traveler Bennet Stevenson, who described the festivities, said that the students of San Fernando performed four plays, *Catón, Adrómaca, Zoraída,* and *La Araucana* "for the purpose of inspiring love of liberty and the principles of republicanism." He failed to tell who adapted a Chilean epic or translated from the French and English. None had any relation to Ecuador.

Performances followed in other parts of New Granada. In 1746 Jacinto de Buenaventura of Ibague, Colombia, wrote a *loa* for the celebration of the coronation of Ferdinand VI;[8] and another *Loa que*

---

[6] "Loa que representó el Colegio Mayor y Seminario de S. Luis de la ciudad de Quito celebrando la elección del obispo de Santa Marta, hecha en el Doctor D. Juan, nieto Poto de Aguila, natural de Popayán y colegial que fue de dicho colegio, y hoy obispo dignísimo de la Sta. Iglesia de Quito," in *Museo histórico,* V, No. 17 (September, 1953), pp. 132–148.

[7] Archer Woodford, *Obras de Cueto y Mena.*

[8] See *Revista Iberoamericana,* VII, No. 14 (February, 1944), 269–303.

salió a expensas del Sr. Alcalde de Quito, in 1760, is mentioned by Arrom.[9]

At first, theatrical performances in New Granada must have taken place not only on portable stages in the plazas but also on porches of churches and in yards around them, but the *Constituciones sinodales* of 1687 in Venezuela forbade any further such use of church buildings or cemeteries. It also ordered that, no matter where performed, all plays must first be censored by a priest or "persona docta."[10]

The effect on the colony's developing theatre can be guessed by what happened later in Spain, where Cotarelo y Mori blamed the complete decay of the eighteenth-century Spanish theatre on "this war without quarter or truce that is waged in the name of morality in the pulpit, in the confessional, in gatherings, in books, pamphlets, acts of town councils, church censorship, and all sorts of schemes."[11]

Some plays, however, continued to be performed, chiefly in private houses, though so few in number as to cause a later critic, Luis Peraza, to declare: "From 1584 to 1804 was, theatrically speaking, a black colonial night for Caracas."[12] The observation was just as true of Quito, and to a somewhat less extent, of Bogotá. From the latter, however, one play has come down to us: *La conquista de Santafé de Bogotá* (1718), in which Fernando de Orbea introduced Jiménez de Quesada, King Osmún of Santafé, and mobs of Spaniards and Indians. It was a bad play and full of anachronisms.[13] This was also the period when Francisco Cardoso considered it a literary accomplishment to turn out a drama in which the vowel *a* did not appear.

To get an idea of the lost works of this period, one need not go back in the eighteenth century. As the plays of the sixteenth-century Spanish priest Diego Sánchez de Badajoz reproduced his country's

[9] José Juan Arrom, "Documentos relativos al teatro colonial en Venezuela," *Universidad de la Habana*, XXI (1946), 80–101. In *Thesaurus*, XIV (1959), 161–185, Arrom discusses a recently discovered *Laurea Crítica* by Fernando Fernández de Valenzuela, the first Colombian theatrical work.

[10] Arrom, "Documentos relativos," *Universidad de la Habana*, XXI (1946), 80–101.

[11] *Bibliografía de las controvercias sobre la licitud del teatro en España*, p. 28.

[12] Luis Peraza (ed.), *Teatro seleccionado de Leopoldo Ayala Michelena*, pp. ix–xvi.

[13] Fernando de Orbea, "La conquista de Santafé de Bogotá," *Boletín de Historia y Antigüedades* (March, 1925).

dramatic attempts of three centuries earlier, so in Colombia in 1928, a priest, Fray Carlos Gil Rozo, published four plays that could just as well have been a product of some of his fellow clergymen of two centuries earlier, who used the theatre to preach to their parishioners. His *Cosas de ayer* is a short farce about Agapito, a country bumpkin, who puts on the frock of a priest while its owner has gone to administer Last Rites to Agapito's mother. The simpleton mixes the plans for a funeral and a wedding. Rozo's two-act *juguete*, *A quien Dios no da hijos el diablo da sobrinos*, is a preachment for matrimony, with its moral put into the mouth of the *bobo*, Toribio. It concerns Hermenegildo, who decides to ask his niece and nephew to keep house for him so he won't need to get married. They get him carried off to an insane asylum. The three-act *Cosas de hoy* is just as didactic in showing what happens when Julio will not listen to priestly advice.

Some attempt to raise the level of literary tastes was made with the organization of El Círculo de Buen Gusto in Bogotá in 1806 by Manuela Sanz de Santamaría.[14] As a result, one of the circle, José Miguel Montalvo (1782–1816) wrote a tragedy, *El zagal de Bogotá,* one of the earliest attempts at Colombian drama. It was produced in 1806 in the Coliseo Ramírez.[15]

The theatre's greatest handicap was that most people looked with scorn at plays and those who performed in them, especially if the actors received pay. This feeling has not entirely disappeared in Latin America even today. Only actors who performed in foreign products or in operas, after that form of entertainment was introduced into Bogotá in 1848 by Francisco Villalba, were considered cultured and artistic.

Few were the attempts to perform dramas dealing with national themes. Menéndez y Pelayo mentions only *El nuevo Luciano* (1799), which attacked colonial education in Quito. Nor were plays about the lower classes, like the Chilean *Tremendo* or the Argentine *Amor de la estanciera,* duplicated in New Granada, though attempts at realism occasionally occurred. As narrated in the historical novel *El alférez real,* during the performance in 1788 of García de la Huerta's *Raquel*—as part of the ceremonies of allegiance to Charles IV in

[14] José Sánchez, "Círculos literarios de Iberoamerica," *Revista Iberoamericana,* No. 18 (May, 1945), 297–323.
[15] Ortega Ricaurte, *Historia crítica,* 1st ed., pp. 47–49.

Cali, Colombia—the audience was horrified to see the ensign fall with blood streaming from his wound. Women fainted before they realized that the actor had squeezed it out of a bladder hidden under his uniform.[16]

Of all the division of New Granada, Bogotá appears to have been the most active in the field of drama and was at least one place where women appeared on the stage. There they had a long tradition. In 1594 a group of Spanish citizens founded a dramatic group and performed behind a fence of curtains, two blocks from San Francisco Plazuela. They used no scenery. At the beginning of the show, the leading lady appeared before the audience to describe what it was supposed to be seeing. Two centuries later, the wife of the Marqués de San Jorge, Rafaela Isazi, made a reputation under the stage name of "La Jerezana," derived from her birthplace in Spain, while the wife of the Spanish Colonel Eleuterio Cebollino who was later shot as a rebel, became better known under her stage name of "La Cebollino" than her real one of María de los Remedios Aguilar. Two other ladies of Bogotá society, Andrea Manrique and María del Carmen Ricaurte, performed with the visiting English actor Charles Burman, who had first come for the 1798–1799 season. Their names appear with his in the cast of the first really comic play in Colombian history, *El rey pastor*, in 1808.

When actresses were not available, boys took the female roles here, as elsewhere, even into the nineteenth century. As late as 1853, when Lorenzo María Lleras enlisted his friends into a company of actors, two ladies played parts in private performances but were replaced by boys when the public was admitted. On one such occasion, a boy who later became a famous politician played an old lady and gave such a convincing performance in the sentimental role that the audience dissolved in tears, and even he wept. He fumbled around till he got his handkerchief from his trousers pocket, completely forgetting that until that moment it had been covered by a long black skirt.

Another comic moment in Colombian dramatic history was made by the fifteen-year-old José Caicedo Rojas (1816–1898) before he began writing his own plays. As the heroine, Palmira, in the tragedy *Mahomet* "she" committed suicide too close to the front of the stage,

---

[16] John L. Martin, "El alférez real," *Hispania*, XXIV (1941), 195.

and to escape a real death from the heavy descending curtain had to roll back from the footlights. Spectators leaving the theatre were heard to comment that the poor princess was still in her death convulsions even while the curtain fell.

Occasionally colonial Bogotá was also visited by foreign companies, like the group of six actors and two actresses who appeared before lawyer Pedro de Bustamante on November 3, 1618, to draw up articles of consolidation. The leading actor was named as Martín Calvo and the leading lady was his wife, María de Sandoval, whom he had married while performing in Guatemala. According to the contract, as discovered by Harvey Johnson, they arranged to remain in Colombia till after the 1619 Corpus Christi.[17] This was doubtless the company that performed the work of the first Colombian playwright whose name is known and whose product is preserved: Bruno de Valenzuela, author of a religious comedy, *La vida de hidalgos* (1617). As one way to insure its success, he made a public vow that if it was applauded by theatregoers in Spain and in Bogotá he would build a hermitage to Our Lady of Monserrate. The play was performed first in Seville and Valladolid, Spain. The only clue to its acceptance in Quesada and Bogotá is the record of the construction of the hermitage in 1620 and the fact that Valenzuela was encouraged to write a later play, *En Dios está la vida* (1622), before leaving the world and entering the monastery he had built.

Less successful with its plans was the Calvo company. The actors had intended to continue on to Peru and later to Mexico, but records reveal that Calvo remained in Peru after his arrival, piecing out his income by becoming a jailer, and died there in 1626. His wife survived him, and became known for her masculine roles, thus reversing the customary practice. In Peru the Calvos had the use of a permanent theatre, El Corral de Morales, built in 1598, an improvement over impoverished Bogotá where they had only makeshift quarters. Indeed Colombia had to wait till 1793 for a permanent theatre, but when it came, it was quite a structure.[18] Its location was the spot picked out by the amateurs two centuries earlier, near San Francisco

---

[17] Harvey L. Johnson, "Una compañía teatral en Bogotá en 1618," *Nueva Revista de Filología Hispánica*, II, No. 4 (October–December, 1948), 377–380.

[18] For description and details see Ortega Ricaurte, *Historia crítica*, 1st ed., pp. 14–17.

Plazuela. It was supposed to copy Madrid's Teatro de la Cruz and to cost six thousand pesos. Before it was finished, the manager, José Tomás Ramírez, had to spend nearly sixty thousand pesos, and went bankrupt. Citizens of Bogotá, however, came to his rescue by buying shares in the theatre at twenty-five pesos apiece. Viceroy Mendinueta personally subscribed for four shares.

As always, talk of a theatre brought protests from the clergy. The archbishop prophesied from the cathedral pulpit that Ramírez would be damned as well as penniless, and that the roof would collapse on the wicked spectators. But unawed, the manager opened it, still incomplete, on January 6, 1793. General admission for its 1,200 spectators was two *reales*, with half-price for soldiers. Seats in the bleachers cost another half *real*, and orchestra seats a whole *real*. The main boxes brought eight *reales* apiece, except for the viceroy and the council, who got theirs free. But when the councilors discovered that the viceroy's box was carpeted, they refused to occupy theirs with its bare floor, and sat in the orchestra. The name of one play has come down to us, the first one after the completion of the building on November 4, 1793. It was *El Conde de Alarcos*, the same as Bogotá's first play, 213 years earlier; and so the drama cycle in Colombia had come back to its beginning.

The other divisions of New Granada got their first theatres at about the same time. There seems to be no record of the date of Quito's earliest playhouse, but during the governorship of García de León y Pizarro, between 1770 and 1790, Guayaquil built the first of its many bamboo-and-'dobe theatres to go up in smoke.[19]

In Venezuela, citizens also sought to provide themselves with entertainment. This desire for drama brought a clash with the clergy in 1771. A priest in Guanare banned all plays and dances, declaring that they "encouraged impure desires, adultery, quarrels, and other pernicious consequences." Protesting citizens of Caracas drew up a petition directed to Governor Felipe de Fonsdeviela, requesting the annulment of the ban on the grounds that after their hard work on farms and ranches they deserved diversions. Though the Governor's

---

[19] José Torre Revello, "Orígenes del teatro en Hispanoamérica," *Cuaderno,* No. 7 (1937), p. 49, speaks of an important theatre in Guayaquil in 1779–1790, but Chávez Franco declares that plays during that period were performed in "la lechería de Polo Chavarría."

sympathies were certainly on the side of the drama lovers, as he later proved in Havana, he was transferred to Cuba before he could make a ruling in Venezuela.

His successor, José Carlos Agüero, was already disliked by the clergy because he had given permission for the performance of plays while in charge of the port of La Guaira. Not trusting to his impartiality, therefore, the priests went over his head in a direct appeal to Charles III. Unfortunately for them, they had to wait five years for his reply; meanwhile the Venezuelans continued to enjoy their plays. To supply them, Simón Berben petitioned to give five plays, using soldiers from the garrison. The performances probably took place in the plaza, for the first Caracas theatre was still twelve years in the future.

Again protesting, one priest suggested to Agüero that because of Spanish military reverses in Africa, prayers would be more in order than plays, but the Governor replied that the defeat of the Spaniards had occurred far away, while it was to the interest of the Venezuelan clergy to acquire an income from the theatre right there at home.[20]

When the King's reply finally reached Caracas, it declared that the clergy had jurisdiction over the prevention of immorality on the stage, through their censorship, but permission for performances was the business of the governor. Charles also added shrewdly that since the clergy might try to delay or prevent performances by refusing to read play manuscripts submitted for censoring, any play that had ever been cleared by any religious body could be performed without further clearance. New plays, however, or those that because of title or author might arouse suspicion, ought to be carefully scrutinized, he added. The only recourse left to the clergy was their threat to excommunicate parents who let their children attend plays.

The next governor, Manuel González Torres de Navarro, showed that he sided with the theatregoers of Caracas by building at his own expense in 1782 an "hermoso y cómodo" theatre capable of holding 1,800 spectators. It was located between the squares of El Conde and Carmelitas.[21]

The citizens of Maracaibo also had their clashes with the Church. Padre Arcos objected to their petition to perform a play, the first

[20] Juan José Churión, *El teatro en Caracas,* pp. 78–86.
[21] Arrom, "Documentos relativos," *Universidad de la Habana,* XXI (1946), 80–101.

since *La vida es sueño* in 1760. He insisted that Lope de Vega and Calderón had done as much harm in Spain as Martin Luther had done in Germany. But the officials disregarded him and the play was performed. Less fortunate were the people of La Victoria, in 1791. When the clergy discovered that *los pardos* were rehearsing an Easter play, they protested so strongly that the city fathers sided with them and *los pardos* went playless.[22]

In 1792 two partners leased the Caracas theatre for a three-year period for five hundred pesos a year rental and a promise to perform a minimum of four plays a month. For Church holidays they would offer "outstanding plays, complete with *loas* and *sainetes*," and a 6:30 curtain. Since Caracas had no newspapers till Gallagher and Lamb brought a printing press there in 1808, investigators can find no record of the partners' repertory or fate.

Still another theatre opened its doors in Caracas in 1797. Boys played the female roles and received a strange sort of applause: the performance of one locally written *sainete criollo*, *El café de Venezuela*, brought "showers of lemons, green apples, oranges, and other projectiles."[23]

Perhaps the local standards of excellence were low, or the fruit may have had another significance. European visitors were not so well impressed. Francisco de Pons, who visited Venezuela in 1801, declared that the plays were "impiously performed," with the actors as monotonous as a ten-year-old child reciting a poem. He reported that in gestures, intonation, and stage presence they were worse than the worst barnstorming troupe in Spain; yet the cultured citizens paid their admission price of a *real* apiece and on feast days thronged the theatre—"a fact that indicated the poor taste of Venezuelans."[24]

About the same time, Humboldt visited the Coliseo, or Teatro del Conde. He noted that the city had eight churches, five convents, and only one theatre. In it the men and the women were separated, and though there was room for 1,500 spectators, they had to bring their own chairs. But the chief objects of Humboldt's criticism were the candles and the odorous and smoking olive oil lamps. The canvas roof that had originally protected the audience had rotted away, and

[22] Pérez Vila, "Polémicas sobre representaciones dramáticas, 1775–1828," *Revista*, No. 127 (March, 1958), 98–101.

[23] Churión, *El teatro en Caracas*, p. 86.

[24] Francisco de Pons, *Viaje a la parte oriental de Tierra Firme*, p. 397.

he declared himself more entertained by the stars overhead than by the stars ranting on the stage.[25] This Coliseo was destroyed by the earthquake of March 26, 1812.

Apparently its audiences saw no local plays. The first one was presented in 1804 when Andrés Bello (1781–1865), later to become the grammarian and pedagogue of Chile, wrote a brief *juguete cómico*, in homage to F. X. Balmis. Bello's offering was not only to honor Balmis, who had just brought vaccination to Venezuela, only eight years after Edward Jenner first used it in England, but it was also propaganda to persuade his fellow citizens to be vaccinated. More literary was his serious elegiac *loa, Venezuela consolada,* dedicated to Charles IV, that, in spite of flaws as the work of a twenty-three-year-old, marks the beginning of the Venezuelan national theatre.[26] Later, Bello also made a translation of Byron's *Marino Faliero,* and around 1840 he started to translate Sheridan's *The Rivals,* under the title *Una posada en Valencia.* For a long time it was considered an original work by him. Identified later, it was completed by José Nucete Sardi and performed on Andrés Bello Day, 1955, by the Teatro Universitario of Caracas.

Bello's *Vacuna* was staged in El Conde, as was probably *Aníbal* by the poet Vicente González, though in a letter he speaks of dramas performed in the hall of the Sociedad Patriótica, with women occupying "las tribunas," and applauding, sometimes serious dramas, sometimes picaresque *sainetes.*[27] At this moment, on the eve of independence, José Domingo Díaz, a realist, wrote *Juana, recuerdo de la revolución en Caracas.*

Revolution was in the air and according to the usual pattern throughout Latin America the imaginary world of the theatre gave way to the drama of real life, except for such performances as could whip up the spirit of revolt. But such plays were propaganda, not literature, and alien to this study.

The government's treatment of rebels followed a parallel course in the three regions of New Granada. The army of patriots marching to Caracas under Francisco de León in 1747 to protest against the Guipúzcoa Company that stifled trade and kept the price of living

[25] Alejandro de Humboldt, *Viaje a las regiones equinocciales,* p. 314.
[26] Aristides Rojas, "Orígenes del teatro en Caracas," *Estudios históricos, Serie* I, p. 320.
[27] Quoted by Churión, *El teatro en Caracas,* Chapter XI.

high, was pacified with promises till its leaders could be seized and executed, just as the Quito Creoles were deceived and slain in 1765 when they sought economic and social equality with the Spaniards, and the Bogotá advocates of a *común* or *junta* were tricked and defeated in 1781. But, eventually, under Bolívar independence was achieved, and in December, 1819, Colombia and New Granada became the Republic of Great Colombia, with the Presidency of Quito added in 1821. By Bolívar's proclamation of May 29, 1822, some two and a half million people tried to live together as the Republic of Great Colombia, under a tricolor flag.

Varying interests and ambitions, political jealousies, and the old problem of difficult communication caused rifts even before the ailing Bolívar died of tuberculosis in Santa Marta, Colombia, in 1830. After the split, as someone has written, Ecuador turned to the liturgy of the Church, Venezuela applied itself to law, and Colombia cultivated literature. And so came to an end the theatre of the viceroyalty of New Granada.

CHAPTER 19

The Theatre in Independent Ecuador

The development of the theatre in the different segments of the separated New Granada followed a common pattern, but each needs to be considered separately.

Jorge Carrera Andrade, contributing a thirty-page chapter to *Panorama das literaturas das Américas* about Ecuadorian literature during the past century, does not even mention drama. If the vice president of the Casa de Cultura Ecuatoriana thinks so little of the theatre of his country, how can outsiders esteem it very highly?

However, in the century and a half since Ecuador proclaimed its independence a few moments of theatrical activity have been worth recounting, even though drama in Ecuador is a waif with little known or recorded about its ancestors. In this nation of politicians, poets, and journalists, the dramatist is hard to find and usually unhonored.

Earliest plays of the national period by Ecuadorians on Ecuadorian themes were probably *Huainacapac* and *El insurgente* by José Antonio Yáñez, and the plays by José Joaquín de Olmedo (1780–1847), who is called the "Father of Ecuador's Modern Theatre."[1] Olmedo, one of the greatest of American poets, returned from exile in 1830 and afterward wrote his first play. For the tastes of today, his dramas are bombastic and flamboyant, but the audiences of his time were charmed by his rhetorical flights.

Chief source for a study of Ecuador's drama is the Rolando bibliography.[2] Unfortunately its author listed only published plays, and only a small percentage of the plays written got into print. Publication in Ecuador depended on many factors, least of which was dramatic excellence.

Dr. Rolando's records begin with a two-act anonymous comedy, *La magajuilla*, that appeared in the pages of *El Popular Guayaquil* in

[1] Enrique Avellán Ferrés, "La evolución del teatro ecuatoriano," read over Radio Quito, January 14, 1941.
[2] Carlos A. Rolando, *Las bellas artes en el Ecuador*.

1849. His next entry chronologically is *La honradez militar* by Francisco Santur which, though dealing with events in Quito, was published in France in 1854. It is followed by the religious *El bello ideal* (1857) by Carlos Augusto Salaverry, with its prolog set in Peru and its action in Mexico. The pedagogue Juan Rodríguez Gutiérrez published his five-act tragedy *Bellini* in 1862, but his later tragedy "Clemencia Lavalle" apparently never got into print. *Una mujer vengativa* by José Matías Avilés was also published in *La Unión Colombiana* in 1862, and reprinted seventeen years later in another newspaper, *El Comercio.* For some reason Avilés never published it in his own literary review, *El Rosicler.*

Meantime, inland Cuenca was witnessing performances of plays by such native sons as Luis Cordero, José Peralta, and Octavio Cordero Palacios, but these manuscripts were lost for want of a wealthy patron to get them printed. There were never enough potential play purchasers to tempt a regular publisher. One of these early plays that was preserved, however, is Sixto Juan Bernal's tragedy, *El último huancavilca y el primer guayaquileño,* undated in its first edition, then reprinted in 1871 in the newspaper *La Patria.*

To reproduce Dr. Rolando's list would be fruitless. Even the printed copies of most of the plays mentioned have disappeared. But his bibliography does serve to show that about every two years a play by some Ecuadorian achieved print, and that in 1878, 1883, and 1885 two plays per year came off the presses.

Some plays went unmentioned because they dropped from sight. Not until after his death was all the dramatic activity of the essayist Juan Montalvo (1832–1889) discovered. During his lifetime *La leprosa* and *Descomulgada* (finally published in Ambato in 1931) were performed, but his best is probably the tragedy *El dictador* (1873), only recently found.[3] Five of his Platonic dialogs can now be read in his *Libro de las pasiones* (University of Havana, 1930). To modern readers all have a pompous air, but Barrera insists on their greatness when judged by the literary tastes of Montalvo's time.[4]

Representative of the historical drama was *Diez de agosto* (1883)

[3] Printed in *Universidad de la Habana,* IX (July, 1934), 77–109, and X (January, 1935), 49–66.
[4] Isaac J. Barrera, *Historia de la literatura ecuatoriana,* p. 144. See also Manuel Pedro González, "Los dramas de Juan Montalvo," *Estudios sobre literaturas hispanoamericanas,* pp. 347–350.

by Abelardo Moncayo, a forerunner of spectacles like José Luis Velasco's *El nueve de octubre de 1820*, a poetic play in five acts prepared for the centenary of Ecuador's independence. Some dramatists looked even farther into the past for inspiration, as, for example, Guillermo Dávila in his three-act tragedy-with-music *Atahualpa* (1920), and Filemón Proaño in his "prehistoric drama" *El príncipe Cacha* (1931), that won a gold medal in Sevilla.

Most repeated names in Dr. Rolando's bibliography, however, are Nicolás Augusto González (1858–1918) and Juan Eusebio Molestina. The poetic dramas of González were written so fast that their literary quality suffered. *Hojas secas* (1878) and *El Mundo del hombre* (1880) were published in Quito. *Fuegos fatuos* came later, as did *Amor y patria* and one that appealed to young people, *Primavera*. The dramatic career of Molestina crossed the year 1895 which marked the end of romanticism and the beginning of modernism, with General Eloy Alfaro. In the seventy years since, there has been only occasional activity.

Molestina produced poetic dramas, set far from the national scene: *Las penas del trovador* (1883), *El poeta y la coqueta* (Guayaquil, 1885), and *La duquesa y la aldeana* (1910). But a couple of women dramatists looked closer to home for their material. Doña Carmen Pérez de Rodríguez (1828–1898) of Guayaquil was author of a comedy, *Los montuvios*; and Mercedes González de Moscoso (1860–1911), produced in Quito in 1905 her poetic tragedy *Martirio sin culpa*, concerning the evil daughter of a noble mother. Her only surviving drama, however, is *La abuela*, with editions in 1903 and 1907.

Another productive dramatist was "Américo Hispano" (José Miguel Pozo) who within a month sold out one printing of *Alba de sangre* (1923) and required a second edition. His three-act *Regeneración o catástrofe o La invasión peruana del Ecuador* stirred the blood in Guayaquil in 1923. Later, from Riobamba, came an undated edition of another of his patriotic appeals, *Víctimas del siglo*, in four acts. From Riobamba, too, came Juan Félix Proaño, author of five-act Indian dramas like *Quizquiz o Desastre de la raza* (1919) and *Condorazo* (1925). "Brigadier Alfa" (César Augusto Velarde) of Guayaquil published a similar Indian drama, *Viracocha* (1925).

Two other dramatists whose work rose above the low level of their time were Victor Manuel Rendón (1859–1940) and Alfredo Baquerizo Moreno. Rendón's collected *Teatro: 1922–1936* (Guayaquil,

1937) includes a number of children's plays written for the use of the school associates of his two daughters, and some for adults, like *Hoy, ayer, y mañana* (1922) and *Salas populi* (1928). The title of this last indicates Dr. Rendon's classical training. For these plays not only were there few actors, but the quality of acting during the early days of the century was low. Local dramatists had to count on friends or on students in the various academies of dramatic art, who had not learned Hamlet's advice to the players.

In 1927 an actor, Eduardo Beltrán, came to Guayaquil from Spain with ambition to improve the quality of acting by training children. He founded the Compañía Infantil with actors under twelve, including five of his own children. Though it lasted only three years, it long influenced the theatre. Paco Villar, one of its juvenile stars, has dominated the theatrical and radio scene of Guayaquil ever since. Most of his youthful associates, however, went into more lucrative professions.

In contrast to Villar, who acted with restraint, was one practitioner of the "moans and tears" school, Guillermo Cabezas, who performed tragedies under the Anglicized name of William Head. When his agonizing turned away people with taste, he appealed to the galleries by spicing his offerings and taking such liberties with his scripts that he often shocked those who knew the originals.

At this time Quito, the capital, separated from Guayaquil by more than the miles of mountainous roads, was developing its own interest in the theatre. One cause was the arrival about 1930 of a Spaniard, Abelardo Revoredo, to teach in the conservatory. His comments in class about the French and Spanish theatre inspired some of the students to form a group of traveling players, as Lope de Rueda had done in Spain in the sixteenth century, to take drama to the villagers. Marina Moncayo became the leading lady, with her husband, Jorge Icaza (1906–),[5] and Gonzalo Proaño as the leading men.

Icaza had already started writing plays, influenced by his study of the French theatre. A foreign company had performed his three-act *El intruso* (1928), a farce about marital infidelity. The same year his *Comedia sin nombre* had set Quito laughing at Ecuador's bureaucratic system. And now that he had completed a new farce, *Por el*

[5] Albert Franklin, "A Versatile Ecuadorean," *Inter-America,* I (November, 1942), 33–35.

viejo (published 1928), the group selected this play by their twenty-one-year-old leading man as their first offering for the 1929 season. By horse and muleback they took it to small towns around the capital, not making much money but gaining the experience that Ecuador actors and dramatists find so hard to acquire.

Deciding he wanted to make people think as well as laugh, Icaza next wrote a one-act tragedy in three scenes, *¿Cuál es?* This serious production in 1931 by a supposedly funny writer shocked Quito. They wanted no problems from Freud and Marx about children who killed their father. When Icaza went on to write another gloomy experimental play, *Como ellos quieren* (1932), about feminine hysteria, the public, which had demanded he be jailed after the one-act play, now clamored that the new play be prohibited. The Moncayo players decided not to present it in their 1932 season, but a published volume containing it and its predecessor sold out within a week. His *Rumbo al sur* deals with the most popular passenger during a voyage to Panama: she turns out to be a prostitute. *Sin sentido* was also written for 1932.

Icaza's next theatrical venture was also disheartening. Reading Jules Romains' *Le Dictateur* (1926) had decided him to make a Spanish version with which to open his 1933 season. But Dictator Páez of Ecuador suspected an innuendo against his Administration and refused to license it. In a discussion among Icaza's associates, some wanted to abandon attempts to present local plays, arguing that profit would come only from foreign offerings. The "arty" ones wanted tragedies; the rest wanted to bask in guffaws from the galleries—and so the troupe split. Icaza and his wife Marina persisted for a time, and their repertory included: *Como los árboles* and *Manos de criminal* by Avellán, *El último bohemio* by San Miguel, *El milagro de una culpa* by Mayar Francisco Villavicencio, *Bambalinas* and *Bajo la zarpa* by Salvador, *Potaje comunista* by Manuel Antonio Salgado, and *Suburbio* (1931) by Raúl Andrade.

While running into debt themselves it was discouraging to watch the success of their former associates, who filled their seats with those who believed that any play from abroad was better than anything from their own country. Meantime Icaza had turned to fiction about the downtrodden Indians and had won international recognition with his novel *Huasipungo* (1934). Faced with a choice between constant struggle as a dramatist and wide glory as a novelist, he abandoned his first love and dissolved his company. Later, when he tried to collect them to perform one more work, his brief ballet-like *Flagelo* (1942), he discovered that one player had shot herself and another hanged himself in Lima. Sure now that he was not destined to be a dramatist, especially when he had to wait six years for a production of this gloomy thesis play showing the Indians suffering at the hands of both clergy and landowners, Icaza opened a bookstore in Quito and concentrated on writing novels. Gonzalo Proaño tried to find a producer for his own four-act, pre-Inca melodrama "El príncipe Cacha" of 1931, then also gave up.

Ecuador has had other national *elencos*, the most famous being the troupe of Chavica Gómez and her husband, Ernesto Albán Mosquera. They have performed such national plays as *Sátiro encadenado* and *Lázaro* by Aguilera Malta, and others by Descalzi, Moscoso Vega, San Miguel, and Avellán Ferrés. To provide laughs they have staged Aguirre's *Receta para viajar* and frequent *estampas*, local-color sketches so full of slang and local allusions that only native-born Ecuadorians can understand them. Many were written by "Rodrigo de Triana" (Professor Rodrigo Chávez González of Guayaquil). Others were the work of Albán, who created the typical lower-class Evaristo to ridicule customs and situations. *Evaristo, autor*, for instance, pokes fun at the vanguardists, etc. During the Galo Plaza elections, Albán presented *Evaristo, presidente*. Some of these *estampas* were published in book form in Quito in 1949.

The Gómez-Albán troupe does not need to depend on Ecuador for patronage. Their annual tours with Spanish and Argentine repertory cover the Spanish American world. One of their most popular offerings has been a Spanish version of *Charley's Aunt*.

Another Quiteño who wrote plays was Humberto Salvador (1908–   ), professor of Comparative Literature at the University of Quito. Professor Salvador wrote *Canción de Rosas* (1925), *Amor prohibido* (1926), *Bambalinas*, *Bajo la zarpa*, and *El miedo de amar*. Unable to get directors to produce them, he turned to writing psychological novels of protest, and made himself much better known as a sociological novelist.

Cuenca, too, has had its theatrical seasons. Here at the beginning of the twentieth century lived Octavio Cordero Palacios, writing Calderonian dramas like *Atahualpa*; and Nicanor Aguilar, whose play manuscripts were gladly lent to school dramatic groups that promptly lost them. Here Alfonso Andrade Chiriboga, in his unpublished national plays, filled his dialog with Indian dialect.

Later César Andrade Cordero and Arturo Montesinos Malo developed their radio dramas, and inspired four amateur groups to perform in the Teatro Andrade. In 1944 the University of Cuenca built its Little Theatre, with 650 seats, where Paco Estrella directed six foreign and national plays a year.

Cuenca's most active dramatist as well as artist and journalist is Luis A. Moscoso Vega (1909–   ). As a newspaper editor, he prints his plays on his own presses and issues them in small volumes, the width of a newspaper column. Among his score of titles, half of them comedies, is *Conscripción* (1941), which shows his sympathy with the Indians and hope for eventual justice. Introduced first by Gómez-Albán, it has been played more than 150 times. Even more frequently performed is Moscoso's comedy *Los mellizos de doña Amada* (1945), in which the characters try to find babies so as to be eligible for the wealth of Don Ramón. *Anselmo el boticario* is the humorous account of a hypochondriac who is cured by a druggist disguised as a famous specialist. Moscoso Vega's most recent play, *El ataúd de cristal* (1952), is a morbid study of a patriarch's attack on parental domination. Its title is derived from the glass coffin through which one of the characters, Mateo, expects to watch the process of putrefaction.

Outside Cuenca, within sight of the jungles, is the little town of Azogues, with one main street. When movies are shown at its single theatre, everybody attends. Between times, its stage is used by a group of young people. Their only reported experiment with an Ecuadorian play was the production in 1945 of *Lázaro* by Aguilera Malta, but between 1946 and 1950, these amateur actors performed all the plays of the Uruguayan Florencio Sánchez, a feat perhaps unique in the history of the Latin American theatre.

Guayaquil, meantime, was not inactive. In 1928 Carlos Arturo León published his *Obras*, containing dramas. A woman, Rosa Borja de Ycaza, witnessed a production of her three-act comedy of customs, *Las de Judas*, in 1932, at the seventy-five-year-old Teatro Olmedo, and saw the play published in 1933. In 1935 a poetic comedy in six scenes, *Paralelogramo*, brought Gonzalo Escudero to public attention.

In 1941 Ecuador saw the beginning of the playwriting career of a man who, if the country had possessed a thriving theatre, would have been one of the most active dramatists of the continent. Demetrio Aguilera Malta (1909–   ) had for ten years been known as a skilled novelist. He was also teaching in a new boys' school, Colegio Vicente Rocafuerte, whose building appropriations had been exhausted before the school theatre could be equipped. In 1940 the students persuaded Paco Villar to help them raise funds for scenery by producing a play from Spain; but the electric equipment was still unpurchased, so Aguilera Malta offered to write a play for them. The result was *Lázaro*[6] the study of a school teacher, that became one of the most frequently produced of Ecuador's plays.

Once their theatre was equipped, the boys performed thirty-one plays during the first five years of their activity and even made a barnstorming trip to Quito during a vacation period. But though this group, like the Gómez-Albán company, occasionally selects national plays, most of Ecuador's dramatists, as Professor Adolfo S. Simmonds laments, have given up the struggle to find someone to put their manuscripts onto the stage.[7]

Aguilera Malta kept on experimenting with various types of plays. *Sátiro encadenado* was followed by *Sangre azul* (1946), about the clash of ideas between Guayaquil aristocrats and gringo visitors. *El pirata fantasma* the same year, set in colonial Guayaquil, is probably the first mystery play written by a Latin American.[8]

Giving up the idea of finding outlets in Ecuador, Aguilera Malta went to Brazil and finally to Mexico, earning a living by adapting scenarios for the movies, but continuing to produce original plays. *Dos hombres y mil mujeres* (1948) was a fantasy about an airplane accident on a tropical isle of Amazons. *No bastan los átomos* was a modern pacifist play, published in 1955 with the brief, satirical *Dientes blancos* by Ecuador's Casa de Cultura. More recently (1959) three of Aguilera Malta's one-act plays were enthusiastically received in a Mexican publication, *Trilogía ecuatoriana*. One was *El tigre*, a folklore study of brute power and superstitious fear, already three times published. Another was his recent *Honorarios* (1958), a dramatization of a story of villainy and sacrifice by his fellow country-

[6] Published in *Revista del Colegio Nacional Vicente Rocafuerte*, II, No. 3 (October, 1941).

[7] *Ibid.*, No. 1 (January, 1941), 3–14.

[8] *Sangre azul* was published in Spanish, Portuguese, and English by the Panamerican Union in 1948. It, with *Pirata fantasma*, appeared in textbook form as *Dos comedias fáciles* (Boston: Houghton Mifflin, 1950).

man, the novelist Cuadra. Among other still unpublished plays are "Fantoche," one of whose characters is a ventriloquist's dummy, and "La muerte es en gran negocio" (1962), a fantastic but ironic satire about a medicine man with an elixir of life. This dramatist is both skilled and tireless and can contribute greatly to any theatre that Ecuador may eventually develop. With his wife, the Mexican actress Velia Márquez, he wrote the three-act play about the theatre, *Una mujer para cada acto* (1960). It has only two characters.

Another who might have made a career of playwriting was Augusto San Miguel. Being wealthy, he was able to visit Europe and study its theatre first hand. On his return to Guayaquil he began writing. His sketch *Almas bohemias*, also called *El último bohemio*, was well received. *Una tristeza más en mis tristezas* provided Carmen Méndez with a triumph in the Teatro Olmedo. But San Miguel did not have to write plays for a living and, disillusioned by the efforts to get them produced only to draw criticism, he took to drink. *Sombra*, his autobiographical tragedy about the effects of alcoholism, is still remembered by those who saw its only presentation. Then, himself a volunteer fireman, San Miguel dashed off a comedy, *El tercer cuartel*, about firemen, whose riotous performance was a high point in Ecuador's theatrical history. He probably wrote other plays but when he died prematurely, his mother and his brother destroyed all his papers. Nothing but his reputation remains, since none of his plays ever got into print.

More recently a few dramatists from the coast have had better luck. Pedro Jorge Vera (1912–   ), a bookseller like Icaza, began with three volumes of poetry that firmly established him. After a stay in Russia, he switched to the novel and wrote the powerful *Los animales puros* about Guayaquil laborers, followed by *Luto eterno*, one of Ecuador's finest collections of long and short, but humorless, fiction. But all the time he was reading and thinking theatre. His bookstore is the country's biggest deposit of plays. Eventually, in 1938, he wrote *El dios de la selva*, a four-act drama of the jungles, not published till 1943. A technical feat, it protests the tremendous power of the Green Moloch in a sort of dramatic Green Hell, except that man is victorious. *Hamlet resuelve sus dudas* (1950) follows a political career from rebellion to oppression. Retitled *Los ardiente caminos*, and with Indians from Icaza's novels, it suggests Romains' *The Dictator* and Giraudoux's *Siegfried*, and harks back as well to the justice administered by the people in Lope's *Fuenteovejuna.* However that does not deprive it of originality or detract from the skill of Vera the dramatist. It was succeeded by *La mano de Dios,* his best, and the winner, in spite of its brevity, of the 1953 Sociedad Amigos del Teatro prize. García Lorca is its spiritual parent.

Most recent is *Luto eterno* (1955) which Vera termed "espectáculo grotesco," a dramatization of the title story of his book collection. He and his friends performed it under the direction of Telmo Vascónez, in the Teatro Intimo of Quito, with the usual disheartening attendance. However, this present-day social analysis, for its fluid dialog and well-rounded characters, can stand with the best of Ecuador's theatre.[9]

In 1950 Enrique Garcés, a physician from Otavalo, published *Alondra,* in which psychiatrists decide what is wrong with a woman. But his attempt to find an audience for it was reminiscent of the experience recorded in the diary of the Frenchman Wiener, who visited Guayaquil in 1879. He bought a ticket for a play but was told at the door that the prospect of an audience of only four had decided the actors to cancel. Nor have conditions improved since. In 1946 a Colombian company arrived with the interesting *Manuelita la libertadora,* by Genecot, for a week's run. It should have attracted throngs, since it dealt with the mistress of Ecuador's national hero, Simón Bolívar; but not enough tickets were sold for even one performance. Even a program of Ecuadorian farces by Paco Villar that year could not fill the tiny Teatro Aladino, but in the next block customers stood in line to pay twice as much for a movie in English that they could not understand.

Yet Garcés did not give up. By 1958, when his *Teatro* was published in Quito, he had completed three genuinely national dramas, though his inability to work with them in production gives them an air more literary than scenic, as the hand of the author moves the puppets. Besides *Alondra,* with a first act rising to dramatic heights, the volume contains *Boca trágica* (1943), another psychopathic study; and a moral comedy, *Lo que no puede ser,* in which the bad brother rises through knavery, but the virtuous brother triumphs in an excellent final curtain. These plays of Dr. Garcés point the way to what may some day be good national drama.

[9] Vera's complete *Teatro* was published (Quito: Casa de Cultura Ecuatoriana, 1957).

Another playwright who has refused to be discouraged is the man about whom the Chilean actor Gabriel Martínez declared: "Anyone who says that Ecuador has no theatre does not know what he is talking about. It has that masterly author Avellán, and that is plenty." He was referring to a native of Guayaquil, Enrique Avellán Ferrés, born in 1908, whose first play, *Como los árboles* (1927), performed before he graduated from the university, was called "audacious" but pleased both public and critics. It concerns two children whose father brought them up to believe their mother dead, so that he would not have to explain about her unfaithfulness or his refusal to get a divorce. The handling of suspense, and the character development show the skill of the young dramatist, as the wordiness of some of the scenes betrays his inexperience.

In *Sin camisas* (1934), a one-act play with unconvincing psychology, Avellán had difficulties about the passage of time, allowing some characters to leave for Mass and return after only two pages of dialog, while the easygoing hero goes job-hunting and gets back in less than a minute of conversation.

El mismo caso (1938) tries in a single play to describe conditions in Guayaquil's shipyards, to preach against adultery, and to debate universal mechanization versus socialism, communism, and syndicalism; he relies on a coincidental gasoline explosion to solve everything. But little Graciela is a real character and so is her grandfather; the dialog is agile; and there are moments of great dramatic power.

By the time Avellán started on his fourth play, *Manos de criminal* (1939), he had a better grip on his technique, and his first act is thoroughly convincing in its setting, a typical Guayaquil *covacha* where the life of its tenement dwellers go on as usual though Petra is having a baby. The huge hands of the infant earn him his nickname. Their effect in shaping his character is shown in the last two acts. Much of the play is concerned with labor problems which, in dramas by the coast dwellers, take the place of the Indian problem in the plays of writers from Quito. Later, Avellán moved to Quito and became occupied in the law. No works by him have appeared since then. However the problems of the laboring masses have also been treated in such plays as *Crimen social* (1905), *Frontera* (1910), *Honra de obrero* (1911), and others by Emilio Gallegos del Campo (1875–1914).

One other playwright, César Ricardo Descalzi (1912–   ) of Quito, deserves mention. While a student of medicine, he wrote the three-act *Anfiteatro* (1936) for a Student Day celebration. It grew out of his own experiences and was set in the dormitory of a medical student. This combination of criticism and romanticism had five performances in Quito and several in Guayaquil and Cuenca, but not till 1950 was it finally published, and then more because of the interest in its theme than for its technical excellence.[10]

Much better in construction are Descalzi's later plays. His medical interest in tuberculosis is shown in *Los caminos blancos* (1938), about the invalid Luna, vainly seeking to cure her tuberculosis. Descalzi is best known, however, for his tragedy in twelve scenes, *Portovelo*, written in 1938 while as a medical student he was visiting gold mines run by foreigners in Portovelo. Sometimes described as anti-Yankee, the play is just as vitriolic in condemning Dictator Enríquez for permitting poor working conditions. Its content is superior to its form: the dramatist's belief in the inherent goodness in man is shown. And Pan Americanism is served by the pairing of Dolores, daughter of an Ecuador doctor at the mines, with the young American doctor of the company. One ironic scene takes place in New York where financiers are worrying about the falling value of their stock because of what is happening "in some far-off place called Ecuador." The play was finally published by the Quito Casa de Cultura in 1951.

Most recent is his "intellectual play," *En el horizonte se alza la niebla*, which reveals a mystic side to Descalzi. Its performance by a visiting Chilean company in 1945 won it the prize of the Play of the Year by the Guayaquil branch of the Casa de Cultura, but it has never been published.

Following these dramatists came Augusto Sacotto Arias, who as a young writer in 1942 placed first among twenty-five entries for the Ecuador National Prize of Literature, with his two-act *La furiosa manzanera*. It combines the modern García Lorca and Spain's sixteenth-century Jorge Manrique, in that it is more a work of poetry than drama—it has one character who can talk only in verse. Some critics view this artificial play as an attempt to establish a new trend, away from the proletariat,[11] but, if so, Sacotto had no followers. Following this success, Buenos Aires' Teatro del Pueblo contracted in

---

[10] Published by Casa de Cultura Ecuatoriana, Quito, 1951, as part of its attempt to give permanence to important national works.

[11] "Sacotto Arias," *Revista del Mar Pacifico*, Quito, June, 1943.

1945 to produce three of his plays and he went to Argentina. There seems to be no record of what he did there.

After 1945 the theatre seemed dead within the nation of Ecuador. The novelist and essayist Leopoldo Benítez Vinueza, author of one play, had to enlist the Uruguayan National Players to produce his *Cuzunza o Aguas turbias* in Teatro Solís in 1950. This tragedy of the jungle's overcoming and devouring its protagonist was very difficult to mount and had only a short run. Alberto C. Saltos' four-act drama, *El precio de amor*, was published by the Casa de Cultura in 1955, with no indication of any previous performance.

The names of José Trajano Mera, César E. Arroyo, Carlos Granados Guarnizo, and Luis Paz y Miño have appeared briefly as authors of plays, but even the Casa de Cultura's move into new quarters in Quito, with a good theatre attached, was not enough to bring new life to the world of drama there. Ecuador's dramatists' had moved away or entered other professions.

Then, unheralded, appeared a new dramatist. Francisco Tobar García (1928–   ), lawyer and professor of literature at Quito's Catholic University, turned to the theatre. His first produced attempt was discouraging: *Yanaqui* (House of Cards), intended as a tragedy, was misunderstood by the amused audience, so the author destroyed it and dates his career from a one-act play, *Miedo* (1954). Fear was to loom large in all of Tobar's drama, along with anguish and internal mystery. His characters from both upper and lower classes are portrayed as denying spiritual values. But they show dramatic power. His next attempt, the one-act *Mariposas* (1955), written to be acted by his Teatro Independiente at the University of Quito, had four performances. Then he extended himself to three-act dramas. *En una sola carne* (1955) is a triangle play in defense of the middle class and its intellectual corruption. Critics saw the influence of O'Neill till Tobar insisted he had never read O'Neill.

Quito in the 1950's had a few struggling theatres: the Pichincha Play House; Amigos de Teatro, run by Matilde de Ortega; and Teatro Intimo, later the Teatro Moderno, which was established in 1953 by a German drama enthusiast, Dr. Karl Loewenberg, who with Vera Kohn was trying to develop a theatre-going public by producing plays in Cueva de Buho. For this last group, Tobar wrote *Las res* (1956), a one-act suspense play set in a jungle town. An escaped convict plans to kill the shopkeeper Ursula, and a passerby is too cowardly to come to her help. This was the last play directed by the discouraged Dr. Loewenberg before he returned to Hamburg.

That same year Tobar mingled prose and poetry in a four-act historical play commemorating the founding of Quito. In addition he directed it and played the part of Padre Rodríguez. Its title, *Los dioses y el caballo* (1956), describes the attitude of the Indians toward the white invaders. A dozen of Tobar's plays, published by the Casa de Cultura Ecuatoriana in his two-volume *Teatro* (1962), serve to show his increasing ability. In *Atados de pies y manos* (1947) he abandons the restraint of his earlier plays and lets the money-worshiping chief character rebel against God. His own favorite, and well received by audiences, was *Todo lo que brillo es oro*, retitled *El limbo* (1958), but his big moneymaker was an "abusive version" of Molière's *The Miser* (1958).

The playwright confesses that his admiration for English literature influenced his next play, *Parábola* (1958), preferred by many Ecuadorian critics. *La noche no es para dormir* (1960) shows the effect of Fry and James. His masterpieces are this one and *La llave del abismo* (1961), for which Tobar gives credit to his greatest inspiration, Sophocles. It takes its title from *Revelations*, Chapter 9, where the Fifth Angel delivers "the key of the pit of the abyss." His newest play in verse, *En alguien muere la víspera* (1962), called a "burlesque detective play" and influenced by Meredith, surpassed anything he had written previously when performed by the Ecuadorian actor Ernesto Albán in Quito in 1963.

All these dramas and comedies with their poetic touch definitely establish Francisco Tobar García as one of the authentic playwrights of the continent. Though not realistic theatre, the plays of Tobar deal with realities, and irony is always their spring. Perhaps he can breathe new life into the Ecuadorian theatre.

Certainly even the activities of the dramatic groups in schools and universities have done little to improve the situation, for too often the enthusiasm disappears upon graduation, or the students move away. The promising Gregorio Cordero y León moved to Mexico, where he published *Tres tragedias rurales*.[12] Aguilera Malta has left; Avellán Ferrés has stopped writing; but others persist. Under Tobar, El Independiente has been functioning for ten years. El Teatro Ex-

---

[12] Gregorio Cordero y León, *Tres tragedias rurales*.

perimental de Alianza Francesa came into being in October, 1959, with Jean Zune and Jacques Thiériot. And Teatro Experimental de la Universidad Central (TEU), under Sixto Salguero, even made a tour, although with a repertory of foreign plays. In 1961 Benjamín Carrión and the Casa de Cultura Ecuatoriana founded Instituto Nacional del Teatro. It has not done much yet, but it promises to awaken local authors and stimulate Ecuador's theatre. ¡Vamos a ver!

CHAPTER 20

The Colombian National Theatre

By 1831, when Colombia resumed the name of New Granada as its exclusive title and a political struggle began between liberalism and conservatism, the influence of France had already become evident in the many pseudoclassical tragedies performed since the beginning of the century, like *El soliloquio de Eneas* and *El sacrificio de Idomeneo* (1803) by José Mª· Salazar (1784–1830). While occasional traveling players stopped in Bogotá, one in 1798 and one in 1833, it was mostly amateur groups that brought plays by Moratín and Gorostiza and translations from Alfieri and others to the Ramírez Coliseum. Occasionally a play by a Colombian author saw the boards. The pioneer, *El zagal de Bogotá* (1806) by Montalvo, has already been mentioned. Later came *La ilusión de un enamorado* (1813), a preromantic blending of prose and poetry by Mario Candil (1789–1841), also performed at the Ramírez. It was a surprise-ending fantasy in which the twenty-four-year-old lover dreamed he was caressing his sweetheart. It was dedicated to the patriot Antonio Nariño, and some of the socialites of Bogotá performed it. Another fanciful play by Candil was *Amor y desdén* (1826). It was in verse with a fairy-tale plot more suitable for children's theatre, about a princess truly loved by a dwarf but charmed by a faithless giant. When Candil tried to handle a more adult theme and wrote *El fulgor de los escombros* (1827), critics disapproved of his dialog and wooden characters.

The first writer deserving of a place in independent Colombia's theatrical history, however, was the short-lived genius Luis Vargas Tejada (1802–1829). This student of German, English, Italian, and French, wrote his first five-act classical play on an Indian theme at the age of sixteen. Of all his tragedies, only two survive. *Sugamuxi* (1818) takes its title from the Indian temple of human sacrifice. The drama *Doraminta* (1819) deals with a disinherited prince whose fiancée gets control of the throne and invites his rival to help run the government. The slow pace of these plays is due in part to their meter of unrimed, eleven-syllable lines—Shakespearean blank verse ill-adapted to Spanish. The lost tragedies *Aquimín* (1819) and *Saquesa-zipa* (1819), and the drama *Witikindo* (1820) also had Indian themes.

Local and contemporary—even though derived from Lope de Vega's *Acero de Madrid* by way of the Italian Francesco Abergati Capacelli's *Convulsioni*—was Vargas Tejada's inconclusive one-act *Las convulsiones* (1829). Full of Santa Fe characters, it pokes fun at the aping of French customs and narrates the antics developed around Crispina's feigned fainting spells.

Once an admirer of Bolívar, Vargas Tejada praised the Liberator in a number of early poems and in the one-act comedy-in-verse, *El Parnaso transferido* (1820), in which the dwellers in Parnassus flee from its tyranny to seek the liberty enjoyed in independent Colombia. However, later seeing Bolívar as a tyrant, Vargas Tejada attacked him in a lyric monolog *La madre de Pausanias*, and then, convinced that the sword was mightier than the pen, died in an attempt to assassinate Bolívar.

The other dramatist who helped establish the Colombian stage was the physician José Fernández Madrid (1789–1830), President of Venezuela and New Granada in 1816. Later, while an exile in Cuba, Fernández Madrid wrote and published a neoclassical tragedy, *Atala* (1822), based on Chateaubriand's novel of 1801 about the daughter of a North American Indian chief. She saves the captive, Chactas, then flees with him and hides in the cave of a hermit, Obrí. She takes poison to keep her reputation unsullied. It was performed by students in Bogotá to entertain Bolívar. Under the influence of Nicolás de Moratín and of Jovellanos, this facile versifier also wrote the classical *Guatimocín* (1824), dealing with Cortés and the overthrow of the Aztec empire. Fernández Madrid believed in the usefulness of the stage to teach a love of liberty, and although he wrote too rapidly to create masterpieces, and critics consider his dialog heavy and stage movement elephantine, he did create characters and moments of high drama, and he helped provide impetus for the developing Colombian theatre.

Between the classicists and the romanticists can be found "José Negreros," (José Joaquín Ortiz, 1814–1892), teacher, journalist, poet, and religious leader, who improved on *Sugamuxi* in his popular tragedy *Sulma* (published 1870), and who also wrote a comic piece, *El hijo pródigo*.

The five-act tragedy *La Pola* (1826) by José María Domínguez has already been mentioned. This heroine of Colombia's struggle for freedom, Policarpa Salavarrieta, has been a favorite with dramatists, not only in her native Colombia, but elsewhere.[1] From the time that General Santander told José Domingo Roche to dramatize her tragic story in order to stir up anti-Spanish feeling, at least seven other dramatists have used her in their tragedies, including four other Colombians, the Argentine Bartolomé Mitre, and the contemporary Uruguayan poetess Sarah Bollo.

For lack of visiting actors, local lovers of the theatre began organizing their own companies, with boys to play the feminine roles. Earliest of these, formed by Juan Granados in 1833, included the dramatist Constantino Franco, his father, the comedian Losada, and, as "señoritas," Venancio Ortiz, Antonio Vargas Reyes, and the future lawyer, Ignacio Ospina. Joaquín Salgado was billed as the "dama característica." The repertory was largely Colombian: *Aquimín* by Vargas Tejada; *Don Gonzalo de Córdoba* and *El conde don Julián* by Francisco de Paula Torres; and *Miguel* by Alvarez Lozano. That same year Francisco de Villalba brought to Bogotá a traveling company with an Argentine leading lady.

For the national company that year of 1833, Francisco de Paula Torres, one of Colombia's earliest romanticists, provided history in sugar-coated doses, with his *Don Gonzalo de Córdoba* about the fifteenth-century "Great Captain" in Italy, and *El conde don Julián* about the Moors in Spain. His plays supplanted Ortiz' *Sulma* (1870) in popularity.

Also in 1833, the eighteen-year-old Manuel María Madiedo (1815–1888) wrote the five-act tragedy *Coriolano* (published 1849), and then went on to investigate the Roman scene in the neoclassic tragedy *Roma libre*, not performed, however, until 1849. *Lucrecia* and *Bruto* were also by him, as well as the comedy *Una idea abismo*, and several popular comedies: *El doctor Berengena*, *Una mujer de las que no se usan*, and *Tres diablos sueltos*. In 1834 Colombia saw the first performance of *Miguel* by Rafael Alvarez Lozano, who is also

[1] Agustín del Saz, "El teatro hispanoamericano del siglo XIX," *Historia general de las literaturas hispanoamericanas*, IV, 432–433.

remembered for his successful preromantic tragedies: *Los proscritos* and *El corsario.*

A group of touring Spanish actors under Alfonso Torres, arriving in Bogotá for a four-year stay, put an end to the classical-theatre movement by introducing samples of Spain's romantic plays that had been playing in Madrid since 1833. The old Ramírez Coliseo was reconditioned in 1840 with a new curtain displaying Apollo and Pegasus. The curtain was painted by Eladio Vergara, who later wrote several dramas for the Coliseo: *El oidor de Santafé* (1857), *El bandido de San Lotario* (1858) and *El misionero* (1858). As El Teatro Maldonado, renamed for its new proprietors, it opened with an announcement of free tamales between the acts. Unexpectedly, the smell of the meat pies kept spectators away. The era of popcorn and banana chips had not yet arrived.

Inspired by the thrill and vivacity of Spanish romanticist plays by García Gutiérrez and Larra, several local writers also joined the new movement. One who did was José Caicedo Rojas (1816–1897). This senator, Cabinet minister, diplomat, and university professor achieved his first success with the drama *Miguel Cervantes Saavedra* (1849) and followed it in the Teatro Maldonado by three more: *Selos* (1858), *Amor y ambición* (1868), and *Gratitud de un artista* (1869). As Ortega points out, these plays no longer have an appeal, because they are more literary than dramatic and deal with past events rather than current problems.[2] But Caicedo's work established him among important Colombian dramatists, and marked a turning point in the life of Colombia's stage, as it popularized his brand of realistic romanticism. His book, *Recuerdos y apuntamientos* (1868) contains a large amount of material useful to a historian of the Bogotá stage.

Caicedo Rojas was followed by Santiago Pérez (1830–1900), whose romantic *Jacobo Moloy* (1851) was to break up the Centro de Autores Dramáticos. Pérez was also rector of the University, and for two years President of Colombia, but he is best remembered for his melodramatic plays of suicide and assassination. According to one critic, they "killed off everybody on the stage but the prompter."[3] In his day his 1853 *Castillo de Berkeley* (published 1885), about Ed-

[2] José Vicente Ortega Ricaurte, *Historia crítica del teatro en Bogotá*, 1st ed., pp. 95–97.
[3] Javier Arango Ferrer, "Medio siglo de literatura colombiana," *Panorama das literaturas das Américas*, I, 338.

ward III and fourteenth-century England, and his *Leonor* were called the "two majestic condors of Colombian literature."[4] *Nemequene* (1855) was another of his dramas. Its chief character was the Indian witch doctor of Chief Osmún's court, already introduced in Orbea's *La conquista de Santafé* (1718).

His diplomat brother, Lázaro Mª. Pérez (1824–1892), who represented Colombia in Germany as well as directed the Bogotá theatre, tried to encourage Colombian plays in his theatre. But he himself wrote such non-national plays as a romantic tragedy of Italy, *Teresa o La cordelera* (1854), performed by the Lleras company; *Elvira* (1856), about the humiliation of Spanish King Felipe IV by his vassals; *El gondolero de Venecia;* and *El corsario negro.* But he did at least write *El sitio de Cartagena en 1815.*

Still another Pérez, Felipe Pérez (1836–1891), was author of *Gonzalo Pizarro* (1857), a romantic tragedy in verse about the early days of Peru. It received high praise from the drama lovers. The drama *El ladrón* (1856) and the comedy *Cuando el río suena* (1857) were also by him.

Leopoldo Arias Vargas (1832–1884) won a temporary popularity with the passionate *Besos que hieren* (1856). He repeated with his adaptation from Dumas, *Pascual Bruno* (1857), which was several times revived. He also wrote the melodramatic *La gema de Castelnovo.* Another interesting play of this period was the amusing one-act *Los alfandoques* (1856), which appeared under the signature "D. R. i Caro." Before it was published in 1876, the Colombian novelist Ricardo Carrasquilla (1827–1886) confessed that the signature was his anagram from "Ricardo."

But all the melodramatic plays failed to create a theatre-going public. That did not come till the beginning of the *costumbrista* movement brought national themes onto the stage.[5] To do what Lázaro Pérez had advocated but had failed to do—write about Colombia and Colombians—came José María Samper (1828–1888). Among his plays were his first and best drama, *El deber cumplido* (1854), and also *El hijo del pueblo* (1855), *Dios corrige, no mata* (1857), and *La conspiración de setiembre* (1860). He wrote three comedies: *Un día de pagos* (1857), *Percances de un empleo* (1857) and *Los aguinaldos* (1858). Best of his output, however, was the libretto of

[4] *Ibid.*
[5] Javier Arango Ferrer, *La literatura en Colombia*, p. 65.

a national opera, *Un alcalde a la antigua* (1874), with music by José María Ponce de León.

The most important contribution of Samper to the Colombian stage was his organization in 1854 of the Centro de Autores Dramáticos. Sadly, after some years of encouraging writers, the Centro came to a violent end in a split over a benefit performance for the popular actor of the Bogotá stage, Guillermo Eloy Izásiga. The play originally selected was Pérez' *Jacobo Moloy*, earlier awarded a prize by the Centro. However one of the associates, Vicente Osuna, schemed for the selection of something by his uncle, Constancio Franco (1842–1894), who, with his fifteen titles, was, next to Juan José Botero (1840–1926), the most prolific of Colombian dramatists. Franco's comedy *Los próceres* (1868) and *El telón descubierto* (1892) have some merit, but most of them, like *El demonio alcohol* (1876), are only dramatized sermons. After an argument, the popularity and better technique of Pérez caused the selection of his play, at which about half of the members of the Circle resigned, and the organization came to an end.[6] Its demise is one reason why the second political period of Colombia's history, 1861–1880, during which the Liberals were in control, is not marked by much dramatic activity, even after the Maldonado Theatre was replaced by the New Colón. Contemporaries were contemptuous of the Colón. It had boxes, but those who rented them had to bring their own chairs. The use of candles for footlights created such an intimate atmosphere that it tempted spectators to chat with the actors, and often made the dialog unintelligible.

There was no lack of actors for the new theatre, thanks chiefly to the activity of Lorenzo Mª. Lleras (1811–1867). Not only did he form a troupe among his friends, to perform first in his patio and, after 1856, in a small theatre which he built, but he inspired the formation of other groups of cultured amateurs, like El Pesebre Espina in the home of Antonio Espina. It was in Dr. Lleras' own theatre that Izásiga achieved his popularity. For two years, Lleras produced five plays a month, from manuscripts supplied by his dramatist friends and his own translations of foreign romanticist plays. Even his son, José Manuel Lleras (1843–1879), was inspired to write a zarzuela, *La guardia del campamento*, and comedies like *El en-*

---

[6] For names of other drama groups, see del Saz, "El teatro hispanoamericano del siglo XIX," *Historia General*, IV, 426.

demoniado (1861), *El domingo* (1863), and his masterpiece *El espíritu del siglo.*[7]

Angel Cuervo (1838–1896) and Carlos Sáenz Echeverría (1853–1894) also wrote some unimportant local-color plays during this period. The latter was professor of geography, Colombian history and law, as well as a judge and diplomat, but he also had time to write three zarzuelas, like *El Estudiante.*

Of this period, the greatest for his comic spirit was Adolfo León Gómez (1857–1927), who has been called the Colombian Vital Aza, though he did not have the productivity of the Spanish dramatist. His volume, published in 1887 and containing *El soldado* and *Sin nombre,* provides an explanation for the scanty number of his plays. His preface charges that the censors refused to read them and that the Colombian stage was inhospitable to national dramatists. So Gómez' thirteen *Juguetes escénicos* and his *Corazón de mujer* (published 1919) remained unperformed. Only *La política exaltada* (1877) and *Globos ilustrados* (1888) are known to have been seen by the public.[8]

In 1890 the Conservatives regained power, with no great effect upon the nation's drama. The dilapidated Ramírez-Maldonado Theatre was replaced in 1890 by the Teatro Municipal, with oil lamps that ended conversation between audience and actors, but now the country had few dramatists to provide plays for it.

There was one belated romanticist, the sociologist Carlos Arturo Torres (1867–1911), whose *Don Lope de Aguirre* (1891) has been called Colombia's best cape-and-sword play. In the best tradition of Spain's Golden Age, this tragedy in verse tells of a satanic old explorer of the Amazon who kills his daughter rather than see her fall into the hands of her enemies. In 1894, Federico Rivas Frada (1858–1922) offered two plays: *La más allá* and *Entre la tierra y el cielo.* Two brothers were also writing charming local-color zarzuelas in the style of the Quintero brothers: Federico and Victor Martínez Rivas together wrote *Generales en compañía* (1899) and *Very Well* (1903). Later Victor alone wrote the amusing *Cosas de oficio* (1917),

---

[7] This play and two zarzuelas by Carlos Sáenz Echeverría, *Similia similibus* and *El estudiante,* appear in *Selección Samper Ortega,* Vol. 93.

[8] A number of other occasional dramatists of minor importance during the 1870's and 1880's are listed by del Saz in "El teatro hispanoamericano del siglo XIX," *Historia General,* IV, 439–440, and by Ortega Ricaurte in *Historia Crítica,* 1st ed., pp. 121–137.

criticized by many as immoral but revived a half century later by the Atenas group for performance in Bogotá. Based on one of his brother's poems, Victor also wrote his best drama, the sentimental *Sol de diciembre* (1925), reminiscent of another Martínez (Sierra). Alfonso León Gómez (1857–1927) had a foot in both centuries. His *La política exaltada* (1877) was followed by a drama, *Corazón de mujer* (1919).

The early years of the twentieth century saw a tragedy about the Chibcha Indians, *La raza vencida* (1905), by Maximiliano Grillo (1868–1949), who later wrote the more optimistic *La vida nueva* (1909). However, one may say that the turn of the century saw Colombia without any dramatist with box-office appeal. Bogotá, for so long the "Athens of America," one of the active theatrical centers of the New World, now had only her poets to maintain her reputation. The Teatro Colón staged only concerts, poetic readings, and a few operas.

Between 1910 and 1920 came a brief flurry of dramatic activity. An actor, Arturo Acevedo Vallarino (1874–   ), was largely responsible. He founded the Society of Authors of Bogotá in 1911, an act imitated by the socialites of Medellín with El Grupo Escénico. Ortega Ricaurte considers Dr. Acevedo Vallarino one of the greatest contributors to the development of Colombia's theatre.[9] In addition to his organizing ability, he had talent as an author and wrote a delightful one-act play, *Retazo de vida* (1917) in which a kindly priest plays Cupid.

A couple of players of Bogotá, Manuel Castelló and Luisa Martínez Casado, deciding to try to revive an acting company which dated from 1904, established Teatro del Bosque, to perform local plays. During rehearsals one afternoon, they were interrupted by the appearance of a seventeen-year-old student with a manuscript. Thus onto the scene came the dramatist called by del Saz "the initiator of the modern Colombian theatre."[10] Antonio Alvarez Lleras (1892–1956), grandson of the earlier dramatist, showed in *Víboras sociales* (1911) that he had profited from a study of Echegaray and Benavente. His tragedy of an avaricious and hypocritical husband and

---

[9] Ortega Ricaurte, *Historia Crítica*, 1st ed., p. 213.
[10] Del Saz, "El teatro hispanoamericano del siglo XIX," *Historia General*, IV, 452–457.

the vengeance of the wife, Inés, makes one of the best plays of Colombia.

This was not his first play, because at fifteen Lleras had written an amateurish school play, *El doctor Bacanotas,* but there was little immaturity about his new manuscript, and he continued experimenting and improving in *Alma joven* (1912), with its touch of Alvarez Quintero, and *El fuego extraño* (1913). This story of a family clash won the Society of Authors' prize contest and was performed not only in Colombia, but in Venezuela and Spain, in testimony to its universal appeal. Additional proof of the young dramatist's ability to plot and to develop character came in his *Como los muertos* (1915), a tragic triangle about Blanca, torn between her warm-hearted cousin, Alfredo, and her austere husband, Manuel, a victim of leprosy. A hundred performances in Bogotá, others in Spain, five printed editions, and a movie version starring Matilde Palou testify to its popularity. Although theatrical, it has its sentimental and inspirational moments. Some find in it suggestions of Joaquín Dicenta's *Sobrevivirse.*

When *Los mercenarios* was performed in 1924, local critics compared the author with Ibsen. Certainly the character of wealthy Esteban, with his savagery and kindness, his humble origin and sovereign pride, is one of the greatest creations of Alvarez Lleras.

Camila Quiroga preferred his realistic *El zarpazo* (1927). She gave it a prize and performed it in a half-dozen countries. The story is of oil-seeking José, who returns to kill Linares for replacing him with his mother and his sweetheart, and then demands that his mother share the responsibility for his crime. Other plays followed, several for children; *Alma de ahora* (1941), originally called *La defraudada,* which won prizes and was given several hundred performances; and a historical play, *Alejandria la pagana.* Finally came what has been called the best historical drama of Latin America, *El virrey Solís* (1948)[11] It deals with the love of an eighteenth-century colonial governor for María Lugarda, and the retirement of both from the world. Solís, a combination of Don Juan in sinning and Oedipus in repenting, lets the dramatist combine the poetry of a romanticist with a realistic and psychological treatment. With the number and the merit of

[11] Nicolás Bayona Posada, *Panorama de la literatura colombiana.* For detailed plot and analysis, see del Saz, "El teatro hispanoamericno del siglo XIX," *Historia General,* IV, 459–461.

his plays, Alvarez Lleras has won an important place in his country's theatre.

There were others writing, inspired by his successes and by the prizes offered by several groups. Pedro Gómez Corena (1882–   ) won first prize in the 1913 contest of the Society of Authors with his *Hacia la vida*. His *La misma sangre* (1921) was a more finished product. Lorenzo Marroquín (1856–1918), best known for his novel *Pax*, collaborated with José María Rivas Groot (1864–1923) in *Lo irremediable* (1913).

In 1915 came several attempts at lyric theatre, especially by Angel María Céspedes (1892–1956): *Escenas de la escuela, El congreso de las musas*, and *El regimiento pasa*. The next year he wrote what Leguizamón classifies as "cuento escénico en verso," *El tesoro*, reminiscent of Rostand.[12] Eventually Gerardo Valencia was to perfect this form in *Chonta* and *Cuento de miedo* (1940), translated and produced in New York.

Now came the three outstanding examples of Colombian drama. *Madame Adela* (1913) by Miguel Santiago Valencia, performed by Virginia Fábregas, was the first. The other two were *Juventud* (1920) by the short-lived Meza Nicholls, and the three-act drama *El escollo* (1925) by Samper Ortega.

Alejandro Meza Nicholls (1896–1920) won the 1917 Society of Authors' Prize with *Nubes de ocaso*, which was somewhat faulty in psychology. His *Golondrina errante* and the bombastic *Lauro Candente*, both of 1920, are not important, but his *Juventud* (1920) is another bright spot in the theatre. Young Antonio, grown sour from reading pernicious philosophy, is cured by the insistence of his Uncle Julian that youth is meant to be used like light and air, and his pretty cousin proves that Uncle Julian is right.

Daniel Samper Ortega (1895–1943), director of the National Library, and moving spirit in the *Selección Samper Ortega* collection of Colombian classics, first wrote *El culto de los recuerdos*, a comedy performed by an amateur group in 1923 but never published. Then came another of the plays to be starred in Colombian theatre. His *El escollo* has only three characters. Salvador loves Ana, the model for his masterpiece, which his jealous wife has destroyed. Ana, refusing

---

[12] Julio A. Leguizamón, *Historia de la literatura hispanoamericana*, II, 543.

to be Salvador's *escollo*, gives him up. It has several times been revived, once in 1932.

It would be dull to catalog authors of this period who turned out a play or two.[13] However, one should be cited: Dr. Germán Reyes. His medical training inspired *En la clínica*, which had not much importance, but *Margot* (1924), with its simple plot but moving story, is considered by Ortega Ricaurte one of the excellent plays of the Colombian theatre. It is contemporary and pictures national customs, with pleasant and witty characters. *Uno de tantos* (1924), his comedy that followed it, had a few performances, as did *El amor manda* (1926). But *La racha* (1925), for political reasons was forbidden a performance.

In lighter vein is *La llama*, by José Luis Restrepo. Winner of the 1925 Medellín Little Theatre competition it deals with the examination preparation of three students in a boardinghouse. Restrepo has also gone on with other plays to make his place in the national theatre.

Rather like vaudeville sketches are three *costumbrista* plays[14] of the country people of Antioquia, by Carlos Mejía Angel (1894–   ), writing under the pen name of "Ciro Mendía." Like its title, *Pa' que no fregue* is rustic and full of folklore, as Pedro courts the daughter of a blacksmith. *Arrayanes y Mortiños* concerns trouble about a calf not yet born. *El papá de Trini* expresses the objections of Gregorio to his daughter's marriage to Marcos. He finally explains: Marcos is his illegitimate son. But Trinidad's mother has the answer: the girl is not Gregorio's daughter! Like many similar dialect plays in Latin America, some of the dialog is all but incomprehensible to an outlander. "Ciro Mendía" is still active. His *Prometea desencadenada* (1960) was refused permission for a performance in Bogotá, without explanation. Finally Gaitán Gómez and his Atenas group performed it in 1962 without any shocking results.

More significant is the work of Luis Enrique Osorio (1896–   ), an experimenter in the theatre. His first comedy, *La ciudad alegre y coreográfica* (1919), performed by the Lizardo Planells troupe, roused the wrath of people who thought they could identify one of

---

[13] For the names of some who may be important in the future, see del Saz, "El teatro hispanoamericano del siglo XIX," in *Historia General*, IV, 450–451.
[14] Published in *Teatro*, No. 6 (Bogotá, 1945).

the characters in Bogotá's high society. His *Flor tardía* (1920), though revealing dramatic feeling and a flare for dialog, brought charges he had imitated Insúa's *Amor tardío*. To obtain a performance of his third play, *Al amor de los escombros* (1920), which he called "an American drama adapted to the Colombian scene," Osorio had to go to Mexico, where María Tereza Montoya put it onto the stage. Then he continued on to Europe.

In Spain his *Sed de justicia* (1921) had a more friendly reception by those who recognized its logical development and excellent technique. After writing two more comedies, Osorio went to Paris and there departing from his *costumbrista* plays, he wrote in French the universal *Lest createurs* (1926), whose performance in the Theâtre Michel marked the first play in France by any Latin American. That same year he visited Madrid and saw it performed in Spanish.

Returning home in 1929, the disillusioned author published his satire on Latin American politics, *El iluminado* (written in Paris in 1926), prefacing it with the comment: "The weakest thing about this is that it is a play. A Colombian has no excuse for writing a play. He will never see it performed." So he gave up the theatre and took to teaching till on a trip to Venezuela he was encouraged by sight of the flourishing theatre there, of Certad and others. Perhaps drama could still be a vital force in Colombia, he thought, provided it took the form of something deep-rooted in the native soil, like the national drama of England.

With the cooperation of the mayor of Bogotá and the subsidy of a few thousand pesos, Osorio organized a national company to present one Colombian play a month in the Municipal Theatre. His own high comedy *Nudo ciego* opened on July 23, 1943. Its run of twenty-five performances encouraged the company to perform another Osorio comedy, *El doctor Manzanillo*, which held the stage for fifty nights.

As a further stimulus to drama, Osorio founded a quarterly, *El teatro*, of fifty pages, each containing a complete play and selling for a few cents. The first issue offered *Nudo ciego*, in which Fanny declares her marriage is a "hard knot" that cannot be untied. In the second, *El Doctor Manzanillo* (1943) deals with a professional politician who believes in the spoils system. Both these plays contain elements of Osorio's earlier efforts, *Los creadores* and *El iluminado*, but with more quiet humor. A sequel, *Manzanillo en el poder* (1944), is more bitter than amusing with its warning to unscrupulous politicians of their eventual discovery and punishment. Serious, too, is his *Tragedia íntima* (1944).

Then followed a number of lively comedies. *El hombre que hacía soñar* (1945) depends on Freud and hypnotism. *Adentro los de Corrosca* (1945), *Rancho ardiendo* (1946), *El rajá de Pasturacha* (1947), *El cantar de mi tierra* (1950), and *Pájaros grises* (1960) are samples of the comedies that Osorio turned out, about one a year. They were based on the foibles of his countrymen. Many were presented in the Teatro Municipal in Bogotá, and others had their showing in provincial towns visited by his touring company. In 1952, supposedly to provide a better view for the presidential palace, President Laureano Gómez ordered the Teatro Municipal demolished, and drama was homeless in the capital. However, through the efforts of Osorio the Teatro de la Comedia was built. It opened December 11, 1953, with a sort of classical *loa* provided for the occasion by Benavente, followed by an almost Lope de Vega *comedia, Sí, mi teniente,* by Osorio. Perhaps this play has more action than psychology, and it has types, rather than characters, but it was in the Osorio popular national vein, and continued for a hundred performances before being replaced by his *Que tu esposa no lo sepa* (1954). About then, as Colombian politicians seemed bent on destroying drama in their nation, Osorio had to flee to political exile in Mexico. His theatre was turned over to movies.

During the period of Osorio's activities, several literary groups of Bogotá ran their courses. Los Nuevos, a postwar group that took its name from the Leon de Greiff magazine in Bogotá, used to meet in the Café Windsor to discuss the various "isms" from Europe, while an association calling itself Piedras y Cielo got started in 1935.

Typical of the changes in the theatre brought about by these students of the European scene was the work of Jorge Zalamea (1905–), later a diplomat. *El regreso de Eva* (San José, 1927; Bogotá, 1936) combines Freud and Proust in a dramatic farce about people impelled by their libidos. Its mingling of fantasy and reality challenged actors who had to use a light touch to make it seem serious; otherwise its violence and assassinations would make it ridiculous. Zalamea's next effort, *El rapto de las Sabinas*, a *costumbrista* piece about the Civil War of 1880, written for a radio play contest in 1941, won a prize which the dramatist refused.

Two Christmas radio plays by Zalamea also came in 1941: *Pastoral,*
noteworthy only as the product of a poet, and *El hostel de Belén,* a
charming Yuletide play with its realistic picture of the Nativity,
though neither Joseph nor Mary appears.

Products of the Piedras y Cielo group—and admirers of García
Lorca, Claudel, and Giraudoux—are: Arturo Camacho Ramírez,
author of *Luna de arena*; Jorge Rojas, *La doncella de agua*; and especially Gerardo Valencia, inspired by folklore to describe a tropical
hacienda in *Chonta.* He is also the author of *El hada imprecisa* and
Cuento de miedo.

The Colombians have always been proud of their culture. They
have considered their speech the purest Spanish in the New World,
and Colombian presidents have boasted about the success of their
volumes of poetry more than about their political triumphs. Therefore the low state of the theatre was particularly galling, and after
1941 the government took steps to remedy conditions. Open-air theatres were established in a number of cities. Osorio, as already noted,
in 1943 got the use of Bogotá's Municipal Theatre for national plays.
Hernando Vega Escobar (1907–   ), who at the age of fourteen had
performed in Osorio's *Sed de Justicia* and *La culpable,* and later in
Samper Ortega's *El escollo,* returned after years in Venezuela to
share in the national movement. Actors under his direction took plays
by Gerardo Valencia, Rafael Guizado, and Arturo Camacho Ramírez
on a tour of the nation. Ernesto Albán and his actors came from Ecuador and performed José Vicente Arias Olaya's *La esposa del diablo*
(1943). Arias also wrote *Lo que importa es casarse* (1940) and *Sin
perdón y sin venganza.* The Argentine actress Nélida Quiroga introduced the latter to the capital in 1960.

While the activity was not enough to spark a golden age of the
theatre, it did get others interested in the stage. Since Colombia's
coffee crop failed to provide wealth to lavish on culture, a cheaper
way of putting on plays was discovered—the radio. Zalamea wrote for
it, and Vallarino also completed a number of plays to be performed
over the air. Colombia vied with Paraguay in its airing of drama.
Rafael Guizado took charge of one station, broadcasting his own plays
and those by other national dramatists. He is author of *Cumplemento*
and *La mujer de Loth.* When television came in later, Colombian
dramatists began experimenting with that, too.

Another source of activity has been the experimental theatres in even the smaller centers.[15] Bogotá began activity under Fausto Cabrera and actor-author Bernardo Romero Lazana. The National University founded a School of the Theatre and an experimental group under Victor Mallarino in the Teatro Colón. At the University of America, Dina de Gaitán was in charge. Medellín boasted a Little Theatre with Sergio Mejía in charge, and Barranquilla drama lovers banded together under Espriella. Cali, too, began dramatic activity, thanks to the dramatist Enrique Buenaventura.

Prize contests were held for playwrights. The 1951 Premio Espiral went to Oswaldo Díaz Díaz for *Los sueños, sueños son,* although it was criticized for its slow start. He listened to criticism, and when Osorio announced a competition for his Teatro de Comedia in 1953, Díaz Díaz won it with a serious play of the revolution, *Diana Valdés.* Its failure on the stage convinced Osorio that Bogotá theatregoers did not like to think; so he substituted one of his own comedies to bring back the spectators and make up the deficit. Undiscouraged, Díaz Díaz completed *Galán* (1954). Though classified as an historical tragedy, it is really a pageant dealing with the Colombian patriot José Antonio Galán. Now one of the hopes of Colombia's stage, Díaz has written at least a score of plays, even some for children. Among the most recent, still in process of publication, are "Caín y Abel" (1958), "Cada mayo una rosa," "Desdemona ha muerto," and "Hora azul, 3 A.M."

Another dramatist, encouraged by Osorio, was Mariano Lemos López, a lawyer of Cali, who founded the Compañía Colombiana de Comedias in 1952 to try out his own initial effort, *Bigamia oficial.* The next year his three-act comedy *Sangre verde* won Osorio's Teatro de Comedia competition. Critics who saw it at the Cali Municipal Theatre in 1960, proclaimed it one of the excellent plays of Colombia. It has not been published. Dr. Lemos directed two of his plays in the United States, *Préstame tu marido* and *Baile,* and won in competition against a dozen Latin American directors.

The Lemos group presents national plays, but another group, the Escuela Departmental de Teatro, was founded in Cali to introduce semiclassical drama. Pedro Martínez originally directed the group, which achieved a reputation by winning the first National Theatrical Festival in Bogotá in 1956. They presented *The Madwoman of Chail-*

---

[15] Arango Ferrer, "Medio siglo de literatura colombiana," *Panorama das literaturas das Américas,* I, 385–386.

lot and an adaptation by Enrique Buenaventura (1925–   ) of *Oedipus Rex* before thirty thousand spectators in the Bogotá Coliseum. Then emboldened, they attempted no less than a European tour, to appear at the Paris International Theatrical Festival in 1960. Financed by a grant from the municipality and by contributions from firms in the Cauca Valley, they set out in 1960 with *A la diestra de Dios*, Buenaventura's dramatization of a story by the Colombian fiction writer Tomás Carrasquilla. Rave notices followed their appearance in Paris, as well as their tour to Holland and other countries. The play is a modern-day fantasy with Biblical and folklore elements, set in a low class café in Colombia. Peralta, trying as best he can to cure the sick, is given help by Jesus, who sits on a cloud. Jesus helps him restrain Death; he even beats the Devil at cards and turns him into an ant. Jesus is then amazed at the chaos that results from attempts to achieve perfection on earth. In the play, the devils and Jesus wear masks. The modern-day people do not. Buenaventura had careers as architect, painter, sailor, cook, journalist, and itinerant actor before he settled in Cali, where he founded a theatre. After the success of his play in Paris, he received further honor from the UNESCO Theatre in Paris for *La tragedia del rey Cristophe*. His most recent drama is *Un réquiem por el padre Las Casas*. Irony, humor, and closeness to the soil are characteristic of this increasingly important figure of the Colombian theatre.

Other activities can be observed elsewhere in Colombia: In Manizales, the Experimental Theatre, under Dorián Mejía, a movie actor and director with experience in North America and Europe, came into being in 1958. The next year it won second prize in the Bogotá Drama Festival with its performance of *El hombre que hacía llover*. In 1960 it competed again, with Tennessee Williams' *A Streetcar Named Desire*. One 1961 production was *Pago a todos* by Adel López Gómez, whose daughter Gloria was in the cast.

Barranquilla, beginning in 1955, has been holding competitions among high school groups performing national plays. The third meeting, late in July, 1960, welcomed groups from five Colombian cities.

Of course the greatest activity can be observed in Bogotá. A group, Sociedad de Amigos del País, under the presidency of Carlos Lleras Restrepo made the old Teatro Odeón available for the Atenas group directed by Jorge Gaitán Gomez. His *Los idiotas son otros* and *Bernabé* figured in the programs. *La mariposa* by Juan Bautista Castro, which drew praise and admiration from Benavente, as well as his *El Cristal*, winner of the 1958 National Comedy Prize, have also been seen by Bogotá theatregoers. The School of Dramatic Art, performing at Teatro Colón under Victor Mallarino, is another possibility for local dramatists seeking to get a try-out.

The Colombian stage, as in other countries, has passed through four steps in its evolution. After the religious plays came pseudo-classical tragedies, followed by melodramatic romanticism. Then came *costumbrismo* and a nationalized stage that brought an era of social criticism. Osorio pessimistically decided that amusement was all that the Colombian theatregoer sought. Some of the contemporary offerings in Colombia make it seem that the audiences are more mature and are willing to face reality. Perhaps the "Athens of America" is beginning to live up to its boast of national culture.

CHAPTER 21

Independent Venezuela and Its Theatre

The celebration of Venezuela's independence, according to Manuel Palacio Fajardo, made full use of the theatre. "Small stages in different parts of Caracas offered new pleasures to the populace, drunk with enthusiasm."[1]

More permanent theatres did come eventually, but only after the same sort of disputes with the Church as had happened in its colonial period. In 1829, there was an attempt to perform a kind of spectacle called "Entradas a Jerusalén," but Archbishop Méndez offered objections, claiming it was only a way of getting around the prohibition of comedies during Lent. General Arismendi sided with the people, and allowed them their Lenten entertainment.[2]

For the other types of plays a series of theatres was constructed: El Maderero, Teatro Principal, Teatro Coliseo, and the Teatro del Puente de Hierro, especially popular among the *aficionados* because of the unforgettable Emma Soler, and Téofilo Leal, Lucio Delgado, and Guillermo Bolívar. Churión tells of a projected season there, twenty-four performances on Thursdays and Sundays supposed to begin after Easter, 1834, with general admission set at ten pesos and boxes at thirty-six pesos more; but political unrest upset the plan.[3]

In general, one might say that after a slow start, Venezuela's theatrical activity increased after 1850. Between then and 1900 more than a hundred plays by Venezuelan authors were performed or printed. Some were even taken to Spain.[4] In the next fifty years,

[1] Manuel Palacio Fajardo, *Esquisse de la Revolution de l'Amerique Espagnole*, quoted in Juan José Churión, *El teatro en Caracas*, Chapter XI.

[2] Manuel Pérez Vila, "Polémicas sobre representaciones dramáticas: 1775–1829," *Revista Nacional de Cultura*, No. 127, (March, 1958), 102–104.

[3] Churión. *El teatro en Caracas*, pp. 90 ff.

[4] Rafael Pineda, "Pasado y presente del teatro en Venezuela," *El Faro* (March, 1954), pp. 32–33. Juan Piñango Ordóñez made a list of national plays, quoted in Churión, *El teatro en Caracas*, pp. 204–214. See also José Juan Arrom, "Bibliografía dramática venezolana," *Anuario Bibliográfico Venezolano, 1946*, pp. 199–209, where ninety-four authors and about two hundred plays are listed.

though there were flurries around 1914 and 1930, more actors were available than Venezuelan plays. The complaint of Goethe that he would have written more plays if there had been more actors and more public interest, a situation common enough to most of Latin America, is only half true about Venezuela.

One of the first plays of independent Venezuela was an anonymous *Virginia* (1824) by "un caraqueño." On Febuary 10, 1833, the bashful "Sr. J. M. G.," presented a one-act drama in verse, *La restauración de Venezuela*, and Domingo Navas Spínola provided *La Ifigenia en Aulide*, based on Racine. Dr. Pedro Pablo del Castillo, after his *El fanatismo druida o La sacerdotista* (1839), in three acts, got closer to home with *El 19 de abril o Una verdadera patriota*, a two-act prose comedy performed in El Coliseo in 1842. Its actors had a better reception than one which was earlier accorded during what the people called *Bajada de los reyes*. In this traditional accompaniment to the Epiphany celebrations the audiences indulge in horseplay. A Negro, Casto, playing the part of the Black King on January 6, 1830, was knocked off his horse. He fell on his head, and died.

Meanwhile the state of Zulia had begun developing its own local theatre.[5] As early as 1830 a group of amateurs built a stage in the patio of a private house and undertook to produce a play a week, with admission free. Other play lovers followed their example. In 1840 Miguel Antonio Baralt erected the first theatre in Maracaibo, in the vacant lot next to his house. The stage was roofed, but spectators had to bring their own seats. The city fathers agreed on another playhouse where the Baralt Theatre is today, with covered stage and dressing rooms, but no roof for the spectators. With money earned by amateur performances, it was completed and opened on October 28, 1853, with a performance of the Gil y Baus translation of *Lázaro o El pastor de Florencia* from Bouchardy, repeated by request three days later. Martínez de la Rosa's *Lo que puede un empleado* and Gil y Zárate's *Guzmán el bueno* came next, with a new play by the group once or twice a month. During their first season the amateurs put aside, toward a better and more adequate theatre, the sum of three thousand bolivares. For two more seasons they raised money through performances, though never using the works of local playwrights. When time came for an accounting, however, the money had dis-

[5] M. M. Marín, *El teatro en el Zulia*; also discussed by Aida Cometta Manzoni under the same title in *El Universal*, Caracas, September 18, 1954.

appeared, "on account of circumstances which we must not mention." Discouraged, the troupe disbanded, but public demand caused it to reassemble shortly around Luis Otazo, an actor from Caracas. At the end of this season, however, the profits were divided among the actors.

Eventually they got around to performing a locally written play, *Sinvergüenza, avaro y flojo*, by Manuel María Fernández. According to the critics, it was the effort, rather than the result, that earned the audience's applause. Much later, a woman of Zulia, Julia Añez Gabalón, was more successful with *El premio y el castigo* and *El sacrificio por oro*. In the twentieth century a dentist of Maracaibo, Dr. Gabriel Bracho Montiel, wrote a comic *sainete*, *Los sin-trabajo* and a tragedy, *El dolor de los otros*, which posed the problem of marriage between lepers.

From 1853 to 1855 the company of amateurs in Zulia used their collected money for the restoration of the Church of San Juan de Dios. Only after its completion did the new priest learn where the funds had come from; he forthwith demolished the new sections. Church and stage were still not partners in Maracaibo.

Not till July 24, 1883, did Maracaibo get its first real theatre. With the help of the president of the state, General Rafael Parra, the building was completed and inaugurated with a competition for national plays. Seven authors competed. The opening of a national theatre with national plays is so unusual in Latin America that the details are worth repeating. The prose entries numbered three: *Sufrir por culpas ajenas* by Eduardo Gallegos Celis, *A donde lleva una falta* by Simón González Peña, and *Un bobo como hay muchos* by Ramón Antonio Infante. Since the committee did not like any of them, the authors drew for the prize and Gallegos got it. The judges were better pleased with the dramas in verse. The first prize went to *Qué mujer* by Octavio Hernández, and a second award to *En el borde del abismo* by Manuel Antonio Marín. The other entries were *Una noche de baile* by Pablo Antonio Vilches, and *El hombre de los tres nombres* by Juan Canujo.

Vilches continued writing and published *Lo irreparable* in 1893; Marín not only published his prize play in 1887, but wrote four other dramas, all in verse, and all published in Maracaibo. That concludes the narrative of Zulia written by Marín's son and resurrected by Mrs. Cometta.

One reason for the renaissance of drama in Caracas was the eventual completion of the capital's first comfortable theatre. In 1820, to celebrate the new constitution of Spain, Ambrosio Cardozo had set up a stage in his house, where comedies and *sainetes* were performed till he completed the Coliseum in 1831. For the next twenty years it was managed by Colonel Juan José Ponce. Then the government underwrote the cost of the well-appointed Teatro Caracas; it opened Sunday night, October 22, 1854, with Verdi's *Hernani*, performed by singers brought from Paris. The venture changed Caracas' eating habits because its seven-o'clock curtain required dinner at five.

Guzmán Blanco, who became President in 1870, was a drama enthusiast. He imported a troupe under Grifell in 1877 to train local actors and perform local plays, and in order that they might have a theatre, he destroyed the Church of San Pablo to provide space for Teatro Guzmán Blanco. It opened Sunday, January 2, 1881, again with an opera, *Il Trovatore*. Realists like General de la Plaza declared it was much to ambitious for the limited number of Venezuelans to whom the drama appealed. Here, on October 27, 1884, during a performance of *Faust*, electric lights were used for the first time. The generator broke down the next day. After Guzmán was deposed in 1888 his pride was renamed Teatro Municipal.

Teatro Nacional was the work of President Cipriano Castro after he came into power in 1899. It was shoddily built and by 1950 was so dilapidated that it rattled with the passing buses, making the voices of actors inaudible.[6]

The craze for romanticist plays at the middle of the nineteenth century was responsible for works like *La víctima de la libertad o Policarpa Salavarrieta*, by Lisandro Ruedas, performed in Valencia, April 19, 1850; *Poncio Pilato en Viena*, a one-act historical drama in verse by Domingo Ramón Hernández; and Dr. Guillermo Michelena's *El hombre justo y el ambicioso o sea La libertad sin límites* (1859).

By the middle of the century a change in thinking had brought modern drama, by writers concerned with social problems. Some plays were light in tone, like Felipe Esteves' *Para un celoso un prudente* and Francisco Sales Pérez' *Jugar con dos cartas*. Four dramatists were especially active. Heraclio Martín de la Guardia began as

---

[6] Pineda, "Pasado y presente del teatro en Venezuela," *El Faro* (March, 1954), p. 32. Its restoration in 1955 was the subject of a nostalgic article about it and the national plays, 1875–1950, in *El Universal*, April 19, 1955.

a romanticist. His *Güelfos y gibelinos,* four acts with a *Romeo and Juliet* theme, published in 1859, was very popular. Of his eight-volume *Obras* (Caracas, 1903–1905), Volumes III, IV, and V contain seven plays. He began writing with no conception that dramas were any different from any other kind of writing. Foreign history provided themes for his romantic plays, but without filling him with passion. This detachment was just as true about most of his contemporaries, but at least Guardia continued writing enough to bring improvement in his last works, especially when he dealt with local problems, as in *Luchas del progreso* (1863) and *Fabricar sobre arena* (1878).

A contemporary was a lawyer, Anibal Domínici, who broke with European fashions and ran counter to the nineteenth-century Spanish code of honor in his three-act *Honra de la mujer* (1880) by insisting that it is a woman's right to save her honor, even though it involves freeing herself from her husband and breaking up her home. Another Domínici, Pedro César (1877–   ), wrote and produced the comedies *La jaula de oro* and *La Venus triste,* and the dramas *El hombre que volvió, La casa,* and *Amor rojo.*[7]

José María Manrique suggested Dumas in his romantic *Mátata,* but *Un problema social* and *Los dos diamantes* (1879), dealing with adultery, and *El divorcio* (1885) are in the more modern spirit. He also published a volume of children's plays from Curaçao in 1892.

Finally Manuel María Fernández ("El sordo don Simón") wrote the first Venezuelan play performed in Maracaibo and eight other comedies, including *El que despabila pierde* (1879), *Dos mujeres como hay pocas y dos hombres como hay muchos,* and *Lo que siembres, cojerás.*

Nicanor Bolet Peraza began in 1873 with the satirical one-act *A falta de pan buenas son tortas* (published 1881) about Toribio Zurcelatas, a tailor who wanted to be Minister of Finance. The first performance aroused great enthusiasm, but fearing political repercussions, people stayed away from its repetition the next day. Bolet was not discouraged from writing *Luchas del hogar* (1875), a three-act drama which also won audience approval.

A cosmopolite among Venezuela's plays is *El Moctezuma* by Joaquín María Pérez. First produced in New York in 1877, it was printed

---

[7] Raymond Grismer, *et al., Vida y obras de autores venezolanos.*

at 40 Broadway by E. Pérez, but dated "Panama, 1877." It tells of the attempt of the Peruvian Leoncio Prado (1853–1883) to get passage on the Mexican steamship *Moctezuma* with ten Cuban conspirators to seize the ship in the name of the Republic of Cuba. The only available version of this Pan-American play is in the 1942 *Ediciones Peruanidad*.

In the next quarter century, when dramatic monologs were in style, José Antonio Calcaño published his *Bolívar en Santa Marta* (1886), and Eduardo Calcaño (1831–1904) appeared as author of *Policarpa Salavarrieta* (1891) to lay the foundations for Venezuela's modern theatre.

Some of the young people of Caracas with theatrical ambition founded Liceo Artístico, under Pedro Emilio Coll. Their performance of *Parada y fonda*, with D. Emeterio as their director, brought down the house. They received some good training and introduced a number of local plays before enthusiasm declined and their director was called to other duties. In 1897 Alberto Smith, one of the Cabinet, tried vainly to rouse interest in an amateur group again.

After this came a long dull quarter-century, not broken till 1914 when two actor-authors, "Leo" (Leoncio Martínez) and Rafael Guinand, and dramatist Leopoldo Ayala Michelena, were responsible for an active and successful season.[8] The only published play by Martínez is the *sainete*, *Salto atrás* (1925). Even Guinand, most popular of Creole *sainete* actors, has had published only one of his many local-color *sainetes*: *El rompimiento* (1930) in the dialect of central Venezuela.

In 1914 the Teatro Caracas offered plays by such Venezuelans as Enrique Soublette (1886–1912), already known for *El brujo* (1908), *La selva* (1911), and *Las sombras* (1911); and Angel Fuenmayor (1883–), author of *Don José*, in three acts. It also offered the dramas *Víctimas* and *Gesta magna* (1912), four acts; a comedy, *Pacto de bodas*; and *Llegará un día* (1920). Other dramatists producing, if not publishing, around 1914 included Juan José Churión (1876–), Luis Churión (1875–), José Santaella (1883–1927), Ildemaro Urdaneta (1885–1912), Humberto Tejera (1892–), and the famous actor Téofilo Leal Berra, author of *Caín*.

Simón Barceló, with better luck, had two plays published: *El hijo*

---

[8] Churión, *El teatro en Caracas*.

de Agar (1907), in two acts, and *Cuento de Navidad* (1909), in one act. Andrés Eloy Blanco (1899–1955), the great poet and politician, later a member of the Sociedad de Amigos del Teatro, also tried drama during this period. The beauty of his lines made a success of his *Abigail* (1937), a lyrical tragedy in three acts based on a Biblical theme, and it was both produced and published. It was revived as one of the showpieces for the Festival de Teatro Venezolano, held in Caracas, September–November, 1959. Also by Blanco are *El Cristo de las violetas* (1925), *El pie de la virgen*, and *Los muertos las prefieren negras* (1950), which were published with *Abigail* in 1960. His "Fajardo" and "Caoba" never developed beyond the manuscript.

Even a President of the Republic felt the urge to turn dramatist. Dr. Manuel Antonio Díez began with two one-act comedies, *Carnaval en Caracas* and *Delicias de la vida* in 1911, and followed with two longer plays, *Fotografías parlantes* and the immortal *Queso frito* in 1912. Dr. Díez also wrote a number of other *sainetes*.

Considered dean of Venezuela's theatre at this time was Angel Fuenmayor, though his chief works, *Pacto de bodas* and *Don José*, were rarely performed and are now forgotten. Juan del Llano wrote a satirical political allegory, *La sagrada familia*. Juan Saturnino Canelón even won a prize from Ateneo Caraqueño for his middle-class *Nunca somos los mismos*, but he had to go to Mexico to get it published.

The most popular of the dramatists around 1914, however, was Leopoldo Ayala Michelena (1897–   ). Largely self-taught and a rent collector by day, by night he turned dramatist, although he was unacquainted with world drama. One evening, as Peraza describes it,[9] he read to his friends his first attempt, *Emoción*. Its combination of sentiment and humor along with its lyrical quality, in its story of a paralytic in love with a beautiful girl, made them urge him to offer it to a manager. Afraid of its reception by the public, however, Ayala held off till he had finished a second play, *Al dejar las muñecas*, and the two were performed together, July 22, 1914. The second contains poetic descriptions of dawn in the garden, a likable old grandmother, and a twelve-year-old heroine, Orilia. When the enthusiastic audience called the bashful author before the curtain, he was so upset that he forgot to take off his hat. After several sentimental plays

[9] Preface to *Teatro seleccionado de Leopoldo Ayala Michelena* (ed. Luis Peraza), pp. xii–xiii.

about children, he ventured into the adult world with *Bagazo* (1933), contrasting honesty and trickery in a department store. *Almas descarnadas* has a father resorting to a fake telegram about a factory fire to reveal his selfish son, who has stolen the fire-insurance money to further his career as a doctor. It was selected as Ayala Michelena's most representative play for the 1959 Venezuela Theatre Festival.

Among his plays are also farces. *La respuesta del otro mundo*, entirely in dialect, tells of a medium trying to tune in on the bawdy days of ancient Rome. In *La perra* a wife tries to get rid of her husband's destructive dog. Amusing, too, is *La barba no más*. Though intellectuals scorn these plays for their lack of culture, distortion of language, and plots which one critic characterized as "corny," their humor and sentiment have made their author popular.

In serious drama, as Dr. Picón Salas complains in the few words devoted to drama in his study of Venezuelan literature, his countrymen have imitated "y con suma debilidad" the European fashions.[10] An example is one of the earliest women of Venezuela to have her say on the stage, Narcisa Bruzual (1900–   ), author of many romantic novels. Her *Amor y . . . dolor* is a three-act drama in verse based on Dumas' *The War of Women*. Her others are in prose: *La causa del mal*, a psychological comedy, and two tragedies, *Los náufragos* and *El veneno del pecado*. Most recent is her *Horas sentimentales*.

The 1930's brought another burst of theatrical activity to Venezuela, chiefly because of the formation of the Asociación de Escritores Venezolanos, whose headquarters provided a center for lectures, concerts, and theatrical performances. Its prizes for plays and its printing facilities encouraged play writing and gave the rest of the world a glimpse of the country's new theatrical activity. Later, in the 1940's, came further theatre stimulus. Under the sponsorship, appropriately, of the Ministry of Labor and Communications, a "people's theatre" was founded. In Teatro Bolívar, renamed Teatro Obrero, and with the help of some of Venezuela's outstanding actors, several performances a week took place. Explanatory comments by loudspeakers during the performance and discussions after the final curtain provided education in good drama and good acting for people of Caracas who had never before attended a theatre.[11]

[10] Mariano Picón Salas, *Formación y proceso de la literatura venezolana*, pp. 14–15.

[11] *Revista del Caribe*, November 1941, p. 19.

For others who knew drama, some local authors and actors and a few wealthy patrons of the theatre formed the Sociedad Amigos del Teatro in 1941. Rómulo Gallegos was a member. During its brief existence, with Certad and Meneses as presidents, it performed a number of national plays,[12] though critics like Feo Calcaño believed it was wrong in stressing *costumbrismo*. This was the time when such dramatists as Mariano Medina were using a local dialect in plays of customs like *Cara 'e santo*. Feo Calcaño failed to see the tenderness and artistry in this play. The Sociedad believed that local color as well as local problems were necessary in a national play, and they wanted something beyond farces written to bring guffaws from the lower classes. In a period when Venezuela's other literary activities— the novel, poetry, and essays—were attracting attention beyond the national frontier, they wanted to raise the quality of drama, too.

The first plays presented by the Amigos were *Dial M for Murder*, by Frederick Knott, and Lorca's *La casa de Bernarda Alba*, but then they turned to the Venezuela scene and, while waiting for plays on social and postwar problems, performed Certad's *Lo que le faltaba a Eva*.[13] They did not always get nationalism, but the product of Venezuela playwrights improved. Pablo Domínguez earlier interpreted some of the local problems in his *Tremedal* (1933; published 1952). It takes place about 1905, with Julio, the hard-working man; Miguel, psychologically maladjusted because of the civil wars; and Don Prudencio, the old landlord.

Julio Planchart (1885–1948), a politician, scholar, and under the pen name of "Maestro Solnes" dramatic critic of *El Tiempo*, wrote *La república de Caín* (1936), one of the most powerful satires in Venezuelan letters, though he labeled it a "vile and unperformable comedy in prolog and five acts, written in verse against Caudillism." In 1938, Julián Padrón (1910–1954), best known as a novelist, had his three-act farce, *Fogata*, published by the Writers' Association, followed by a *sainete*, *Parásitas negras* (1939), and the short tragicomedy *La vela del alma* (1940).

Luis Peraza ("Pepe Pito") though born in Spain in 1908, has been so long associated with Venezuelan letters as to be regarded a native.

---

[12] Walter Rela, "Literatura dramática suramericana contemporánea," *Revista del Instituto de Estudios Superiores*, I (1957), 123.

[13] Published in *Cuadros de la Asociación de Escritores Venezolanos*, No. 85 (1954).

He began his writing career with the two-act social comedy *El hombre que se fue* (1938), one of the most frequently produced of Venezuelan plays. It has had at least 150 showings. *Cecilio*, a one-act comedy written by him in Yale in 1940, and a musical play, *Una para dos* (1940), in collaboration with "Leo," preceded his best effort, *Mala siembra* (1940), a plea for progressive education. The narrow-minded religious bigots who bring tragedy to Carlota are reminiscent of Benavente's *Malhechores de bien*. Also well received were Peraza's *Tres cariños*; *Matador de palomas*; *La gota de agua* (1943), a three-act comedy; *Olaya Buroz* (1950); and *Inocencia* (1953).

In 1940 a guignol by Luis Barrios Cruz was performed by Ateneo de Caracas; Rodolfo Quintero had his *Huanachone* published in Chile; and the diplomat Victor Manuel Rivas Lázaro (1909–   ) won the Ateneo drama prize with *Antesala*, a slice of contemporary Venezuelan life about the bureaucrats of Caracas. It was first published in the *Repertorio Americano* of San José, Costa Rica. Having turned to production of petroleum, Rivas Lázaro now writes in his spare time such hits as *El puntal, El pueblo, La Zamurada*, and *Tres tardes en los Robles* (1943). He has also directed a production of his *Miss Pickerton*.

In 1941 the Writers' Association published together the two-act comedy *Virgen del Carmen* and *Vivir por los demás* by Eduardo Innes González (1883–   ). Besides *Cuento de otoño*, this diplomat wrote *Una señorita de Caracas, comedia en tres momentos*, of which the final *momento* was published in *Revista Nacional de Cultura*, No. 38. It is the ironic story of Elisa, deceived by a sweetheart to whom she was too kind. She is sure now that cold treatment will bring back a second suitor.

Another Eduardo Calcaño, a lawyer born in 1913, published his *Polo negativo* (1942), showing the clash between dreams of artistic creation and the realities of everyday life. Its title comes from the name of a group of intellectuals. The painter hero wants to be ultra-modern, but to marry his sweetheart he must paint a realistic portrait of her uncle. The play was published by Amigos, which also performed his next play, *Casa de arena* (1943). Calcaño has written twenty-eight more plays.

The plays of three excellent Venezuelan dramatists were introduced in 1943. The painter and poet César Rengifo (1911–   ) turned to the stage with *Soga de niebla* (1943), about a weak man forced to serve as public executioner. It was followed by *Curayú* (1949) and *Los canarios* (1953). His later *Vendaval amarillo*, along with *Soga de Niebla*, figured in the First Venezuelan Theatrical Festival. Since then he has shown increasing promise with *Obcénaba*, an Indian-white man struggle, and *Joaquín Sánchez*, a historical drama. His earliest effort was *Manuelote*, about a Negro slave during the violence of the "War to the Death." Rengifo is a new and promising playwright.

Guillermo Meneses (1911–   ), who began as a short-story writer, dramatized his grim *La balandra Isabel llegó esta tarde* (1943), which was later performed at the 1959 Festival and made into a movie, and followed it with the three-act comedy *El marido de Nieves Marmol* (1944).

The third dramatist is Rafael Angel Díaz Sosa (1926–   ) better known as "Rafael Pineda," a poet with five volumes of verse and several of essays, who studied drama at the University of North Carolina. His *Los conjurados* (1950) won a prize at the Teatro de la Universidad Central, his alma mater. It is a violent drama in two acts, one of which is set at the end of the nineteenth century and the second fifty years later. *La inmortalidad del cangrejo* (1953), another successful work by this versatile writer, won the first prize at the Ateneo de Caracas. Several other works by him have been reported completed.

Best-known Venezuelan dramatist in theatres outside his own country is the journalist, poet, and diplomat Aquiles Certad (1914–   ), basically an impressionist in the modern theatre who sometimes lowers his literary standards in his endeavor to amuse. For this reason the public flocks to performances of his plays in Buenos Aires and elsewhere. Sociedad Amigos del Teatro performed and published his first three plays: *Tres maridos al azar, Lo que le faltaba a Eva* (1943), and *Cuando quedamos trece* (1943). The play about Eve, a charmer of Caracas, introduced an international crowd in what came nearer to high comedy than anything previously written in Venezuela. Eve lacks a number of things: an ability to thrill her suitor Adam Páderes; an assurance to say "no" to the lawyer who wants to marry her; and especially two toes on her left foot, the lack of which, as she confesses to the philosophic bartender, makes her "antiaesthetic."

Cuando quedamos trece deals with a superstitious family whose head, Gaspar, supposedly flew on a business trip. His wife's "oracle book" gives her no help when news arrives of the airplane's crash. Gaspar, who has used this trip as an excuse to steal a weekend with his mistress, is equally at a loss for an explanation of where he has been.

Certad's volume, *Tres obras de teatro* (1953) contains *Cuando Venus tuvo brazos*, a slight work with forced humor introducing an archaeologist and a secretary whose arms make him forget his theories about Venus de Milo. At least one critic selects as Certad's masterpiece *La serpiente sobre la Alfombra*, about a genius destroyed by a woman's love. To some it makes boring reading, however it may play. The third play of the volume, a fantasy suggesting Casona's *Prohibido suicidarse en primavera*, is *El hombre que no tuvo tiempo para morir*, about a philosopher who fills hopeless people with dreams and ambitions.

Certad's later plays are more substantial, but though he upholds the thesis that it is the duty of a dramatist to point out the defects of humanity in general, social criticism plays only a small part in the plays. In *Julieta engaña a Romeo* (1952), about two rival phonograph record companies, Julieta of the Shakespeare Company gets a job with the Orfeo Company to steal its secrets. Marriage is the theme of a trio of Certad's recent comedies: *Tres maridos al azar*, *El caso de divorcio*, and *Mamá se casó en París*.

Three outstanding Venezuelan novelists have also tried their hand at drama. Arturo Uslar Pietri (1906–   ) began with *El día de Antero Albán* (1944), using abstract rather than human characters, and *El dios invisible* (1957). Both have been criticized as being too intellectual. The two, along with *La tebaida* and *La fuga de Miranda* were collected in his *Teatro* (Caracas, 1959). *Chúo Gil y las tejadoras* (1959), about a mythological character who appeared in town, was better received and was chosen for performance in the 1959 Drama Festival. Rómulo Gallegos (1882–   ) is the author of *El milagro del año* (1915), *La doncella* (Mexico, 1957), and of a script for the movie *Juan de la calle* (1942).

Ramón Díaz Sánchez (1903–   ) saw the first performance of his drama *La casa*, a conflict between traditional and modern Venezuela, in the Teatro María Guerrera of Madrid in 1956, under the title *Bajo estos aleros*. It brought more violent polemics than any of the novels or short stories he had previously written. His most recent, *La virgen no tiene cara*, opened the 1959 Theatre Festival. While Gallegos did not persist in writing for the stage, Uslar Pietri and Díaz Sánchez have continued alternating plays with their novels, short stories, and histories.

Another recent name in the Venezuelan theatre is Alejandro Lasser (1916–   ). Political and sociological significances are emphasized in his two historical plays: *El general Piar* (1945; published 1946) and *Catón en Utica* (1945). Pedro Rial produced Lasser's drama *Nuramí* (1945). In spite of the heavy dose of Freud and long poetic dialog it maintains mood and is good theatre.

Enrique Azaguirre, too, author of *La esperada*, and Humberto Orsini, who wrote *Precipicio*, got a chance to direct their own plays in 1954 at the Teatro Máscara. Luis Colmenares Díaz was encouraged by the increased theatrical activity to finish *Un día en Nueva York* (1959) and other plays. Isaac Churión (1932–   ), who put *Look Back in Anger* into Spanish, wrote *Mónica y el florentino* about a mixed-races group in an Italian boardinghouse, each member with his national characteristics. Another of his plays, *El quinto infierno*, typical in its withdrawal from reality, was performed by Venezuela's first stable professional theatre, Teatro Los Caobos, founded by Pedro Hurtado and the Argentine actress Juana Sujo, whose death in 1961 was a great loss to Venezuelan drama.

El Teatro del Buho gave opportunity to its imaginative director, Román Chalbaud (1930–   ). He wrote *Muros horizontales* (1953); *Caín adolescente* (1955), a tragedy of country people in a metropolis; and for the 1959 Venezuela Theatre Festival, he wrote an experimental *Requiem para un eclipse*, in verse. It deals with homosexuality and the narrow line between right and wrong. His *Sagrado y obsceno*, intended for the Second Theatre Festival, was closed by the police for its satire against the government.

After drama enthusiasts at the university started off with Goldoni, though with a promise to perform local works, the University Theatre was founded in Caracas in 1958. It started fulfilling its promise by sponsoring Venezuela's First Theatre Festival in 1959. A dozen national plays made up the offering. Among them were *La tempestad* by César Rengifo, and *Los insurgentes* by Juan Francisco León, whose excellent technique was again displayed in *Un extraño viaje de Simon el malo* (1952). Alfredo Terrero Atiezo (1907–   ) wrote *Don Francisquito*. Some critics complained that 60 per cent of the Festival plays and audiences were leftists.

Another Theatre Festival was held the following year, and a third was announced to celebrate the fifth anniversary of the organization. So successful has the group been under Nicolás Curiel that its members have taken plays not only to the provinces in its Teatro Rodante program, but to Mexico, the United States, and Europe. Its activities include a school of the drama and three experimental theatres: U.C.V. of the Universidad Central, the T.E.H. under Rafael Briceño of the Facultad de Humanidades, and the T.E.A. directed by Pedro Velazco at the School of Architecture.

Other theatrical groups, which have shown sporadic activity, are: Teatro el Duende, of Gilberto Pinto; Teatro Popular de Venezuela, of Alfonso López; Teatro Compás, of Romeo Costas; Grupo Cervantes, of Carlos J. Ortiz; Teatro Nacional Popular, of the Ministry of Labor; Grupo Máscaras, of Humberto Orsini; Teatro del Ateneo de Caracas, directed by Horacio Peterson; and Teatro de la Comedia, of Natalia Silva. Most of them have, at least occasionally, used national plays.

Contrasting with these struggling groups is the Caracas Theatre Club, established by a petroleum company in 1951. Its million-dollar plant includes a swimming pool, bowling alley, bar, and a theatre in which its members present from four to eight plays a year. But it offers no help to local writers since its program is comprised of Broadway successes.

Still, the number of dramatists in Venezuela during the last ten years has been increasing. One of them, Pedro Berroeta, had his *Los muertos no pueden quedarse en casa* (published 1959) performed in the First Festival. It introduces a dead man returning as a ghost to declare: "An adult is a child who has learned to lie. If he does not lie, others learn his secret and can dominate him." For the Second Festival he offered *La farsa del hombre que amó a dos mujeres*, actually his sixth play, all performed. Many of the other new dramatists, still unpublished, are only names to the outside world, among them: César E. Aroyo, Carlos Granada Guarnizo, Luis Paz y Miño, Román Rojas Cabot, José Trajano Mera, and the critic Guillermo Feo Calcaño, author of *El último mensaje*.

Venezuelan women too are getting curtain calls as successful playwrights. Leticia Maneiro wrote a two-act comedy, *Sangre mestiza* (1943). Elizabeth Schon, whose *Intervalo* won second prize in the 1956 Ateneo contest, revised its over-poetic speeches following a showing the next year, and had it performed in the 1959 Festival. The greatest Venezuelan poetess, compared by some to Sor Juana Inés de la Cruz, has also written excellent dramas in verse. The first work by Ida Gramko (1924–   ), was an oratorio-ballet, *Loma de ángel,* dramatized the Cuban novel about the mulatto Celia Valdez, loved by her own half-brother. Music was provided by the Cuban Hilario González. In 1943 Miss Gramko wrote two plays blending pagan superstitions and Christianity, *Belén Silvera* and *María Lionza.* The latter, a story of a legendary witch, was successfully performed in 1957. A children's play, *La hija de Juan Palomo* (1944) was included in her *Poesía y teatro* volume in 1955. Her three-act comedy *La rubiera* won the 1956 Ateneo contest, and her adaptation of a legend, *La dama y el oso,* represented her work in the 1959 *Teatro contemporáneo* series. All her works were collected in 1961 in *Teatro* with a foreword by Rafael Pineda.[14]

The children's theatre has been active in Venezuela since the visit to Caracas in 1938 of the Díaz-Collado Company, directed by Alejandro Casona. Dr. Sabas Oliazola, of the Venezuela Experimental School, began in 1939 writing plays for school use which were published in the monthly *Tricolor.* Established dramatists like Victor Manuel Rivas, author of *El puntal,* and Fernando Paz Castillo, known for *Huerta de Doñana,* have also provided scripts for children.

One of the most active dramatists for children, however, has been "Lucila Palacios" (Mrs. Mercedes Carvajal de Arocha, 1902–   ), who turned from novels and short stories to this new field. Her *Orquídeas azules* (1942), which she called "sinfonía tonta y ballet sobre una leyenda venezolana de la selva guayanesca," had music provided by María Luisa Escobar. *La gran serpiente* (1943), in three acts, takes Snake Princess Con to the infernal regions. *Juan se durmió en la torre* won the Municipal Prize in 1949. Among her other works are *Niebla* (1948), *Hay que pintar los verdes,* and *Tres palabras y una mujer.* A new dramatist, Vicky Franco, began with *Merecure* (1959) and *Lo que arrastró la creciente* (1960). Also in 1960 a young dramatist Elisa Lerner created a very favorable impression with *La bella de inteligencia.*

As part of the children's program, the actor Ramón Zapata began producing plays in 1939, especially musicals, with youthful actors. Eighty children selected from 370 candidates comprised his com-

[14] Ida Gramko, *Teatro.*

pany which in the last half of 1939 produced four plays. The following year they moved to a larger theatre and eventually took over Teatro Municipal. But the turnover of young actors and the loss of interest in this novelty sent Zapata back to the adult stage and the venture ended, though children's theatres still exist in the provinces, encouraged by occasional visiting groups from the capital.[15] Under government sponsorship the *Retablo de Maravillas* took a portable stage on tour in 1952, playing 114 times before more than a million spectators. The following year it drew even bigger audiences.

Arrom declares that the chief handicap of Venezuela's theatre has been the nation's scanty population and its many small towns that cannot support a theatre.[16] Picón Salas adds that the Venezuelan theatre in formation may never finish forming because the movies are such a formidable adversary.[17] But the government and a number of the Federation of Independent Theatrical Groups are waging an active campaign.

[15] Eduardo Calcaño, "El teatro infantil y sus proyecciones en Hispano-América," *Educación* (July, 1940), pp. 12 ff.

[16] José Juan Arrom, "En torno al teatro venezolano," *Revista Nacional de Cultura*, No. 48 (January, 1945), 5.

[17] Picón Salas, *Formación y proceso*, p. 15.

CHAPTER 22

The Theatre in Panama

Panama, in its position of linking, yet separating, the two continents, had no independent existence for a long time, being merely the shortest passage between Atlantic and Pacific oceans. The chaplain of Emperor Charles V scorned suggestions of a canal there, with the words from Matthew 19:6, now familiar in marriage ceremonies: "What therefore God hath joined together, let not man put asunder." Following the founding of the city of Old Panama in 1519, the Isthmus of Panama was soon made part of the viceregency of Peru. Later, in 1740, it was transferred to New Granada. Only since its revolt against Colombia in November, 1903, has it been independent. In the early colonial period its culture was most scanty; yet there was at least one slight stirring of the drama.

On the night in January, 1544, when gruff Viceroy Blasco Núñez Vela reached the city of Panama en route to Peru, he was entertained, according to Cieza,[1] "con gran bullicio y alboroto," and "se le recitó una comedia en su posada." This was probably some farce, *coloquio*, or slight musical piece, such as would appeal to the crude tastes of a lusty soldier. All records of other theatrical activities, such as may have accompanied celebrations in Panama of royal coronations or birthdays, perished when Drake sacked and destroyed Old Panama in 1572.

In a rebuilt city in its new location, trade guilds of Panama helped celebrate the oath of loyalty to Ferdinand VI in May, 1747,[2] by performing four plays from Spain in the Plaza Mayor. The Tailors' Guild was in charge of Calderón's *Amado y aborrecido* and *Lances de amor y fortuna*. Members of other guilds played in *El montañés*

---

[1] Pedro Gutiérrez de Santa Clara Rodríguez, *Historia de las guerras civiles del Perú* (1544–1548), I, 57, quoted by Armando de Maria y Campos, *Entre cómicos de ayer*, p. 12.

[2] Diego Angulo Iñíguez, *Planos de monumentos arquitectónicos de América y Filipinas*, I, 63; Guillermo Lohman Villena, *El arte dramático en Lima durante el virreinato*, pp. 400–407.

más hidalgo and *Solo el piadoso es mi hijo* by Matos Fragoso, Ave-llaneda, and Villaviciosa.

The first recorded performance of a work by a Panameño did not occur until after Panama became part of Colombia. Then *La política del mundo* by Victor de la Guardia y Ayala (1772–1824) was per-formed in his home town of Penonomé in 1809.[3] This three-act trag-edy in verse followed the classical tradition and was set in Rome during the time of Caesar and Calpurnia, but it had a "modern" appli-cation in that the final scene contained allusions to Napoleon, the "Modern Caesar," and criticisms of Ferdinand VIII. While not great drama, its date makes it of interest. Lost for nearly a century after its author took it with him to Costa Rica, it was discovered here in 1902 and published by the dramatist's grandson, himself an important writer.

In 1821, when the rest of Middle America was making the first of its many attempts to achieve unity, Panama looked southward, threw in its fortunes with Colombia, and was speedily eclipsed in culture by the wealthier Bogotá, that already called itself "The Athens of America." Several times Panama seemed on the verge of an economic boom. Once its hopes were unduly aroused, when the Panama Rail-road was constructed in 1855 to help in the California gold rush. Later the failure of the French Canal Company to complete its dig-ging disappointed the region's hopes of becoming a port for the world's shipping. Those disappointments lay back of Panama's deter-mination not to let Nicaragua steal its chance of a canal, when Co-lombia refused to complete its right-of-way treaty with the United States. And so the Isthmus demanded its freedom and negotiated its own treaty. After that, money began to flow in from sale of supplies and the wages of canal workers, and the level of culture mounted. Part of the new wealth was used to build the Teatro Nacional in 1908, in imitation of the Paris Opera House, though Panama had neither local actors nor playwrights to use it.

Poets had long been plentiful in Panama. Being the easiest form of literature to write and disseminate, poetry had flourished on the Isthmus, changing with the fads and becoming modernistic toward the end of the century, when Rubén Darío twice visited Panama and the great Darío Herrera was active. Those writers without poetic

[3] Rodrigo Miró, *La cultura colonial en Panamá*, pp. 61–69, quotes part of it. See also Hubert Turbyfill, *My Panama Canal Theatre Adventure*.

talent were attracted to short stories, as a form that could be written fairly rapidly, with copies easily provided for distribution.

The only form of theatre cultivated in Panama was something called "dance stories" such as were performed in the 1920's during the Presidency of Dr. Arnulfo Arias. They were short *costumbrista* sketches ending with regional dances. Groups of students took them to the back regions of Panama for educational purposes. At this same time a School of Dramatic Art and Declamation was founded, but little came out of it.

The government did nothing to stimulate national drama. In 1942, to encourage the writing of novels, it offered a prize in the name of Ricardo Miró, a literary figure, and the result was so fruitful that the competition for novels became an annual event. The impetus of the prize has helped produce a respectable list of excellent Panamanian novels. But playwrights had to provide their own inspiration.

One dramatist, José de la Cruz Herrera (1876–   ), who completed his studies in Bogotá while Panama was still a part of Colombia, translated six Greek tragedies and the comedy *The Knights* by Aristophanes, but no crowds flocked to witness them. Disappointed, he moved to Buenos Aires, where he published his translations in 1949 and wrote a history of the Greek theatre, since his own country had no theatre worth recording.

Joaquín Darío Jaen (1893–1932), actor, magician, and hypnotist, also turned dramatist and performed in several of his efforts, but he could not get them published. Novels were more popular; so he wrote and published four, as well as three collections of short stories.

Musical-comedy writing at least got a hearing. The poet and fiction-writer "Rogelio Sinán" (Bernardo Domínguez Alba, 1904–   ) made theatrical history when his folklore play *La cucarachita mandinga*, written in 1937, with music by Gonzalo Brenes, had a successful performance at the Teatro Nacional in 1938. "Sinán" later turned to the children's theatre with *El desquite de la caperucita*, giving a novel twist to the story of Red Riding Hood.

Juan O. Díaz Lewis (1916–   ), an English-speaking lawyer, also had several successful performances of his plays, especially *El señor ministro*, about politicians and their followers, but only his short stories found a publisher before he departed for Paris and a position in UNESCO.

The only dramatist with published works seems to be Renato

Ozores (1910–   ), university professor, journalist, and author of two volumes of delightful short stories and at least one good novel. Following his initial venture into the theatre came his *Teatro* (1945), which contains the drama *Un angel* and the comedy *Una mujer desconocida*. In 1957 the Ricardo Miró competition was opened to playwrights, and first prize was awarded to Professor Ozores' *La fuga*. It was performed successfully in spite of its wordiness at the Teatro Nacional, June 30, 1958, and published in 1959 with a preface by Dr. Mariano Górriz. The dramatist's interest in psychiatry is evident: the chief character, Daniela, brought up by her father after her mother's death, has an Oedipus complex. Her marriage causes her flight into insanity, from which the tragedy gets its title.

Another playwright, starting somewhat later, was Mario Riera Pinilla (1920–   ) who began with *La conciencia* (1949), followed by *La muerte va por dentro* and *La mujer del alcalde*. His best work is a thoroughly national tragedy contrasting the wealth of the Canal Zone with the poverty of inland Panama. *La montaña encendida* takes place in the Panamanian uplands where the mestizos labor for the *criollos*, with no hopes of being able to possess land of their own; the chief character tries to get them to rebel and seize some. The play is serious and well written.

The new writers have, since the war, been dealing with social problems and the relationship of Panama to the rest of the world. To help them and other ambitious beginners, the University Theatre was established in 1959 with the help of several experts from the United States.

In 1941 a Theatrical Congress in Montevideo declared that only in Paraguay and Panama of all the Latin American countries was the theatre dead. These details show that the accusation is no longer true in Panama. Especially active is José de Jesús Martínez (1929–   ), master of the short play, concise in exposition of even metaphysical themes, and author of *La mentira* (1955), etc. His best play is *El juicio final* (1962).[4]

---

[4] Charles A. King, "Apuntes para una bibliografía de la literatura de Panamá," *Inter-American Review of Bibliography*, XIV (1964), 262–302, 264–265, 300.

CHAPTER 23

The Theatre in Puerto Rico

Although Puerto Rico is one of the smallest of the Caribbean regions, its theatre deserves a chapter, not only because of its present activity but because of all that is known of its past.[1]

Because of the destruction of Puerto Rican archives by the Dutch in 1625, all records of early sixteenth-century dramatic performances on the island have been lost. The earliest surviving date is September 27, 1644. On that day the Trinitarian bishop of Puerto Rico, Damián López de Haro, wrote to a friend in Spain that he disembarked on the island in the midst of dances, bullfights, and comedies arranged for the observation of the Day of San Antonio. The plays that roused the cleric's wrath may have been secular plays or *autos de pasión* like those in Spain.[2]

This spoilsport bishop convened a council in the cathedral, and in 1645 issued his *Constituciones sinodales*, which, like the decrees of the Council of Lima in 1582 and the Third Mexican Council of 1585, sought to reform social and ecclesiastical customs. The first section forbade the use of alms collected by the Cofradías for *fiestas profanas*, plays, or bullfights. The fifty-seventh prohibited the participation of the clergy in *comedias y autos públicos*. Number 71 declared: "In mysteries dedicated to the worship of God, no profane matter shall enter, nor shall temples . . . become theatres of laughter and vanity." The seventy-eighth, though permitting performances of plays for Corpus Christi, since that was the custom in Spain, stipu-

---

[1] Cesáreo Rosa-Nieves, "Notas para el origen de las representaciones dramáticas en Puerto Rico," *Asomante*, VI (January, 1950), 63–77; Rosa-Nieves, *La lámpara del faro*, pp. 197–219; Antonia Sáez, *El teatro en Puerto Rico*; Wilfredo Braschi, "Treinta años de teatro en Puerto Rico," *Asomante*, XII (January–March, 1955), 95–101; Francisco Arriví, "Perspectiva de una generación teatral puertorriqueña, 1938–1958," *Revista del Instituto de Cultura Puertorriqueña*, No. 1 (October, 1958), 41–47; Arriví, *La generación del treinta: el teatro*; Emilio Pasarell, *Orígenes y desarrollo de la afición teatral en Puerto Rico*.

[2] Alejandro Tapia y Rivera, *Biblioteca histórica*, p. 441.

lated they be *a lo divino* (approved by the bishop), performed outside the church, and unaccompanied by *entremeses deshonestos*.[3]

However such severity did not last long. From 1685 on, plays, bullfights, and jousting with lances were part of the fiestas of Santa Rosa, San Juan, Santiago, and Corpus Christi, with the *ayuntamiento* footing the bills. There is a record of plays to celebrate the coronation of Philip V in 1701. By 1712, Bishop Pedro Urtiaga was complaining in vain that more money was being spent on *comedias, danzas y profanidades* than on the adornment of the saints in the churches. The celebration of the coronation of Ferdinand VI, in 1747, under Governor Colomo, though postponed for several months because of an epidemic, was very elaborate. The plays included: Calderón's *El conde Lucanor* (May 2); *Los españoles en Chile*, by González de Bustos, based on *La araucana* (May 3); *El villano del Danubio y el bien juez no tiene patria*, by Hoz y Mota (May 5); and Moreto's *Primero es la honra*, about the love of a married king for the daughter of a noble (delayed till May 29 because the soldier actors could not get it ready earlier). Different groups were responsible for performing each play. The municipality hired actors for the first, the Church provided players for the second, and the *pardos*, or mulattos, fittingly enough put on *El villano del Danubio* which dealt with protests

---

[3] Rosa-Nieves reprints in *La lámpara del faro* part of the *Constituciones sinodales hechos por el Ilustrísimo y Reverendísimo Sr. Dr. Fray Damián López de Haro, Obispo de la ciudad de San Juan de Puerto Rico* (published in Madrid, 1674) that deal with the theatre:

"Const. I, p. 1: que las cofradías no pueden hacer fiestas profanas, comedias, ni banquetes ni correr toros con las limosnas de la cofradía ni que se recogieran entre los fieles.

"Const. LVII: no se debe permitir en ninguna manera que los sacerdotes y ministros de Dios tengan ocasión de distraerse en punto se entremeten a representar en las comedias y autos públicos. Por tanto mandamos que ningún clérigo de Orden Sacro de este obispado represente ni entre en comedias, autos, danzas, fiestas, músicas ni regocijos ni máscaras o vestirse de mamarracho, aunque las tales fiestas sean en el día Corpus Christi o de otras solemnidades de la Iglesia, lo cual así cumplan pena de excomunicación mayor y de un mes de cárcel y de seis pesos de la primera vez.

"Const. LXXVIII, titled "Como se han de hacer las comedias en las fiestas del Corpus y en otras": En cuanto para regocijar y solemnizar la gran fiesta de Corpus Christi y otras fiestas que nuestra Madre la Iglesia entre año celebra, hay costumbre de hacer y representar comedias y autos, permitimos y toleramos tal costumbre con tal que los autos y comedias . . . sean a lo divino y vistos y aprobados por Nos o nuestro provisor, con tal que no se mezclen en ellos entremeses, bailes, ni otras cosas que toquen a deshonestidad y con que no se hagan dentro de la Iglesia."

against slavery made to the Roman Senate by Germanic peasants. Each performance began at 9:00 P.M., with elaborate costumes and stage decorations, equal in painting and lighting, according to the historian, to anything in the coliseums of Italy.[4] One performance lasted till 2:00 A.M.

Later plays must have become quite earthy, because in 1750, with the explanation that theatrical performances provided temptations, Bishop Antonino de la Ribera prohibited plays anywhere in Puerto Rico,[5] and in 1770 the Church authorities even forbade the attendance of priests at dances.

There was nothing local about Puerto Rico's first plays. Priests had no incentive to dramatize Bible stories or Indian legends for the Indians, because most of the native Boricuas had disappeared soon after the arrival of the white man; besides, their "Taíno" dialect had no written form and was too primitive for drama. Early records, however, do speak of their *areytos*, or ceremonial representations in song and dance of the tribal history. And so, though these people were without the cultural background of the Aztecs or the Incas, they still had a sort of theatrical tradition. Belaval thought so when he gave the name "Areyto" to his drama group in 1938. But the early Spaniards cared nothing for these primitive performances. For entertainment they preferred the works of Spain's Golden Age dramatists, but they probably saw very few productions of them. As Rosa-Nieves indicates, because of the poverty of the island, education was scanty and there was almost no cultural interchange with the rest of the world. During the sixteenth and seventeenth centuries few books were available and few were required in Puerto Rico. Its first printing press did not appear till 1806.[6]

The earliest known play written locally has come down to us in fragments, only sixteen pages of a poetic drama, saved because it formed part of the binding of another volume. It bears no title and the author's name is unknown. The action takes place in Puerto Rico between 1795 and 1805 during the war of Spain and France against

[4] Cayetano Coll y Toste, "Relación verídica de lo acaecido en Puerto Rico a fines del año 46 y principios del 47 con el motivo de llorar la muerte de Felipe Quinto y celebrar la exaltación a la corona de N.S. don Fernando Sexto," *Boletín Histórico de Puerto Rico,* V, No. 3 (May, 1948), 148–192; also quoted in Rosa-Nieves, "Notas," *Asomante,* VI (January, 1950), 67–68.

[5] Pasarell, *Orígenes y desarrollo,* p. 5.

[6] Rosa-Nieves, "Notas," *Asomante,* VI (January, 1950), 68.

England, and it concerns a bigamist husband whose wives finally meet. Pasarell deduced that some local dramatist completed it shortly before 1811.[7]

The French Revolution and the abdication of Charles IV in 1806 produced political disturbances in Puerto Rico, as they did in the rest of the world, and the theatre suffered, as it always does during unrest. Puerto Rico's citizens, however, enjoyed a series of performances in 1811 by a visiting company of actors in a provisional theatre, El Corralón, on Calle del Sol. In spite of objections by the bishop, Governor Meléndez permitted their season to open on Sunday, October 21, with a benefit play for the Hospital de Caridad; it netted five hundred pesos—money, by the way, that the stubborn bishop refused to accept.

After that, the Church clamped down and there were no more plays for awhile in the capital. Actually, the first theatre in Puerto Rico was built at Caguas in 1820 by private individuals, at a cost of six hundred pesos.[8] It was large enough to seat "the elite of the town," and housed sixteen performances during the first season. That same year Ponce erected a provisional theatre, though its permanent playhouse was delayed for twenty-five years. Elsewhere on the island, Arecibo had a theatre as early as 1826. The first provisional theatre in Mayagüez dates from 1834, eleven years after the first recorded performance in that city. Its permanent theatre did not come till 1859.

Meantime, back in San Juan the citizens decided in 1822 to build their own coliseum. They were stimulated by the visit of an impresario, with two professional actors, who recruited local talent for lesser roles. In spite of two postponements because of bad weather, open-air performances were finally given, but the delay had proved to the citizens the importance of having a covered amphitheatre, and they so petitioned the government. Anxious to distract attention from tyrannical practices, the authorities encouraged the building attempt and allowed shares to be offered for sale beginning in September, 1824.

The prospect of a theatre in the capital brought on a battle of plays. A Puerto Rican exile, Félix Mejía, published the five-act, anti-

---

[7] Reprinted in Pasarell, *Orígenes y desarrollo*, pp. 14–25; see also *Puerto Rico Ilustrado*, April 22, 1941.

[8] Pedro de Angeles, "Curiosidades puertorriqueñas," *Revista Blanca*, I, No. 26 (January 10, 1897), 339–340.

government *Rafael del Riego o La España en cadenas* in Philadelphia in 1824 and tried to smuggle copies into the island. The government countered with *Triunfo del trono y lealtad puertorriqueña* by Pedro Tomás de Córdoba, secretary to Governor Miguel de la Torre.[9]

Alejandro Tapia must have been referring to this theatre when he wrote that before he was born (1826) or shortly afterward, a *corral de comedias* existed near the site of the military hospital.[10] As a boy, he had heard talk of an amusing Andalusian actor, Cándamo, and his leading lady, "La Chicha," who performed in plays by Gorostiza and Moratín, and in some in the style of Comella, as well as in *sainetes* by Ramón de la Cruz. Tapia mentions another play with local color, probably the work of Cándamo himself, called *Velorio en Bayajá y pendencia en Culo Prieto*. With a title like that, embodying that disrespectful name for what must have been a San Juan slum, this could only have been a farce.

The San Juan Municipal Theatre, later Teatro Tapia, begun in 1824, was not completed till 1832, after the grandiose plans for the building had been reduced from three stories to two so as to fit within the budget. Even at that, it cost 134,974 pesos. A raked stage was included. The theatre was dedicated by an English opera company and indeed for most of the time its 956 comfortable seats were more frequently filled for music than for drama.[11] However the year-by-year listing by Pasarell does show a few plays that passed the Church censorship.[12] Gil y Zárate's *Carlos II el hechizado* was forbidden here because of its unflattering portrait of royalty. The José de Vicente y Caravantes' translation of the five-act French *La abadía de Castro* was also turned down in 1840 because of its criticism of Pope Sixtus V. One early tragedy produced was *Mucen o El triunfo del patriotismo* (1833) by Luis Nebot Celedonio. José Simón Romero published in 1834 what was called a Chinese tragedy in three acts, *El arrogante Gullerón, reina de Nangán*. In 1841–1842 there were per-

[9] Córdoba, *Memorias* (1832), as quoted by Rosa-Nieves, in "Notas," *Asomante*, VI (January, 1950), 75.

[10] Alejandro Tapia y Rivera, *Mis Memorias*, pp. 91–92.

[11] Cristóbal Real, "Gran alboroto en Puerto Rico al establecer el primer teatro," *El Mundo* (November 30, 1947), quotes a letter from Bishop Juan Arizmendi to Ferdinand VII objecting to the governor's permission to produce plays in the Teatro.

[12] Pasarell, *Orígenes y desarrollo*, 306–314, names about fifty minor dramatists who created a play or two, usually neither performed nor published.

formances of Dumas' *El marino* and a translation by García Gutiérrez of his *Mancha de sangre*, as well as *El pilluelo de París*, a comedy in two acts, and *La familia del boticario*. Governor Méndez de Vigo took advantage of this theatrical activity to raise money for an orphan asylum by putting a tax of one peso on musical events and five pesos on plays. Amateur actors helped him by staging benefit performances. Fifteen dramas were performed in 1842–1843 alone. The Governor's sons Ramón and Felipe acted in several of them.

The quarters of the Philharmonic Society, founded in 1846 under the patronage of the next governor, Aristegui, made available another stage, used chiefly for lectures and concerts, though the Society's members also formed their own company. They produced Arrieta's zarzuela, *El dominó azul* only four months after it opened in Madrid, and gave the great Puerto Rican dramatist Alejandro Tapia his start with a performance of his three-act opera *Guarionex* (1848), with music by Felipe Gutiérrez.

Among the dramatists of this early period were Carmen de Araújo, Tapia, and Salvador Brau. Carmen Hernández de Araújo (1832–1877), the first woman dramatist of Puerto Rico, provided three plays for the legitimate stage. In her teens she wrote *Los deudos rivales* (1846), in five acts. It is set in Sparta about 219 B.C., but its use of destiny and romantic passions removes it from classical drama. *Hacer bien al enemigo es imponerle el mejor castigo* (1847) sounds like a Golden Age title. Her third play, *Amor ideal* (1863), published with the others in 1866, is the one of highest literary quality, but she forced a happy ending in its story of seventeenth-century Seville. No indication remains of the reception of her plays by the public.

María Bibiana Benítez (1785–1873) another long-lived woman writer, was author of a historical two-act play more sentimental than dramatic, *La cruz del morro* (1862), about the Dutch attack on Puerto Rico in 1625; it included a duel between the Dutch admiral and the commander of the fortress. *La cruz* was performed again in 1900, on the two hundred seventy-fifth anniversary of the event, and was published in 1919. Miss Benítez was a disciple of Calderón.

The outstanding figure of this early period, however, was Alejandro Tapia y Rivera (1826–1882). At the age of twenty-two, before being exiled to Spain for dueling, he attempted a literary tragedy, but realized its weakness and suppressed it. When he was permitted to return, he rewrote it as *Roberto D'Evreux* (1856), a his-

torical play in four acts. Though it had nothing to do with Puerto
Rico, being set in the court of Queen Elizabeth in 1602 and dealing
with the conspiracy of Essex and James of Scotland, the censors had
a feeling that its implication that kings are human might, at least in-
directly, encourage the antimonarchical feeling in the island. They
therefore refused publication or performance till 1862.

The next year Tapia wrote another play, *Bernardo de Palissy o El
heroísmo del trabajo* (1857). There was no official objection to its
performance or publication because in dealing with the St. Bartholo-
mew massacre of 1572 it put the French in a bad light. Critics like
Menéndez y Pelayo declare it the best play by Tapia; certainly it is
the most faithful to history.

This author's romanticism was underscored by his *Camoens* in
1868. In a revision in 1876 he reduced this tragedy of an ill-starred
figure from four acts to three, intensified the emotion, and retouched
the beautiful verse. The ghost of the famous Portuguese explorer appears in it.

One other historical drama, *Vasco Núñez de Balboa* (1872), came
from Tapia's pen. Its violence and villainy tending toward melodrama weaken the emotional appeal and the development of its
theme that great deeds are more important than social rank.

Tapia's other plays show his interest in social problems. *La cuar-
terona* (1867), though set in Cuba, where he spent part of his exile,
deals with the equally Puerto Rican problem of interracial marriage.
It was selected to dedicate the remodeled Municipal Theatre of San
Juan in 1950 when it was renamed Teatro Tapia. The tragedy is
heightened by making the two girls, one white and one quadroon,
daughters of the same father. The sudden and undramatic end gives
the impression that the author suddenly tired of writing it. It was not
performed in Puerto Rico till 1878, five years after the abolition of
the slavery it attacks.

Finally, to prove his sense of humor, Tapia wrote *La parte del león*
(1878; published 1880), set in contemporary Madrid. He used prose,
which he considered good enough for contemporary subjects, and
preached a single standard for both partners in a marriage. As Justo
puts it: "The soul has no sex." His native San Juan gave Tapia a gold
medal at the première and compared him to Echegaray.

The next important dramatist of Puerto Rico was Salvador Brau

(1842–1912).[13] After organizing and directing a dramatic group for three years, this accomplished lyric poet began his career as a dramatist in 1871 with *Héroe y mártir,* whose first performance inaugurated the theatre in his home town of Cabo Rojo. It deals with the love and death of a sixteenth-century fighter for Spanish independence, Juan de Padilla, but is somewhat melodramatic.

Brau allowed a touch of farce to creep into his *De la superficie al fondo* (1874), in which an extravagant Puerto Rican mother beggars her family to supply a husband for her daughter. The fiestas in it give it local color, but its comedy is universal. Local, too, is his *La vuelta al hogar* (1877), a three-act drama in lyric poetry, about a well-known local pirate. In its story one finds all the trappings of romanticism.

For his last play Brau dramatized the Sicilian vespers theme. It was his best work, the romantic three-act *Los horrores del triunfo* (1887). The authorities, remembering Brau's earlier appeal for freedom through the speeches of Juan de Padilla were afraid this new play of a people's conspiracy against the Count of Anjou might offer further incitement to rebellion against Spain. So after its first performance it was forbidden and not repeated till 1890. The disillusioned dramatist never tried again.

Puerto Rico had other playwrights even while Brau was writing. Eleuterio Derkes (1834–1883), a poet, was author of the four-act prose drama *Ernesto Lefebre o El triunfo del talento* (1871), and two one-act comedies, *Don Nuño Tiburcio de Pereira* (1877) and *El tío Fele* (1883), of lesser importance. The Code of Honor, as interpreted by Echegaray, inspired Manuel María Sama (1850–1913) to write *Inocente y culpable* (1877), a drama in verse, in which a father tries to preserve the good name of his guilty daughter by casting suspicion on his daughter-in-law, but justice finally triumphs. Derkes followed it the next year by another drama along similar lines, *La víctima de su falta.*

One reason for all this playwriting activity was the presence in Puerto Rico of the celebrated actor Eugenio Astol (1843–1904). Astol created the lead in all the previously named plays, as well as the re-

[13] Darío Córdoba Landrón de Guevara, *Salvador Brau, su vida, su obra, su época.*

vised edition of Tapia's *Camoens,* which he used to inaugurate his own Teatro Moratín, founded because the fifty-year-old Municipal Theatre needed repairs. It was for Astol, too, that Brau wrote *La vuelta al hogar.* After dominating the island theatre for a long time Astol eventually went to Bolivia, where he died.

A new type of Puerto Rican drama was just beginning. As Ramón de la Cruz of Spain had dramatized lower-class people in his *sainetes,* so Puerto Rican dramatists began using the *jíbaro,* rural farmer. The *jíbaro* first appeared on the stage in *El juego de gallos* (1852) by Roberto C. T. Caballero, a Venezuelan who lived in San Juan and in the works of Ramón Méndez Quiñones (1847–1889). *Un jíbaro como hay pocos* (1878; published 1881) begins the story of Leoncio, who is trying to marry his daughter to the sophisticated Canuto. Its sequel, *La jíbara* (1881) finally reveals the outcome: the bride solves her own marital problems and by her nobility wins the love of her husband. Though light, both plays have good local color and embody the psychology of rural Puerto Rico.

Méndez developed this vein in other famous plays: *Los jíbaros progresistas* (1882), with its spirited cockfight scene at the Ponce Fair, and its sequel, *La vuelta a la feria* (1882); *Un comisario del barrio,* where the civil guard breaks up a card game; *La triquina,* a farce about fake doctors and a wife who repents her immoral life; and others whose titles reveal their local color: *Un casamiento, Un bautismo, ¡Pobre Sinda!,* etc. In 1889 this dramatist went to Honduras to act in the troupe of Asuaga but died there shortly after his arrival.

Another poet and novelist, Manuel M. Corchado y Juarbe (1840–1884), had a brief fling at the stage, which he had known as a law student in Barcelona. He began with a dramatic *cuadro, María Antonieta* (1880), first performed in Barcelona. His other plays, *Desde la comedia al drama* (1887), about the Honor Code, and the patriotic *El capitán Correa,* were published after his death. Neither was of much importance.

From then on Puerto Rican drama went into a decline. The few authors of sporadic plays provided pale reflections of European drama traditions, and most of them revealed little knowledge of theatrical technique. The struggle for independence and the imposition of a new culture following the Spanish American War partially explain the dearth of drama. Lack of actors, the feeling that plays were difficult to write, and the competition of the movies further handicapped the rise of a national theatre.

In 1912, however, the six months' stay of Virginia Fábregas in Puerto Rico provided new impetus for drama. Rosa-Nieves dates the modern Puerto Rican theatre from the time of her visit.[14] Besides her repertory of Spanish plays and French plays in translation, she performed two by José Pérez Losada (1879–1937), a Spaniard by birth but a resident of San Juan since 1895. He set most of his musical comedies in Spain, including his masterpiece *La cantaora*; but his three-act high comedy *La crisis del amor* (1912; published 1925), one of the best of Puerto Rico's plays, gives humorous dramatic treatment to the differences in marriage customs of Puerto Rico and the United States. Maeterlinck and Benavente were its predecessors. With no attempt to provide any solution except philosophic acceptance of loneliness, Pérez Losada provided good satire and lively dialog. Another produced play, the drama *La rabia* (1912) was immediately published. Later he wrote the three-act comedy *Los primeros fríos* (published 1915), winner of an Ateneo prize, and *La vida es ácida o Las industrias de la prohibición* (1925).

The first modern play by a Puerto Rican, according to Rosa-Nieves, was the romantic *El grito de Lares* (1914; published 1929), by the lawyer Luis Llorens Torres (1878–1944). Having completed his graduate studies in Spain, he was familiar with the European stage. This outstanding historical drama in prose and verse about the first, and unsuccessful, organized rebellion against the Spanish domination, though setting no definite trend, started a movement that developed along various paths. Most of them had no relationship with contemporary life. However Juan B. Huyke (1880–) scrutinized rural politics and education in *El batey* (1926). It has more appeal than technique. Indeed all the plays by this educator have a didactic slant.

Along historical lines and involving real people was the romantic *Juan Ponce de León* of 1932 (published 1934) about Puerto Rico's colonizer and first governor and his struggle against the Taínos and Boriqueños Indians of the island. Influenced by Villaespesa and Marquina, it was the patriotic and modernistic collaboration of José

---

[14] Rosa-Nieves, "Notas," *Asomante*, VI (January, 1950), 70; Josefina Rivera de Alvarez, *Diccionario de literatura puertorriqueña*, pp. 340–345.

Ramírez Santibáñez (1895–1950) and Carlos N. Carreras (1895–), and was first performed by María Guerrero and Díaz de Mendoza in the city of Ponce.[15]

Along humorous lines came *El héroe galopante* (1923; published 1935) by United States–educated Nemisio R. Canales (1878–1923), about the modern, eighteen-year-old Marisabel and her feud with her guardian. Suggested by Shaw's *Arms and the Man* was the psychological comedy *Un hombre de cuarenta años* (1928), by Antonio Coll y Vidal (1898–), it was an early vanguardist attempt, with thought substituted for action. Coll had to take it to Havana to get it performed. In fact, Spanish actors performed in all these plays except the Canales farce. Perhaps the nearest to high comedy was the work of Arturo Cadilla (1895–) who gave satirical treatment to local problems. *El oro de la dicha* (1933), *El dictador* (1935), the *entremés Gatilandia* (1935), and others in prose and poetry came from his pen.

The founding by the lawyer, critic and short-story writer Emilio S. Belaval (1903–) of a group of amateur actors in 1938 is credited by Solórzano with the birth of the national theatre in Puerto Rico. He calls it the most organic, homogeneous, and interesting national theatre of Latin America.[16] Belaval called his group "Areyto," a name taken from the earliest dramatic dance-shows of the island. Though it lasted only three years and performed in a small and obscure theatre in San Juan, Areyto was the stimulus for several successors.

Beginning in 1926, Belaval had himself written several one-act plays. For his group he dramatized a folk ballad under the title of *Cuando las flores de Pascua son flores de azahar* (1939) and wrote *La presa de los vencedores* (1939), an ironical look at the will to conquer. *La hacienda de los cuatro vientos* (1940) was nearer to the ideals of the Areyto; it goes back to the days of Father José de la Paz, who struggled to free the slaves and persuade the Spanish landowners of the equality of man. Spanish hidalgos, Creoles, and slaves steeped in Martinique witchcraft appear in a well-constructed drama with an excellent second-act curtain, though its long romantic speeches get a bit tedious. First performed the year it was written, this play later represented Belaval at the first Puerto Rican Drama

---

[15] Braschi, "Treinta años de teatro," *Asomante*, XII (January–March, 1955), 95–101.
[16] Carlos Solórzano, *Teatro latinoamericano del siglo XX*, pp. 63, 83.

Festival. He is not always concerned with the national scene. *La muerte*, originally written for his own Areyto group, was considered too difficult for amateurs and did not get a performance till the University Players produced it in 1957.[17] In it, an Italian count, a Spanish priest, and a Latin American heiress, guests in a Riviera hotel, after fear of dying from lobster poisoning, revert to their primitive selves. *La vida* (1959)—"tragedia de la vida útil"—published in Madrid, has no national note. Set "anywhere that the city dominates man," it is a thought piece, with the mysterious "La enajenada" wandering through the scenes. Published in 1961 is Belaval's *Cielo caído* (1959), "una tragedia del bello cuerpo" set "anywhere that the lights have begun to devour man." These newest plays by Belaval, who in the meantime had been appointed to the Puerto Rico Supreme Court, probably read better than they play.

It is not as a playwright that Belaval has chiefly influenced the Puerto Rican theatre. He preached, if not practiced, the importance of using local characters and national themes and held his Areyto group ready to perform any forthcoming results. Even though some of the dramatists that he encouraged into activity had their works performed elsewhere, or later, their attention had been focused toward the possibility of Puerto Rican subjects. An Ateneo Puertorriqueño drama contest in 1938 gave them more spur, with the Grupo Areyto ready to perform the winning plays. And so came into being a group of enthusiastic young amateurs, all born between 1900 and 1910. They were unsure of their technique and sometimes even of their purpose: *Mi señoría*, by the oldest of them, Luis Rechani Agrait (1902–), begins as a serious consideration of political problems but turns into a grotesque farce; the epilog of Méndez Ballester's *Encrucijada* destroys its effectiveness. But they had in common a love of the theatre and an appreciation of its value as a mirror to make their fellow islanders confront their problems.

One of the many plays offered to Areyto dealt with a middle-class Puerto Rican family in the United States. *Esta noche juega el jóker* (1939) was written by Fernando Sierra Berdecía (1903–). During its three acts, a husband with an inferiority complex wins a game of poker against men who covet his wife. On a broader canvas, the drama presents the cultural clash of family patterns—the Latin

[17] Published in *Biblioteca de Autores Puertorriqueños*, 1953. See René Marqués, "Apuntes para una interpretación de *La Muerte*," *Asomante*, X (1953).

paterfamilias and the North American matriarch—along with the psychological transformation of the Puerto Rican immigrant in the United States. It ends on an optimistic note. The play won for its author a prize of $1,000 as the best book of the year. Sierra's later experimental *La escuela de buen amor* (1941) was not up to the standard of its predecessor.

Other aspects of the expatriated Puerto Rican were also dramatized. The poet and novelist Pedro Juan Labarthe (1906–   ) wrote *Los nietos antillanos* (1940), which has been performed in Bayamón, Santo Domingo, Cuba, and New York, and translated into English. It tells of the wrong uses of liberty by a family of immigrants and of their return to Puerto Rico with their illegitimate children, all *nietos antillanos*. Mexico and Paris have seen performances of Labarthe's *Los eternos tres en uno* (1940) about a split personality.

Other dramatists turned their attention to the Puerto Rican in his native land, harking back to the earlier *jíbaro*—comedies which are now given serious treatment.[18] In *El clamor de los surcos* (published 1940) Manuel Méndez Ballester (1909–   ), enticed into playwriting by the 1938 Ateneo Puertorriqueño competition, tells of a hard-working family dispossessed of its sugarcane fields. In *Tiempo muerto* (1940), its title derived from the name of the dull period when the farmer has no income after the harvesting of the cane, the *jíbaro* Ignacio and his family leave their mountain home for an even more miserable existence working in the sugar factory.[19] An eager exponent of the national theatre, Méndez Ballester founded Sociedad General de Actores. In 1943 it performed his tragedy *Hilarión*, a modernization of Sophocles' *Oedipus*, and his shorter *Nuestros días* (1944), in which he brought Chekhov to Puerto Rico. A couple of amusing plays, *El misterio del castillo* (1946) and *Un fantasma decentito* (1950), preceded his farce *Es de vidrio la mujer* (1952), which had its sources in Cervantes.

With *Encrucijada* (1956), about the fates of Puerto Ricans in New York, Méndez Ballester resumed his serious drama. The different moral values in their new home destroy the family. This play reveals the weakness of its author: he merely narrates. There is no stressing

[18] Sáez, *El teatro en Puerto Rico*, pp. 75–76.
[19] *Tiempo Muerto* and *El clamor de los surcos* were published in San Juan in 1960.

of fate or pondering of reasons. He does not study the clash of cultures, however, to the extent done by the later René Marqués.

Other dramatists continued exploiting rural problems. *El desmonte* (1938; published 1940), about coffee growing, was written for the Ateneo contest by Gonzalo del Toro and was performed by Areyto. *Tierra y honor* (1943) by Raúl Gándara (1910–   ), a drama about the economics of farm labor, was followed by his impressionistic *El padre Damián* (1948) and *Por orden del doctor* (1948). Inspired by *Tiempo muerto* were other rural plays, like the poetic tragedy by Edmundo Rivera Alvarez (1917–   ), *Camino del silencio* (1944). It was better received than his staged radio soap-drama *La cárcel de yedra* (1950).

In 1940 Areyto performed an amusing political and social comedy, *Mi señoría,* by the journalist Luis Rechani Agrait (1902–   ). It was revised for the 1959 Puerto Rico Drama Festival. Less enthusiastically received were *El eterno anhelo* by Angel F. Rivera, or *He vuelto a buscarla* (1940), a psychological study of a modern woman, and *La hormiguela,* both by María López de Victoria (1893–   ), who writes under the pen name of "Martha Lomar." The historian of the Puerto Rican stage must also consider René Jiménez Malaret (1903–   ), for his social drama of ideas, *Cosas de familia* (1941); and Julio Marrero Núñez (1910–   ), both for his *Borikén* and *La doncella del flamboyán* (1946) and for his direction of the best plays by Méndez Ballester, Marta Lomar, and Rechani. There are also the youthful Pedro Juan Soto, whose naturalistic one-act *El huésped* was performed by Teatro Experimental del Ateneo in 1956; and Gerard Paul Marín, whose dramatic qualities were first apparent in his fantastic *Retablo de Juan Canelo* (1958). As a surrealist he wrote *En el principio la noche era serena* (1960), about the final moments of the protagonist, filled with impressions that sum up his whole life.

By midcentury Puerto Rico had a number of acting companies. In 1944 the University Players performed the nostalgic *La resentida,* about the reaction following independence from Spain. It was written by Professor Enrique A. Laguerre (1906–   ), novelist and radio commentator, who also wrote a volume, *El pulso de Puerto Rico* (1956), concerning local dramas and the six hundred plays of all periods and lands broadcast by the government stations with which he is connected.

The outstanding poet and critic Cesáreo Rosa-Nieves (1904–   ) also turned his attention to the stage.[20] Though critics praised his romantic *Baldorioty de Castro* (1947) in verse, about the patriot who in 1887 revolted against the political corruption of tyrannical Governor Palacios, the spectators considered undramatic its solution through a general Christmas amnesty. Later plays by Rosa-Nieves were more favorably received. Three of them are collected in *Trilogía lírica* (published 1950). *El huesped del mar* recounts an adventure of Puerto Rico's Robin Hood, Roberto Cofresí, with a siren. *Flor de Areyto* goes back to 1514: Pedro Mejía and his Indian sweetheart Luisa are slain together, accused of the death of Pedro's rival. The third play is contemporary. *La otra* is a monolog by "Ella," (which translates "She") against her roommate "La otra" ("The other"), who is leaving her to get married. The author defends his choice of a homosexual theme by having Ella shoot herself. Dr. Rosa-Nieves' latest, an experiment in prose, is the rural drama *Norka* (1957), not yet published.

The founding of Teatro Universitario in 1941 following the collapse of Areyto created a new generation of younger dramatists. University trained, they know about psychology, dramatic technique, and the art of dialog. The principal ones have even studied abroad. The oldest of them is Francisco Arriví (1915–   ), who studied playwriting at Columbia University, New York. Professor Enrique A. Laguerre gives him an important role in the theatrical revolution in Puerto Rico.[21] Besides translating plays for a radio program and for the University Theatre, he founded El Tinglado Puertorriqueño, an experimental group that performs many of his plays. His writings have also contributed to the history of his country's theatre.

The plays of Arriví fall into two divisions. His first attempts are characterized by a veil of fantasy and a departure from the problem plays about Puerto Rico which are being produced by most of his contemporaries. *Alumbramiento* (1945) is concerned with birth, life, and dreams. The title of *El diablo se humaniza* shows its theme. A soul in crisis and a narrator sitting in the audience are part of *Caso del muerto en vida* (1950), performed, like Marqués' earlier *El sol y los*

[20] Arriví, "Perspectiva de una generación teatral," *Revista*, No. 1 (October, 1958), 41.

[21] Professor Laguerre is quoted in Frank Dauster, "Francisco Arriví: The Mask and the Garden," *Hispania*, XLV (1962), 637–643.

Macdonald, with split-level stage, area lighting, flashbacks, and other modern techniques.

The one-act farce *Club de solteros* (1940) which initiated Arriví's career was expanded to three acts in 1953. It tells of an antifeminist who founds a bachelor's club and starts a war between the sexes. It was first performed by Arriví's group at the University of Puerto Rico.

The most substantial play of Arriví's first period, however, is *María Soledad* (1947), retitled *Una sombra menos* when published in 1953. Dauster points out the various planes of the action and the psychopathic symbols of dragons and lilies, but most of the audience would miss them. They could not miss, however, the basic psychology that gives the play substance.

In his second period, Arriví turned to realistic treatment of Puerto Rico, especially racial discrimination and its psychological complexity. Most of his characters are human beings isolated by walls of solitude. His trilogy, *Máscara puertorriqueña,* involves the dramatist's own countrymen, sometimes in their own land, sometimes in the United States. Part I, *Bolero y plena* (1956)[22] takes the names of its two plays from two folk dances. The bolero "Silencio" is used as the theme of the first play, *El murciélago.* Juan, rejected by father and stepmother, drives away his sacrificing wife. *Medusas en la bahía,* the second play, based on a *plena,* tells of the suicide of a quadroon unable to associate with either blacks or whites.

Part II, *Vejigantes* (1957), selected as Arriví's best play for the Puerto Rico First Drama Festival,[23] stresses the theme that by denying their African heritage the Puerto Ricans reject true happiness. Part III, *Sirena,* repeats the theme that one's Negro ancestry cannot be concealed by surgery and make-up.

Best of the island's dramatists, and deserving a place among the best in Latin America is René Marqués (1919–   ), also a critic and short-story writer. He, too, became interested in the racial problem, but he adds a political interpretation. He is a nationalist in both art and politics. Marqués' first play, *El sol y los Macdonald* (1947) was written while he was a student at the University of Madrid and was first produced in 1950 by Teatro Nuestro, a troupe he recruited from University of Puerto Rico students. Set in the southern United States,

[22] Published in *Asomante,* XII, No. 2 (1955) and XIII, No. 1 (1956); both together in *Bolero y plena* (San Juan, 1960).

[23] Published in *Asomante,* XIV, No. 1 (1957), 8–42.

it deals with an attempt by Gustavo MacDonald, last of the family, to keep the line uncontaminated by foreign blood. Then Marqués wrote a universal play, *El hombre y sus sueños* (1948), published in *Asomante*. Showing his acquaintance with Unamuno, he seeks to express man's hunger for immortality and the "tragic sense of life." Solórzano says that protection as a destroying force is Marqués' favorite theme, which is why he protests against United States protection of Puerto Rico.[24] This feeling is back of Marqués' *Palm Sunday* (published 1949), written in English for a playwriting class at Columbia University and dealing with the 1937 Easter massacre of a score of nationalists in Ponce. It attacks the blindness of United States officials in Puerto Rico. The author directed its first performance in 1956 at the Tapia Theatre, amid a storm of newspaper controversy.

Next, accomplishing what Sierra Berdecía and Méndez Ballester could not do because of their sympathy for their protagonists, Marqués in *La carreta* (1950) wrote the utter tragedy of an old *jíbaro*, Chago, forced from the land he loves, and of his descendants unable to adjust in New York.[25] The play is more than *costumbrismo*. In Marqués' handling of the tribulations of the family, it becomes clear that the influence of Sartre and Camus have reached Puerto Rico. A number of critics consider this symbolic play not only the best in Puerto Rico, but outstanding in Latin American drama because of its deep feeling, dramatic action, and brilliant dialog. The play was first performed in New York, in May, 1950, then in December by the Ateneo Experimental Theatre founded by Marqués, and finally in the Teatro Tapia in January 1951.

After a pause, Marqués experimented with "a Puerto Rican pantomime for an occidental ballet," and wrote *Juan Bobo y la dama del occidente* (1956).[26] Like its nationalist author, the traditional folklore character prefers his island sweetheart to the western charmer. In *La muerte no entrará en palacio* (1957), a man given power by the people and getting protection from "a powerful country in the north," is the chief character. When he turns his power against the people, his own daughter kills the despot, then commits suicide. One

[24] Solórzano, *Teatro latinoamericano*.
[25] Published in *Asomante*, VIII, No. 4 (1951), and IX, Nos. 1 and 3 (1952). See also Maria Teresa Babín, "Apuntes para *La carreta*," *Asomante*, X, No. 4 (1953).
[26] Published in *Asomante*, V, No. 2 (1948). His volume, *Teatro* (Mexico, 1959) contains three recent plays.

admiring critic referred to this play as "one of the most solid of Latin American dramas."

A theatre, to be national, must reflect its country's conditions, and Puerto Rico during the last two decades was in a state of turbulence. Once the poverty spot of the Caribbean, with festering slums, it was going through an economic revolution that they called Operation Bootstrap, and with Governor Muñoz Marín as its impetus, money and manufacturers poured into the island. The flight of ambitious citizens to New York slackened, and some began returning. The cultural level also rose. Pablo Casals has been largely responsible for the increase in interest in music, and his festivals have been attended by great musicians and musical organizations. The theatre, too, has showed increasing tempo. In 1958 the Instituto de Cultura (established 1956), both to encourage the new group of rising dramatists and to recognize the efforts of the four dramatists whose endeavors had kept the theatre alive for the past twenty years, organized the First Puerto Rican Dramatic Festival. Honored were Méndez Ballester, Belaval, Arriví, and Marqués, and each was asked to provide a play for presentation.[27]

As his contribution, Marqués turned an incident in his home town during his childhood into his best play and the most successful of the four performed at the festival. *Los soles truncos* (1958) was based on an earlier short story, *Purificación en la Calle de Cristo*, about three elderly sisters, scions of an ancient family, living in their family mansion in one of the old streets of San Juan. In addition to the dramatist's preoccupation with the philosophic concept of time, the play seemed to most spectators the expression of an ardent nationalist's loyalty to his Spanish culture.

The next play by Marqués, *Un niño azul para esa sombra*, written for the 1959 Festival, won the Ateneo prize of $500 for the best unproduced play of 1958. Again it exhibits symbolism in its story of rebellion and patriotism and death as the only way to achieve liberty. The small son of the title, believing in his father's principles, kills

[27] Plays from the First Festival, and the Second, in 1959, were published in the two-volume *Teatro puertorrequeno*. Vol. I includes the four plays of the First Festival: Méndez Ballester's *Encrucijada*; Belaval's *Hacienda de los Cuatro Vientos*, Arriví's *Vejigantes*; and Marqués' *Los soles truncos*. Vol. II contains plays presented the following year: Laguerre's *La resentida*; Rechani's *Mi señoría*; and Sierra Berdecía's *Esta noche juega el jóker*. Volumes for the next three festivals have also been published.

himself. Three of Marqués' recent plays were collected in *Teatro*, published in Mexico in 1959. Most recently came *La casa sin reloj, comedia antipoética en dos absurdos y un final razonable* (1962).

With enthusiasm begetting enthusiasm, other younger dramatists are appearing in Puerto Rico. In the five plays of Juan Bautista Pagán's published *Teatro* (Puerto Rico, 1957) only the three-act *Angel* concerns modern Puerto Rico, *La libertadora* deals with Manuela Sáenz in Bogotá in 1828. *El gallo de Esculapio* concerns the death of Socrates, and *El círculo de tiza* reworks a Chinese play by Li-Hsing-tao. But other authors of still unpublished plays remain nearer their local scene. The presence for the first time in San Juan of a professional company looking for plays by Puerto Rican dramatists is one stimulus. Frequently in the Latin American countries a playwright must provide his own performers, and a performance depends more on the energy and ambition of the author than on the quality of his manuscript. This system has one advantage: plays unattractive to impresarios who look first for monetary returns have been successfully produced. But drama festivals offer a better way, and in Puerto Rico they have already inspired even more activity in what was already the lively theatre world of Puerto Rico. One of the newer figures is Eugenio Sánchez de Fuente, author of *Sacrificios*.

CHAPTER 24

The Theatre in the Dominican Republic

Baptized Española when Columbus settled the island in December, 1492, Santo Domingo was later given the Latinized name of Hispaniola by Pedro Mártir de Anghiera. Not till 1505, when a new capital replaced Nueva Isabel, destroyed by a hurricane, did it and the colony get the name by which it was long known. Actually Santo Domingo was the whole island, including Haiti.

As the first center of European culture in the New World and the administrative base for the political and religious conquest of Spanish America, Santo Domingo was probably the scene of the first European-type plays performed in this Hemisphere. At least it should have been. Christopher Columbus' son, Diego (1474–1526), arriving as its governor in 1509, brought his wife, María de Toledo, niece of the Duke of Alba, for whom Encina had written Spain's first colloquial play, a Christmas eclog, in 1492. It is well known that some of Spain's earliest dialogs were performed for the entertainment of seminary and university students. Santo Domingo, too, had seminaries and universities. The Dominicans, after their arrival in 1510, established here America's first seminary as well as its first university, St. Thomas Aquinas, in 1538, followed shortly by the University of Santiago de la Paz y de Gorjón, named for its wealthy founder, Hernando de Gorjón.[1] Who can doubt that some of its students had ambitions toward the stage?

The visits of dramatists from Spain provided additional incentive to develop its theatre. One of the first was Micael de Carvajal (1490–1545?), who reached Santo Domingo in 1534, having already dealt dramatically in Spain with Joseph in Egypt in his *Tragedia Josefina*. And Tirso de Molina (1583–1648) could very well have put a couple of plays on paper before he arrived in 1616 with the Mercedarian friars to extend the religious work of his order into America. In Santo

---

[1] Cipriano de Utrera, *Universidades de Santiago de La Paz y de Santo Tomás de Aquino*, pp. 56–75.

Domingo, Tirso got public recognition when in September, 1616, he was awarded first prize in a poetry contest to honor the Virgin. The mention of tropical customs and fruits in his later *Villana de Vallescas* (1620), and the New World plots of *Amazonas de las Indias* and *La lealtad contra la envidia*, both of 1635, show that dramatically Tirso profited by his visit. Perhaps the island did too.

None of Santo Domingo's theatrical activity was considered worth recording, however, prior to a performance on June 23, 1588. That one achieved immortality only because the local authorities disapproved of it so strongly that their complaints in writing were sent to the king.

Cristóbal de Llerena (c. 1545–c. 1610) was a canon and music director of the cathedral. As professor of Latin at the University, he was accustomed, according to the testimony of the archbishop, to compose "comedias con que suele solemnizar las fiestas y regocijar al público." However the play written in 1588 and performed by university students from his class was a different sort. In it, a *gracioso* asks Cordellate, a typical Spanish *bobo*, supposedly meant to represent the populace, what has happened to his previously fat stomach. Cordellate explains that he has given birth to a horrible monster with a woman's head, a horse's neck, a bird's body, and a fish's tail.[2] Since the times were critical—only two years earlier Sir Francis Drake had sacked the city—*gracioso* and *bobo* think the birth may be an omen and decide to consult soothsayers. One such, Proteo, calls it retribution for capricious and wanton women in the city and for the venality of lawyers and theologs; another, Calcas, fears it forebodes another invasion. Under pressure the alcalde promises to take up the "unimportant" detail of defense with the next *cabildo*.

This not too subtle attempt at reform by the patriotic author galled the city fathers so much that two weeks later Llerena was dragged out of bed and shipped off to New Granada, while an account of the affair, with a copy of the play, went to Philip II in Spain. There it was found in 1921 by the Mexican Icaza.[3] The exile of Llerena did

---

[2] José Juan Arrom, *El teatro de Hispanoamérica en la época colonial*, pp. 59–62, finds a source for this creature in Horace's *Epistle to the Pisones*.

[3] Francisco A. de Icaza, "Cristóbal A. de Llerena y los orígenes del teatro en la América Española," *Revista de Filología Española*, VIII (April, 1921), 121–130. See also Pedro Henríquez Ureña, *La cultura y las letras coloniales en Santo Domingo*, pp. 93–95, 153–157; Antonio J. Pasquariello, *El entremés, sainete, y*

not last long. His versatile talents were required by the student body of the University of Santiago and by the cathedral choir, and he was soon forgiven and brought back. He was not again tempted, however, to turn dramatist.

As in Paraguay, after its one evidence of activity the dramatic life in Santo Domingo languished. Of the 337-page study of Dominican authors by Max Henríquez Ureña, only seven deal with the theatre.[4] However, there are occasional references elsewhere. In 1610 the synod gave permission to prelates to perform "farsas, autos, y comedias" in their churches, provided they were "santas, católicas y honestas." They also allowed "entremeses graciosos" and even "cosas profanas," provided they were not "deshonestas o muy profanas."[5]

Seminary inmates were evidently performing plays before public audiences, as proved by Churchly threats of excommunication for some students who stole time from their studies to prepare a play for the Feast of Our Lady of the Rosary in October, 1663; indeed, Archbishop Francisco de la Cueva y Maldonado ended by refusing to let students perform "comedias ni otros actos en tablado ni fuera de él."

Sixteen years later, he was still fulminating, with the backing of the captain general, this time against plays and bullfights that were keeping the women out late, "de lo que no podía esperar nada bueno." Unfortunately for historians, he made no mention of the authors of these plays, though Américo Lugo, investigating in the Archives of Seville for his *Historia Colonial de la Isla,* reported seeing a faded copy of an anonymous play written in Santo Domingo in the seventeenth century.[6]

By the eighteenth century stage shows in private homes had become a popular entertainment. At the urging of his wife, José Solano y Bote, governor of Santo Domingo from 1771 to 1778, sponsored per-

---

loa en el teatro colonial de Hispanoamérica, pp. 57–80; and Flérida de Nolasco, *Días de la colonia,* pp. 31–51.

[4] Max Henríquez Ureña, *Panorama histórica de la literatura dominicana.* However, see Manuel de Jesús Goico Castro, "Raíz y trayectoria del teatro en la literatura nacional," *Revista de la Universidad de Santo Domingo,* IX (1945), 71–90; X (1946), 155–202. Joaquín Balaguer has little to say about the theatre in his *Historia de la literatura dominicana.*

[5] Max Henríquez Ureña, *Panorama de la literatura dominicana,* as reviewed in *Panorama,* No. 31, pp. 27–29, traces drama from del Monte to 1928.

[6] See Pedro Henríquez Ureña, *Literatura dominicana,* p. 17, n. 2.

formances in the Palace, not only of plays sent from Spain but of a few local writers.[7]

Shortly afterward the political status of the island changed. Spain and France clashed over it but, finally, by the treaty of 1795 Spain relinquished its claims and Santo Domingo came under French domination. France's cruel treatment of Toussaint L'Ouverture in 1801 alienated even its defenders, and in 1804 the island became independent, first under the Haitian Dessalines, then under Henri Christophe.

One result of the French domination was a period of theatrical activity. Part of the crew of a French squadron, defeated by British warships off Santo Domingo harbor, managed to swim ashore. To occupy their spare time they founded the Dramatic Society of Santo Domingo and took over the Nuestra Señora de Regina Convent, putting a theatre sign over the entrance where a saint's image had stood. Though the sailors were not great actors and their repertory not very extensive, they gave the citizens opportunity to see some plays.

In 1809 the Spanish inhabitants reconquered their section of the island and for a time maintained their colonial relations with Spain; then they declared for independence and in 1821 tried to join Greater Colombia, but Jean Pierre Boyer, president of Haiti, determined to unify the whole island and in 1822 conquered and absorbed Santo Domingo.

The imposition of the French language and the attempt to obliterate all Spanish atmosphere decided many of the aristocratic families to flee to Venezuela, Puerto Rico, and Cuba. For that reason, Cubans rather than Dominicans had the honor of witnessing the first play of the new romantic movement in America.

Among the exiles from Santo Domingo were the parents of Francisco Xavier Foxá y Lecando (1816–1865). Eventually they settled in Havana, where Francisco's Hugo-esque *Don Pedro de Castillo* was first performed in August, 1838. If written in 1836, as generally believed, it makes the Dominican Foxá the first romanticist playwright of the New World, even though *Guillermo*, a play by the Cuban José María de Andueza was performed in Havana a month earlier.

Foxá lacked spontaneity, not only in *Don Pedro de Castillo* but in his other attempts—the four-act poetic drama *El Templario* (1838)

---

[7] José Gabriel García, *Historia de Santo Domingo*, I, 221.

and *Ellos son*, a one-act comedy in verse. However he did win for Santo Domingo the honor due a pioneer.

On the island the theatre had practically gone underground. During the twenty-two years of Haitian domination (1822–1844) a few dramatic societies, such as La Filantrópica sprang up. To give the people something to do besides conspiring against Haiti in the secret society La Trinitaria, President Boyer permitted Manuel Guerrero to turn the old jail into a theatre. While forbidding any locally written plays for fear of propaganda, he thought it safe to allow the performance of plays from Europe, provided no changes were made in the lines. However, by selecting plays dealing with situations analagous to their own, the patriotic amateur actors could keep alive the desire for independence. One choice was *Un día del año 1823 en Cádiz* by Eugenio de Ochoa, set during the French domination of the Iberian Peninsula. Martínez de la Rosa's patriotic *La viuda de Padilla* and a translation of Alfieri's *Bruto o Roma libre* were other favorites. After such stimulus, the citizens, under General Juan Pablo Duarte, eventually defeated President Boyer and on February 27, 1844, achieved independence.[8]

The father of drama in independent Santo Domingo was Felix María del Monte (1819–1899), remembered as author of that country's national anthem. In La Republicana, a theatre erected by Los Amantes de las Letras on the site of an old Jesuit monastary, del Monte witnessed a performance of his *El general Antonio Duvergé o Las víctimas del once de abril* (1856); the story was based on a national catastrophe. Of all his plays, only this and part of his musical *Ozema o La virgen indiana* (1870) still survive, along with one act of his dramatization of Chateaubriand's *El último Abencerraje* (1872). In addition, he wrote a dramatic legend, *El artista Antonio Brito*, and three romantic dramas in verse set in different sections of Europe: *El mendigo de la catedral de León*, *El vals de Strauss*, and *El premio de los pichones*. Since they were never performed, the only joy their author got from them was reading them to the La Juventud Literary Society.

Like Foxá, Javier Angulo Guridi (1816–1884) was almost lost to Santo Domingo. His parents became voluntary exiles, and both he and his brother were born in Puerto Rico. They were in Cuba when

[8] *Ibid.*

Javier published his first book, *Ensayos poéticos,* in 1843, but he came back to his homeland to fight in the War of Restoration (1865), and drew on his war experiences for the *entremés Cacharros y manigüeros,* which is thoroughly national in its use of rural dialect. Symbolizing his desire to remain independent instead of rejoining Spain, he wrote a three-act romantic drama in verse, *Iguaniona* (1867; published 1881), whose sentimental plot had a political purpose of hinting that military domination need not mean spiritual domination.[9] Its Indian princess heroine loved a Spaniard but, with the psychological motivation of a Spanish lady of the Golden Age, she poisoned herself because she felt that she and her white sweetheart could never achieve a community of interests. Though a propaganda drama it must be classified with other Indian plays by the early *costumbristas,* like *Ozema* by del Monte, already mentioned; *La sacerdotisa del sol* by Juan Manuel Losado; and some by Manuel de Jesús Rodríguez Montaño (1847–1915). Rodríguez Montaño also dramatized his war experiences, and was the author, in collaboration with the great orator Federico Henríquez y Carvajal (1848–1951), of the poetic drama *Tilema* (1873), and of such zarzuelas as *Amores de dos zagalas o Los cálculos de un tutor* (1871) and *La promesa cumplida* (1874). The long-lived Henríquez went on to develop national themes in his own one-act comedy *El hombre epopeya o De flor en flor* (1870) and *La hija del hebreo* (1878).

Guridi, between his professions of journalist and politician, also turned a short story into a poetic drama *El conde de Leos* (1868), and wrote the comedies *Don Junípero* (1868), *Los apuros de un destierro* (1869), both full of dialect, and the prose plays *La ciguapa* and *El fantasma de Higuey.*

Contemporary with them was the lyric poet and President of the Republic, Francisco Gregorio Billini (1844–1898), who contributed to the theatre in verse *Una flor del Ozama* (1867) and the historical *Amor y expiación* (1882). About this time Pedro Alejandro Piña (1821–1879) built his own *teatrillo* for plays by him and his friends.

Across the island, in Haiti, A. Fleury-Barrier (1841–1882) had written a tragedy in French about the sixteenth-century Indian Queen Anacaona, who was betrayed and hanged by the Spaniard Ovando, whom she had considered her friend. Inspired by it, José

[9] Fragments of this play are reprinted in *Antología de la literatura dominicana,* I, 25–39. It was first published in 1881, and republished about 1953.

Joaquín Pérez (1845–1900) started in 1874 to write a Spanish version. Halfway through, discouraged by the inactivity of the theatre in his nation, he decided he would have a wider audience by putting the legend into poetry; so the play was never finished.

Some of his countrymen were more optimistic. "El Vate" José María Jiménez (1862–1942) enjoyed performances of both *Maldito amor* (1886) and a comedy of manners, *Pedir peras al olmo* (1887). Felix Francisco Rodríguez wrote several plays performed in Cibao, though never published. César Nicolás Pensón (1853–1901), besides writing *tradiciones*, as did Ricardo Palma, is remembered for his amusing *Los viejos verdes* (1879).

A few writers persevered, though they possessed greater talent in other directions. Gastón Fernando Deligne (1866–1913) provided lyrics for the opera *María de Cuéllar*, for some of Pablo Claudio's music, and for a comic *paso*, *Soldado, pulpera y comendador*. His brother, the excellent short-story writer and critic Rafael Alfredo Deligne (1863–1902), though he was bedridden most of his life and eventually died of leprosy without ever having seen a theatrical performance, wrote a poetic drama, *La justicia y el azar* (1894), and the superior *Vidas tristes* (1901) in prose.

The performance of this last play was severely criticized by Ulises Heureaux, Jr. (1876–1938), son of the cruel Negro dictator. Because of knowledge gained in his attendance at French theatres during his studies in Paris, Heureaux felt capable of pointing out its flaws. To show how it should be done, he wrote *Consuelo* (1902). Its technique was superior to its inspiration, but with it he embarked on a fertile career and turned out more than a dozen plays that were performed at La Republicana and Colón. Among other titles by this most prolific of Dominican playwrights are the three-act *El grito de 1844, Genoveva, Lo inmutable, El artículo 291, El jefe, La fuga de Clarita, Entre dos fuegos, La noticia sensacional, El enredo, Blanca, La muerte de Anacaona, En la hora superior, Alfonso XII*, and *De director a ministro* (1926).

Perhaps heredity can explain the playwriting of the Pellerano family. José Francisco Pellerano (1844–1879) wrote a comedy of manners, *El que menos corre, vuela* (1871). The romanticist poet Arturo Bautista Pellerano Castro (1865–1916), who signed his verses "Byron," followed Echegaray in his plays as the Dominican theatre moved out of its romanticist phase in the last decade of the century.

Stronger in their lyrical qualities than in situation or character development were his efforts, beginning with *Fuerzas contrarias* (1892)
written for the fourth centenary of Columbus; followed by *Antonia*,
produced by the Roncaroni Company in 1895. Then came *De mala
entraña* (1902) and his masterpiece, *De la vida* (1912). After its successful première some of the high lights were printed in *Ateneo*. They
reveal energetic characters, lively action, and good dialog. His son,
Fernando Arturo Pellerano Amechazurra (1889–1933), also inclined
toward the theatre and wrote several comedies. The Moncada
Fuentes troupe performed his *Grandezas efímeras*, a comedy modern
in time and theme, in the Colón Theatre in 1927. The next year he
produced *El más fuerte*, a realistic tragedy set in a sugar plantation.
Other works by him include *La hez* (1925); *En la casa del loco*
(1928); *Un cobarde*, a drama; *Los defensores del pueblo*, a comedy;
a couple of *entremeses*; and *Bueno es cuidar la pierna . . . pero*.

Another writer whose nationalist plays reveal traces of realism was
Rafael Damirón (1882–?). His *Alma criolla* (1916) and *Mientras los
otros ríen* (1917) were performed by the Recalde Brothers and repeated in 1919 by Velasco's Compañía de Revistas. In 1917 the Recalde troupe performed in El Colón the first plays by a trio of promising dramatists. They were the comedy *El castigo* by Enrique Montaño, Jr.; the comedy of customs, *Cuento de amor* (1917), and a
drama, *En la hora del dolor* (1917) by the lyric poet Apolinar Perdomo (1882–1918); and the three-act comedy *El trino errante* (1917)
by Emilio Morel (1887–   ). Perdomo died the next year, and Montaño gave up literature, but Morel went on to produce *La copla
triste*, *El domador*, *El pésame*, and others. Damirón, too, continued to
provide the stage with a number of plays: *La trova del recuerdo*, *Tres
minutos de otro tiempo*, *Como cae la balanza*, and, with Arturo Lo-
groño, the contemporary comedies *Una fiesta en el Castine* and *Los
yanquis en Santo Domingo*.

For the first century of its independence, the Dominican Republic
had only one theatre of any size. At economic sacrifice, since there
was little hope of a play-purchasing public, about thirty plays were
published. Others had a brief life in some small theatre developed by
one of the amateur societies, like La Juventud in 1868, and Amigos
del País in 1871. There were also a few school theatres. When Padre
Francisco Xavier Billini founded the San Luis Gonzaga College in
1867, he arranged for a stage there. The educator Eugenio María de

Hostos (1839–1903) turned part of his residence into a theatre to present, in his words, "tentativa candorosa de niños grandes en favor de niños chicos." He himself wrote brief didactic plays: *La enferma, El naranjo,* and others which he hoped would inspire a national theatre.

The tiny theatres and the small chance for a production determined the trend of writing and resulted in what some critics termed "miniaturismo teatral." Most of the plays in *Ensayos dramáticos,* published in 1906 by the lawyer and historian Américo Lugo (1870–1952), are lyric monologs with romantic coloring. Their titles carry out the idea: *Víspera de boda, Elvira, En la pena pobre,* and *El avaro.* Later, in this island of no Indians, Lugo wrote an Indian drama, *Higuenamota* (1907), and *Don Pedro el cruel,* set in Spain but never published. Max Henríquez Ureña lists half a dozen other writers of closet drama,[10] including Tulio Manuel Cestero (1877–1955) better known as poet and novelist who, while secretary to the President of the republic, wrote *La enemiga* (1905) and the realistic *El torrente* (1907), both published in *Citerea* (Madrid, 1907), along with his *Medusa* and *La sangre.* Later he retired to Chile.

Drama progressed slightly in 1907, with the publication of some dramas, although some were never produced. Rafael Octavio Galván wrote the one-act *El príncipe travieso,* set during the Renaissance, which was judged one of the best Dominican dramas up to then. Other playwrights managed a production, even if only as a means of collecting money for some charity or as a performance by visiting troupes to tempt audiences to their programs. Alfonso Matos and Telésforo Alfonseca's comedy of customs, *Sin padre,* was mounted for this reason in La Republicana in 1907 by the Leopoldo Burón company. Matos was thus encouraged to continue and later produced *Rasgos de nobleza, Al fondo de un abismo, Una terrible pasión,* and *Es igual.*

In 1910 the Díaz-Perdiguero troupe performed *Lesbia* by Vetilio Arredondo and *La cita* by the poet Fabio Fiallo (1866–1942), friend of Rubén Darío and disciple of Bécquer and Heine. *La cita* was not published till 1924. Outside the capital, in Puerto Plata, a zarzuela, *Las feministas* by Virginia Elena Ortea (1866–1903) was staged, and the citizens of Santiago also saw a zarzuela, *La bruta de la loma,* the

---

[10] Max Henríquez Ureña, "Las letras en la República Dominicana," *Panorama das literaturas das Américas,* III, 1312.

only theatrical attempt by Pedro María Archambault (1862–1944) among his histories and novels.

The presence of North American soldiers in Santo Domingo after 1916, originally there to refund the foreign debt through the collection of import customs, brought renewed dramatic activity, first as a means of patriotic protest, then to supply plays, as foreign actors arrived when the country became stable. In 1916 Pedro Henríquez Ureña (1884–1946) published in New York *El nacimiento de Dionisos*, dramatized as he thought a Greek would have handled the theme. While there is nothing national about it, the Uruguay classicist Rodó called it "one of the most beautiful creations of the New Hispanic American Literature."

After this flurry, one must go searching for awhile to find activity. The folklorist Miguel Angel Jiménez (1901–   ) turned out a number of national plays, mostly set in Cibao. One of his best is the drama *Orgullo de raza*, about North American military occupation. Two recently revived by TEAN are *Tus ojos no deben llorar* and *Por la buena o por la mala*. In addition, Angel Jiménez is remembered for *El novio con faldas* (1924) *Cuatro cibaeñas en Ciudad Trujillo, Los amores de Ezequiela*, and *El secreto de las teclas* (1930). Among his dramas are *La mensura* and *Amor de madre*; and he was also librettist for the satirical *sainete, Las mujeres mandan* (1933), written when President Trujillo was making plans for woman suffrage.

A contemporary of his was Julio Vega Batlle (1899–   ) author of the comedies *La calandria* (1923), *Cristales rotos, La silla vacía* (1924), *El hombre superior, De Santo Domingo a Broadway*, and the drama *La venganza del sol*. He called himself a "Postumista." Franklin Mieses Burgos (1907–   ), poet and editor of the influential magazine *La Poesía Sorprendida*, wrote *La ciudad inefable*. Christián Lugo offered *Una gira en Boca Chica, La alegría de la vida, Un hombre*, and *Un civilizado*. Nestor Caró wrote in dialect *Dolore la enamorá* and *Los apuros de don Simón. Mi hijo mayor* and *Una aventura de don Lorenzo* by Freddy Miller Otero looked vainly for a director.

Whatever may be one's opinion of the late Dictator Rafael Trujillo and his motives, one result of his assumption of power, beginning in 1930, was economic and cultural progress, and one place it showed was in the theatre. In 1940 the University Theatre came into being to lead a sporadic existence, with especial activity during the centenary celebrations of 1944. Girls at the Salomé Ureña High School established an experimental theatre in 1945 that fostered an interest in drama and provided actresses and directors for later years.

On May 3, 1946, to raise money for the Red Cross, a group of amateurs presented in Teatro Olimpia the two-act *Falsa amistad* by María Martínez de Trujillo, wife of the dictator. It was a great social success, and in appreciation Trujillo announced a few days later the establishment of the Teatro Escuela de Arte Nacional (TEAN). This center was largely responsible for the subsequent remarkable activity among Dominican dramatists. *Falsa amistad* was revived the next year when María Tereza Montoya visited the Dominican Republic, again in 1953 by the Salomé Ureña High School group, and in 1959, when it was performed before 1,500 people to celebrate the author's birthday.

Madame Trujillo was not the only woman experimenting with drama, but merely the most influential. Margarita Vallejo de Paredes has written children's plays like *Historia de caracoles*, second-prize winner in a 1957 competition. So have Delia Quezada, author of *Teatro infantil*, and Ana Jiménez Yépez, with *Independencia o muerte*. Delia Weber (1902–   ) wrote *Los viajeros* (1944), *Los bellos designios, Salvador y Artemira*, and *Lo eterno*.[11] Melbe Marrero de Munné (1911–   ) is the author of several successful children's plays, and at least one of her plays for adults has been performed.

Based on the original TEAN, other theatre groups were formed. One in Santiago performed a poetic drama in three acts, *Cuando el otoño riega las hojas*, by Mariano Lebrón Saviñón (1922–   ). He is also author of *Mirtha Primavera* a "poema en cuatro sueños."[12] Looking for folklore, as expressing truly national drama, they turned to Manuel de Jesús Javier García, author of *Leyenda india, Batey, Le cuaite si valen, Cosas del llano, La jornada redentora, El niño juez, En el bohío de Bonifacio, Almas infantiles*, and *Yo soy el amo de casa*, a prize winner in 1952.

Many other ambitious dramatists had plays ready for their consideration: Horacio Pérez Licairac, *La isla de la leyenda* (1939); "Carmen Natalia" (Martínez Bonilla, 1917–   ), *Luna gitana*, in verse;

[11] *Los viajeros* was reprinted in *Cuadernos domínicos de cultura*, April–May and June–July, 1951; *Los bellos designios*, appeared in July–August, 1950.
[12] Published in *Cuadernos domínicos*, March, 1949, pp. 23–44.

Pedro René Contín Aybar (1910–   ), *Raíz* (1947); and Carlos Curiel, *Alino* (1949). Bienvenido Gimbernard was fortunate enough to persuade the Dominican actress Divina Gómez, later director of Santiago's Teatro-Escuela, to perform his *Casta de hombres* (1942), *La campesina*, and *Cuatro palabras*. He is also author of the comedy *El premio mayor cayó repartido* and the drama *Espera honor de aquel a quien haces desprecio*. Jose María García Rodríguez, author of *Zombi* and *Ya viene el general Campuzano*, had his *Los encantadores del halcón azul* produced by Pro-Arte in 1956. The diplomat Virgilio Hoepelmen (1915–   ) was brother and uncle of actors whom he depended on for his *Rosalía*. Manuel Resumil Aragunde waited long to see his *Alejandro el grande*, that won first prize back in 1935. Early dramatists profited little from their predecessors, since with the exception of Guridi and Del Monte, they only copied the outmoded style brought from Europe by visiting actors. Even dramatists trying to be national imitated other Latin American writers, also striving for regionalism. As Máximo Avilés Blonda, himself a practicing dramatist, wrote, most of the Dominican dramatists for a century wrote with no acquaintance with stage technique. Their chief desire was to be "literary," and their dialog, instead of depicting character or advancing the action, was prettily turned phrases loaded with moral, political, or patriotic ideas, and usually further handicapped by being expressed in verse.[13]

To know the present state of drama, at least up to the end of the Trujillo dynasty, four dramatists should be examined. The only Dominican who might be called a professional playwright is Franklin Domínguez (1913–   ), though he, in spite of his score of plays, has to earn his living as a magazine editor and government employee. This writer about psychological problems of people badly adjusted to the world was a student of dramatic art at TEAN, under the Spanish actor Emilio Aparicio. Upon graduation in 1949 he sought experience in every phase of the theatre, even though at the same time he was studying law at the University of Santo Domingo. While a member of the National Comedy troupe in 1951 he attempted his first play, the Biblical *Exodo*. In 1952 he helped found the María Martínez de Trujillo Experimental Group. This year he also received his first drama

[13] Preface to Franklin Domínguez, *El último instante*, pp. 7–36.

prize, for *El vuelo de la paloma*, about Juana and her departure from conventional morality. As an expression of new currents in world drama, it received honors at the 1952 Juegos Florales.

In 1953 Domínguez graduated from the University with honors in philosophy, and wrote *Alberto y Ercilia* (1954); it has exaggerated and almost farcical characters. The next year his psychological *Extraño juicio*, breaking with romanticism, was introduced at the First Drama Festival. Then he went to Texas to study international law. Even at The University of Texas, half his efforts were devoted to the theatre. Several of his plays got stage presentations and others were read in a drama class. The one-act *Un amigo desconocido nos aguarda*, voicing the belief that the past controls the present, was later presented over the Dominican radio station and on the stage before being published in 1958. Based on the Platonic conception of a soul mate, it describes strangers meeting briefly in New York on a New Year's Eve and attempting to solve each other's problems. *Tertulia de fantasmas* (1956), his next play, was performed by the Dominican-born Hollywood actor Rafael Campos, who has appeared in *Blackboard Jungle* and *Trial*.

In another field, Domínguez won the 1957 puppet play competition with *La niña que quería ser princesa*, a simple skeleton of a play clothed in poetry and poetic prose.

Each year since has brought more plays by this industrious dramatist, and they show an increasing mastery of techniques. A volume in 1958 offered a monolog, *El último instante*, about subjective morality and unattractive tranquility, delivered by a woman hurt by an incomprehensible world. *La broma del senador* is a fast-moving farce about a will that leaves a fortune to a widow if she will marry one of her old suitors yet keep her first husband's portrait in the living room.

This Dominican author completed six plays in 1959, but only one, *La espera*, was published. A universal problem and human characters, most of them with a spiritual defect, are presented. But Domínguez is too good a dramatist to forget that drama, not philosophy, is the requirement of a successful play, even though he may combine the two, as in the poignant exclamation "¿Quién?" which provides the final curtain for *La espera*.

His *Espigas maduras* (1960), having to do with a motherless family controlled by a domineering father embodies mankind's never

ending search for an individual self. First performed in Ciudad Trujillo, it was repeated in a half-dozen other cities of the republic.
Critics called it the best of Domínguez' plays so far.

Somewhat older is the poet Manuel Rueda (1912–   ). He only recently turned to the stage, but his *La trinitaria blanca*, performed by
TEAN in 1957, was considered the outstanding work of the year.
Some critics objected that it was not national because it could take
place anywhere. Yet Avilés Blonda points out that the essential universality, the theme of frustration, is developed through what may be
the usual Latin American reaction, but is set in what can only be
Dominican surroundings.[14] And so the play is national in the best
sense of the word.

Rueda completed another play, *Vacaciones en el cielo*, contrasting
the fanaticism of a layman with the true piety of a couple of charming priests who visit him. Containing religious overtones also are his
other new plays, *La tía Beatriz hace un milagro* and *María Trinidad
Sánchez o La noche de los mártires*.

An older writer only recently attracted to the theatre is the well-
known poet Hector Incháustegui Cabral (1912–   ), who modernized
and Christianized Aeschylus' version of the Greek legend in *Prometeo*
(1959). In his tragedy, he portrays the industrial revolution as it
clashes with the modern concept of Christian living. The writer has
announced this play as the first of a trilogy, to include a reworking of
Sophocles in *Filoctetes* (1960), and of Euripides in *Hipólito*, all in
verse.

The poet and critic Máximo Avilés Blonda Acosta (1931–   ) the
fourth of the quartet, began his dramatic career auspiciously in 1959
with *Las manos vacías*, performed by the Teatro-Escuela and published in 1960. Following the classical unities and using a plot about
a Roman Catholic priest who recovers from an attack of amnesia to
find himself with a wife and child, and about a German officer of a
concentration camp, this new dramatist stresses the consequences to
innocent people of selfishness and the responsibilities inherent in the
gift of freedom of choice. The enthusiastic reception of this powerful
first play has encouraged Avilés Blonda to continue writing during
what time he can snatch from his responsibilities as director of the

[14] *Ibid.*, p. 24.

Teatro Universitario Dominicano. His *Las manos vacías* was revived in El Palacio de Bellas Artes late in 1961.

In 1952, after the Teatro-Escuela had proved successful, members of the Comedia Nacional and others, including Domínguez, organized an experimental theatre sponsored by and named for "La Primera Dama de la República." Not only did its actors perform representative plays from a half-dozen different foreign countries, but in 1953 it sponsored a conference of drama lovers from all over the nation. The purpose was to establish groups of amateurs throughout the country, but it was a vain attempt.

Several companies did organize in Ciudad Trujillo. Since 1946 Canadians and North Americans, along with English-speaking Dominicans calling themselves the Quisqueya Players, had been giving plays in English. Now the Círculo Cultural introduced the theatre-in-the-round. The Tirso de Molina troupe, representing the De la Salle School, concentrates on foreign plays. La Comedia de Arte is another active group. *Noche de farsa* was its 1959 success, and *Espigas maduras* by Domínguez was its most popular play of 1960. El Ateneo Dominicano offered a performance of *El amor se va de vacciones* (1959), by its lawyer-president Armando Oscar Pacheco and the Department of Education also published it that year. His earlier plays, "La góndola azul," "Como las demás," "Amatista," and "En la boca de lobo" remain in manuscript.

Although, as in most Latin American countries, the movies have dulled the enthusiasm of audiences so that the Dominican Republic has a drama of the minority rather than a drama of the masses, the impetus given by the state and the press has started the development of a theatre-going public. One can only guess what will happen when the present political turmoil settles.

CHAPTER 25

Cuban Drama

José Juan Arrom found sufficient theatrical activity in Cuba to devote an entire volume to its study.[1] Though he discovered literary activity as early as 1512, when a Spanish sailor taught the Indians to reverence the Virgin in *areytos*, action dances, the earliest mention of actual Cuban drama were reports of *invenciones*—which usually means "plays"—under the supervision of Pedro Castilla during the Corpus Christi celebrations in Havana in 1573. The same Castilla contracted to manage the festivities of 1576. José Pérez de Vargas furnished the entertainment in 1577.

The *actos* of the *cabildo* for August 26, 1588, report payment of twenty ducats to Gaspar Dávila for the *farçantes* for that year; Francisco Mojica is mentioned as its author, the first named writer of Cuba. Two years later Juan Bautista Siliseo collected payment for performing a couple of *comedias*; however the often repeated account of an evening theatrical performance of *Los buenos en el cielo y los malos en el suelo* on June 24, 1598, must be pure fiction. Even in Spain at that early date, the Church safeguarded public morals by restricting performances to daylight hours.

Besides, there were no theatres in Cuba. The occasional plays took place in the church, the plaza, or private homes, such as one on Callejón de Justiz. They were brief and probably unliterary. For the first long drama with literary finish written by a Cuban, Arrom can go no farther back than a play by Captain Santiago de Pita (?–1755). Called *El príncipe jardinero y fingido Cloridano*,[2] it is so close in spirit to the Golden Age products of Spain, though written about 1730, that some previous scholars ascribed it to Lope de Vega. Ac-

---

[1] José Juan Arrom, *Historia de la literatura dramática cubana.* See also Arrom, "Primeras manifestaciones dramáticas in Cuba: 1512–1776," *Revista Bimestre Cubana*, XLVIII, No. 2 (September, 1941), 274–284; and Juan J. Remos y Rubio, "Letras y artes en los siglos XVI y XVII," in *Historia de la nación cubana*, ed. Ramiro Guerra y Sánchez, I, 345–366; also IV, 349–388.

[2] Edited with Introduction and notes by José Juan Arrom (Havana, 1951).

tually it is based on a play of the same name by the Italian Giacinto Cicognini (1606–1660). The original setting was Valencia and the Prince of Aragon was the suitor, but when Pita rewrote it, he changed the protagonist to Fadrique, Prince of Athens. It is told in a variety of meters. The earliest known performance in Cuba took place in 1790.

Havana had an excellent theatre by then, thanks to Don Felipe de Fonsdeviela, Marqués de la Torre. He had been governor of Venezuela, but when he refused to uphold the 1771 decision of the ecclesiastical court to banish plays, Church influence forced his transfer to Cuba. Here, ironically, he found himself in the midst of more theatrical argument. The cultured Cubans wanted a theatre. The clergy insisted that any available money be used to support an orphan asylum. Appealed to by both sides, the Marqués pointed out that both were possible if the income from the theatre was used to support the Church's charities. So, in 1776 El Coliseo, the finest playhouse in America up to that time, came into being to support La Casa de Recogidos de San Juan Nepomuceno. The coliseum was so handsome, in fact, that it inspired the jealous viceroy of Buenos Aires to equal it in his domain.

The list of plays witnessed by the Coliseo audiences in 1791 is of value as evidence of the favorites of the New World. Of the eighty-six titles, fifty-one dated from Spain's Golden Age, twenty-three came from contemporary Spain, one was the Cuban *Príncipe jardinero*, and the rest were translations.[3]

It was in this Coliseo, later called El Principal, on Alameda de Paula, near the Plaza de Armas, that Cuba's first great actor-author began his career. Francisco Covarrubias (1775–1856) was the son of a wealthy family that went into mourning in 1793 when Francisco gave up his medical studies and decided to devote himself to the theatre. But it was a decision that brought a half century of pleasure to Havana drama lovers.[4] As a playwright, Covarrubias determined to write about types he knew, and his *Elegir con discreción y amante privilegiado* (1792) is considered the first play of Cuba with a local setting. Though only a few *décimas* from his writing remain, the titles of some of his lost plays show how he brought amusing Cuban types onto the stage. Among them are *El peón de tierra adentro, El*

[3] Arrom, *Historia*, pp. 21–24.
[4] José Agustín Millán, *Biografía de don Francisco Covarrubias*.

guajiro sofocado, Las tertulias de la Habana (1814), *La feria de Ca-rraguas* (1815), and *El tío Bartolo y la tía Catana* (1820).

Writing a little later was José María Heredia (1803–1839), one of the greatest poets of his epoch. When only fifteen he composed *Eduardo IV o El usurpador Clemente* and also acted in it, along with Gertrudis Gómez de Avellaneda. Before he left Cuba for France in 1837 Heredia had completed several original plays and had translated others from French, to be produced when he could gather his friends as actors. The first serious play by a Cuban which was performed professionally in Havana was *La prueba o La vuelta del Cruzado* (1837), the work of Heredia's contemporary, Ramón de la Palma (1812–1860).

El Gran Teatro Tacón, where it was performed, came into being because of the arrival of a drama-loving governor, Miguel Tacón. In his ambition to provide his new subjects with the best and largest theatre in the New World, Tacón imposed a tax of seventeen pesos on every slave imported into Cuba, and by this means amassed so large a sum that he could not only pay for a theatre with 4,000 seats and 150 boxes, but had a surplus to build Cuba's first railroad across the island, and to provide drinking fountains for his capital.

In the Tacón Theatre in July, 1838, the first New World performance of a romanticist play, *Guillermo*, took place. A twelfth-century Catalonian tragedy by the Basque José María Andueza (1809–?), it came two years after the presentation in Spain of García Gutiérrez' *El trovador,* also about a gypsy's curse; but Andueza borrowed also from Dumas and Hugo for his tragedy. He later wrote *María de Padilla* and *Blanca de Navarra.*

What is believed to be the first romantic play written in America, *Don Pedro de Castilla,* had its performance a month later in the same theatre. Its author was Francisco Foxá y Lecanda (1816–1865), an exile with his parents from Santo Domingo. Though Foxá wrote it in 1836, his hesitancy in looking for a producer lost him the honor of being the first romanticist dramatist to have his work performed in America. But the first night of *Don Pedro* was, as Mitjans declared, "as famous in Cuba as the first night of *El trovador* in Madrid. Such a tempestuous theatrical occasion had never been seen before. Plácido dedicated a sonnet to the event."[5] Arguing conservatives and radicals

---

[5] Quoted in *Revista de la Habana,* 1953. The first night is described in Arrom, *Historia,* p. 49.

in the audience indulged in fights that resulted in the death of one spectator. The authorities, with the excuse that the script contained an attack on Spain, closed the play after the first showing, at no great loss to Cuban letters, for the play was weak both poetically and technically, as could be seen after its publication in 1838. It lacks the spontaneity of Foxá; its importance is that it was a pioneer.

Another Cuban dramatist also began his activities in 1838. José Jacinto Milanés (1814–1863) revealed romantic tendencies when he produced one of the most important plays of this first period of Cuban drama, *El conde Alarcos*.[6] The tragic old Spanish ballad about a noble who had to see his wife killed so that he could marry a princess had been put onto the stage previously. Colonial Colombia had seen one dramatization, though it remained for Jacinto Grau of Spain to produce the best version. Milanés' play was so well received that he went on to write other dramas, all set outside of Cuba. *El poeta en la corte* (1840) is a cape-and-sword story of the time of Philip IV. *Ojo a la finca* introduces Cervantes and his wife and *Por la puente o por el río* follows the style of Lope de Vega. *A buen hambre no hay pan duro* dramatizes a proverb. Milanés' series of satirical dialogs came to an end when he became insane through love for his cousin Inés Ximeno, as legend has it. His *Obras* were published in 1846.

After romanticism became well established in Cuba, more than eighty romantic plays were composed in ten years; forty of them were performed and published in one year![7] Others, like José Francisco Broche's *Mendoza*, were refused permission to print "por considerar la obra inmoral e irreligiosa," while *Los cruzados* by Christiano Kruger was banned because it was set in a convent.

One of the 1841 crop was *El médico lo manda* by José Agustín Millán, born early in the nineteenth century and author of a number of one-act plays set in Cuba. In contrast to the writers who used only European personalities, the works of Millán offer a gallery of amusing Cuban types, such as the gold-hunting miner of *El californiano*, and the onlookers in *El comete del 13 de junio* (1857). But unfortunately for the theatre, Millán received a government appointment and stopped writing. He did preserve, in two editions of *Miscelánea dramática* (1848 and 1857), his plays that amused a generation of

[6] Published in *Alma Cubana*, Época II (May, 1929), 31–64.
[7] Francisco González del Valle, *La Habana en 1841*, pp. 304, 358–370.

theatregoers. They extend from *El novio de mi mujer* (1842) to *El velorio de Jesús María* (1857).

Of the rest of this decade of productivity, all but a few titles and authors have lapsed into obscurity.[8] *Cora* (1839) and *Ginebra* (1839) by Ramón Francisco Valdés are remembered, along with six comedies and the tragedies by the polished poet and invalid, Joaquín Lorenzo Luaces (1826–1867). Lorenzo was a disciple of Milanés and a self-educated student of Greek. His *El mendigo rojo* (1865) takes place in Scotland, and his *Aristodemo* (1867) is an involved tragedy set in Greece.[9] The violent criticism it received at its first performance is believed to have caused its author's death. None of his other plays was published.

Cuba had one other native-born dramatist at this time, Gertrudis Gómez de Avellaneda (1814–1873), but her only connection with the stage in Cuba was an appearance in *Eduardo IV*, by Heredia. Her writing of plays began after her family had taken her to Spain. There her first effort, *Leoncia* (1840), though performed in both Granada and Sevilla, was later disclaimed by her, and she cited as her initial venture *Munio Alfonso* (1844), a tragedy of twelfth-century Toledo, whose chief character was one of her ancestors. Written originally only for her pastime, it was submitted to a manager at the insistence of friends, and accepted. Encouraged, that same year she wrote *El príncipe de Viana*, another excellent tragedy.

Besides adapting several French plays, Avellaneda wrote a Biblical tragedy, *Saul*, in two versions (1846 and 1849). She dropped into light prose comedy with the brief *El millonario y la maleta*, successfully revived in 1940, but her fame rests chiefly on her poetic comedy *Hija de las flores* (1852) and the Biblical *Baltasar* (1858).

In 1858 one of her two plays in prose, *Tres amores*, opened in Madrid. The audience reaction was so violently abusive that the dramatist's husband got involved with some of the spectators, and the injuries he received made him a permanent invalid. When the theatre manager withdrew the play, Doña Gertrudis quickly offered to substitute *Baltasar*, which, though named for King Belshazzar, really deals with two Hebrew captives, Ruben and Elda. She had submitted

---

[8] Miguel de Cárdenas y Chávez, "La literatura cubana," *La Prensa*, October 29, 1841.

[9] Published in *Alma Cubana*, Época II (May, 1929), 19–29.

it previously to various producers but the theme and the cost of costumes and scenery had appeared prohibitive. However, to keep the theatre open, it was now put into rehearsal and proved a great success with a long run. Critical opinion proclaimed it among the best romantic works written in Spanish. Her Cuban countrymen claim it and her and the rest of her sixteen plays.

In her writing, Avellaneda showed a masculine strength that won the admiration of her contemporaries and gave her a lasting place in literature. After 1868, however, Cubans had more serious matters to consider. The swelling spirit of independence dulled their interest in drama. The few who did write rarely completed more than one or two plays. Difficulties in production or publication were too disheartening. Among the writers was a revolutionary leader of Cuba. At the age of sixteen the patriot and liberator José Martí (1853–1895) wrote a poetic tragedy, *Abdala* (1869).[10] Set in Nubia, to avoid troubles for himself, it managed to reflect the author's love of freedom, and its final verses might well be Martí's own epitaph:

> Oh ¡qué dulce es morir cuando se muere
> luchando audaz por defender la patria!

Exiled to Spain as a rebel, Martí there wrote an Echegaray-like tragedy, *Adultera* (1872), and later, while a fugitive in Mexico, he dramatized a proverb in *Amor con amor se paga* (1875). Through his writing can be glimpsed his interest in the theatre. While in Guatemala he started another play, attacking the Spaniards for enslaving the Indians. But he realized that his greatest contribution to the fight for Cuban independence lay not in the theatre but in his oratorical ability; so he put behind him his love for the stage.

Not till Cuban independence was achieved was there any serious new attempt to revive the theatre. Federico Edelman took the first step by founding El Círculo de Bellas Artes in 1910. Then in a spirit of national pride, three lovers of the stage, José Antonio Ramos, Bernardo Barros, and the Dominican Max Henríquez Ureña (1885–) founded the Sociedad de Fomento del Teatro. For the tenth anniversary of Cuban independence, November 20, 1910, it

[10] Willis K. Jones, "José Martí dramaturgo," *Memoria del Congreso de escritores martianos*, pp. 718–728.

sponsored the performance of Avellaneda's *Hija de las flores* and Martí's *Amor con amor se paga*, starring Luisa Martínez Casado.[11]

The public, however, had not yet developed a taste for serious drama. The entertainment most popular with Cubans was a form called *bufo*, from the Italian verb "to puff out one's cheeks in mockery." As an artistic form, it originated in Paris and passed by way of Spain to Cuba during the Ten Years War (1868–1878). Critics argue about its status, some considering it the only purely Cuban theatre, others scorning it as carelessly written sketches appealing only to an uncultured taste. The Negro is its chief character. As Ortiz explains, they are the masters of satire, who brought a fresh breath to the suffocating tropics.[12] Of course, the Negro had long existed as a figure in the theatre. As early as 1838, the Galician Professor Bartolomé José Crespo y Borbón (1811–1871), under the pen name of "Creto Gangá," used Negroes with their broken Spanish for humor in his *paso, El Chasco*. Other *sainetes* by him include: *Un ajiaco o La boda de Pancha y Canuto* (1847), *Debajo del tamarindo* (1864), and *Los apuros de Covarrubias*. Francisco Fernández introduced the obsequious Negro around 1868 in a series "Los negros catedráticos." *El bautizo* and *El avaro* were some of many sketches by Fernández, performed between musical numbers and ending with a band number by the whole company.

The twentieth-century version of the *bufo*, however, acquired a formula in which the quick-witted and unscrupulous Negro, frequently aided by his mulatto girl friend, got the better of a stupid and parsimonious Galician immigrant, usually owner of a grocery store. Occasionally La Gallega and Liborio, a backwoods farmer, were added to the cast.[13]

On this pattern many changes could be rung, and actors took occasion to display their versatility with "specialties." The authors could introduce topical references. Carlos Robreño (1903–), who acted in his own *bufos*, stated that he wrote them as one would con-

---

[11] Arrom, *Historia*, pp. 54–57; Edwin B. Williams, *Life and Dramatic Works of Gertrudis de Avellaneda*; Emilio Cotarelo y Mori, *La Avellaneda y sus obras*; Mercedes Ballesteros, *Vida de la Avellaneda*.

[12] Fernando Ortiz, *Los bailes y el teatro de los negros en el folklore de Cuba*, p. 418.

[13] Ruby Hart Phillips, "Drama and Burlesque on the Cuban Stage," *Inter-America*, II (January, 1943), 24–25.

coct a newspaper article, but dramatizing instead of describing the events, and confessed that he could pound out a *bufo* on his typewriter in five or six hours.[14] *El lío de los teléfonos* and especially *Jalisco* and *Rancho grande* (1933) were among his greatest successes. His father, Gustavo Robreño (1873–1957) completed two hundred of these playlets: *Napoleón,* attacking the presidency of Estrada Palma; *Ciclón,* about North American intervention; and *La madre de los tomates* were among his most popular. Following Gustavo Robreño's death, Rafael Suárez Solís called him "uno de los cuatro grandes fundadores del teatro cubano."

Twice as productive was Federico Villoch (1866–1954), greatest of *bufo* writers, who won fame and fortune with such plays as *La cruz de San Fernando* (1897), *El peligro chino* (1924), *La mulata María,* and *La isla de las cotorras.* Best known (performed more than four hundred times) is his *La casita criolla* (1928), a political attack that destroyed the presidential hopes of José Miguel Gómez and won the election for Menocal. Agustín Rodríguez also wrote *bufos.* These men wrote for the Alhambra Theatre, which beginning in 1902 became the center for this type of play "for men only," except for an annual program of censored *bufos.* Until its roof caved in, in 1934, the Alhambra was the home of the *bufo.*

In 1909 the Moulin Rouge Theatre opened for bufo plays with music, with Mario Sorondo (1885–) providing many of the scripts. *Cantos de Cuba* and *Lydia en el convento* were two of the offerings of this dramatist, who was dedicated to the establishment of an inexpensive popular theatre. He also wrote serious plays like *El esclavo* (1931), which dealt with labor problems.

Some actors devoted their lives to performing *bufo* roles. Most famous of the interpreters in the 1930's were Regino López, Adolfo Otero ("El gallego"), and Sergio Acebal ("El negrito"). Others remembered for their interpretation of an individual character after 1937 in the Comedia Theatre are Piñero (El gallego), Cándida Quintana (La mulata), and Alberto Garrido, in blackface (El negro).

Protests against this form of theatre began early. One of those who tried to raise the standards of taste was José Antonio Ramos (1885–

---

[14] Antonio Ramírez "Un autor que ha estrenado 100 obras," *Carteles,* XXXII (August 28, 1936), 42–45.

1946),[15] called by the Spanish critic Custodio "Solitary Star of the Cuban Theatre." Inspired by a visit to Havana by the Italian actor Roncoroni, Ramos was moved at the age of twenty to write for the stage. In 1906 he wrote "Almas rebeldes" and "Una bala perdida" but, unable to find a publisher, he sent the manuscripts to some of his family in Barcelona. Two others, *Nanda* (1907) and *La hidra* (1908), were printed in Havana later, while Ramos was traveling in France and Spain. After meeting Villaespesa and Jacinto Grau, he returned to Cuba full of enthusiasm to organize a group of theatre lovers. They called themselves Sociedad de Fomento del Teatro.

To prove the low quality of the *bufo*, which he claimed required no skill, Ramos dashed off a script overnight and sent it to a manager. Performed in 1910 by Regino López as *A la Habana me voy*, it proved so successful that Ramos fled to Spain to escape the omnipresent monster he had created. He got an appointment as Cuban consul in Barcelona, where he spent most of his time reading Strindberg, Bjoernson, and Ibsen. He wrote *Liberta* in four acts, and the brief *Cuando el amor muere*, to show he had assimilated his models' techniques, but he could find no producer in Spain. *Liberta* (1911), with its attack on the double standard, had an enthusiastic author's reading at Madrid's Teatro Español, but the Spaniards' dislike of Cubans and the eventual victory of subservient Mercedes Morales, the heroine, kept it off the stage, though Benavente, whose influence Ramos reveals, wrote a laudatory preface when the two plays were published together in 1911. The other play, translated into English as *When Love Dies*, gives the impression of being only the first act of a drama.

Still apparently attracted by unpopular ideas, Ramos completed *Satanás* (1913), which is reminiscent of Galdós' *Doña Perfecta*. At performances in Barcelona and Havana audiences were shocked by the ideas of the free-thinking artist, Esteban, and his murder by his protegée, Lissette. Indeed, Ramos thought it best to get out of Barcelona; he transferred to the consulate in Lisbon and eventually back to Havana, just in time to see a performance of his earlier political satire *Bala perdida*—by then revised as *Calibán Rex* (1914)—in the same Teatro Payret that had introduced his *bufo*. Like *Satanás*, its

[15] Angel Custodio, "José Antonio Ramos," *Hoy*, March 7, 1943; José Juan Arrom, "El teatro de José Antonio Ramos," *Revista Iberoamericana*, XII, No. 24 (June, 1947), 263–271.

long speeches sometimes make it more preachment than play. However Ramos' *El hombre fuerte* (1915), in its frightening portrayal of the instinctive wilful politician Vicente Inclán, delivers its theme dramatically.

Now another Cuban took up the fight for good drama, Sánchez Galarraga in 1916 voiced an appeal for beauty and inspiration on the stage, in which he was joined the following year by a young university professor, Salvador Salazar, and by Lucilo de la Peña, who organized Sociedad del Teatro Cubano. In striving for a national theatre they sponsored a season of a dozen plays, some of which were published in their short-lived magazine, *Teatro Cubano*. One was Ramos' *Tembladera*, a 1918 revision of *La hidra*. In its new version it won the prize of the National Academy of Arts and Letters.[16] This excellent example of Cuban realism takes its name from a sugar plantation in which colonial customs and modern progress clash over the sale of land to foreigners.

Following this success Ramos spent ten years as a consul in the United States, and later got an appointment to Mexico, where the attitude of its easygoing inhabitants inspired *En las manos de Dios* (Mexico, 1935). In its prolog, prayer is pitted against medicine as a means of curing disease.

Two other brief plays ended Ramos' career as a dramatist. Jupiter and the nymph Calisto figure in the quiet poetic *La leyenda de las estrellas* (1935). In contrast, the plotless *La recurva* (1939) shows a clash of conservative old folks and revolutionary youngsters against the background of a hurricane. The two were published together in 1941. At the time of his death, Dr. Ramos was working on a three-act comedy, "FU. 3001," an ironical portrait of Cuban aristocracy and dishonest politicians. It took its name from a telephone number.

Ramos' theatre is one of ideas, even though in expressing them his speeches frequently are long and sermonizing. Another of his flaws is a lack of humor, due perhaps, as Salvador Bueno suspects, to Ramos' keen feeling of the anguish of his homeland.[17] As a person, Ramos impressed others as being genial and charming, with a keen sense of the comic.

His long and eventful life bracketed the formative period of his

---

[16] Published in *Anales de la Academia Nacional de Artes y Letras*, III (January, 1918), 31–158.
[17] Salvador Bueno, *Medio siglo de literatura cubana*, p. 127.

country's theatre, in contrast to the brief existence of the wealthy
traveler and bohemian, Gustavo Sánchez Galarraga (1893–1934),
already mentioned. Galarraga's output of twenty-four plays, later collected in eight volumes, were written too quickly to achieve much
depth. He frequently fails to get inside his characters. He criticized
the upper class in his two popular plays, *El mundo de los muñecos*
and *El grillete* (1920). The latter is about the troubles resulting
from marrying out of one's social class. He wrote an amusing
husband-wife farce, *La máscara de anoche* (1912), which was influenced by Benavente, and won prizes for a war zarzuela, *El recluta
del amor* (1919), which marked the entry of Cuba's great composer
Ernesto Lecuona into the field of musical comedy, and gave full play
to his librettist's lyrical gifts. *El héroe* (1919), idealizing the war
spirit, presents a younger brother who gives up Adela so she can care
for his battle-blinded brother. The plot is childish, the characters
preposterous, but, except in the melodramatic passionate parts, the
dialog is excellent. This disciple of Benavente, and the most prolific
of modern Cuban dramatists, considered his best dramas to be *La
verdad de la vida* (1912), *Un caso, El garrote, Tierra virgen, El
abandonado*, and *El egoísmo de la honra*, in most of which he criticizes the idle aristocrats. He preferred, however, to be recognized as
a lyric poet, and published twenty volumes of verse.

José Arrom, after contrasting the thinker Ramos with the poet
Galarraga, calls Ramón Sánchez Varona (1883–   ) the best of
Cuba's modern dramatists.[18] He was noted for his gift of observation,
his skilful dialog, the self-revelation of his characters, and the balance of his scenes. His career began with three plays: *Quiebras de la
osadía, Rosa*, and *Las piedras de Judea* (1915). The last, discussing
whether a wife may seek love elsewhere if her husband does, really
launched him on his career. It was followed by *El ogro* (1915), in
which the uncouth Carlos is civilized by jealousy. Two entries represented this playwright in the 1918 competition of the Cuban Theatre
Society. *María*, a play about war fever, won first prize. In the opinion
of Arrom it is one of the best comedies of Cuba's theatre. Sánchez
Varona's second offering, *Con todos y para todos*, recreates the revolutionary days and, based on a poem by Martí, presents rural Cubans
as the bulwark of the future. It received honorable mention for its

---

[18] Arrom, *Historia*, p. 81.

traditional and patriotic qualities. For the next few years Sánchez Varona tried to make a living as a dramatist. Each of his next four plays received some sort of award, but more honor than cash.

The Cuban Theatre Society succumbed in 1924. People blamed the movies, and dramatists' attempts to create local plays by insinuating a few local words or customs into foreign plays, and the competition of a company of actors from Spain. But Sánchez Varona continued awhile longer, trying to bridge the gap between the literary theatre and the popular *sainete* with artistry but not chilly intellectualism. *La cita* (1918), *La hipoteca*, and *El pequeño tirano* are some of his efforts.[19]

Unable to make a living from serious drama, he finally turned to writing radio sketches, where his ability to concoct plots and provide amusing dialog permitted him to complete nearly two hundred sketches in ten years. However, for a Department of Education competition in 1938 he took time to write an outstanding tragedy, *La sombra*, whose chief character never appears on the stage. The shadow of the dead wife keeps the lovers forever apart. *La sombra* was awarded first prize as a play that was Cuban in externals but universal in substance. Sánchez Varona also completed a Benaventian rural comedy, *El gavilán* (1935), still unpublished, and Arrom mentions a later historical tragedy, "Pintó," about the victim of the 1854 conspiracy, but it has been neither produced nor published. Meanwhile Sánchez Varona writes for the movies and awaits the arrival of a more active Cuban national theatre.

One of Cuba's outstanding national playwrights is Luis A. Baralt (1892–   ), already mentioned as a sponsor of drama. Educated in Spain, he first wooed the stage with *Taowami* (1920), about a biology professor who tries to escape into a simple life only to find on a foreign island a civilization even more complicated and deformed. This same idea pervades *Tragedia indiana*, written at about the same period but not performed till 1952. The extremes of piety and violence are exhibited by Padre Bartolomé de las Casas and the conquistador Porcallo de Figueroa. One falls on his knees, the other on the aborigines.

Baralt's best plays are *La luna en el pantano*, which won first prize in the 1935 Ministry of Education competition, and *Junto al río*, which

[19] *Ibid.*, p. 83.

received honorable mention in 1938. Both are set in contemporary Havana, and both bring present-day technique and ideas onto the Cuban stage. Scenery and stage lighting play an important part in the denouement of the first.

There is more violence in Baralt's *Junto al río* about sixty-year-old Juan, a squatter "beside the river," where he raises his adopted daughter, Sol, and where he provides refuge for an escaping anti-Machado revolutionist. The play is noteworthy for introducing lower-class but typically Cuban individuals, and reveals that the dramatist has studied J. M. Synge and Dunsany, whom he has translated. Baralt's other works are symbolic and philosophic but without Cuban roots, like *Mariposa blanca* (1948), set in Peru, and the most modern and representative. *Meditación en tres por cuatro* (1950), which treats of four symbols: Materialism, Poetry, The Whole Life, and Existence.

Other dramatists sought the country outside Havana for their inspiration. Marcelo Salinas (1889–   ) made his reputation with *Alma guajira o Charito* and *La tierra . . . tu tierra,* both of 1928. They idealized the Cuban country dweller and marked the reawakening of the national theatre, according to Natividad González Freire.[20] Most of Salinas' other plays deal with politics. *El mulato* (1940), about the mulatto secretary of a crooked senator, also introduces racial discrimination. Solórzano sees traces of Florencio Sánchez in this study of the moral problems of two different generations,[21] but the presence of the mulatto helps it retain its Caribbean atmosphere.

Farmers figure in two tragedies by José Montés López. *Chano* (1937) deals with the subjugation of rural Cubans. *La sequía* (1938), superior as a drama, presents both man and nature as foes to the farmer. When the drought lasts too long, fortune, happiness, and even honor may be lost.

After an apprenticeship dramatizing the precepts of his Socialist party, Paco Alfonso (1906–   ) produced in *Sabanimar* (1943) a Cuban *Tobacco Road* for the Teatro Popular. He did the same for sugarcane workers in *Cañaveral* (1950). Experimenting in other directions, he wrote a tear jerker *Ya no me dueles, luna* (1946) about a wronged woman; *Los surcos cantan la paz* (1951), a protest against war; and *Hierba hedionda* (1951), a fight for social equality and a

---

[20] Natividad González Freire, *Teatro cubano contemporáneo: 1928–1957.* She also lists Cuba's theatrical groups and their repertoires, pp. 28–39.

[21] Carlos Solórzano, *Teatro latinoamericano del siglo XX,* p. 18.

protest against racial discrimination. This mediocre dramatist, who writes badly, produced an interesting experiment of popular lyric drama in *Yari Yari Mamá Olúa,* under the influence of Brecht.

Dramatist by avocation, but with a long list of successes is Judge Miguel Angel Macau (1886–   ), whose first play was produced in 1909. *La justicia en la inconsciencia* (1909), about the troubled times of 1896, shows the influence of Echegaray. It deals with Leonor, the daughter of a revolutionist, who is courted by a loyalist. Five full-length plays and six shorter plays, many reprinted in several editions, comprise Judge Macau's list. *La maternidad es amor* was very well received, and his literary *bufo, Soledad* (1933), was a stage success.

Tiempo muerto by Jorge Mañach (1899–1962) represents momentary interest in the Cuban theatre by a literary figure with greater reputations in other fields. Also worthy of mention are José Cid Pérez (1906–1953), who wrote *Altares de sacrificio,* about Cuba's revolution, and Felipe Pichardo Moyas (1892–1957), author of *La oración,* which pictures nineteenth-century Camagüey.

This enumeration does not exhaust the list of Cuban dramatists. Professor Salvador Salazar Roig (1892–1950), best known of Cuban *costumbristas,* dealt sentimentally with local customs in such plays as *El amor detective* (1918), about the robbery of a wealthy banker and a young man who poses as a detective to woo the banker's daughter, and *La torpe realidad* (1919), about middle-class Cubans. His plays range from the intense drama of a wife's sacrifice for her politician husband and the deceits necessary to achieve power, in *El precio* (which he wrote in 1924, although it was not produced until 1940), to *Estampas de Cervantes* (1950), one of the few national plays performed by the Teatro Universitario. Salazar's technique follows the Spanish Golden Age, but his dialog is lively and his themes deal with present-day Cuba. The collaboration of Julio Sanz and León Ichaso resulted in several Quintero-like *sainetes,* such as *Rosalba* and *Flor de camino* (1918).

Also to be mentioned as a hope for Cuba's theatre is César Rodríguez Expósito (1904–   ). Beginning to produce just as the stagnation of the Machado dictatorship ended, he provided realistic pictures of the flaws in Cuban society as viewed by a trained newspaperman. *Huyendo de la verdad* (1932) attacks those refusing to face reality. *Humano antes que moral* (1933) offers a gallery of symbols. Many of Rodríguez Expósito's other plays conceal propaganda: *El poder del sexo* (1933), for good politics; *La superproducción humano* (1937), for birth control; and *Multitudes* (1944), against Hitler. In 1937, elected president of the Sociedad de Autores Teatrales de Cuba, he went on to dramatize social problems with fire and technical excellence. Unfortunately, the impossibility of making a living in Cuba from even theatrical successes drove him to become drama director of a Cuban radio station, where, at least, he has contributed a dozen plays of professional caliber to Cuban drama of the air.

The bibliography of published plays in Arrom's volume, *Historia de la literatura dramática cubana,* covers thirty-three pages and includes 1,500 titles, but in spite of its heritage, the contemporary Cuban theatre shows few signs of life. Many writers, influenced by European plays, have thought the inclusion of a Cuban character or two enough to create national drama, even when spirit and theme have been alien to the soil.

The public, tired of seeing old material rehashed, turned its back on the theatre, even on the world's largest theatre, Blanquita, with 6,500 seats. There were a number of attempts by lighting, decoration, and theme to give drama a new look so that the public would also take a new look. A group calling itself Pro-Arte Dramático flourished briefly in 1927, and Luis A. Baralt founded the art theatre, La Cueva, in 1936 to bring European currents to the attention of Cubans. Its choice of an opener was Lope's *Fuenteovejuna!* In 1938 the Department of Education made its contribution through its Teatro Cubano de Selección.[22] Two years later, Juan J. Remos, then Minister of Education, sent a road company through the provinces with plays for both children[23] and adults. Rafael Marquina was the leading actor. Marquina, by himself and with the drama critic Félix Lizaso (1891–   ), was author of eight plays, around 1940. *Contra el deber* and *Divertimiento alfabético* are typical. When M. M. Chacón became Minister, he continued Remos' policy. In 1941 the troupe gave forty performances, among them Remos' own *Las Corrientes del siglo*, about a weary man seeking himself in the labyrinth

[22] González Freire, *Teatro Cubano.*
[23] An idea of the available children's plays may be obtained from an undated catalog of Librería Cervantes, Havana. Twenty of its ninety-two pages list Teatro Infantil, giving ages and sex of the required actors. Many plays are only for boys or only for girls. Adolfo Cortada is listed as author of eighteen of them.

of the world. He has also written *Adaris* (1916) and *El destino de Israel* (1929).

Those were the antecedents of the Teatro Universitario, organized in 1941 under the Austrian Ludwig Schajowicz, originally to perform plays from the Greek. Six years later Schajowicz left for Puerto Rico, and Professor Baralt became the Teatro's moving spirit. In the first twelve years of its existence, forty dramas with an international reputation were performed, and half that many experimental plays. Only a few, however, were by local authors.[24] *La hija de las flores* by Avellaneda was revived, April 8–9, 1953.

There continue to be local dramatists, producing sporadically. Alfonso Portuondo (1882–   ) at the age of fifty began studying Greek tragedy and the romanticists. Then after a bout with Ibsen and Macaulay's criticism of the Restoration dramatists, he started writing. *La voluntad hace milagros,* a revealing title, and *Los amores* are some of his works.

Arrom lists the Cuban dramatists through 1942, José Cid Pérez continues to catalog them through another ten years, and Natividad González Freire brings the record down to 1958.[25] She divides the twentieth century into generations, with the third generation beginning about 1944 with such student groups as ADAD and the Teatro Popular troupe. The fourth generation began its work in 1952–1953. González Freire's doctoral dissertation takes nearly a hundred pages to describe them and their works, and since hardly any of them have been published, her opinion must be followed, and need not be echoed here.

One of the most prolific among contemporary Cuban dramatists is Oscar Valdez Hernández (1915–   ), among whose politico-social works, set in many countries, is *Guerrilla del pueblo* (1943). Another Cuban dramatist to be watched is "Carlos Felipe" (Carlos Fernández, 1914–   ). Starting with the amateurish *El divertido viaje de Adelita Cossí* (1938), he was able by 1959 to achieve sufficient promi-

[24] J. M. Valdés-Rodríguez summarized its achievements in his column "Tablas y Pantalla," *Mundo,* February, 26, 1953; see also Humberto Sumel, "Teatro cubano," *Policía* (November, 1942), pp. 3–33.

[25] Arrom, *Historia,* pp. 84–91; José Cid Pérez, "Cincuenta años de teatro cubano," *Carteles,* XXXIII (May 18, 1952), 110–113, 188–189; González Freire, *Teatro cubano,* pp. 115–228; Francisco Ichaso, "Medio siglo de teatro en Cuba," *Diario de la Marina,* September 15, 1957; Cid Perez' article serves as foreword to *Teatro Contemporáneo: Cuba,* Madrid: Aguilar, 1959.

nence to be picked by José Cid Pérez for his *Teatro contemporáneo: Cuba.* Coming from a poor family, he went to work at sixteen, but his ambition drove him to language study, a good position in the Customs Bureau, and time to write. *Esta noche en el bosque,* which won him the 1939 National Theatre prize, shows his key quality to be tenderness. *Tambores* (1943) presents a group of typical Cubans. Then Carlos Felipe became interested in individuals. *El chino* won the 1947 A.D.A.D. prize, and *El travieso Jimmy,* introducing the elderly Leonelo trying to relive the important moments of his life, won for its author the 1949 National Prize and was selected by Cid Pérez as Carlos Felipe's greatest play. *Capricho en rojo,* in which several women wearing the same style of clothing confuse Pablo, won him the A.D.A.D. Theatre competition in 1950. The mastery of psychology by this self-taught dramatist was not apparent in *Ladrillos de plata* (1952) in which Lisia, the adulterous mother, turns silver into dross for her family. It is one of three reprinted in the author's *Teatro* (Santa Clara, 1959).

Of a different sort is Marcelo Salinas (1889–   ), a laborer who became an anarchist, frequently arrested by the police. He is author of social plays of both city and rural districts: *El mulato, La santa caridad, La tierra. . . tu tierra* (1928), and *Alma guajira* (1928), the best of his early period. *Ráfaga* (1939) and *El poder* are political plays. *El vagón de tercera* is a surrealist play in one act, and *Llegan los bárbaros* (1941) shows the power of boycott.

Women, too, are achieving a place in Cuban drama. The most important is a schoolteacher, journalist, and prize-winning poetess, Renée Potts (1908–   ), whose chief theme has been women characters fighting their environment to achieve happiness. Her plays include *El amor del diablo* (1931), *Buen tiempo de amor* (1934), and *Las Hopalandas,* about an elderly couple on a farm of that name. In 1934 Miss Potts turned to history in *El conquistador,* about the epoch when England controlled Havana. Women aboard a transatlantic liner are characterized in *Imagíname infinita*; *Canela o La muñeca de cartón,* dealing with adolescent love, received popular acclaim; but both are over-sentimental and weak.

Among other Cuban dramatists are Teté Casuso; Isabel Fernández (1910–   ) who collaborated with Cuqui Ponce (1916–   ) in *El que dirán* (1944) and *Lo que no se dice,* both of which show United States influence; and María Alvarez Ríos (1919–   ), disciple of

García Lorca, who wrote *Martí 9* (1944), *Según el color* (1953), *La víctima* (1956), and others. Her *Funeral,* an all-women symbolic play developed in monologs, was part of the Semana de Teatro Cubano held in Madrid in 1957.

Also on that program was *Mañana es una palabra* (1947) by Nora Badía (1921–), a dramatic monolog in which a woman unburdens her soul to her sweetheart, only to discover that he is dead. It is excellent. She also wrote *La alondra* (1948). One of a trilogy is *Scherzo* (1948), a poetic fantasy of self-searching by Eduardo Manet (1927–), which was produced in Madrid. The play judged best by Madrid critics was a sentimental picture of Havana, *Una vieja postal descolorida* by Alfredo Marquerie, a Spaniard living in Cuba.

Jorge de Busto (1918–) pre-empted a different field, the innocence of man and the need to believe in a divinity. But he also mocked that idea in his bitter farce *El Cristo* (1948), treating ironically the events up to the death of Christ, then announcing they were merely a rehearsal for a theatrical performance. Emilio Bacardí and Virgilio Varela Zequeira have also dealt in satire.

Along with the reaction against Dictator Fulgencio Batista, the theatre of Cuba began to experience a revolution, so that Dr. González could write about a "fourth generation" and René Leal could report on the waning influence of García Lorca, who was being replaced by Tennessee Williams and other North American dramatists.[26] Miller's *Death of a Salesman* had not reached Cuban audiences, and the man-and-God theme of O'Neill had little influence, except perhaps for the effect of his *A Long Day's Journey into Night* on the first act of *Aire frío* by Virgilio Piñera (1914–),[27] but the Freudian concepts of Williams have attracted a number of the new Cuban dramatists, appearing since the revolution.

So has the delicate psychological realism of Chekhov. One of the most promising of recent dramatists, Fermín Borgés (1931–), has confessed his ambition to become a "Creole Chekhov." He has trav-

[26] René R. Leal, "Actuales corrientes en el teatro cubano," *Nueva Revista Cubana,* I, No. 1 (April, 1959), 162–170; Sumel, "Teatro cubano," *Policía,* (November, 1942), pp. 30–33. Four volumes of contemporary theatre have been officially published in the *Escena Cubano* series, 1959; No. 1, C. Felipe, *Capricho en rojo*; No. 2, M. Álvarez Ríos, *La víctima*; No. 3, V. Piñera, *Aire frío*; No. 4, P. Alfonso, *Yerba hedionda.* Each is in three acts.

[27] Published, in *Lunes de Revolución* (1958); the complete play appears in his *Teatro* (1964).

eled in Europe, and from his study of neorealism in the Italian theatre he is trying to portray Cuba's soul. He began with the one-act *Escenas de gentes desconocidas o Treinta grados sobre cero* (1953), a picture of life in the wreck of a colonial mansion in Havana. *Pan viejo* (1954) concerns two old people with no money to bury their dead boy but with hopes of winning enough in the lottery. In the course of the action most of the problems of Cuba's poverty are revealed. *Doble juego* (1954) stems from Kingsley's *Dead End;* a couple of juvenile delinquents confess to each other the crimes they have committed to get money for their vices. On another plane, Borgés wrote poetic children's plays, but he returned to Chekhov in the long and interesting, but somewhat imperfect, play about Havana, *Con la música a otra parte* (1958).

Another follower of Chekhov, though prevented by the psychological quirks of his characters from picturing the real Cuba, is José Enrique Montoro Agüero (1930–   ). He revealed his talents in *Cumbre y abismo* (1950) and *Lo verdadero muestro o Desviadero 23*, which won the 1956 Soto Theatre prize. Celia, its melancholy, transplanted-Chekhov heroine, scorns the city. In Montoro's *Tiempo y espacio* (1956), however, one can find a trace of *A Streetcar Named Desire*. The dialog is fluid, though the characters are frustrated and maladjusted. The crude language is in keeping with its brutal plot.

Manuel Reguera Saumell, in his three-act *El jardín de los cerezos* shows a trend toward the presentation of these frustrated people, not only among the protesting laborers, but among the middle class in provincial Cuban towns. Two similar plays by Montoro, "Mamaíta Zapatón" about the rights of the lower classes, and "El hombre honrado" dealing with Cuban politics, have been judicially kept off the stage for the present.

The theatre-in-verse has not made much progress in Cuba. Jorge Antonio González wrote a comic *Fedra*, with apologies to Racine, but he had little poetic talent. The authentic Cuban poet Nicolás Guillen (1902–   ) has been tempted by the stage only in *Floripondito o Los títeres son personas,* completely atypical. Expressionism has been tried only by Matías Montes Huidobro (1931–   ). After beginning with the Shakespearean *Las cuatro brujas* (1949), he turned to social plays like *La botija* about a widow and a druggist struggling for a treasure that belongs to the village, and *Los acosados.*

Professor Leal speaks of the "theatre of the absurd," as practiced by Gloria Díaz Parrado in *El juicio de Aníbal* (1958); *Las buhardillas de la noche* (1951), set in the Paris of 1930, by Roberto Bourbakis (1919–); and *La boda* (1958), by the "intellectual idealist" Virgilio Piñera. Bourbakis also wrote *M. Hirbú* (1949), *Survey* (1950), and *La rana encantada* (1951). His brother wrote *La hostería de la sirena* (1947) and *La columna y la vida* (1949), both symbolic dramas.

Part of this new activity in Cuba was the result of attempts to encourage local dramatists by various devices. In February, 1958, Cuban Theatre Month was announced, and each of the eight active theatres at the capital mounted a national play. The only old-timer honored was Ramos, with *La recurva* and *La leyenda de las estrellas*. Two theatres selected plays by Piñera: *La boda* and *Electra Garrigó*. Paco Alfonso's *Ya no me dueles, luna* and the farce *Gracias, doctor* by Enrique Núñez Rodríguez were well received, as were two plays by women: *La víctima* by María Alvarez and *Lo que no se dice* by Fernández and Ponce de León. The Theatre Month was well supported by press and merchants, and one was planned for the following year, but by then a new government had taken over.

Another highlight of the 1958 season was *Un color para este miedo* by Ramón Ferreira (1921–). He had become known through *Dónde está la luz* (1952), originally called *Marea alta*, a study of the racial problem. The drama was seen by four thousand people during its three performances by the Instituto de Cultura Nacional. In it, Ferreira said he was seeking the reality in the Cuban spirit. Ferreira was also author of *El hombre inmaculado,* about a corrupt chief of police during the Batista period. It earned him the vote as the best dramatist of 1959.

The most talked-of play of 1959, however, was *El flaco y el gordo* by the young writer Virgilio Piñera (1914–). His experimenting with O'Neill has already been mentioned. His *Falsa alarma* (1957) and *La boda* (1958) are indebted to Eugene Ionesco. His earlier *Jesús* (1950) was a well-made play with French ancestry. Its protagonist is a barber, regarded as a new Messiah by the villagers. In his attempts to deceive the people, he plays out this drama of the Passion. While lacking any metaphysical implications, the play does attack hypocrisy and schemes to deceive the public. *Electra Garrigó* (1945) when performed at the 1958 Cuban Theatre Month, introduced a Cuban Electra and transplanted the treachery and crimes of

Argo to Havana. A "Guantanamera," or rural ballad singer, replaced the Greek chorus to open and close each act, Clitemnestra was poisoned by a papaya fruit, Electra and Orestes were suggested by a mare and a stallion, and the death of Agamemnon was visualized through a fight between an old black rooster and a young white cock.

In *El flaco y el gordo* Piñera now fell in with the Castro line of denigration of human dignity. "El flaco," the exploited man, devours the fat man and so maintains the social level. By the critics, it was declared very boring. The average spectator considered it shockingly cannibalistic, but the official publication of "liberated" Cuba lauded it as the outstanding play of the year.

Well, art is long and the span of a dictator is short, but meantime, in its search for culture Cuba offered more concerts and recitations than drama, in theatres being established throughout the island "at reduced prices for students and laborers, and free to soldiers." A twenty-five-cent admission is the going rate.

To develop a cultural program, various steps were taken in 1960. One theatre, La Sala Arlequín, instituted El Lunes de Teatro Cubano in April, 1960, with the intention of performing a local play every Monday. If the play caught on, it might run longer; otherwise some other play would replace it. The first two plays, both by Matías Montes Huidobro, were *Los acosados* and *La botija*.

El Teatro Nacional Gómez de Avellaneda had a second Mes del Teatro Cubano. Several selections had been performed previously. Two were announced as pre-Revolution plays dealing with situations remedied since then. They were *Sara en el traspatio* by Manuel Reguera Saumell and *Árboles sin raíces* by Raúl González de Cascorío (1922–   ). The first, attacking bureaucracy and false pride, tells of the family of Sara, who tries to keep her family of three daughters united. It deal with the sugar industry.

González de Cascorío got most of his dramatic experience abroad. His *Parque-Bar* was a success in Madrid in 1957. *Árboles sin raíces* was a realistic yet lyric tragedy of a tenant farmer driven from his land by a minor politician. It was experimentally mounted, and *Boletín Cultural*, No. 6 (May, 1960) announced it was a tremendous success.

Ferreira's *Un color para este miedo* was repeated among the offerings of the Mes del Teatro Cubano. The only light touch in the month of plays was *Función de gala*, a comedy by the only woman writer participating, Clara Ronay. It concerns a foreign actress passing through Havana, where she is faced by the emptiness of her existence. In its solution it achieves universality.

Except for these moments, as Ruby Hart Phillips declared, most of Havana's experimental theatres present only foreign plays. A recent contest for local dramatists brought many entries, all from amateurs, but the judges did not find one worth accepting. As one literary man explained his reason for not attempting drama: "Why make glasses for people who do not wear them?"[28]

Just before the Castro era, Dr. González Freire, discussing the lack of trained actors and actresses, declared there would be no national theatre till the Cubans of all social classes played their part.[29]

In subsequent years, as the dramatists began seeing an opportunity for performances, the theatrical activity was augmented considerably and the quality has improved. Among those showing exceptional promise is Antón Arrufat who satirizes the Latin American backward glance and resistance to progress in his farce, *El vivo al pollo*, about a widow who has her husband's body embalmed and kept as a member of the family. One of the youngest dramatists is Rolando Ferrer, whose *sainete Taza de café* deals with the clash of social classes, in the meeting of a wealthy, aristocratic woman and her poor relative. Their caustic conversation reveals their hatred of each other.

Dramatist of class struggle with evident sympathy for the lower class is Fermín Borges (1931–) whose technique follows that of the Italian movies that discover poetry amid squalor. *Gente desconocida* shows the regression of impoverished, unimportant sweethearts. *Pan viejo* deals with two elderly people, always hungry, and *Doble juego* shows to what extent a couple of young people can be driven by a mortal craving.

Frustrations in the middle class are revealed by René Buch (1926–), a psychologist, in *El agua de la vida*. The general Cuban spirit of revolt runs through his other plays, *Nosotros los muertos* (1948) and *El joven y el mar* (1947). His anguished characters revolt against their surroundings and each other.

Abelardo Estorino (1925–) is a dentist turned playwright and actor. After *El peine y el espejo* and *Hay un muerto en la calle*, he was recognized by an Honorable Mention in the second Concurso

[28] Ruby Hart Phillips, *Cuba, Island of Paradox*, p. 359.
[29] González Freire, *Teatro cubano*.

Literario Hispanoamericano for his *El robo del cochino* (1961). It deals with an exciting moment in the overthrow of Batista and concerns a provincial family and its worries over the son, among the guerrillas fighting in Sierra Madre.

As a propaganda gesture in connection with the Third Concurso Literario Inter-Americano de las Américas de la Habana in 1961, a Latin American drama contest was announced for October, 1961, by the Casa de Las Américas. The first prize, a thousand pesos, went to the Guatamalan Dr. Manuel Galich (1913–   ) for *El pescado indigesto*. The Argentine Osvaldo Dragún won second prize with *Cuatro historias para ser contadas*. Third prize went to the Brazilian Suassuna for *Auto de la compadecida*. Chile and Mexico were also represented and the judges, Virgilio Piñera and Sergio Beltrán, gave honorable mention to four Cubans, two of them women: María Irene Fornés, *La viuda*; Gloria Parrado, *La paz en el sombrero*; Antón Arrufat, *El hoyo*; and Abelardo Estorino, *El robo del cochino*.

Since then, though there has been aerial survey to supplement sparse political and military news, little has come out of Cuba concerning the activity of its stage.

CHAPTER 26

Costa Rican Drama

Literary historians of Costa Rica take a dim view of their national drama. After Adolfo Herrera García's pessimistic prefatory declaration: "No existe el teatro costarricense," the newspaperman Borges Pérez devoted a hundred pages to San José's theatrical activities, then added: "They have their theatres—Puntarenas, Cartago, San Ramón, Alajuela, etc.—and their theatrical enthusiasm."[1]

Enrique Rodri-Mur, feeling that the theatre was at a low ebb, tried to resuscitate it by a series of newspaper articles.[2] And most recently, Ulloa Zamora has written: "Drama has not played a very important role in Costa Rica, being always secondary to poetry and the novel."[3]

None of them finds early evidence of plays. Borges noted the appearance of the first permanent theatre in 1837, a "galerón de paja para la diversión de la sociedad josefina, con el espectáculo de representaciones teatrales." But there cannot have been a wide interest, for the playhouse held only seventy spectators, who had to provide their own seats. The venture did have the enthusiastic support of the Church, however, inasmuch as the performers were all male and the plays were generally *autos sacramentales* written by the poet and Latinist Dr. Daniel Castillo. Performances were twice a month.

For nine years these supervised presentations represented the total dramatic activity in San José. In 1846, against the protests of the clergy, another playhouse was built, with two hundred seats, to offer plays imported from abroad. On its stage Costa Rica's earliest-mentioned actress, Lelia Castillo, made her first appearance. So often was the house filled to capacity that one of the first official acts of President Juan Rafael Mora after his re-election in 1849 was to order

---

[1] Fernando Borges Pérez, *La historia del teatro en Costa Rica*, especially p. 106.

[2] Enrique Rodríguez Murillo, "La historia del teatro," *Diario Nacional* (San José), June 9, 1955, to February, 1956, especially November, 1955.

[3] Alfonso Ulloa Zamora, "Panorama literario costarricense, 1900–1958," *Panorama das literaturas das Américas* III, 976.

a much larger theatre. It was built by Colonel Escalante, whose chief qualification seems to have been that during his travels he had seen the theatre in Lima which he was directed to reproduce in Costa Rica.

In anticipation, Larriva, a Spanish actor living in San José, was asked to recruit and train a company of amateurs in a play to inaugurate the building. His choice was *El Pelayo*, the Jovellanos play of 1792, or more likely the Quintana version of 1805. Either the amateurs were too eager, or the builders were slow, because the play was ready before the stage was. Instead of waiting, they performed it at the university with the idea that they could then prepare Zorrilla's *Caín Pirata* (1842) with which to open the theatre. That was their mistake. Critics saw their performance and decided to invite a German magician and his singing wife to open the Mora Theatre.

These amateurs got their moment on the stage, however, and performed in another Zorrilla play, *La gran comedia del caballero del rey D. Sancho* (1849), just arrived by galleon, and then went on to the Eugenio Ochoa translation from French of *El campanero de San Pablo*. The local actors were followed between June 5, 1851, and October 11 by a Spanish company, en route from Guatemala, which introduced Eugene Sue's *Wandering Jew* and other European successes.

Other foreigners followed. One interesting evening was provided by a group of eighteen North American soldiers of fortune. Captured during the attempt of William Walker to take over Central America, they had been released with no funds to pay their passage back to the United States. By their singing, dancing, and dramatic sketches they took in enough at the ticket window to let them sail for California on December 28, 1857, though without their filibuster leader, who was shot in 1860.

A different kind of performance took place in the Mora Theatre on August 14, 1859. The Gil y Baus translation of *Carcajada* was the stage attraction. At the end of the first act, however, followers of Colonel Lorenzo Salazar provided an *entremés* and signaled the end of the *Carcajada*, by circulating through the audience distributing anti-Mora leaflets. Chairs flew. One actress was trampled and had to be rescued by the police.

The revolt thus touched off was successful. Mora was ousted and his theatre was refurbished and renamed Teatro Municipal. But there was little municipal about its artists or their offerings. Adolfo Blen, an actor from Spain, tried to make money performing zarzuelas and dramas. Failing, but still enchanted by the country, he became a citizen and eventually earned his living as national librarian.

In 1865, according to Rodri-Mur, not a single play was performed in the Teatro Municipal.[4] Some blamed President Jesús Jiménez Zamora because of his order that every performer or group of performers entering Costa Rica had to deposit enough money for the return trip home, so they would not become a burden on the state. Records for the theatre for 1866 and 1867 show only operas and performances by acrobats.

When President Tomás Guardia came into power in 1870, he insisted that the increasing wealth and population of Costa Rica deserved a playhouse better than the tiny Municipal Theatre. He proposed a tax of five centavos on each *arroba* (twenty-five pounds) of coffee exported, to raise an estimated construction cost of seventy-five thousand pesos.[5] Unfortunately he died in office in 1882 before the total was collected and his successor used the money for other things.

In 1888 the destruction by fire of the Municipal left San José without any theatre. That was when another actor, Tomás García, who had arrived with the touring Luque players and remained to become a Costa Rica citizen, was moved to build Teatro Variedades, with 185 seats on the main floor, 96 in the boxes, and room in the gallery for another 100 spectators. But there were no local players or plays to entertain its audiences, so García had to import foreign artists, including his old comrades Luque and his associates for several visits.

The nineteenth century was almost ended with hardly an original Costa Rica play produced. There had been one valiant attempt made in 1885 to put an amusing local-color skit, *Un duelo a la moda* by Rafael Carranza (1840–?), onto the stage. It satirized the military and had possible autobiographical touches in descriptions of the sad lot of a writer. Though Borges Pérez called it "a humorous satirical *sainete*," a politician, suspecting himself the lampooned victim, threatened the dramatist with a real duel. Rehearsals ended, and the play was not published till 1890, after the death of the politician. It

[4] Rodríguez Murillo, "La historia del teatro," *Diario Nacional.*
[5] Armando de Maria y Campos, *Entre cómicos de ayer.* The beauty of the National Theatre is described, p. 199.

was also finally performed. About the only thoroughly national products were a couple of zarzuelas. Mateo Fournier provided the libretto for one, *Los huérfanos,* with music by his son, Mateo, Jr. It was performed in the Teatro Variedades in 1885. In 1890, Carlos Gagini wrote the brief *Los pretendientes.*

Meantime, in San José Padre Hubert Prause had taken charge of the Colegio Seminario, where sons of many of the leading Costa Rican families received their education. In 1895 the students staged the locally written *El triunfo de la religión* with President Rafael Yglesias in the audience. The event was enough to spark his enthusiasm for drama, and while the boys in the school were staging other plays, written by Padre Rosendo de J. Valenciano of the faculty, President Yglesias gave orders to build the Teatro Nacional. It was completed in October, 1897. Actors and world-famous musicians who have performed in it proclaim it one of the best in Latin America acoustically, and although others are larger, for beauty and convenience for actors and audience it has few rivals.[6]

Yglesias determined that no German magician should dedicate this temple of Thespis. He ordered the Costa Rican Minister in Paris to recruit singers for an inaugural performance of *Faust,* October 21, 1897. It was not his fault that the famous tenor was incapacitated by a common tropical disease on the opening night or that the substitute and his fellow singers received more abuse than applause from the spectators.

With the arrival of the twentieth century, however, the Costa Rican stage showed more signs of vitality, thanks to the arrival in 1902 of a company of Spanish actors headed by Esteban Serrador and Josefina Mari. They located in the National Theatre with the announced purpose of welcoming local playwrights. One of the first plays performed was *Ñor Concepción* (1902), a short, rural, local-color skit in prose by Carlos Gagini (1865–1925), who was already known for his short stories. He had also written the books, and Eduardo Cuevas the music, for the brief musical *Los pretendientes* (1890) and for *El Marqués de Talamanca* (1900). *El Marqués,* set in Cartago in 1663, was the first full-length Costa Rican zarzuela. All three plays were published together.[7] After that, Gagini turned to regional novels

---

[6] *Ibid.*
[7] Carlos Gagini, *Obras dramáticas* (1905), and *Teatro* (1963).

with melodramatic plots, and to textbooks on grammar, and forsook the stage.

When Serrador and Mari performed the poetic drama *Venganza de un poeta* (1902), by Emilio Pacheco Cooper, his home town of Cartago presented its author with a laurel wreath, and the critics crowned the play with praise. The presence of these foreign actors in San José also moved Ricardo Fernández Guardia (1867–1950) to turn from his histories and his *Cuentos Ticos* to complete a three-act drama in prose, *Magdalena* (1902). His five years in Europe (1885–1890) as diplomatic representative of his country had given him an acquaintance with the stage in England, France, and Spain. This single play, the culmination of his literary productions, seems to have been his only attempt, though that same year he did edit, as a literary curiosity, a poetic tragedy in two acts, *La política del mundo*, by his great grandfather, Victor de la Guardia (1772–1824), originally performed in his birthplace of Penonomé, Panama, in 1809.

With the passing of Serrador-Mari, drama in Costa Rica hibernated till another Spanish actor, Emilio Thuiller (1868–1921), originally with the Guerrero-Mendoza company, arrived in Costa Rica in 1905. He performed several local manuscripts. One of them, the one-act *El grito de la conciencia* by Joaquín Barrionuevo, was better received by the critics than by the public. After publishing it in his volume of essays, *Albores* (San José, 1906), Barrionuevo revised it and tried it out with greater success in April, 1910. He later wrote a three-act drama, *El cuarto mandamiento*, performed in San José in 1916, but never published.

Another Costa Rican, Daniel Ureña (1876–1932), also provided Thuiller with several plays. Having studied drama from the shelves of his father's bookstore, he wrote a *juguete* in verse, *De la estación al hipódromo* (1903), and a humorous local-color revue, *San José alegre* (1903). And he also had the manuscript of a three-act prose drama, *María del Rosario*, to show Thuiller, who performed it May 3, 1906, and provided the prolog for its printed version (San José, 1907). Ureña was invited to take a part in his own one-act poetic drama *Sombra y luz* (1907). Thuiller and his leading lady, Ana Ferri, also successfully introduced Ureña's three-act drama *Los huérfanos* (1909), which was printed in 1910.[8] Other plays by Ureña, well-

[8] Excerpts were published in Eduardo de Ory, *Los mejores poetas de Costa Rica*, p. 267.

received but never published, were *Muñequerías* (1908) and *El sueño de una noche*.

To this period also belong Ernesto Martín Carranza (1879–   ) and Manuel G. Escalante Durán. Carranza, a lawyer and diplomat, saw his two-act local-color comedy *Cuento de amor* performed at the Nacional, November 3, 1910, and published the same year. Escalante's first endeavor was a dramatization of Alarcón's romantic adventure novel *El final de Norma*. As a comedy in three acts and twelve scenes, he and his friends performed it in 1911 at a family gathering to which a few critics were invited. The high praise it received was repeated when it was printed that same year. After a long interval, Escalante wrote the light romantic *Jeannine* (1945) and the much more impressive *Bruma* (1948), a drama of metaphysical love, consumed in its renunciation. It is generally considered one of the best of Costa Rican plays.

The visit to San José in 1912 of Díaz de Mendoza and his company encouraged playwrights. One such was a young actor, Francisco Soler (1885–1920), who was inspired to write *Pecados capitales*, completed in 1913.[9] The next year, in collaboration with the Colombian Camilo Cruz Santos (1888–   ), Soler wrote a three-act comedy, *La iniciación* (1914). His best play was *El último madrigal* (1918), in which he played a part. It had a second edition in 1919, the year before he died in Paris. In all his plays, Soler combined irony with a light touch. His early death was a great loss to Costa Rican letters.

The arrival of Díaz de Mendoza also encouraged a soldier, poet, and journalist to make another effort at drama writing. Eduardo Calsamiglia (?–1918) had seen his one-act drama *Vindicta* performed by Cuevas in 1910, and Múñoz and his associates had put on the stage his three-act drama in prose, *¡El!* (1911). But it was Díaz de Mendoza who really started him on a career by performing the brief *El hombre malo* and the poetic *Los pecados capitales* in 1912. Three brief fantasies in verse, reminiscent of Poe, are *Poderes invisibles*, *Ni en el cielo*, and *Un pecado mortal* (1914).

A half dozen of Calsamiglia's experiments were collected in book form in 1918 under the title of one of them, *El combate*. This grim

---

[9] Unpublished except for an excerpt in Rogelio Sotela, *Valores literarios de Costa Rica*, pp. 238–239. Other volumes for the study of Costa Rican drama include: Luis Robles Segreda, *Índice bibliográfico de Costa Rica*; Rogelio Sotela, *Escritores y poetas de Costa Rica*; and M. Vincenzi, *Los ídolos del teatro*.

struggle of a doctor between marriage and his professional duties is considered the author's best. Six others, all performed at the Teatro Nacional, were never printed, though those who saw them praised their perspective, even while qualifying them as showing little improvement over the technique of the time. One, however, and the most famous, the poetic *Bronces de antaño* (1919), which dealt with the Spain of Ferdinand and Isabel, was published after Calsamiglia's death by his friend Joaquín Vargas Coto, who provided data about the playwright in the preface.

Another experimenter, and one of the most productive of Costa Rican dramatists, was José Fabio Garnier (1884–1956). Sent to Italy to be trained as an engineer, Garnier did write a mathematical study, but was more interested in literature, and between 1904 and 1906 he completed three realistic novels with sentimental overtones. This development was nothing unusual. One Costa Rican humorist has commented that every Costa Rican has either written or planned a novel. But Garnier was also experimenting with the theatre.

His earliest attempt at drama was a *boceto de comedia, Nada,* written in Venice in 1904. There is no record of any performance. However his second attempt, *La última escena,* turned out in Bologna in 1905, was performed in 1912 by Díaz de Mendoza, and again in 1915 when Serrador y Mari returned to San José. A third product from his Italian stay was *El retorno*, from Ravenna, 1906, performed by Evangelina Adams in 1910. All three appear in the volume *Teatro* (San José, 1912).

Garnier's Italian phase ends with *Boccaccesca*, written in 1910. Though several printed versions of it exist, its theme makes a performance seem doubtful. It deals with the beautiful Violante who persuades her husband to let her spend a half hour with another man, and though the husband picks a supposedly safe candidate, the naked charms of Violante make the temptations too great for his control.

One of the longest and best plays by this modernist, with touches of what has been called "suave romanticism," is *A la sombra del amor,* performed by Fernando Soler, Evangelina Adams, and Bernardo Jambrini in 1921. Fernando, to keep Clara's husband from learning of their affair, has to marry her daughter Magdalena. When the girl discovers the situation from some old love letters, she commits suicide. When this play was published in 1921, two other plays were included in the volume: *El segundo coloquio que pasó entre Cipión y Breganza*, a satirical sequel to Cervantes' dialog between two dogs, and a three-act, undated comedy, *Sombra de la hermana*.

Generally considered Garnier's best is *Con toda el alma* (1929), performed in 1933 by María Montoya. It deals with a disrupted family in which the mother becomes a prostitute.

Fifteenth and last of Garnier's plays was the three-act comedy *El talismán de Afrodita* (1929). The fact that all characters in the play are symbolic, and that no one has a name, confuses still more a confusing play. But the work of Calsamiglia and Garnier, though colored by their foreign influence, had a good effect on the dramatists who were to come later.

Most of the playwrights who followed and who are mentioned in histories, have produced only one or two titles, frequently unpublished. One explanation is the few potential purchasers to absorb even a small printing, which must be done at the author's expense. Dr. Julián Marchena, director of the National Library, and himself an author, confesses that though his library is the best in Central America, there is hardly a handful of local plays among its eighty thousand volumes. So the reward for a dramatist's weeks of composition can only be one or, rarely, two performances at the huge Teatro Nacional when some touring company can be persuaded to perform his creation. The smaller Teatro Variedades has since 1920 concentrated on the more remunerative movies. No other space is available for local playwrights except the América, built in 1915, the little theatre built in 1947 for the University of Costa Rica players, and the Teatro de Cámara de la Prensa, inaugurated in 1956. In September, 1954, the Aquileo J. Echeverría Theatrical Company was created to perform plays by national authors. The Rotary Club gave it a send-off with a banquet for its three leading actresses, Marita Hine, Ester Ureña, and Julia Cordero. Some of the older actors who helped the local writers get a start were also lauded, among them Adolfo Blen and Eduardo Cuevas. And Octavio Castro Saborío, who had directed the Teatro Nacional for thirty-three years, displayed his scrapbooks about Zelmira Segreda, Melico Salazar, and other great figures. But nothing of that has been put into print and most of the national plays in which they appeared have disappeared for lack of interest, though some of the names and items survive.

The poet Raúl Salazar Alvarez is remembered because of his humorous plays at the beginning of the century. His political revue *San Juan en camisas* broke local records with a run of 110 performances in the Trébol Theatre, which alternated between drama and movies till it burned in 1924. A sequel was *Costa Rica en B.V.D.* Salazar's *Flor de almas* (1924) raised a large sum for victims of an armory explosion. In 1929 he published *El hombre que buscaba el verdadero amor* (eleven scenes about an aging actress and her ridiculous English doctor who murders Spanish), and *La mujer que tenía en la boca el corazón*, for which he gave credit to Conan Doyle.

In this land of novelists, one of the few Costa Rican novels that ever sold enough copies to make money was *Pedro Arnáez* by José Marín Cañas (1904–   ), the son of Spanish parents and educated in Spain, but author of works redolent of the soil of Costa Rica. His earliest attempt at drama, a one-act drama, *Como tú*, was first performed by Antonia Herrero in 1929 and published under the pseudonym of "Juan de Espinel." Later it was expanded to a three-act drama and performed by Herrero Tordesillas. The woman's role is especially powerful but the man makes the final curtain memorable as, defeated and stupefied, he surrenders with a muttered: "¿No ves que estoy fumando?" Marín Cañas also wrote *Una tragedia en ocho cilindras* and several light comedies of great agility but less importance.

Gonzalo Sánchez Bonilla (1884–   ) came into prominence when his philosophic novelette *El pobre manco* won the 1909 Juegos Florales, and was published in 1910. He began his playwriting career with a two-act zarzuela, *La bachillera* (1916), and a one-act comedy, *El amor es triunfo*, first performed in Alajuela in 1917. But the greatest contribution of Sánchez Bonilla to the serious Costa Rican stage was his dramatization of *El pobre manco*. This outstanding tragedy deserves to be published.

In 1921, the centenary of Costa Rican independence, there was enough literary activity to cause critics to speak of the "generation of '21." One member was Alfredo Saborío Montenegro, whose two historical dramas, *Santa María* and *Auto místico de la Virgen de los Angeles*, were written and performed at this time, though neither was published till 1942.

Shielded by the pen name of "Juan Calvani," José Fernández

Morúa launched the amusing one-act *Lo que no sucede*. Ricardo Jinesta (1891–   ) published his two-act drama, *La mueca del destino*.

For children, and she was the first in her country to devote herself to this branch of drama, María del Rosario Ulloa Zamora (1901–1935) wrote and published two volumes: *Dramatizaciones infantiles* (1925) and *Teatro infantil moderno* (1928). Rewarded by a scholarship to the United States, she remained there till 1932, then returned to devote the last few years of her brief life to this field. Assisting her in her efforts was a judge of the Supreme Court, Victor Manuel Elizondo, who not only wrote children's stories but published a volume of plays for children under the title *El granuja y otros dramas y comedias* (1936).

Since then, only one name has achieved prominence in Costa Rican drama: "Marizancene"—a pen name that covers the identity of Hector Alfredo Castro Fernández, conscious dramatist. As Garnier was indebted to Italy, Castro Fernández reveals the influence of Proust and of French existentialists. In fact, many of his plays were originally written in French and put into Spanish by other hands. The first of his plays to be published was *Pounette* (1937), about a dramatist and his jealous mistress. *Un soir, ce soir, El espíritu de rebeldía* (translated by Fernández Callejas), and *La horma de su zapato* (put into Spanish by Chacón Trejos), appeared together under the French title *Théâtre* (San José, 1938). In one, Andrés tries to arouse the "spirit of rebellion" in the laboring masses, with the result that Clara, the consumptive whom he loves, and her prostitute roommate are both killed by the laboring masses. *La horma*, by contrast, is a farce: Alfonso, the doctor's servant, masquerades as the doctor to give physical examinations to two girls, but the doctor returns and takes over the treatment.

Le vitrail (1937), also originally written in French, deals with the psychoanalysis of the sick soul of a jealous wife who destroys her artist husband's masterpiece. The disillusioned artist has no future except in commercial art, painting bouillon cubes. *Fragata Bar* presents a woman of the French Resistance who, driven mad, takes revenge on an innocent person.

Another play by Marizancene in that frenzied publication period of 1937–1938 was his only departure (and then only partial) from the French scene: *L'Ameró*, from the name given in Argentina to an Indian wet nurse. Sixty-year-old Tonton, married to the charmer Henriette, selects an attractive lad to father his son, and confesses as much to the guests at the christening.

With the most productive of Costa Rican dramatists setting their plays in Europe, the future national theatre lies in the hands of a few occasional authors.[10] Carlos Orozco Castro has written three excellent dramas. *Río de sangre* was performed in 1933 by María Tereza Montoya, but like his other two excellent plays, "Ya no iré a tu casa" and "El embrujo de la tierra," it remains unpublished.

Alberto Cañas, writer and outstanding critic, is also author of three good plays: *Don Juan pusilánime, Hay que besar a la niña,* and *Donde termina la calle.* Other dramatists waiting for recognition include José Neri Murillo, Eduardo Chavarría, and Alfredo Mata. Ricardo Jiménez Alpízar whose *Alacrán* (1934) was ruined by its actors, is also mentioned as critics' choice should the theatre ever really go looking for dramatists. Victoria Urbano had to take her *Hija de Charles Green* to Madrid, where it was successfully performed in 1945.[11] And along more modern lines, Alfredo Sancho attempted a surrealist drama, *Débora,* based on the Bible story, and supposedly published somewhere.[12] Castro Fernández tried to produce a thoroughly national movie by filming his script of Garnier's *El retorno,* but lack of financial returns discouraged further attempts.

And so, slow in starting, Costa Rica is still far from achieving her national drama.

---

[10] Ulloa Zamora, "Panorama literario," *Panoramas das literaturas das Américas,* III, 978, lists some of them.

[11] Agustín del Saz, "El teatro hispano-americano del siglo XIX," *Historia general de las literaturas hispanicas,* IV, 440; Armando de Maria y Campos, "El teatro nacional de Costa Rica," *Hemisferio* (June, 1944), pp. 25 ff.

[12] *Ibid.*

CHAPTER 27

Nicaraguan Drama

The theatre of Nicaragua began with folklore in *El baile de Güe-güence*,[1] which blended Spanish and Nahuatl Indian currents, and took its name from *huehue*, which is Nahuatl for "old man." The hero is a sort of Nicaraguan Till Eulenspiegel with a name, Macho Ratón, that makes him as an early "Mickey Mouse."

Combining ballet and dialog, the performance starts with the dance of the old man and his sons. The governor arrives, and after the exchange of some wisecracks about mules and girls, his daughter is betrothed to one of the sons, with an exchange of wine. This rather pointless play combining Indian legends with a satire against the Spanish system of taxation existed long before it was written down and modernized. Arrom cites, as proof of its antiquity, the mention of such coins as doubloons and maravedis, the ancient dances interspersed in the play, and the many obsolete words, Spanish as well as Aztec, in the speeches. In its repetition of dialog it harks back to the Indian technique of *Rabinal Achí*.[2] The humor of the play lies in puns, and in the horseplay of the old man. The first scholar to set it down reported that it had been frequently performed since at least the sixteenth century.

The setting for this play was the first region of Central America seen by white men, where Columbus, during his fourth voyage, sought safety from a storm on September 12, 1502, at a place he called Cape Thank God. And folklore drama has been part of Nicaragua's cultural life ever since. In fact, till recently, other kinds of plays have been largely lacking.[3]

The printing press, first brought to Managua in 1835 by José Ze-

---

[1] Marshall Elliott, "El baile de Güegüence," *American Journal of Philosophy*, V (1884), 50 ff.

[2] José Juan Arrom, *El teatro de Hispanoamérica en la época colonial*, pp. 117–118.

[3] Pablo Antonio Cuadra (ed.), *Tres obras de teatro nuevo*. See especially "Breve nota sobre el teatro nicaragüense," p. 218.

peda, president of Nicaragua and founder of its first newspaper, *El telégrafo nicaragüense*,[4] has been a great boon to poets and dramatists, permitting them to earn a living as journalists while devoting their free hours to literature.

Citizens of neighboring nations have helped develop the national drama. Not only have traveling companies of actors performed local plays, but the dramatist Alejandro Angulo y Guridi (1826–1906), born in Cuba of Dominican parents, spent the last years of his life writing in Nicaragua. Francisco Gavidia (1864–1955), Salvadoran dramatist, collaborated with Nicaragua's Román Mayorga Rivas in *El misterio de un hogar* before Mayorga embarked on his own career as author of humorous plays.

There was reciprocity, too. Feliciano Gómez H. was an exile in El Salvador when he wrote the two-act, bitter political satire *No es el león como lo pintan*, and Francisco Quiñones Sunzín, mentioned by Leguizamón, did most of his writing outside his native Nicaragua.[5]

Nicaragua really achieved its literary majority with the advent of Rubén Darío (1867–1916). Darío's career as a modernist poet is, in general, alien to this study, but he did twice attempt the theatre. Once was with a comic one-act play in verse, *Cada oveja . . .*, performed in Managua on April 1, 1896, by the Spanish company of José Blen. A little later he tried again with *Manuel Acuña*, in which one poet interpreted the tragedy of another. According to newspaper reports it was successfully performed. Unfortunately, both plays have completely disappeared.

Ten years pass before there is a record of the next local play, a three-act romantic drama, *Ocaso*, by Santiago Argüello (1871–1940), "estrenado en el Teatro Municipal de León con éxito extraordinario," according to the printed version (León, 1906). Its author was one of the best poets of Central America and a friend of the slightly older Darío. At least the tragedy was liked well enough to be repeated several times, though each announcement of a performance brought argument between the religiously inclined people and those who believed that religion and conservatism ought not to sway literary criticism. The plot deals with a frivolous and unfaithful wife—a universal theme—even though the characters are representative

[4] Juan Felipe Toruño, "Sucinta reseña de las letras nicaragüenses," *Panorama das literaturas das Américas*, III, 1095 ff.

[5] Julio A. Leguizamón, *Historia de la literatura hispanoamericana*, II, 186.

Nicaraguans. Unfortunately its performance did not encourage Argüello to follow a dramatic career. His poetry, and later his philosophy and essays, occupied his attention.

A brother, Solon Argüello (1880–1922) also ventured into the theatre as a writer of children's plays, and two of his works are preserved: *La venganza del héroe* and *La toma de Churubusco*. They have only a local interest.

Next milestone along the course of Nicaraguan drama is the 1919 performance of *La rifa*, by Anselmo Fletes Bolaños. The printed version (Managua, 1919) of this present-day political comedy in two acts boasts it was "representado con extraordinario éxito en todos los teatros sociales, morales, y políticos de la gran patria." It is a story about a man who used patriotism as a screen for crooked dealing.

With such a start, one might expect a succession of comedies by this writer of biting satires, but for the rest of his life, though he wrote witty poetry and prose under the pen name of "Gil Blas" and even founded a magazine with this title, for him the stage had no further attraction.

The twenties saw a minor flurry in the Nicaraguan theatre. Marcial Ríos Jerez (1897–   ) wrote several romantic dramas, like *Marta* and *El triunfo de la inocencia*, in which love and virtue conquer materialism; and Manuel Tijerino and Belisario Salinas collaborated in a couple of zarzuelas, with music by Jesús Sequiera. They were *Junto a la clara fuente* and *El debut*.

This period also saw the early efforts of the most active and prolific of Nicaragua's writers, Hernán Robleto (1893–   ). Besides a succession of novels, some about the jungles, and two anti-American yarns, he began playwriting in 1918 with *La rosa del paraíso* (Managua, 1920), his most frequently performed comedy of customs. During the next twenty years, while working on a Mexican newspaper, he completed fifteen plays. Though he was not experimental in the modern sense, Robleto knew enough about world drama to use modern technique against a local background. His dramatic comedy *El vendaval* won the Central American Theatre Contest in Guatemala in 1925. His earlier *El milagro*, a religious drama, was performed and published in Tegucigalpa, Honduras, in 1922, and one of his popular comedies, *La señorita que arrojó el antifaz*, found a publisher in Mexico in 1928. Others were performed in Nicaragua by Paco García and other actors enlisted by the playwright in an attempt to stimulate the national theatre. His published volume, *Tres dramas nicaragüenses* (1948), contains *Muñecos del barro* (1938), *La cruz de ceniza* (1939), and *La niña Soledad,* not performed till 1953.

By contrast, the plays of Manuel Rosales, *Alegría dolorosa* and *Un posible,* were given their premières by visiting troupes before Adán Castillo of Nicaragua put them in his repertory for frequent performances.

In 1928 the magazine *Vanguardia* was founded, and began to influence all phases of literature. A group of amateur actors, borrowing that name, combined in 1935 to restore the national theatre, using local problems and vernacular language, especially folk poetry. They were responsible for a number of plays performed and published about then. Little theatres springing up also encouraged the writing of plays. The social critic Pablo Antonio Cuadra (1912–   ), the other active and important figure in Nicaragua's drama, followed the performance of his earliest plays by Vanguardia with the founding of El Teatro Lope in Granada, where some of his other plays had their try-outs.

Among the better-known works of Cuadra, written between 1935 and 1953 and given their first showings largely in Granada, are: *El árbol seco* (1938); *Satanás entra en escena* (1938), a religious mystery; a Christmas *Pastorela* (1939); *El que parpadea pierde* (1942), a one-act dramatization of a Mexican story; *La cegua,* prepared in Spain as a movie; and *Máscaras exige la vida,* a three-act comedy produced in Managua in 1952. *Por los caminos van los campesinos,* the only one published,[6] was written in 1937, "for strolling players on street corners, to carry a message of rebellion against the routine politics imposed by governments and revolutions."

The Nicaraguan actor Adán Castillo portrayed the character of fatalistic old Sebastiano, accustomed to bad luck but proud and jealous. The play has been produced in all parts of Central America. The villain of the piece is the lawyer Fausto Montes, whose first name was chosen to symbolize his Devilish connections. Lieutenant Comfort of the U.S. Marines is another character in this play, which is set during the *intervención* of the 1920's. The most important "personage," however, is the nomadic thatched cabin of Sebastiano whose

[6] Cuadra (ed.), *Tres obras.* Other examples of Nicaraguan drama were reprinted in *Revista de America* (Mexico: Instituto Panamericano de Geografía e Historia), No. 23, June, 1947.

land is stolen through trickery. This powerful and thoroughly national play is made universal in its expression of the bitterness and hopes of simple people. It points out the misery war and injustice bring to the landless and impoverished lower class, but its ending heralds the approach of a New Day. In its six characters and single situation, Cuadra tries to epitomize most of the problems of his country.

Contemporary with this play, and also published in the *Tres obras*, is a collaboration, *Chinfonía burguesa*, by two literary men who studied abroad. Joaquín Pasos (1915–1947) was educated in France, and José Coronel Urtrecho (1906–) lived in the United States long enough to interest himself in the theatre and want to help with the Teatro Experimental Lope. In their play the two tried to follow the example of García Lorca and mold the burlesque popular poetry of their country into what they called the *género chinfónico*. The prototype, *Chinfonía burguesa*, began as a poem in 1932, and was then dramatized as a farce in 1939, and published in the magazine *Centro*, as a "comedia bufa basada en rimas populares," like Lorca's *Pájara pinta* or *Los amores de don Perrimplín y Belisa en el jardín*. The authors themselves acknowledge that "the plot is completely silly." Among the characters are "Don Chombón, el mismo Don Trombón y Don Bombón," and his fat wife. Inter-riming lines like "como una loca oca cocoroca foca foforoca" suggest Dr. Seuss. And no play can be taken seriously when the character Death declares at the end: "Yo soy la muerte fuerte, sorda y gorda, y los llevo a la tumba, a la zumba marumba."

Both poets have done better and more serious work as members of the Vanguardia poetic movement, but this slight play serves as a reminder that Nicaragua's theatre began with folk legends and was nourished on *logas*, *posadas*, and *pastorelas*, along with the *teatro callejero* and its Bible themes.[7]

Playwriting for children has had other practitioners in Nicaragua since Solon Argüello. A teacher of long experience, Josefa Toledo de Aguerri, published *Personificaciones en la historia de Managua* (1942), and there have been many other children's plays written, but none published.

In 1940 the initials "G. R. N." attached to the political comedy *El*

---

[7] Cuadra, (ed.), *Tres obras*, p. 217. See also Francisco Pérez Estrada, *Teatro folklórico nicaragüense.*

congreso se divierte, published by *La Estrella de Nicaragua,* concealed the identity of the humorist Gonzalo Rivas Novoa. In 1941 *Ya: Magazine Popular Nicaragüense* printed *La novia de Fola,* by Alberto Ordóñez Argüello (1914–), but its author became too busy with politics and travel to follow it up, and finally settled in Guatemala. Enrique Fernández Morales, unable to find an outlet for his *Niña del río,* had to make it known through author's readings.

Francisco Pérez Estrada, working the vein of legends and folklore, published his plays in *Los Cuadernos del Taller San Lucas* (1942–1951), a publication named for a printing shop where the literary people of Managua met, and in *Teatro folklórico nicaragüense* (1946). Later, Manuel Antonio Zepeda appeared as author of the four-act drama *La ley castrillo,* published, undated, in Managua.

Chief among Nicaraguan contemporary dramatists is José de Jesús Martínez (1928–), educated in Mexico, Madrid, and Heidelberg, and at present teaching in Panama. His first dramatic efforts were published in Madrid in 1954: *La mentira, La perrera,* and *La venganza.* For some reason the volume was at once removed from sale. However *La perrera* was performed in Teatro de la Comedia, Madrid, in 1957, and became No. 197 of the Alfil Dramatic Series. His most recent play is the cynical *Caifas,* with a prolog and three acts, performed in Panama in 1961 under the direction of the vanguardist Rogelio Sinán. Caiphas, the high priest, feels that only by developing a general feeling of guilt can a people regain its faith. With Saul's help he arranges that one of the many people with hallucinations will be recognized as the Messiah. The dramatist shows his skill in his tight control over his material.

In this nation of Nicaragua, where *costumbrismo* seems best expressed in poetic plays, Rolando Steiner (1935–) wrote *El ángel extraviado de Judit* (1948; published 1958), about a man who cannot separate dreams and reality. Julián dreams that he has picked up a girl, Judit, but wanting no son by her, he kills her. When dream has become reality, he finds he has strangled his own wife.

So Nicaragua continues to produce two kinds of plays: a fanciful sort, which Broadway producers tend to associate with Latin America —and because of which they refuse to look in that direction for manuscripts—and plays dealing with reality. The hope for a permanent and vital Nicaragua theatre seems to lie in the hands of those who can produce plays of reality based on the nation's folklore.

CHAPTER 28

Drama in Honduras

To Honduras, a nation about the size of Ohio, on the Atlantic side of Central America, goes the honor of Americanizing the European pastoral (*pastorela* in Spanish). The French troubadour Adam de la Halle (c. 1237–1286) took the uncomplicated lives of shepherds as delineated in the third-century-B.C. poetry of Theocritus, and wrote the first comic opera, the witty *Jeu de Robin et de Marion*. Its songs made it a sort of melodrama that antedated Politian's *Orfeo* (c. 1471) and Shakespeare's *As You Like It*.[1] In Honduras the humanist and educator Fray Juan José de la Trinidad Reyes Sevilla (1797–1855), student of the classics at the San Román de León College in Nicaragua, was inspired to introduce this form of drama into the New World in an attempt to correct the social and political vices of his time.[2] This mestizo, who founded the University of Honduras, knew music well enough to compose two masses and more than a dozen songs. He imported the first piano into Honduras, and the first printing press. He is best remembered, however, for his poetry and his nine *pastorelas*. Some, with the slapstick appropriate to the season, are still performed at Christmas, not only in Honduras but in other nations of Central America.[3] However, they do deal with Christian doctrines, though with sugar-coating. Most previous eclogs or dialogs of shepherds had no Christian application, except where Spaniards like Juan del Encina of the fifteenth century added it. It was even largely absent in the Golden Age pastoral plays by Lope de Vega,

---

[1] Walter W. Greg, *Pastoral Poetry and Pastoral Drama*.

[2] M. Menéndez y Pelayo, *Historia de la poesía hispanoamericana*, I, 206, states that Reyes wrote "representaciones dramáticas de Nochebuena," representing a prolongation into the nineteenth century of the fifteenth-century "auto de Navidad." See also Rafael Heliodoro Valle, "Las pastorelas de José Trinidad Reyes," *Universidad*, pp. 23–48; and Agustín del Saz, "El teatro hispanoamericano del siglo XIX," *Historia general de las literaturas hispánicas*, IV, 440. One *pastorela* reprinted in Alfonso María Landarech, *Honduras Literaria*, III.

[3] Alfonso María Landarech, *Estudios literarios*, p. 205.

Tirso de Molina, and Calderón. Padre José Trinidad Reyes, however, composer of *villancicos*, or Christmas carols, was naturally led to associate shepherds with the visit to Bethlehem and wrote nine "shepherd" *pastorelas* with such titles as *Micol* (his first, composed in 1841), *Elisa, Zelfa, Nebtalia, Rubenia,* and others. Though *Noemi* was written before 1838 and *Olimpia* in 1855, none was printed till eight of them were published in 1905 by Dr. Rómulo E. Durán. The ninth, *Flora o la pastorela del diablo,* was omitted because among the many versions the learned editor could not decide what was the work of the original dramatist, and what had been added by the many later producers. Some satirize politicians, doctors, and bachelors, and present only thinly disguised local people.

Most popular and the one most frequently produced is *Olimpia,*[4] in four acts and ten-syllable verse, written in a village near the capital to which "El Padre Trino" had fled during a revolution. Dedicated to Señorita Borjas, it was performed in Tegucigalpa in 1855, the year of Reyes' death. Then it disappeared for half a century. The words were finally discovered in the author's handwriting in a copybook, but without music. When Dr. Durán began collecting the *pastorelas,* he found some of the old people who remembered enough of the catchy tunes of the nine plays to enable a musician to partially restore them. The other songs were given new settings by local musicians. Of the seven musical numbers in *Olimpia,* only one is by the original author.

Its plot is simple. Olimpia, a shepherdess, has been visiting her patroness, St. Isabella, who sings the first solo. Shepherdesses sing a chorus and a duet, and then Olimpia reports she has heard a prophecy about Christ's birth. Her solo uses the one undoubtedly authentic musical setting. While all the shepherds join in singing the Magnificat, Nicodemo arrives, having learned from an angel of Christ's birth, and the play closes with a farewell song at the door as they leave to worship Him. It is all done in authentic rustic language and good taste. These works of Reyes served as models in many lands for other shepherd plays with music. But he seems to have had few followers in Honduras—none in the early *costumbrista* period. Whatever dramatists used Honduran subjects did it to plug nationalism or for social protest, and their works have been lost.

The Doyle bibliography contains a mention of José M. Tobías

[4] Published in *Revista de Archivo,* June 30, 1936, pp. 707–766.

Rosas, as author of children's plays between 1902 and 1930,[5] but he did more than that. He was writing short plays with a moral purpose. In *Con la vara que midieras* (i.e., "Judge not that ye be not judged") in 1910 he made a plea for tolerance. *Las intrigas de un malvado* was another didactic play. He made a sentimental appeal for pity for the poor schoolteacher in *Los sufrimientos del maestro*. And he was author of *Un mártir de la tolerancia*, described as "without characters and with simple and direct action."[6]

Rivera mentions the *Radio Teatro Infantil* collection by Mercedes Agurcia Membreño and some folk plays by Mary Isabel Rodríguez, published under the title *Fantasías teatrales*, with the comment: "The majority of folklore dramas have not been performed and in general are little known."[7] Indeed the only playwright mentioned in his seventy pages devoted to Honduran literature is Luis Andrés Zúñiga Portillo (1880–   ), friend of Darío and Enrique Gómez Carillo. His only play is *Los conspiradores* (1916), a dramatization of the eternal Central American conflict between conservatives and liberals. It got its recognition in the 1916 Juegos Florales in Guatemala. Its chief flaws, which prevent its receiving the performances it deserves as a fine melodrama, are its traces of the colonial past and its loading of the scales against conservatism.

In the drama pretty Rosario is sought by the son of an aristocratic Spaniard who is plotting the assassination of Morazán. He betrays the girl, but to save her otherwise illegitimate son, Jenero, a country lad and preserver of Morazán's life, gets the young man freed to marry her. This play served on August 15, 1916, to inaugurate the Honduras Teatro Nacional. It was also published, with illustrations, by the Honduras Ministry of Public Education in 1954. Though there have been many volumes of poetry compiled and published in Honduras, few dramas or practitioners of drama have been so honored. Marcos Carias Reyes eulogized the play as a "postmodernistic historical drama with romantic qualities," and he sees social and theatrical ele-

[5] H. Grattan Doyle, *A Tentative Bibliography of the Belles-Lettres of the Republics of Central America*.

[6] Carlos Solórzano, *Teatro latinoamericano del siglo XX*, p. 36. A brief section on the theatre of Honduras also appears in Eliseo Pérez Cadalso, "Panorama de la literatura hondureña," *Universidad de Honduras*, July–August, 1961.

[7] Humberto Rivera Morilla, "Literatura Hondureña en el siglo XX," *Panorama das literaturas das Américas*, II, 673–736.

ments in it, as well as a loud defense of democracy at a period of rapid transition.[8]

A later figure, Jorge Fidel Durón (1902–), diplomat, representative at the United Nations, bibliographer, and rector of the National University, also turned to the stage briefly and wrote *Prisión y fuga de Francisco Morazán* and *Ultimos días de Morazán,* patriotic dramas; but otherwise dramatic life in Honduras has been very dull.

[8] Marcos Carias Reyes, *Hombres de pensamiento,* p. 79. See also Agustín del Saz, "El teatro hispanoamericano del siglo XIX," *Historia general,* IV, 440; and Jorge F. Durón, "Sobre el teatro en Honduras," *Honduras Rotaria,* June, 1958, pp. 12–13.

CHAPTER 29

Drama in El Salvador

Salvador contains no records of the sort of early dramatic performances characteristic of other Latin American regions. Surely there must have been some activity in a colony whose governor from 1585 to 1589 was the celebrated poet from Andalusia, Juan de Mestanza. Perhaps the seven earthquakes and lava flows that destroyed so many of its earliest buildings also destroyed traces of its beginning drama.

The first capital, Cuscatlán, founded in the Bermuda valley in 1525 by a brother of the bloodthirsty conquistador Juan de Alvarado, was transferred in 1539 to its present site in Las Hamacas within sight of an active volcano after the original city had been destroyed by earthquake. The country became the home of many poets, but no playwrights—at least not till close to the time of its independence.

Concerning the first dramatic performance of independence-conscious Salvador, Maria y Campos provides an interesting sidelight.[1] In the elections of 1814 the patriots elected a majority of the officials; so the captain general of Guatemala (of which it was then a part) nullified the result and appointed José María Peinado as mayor, with a corps of volunteers to help him. The patriots decided to capture the mayor and take over, and to provide opportunity, announced the performance of a play, *Más vale tarde que nunca* (1753) by the Spaniard José López de Castro, to be held in the mayor's house as part of the New Year's festivities. Soldiers and some of the patriots were to be the actors. Unfortunately too many people knew the secret. One with a guilty conscience made confession to a priest, who passed the information on to the captain-general. He planned to let the show go on, seize the conspirators, and kill them on the spot, but his plans, too, leaked and the plot was called off. In a stream of orders and threats that increased the number of his enemies, the governor forced attendance at a play the next Sunday. Eventually Spanish control was bloodlessly overthrown in 1822. In

[1] Armando de Maria y Campos, *Entre cómicos de ayer*, pp. 182–185.

El Salvador, as elsewhere in the New World, the theatre played its role in the colonists' struggle for independence.

In the new nation the theatre was at least respected. In *costumbrista* tradition the poet Francisco Gavidia (1863–1955) declared: "The theatre is the exaltation of noble ideas, the keen critic of our customs, the purifying crucible of our language. Create youth for the theatre and perhaps it will find its path now unfortunately lost."[2]

Tradition points to Francisco Díaz (1812–   ) as author of the first dramatic writing of independent Salvador. This poet—again quoting Francisco Gavidia: "El solo popular chico Díaz está sobre nuestros escritores más encumbrados"—fought beside General Morazán in Costa Rica when he was trying to restore the Central American Confederation. After Morazán's execution in 1842, Díaz immortalized him in *La tragedia de Morazán*. But the play encouraged no other would-be playwright, and even "el divino calavera Díaz" never tried drama again.

When Isaac Ruiz Araujo (1850–1881) introduced romantic poetry into El Salvador, romantic drama should have accompanied it, but it failed to arrive, and the honor of bringing the theatre to this smallest of Central American nations belongs to the schoolteacher Francisco E. Galindo (1850–1955). Of Galindo's writing, only his patriotic verses remain, though his three-act poetic drama *Dos flores o sea Rosa y María* is known to have been performed at the Teatro Nacional in 1872 and published in *El correo de Ultramar* (1873). Gavidia was more fortunate.

Gavidia once boasted that it was he who called the attention of his young friend Rubén Darío to the effect of the Alexandrine lines in Hugo's seaside meditation *Stella* (1853), and made him aware of the symbolist poetic movement in France. The humanist Gavidia wrote poetry and destroyed the tradition in Salvador that literature was only a hobby or part-time occupation. But he is also honored not only as the forerunner of the modern Salvador theatre, but as a generous contributor to its repertory.

When he was only twenty, his political drama *Deuda antigua* was published in *La Juventud* (1883). Ten years later he wrote *Ursino de Orbaneja o Capitán Partideño*, an example of symbolism in five acts, which for a long time was thought lost, since it was not included in

[2] Luis Gallegos Valdés, "Panorama de la literatura salvadoreña," *Panorama das literaturas das Américas*, II, 547 and *passim*.

his collected works (1913–1918). It was finally recovered and published.[3] On one occasion, while discussing the purpose of the plays he had written, Gavidia explained that in *Ursino* he was trying to stress the need of agreement among the social classes by showing what happened when there was no accord.[4] At the same time he provided in it a picture of the period before Central American independence. No one knows why he omitted it from the rest of his writing.

In the play the wellborn Ursino steals the wife of Partideño, who then gathers a gang of bandits to seek revenge and kills some of the aristocrats. Ursino enters a Franciscan monastery, where he becomes an evil and avaricious prior. With identity papers of a captured *visitador*, Partideño gets into the monastery and justice is achieved, even if verisimilitude has to be distorted in the process. The bandit of the play was an actual person of the time of Ferdinand VII and figured in other plays.

In 1894 Gavidia published the three-act drama *Lucía Lazo o Los piratas*, which marked the dramatist as part of what might be considered a second wave of romanticism in the Latin American theatre. Two pirate ships capture a Spanish galleon carrying the new governor to El Salvador. The plot is logical and dramatic, with a love story enlivened by the antics of Parola, a typical Golden Age *gracioso*.

Symbolism came back into Gavidia's theatre with the four-act drama *Jupiter esclavo o Blanca Celis* (1895), in which he stressed education aimed at good citizenship. Some see in the Negro slave Jupiter the personification of the people, and think his love for the aristocratic Blanca Celis represents the quest for liberty. When the Negro's suit is refused, after the triumph of the revolution, he kills Blanca's father and himself, and the play ends with the exclamation by the patriot leader P. Delgado: "Una vez más el esclavo ha dado muerte al libertador. Por dicha no es posible herir la libertad." The play was performed posthumously in 1955 in Gavidia's honor, as his best play.

The symbolic *La princesa Citalá*, in three parts, is also based on a

---

[3] Francisco E. Gavidia, *Ursino de Orbaneja*, in *Revista del Ministerio de Cultura*, July, 1946, pp. 67–109.

[4] *Ibid.*, "Discurso del poeta Francisco Gavidia en la coronación del Hijo Predilecto de San Miguel," in *Boletín de la Academia Salvadoreña*, August, 1940, p. 111.

national theme, the conquest by Alvarado. Young Atlacatl fights back the white invaders, meets Alvarado in battle, and loses his shield of the Golden Sun. The Princess Citalá ("Star"), to recover the Sun and kill the conqueror of her tribe, steals into the Spanish camp, but is so moved by the beauty of the Church service which she witnesses that she is deterred from assassinating the Spanish leader.

The rest of Gavidia's dramatic compositions do not rise to the same level of excellence. *Amor e interés*, which its author calls "a lyric comedy in the style of Terence," was inspired by an election riot in which one of the candidates was killed. The brief tragedy, *La princesa Cavek*, takes place in a Mayan palace in Cuscatlán. *Ramona* and and its sequel, *La torre de marfil*, published without a date, were written against a background of conflict between the Herrera and Almendárez parties, to underscore the weakness of democracy and, as the author declared, to protest the use of the resources of science for warfare and destruction.

Also from the pen of this teacher and originator of the short story in Salvador, after whom a theatre in his native San Miguel was named in 1939, are *Héspero* (1931), "auto sacramental a la moderna," a translation of the one act of Molière's *Misanthrope,* prepared "to accustom the young to the productions of genius and to attract our youth to the studies of great masters"; and *Velásquez,* a reworking of a play by Goethe. He also wrote *Cuento de Marino* (1947) a kind of Erl-king dramatic poem of the colonial times when Alvarado was about to leave Acajutla for the conquest of Peru. The adventurers are gone so long that when they get back the citizens believe them ghosts.

Gavidia's plays might have been more frequently performed had not their large casts and frequent changes of scene made them so costly to mount.[5] His country honored him by publishing some of his poems and plays in quarto in 1913. A government edition of his complete works was begun in 1958.

For a while after Gavidia started writing, the history of Salvador's theatre was little more than a catalog of writers who attempted one or two plays and then turned to some more remunerative form of literature. Among them was Francisco Camprodón, whose *Lola o La flor de un día* had several successful performances.

---

[5] Alfonso María Landarech, *Estudios literarios,* pp. 66–71.

The priest Juan de Dios Saldoval wrote in prose and poetry a half-dozen dramas and two *sainetes*. One, *La puerta del abismo*, three acts in poetry, was published in his birthplace, Santa Ana, in 1895. J. Wenceslao García and José María Gomer collaborated in Salvador's first national zarzuela, *Adela*, performed and published in 1897. For some reason the play *A buena cuenta* by the Mexican Federico Gamboa (1864–1959) is dated "San Salvador, 1907."

Another active participant in the theatre, also from Santa Ana, was Joaquín Emilio Aragón (1887–1938). After recruiting actors for performances in Salvador, he took them in 1908 for a season of performances in Costa Rica. While serving as Salvador consul in Spain, he also wrote plays. In March, 1911, a visiting company including Ricardo Calvo of Spain and Evangelina Adams of Cuba presented his *Los contrabandistas* in San Salvador. Incidentally, it was Miss Adams' son-in-law who established the nation's first dramatic school.

Gavidia greatly admired *Los contrabandistas*, as did Calvo, who praised the dramatic scene of the final suffering of old Leandro. Miss Adams liked her part of Leonor enough to repeat it on her return to Havana. Though simple in plot and marred by the usual long speeches, whose rhymes sometimes dictated their content, it has, according to Gavidia, elevated moral sentiments and charm. Its local color is undeniable: the first act takes place in San Salvador, the second in a volcano, and the final tragedy in a Salvador jail.

A later play, revealing Aragón as a romanticist, was the one-act *La propia vida*, written in three days in 1926. Camilo is a happy-go-lucky character going through life without a plan till he falls in love with his sister-in-law, Angelina. Don Severo, a fat part, was reserved by the author for himself. In 1926 he published *Teatro*, Tomo I, containing *La muñeca rota* and *Los contrabandistas*; two other volumes were promised but never printed. In his last plays Aragón was a vanguardist trying to fit his works into a universal theatre. Eventually he returned to Costa Rica, where he died of cancer.

Another dramatist who crossed the frontier to the benefit of Salvador was José Llerena (1895–1943). Born in Guatemala, he was brought to San Salvador at the age of three. He decided to become a dentist, and was later made head of the National Dental School, but he also found time for drama. Llerena represents the advent of realism in the theatre, but in his early plays he demonstrated little concept of technique and tended toward moralizing.

His *La negación de la naturaleza* was performed in Teatro Colón in 1921, and published the following year. His *Teatro I* (1924) contains *El corazón de los hombres* and *Los tatuados*. His *Los vehículos* was produced in 1925. Virginia Fábregas, a visiting actress from Mexico, added one of his plays to her repertory, and Mercedes Navarro starred in his realistic comedy *Nuestra sombra*. Critics of his four-act "simbolismo escénico" *Raza nueva*, an attack on the customs of the middle class, declared it would have had more bite if written in prose, but admitted that Doña Frívola has some excellent scenes, especially where she turns down her four suitors—doctor, soldier, lawyer, and social butterfly—because they come courting with only selfish interest. The social criticism is found chiefly in the speeches of Inconsciente.

Llerena's obsession was fear of increasing North American influence. He fought the standardization of life, and though he did write *Aguilas civilizadas* for the movies, he felt they were a form of art likely to stultify cultural development. Therefore, though living in an impoverished country where movies were the cheapest entertainment, he vainly fought for a living theatre. The movie scenario was actually an attack on Yankee political and social conquest of Central America. *Amanecer de noche* was one of his final plays. All of them were characterized by good moral principles, patriotism, and spontaneity, even if they were not always well-organized. El Salvador was also indebted to Llerena for the establishment in 1927 of Escuela de Prácticas Escénicas, in cooperation with Gerardo Neva, head of a company of actors, who stayed in Salvador to make his home after the company went broke there.

Contemporary with Llerena was Raúl Contreras (1896–) who is remembered less for his unpublished "Cagliostro" than for his dramatization of Rubén Darío's famous *sonatina* beginning "*La princesa está triste*." Contreras published it in Madrid in 1925 under the title *Sonatina*, with a foreword by the Spanish critic Julio Cejador.

It has three acts and seven *glosas*, each with a subtitle. The princess is bored. Neither her jewels nor the gold from her father pleases her. The court dancers and jugglers leave her cold. That night her fairy godmother visits her to say she is a caged bird who should be set free, and they start out on a visit to the world, whose woes make her a woman. *La princesa está triste* is a poetic fantasy, but interesting as the tribute of one Central American to another.

Gallegos Valdés mentions several other dramatists whose work has not been published and whose reputation has hardly passed the frontiers of Salvador.[6] They include José María Méndez, humorist, author of sketches, a novel, and the play *Este era un rey*, published in *Cultura*; and César Virgilio Miranda, a member of the Salvador Academy who wrote "una obrita de teatro."

General José María Peralto Lagos (1873–1944), the first Latin American to graduate from a military academy in Spain, who also held a diploma in engineering, interrupted his career as a humorous *costumbrista* under the pen name of "T. P. Machin" to write the political comedy *Candidato* (1931), in three acts and an epilog, performed in 1932 by María Tereza Montoya. It is more a series of local-color bits than a plotted play, as he introduces many types from various social classes in describing a "free election." In his preface, Peralto hints that real people are hidden under the disguises and that the play was suggested by the ridiculous farce of the election of President Araújo. Thus it is truly regional, not only in its spirit but in its colloquial language. However, Peralto must have felt that his gifts lay along other lines, for in spite of his confessed ambition to dramatize the "tragicomedy of life," he did not try again.[7]

Later, Dr. Alberto Rivas Bonilla (1891–   ) who, though trained in medicine, had spent his life teaching and writing short stories, branched into playwriting with two feminist comedies, both of which have been performed but not published. They are *Una chica moderna* (1945) and *Celia en vacaciones* (1947).

Salvador has the usual difficulty in finding actors, but it can boast an unusual drama group, numbering nearly a hundred members from sixteen nationalities who for fifteen years have been meeting once a week to read plays in English. Actors from the group perform four plays a year publicly. *Othello* recently ran a whole week in a theatre of four hundred seats. For plays in Spanish, authors must usually depend on university groups or visiting companies. However, one hope is Darío Cossier, who directs the Comedia Salvadoreña–Centro–Americana, and there are occasional performances in the Teatro Nacional Francisco Gavidia.

    [6] Gallegos Valdés, "Panorama de la literatura salvadoreña," *Panorama das literaturas das Américas*, II.
    [7] Landarech, *Estudios literarios*, pp. 109–111; Edmundo Barbero, "El teatro en el Salvador," *Cultura*, No. 3 (May, 1955), 33–40.

Some dramatists persist. *La cadena*, by the great short-story writer "Salarrué" (Salvador Salazar Arrué, 1899–   ) was performed to an audience enthusiastic, perhaps because of the reputation of its author rather than for the dramatic qualities of the drama, though it does have literary appeal.

In the newer generation appear the names of Dr. Ernesto Arrieta Yúdice and Roberto Suárez Fiallos. Another whose successes in competition make him sound promising is Waldo Chávez Velasco (1922–   ), the most polished of the "Grupo Octubre" poets, which came into being in 1950. In 1957 his optimistic *Fábrica de sueños* won second prize in the Juegos Florales Agostinos, and his *La ventana* was similarly honored in another contest. *Un poco de silencio en la tormenta* got honorable mention in the 1958 Juegos, as did his *Ruth de Moab* in the Cuarto Certamen Nacional de Cultura. Several critics criticized the judges of all these contests for penalizing plays that failed to follow the traditional theatrical pattern. The critics called Chávez the best Salvador dramatist today. Lack of publication prevents the world from judging his real ability.

Now, however, the Salvador Ministry of Culture is trying to let the world know about its theatre by a series of printed plays. Appropriately it began with *El paraíso de los imprudentes* (1956) by the Salvador dramatist best known outside his country, Walter Béneke (1928–   ), once the country's ambassador to Germany. It is an existialist play with nothing local about it, being set in postwar Paris amid an aimless "generación sin sentido," and with a pentagon, rather than a triangle, of love. Though without much drama, it presents a frightening picture of modern youth.

Béneke's next play, with the English title *Funeral Home* (1958), is set in the United States on Christmas Eve. It is already rated as one of the good Latin American plays. In poetic language and existentialist tone, it presents a widow watching beside the body of her husband as the undertaker celebrates Christmas Eve. A stranger, who has killed his wife, comes seeking shelter. The murderer comes to believe the widow knows of his crime, and kills himself at midnight, at the birth of Christ. The play has art and drama with an impact felt even when it is read.

Juan Guzmán Cruchaga, though born in Santiago, Chile, in 1895, is also for some reason represented in this Salvador Ministry of Culture series, with *María Cenicienta*.

Roberto Arturo Menéndez was first recognized in Guatemala, where his *Los desplazados* won the "Fifteenth of September Contest." He is represented in the Salvador series by *La ira del cordero* (1959). Having studied Chekhov and some of the modern North American playwrights, he combined the Biblical breaking of the Fourth Seal with the Cain and Abel theme. He lays on Adam and Eve the blame for the slaying of Abel. Unfortunately the inexperience of the dramatist somewhat dulls the incisiveness of his tragedy, but he will bear watching.

Even though there are no masterpieces yet in the series, publication will provide hope for Salvador dramatists and perhaps will stimulate drama in this smallest but most densely populated of Central American nations.

CHAPTER 30

Drama in Guatemala

Guatemala, the northernmost nation of Central America, with an area and a population about equal to those of Louisiana, was explored and settled by Pedro de Alvarado in 1524. One explanation of its name is "stomach ache," allegedly bestowed by some Spaniard, sick from a sulphur-filled stream polluted by one of Guatemala's score of volcanoes. Its present capital, the largest city of Central America, is the result of the fourth attempt to establish a settlement after three earlier ones were shaken down by earthquakes.

Guatemala's original Quiché (or Kiché) Indian inhabitants represented a high cultural level, and they defended their territory so bravely that the conquistadors called it the "Land of War" till Padre de las Casas, put in charge in 1536, made it the "Land of True Peace." Here was the locale of what is generally considered the only surviving pre-Columbian drama, *Rabinal Achí*, discussed in Chapter 1. The ancestors of those Indians treated by Alvarado with such cold-blooded cruelty, had also composed *Popol Vuh* (or Buj), a story describing the creation of the earth and the life history of its earliest inhabitants, a work of literature comparable to the Bible or the Koran.

The early Spaniards in their turn contributed to the existing culture. Bernal Díaz del Castillo retired here to set down his recollections of the conquest of Mexico. And the region became the administrative center of the captaincy general of Guatemala, composed of the five present Central American republics and the Mexican state of Chiapas.

One of Guatemala's early visitors was Padre Thomas Gage, who arrived from Spain about 1635 and reported on the state of its culture in *The English American; His Travail by Sea and Land* (1648).[1]

---

[1] Reprinted in Broadway Travelers Series (London, 1928), and discussed in Harvey L. Johnson, "Noticias dadas por Tomas Gage," *Revista Iberoamericana*, VIII, No. 16 (November, 1944), 257–267.

After commenting on shows he had seen in Mexico, Padre Gage described a festival in Chimaltenango, July 26, comprised of bullfights, horse races and "representaciones de piezas dramáticas . . . hechas por los indios del pueblo," sponsored by its wealthy Indian inhabitants.[2] Centuries later, Oliver La Farge described the same sort of Indian pageantry and dances, witnessed by him on April 12 and 13, 1927.[3]

Padre Gage commented on the many religious festivals in the capital itself, accompanied by plays, such as a cradle scene and dramatic spectacles of the crucifixion of St. Peter, and that ever popular theme on the early American stage, the beheading of John the Baptist. The English priest described in detail the cardboard head of John, the costumes, the music, and the dance that formed part of the spectacle.[4]

There must have been continued dramatic activity in Guatemala. Another priest, Fray Antonio de Molina, described in his memoirs an episode of February, 1640, involving two Mexican actresses, Teresa and Catalina, who were performing in Guatemala.[5] The alcalde, Ignacio de Guzmán, had become friendly with "Cata," the prettier one, to the rage of the ladies' Mexican sweethearts, Sebastián Pérez and Diego Ximenes, who had come to Guatemala after them. The Mexicans decided to inflict a few scars on the Alcalde. Unfortunately his wounds proved fatal, and all four of them were imprisoned and condemned to death. At the very time Pérez and Ximenes were being hanged, the uninterested Cata was reading a playscript. Because of her beauty she was finally pardoned and exiled; but the good Padre recalled that she was soon back in Guatemala performing, and that he had seen her.

In 1660 Fray Payo Enríquez de Rivera brought a printing press from Mexico. In 1667 the Royal and Pontifical University of San Marcos de Borromeo was established by royal *cédula*, and the religious theatre was cultivated.[6] Fairly early came a type of religious play

[2] Thomas Gage, *The English American*, p. 117.

[3] Oliver La Farge, *The Year Bearer's People*, p. 100; S. K. Lothrop, "Further Notes on Indian Ceremonies in Guatemala," *Indian Notes*, VI (1929), 2–5.

[4] Gage, *The English American*, pp. 154–156; Johnson, "Noticias," *Revista Iberoamericana*, VIII, No. 16 (November, 1944), 264.

[5] Fray Antonio de Molina, *Antigua Guatemala, 1677–1678*, pp. 28–30; Harvey L. Johnson, "Nuevos datos sobre el teatro en la ciudad de Guatemala, 1789–1820," *Revista Iberoamericana*, XVI, No. 32(January, 1951), 352–353.

[6] Otto-Raúl González, "Panorama de la literatura guatemalteca," *Panorama das literaturas das Américas*, III, 1021.

unique to Guatemala called *Loas del diablo,* in which the Devil, with firecrackers exploding about his head, came tempting the Christians. When they were just about to succumb, the Virgin Mary would appear and save them. This long-lived type of noisy dramatic entertainment can be seen there occasionally even today.

Salazar dates the beginnings of Guatemala's theatre from the end of the eighteenth century, in connection with the rise in status of the chapel of Antigua to a metropolitan church.[7] As part of the celebration six plays were presented. The students of Tridentino performed *San Francisco de Paula.* Other groups acted in *Afectos de odio y amor* by Calderón, *Acertar donde hay error,* etc.

There were also local contributions to Guatemala's stage, some of which are still preserved, like *Loa del siglo XVIII, Luto y sangre,* and *Santiago de los Caballeros* and which serve to explain why Charles III on June 11, 1765, prohibited all *autos sacramentales.* Away from the supervision of bishops, drama had everywhere deteriorated into slapstick and frequently immoral performances. But that the Church still depended on the theatre for religious instruction is proved by a drama date December 22, 1772, the year before the old capital, Antigua, was practically wiped out by an earthquake. It has been published, with notes by Dr. Johnson.[8]

The preserved copy was made by the Cofradía de Nuestra Señora del Rosario de las Vacas, to accompany its request for a performance on October 22, 1796, a request denied by the commission of Guatemala on the grounds that it would provide an occasion for revelry and robbery. The play, of 1,255 lines in ballad meter, deals with the popular drama theme of the conversion of Saul, an occasion commemorated by the Christian Church.[9] At the bottom of alternate pages is the name "José Aroche," who used to be considered the author, but here he is mentioned as a member of the petitioning society. The play was written twenty-four years earlier.

Its unknown author obviously intended to tell the story of the conversion while blending in such Church doctrines as the Trinity, the Immaculate Conception, and the supreme importance of St. Paul

[7] Ramón A. Salazar, *Historia del desenvolvimiento intelectual de Guatemala,* Chapter XXXIV.

[8] Harvey L. Johnson, "La historia de la combercíón de San Pablo," *Nueva Revista de Filología Hispánica,* IV (1950), 115–160.

[9] For details of early plays about St. Paul as far back as the sixteenth century, see *ibid.,* p. 117, n. 6.

among the apostles, all the while providing entertainment. He managed all three. With Jerusalem at one extreme of the stage and Damascus at the other, action begins with the eager Saul about to set out to annihilate the Christians of Damascus. Their defiance angers Saul, who endures the vision and blindness on his way.

But there is much more to the play. The dramatist has used his imagination to combine the traditions of Spain's plays and the local color of the New World. Though the action is supposed to take place in Palestine, the characters and language are of the Spanish New World. The servant of the messenger, an authentic *gracioso*, is called Zompopo, the Nahuatl name of a big-headed ant; among the Christians he meets a crony, another *gracioso*, Hormiga. Their talk is extremely local. Zompopo borrows phrases from the bull ring to tell what will happen to Nathaniel, the Christian leader, and with typical bravado he boasts that even though there are more Sauls and Romans and Hebrews than the sands of the sea, he will make them quieter than the Negroes of Belize.

By contrast, in this play of contrasts, Ananias and Saul, who proclaims himself a viceroy, employ gongoristic language in their eloquence. And so, Guatemala's earliest preserved play, though simple in plot and with no secondary complications, does have character differentiation and an artistic completeness about it, as well as local color.

The next preserved play, and one long considered the earliest, is *El coliseo*, in three acts published in 1813 as the work of Juan de León, though now generally ascribed to Mariano Rivera Cabezas. It satirizes the Guatemalan aversion to the theatre,[10] and was probably performed in the Oñate Theatre. It makes fun of the attempts of "Archbishop Babilonio" (Arzobispo Casaus y Torres) to prevent the playhouse from being completed. It has no literary value.

Not much is known about the nonreligious theatrical fare in the interim, except for 1789.[11] The previous year Spain had crowned a new king, Charles IV, and since his was the first coronation to be celebrated since the accession of Charles III to the throne in 1759, the loyal colonists of Guatemala, like those all over the Spanish-speaking

---

[10] See Antonio Batres Jáuregui, "Historia del teatro," in *Memorias del antaño*, ed. Manuel Mejía Bárcenas, p. 210; Salazar, *Historia de desenvolvimiento*, pp. 251–253; and David Vela, *Literatura guatemalteca*, I, 306–307.

[11] Molina, *Antigua guatemala*.

world,[12] decided to splurge. Lorenzo María Porras offered to provide three plays for 2,500 pesos, and was willing to let the *cabildo* choose the titles. The deliberate city fathers questioned him about costumes, the number of *entremeses* he would throw in, and many other details. Then, being good Spanish bargainers, they beat down his price and three weeks later offered Porras 2,000 pesos if he would perform Calderón's *El mayor monstruo los celos* and Moreto's *La confusión de un jardín* and *Antíoco y Seleuco*. His reply was that they had delayed so long that it would now cost them 3,000 pesos, and he would have to select whatever plays could be got ready in the brief time left.

Later that same year another impresario, José Guillermo Segura, made a proposition that, to give proper welcome to the new captain general, Bernardo Troncoso Martínez del Rincón, he would perform three plays of popular appeal, and he mentioned three by Moreto: *El desdén con el desdén, Primero es la fineza*, and *Industrias contra fineza*. His terms were that the *cabildo* should provide stage, music, and refreshments, and permit him to accept additional engagements in private homes as a means of paying his actors' salaries.[13]

Their plays from Spain's Golden Age theatre must have been performed on temporary stages, perhaps in the plaza. In 1792 a petition by Juan Pacheco to build a permanent theatre was denied, but in 1793 one was built that cost 8,080 pesos 2 *reales*, and was known as the Coliseo de Camato, after its manager.[14] Probably Governor Troncoso, who ruled Guatemala between 1789 and 1794, sponsored it. At least he wrote to the King in 1794: "Entre las diferentes medidas que he adoptado a fin de suavizar las feroces costumbres de la plebe de esta capital sanguinaria hasta no más y propensa a la embriaguez ha sido proporcionarle un coliseo de dos o tres comedias cada semana."[15] In 1794, a season of eight plays was offered, including *El negro más prodigioso* and *El príncipe tonto*.

The Governor's efforts bore fruit. Dr. Johnson found traces of three

[12] Johnson, "Nuevos datos," *Revista iberoamericana*, XVI (January, 1951), 353.

[13] For the documents covering both these business transactions, see *ibid.*, pp. 355–387.

[14] Salazar, *Historia de desenvolvimiento*, Chapter 34, pp. 248–251; Vela, *Literatura guatemalteca*, I, 303.

[15] Quoted in Batres Jáuregui, "Historia del teatro," in *Memorias del antaño*, p. 208; see also Johnson, "Nuevos datos," *Revista iberoamericana*, XVI (January, 1951), 385.

provisional theatres in Guatemala in 1803: in the Patio del Cabildo y Hermandad de San Juan de Dios, whose renters had to give alms to the Hospital of San Juan de Dios; in the Patio de Gallos, where plays alternated with cockfights; and in the patio of the military head-quarters in the Santa Rosa Plaza.[16] In spite of that profusion, Juan José Núñez had difficulty in 1803 finding a place for his vaudeville troupe, though he was finally allowed to use the Santa Rosa location, contingent upon a six-pesos contribution to the hospital. There he offered circus acts in the afternoon and plays at night, whenever his program did not compete with the cockfights. The plays were mostly *estampas*, amusing scenes of everyday life in local dialect. However, even under such protection, the Patio de Gallos could not make money. It had too much competition. Even though the Camato the-atre had been destroyed by 1818, another provisional theatre had been erected, and besides, there were puppet theatres offering the same plays that the actors from Mexico came to perform. One pup-peteer, Mariano Arriaga, made such a profit on three performances in 1818, for which he charged only a half-*real* admission, that he re-quested permission from the *cabildo* to continue his offerings until the following Lent. He was turned down on the grounds that two other puppeteers had made similar petitions and there wasn't enough business for all three. So only José María Alanes, being the best equipped and with the largest repertory of plays, was licensed to offer his dummies in repertory.

In 1818 Francisco Martínez, manager of the cock pit, petitioned the *cabildo*, which after December 11, 1812, had been given complete charge of licensing, censoring, and keeping order at the perform-ances, for permission to run a season of comedies at his Patio de Ga-llos, to recover some of his losses. He offered to contribute one hun-dred pesos to the hospital. Just before this, however, José Oñate had received permission to build a permanent playhouse, so the council refused the request of Martínez. When he persisted, it sent a commis-sion under the architect Santiago Marqui to inspect the cock pit. The report was most damaging. The doors were too small, the aisles too narrow, and the pillars so weak that a slight earth tremor might easily bring down the roof. Martínez protested the report, claiming that Marqui was prejudiced by virtue of having designed the Oñate the-

---

[16] Johnson, "Nuevos datos," *Revista iberoamericana*, XVI (January, 1951), 345.

atre. Another commission agreed with the owner of the Patio de Gallos, but since the Oñate theatre was almost complete,[17] Martinez' request was still refused. A similar response awaited the petitions of
Cayetano Bedoya, who made his request directly to the captain general in 1820 but was referred, according to arrangements, to the
cabildo. These arrangements lasted as long as the captaincy general
of Guatemala remained a Spanish colony.

Governor Gavino Gainza ended the captaincy general of Guatemala in 1822 when he called a *cabildo abierto,* or town meeting, and
declared for independence. Till 1836 the five regions struggled along
together as the Union of Central American States, but finally Guatemala became independent under a series of dictators who ruled the
overwhelmingly Indian population with its high rate of illiteracy.

Only a few brave souls in the new nation tried to foment a theatre.
The Cuban patriot José Martí, an exile there in 1877, tried to dramatize his concept of America and its love of liberty in a play about the
patriot Morazán, but it was never completed. Martí's mind seemed to
dwell on an original American theatre. While still in Guatemala he
wrote in 1878: "This rich field has not lain fallow, nor is the American
stage bare." He mentioned American plays as forerunners of "a powerful theatre yet unborn, a theatre that will bring fire and warmth, for
it is the destiny of America to vivify and warm everything for the
wearied imagination of Europe." Martí envisioned the American theatre arising from the "rich vein of inspiration which lies almost intact
in the history of the long infancy and harried youth of America."

One of the first to do anything about the vision, and therefore a
pioneer in Guatemala's national theatre, was a woman, Vicenta La-
parra de la Cerda (1834–1905). Her first attempt was a dream, *Angel
caído,* in four acts, written in 1880 but not performed till July 18,
1886, in the Teatro Nacional. The arrival of a company of actors from
Spain caused Señora de la Cerda to revise it hastily into three acts,
with changes in the cast to fit the personnel of the foreign company.
It was published in its original form in 1888. In it, Luisa deserts her
daughter and her husband Alberto to run off with his best friend.
She and her lover get shot. Alberto calls her a "fallen angel," but because of the daughter's tears, forgives her before she dies.

In 1895, Doña Vicenta put another agonizing woman onto the

[17] It was completed and opened in 1819. See Salazar, *Historia de desenvolvimiento,* p. 251.

stage in *Hija maldita*. The "bad daughter" tries to escape the husband of her family's choice. *Los lazos del crimen* (1897) contains more sadness because, to Doña Vicenta, the woman always paid. She created more puppets than real characters, but at least she was a forerunner of Guatemala's female dramatists.

Preceding this lady, however, in getting a play performed about the "harried people of the New World" was Miguel Angel Urrutia (1852–1931), who wrote the poetic tragedy *La expiación* (1884), in four acts. But he ignored Martí's advice to express his nationalism, at least in theme, because he reworked the universal idea of marital fidelity. In this tearjerker, Ernesto learns that his mother is in the garden with his father's best friend, Julian. He kills the fleeing Julian with a shot in the back. Unable to claim self-defense and unwilling to tell the truth, which would shame his mother, Ernesto is condemned to be executed. His mother's eventual confession to the magistrate comes too late. The shots of the firing squad drown her out.

In occasional later recurrences of his ambition to become a dramatist, Urrutia wrote *Un conflicto en el hogar*, performed at the Teatro Nacional in 1903, and a three-act tragedy in prose, *Silencio heroico*, not published till 1924.

To this period also belonged Juan Fermín Aycinena (1838–1898), author of several comedies of customs.[18] He made his theatrical debut in Lima, Peru, where his *El hombre de bien*, a poetic comedy in verse, showing the technique of Hartzenbusch, won the Ateneo de Lima prize in 1887, and was proudly printed in the *Revista* of the Guatemala Academy in December of the next year. Its eight characters are essentially Guatemalan, as is the loss of Uncle Prudencio's coffee crop, destroyed by a hailstorm.

Returning to Guatemala, Aycinena produced several children's plays. *La locura literaria*, written in 1885 but not published till after his prize-winner, pounds home a warning not to try to be a writer unless you possess the gift. *La semilla de bien* (1890), about the orphan Perico brought up by a bandit, points the lesson that he turned out all right because of good seeds sown in his young heart. *Esther* tells the Bible story of Xerxes and Queen Vasti, in three acts; it was later made into a zarzuela. In addition, Aycinena wrote in prose, *Quedarse*

[18] Vela, *Literatura guatemalteca*, II, 204–228.

con los crespos hechos, a *juguete* in two acts about another orphan, and an unnamed *sainete* about women in old Guatemala in the eighteenth century.

Felipe Silva, too, won a brief popularity with a series of Indian plays going back to pre-Columbian times. His three-act, poetic *Hebel o La Virgen de la Isla* takes place in 1480 at the time of the separation of Kachiquel and Tzutujil from Utatlán, under Chief Quicob I. Silva's *Tecun Unan* (1887), about the conquest of Utatlán in 1524, and his two-act *Conquest of Utatlán,* originally published the year of its performance, then reprinted in 1913, complete the sequence.

The Guatemala theatre also owes a debt to the Valle family. Manuel Valle (1861–1913) is known to have written two undramatic dialogs, "Flor del café" and "Del colegio a los quince años"; and two dramas, "Don Pompey de Centellas" and "Las solteronas," though there is no record of their performance or publication. A daughter, the poetess Luz Valle, won the 1920 Juegos Florales in Quetzaltenango with *La revancha,* which was published by the committee. His son, Rafael Valle (1894–1922), published his two-act comedy *El retorno* (1921). Two other plays by him, *Rayo de luz* and *La alegría de producir,* were published posthumously in 1922 by the journalist José Rodríguez Cerna.

The Cernas, too, were connected with Guatemala's theatre. Carlos Rodríguez Cerna, born in El Salvador (1894–   ), published *Mixo: poema dramático en dos cuadros y un prólogo* (1921). And there was Ismael Cerna (1856–1901). According to Vela, if Guatemala ever has a national theatre Ismael Cerna will be regarded as its founder.[19] He lived a romantic life, beset by fate, and his drama expresses that. Autobiographic details can be detected in *Vender la pluma* and especially in *La muerte moral,* both influenced by Echegaray. His greatest play, however, is *La penitenciaria de Guatemala,* "written with blood and fire" while Cerna was a fugitive in El Salvador, and first performed there. Written in verse, it first appeared serially in *La República,* then in book form in 1891.

Another of the family, the diplomat Carlos Girón Cerna, wrote many plays. His *Quiché-Achí* reworked the earlier folkplay *Rabinal Achí.* His *Ixquic* (Cuba, 1935) is a three-act tragedy based on tradition number seven of the *Popol Vuh.* His *Tututicutu* also went back

[19] *Ibid.,* pp. 271–276; see also Agustín del Saz, "El teatro hispanoamericano del siglo XIX," *Historia general de las literaturas hispánicas,* IV, 441.

to the past. Using modern themes, he produced *La fotografía de los signos* and *Al tercer día*, subtitled "una función de teatro en el infierno." It won the 1951 Ministry of Education contest.

Another woman tempted to write for the stage was Trinidad Coronado, whose *Ensayos dramáticos* was published in Antigua in 1893, while her three-act poetic "drama histórico-romántico," *Los héroes de Alcalá*, was printed in Chile in 1897. Later came Mercedes Tejada Milla, author of *Dolor*. Her three-act, prose *Una vida* was performed in Managua's Teatro Variedades, October 9, 1924. It romanticized pure but unlucky Lucía, who slaves to keep her brother in school while she hopes for the return of Juan Luis to marry her. Eventually wealthy Leopoldo comes courting her, and when her hypocritical landlady Dolores drives her from her lodgings, she marries him. Bitter tears permeate all these feminine dramas.

Among the men, several Guatemala writers more proficient in other fields made brief incursions into drama. The poet laureate of Guatemala, Máximo Soto Hall (1871–1944), was the author of *Madre*, performed but unpublished. Rafael Arévalo Martínez (1884–   ), famous for his zoopsychic outlook in *The Man Who Resembled a Horse* and other similar stories, was moved by the abdication of Edward VIII (the Duke of Windsor) to write *Los duques de Endor* (1940), a three-act poetic fantasy about King Guillermo VIII of Terra, who had to choose between the throne and Elena. It contains more good poetry than action, and the author termed it "subjective rather than historic." Sixteen years later, in *El hijo pródigo*, Arévalo told, chiefly in *redondillas*, of the two small children of Juana and Ezequiel who reunite their parents. But Dr. Arévalo decided he was too old to learn a new technique and returned to his poetry, philosophy, and short stories.

However, Guatemala can still claim quantity, if not quality, in its theatre. Adolfo Drago Bracco (1894–   ) started with an ambition to be a surgeon, but, as he confessed, "razones de índole afectiva" turned him into a bookkeeper, with leisure time for the theatre. Beginning with *Entre nieblas* (1918), this writer of high comedy completed more than twenty plays, like *Además del amor* and *Se vende una novia*, all performed. One of his earliest was his charming *Colombina quiere flores* (1928), first performed in Teatro Municipal of Quetzaltenango, Guatemala's second city in size, in December, 1923.

Set in France in the time of the Pompadour, the play employs a clever twist of the *commedia dell' arte* about Colombine's birthday party. In spite of various suggestions, she wants only flowers as presents. This is probably the only Central American play ever performed in an English translation.[20]

In 1928, the year the Guatemala National University was founded, Drago Bracco published several pageants with foreign settings: *En la noche mil y dos*, a farce with a ballet, suggestive of Darío's *Sonatina*, about a sad princess and the arrival of Prince Fairuz; and *La danza de los cerezos en flor*, a tragedy set in a fanciful Japan. His *Se han deshojado en el jardín las rosas*, with prolog and epilog supplied by two other writers, was published in 1938. In few of his plays, however, does he give evidence of his Guatemala nationality.

The same is largely true of Miguel Marsicovétere y Durán (1913–   ), famous as a poet and founder of the Tepeus group among the generation of 1930. He also wrote at least fifteen theatrical fantasies, among them *El evangelio de Odolán, Cada quien con su fantasma, Señorita Dama, La noche sin dioses*, and the best of them, *El espejo roto*. Recently, in a new vein, he published a "grotesque in five cartoons," *El espectro acróbata* (1953). Having finished it, the reader turns the book upside down and starts from the other end with a "tragedy of masks," *La mujer y el robot*, which is practically a science-fiction play, dealing with the last survivor of a cataclysm that has destroyed all the world's inhabitants except one woman and four robots. It is a vast improvement over his "contraposición," *El camino blanco y el camino negro*, published in 1938, in which, according to the stage directions, its two characters, El Amante and La Amante, talk "only when the spectators seem to be getting bored." Then they discuss which path to take into the future. Finally, as the night "howls like a wolf on the prowl," they choose the black path, which is "gentle as an angel," and "illuminated like a star."

Following the overthrow of Dictator Ubico, in 1944, literature in Guatemala, especially fiction, took on new life with Carlos Wyld Ospina, Flavio Herrera and his Green Hell novels, Mario Monteforte Toledo, and the great poet Enrique Gómez Carrillo (1873–1927). Gómez published fifty books in all fields. In 1944, too, the University

[20] See *Poet Lore*, Vol. 56, pp. 144–162.

Theatre was founded under the direction of Carlos and Roberto
Mencos, but there were few authors brave enough to start writing
plays for it. Otto-Raúl González cites them.[21]

One is Carlos Chamier, a political exile, whose plays are not mentioned. José Llerena (1895–1943) might have had plays to contribute
had he not been taken at the age of three to El Salvador. Luis Alberto
Chamier wrote *Mientras camina el reloj*. Others wrote plays for
children. Julio J. Cordero published several in 1914. Daniel Armas
(1897–   ) wrote both for children and adults, and published *Como
los muérdagos y otras obras*. The lawyer, novelist, and great poet
Miguel Angel Asturias (1899–   ) has, at several periods of his life,
turned to the stage. *Fantomimas* was an early attempt. *Soluna* (Buenos Aires, 1955) stems from *Rabinal Achí*: the men of the sun and
the moon—that is, light and shadow, life and death—influence the
people of Guatemala. *La audiencia de los confines* (1957) brings
Padre Bartolomé de las Casas onto the stage. His Indian play *Cucul-
cán* was later imitated as *Kukulkán* (1936) by Valentí Abascal
(1908–   ).[22] Guatemala has produced several dramatists interested
in children's plays. Three of them are Lucila Martínez Sobral, Angel
Ramírez, and Salvador Rodas.

One important contributor to the Latin American theatre whose
Guatemalan birth is not generally known is Carlos Solórzano
(1922–   ). Not only did he compile an anthology of Mexican drama
and write the valuable source book *Teatro latinoamericano del siglo
XX* (Buenos Aires, 1961), but he is also author of seven excellent
plays, written mostly in Mexico. He worked with actors of the National University in Mexico. His combination of poetry and philosophy in *Doña Beatriz la sin ventura* (1953), about the wife of the conquistador Alvarado and her mestizo daughter, and his symbolic and
abstract *El hechicero* (1954)[23] caused the Mexican critic Armando
Maria y Campos to consider Solórzano one of the great dramatists of
America in his calm and courageous presentation of human problems.
Solórzano's plays have simple themes, but both inner and outer
action.

His most recent publication, *Tres actos* (Mexico, 1959), contains

---

[21] González, "Panorama de la literatura guatemalteca," *Panorama das literaturas das Américas*, III, 1055.

[22] *Ibid.*

[23] Performed July 16, 1954, in the Sala del Seguro Social.

three one-act plays. The first, *Los fantoches* (1958), called a "mimo-drama para marionetas," is based on the custom of burning the effigy of Judas during Holy Week, an allegory in the workshop of the maker of these papier-mâché figures. The second, *Cruce de vías*, a "vodevil triste" set at a railroad junction, involves a man looking for an elderly woman who has long been the object of his search, and a train that comes and goes. The play deals with the futility of planning and the blindness of human beings. The final one, *El crucificado* (1958), "farsa trágica en un acto," presents Mexican peasants preparing for a Good Friday observance and a portrayer of Jesus who takes his role too seriously. All these plays are far departures from the traditional offerings of the Latin American stage.

One more important Guatemalan dramatist remains, the realistic *costumbrista* Manuel Galich (1913–   ). In and out of politics, he has been a teacher, Minister of Education, and exile. While teaching, he dramatized great moments of Guatemalan history for the young actors. *El retorno* (1938) was followed by *El señor Gukup-Cakix*, published by the Board of Education in 1939. Based on a chapter of the *Popul Vuh*, it deals with the presentation of new teeth and eyes to Gukup, the Sunbird. Three of Galich's plays which also deal with national history appeared in 1940.[24] *Carta a su Ilustrísima* is set in the early seventeenth century. The head of a convent is censored for her ambitions on account of a letter she has tried to send to the bishop, a letter that really states her unfitness for the position as head of the convent. The other two, *Belem, 1813* and *15 de Septiembre*, dramatize Guatemala's struggle for independence.

Written that same year of 1940 was *El canciller Cadejo*, a protest at loss of liberty under a dictatorship. When refused permission for its performance, the University students published it in their magazine, *Senderos*. The title character, El Cadejo, is like a big woolly dog that insinuates himself into power. El rey Perico, El joven Metusalén, and some legendary Guatemalan figures also appear in what is more propaganda than drama.

That play marked the transition between Galich's plays for students and those concerned with social problems. First in the new vein was the three-act comedy *Papá Natas*, with a surprise ending,

---

[24] Afterward published as *Historia a escena* (Guatemala: Ministerio de Educación, 1949).

performed in the Teatro Palacio, October 26, 1938. Lolo Natas has lost his money through failure of the coffee crop, but his children refuse to readjust, and the father is too spineless to curb their extravagance. Finally, however, Lolo rebels. He goes to the adjoining room. There is the sound of an explosion, but it is only the dropping of a light bulb. Even as a suicide he has bungled. He is only a simpleton, a *papanatas*.

The ending is weak and coincidental, but Galich tried to remedy that with a sequel, *La mugre* (1953), which puts onto the stage crooked politics, labor strikes, and the generally scummy side of a revolution, as the title indicates. As in so many of Galich's plays, wrong eventually triumphs.

Though a teacher, Galich took a dim view of education in his three-act caricature, *M'hijo el bachiller*, first presented on radio in December, 1939. Pedro, the cobbler, has won money in a lottery and can afford to send his son, Angel, to school; but sports and girls take up most of the young man's time. Pedro decides education is useless. He will send his son to the United States for a short course in shoe repairing and then he can advertise that he has a foreign technician in his cobbler shop.

De lo vivo a lo pintado, performed in the Palace Theatre and on the open-air Ministry of Education stage in 1947, also points out the flaws in the educational system, along with the blindness of laws and the injustice toward women in Guatemala just before the 1944 revolution. Eliza, the "good woman," has her many troubles in the clash of reality and imagination of the title. Even more grimness characterizes *Ida y vuelta*, a trilogy picturing the poverty and wars of nineteenth-century Guatemala. It did, however, win for Galich the Central American Drama Competition of 1948.

In 1953 Galich began publishing all his plays, till interrupted by political exile. *Gente decente* and *El tren amarillo* are known only by title. One might guess that, like the others, they present characters who alienate the sympathy of audiences. But at least it can be said of Galich that he has followed the pattern of hopelessness in modern dramas, and if nothing else, he has shaken the theatre of his country out of its rut of nineteenth-century romantic tragedies. In 1961, when Fidel Castro tried to woo the Latin American leftists with a Pan American drama competition, Manuel Galich was awarded the one-thousand–peso first prize for his *El pescado indigesto*, not yet published, but like most of his work, corrosive satire.[25]

A few other dramas and dramatists of Guatemala must be listed, even if dates are unavailable. José Arzú wrote *Diálogo de los bostezos*; Alfredo Garrido Antillón wrote *Nacimiento*; Lorenzo Marrioquín was author of *El doctor Puracé*; and Stalio Spino wrote *Muy siglo XX*. Alberto de la Riva was author of *Un loteriazo en plena crisis*, a farce about the false friends produced by a report of the winning of a lottery. José Arce wrote *El apóstol*; Ligia Bernal, the actress and journalist, ventured into the theatre with *La piedra en el pozo*; and Hugo Carrillo is known for two plays, *La calle del sexo verde* and *El corazón del espantapájaros*. Some of these, though unpublished, are mentioned here on the recommendation of Dr. C. A. Mencos Martínez, director of the Teatro de Arte Universitario of San Carlos University. Like universities elsewhere in the Hemisphere, this three-hundred-year-old institution is laboring to create a theatre-going public and playwrights and actors to entertain and stimulate it.

Others are assisting in the movement. Luis Herrera, an actor whose play *La supra-dama* was performed by the University group and Dr. Mencos in 1953, himself helped found Grupo Artístico de Escenificación Moderna in 1954. In it he directed his play *Quien* in 1961 as part of the sixth anniversary of GADEM. That organization has now branched out with a Little Theatre that produced fourteen plays the first year. And there are other organizations. Domingo Tessier was brought from Teatro Experimental of Chile to found a School of the Theatre in the University's Department of Fine Arts. Héctor Picón and Edmundo Barbeto are also active as directors. Guatemala is taking steps to develop its national theatre.

[25] Manuel Galich, *Obras de teatro*. Contains three plays.

Mexico's Theatre over 375 Years

In 1519 Hernán Cortés landed on the mainland of Mexico and within nine months had reached the capital of the empire of Montezuma. After a temporary setback, he took permanent possession of the city in 1521. In October, 1522, it became the center of the captaincy general of New Spain and the headquarters from which to conquer the rest of Middle America.

That Cortés believed in theatrical entertainment for his men has already been shown by his decision to take a puppeteer along on his expedition to conquer Hibueras in Guatemala (October, 1524). The beginning of that form of entertainment, therefore, can be dated with certainty in the New World. No one can be sure, however, when living actors first performed in Mexico in European-type plays. The first Franciscan priests reached there in 1524 to join the friars who had accompanied Cortés, and since Franciscans leaned heavily on visual education, they probably began at once to present Bible stories in pantomime, with dialog added as soon as they could learn the language of their Indian parishioners. According to García Icazbalceta, the minutes of the Mexican *cabildo* for January 9, 1526, contain references to a showing of the Christmas *Los pastores* in Spanish for the soldiers, and the entry is so worded as to suggest that there had been earlier performances.[1]

Los pastores has had a long history. Brought from Spain, it became acclimatized and was elaborated through the inclusion, as Manuel Cañete pointed out, of parts of *Las pastorelas, Raquel, Stella, Anuncio a Zacarías,* and other older religious plays.[2] For more than four centuries, it has continued to be performed in Mexico and the southwestern United States between the mid-December Fiesta of Our

---

[1] Joaquín García Icazbalceta, "Representaciones en México en el siglo XVI," *Obras,* II, 307–368.

[2] Manuel Cañete, *Teatro español del siglo XVI,* pp. 45 ff.

Lady of Guadalupe and Twelfth Night.[3] Sometimes an all-girl cast has been used, for men were not considered pure enough for so holy a play; but other performances have employed only men, with Gila played by a boy.

"En el portal de Belen" is the opening line of the best-known version of this ancient play.[4]

> In the gates of Bethlehem town
> Shines a glorious brightness. See,
> For it tells Messiah's birth,
> He who'll bring us liberty.

Today as in colonial times the shepherds then troop in, wearing their everyday clothes but with skins over their shoulders to suggest their stage characters and with tinfoil or mirrors on their lunchboxes to glint in the bonfire that is frequently the only illumination for the performance. Gila, wife of lazy Bartolo, is told to rustle up tamales for food on their trip to visit Jesus, of whose birth they have just learned. Lucifer bursts in to prevent their pilgrimage. He explodes firecrackers at the feet of the remonstrating hermit, but is helpless against the sword of the Archangel Michael; so off go the shepherds to Bethlehem.

The conclusion of one published version escapes farce only because of its deep sincerity. The shepherds reach the manger with their gifts: Mexican silverware, Dutch linen, a string of spools from the hermit, a put-and-take top from Cucharón, the youngster, and a lullaby from Bartolo, who has eaten his tamales. Then they remember that they have made no provisions for the care of the sheep they have left behind them; so homeward they go, with shouts of "Goodbye, Aunt Mary!" and "So long, Uncle Joe!"

There are other versions.[5] One discovered in Saltillo, Mexico, and

---

[3] Marcus Bach, "Los pastores," *Theatre Arts*, No. 24 (April, 1940), 283–288. I saw a performance in New Mexico as late as Christmas, 1962.

[4] Translated by M. R. Cole in *Memoirs of American Folklore Society*, IX (1907), and also published separately (Houghton Mifflin, 1907). A translation by Aurora Lucero-White has also been published (Santa Fe Press, 1940).

[5] Francisco Monterde, "Pastorals and Popular Performances: The Drama of Viceregal Mexico," *Theatre Arts Monthly*, No. 22 (1938), 597–602.

called *Cuaderno de pastores para selebrar* [*sic*] *el nacimiento del Niño Dios,* begins:

> Bamos pastores por esas bejas,
> bamos arriando nuestras hobejas.

In it Gila is the virtuous heroine and Bato her simple-minded sweetheart; Bartolo, the villain, is on the side of a host of devils that include Zatanaz, Belsebut, and the symbolic Pecado and Astucia. The devils scorn the idea that any woman could be the means of bringing salvation to the world; yet they are willing to use Gila for the undoing of the hermit. A local touch is the arrival of an Indian from his remote village to beg Jesus for divine help for the local priest and the mayor and for good government for his village.

Modern performances demonstrate how in the course of centuries the *pastorela,* or Christmas story, has developed from a short trope of a couple of lines of dialog in the Church service into an involved religious drama, from a brief question-and-answer in Latin into a poetical play in Spanish, revealing in its misspellings the contributions of many untutored collaborators. From a pageant it has become a sort of operetta. It has been described at length here, not because it was the only religious play in the New World but because it was the forerunner of so many.

Constantino Bayle mentions a performance in Mexico in 1530 of *La conversión de San Pablo.*[6] In some of those religious plays the Indians took the roles. As discussed in Chapter 1 of this book, they had been conditioned to an appreciation of plays through their own forms of dramatic entertainment, and it was not hard to find actors among them. Fray Toribio de Benavente (1499–1568), who took the name of Padre Motolinía ("Poor Man"), after his arrival in Mexico, described such a play, "The Last Judgment," performed in the language of the Nahuatl Indians in 1533, sixteen years after the first priests reached the American mainland and eighty-seven years before the Pilgrims landed in North America. "Fue dada en Santiago Tlatilulco una representación del fin del mundo."[7] It was supposedly written by the Franciscan friar Andrés de Olmos (1491–1571), who had come to

---

[6] Constantine Bayle, "El teatro indígena en America," *Lectura,* LII (June 15, 1946), 219.

[7] See "Historia de los indios de la Nueva España," Tratado I, Capítulo 15; reprinted in Joaquín García Icazbalceta (ed.), *Colección de documentos para la historia de México,* I.

Mexico in 1528 in company with Fray Juan de Zumárraga. This play was probably repeated in 1535 to welcome Mexico's first viceroy, Mendoza, though the later performance may have been the version attributed to Padre de las Casas and published in 1546 by Juan Pablo Lobardo, "primer impresor en esta isigne [*sic*] y leal ciudad de México."

The importance of Corpus Christi in the development of the New World theatre has never been thoroughly studied. This commemoration of the institution of the Holy Sacraments, authorized by Pope Urban IV in 1264, was one of the most important of the Church holy days and intensively and universally observed. The theme of the ceremony was fixed: the power of the body and the blood of Christ. Its symbolic restatement was open to an infinity of variations. Calderón in Spain wrote two Corpus Christi plays a year for forty years, pouring into them the best of his lyric gift. And to a lesser degree the priest in each small town was tempted by the holy day to prove his dramatic ability. In America there were always parishioners to interpret the various roles.

In Tlaxcala, June 24, 1538, in a combined celebration of Corpus Christi and the city's grant of incorporation by Charles V, four plays were planned, though because of the lengthy speechmaking some had to be postponed till Incarnation Day. Padre Motolinía, a spectator and possibly author of at least one of the offerings, described the play about Adam and Eve.[8] In its beautiful setting, near the hospital gate, the spectacle of the expulsion from Eden, according to the historian, left the audience in tears. Actual animals were included in the scenery, among them fourteen parrots so noisy that they occasionally drowned out the actors. Two captive ocelots were tied to trees. Once Eve was careless enough to approach one, but the fierce mountain cat moved out of her way and did not bite her. "This," Motolinía added with what must have been an inward smile, "happened before her fall. If it had occurred afterward, Eve might not have fared so well."

After their success in 1538 the amateur actors were inspired to greater efforts the following year to celebrate the peace between Charles V and Frances I. The Indians of Tlaxcala combined history

---

[8] Quoted by Salvador de Madariaga, *Rise of the Spanish American Empire*, p. 182; see also Padre Motilinía, "Adán y Eva," *Boletín de Estudios de Teatro*, No. 27 (October, 1949), 168.

and religion in *La conquista de Jerusalén por el Emperador Carlos Quinto*. Against a setting of five towers, the Spaniards under Count Benavente and their New World allies—Mexico, Tlaxcala, Cuba, Santo Domingo, and Peru—under Viceroy Mendoza, twice attacked Jerusalem, only to be repulsed. Then they paused and held High Mass. Finally an angel appeared to tell them to attack again, for God had heard their prayers. Under St. James, who appeared miraculously, they moved forward to victory and set fire to the towers. Then the Archangel Michael descended to preach to the defeated Moslems, so effectively, according to the chronicler, that many of the actors clamored to be baptized.

Along with plays in the Indian tongues, performances in Spanish were also being given in Mexico. According to the preface to the Eslava *Coloquios* (Mexico, 1877), in the Actos of the Ayuntamiento for March 27, 1539, appears an order to reimburse Alonso de Avila for "104 gold pesos" spent for "nueve varas de damasco y nueve de tafetán y de paño y una gorra de terciopelo," to costume *La conquista de Rodas*, for the Mexican celebration of that same peace treaty of June 18, 1538.[9]

In spite of their success, gloomy Bishop Zumárraga felt that plays were unfit to honor these occasions. He talked of the "representaciones poco honestas que se hacían en la procesión general de la fiesta de Corpus Christi," and finally banned all religious plays unless they had been censored a month in advance by some high Church dignitary. Till his death in 1548 the conversion of the Indians had to proceed through the ear instead of the eye.

Zumárraga's successors in Mexico reacted in various ways to the idea of permitting masked and bedecked Indians to combine Christian preachment with pagan beliefs. Some even gave awards for participation: on May 18, 1565, the Ecclesiastic Council started the practice of offering a prize of jewelry worth thirty escudos for the best Corpus Christi play. The first recorded winner was Diego Juárez in 1575. At other times the Church fathers forbade the use of Church

---

[9] For details and summaries of many other religious plays, see Antonio Magaña Esquivel and Ruth S. Lamb, *Breve historia del teatro mexicano*, pp. 16–17; and the chapter "El teatro catequístico" in Pedro Angel María Garibay K., *Historia de la literatura Nahuatl*, II, 121–159. The same volume in *Historia*, pp. 28–36, and 131–132, provides the text of the Olmos' "El juicio final." See also J. Luis Trenti Rocamora, *El repertorio de la dramática colonial hispano-americana*, pp. 16–22.

buildings and grounds and the plays had to be performed on platforms before the church door or on street corners. However, for
awhile the city administrators were proud enough of their early history to sponsor a commemorative performance of *Conquista de la
Nueva España* in the plaza every August 13.

In 1572 the Jesuits arrived in Mexico. Better educated than the
other religious orders, they saw the value of the theatre and even
wrote plays in Latin. Juan Sánchez Boquero and Vincencio Lannuci
are supposed to have written "The Triumph of the Saints," in five
acts, as part of a week's celebration in 1578 when religious relics of
martyrs arrived in Mexico from Pope Gregory XIII.[10] Students in the
Jesuit seminary took the roles of Faith, Idolatry, and the Christian
martyrs and their persecutors. Though its contemporaries praised it,
the play is lacking in action and literary quality. It is one of many
Latin plays written then and even into the next century intended for
presentaion but not for permanence.

The first lay dramatist of Mexico was Fernán González de Eslava
(1544?-1601?) about whose life little is known with certainty.[11]
Most scholars believe he came from Andalusia to Mexico in 1567 at
the age of twenty-three. However, from his use of dialectal words in
his fourteenth *Coloquio*, some critics suspect he was Leonese. Mention of a stonecutter by his name on a passenger list for Nicaragua in
1557 induced some investigators to assign his birth to 1534, though
his knowledge of theology seems more extensive than a mere artisan
would possess (he later became a priest). But whatever his birth and
nationality, it is as "the first dramatist in America" that González de
Eslava is important.

Sixteen of Eslava's plays, written between 1567 and 1600, were
published after his death, by the Augustine friar Fernando Bello de
Bustamante, under the title *Coloquios espirituales y sacramentales.*

[10] See Harvey L. Johnson (ed.), *An Edition of "Triunfo de los Santos."*
[11] Joaquín García Icazbalceta (ed.), *Los coloquios espirituales de Eslava,* Intro-
duction; Amado Alonso, "Biografía de Fernán González de Eslava," *Revista de
Filología Hispánica,* II (1940), 213-319; Harvey L. Johnson," The Staging of
Eslava's Coloquios," *Hispanic Review,* VIII (1940), 343-346; Arturo Torres-
Rioseco, "El primer dramaturgo americano," *Hispania,* XXIV (1941), 161-170;
Antonio Pasquariello, "The *Entremés* in 16th-Century Spanish America," *His-
panic American Historical Review,* XXXII, No. 1 (February, 1952), 44-58.
Two of Eslava's *coloquios* are reprinted in José Rojas Garcidueñas (ed.), *El
teatro de Nueva España en el siglo XVI,* pp. 143-179; two others are in Rojas
Garcidueñas (ed.), *Autos y coloquios del siglo XVI.*

They were called "a lo divino," and the printer promised that another collection, "a lo humano," would appear shortly. Beristain mentions the two collections as being printed together in a one-volume edition, but no one else has ever reported seeing them. However, of even the 1610 edition of *Coloquios a lo divino* only two copies have ever turned up; so the other volume could well have been completely lost.

Even Eslava's "divine" plays, however, possess human elements, including broad humor. As Eslava comments in his seventh *Coloquio*, "people's wills are so depraved these days that we must give them sacred matters wrapped in humor like sugar-coated pills," and he similarly explains his use of the *simple*, or comic character: "Sale luego un simple a caza no más de para reír." The *simple*, who was always a servant, represents a stage in the transition between the *bobo* of early Spanish *entremés* and the confidential servant who was to appear in the Golden Age *comedia*.

The language of Eslava's plays is simple and colloquial, with a sprinkling of Mexican-Indian words. For exposition of religious dogma the dramatist uses symbolism and allegory to impress an un-tutored public. All except two plays are in one act; they have uncomplicated plots and are written entirely in verse. And there is enough local color and reference to current matters in them to have landed their author in jail for seventeen days in 1574. His criticism of the viceroy's *alcabala*, sales tax, caused the *audiencia* on December 10, 1574, to pass rules for the better censoring of plays. Linguists and students of sixteenth-century customs find in their realistic treatment much material for study.

In the farcical *Entremés del ahorcado*, the ruffian, fleeing from a bully whom he has struck, begs his friend to save him from revenge by pretending to hang him, but his enemy almost stabs him to death anyway. More *a lo divino* is Eslava's *Coloquio de las siete fuertes*, suggested by seven forts built by Viceroy Enríquez as defense against marauding Indians along the road between Mexico and the mines of Zacatecas. In this Pilgrim's Progress, Mankind (Ser Humano) is guided by State of Grace, who is the commander of Baptism Fort, past the lures of Earthly Flesh and the Devil, to the Mines of Heaven.

On that December 8, 1574, when Eslava's *Coloquio de la consagración del arzobispo Moya de Contreras*, in prose and verse in seven *jornadas*, was performed in the Cathedral of Mexico to honor a newly arrived Church dignitary, the program also included the initial play by the New World's first native dramatist. Juan Pérez Ramírez (1545–?), Mexican-born son of a Spanish soldier and an Indian mother, and acquainted with Latin as well as Spanish and Nahuatl, wrote *El desposorio espiritual entre el pastor Pedro y la Iglesia Mexicana* as another welcome to Archbishop Pedro Moya de Contreras.[12] More erudite than Eslava's contribution, this pastoral comedy of the mystic betrothal of the archbishop and the Church mingles real people like the shepherd and the *bobo* with symbolic figures like the Church and the Theological Virtues. The verse is so excellent that Amado Alonso suggests the possibility of help from the Spanish dramatist Juan de la Cueva, then visiting Mexico.[13]

The two plays make an interesting contrast for those who wish to see whether the differentiation between people of Spain and people of the New World, observed later in the plays of Ruiz de Alarcón, had already begun to emerge. The traveler Juan López de Velasco had detected it in 1571, for he wrote in his *Geografía y descripción universal de las Indias* that "los que nacen de los españoles que pasan a aquellos partes que llaman criollos . . . no solamente en las calidades corporales se mudan, pero en las del ánima se alteran también."[14]

The Third Provincial Concilio in 1585, again banned plays in the churches, "except about sacred history or other holy matters useful to the soul," and these manuscripts had to be presented to the bishop a month prior to their performance. *Los pastores* was especially singled out. However this prohibition did not end drama in Mexico. The next year, 1586, Alonso de Buenrostro built a temporary stage in the plaza for the Corpus Christi plays. In 1597 a contract issued to Andrés Laris de Durango mentioned an open-air stage for his performances of *Las profecías de Daniel* and *Nuestra Señora del Rosario*. Possibly these were locally written. It is known that in 1599 Fray Juan Bautista had ready for publication three volumes of religious plays.

[12] Francisco A. de Icaza, "Origen del teatro en México," *Boletín de la Real Academia Española*, II (1915), 57–76; Carlos González Peña, *Historia de la literatura mexicana* (reference is to the English translation, *History of Mexican Literature*, pp. 78–80); Miguel Galindo, *Apuntes para la historia de la literatura mexicana*; José Juan Arrom, *El teatro de Hispanoamérica en la época colonial*, pp. 62–64. Pérez Ramírez' *Auto Desposorio* is reprinted in José Rojas Garcidueñas, *Autos y coloquios del siglo XVI*, and in Ermilo Abreu Gómez et al., *Cuatro siglos de literatura mexicana*, pp. 199–209.

[13] Alonso, "Biografía de Fernán González de Eslava," *Revista de Filología Hispánica*, II (1940).

[14] Quoted in José Juan Arrom, *Certidumbre de América*, p. 10.

Where were they performed? Mañón boasts that Mexico had a theatre built especially for plays long before there was anything comparable in Spain.[15] This statement is somewhat inaccurate. Valencia, the Spanish port for Mediterranean trade, possessed a corral, or open-air theatre, in 1528. The first mention of any stage in Mexico outside the church occurs in a *cédula* of 1553 speaking of "representaciones profanas," but they must certainly have been performed on a temporary platform, like those of Buenrostro and Laris. Meanwhile Madrid had its permanent Corral de la Pacheca in 1568, Sevilla its Corral de don Juan and Valladolid its Corral de la Puerta de San Sebastián, the last two built in 1575. Toledo had El Mesón de la Fruta dating from 1576.[16]

In the New World, only the plazas could accommodate audiences for Corpus Christi plays during the sixteenth century, though there is some evidence that Mexico did have a couple of small theatres. Arias de Villalobos speaks in his *Canto intitulado Mercurio* of "dos extremados teatros de comedias," a reference clarified by the discovery of a suit brought on May 31, 1597, by merchants and residents in Calle Arco (now República del Salvador) against the St. Augustine priests who were trying to close Arco Street. The transcription mentions "Las casas de Francisco de León que es donde se hace la comedia." Rojas Garcidueñas was able to identify their location as the site of present Numbers 111 and 113.[17] These were doubtless like those of Spain, open to the sky, in imitation of the original innyard stages. But if not first to build theatres, Mexico was the first to roof them over as protection against inclement weather. Not till 1742 did Madrid's Corral de la Cruz get a roof, while La Pacheca remained open to the sky till 1745. But when the Order of St. Hippolytus built a theatre in Mexico near the Royal Hospital for Indians, about 1627, it gave complete protection against rain.[18] The brotherhood used the rental from performances to finance the care of their charity patients. Mañón gives details of the theatre and its three performances a week:

[15] Manuel Mañón, *Historia del Teatro Principal de México.*

[16] These dates are from *Boletín de Estudios de Teatro,* No. 16 (March, 1947), 41. Rojas Garcidueñas, *El teatro de Nueva España,* p. 19, gives different datings: Madrid's Corral del Sol, 1568; La Pacheca, 1574; de la Cruz, 1579; Sevilla's de Doña Elvira, 1579.

[17] Rojas Garcidueñas, *El teatro de Nueva España,* 119–129.

[18] Harvey L. Johnson, "Notas relativas a los corrales de la Ciudad de México," *Revista Iberoamericana,* III (1941), 133–137.

Sunday, Tuesday, and Thursday, with an extra free *guanaja* on Mondays for the entertainment of the poor.[19] Because of difficulties in lighting the building, and to discourage immorality, no evening performances were given.

A contemporary, Fray Agustín de Betancourt wrote that two tiers of boxes with latticed fronts were provided for the wealthy. The gallery was spacious and covered by cedar planks to keep off the rain. The stage, raised four-and-a-half feet, was forty-five feet wide and twenty-four feet deep, and decorated with the royal arms.[20]

With the seventeenth century came an increase in quantity and quality of plays. One from this period is *El coloquio de la nueva conversión y bautismo de los cuatro últimos reyes de Tlaxcala en la Nueva España.* This used to be regarded with admiration as the earliest European-type play in America, and was sometimes ascribed to Motolinía. But now, because of the handwriting on the surviving manuscript, and the use of the *décima* stanza, not originated by Espinel till 1591, its composition is assigned to the early seventeenth century where, among competitors of that century, it has now lost importance.

But early Mexico was producing outstanding dramatists. First chronologically came Juan Ruiz de Alarcón (1581–1639), from a wealthy family. Although he frequently claimed the capital as his birthplace, scholars suspect that he was born on the family estate in Taxco. Despite the fact that most of his plays were written in Spain, Mexico claims him on the grounds that his formative years in Mexico gave him those unique personal qualities observed and commented upon by even his contemporaries in Spain.[21] His plays show his pride; his faith in the values of the spirit; his moral sense; his humanity, as revealed in his characters. Technically, he fails to use some traditional Spanish concepts, such as the relationship between old servants and the family.

[19] Manuel Mañón, "El teatro en la colonia," *Máscara*, No. 93 (June, 1948), 11–14.

[20] Fray Agustín de Betancourt, *El teatro mexicano.*

[21] Genaro Fernández Macgregor, "La mexicanidad de Alarcón," *Letras de México*, II, No. 8 (August 8 and 15, 1939); Antonio Magaña Esquivel, *Sueño y realidad del teatro* (see section entitled "Ruiz de Alarcón, intruso en España"). For other details about Alarcón, see José Juan Arrom, *El teatro de Hispanoamérica*, 79–90; Pedro Henríquez Ureña, "Don Juan Ruiz de Alarcón," *Seis ensayos*, 79–89; and Antonio Castro Leal, *Juan Ruiz de Alarcón.*

Undoubtedly Alarcón made his first acquaintance with the theatre in Mexico before he graduated from the University of New Spain and went to Salamanca for postgraduate study in 1600 (the last year that women were allowed in masculine attire on Mexican stages). In Spain he confirmed his degree shortly after his arrival and went on to get a degree in law at the end of 1602. Settling in Seville to practice, his entry in a poetry contest was unsuccessful as was his attempt to find clients. He returned to Mexico in 1608 and, with the intention of teaching, took another legal degree in February, 1609. However, the physical deformities that later made this humped-back dwarf the target of envious Spanish dramatists, prevented his either receiving a teaching appointment or becoming part of the bureaucracy. In May, 1613, he returned to Spain.

No one can be sure how much playwriting Alarcón did in Mexico, though several titles have been suggested as products of the New World portion of his life. Certainly there are very few Mexican touches or references in any of his works. *Las paredes oyen,* one of his best, was first performed in Spain in 1617. Immediately the personal attacks on him began, starting with *El pasajero* by Suárez de Figueroa. Alarcón promptly defended himself in *Mudarse por mejorarse.* Other attacks and slurs followed. In a period when most writers were feuding with someone, Alarcón seemed to be feuding with everyone. Insulting epithets were hurled at him; scenery was weakened to collapse during performances of plays by this "foreigner"; and stench makers were put into the lamps on the stage.

Finally, in 1626, he received an appointment to a post in the Council of the Indies. Financially secure at last, he stopped writing. He did, however, collect and publish his works, eight in the first *Parte* (Madrid, 1628), and twelve more in Barcelona in 1634. A few others, published singly, brought his total up to twenty-six, a small number compared to the product of the other three leading dramatists of Spain's Golden Age.

Details of the plots of plays by Ruiz de Alarcón can be found in histories of Spain's literature. The plays themselves can be divided into four classifications. Beginning with his first arrival in Spain in 1600, he wrote dramas of intrigue, the least important of his production. During the second period, after his return from Mexico in 1613, he showed his interest in psychology, and wrote or rewrote the comedies of character that were to influence Corneille and Molière. His *Mudarse por mejorarse* represents a transition between plays of plot and plays of character, with a touch of autobiography.

The character Don Juan of *Las paredes oyen,* an ugly but noble hero whose sterling qualities are recognized by the Doña Ana he loves, is supposed to represent the author. *Ganar amigos* is also special pleading by a lonely man who dramatizes friendliness as proof of nobility. *La verdad sospechosa* tells of an aristocrat who cultivates lying as a fine art and the punishment that he receives. It is one of the greatest, if not the greatest, by Alarcón. There was a brief period when as a patriot he dramatized national themes. In these three years, 1619–1622, Alarcón wrote *Los pechos privilegiados, El tejedor de Segovia,* and others. Finally, just before his career as dramatist ended, he showed his increasing power and human sympathy in two of his best plays, from a technical point of view: *No hay mal que por bien no venga,* in which two nobles unwittingly save the throne of Alfonso III, and *Examen de maridos,* in which a seventeenth-century feminist puts herself up at auction in her search for a satisfactory husband, a unique concept.

Alarcón's plays had their first presentations in Spain and their Mexican performances were delayed till later, but Mexico did produce some stay-at-home dramatists, most of whom continued to follow the old patterns. Francisco Bramón, in his *Auto del triunfo de la virgen y gozo mexicano* (1620) broke with symbolism in giving his character Pecado the personality of a highwayman; and Matías de Bocanegra (1612–1668) wrote the still readable *Comedia de San Francisco de Borja*[22] with which to welcome Viceroy López Pacheco in 1640. It deals with the sixteenth-century Duke of Gandía, who became a saint. While some of its speeches show the influence of *La vida es sueño* (1638), it also reveals its Mexican roots by employing the *tocotín,* danced to the accompaniment of Mexican musical instruments, for its conclusion.

More dramatists, Agustín de Salazar y Torres (1642–1675), Captain Alonso Ramírez de Vargas (1662–1696), Jerónimo Becerra, and others[23] fill the years between Alarcón and the next important figure

[22] José Juan Arrom, "Una desconocida comedia mexicana del siglo XVII," *Revista Iberoamericana,* XIX (1953), 79–103.
[23] Magaña Esquivel and Lamb, *Breve historia,* pp. 28–39.

of Mexican drama, Sor Juana Inés de la Cruz (1648–1695).[24] While still Juana Inés de Asbaje, she went to Mexico to live with her grandfather, where she became acquainted with the world of literature, even learning Latin so she could find more books to read.

Becoming a nun, she collaborated about 1668 with the priest Juan de Guevara in a three-act comedy, *Amor es más laberinto*, of which she wrote the first and last acts. Set in Crete, the play shows that Theseus could escape the Minotaur, but not the love labyrinth of Phaedra. The lyrical ability of the playwright is demonstrated in the long poetic discussion between Theseus and Minos about life and its hazards. The major dramatic creation of Sor Juana was *Los empeños de la casa*, written between 1680 and 1686, which was the period when Viceroy Count Paredes, the husband of her protector, Doña María Luisa, occupied the palace. With accompanying *loas* and *sainetes*, and borrowing its title from Calderón's *Los empeños de una casa*, she followed Lope de Vega's *La discreta enamorada* in a very complicated cape-and-sword plot. It is full of the disguises and misunderstandings of a Spanish Golden Age *comedia*; some critics suspect it of containing autobiographical elements.

A good example of her *loas* is the one to *El divino Narciso* (c. 1680), written at the request of the viceroy's wife. The characters include The West (a young Indian prince), America (an Indian princess), Religion (a Spanish lady), and Christian Zeal (the Spanish governor). The Indians, celebrating a pagan harvest festival as the Spaniards arrive, are first conquered by Spanish guns, then won over by the charm of Lady Religion, and converted by the one-act "Divine Narcissus" that follows. The sketch ends with the players determining to take the play to Madrid to perform before King Charles II.

Sor Juana's two *sainetes*, inserted between the acts of *Los empeños de una casa*, introduced characters that did not appear in the main play. In the first, called *The entremés of the Palace*, Love, Respect, Flattery, and other abstract qualities are summoned to decide the winner of the prize for exhibiting greatest scorn. No one is found worthy. The second, known only as *Sainete Segundo*, inserted between

[24] Arrom, *El teatro de Hispanoamericano*, pp. 121–137; Ermilo Abreu Gómez, *Semblanza de Sor Juana*; Julio Jiménez Rueda, *Sor Juana en su época*; Sor Juana de la Cruz, *Obras completas* (see prolog to Vol. III by Méndez Plancarte, and notes to Vol. IV by Alberto G. Salceda); Cecilia Gascón de Guilarte, *Sor Juana Inés de la Cruz, claro en la selva*; Magaña Esquivel and Lamb, *Breve historia*, pp. 36–41.

Acts II and III, has been declared one of the most original farces of the New World colonial theatre. In it, Muñiz, believed to be a contemporary actor, and his friend Arias, discuss the flaws of a play by Acevedo, also probably a real person, and decide that if they can encourage enough catcalls, the audience demonstration will discourage the author from further writing. The farce ends with their outcries and the protests of Acevedo.

In addition, this learned and witty woman wrote eighteen *loas* and *autos sacramentales*, one at the age of eight, and one, *El divino Narciso*, good enough, according to Arrom, to win her a high place among the followers of Calderón.[25] Other critics have less respect for her as a dramatist. A fellow countryman, Ermilo Abreu Gómez, declared ". . . her legitimate fame rests chiefly on her lyrical works, essentially amorous."[26]

With this nun-poet's cell the center of Mexico's intellectual life, and with her personal library of four thousand volumes, it is no wonder that Sor Juana was called "The Tenth Muse" by her contemporaries. But she was also conscious of her holy calling, and died caring for the sick during an epidemic. Fittingly, she herself became the subject of at least two Mexican dramas: *Sor Juana Inés* (1876), by José Rosas Moreno (1838–1883),[27] and Octavio Meza's three-act *Diamantino pecho* (1951).

Since comparatively few plays were being written in Mexico during this period, however, others kept arriving clandestinely from Spain. As early as 1531, when Charles V prohibited the importation into America of "*Amadís* y otras desta calidad de mentirosas historias" lest Indians waste their time on "frivolous literature," many a priest brought along in his baggage "dos docenas de comedias," as their baggage lists frequently revealed. Several such lists have been recovered, from that of January 7, 1594, mentioning "coloquios satíricos," "coloquios depo. México," and a comedy by Plautus, to a later list of 504 plays shipped from Spain, May 16, 1713. Details have been collected by Maria y Campos.[28] Besides these legitimate ship-

[25] Arrom, *El teatro de Hispanoamérica.*

[26] Ermilo Abreu Gómez, "Sor Juana," *International Review of Bibliography,* VIII, No. 3 (July, 1958), 272.

[27] José Rosas Moreno, "Sor Juana Inés," *Calendario de la antigua casa de Murguía para 1880,* pp. 33–94.

[28] Armando de Maria y Campos, *Andanzas y picardías de Eusebio Vela,* pp. 3–36.

ments, Cádiz and Sevilla developed a thriving business in clandestine publications, especially plays.[29]

By the eighteenth century theatrical performances were becoming "big business," with the Hospitalers receiving an annual rental of three thousand pesos for their playhouse. But on January 19, 1722, it suffered what was to be the fate of so many tinder-dry, oil-lighted theatres of the Hemisphere. It was completely destroyed by fire during a performance of *Ruín e incendio de Jerusalén* at a time when the billboard outside prophetically announced the coming of *Aquí fue Troya*, a play by Agustín Salazar Torres (1642–1675) which might be translated "That's the End of Everything!"

Under the supervision of the actor-playwright-manager Eusebio Vela (1689–1736), a bigger and better Coliseo was built.[30] In the interest of morality the lattices were removed in front of the boxes and separate galleries were constructed for men and women. This new building escaped the flames for thirty years; long after the death of the Velas, it was replaced in 1753 by El Teatro Principal, that had three tiers of boxes and rows of benches with headrests on the main floor, behind an open space for standing *mosqueteros*. Its stage was so large that for one week in February, 1779, until forbidden by Viceroy Bucareli, bullfights took place there between the acts.[31]

The Coliseo of 1724 was opened by Eusebio Vela, his brother José, and the actresses they had married. Basically these men do not belong to the history of Mexico's drama, since both were born in Toledo and came to Mexico under contract to perform for the theatre owned by the Hospital Real de los Naturales. But both brothers made their contributions to the national drama: Eusebio, besides being the most popular actor of his period, also wrote a dozen plays considered by his admirers the equal of anything by Lope or Calderón. Only three have survived, all in the Golden Age tradition.[32] *El Apostolado de las Indias* is set in Mexico; *Si el amor excede el arte* is Grecian, complete with Cupid and the Furies; and *La pérdida de España* retells the story of King Roderick and the arrival of the Moors.

Before the fire, in 1718, the Vela brothers had taken over the man-

[29] Francisco Escudero y Perosso, *Anales bibliográficos de la ciudad de Sevilla desde el establecimiento de la imprenta hasta fines del siglo XVIII.*

[30] Maria y Campos, *Andanzas y picardías.*

[31] For a description of both playhouses, see Enrique de Olavarría y Ferrari, *Reseña histórica del teatro en México*, I, 29–30.

[32] Jefferson R. Spell and Francisco Monterde, *Tres comedias de Eusebio Vela.*

agement of the old theatre, only to run so deeply into debt that they were back on salary as actors when it burned. In the New Coliseo José had only a year of activity before he died; Eusebio became its manager, continued to be Mexico's chief actor till his death in 1737, which was hastened by smallpox and by his mountain of accumulated debts.

The rest of the eighteenth century was a sterile period for Mexican drama.[33] One reason was that the priests, finding that theatrical performances were cutting into Church attendance, tried to stifle drama, with the help of civil officials. Ordinances were passed against various kinds of plays. Citing laws passed back in Spain as early as 1644 that plays must be founded on fact and must provide moral examples, Viceroy Gálvez in 1786 laid down a series of regulations. Performances must not come at times to conflict with Church ceremonies. Also, not only must morality be maintained by separating the sexes, but good manners must be observed. In the theatre, men had to remove their sombreros! With such handicaps, the theatre dragged along during the final years that Mexico remained a colony of Spain. The only contemporary Mexican dramatist to get a hearing was Francisco Soria, whose three performed dramas, *El duque de Aquitania, La mágica mexicana,* and *La Genoveva* scored mild successes. A few minor writers also had one or two plays staged.

The nineteenth century began without much activity. *El Diario de México,* trying in 1805 to make the theatre bloom in what seemed to be a desert, announced a play contest, but received only two entries. *La Gaceta* tried again in 1806, with slightly better results. When both papers combined their pleas in a contest for prizeworthy tragedies in 1808, only one manuscript was submitted. Opera and *sainetes* were the popular entertainments.

However, José Agustín de Castro (1730–1814) published three volumes of his collected writings (1797–1809), including two plays with authentic Mexican atmosphere: *Los remendones* and *El charro.*[34]

It seems hardly worthwhile to list unpublished and mostly unperformed plays by Juan Wenceslao Barquera (1779–1840), Anas-

[33] For theatrical activities in Mexico in 1790, see *Hispanic Review,* 19, No. 2 (1951); for 1791–1792, see *Hispanic American Historical Review,* 31 (May, 1951).

[34] Luis Urbina, *La literatura mexicana durante la Guerra de la Independencia,* reprints this play, pp. 176–184.

tasio de Ochoa y Acuña (1783–1833), or Francisco Ortega (1793–1849); but José Joaquín Fernández de Lizardi (1776–1827), though more important as the author of the New World's first novel, *Periquillo Sarniento* (1816), does deserve mention as a forerunner of the pre-romantic play. Beginning with *El negro sensible* (1825), a sequel to a play popular during this period, he was also author of a Christmas fantasy, *La noche más venturosa* (1809), witnessed by the patriot Miguel Hidalgo on the Christmas Eve before he uttered his rallying "Grito de Dolores." Besides the religious *Auto mariano para recordar la milagrosa apariencia de nuestra Madre y Señora*, about the Virgin of Guadalupe, and a three-act *Todos contra el payo*, set in Mexico's insane asylum, Lizardi wrote a dramatic monolog about the Emperor Iturbide, and probably was author of the four-act poetic *Tragedia del Padre Arenas* (1827). His plays are all less moralizing, but also less important, than the novel that makes him remembered.

One reason for the dearth of drama was the lack of theatres. El Coliseo Nuevo, renamed Teatro Principal in 1826, was usually occupied by musical plays. So gloomy and dark was it that the populace nicknamed it "Santa Paula" from its resemblance to the cemetery, but it lasted till 1931. El Teatro del Palenque de los Gallos was built in 1823, followed in 1841 by El Nuevo Mexico, which opened with a performance of *El torneo* by Fernando Calderón.

The best playwright of the time, Manuel Eduardo de Gorostiza (1789–1851), was Mexican-born through the circumstance that his mother, wife of the Spanish governor of Veracruz, had reached Mexican soil a week before her baby was due.[35] But five years later, following the Governor's death, Gorostiza and his mother returned to Spain for his education. There, rebelling against the family decision that he enter the Church, he became a soldier and fought against Napoleon.

Gorostiza's first play, *Indulgencia para todos* (1818), was greeted in Spain as the greatest play since Moratín's. With four others, all showing Spanish neoclassic influence, it was published in Paris in 1822. One of the others, *Las costumbres de antaño o La pesadilla*, a little masterpiece of comedy, was the first by him to be performed and published in Mexico (1833).

As a Liberal, Gorostiza and his family had to leave Spain when

---

[35] Armando de Maria y Campos, *Manuel Eduardo de Gorostiza y su tiempo*.

Ferdinand VII regained the throne; so it was in England that his *Contigo pan y cebolla* (1833) was written, supposedly to cure the infatuation of the dramatist's romantic daughter, Luisa, for a penniless Spaniard. It was published in London.

Since Gorostiza, because of his friendship with several influential Mexicans, had been serving as Mexico's commercial and political representative, he returned to Mexico in 1833 with a shipment of farm machinery and a number of French plays[36] in time to see the first performance in Mexico of his *Contigo pan y cebolla*. He settled there as the first national librarian, and in 1844 took over the management of the Teatro Principal, which had been renamed Teatro Santa Ana. For it he rewrote several plays in the manner of those of Spain's Golden Age. He tried unsuccessfully as Mexico's representative to settle the boundary trouble between Mexico and the United States, then fought and was captured in the war that followed.

His death in 1851 was observed with honors for the man "who had restored the Mexican theatre." All but one of his sixty-seven plays were written in Spain or England. Most of them are simple in plot, like *Don Dieguito,* in which Diego's uncle comes to Madrid and pretends to court the gold digger Adelaida to show Diego her shallowness. They contain humor and natural dialog which made Gorostiza the model for Bretón de los Herreros and others; even today some of his plays are occasionally revived.

Long before the death of Manuel Gorostiza, neoclassicism had ended in the Mexican theatre, to be replaced by romanticism. The first example in Mexico was the work of Ignacio Rodríguez Galván (1816–1842), whose life was as romantic as his few plays. Employed in his uncle's bookstore, he not only read the romantic plays of Martínez de la Rosa and others from Spain but taught himself French so as to study the movement in France. In 1838 he seized upon the Mexican Conspiracy of 1566, and with some factual changes, produced *Muñoz, visitador de México*. It has a dramatic final curtain. Inspector Muñoz reveals to Celestina that to free her for himself, he has executed her husband. She drops dead beside him.

Rodríguez Galván's brief *La capilla* (1837), also drawn from the same period of Mexican colonial history, deals with the last moments of Alonso de Avila, executed for conspiring against Martín Cortés.

[36] Jefferson R. Spell, "Some Little Known Plays of Gorostiza," *Romantic Review*, XXIII (1932), 131–141, considers five comedies, two adapted from Scribe.

For his other tragedy, *El privado del virrey* (1842), he adapted a story by Juan Manuel into a drama full of violence and demon-possessed heroes.

His first work, skilfully constructed and revealing a grasp of theatrical technique, is his best and is not only the equal of any of Mexico's romanticist plays, but is on a par with plays written in Spain before *Don Juan Tenorio*. A señorita's rebuffs drove the playwright from Mexico, and he died in Havana of yellow fever on his way to Europe.

Even before Rodríguez Galván began writing in Mexico City, Fernando Calderón (1809–1845) was experimenting with drama in Guadalajara. While still a student he completed *Reinaldo y Elena*, which was performed in 1827. Then, although he went to Zacatecas to practice law, and entered politics to curb the power of Santa Ana, he still had time to write *Zadig*, *Zeila o La esclava indiana*, *Muerte de Virginia por la libertad de Roma* (1832), and other neoclassical plays, most of them now lost. In the last-named, concealed behind its Roman theme was a lament for the loss of Mexico's civil liberties under Santa Ana. This indiscretion was one reason why Rodríguez Galván had to leave Zacatecas for Mexico, where he joined one of the literary circles. The interest in romanticism and the success of *Muñoz, visitador de México* inspired him to write *El torneo*, set in England in the eleventh century. It was first performed in Zacatecas in 1839, then served to dedicate the Teatro de Nuevo México in 1841.

Hernán o La vuelta del cruzado (1842) has as hero a twelfth-century Austrian, Hernán, whose sweetheart, Sofía, marries while he is on a crusade. Hernán turns out to be Sofía's husband's illegitimate son. The unhappy Hernán returns to the Holy Land. Calderón also wrote a magnificent historical drama, *Ana Bolena* (1839), about the wife of Henry VIII.

In Spain in 1831 Bretón de los Herreros had written *Marcela o ¿A cuál de las tres?* about three silly girls unable to please a fussy suitor. As an answer, Calderón wrote, in the only play that he located in Mexico, *A ninguna de las tres*, a contemporary social satire on the inadequate education of women and the craze for French culture. Though a romanticist, Calderón was not blind to the flaws of romanticism, and in thus satirizing them he produced one of the best of Mexico's early comedies, with humor and excellent character portrayal. It has been frequently revived. His four remaining plays were published just before his death, again in 1849, and again in 1882. Menéndez y Pelayo especially admired his poetry as well as the emotion, the noble sentiments, and the character drawing in his comedies.[37]

Mexico had other dramatists mining the vein of romanticism. The majority were of minor importance, but Magaña Esquivel lists a score of them.[38] In his opinion, Mexican romanticism had more impatience, melancholy, disillusionment about the outside world, and desire for freedom than existed in other countries. He sees Mexican romanticism as a synonym of liberalism. The new movement gained impetus though two organizations, La Academia de San Juan de Letrán, founded in 1836, and the Liceo Hidalgo, composed of actors and dramatists opposed to Letrán. Though there was little theatrical activity, because of the troubled state of Mexico's politics, there were hopeful dramatists, among them Guillermo Prieto (1818–1897), poet, teacher, congressman, and founder of the Letrán Academy, who scored a hit with *Alonso de Avila* but was hissed for *Los tres boticarios.*

Pantaleón Tovar (1828–1876), a soldier in exile, and a prolific dramatist, initiated his career with *La catedral de México* (1850) and *Los hijos de Cortés* (1851). He attempted sentimental plays, like *Una deshonra sublime* (1853; published 1870). A performance of this play is described in Juan Díaz Covarrubias' (1837–1859) *costumbrista* novel, *El diablo en México* (1858). The titles of *La gloria del dolor* (1854) and *Misterios del corazón*, also by Tovar, forecast their sentimental themes. His *Justicia del cielo* is a cape-and-sword play.

José Tomás de Cuéllar (1830–1894), one of the cadet defenders of Chapultepec, wrote *Deberes y sacrificios* (1855), which was performed by a Spanish company in a benefit for war victims, and so impressed the actors that they repeated it in Madrid.[39] Pedro sacrifices his life for Fernando, who loves Pedro's wife, Julia, but from a sense of honor the survivors cannot marry. This first Mexican *costumbrista* dramatist also wrote *Azares de venganza* (1856) and *La ranchera* (1859), as well as *Arte de amar* and a play of magic, *Un viaje a oriente* and several others.

[37] *Historia de la poesía hispanoamericana*, as quoted in González Peña, *Historia de la literatura mexicana*, p. 223.
[38] Magaña Esquivel and Lamb, *Breve historia*, pp. 66–67.
[39] Armando de Maria y Campos, *Archivos de teatro*, pp. 177–179.

Francisco González Bocanegra (1824–1861) during his short life-time wrote the Mexican national anthem and a historical play, *Vasco Núñez de Balboa* (1856), which has most of the defects and few of the virtues of Zorrilla's products. He also served as censor for the Mexican stage. At his death he left unfinished a romantic play, *Faltas y expiación*, in which a mother and unrecognized daughter are rivals for the love of the same man.

Zorrilla himself arrived in Mexico in January, 1855. He found the drama in a bad state.[40] In the chief playhouse, renamed Teatro Santa Ana, three performances established a record for a local play. Even with the actress Matilde Díez as the attraction, *Seducción* (1852) by José Ignacio de Anievas opened on July 15, 1855, with so few spectators that it was never repeated and no other Mexican play was offered till October 18, when Cuéllar's *Deberes y sacrificios* held the stage.

March, 1856, marked the opening of the independent Teatro de Iturbide, with seats for 1,800, and with gas illumination. As part of its campaign to encourage Mexican authors, it began with *Y ¿para qué?*. "Why not Bretón, instead?" was the critics' retort. But the management was courageous enough to stage a number of other national plays: *Una deshonra sublime* (June 12), *Ana Bolena* (July 10), *Vasco Núñez de Balboa* (September 14), and *La gloria del dolor* (September 27). A number of Zorrilla's plays were also performed, though Censor González Bocanegra was harshly criticized for passing his *Traidor, inconfeso y mártir*.

In 1857 the Iturbide was acquired and closed by El Teatro Nacional, to reduce competition, since there was too much fighting and shooting in the capital to make theatre-going attractive. There was, however, occasional activity. The most popular offerings of 1861 were collaborations of Vicente Riva Palacio (1832–1896) and José A. Mateos (1831–1913). Many of Mateos' *costumbrista* plays about the high and low classes, first performed in the provinces, have been lost. One such, unfortunately, was *La muerte de Lincoln*. Others were printed and survived: *Los dioses se van*, about student strikes; *El prólogo de don Quijote*; *La monja alférez*; and *Luna de miel*. When Mateos was unable to find actors for them, he and Riva Palacio or-

[40] Luis Reyes de la Maza, *El teatro en 1857 y sus antecedents, El teatro en México entre la reforma y el imperio,* and *El teatro en la época de Juárez.*

ganized their own company and collaborated in plays in a vain attempt to revive the national drama.

Another popular author was the first woman since Sor Juana Inés to write for the stage—Isabel Angela Prieto de Landázuri (1833–1876), who, though born in Spain, grew up in Guadalajara. Five of her fifteen plays are known to have been performed. In *Los dos son peores* (1862), a comedy of customs, the amusing Pepa has two suitors: foppish old Don Lindoro and bookwormish young Samuel. *Las dos flores* contains the Bunthorne type of romantic poet, Carlos, pursued by Magdalena and by the married Julia. *Oro y oropel* was successfully staged, and as a tribute after the death of Mrs. Landázuri, her *Un lirio entre zarzas* was also performed in Mexico.

Even the poet Manuel Acuña (1849–1873) ventured into drama.[41] Encouraged by Altamirano, and in the tradition of the French *Lady of the Camellias* and *Olympia's Marriage*, Acuña wrote *El pasado* (1872), which was performed by Pilar Belaval under the sponsorship of President Juárez. Though classical in its unity of twelve hours, this work by one of the second wave of romanticists calls for a Verdi to put it to music. Eugenia (who would be the soprano) is seduced by wealthy Ramiro (surely the bass). Later she marries the painter David (the tenor?), but when Ramiro reappears, she sees only one solution: suicide. Contemporary accounts reported it a great success, with the author receiving four laurel crowns at its second showing. It was again revived the next year, after Acuña's own suicide, but an inadequate cast doomed it to failure. Its good qualities hint at what might have been had its author lived longer than twenty-four years.[42]

Outside the capital, Guadalajara and Zacatecas had enjoyed drama; now Yucatán developed a native dramatist. José Antonio Cisneros (1826–?) began his career with *Diego el mulato* (1846) performed during the visit to Mérida of the Spanish dramatist García Gutiérrez. It was so well received that he wrote a sequel, *El filibustero,* based on a romantic novel by Justo Sierra O'Reilly, about a mulatto pirate. Cisneros' most famous play is *El cuarto con dos camas.* Besides his plays, Cisneros contributed to the Mexican stage by ending the practice of long monologs and asides. By their omission in

[41] Armando de Maria y Campos, *Manuel Acuña y su teatro.*
[42] Antonio Magaña Esquivel, "El pasado: Drama de Manuel Acuña," *Revista Mexicana de Cultura,* No. 127 (August 28, 1949).

his drama *Mercedes* (1860), and his *Celia* and *Matar al gato*, comedies of customs in prose, he thus preceded Ibsen by forty years in
ridding the drama of that artificiality. Says Magaña Esquivel: "One
can look upon Cisneros as an immature Isben, without Paris and An-
toine, and therefore condemned to an obscure corner of Mexico."[43]

That visit of García Gutiérrez to Yucatán gave impetus to playwriting. Not only did the Spaniard himself write three plays about
local history, based on Sierra O'Reilly novels, but he got a number of
young authors interested in writing for the theatre. One result of this
visit was the emerging of Mexico's most prolific romanticist playwright, José Peón Contreras (1843–1907), also a native of Yucatán.
During his student days, while he aspired to be a physician, he wrote
three plays: *El castigo de Dios, María la loca,* and *El conde Santieste-
ban,* all performed in the San Carlos theatre, Mérida, later to be renamed for him as that city's most famous playwright. With a degree
in medicine and a portfolio of plays, Peón Contreras headed for Mexico in 1863. The producer to whom he submitted his plays discouraged him by returning them unread; so he turned to medicine and
became a psychiatrist in an insane asylum.

In 1875 President Lerdo de Tejada decided to develop Mexican
culture. The year previous, a play, *Martirios del pueblo* (published
1876) by the journalist Alberto G. Bianchi, had been given one performance by María Cañete in the Teatro de Nuevo México. It attacked the President's draft laws. The infuriated Lerdo had its author
jailed, but when eventually Bianchi was freed, unrepenting, he went
on to write other plays of social satire, like *Vampiros sociales* (1887).
In order to show himself a friend of the theatre, President Lerdo put
three hundred dollars into the national budget for drama and hired
Mallorcan actor Enrique Guasp de Peris to produce the works of local
dramatists. Guasp was able to find a few, but to get money to keep
the theatre open, he began offering the more popular foreign plays.
Called to account, he did manage in 1876 to stage about twenty
local plays. Then Lerdo's Presidency and the official subsidy both
ended.

However, the momentary flurry had revived the interest of Peón
Contreras, and the success of his drama in prose *¡Hasta el cielo!,* a
romantic story of the Mexican colonial period, encouraged him. For

---

[43] Magaña Esquivel and Lamb, *Breve historia,* p. 72.

the next three years he worked this period of Mexican history in an endless number of tragedies involving romantic suitors and lovelorn señoritas, all speaking a high-flown language. When pressed, he could turn out a play a week, in verse which, like that of his model Zorrilla, was better than his prose. One product, *Luchas de honra y amor*, performed anonymously in 1876, was immediately identified by the audience through the beauty of its lines.

Among his best works are two of his earliest: *La hija del rey* (1876; published 1896) and *Por el joyel del sombrero* (1878). In the first, Angélica, the illegitimate daughter of Philip II, enters a convent in Mexico. In a duel over her a young man is killed. Angélica goes mad. On its opening night, Peón Contreras received a scroll declaring him the "Restorer of the Mexican Theatre."

The title of the other refers to a hat decoration that identified Don Juan de Benavides when he was discovered in Mencia's room. The lowly Iñigo, son of a squire, takes the blame and dies as a result.

A quicker way of appreciating the skill of this second-generation romantic dramatist is by reading his one-act *Gil González de Avila* (1876), performed in the Teatro Principal the same year as his *La hija del rey*. At its tragic conclusion, all except Violante, the daughter, have been killed. Between 1879 and 1885 Peón Contreras wrote nothing. Then came a few attempts, but the interest of Mexicans in romanticism had dulled, and even of his earlier plays many were never published. One such lost masterpiece was *Antón de Alaminos*, greatly praised at its performance in 1876.

Among several other prolific dramatists who used national themes is Alfredo Chavero (1841–1906), a professor of history and an antiquarian. Between 1877 and 1881 he worked with Indian and colonial themes. About a dozen plays by this popular playwright were published. Besides his own work he translated French plays, collaborated with Peón Contreras in *La ermita de Santa Fe*, and turned out comic operas. *Xochitl* (1877) about the Indian princess loved by Cortés and by his page Gonzalo de Alaminos, and *Quetzalcoatl* (1878), were followed by *La hermana de los Avilas*, and his masterpiece, *Los amores de Alarcón* (published 1879), about the dramatist and Jerónima.

José Rosas Moreno (1838–1883) was the first Mexican to write plays for children. He published three in 1874: *Amor filial*, a farce; *Una lección en geografía*, a drama in prose; and *El año nuevo*, a dramatic allegory in verse. Of his many plays for adults, most are lost, like his Indian tragedy *El bardo de Acolhuacán*. One farce and *Sor Juana Inés de la Cruz* (1882) still survive. In this drama in verse about the youthful Juana and the Count de Mancera, he suggests the reason for her entering a convent.

Juan de Dios Peza (1852–1910) spent much of his life in Madrid, but he criticized the vices of Mexican society in *La ciencia del hogar* (1874; published 1876), and wrote the historical *Ultimos instantes de Colón* (1874), and *Un epílogo de amor* (1875). He is best remembered, however, for his endeavors to found a Society of Mexican Dramatists early in the next century.

One other important dramatist did most of his work in the nineteenth century. The poet Manuel José Othón (1858–1906) first wrote classical poetry, then through Parnassianism he became a romanticist playwright and ended with a historical drama. At the age of nineteen he completed a three-act poetic play, *Herido en el corazón*, which was performed in his native San Luis Potosí. He followed it with *La sombra del hogar* (1878) and a one-act sentimental play in verse, *La cadena de flores* (1878; published 1954), about a wayward husband and two noble women. Then came his best play, the three-act poetic drama *Después de la muerte* (1883), which had its original performance in Potosí. A performance of it by María Servin in 1885 introduced Othón to the capital. Virginia Fábregas later revived it. Echegaray was Othón's model for *Lo que hay detrás de la dicha* (1886), about blemished honor. After several failures, for the 1905 Don Quijote celebrations Othón wrote *El último capítulo*, in which he used the language of Cervantes' contemporaries. The monk Avellaneda, Cervantes' wife, and his thirty-two-year-old daughter Isabel witness the death of Don Quijote. But this play and this author take us into the twentieth century.

Twentieth-Century Mexico and Its Theatre

For no other Latin American nation is the theatre of the last seventy-five years better documented. Not only do general histories of Mexican literature contain sections about it, but volumes have appeared dealing with specific movements and dramatists, and there is even a *Breve Historia del Teatro Mexicano*.[1] There are books surveying the national theatre in Cuba and in Argentina, but the Mexican theatre is unique in originating a volume of single-act sampling of important plays,[2] and a three-volume anthology of complete works by thirty-two authors of the twentieth century.[3] A catalog summarizing plays, several studies listing authors and titles, and a number of anecdotal volumes also provide material for students of Mexico's drama.[4]

At the start of the twentieth century Mexico's few practicing dramatists were blindly following European models, chiefly Spanish, in works characterized by Echegarayan bombast and Benaventian sentimentality, in addition to their shallow nationalism. Teresa Farias de Isassi (1878–19??) won a Secretary of Education prize in 1906 with *Cerebro y corazón*, and later came out with *Sombra y luz* (1912), *Como las aves* (1919), *Religión de amor* (1922), and a one-act tragedy, *La sentencia de muerte* about the Mexican Revolution, that got an English translation.

The novelist-dramatist Federico Gamboa (1864–1939), though one of his social dramas, *La última campaña* was performed in 1894,

[1] Antonio Magaña Esquivel and Ruth S. Lamb, *Breve historia del teatro mexicano;* see also Chris N. Nacci, *Concepción del mundo en el teatro mexicano del siglo veinte.*

[2] Ermilo Abreu Gómez *et al.*, *Cuatro siglos de literatura mexicana.*

[3] *Teatro mexicano del siglo XX.* Vol. I, 1900–1927, edited by Francisco Monterde; Vol. II, 1928–1946, edited by Antonio Magaña Esquivel; Vol. III, 1947–1956, edited by Celestino Gorostiza.

[4] Nacci, *Concepción del mundo*, lists 85 authors and 252 plays for 1900 to 1950; see also *Catálogo del teatro mexicano contemporaneo*, put out by the Secretaría de Educación Pública, 1960.

also deserves a place in the twentieth century, since his first play was not published till 1900, while he was Mexico's ambassador to Guatemala. For his watered-down naturalism, Gamboa had a forerunner in Alejandro Cuevas (1870–19??), author of a half-dozen simple but powerful dramas: *Estrategia militar* (published 1888), *Los muertos que andan,* and *¡Líbranos Señor!,* but Gamboa was greatly superior to Cuevas in sympathetic treatment of the mestizos, who, rather than Mexico's Indians, were his chief interest. Gamboa's early reading of French and Italian drama, some of which he translated, developed his technique, if not his artistic taste. Though his naturalism has been overrated, he was the realist who provided Mexico's first rural drama, in his masterpiece *La venganza de la gleba,* ironically dedicated "To the wealthy people of my country." Foreshadowing the Revolution, the play was completed in Washington, D.C., in 1904, published in Guatemala in 1907, and first performed in 1910. It brings into contrast the selfish landowners and the serfs of the land. The mestizo Damián dares to love Blanca, daughter of the *patrón.* She loves him, too, not knowing that he is her half-brother. *A buena cuenta* (1907; published 1914) was the second part of Gamboa's Mexican trilogy. He left unfinished the third, "La sima." Gamboa's *Entre hermanos* (1928), a tragedy which is technically the best of his plays, concerns the rivalry of two brothers for Pilar. Though performed by Camila Quiroga it was not well received; so Gamboa concentrated on his novels and his diplomatic career and abandoned the theatre. Marcelino Dávalos (1871–1932), singer, painter, lawyer, and politician, was another dramatist whose career began seriously in 1900 with *El último cuadro,* patterned after Echegaray, though some amateurs in his native Guadalajara had previously staged his *Regalo de bodas* in 1898. Starting as a romanticist, Dávalos was finally to turn realist in his treatment of social problems, to the displeasure of his audiences. *Guadalupe* (1903) had a riotous first performance. Realistic and close to the soil are Dávalos' next plays, both of 1904: *Jardines trágicos* and *El crimen de Marciano.* His best play, *Así pasan. . .* (1908), the first important Mexican play of the century, shows him inspired by Galdós in his presentation of three periods in the career of the aging actress Victoria. It is simply told with good characterization, and was performed by Virginia Fábregas.

Then came *¡Viva el amo!* (1910), revealing the happy aspect of rural life. His *Lo viejo* (1911) is a tragedy about social problems.

His political activity against President Huerta brought Dávalos banishment to the United States, where he wrote two more tragedies. *Indisoluble* (1915) and *Aguilas y estrellas,* successfully performed in 1916, about a family ruined by the younger generation, ended his playwriting career in favor of journalism, though his two-volume *Monografía del teatro* (1917) is testimony to his continuing affection for the theatre. Though many of the sixteen plays by this materialist have weak plots, poor character portrayal, and Echegarayan violence, enough are of merit to give Dávalos a place in a study of the Mexican drama.

Another early figure of the twentieth century was Antonio Médiz Bolio (1884–1957), in his time called Mexico's greatest dramatist, because of his national themes and poetic style. He was a follower of Echegaray in *Alma bohemia* (1905), *La guerra* (1905), and *Las dos noblezas* (1906), the last a dramatic debate about whether nobility is achieved through blood or by good deeds. During one period he treated of labor problems. In *La ola* the illegitimate son took over the factory to give the workers what they deserved. The author also revealed his interest in the Indians in *La flecha del sol,* in which the past serves as inspiration for the future. It was published in his native Yucatán in 1918. He also dramatized his own Mayan novel of 1912 in *La tierra del faisán y del venado* (1928). After twenty years in diplomacy he tried to follow Benavente in *Cenizas que arden* (1950), which was bad enough to end his career as a dramatist.

In July, 1910, everything in Mexico faced change. Francisco I. Madero provided the impetus for the Revolution that ended the Díaz dictatorship and formulated a program to solve Mexico's fourfold problem of great estates, landless Indians, foreign exploitation, and Church-State relationship. In the succeeding years the Mexican Revolution made itself felt in every phase of life. Laborers found new hope; artists, musicians, and writers received new inspiration. The theatre, naturally, felt its influence as dramatists turned to the problems of the different social classes. They had vital subjects for their plays. This new activity was not visible at once, nor was it entirely spontaneous. However along with the new accent created by the Revolution came a stress on nationalism, emphasized by the approaching celebration in 1921 of Mexico's century of independence.

Creators were freeing themselves from European influences. Social
scenes and problems, whether of colonial times or contemporary
customs, provided national themes.

Julio Jiménez Rueda (1898–1960), a lawyer attracted toward the
stage, helped develop this social interest in 1921 when he began to
direct the School of Theatrical Art and sponsored a series of plays
by local dramatists in the capital's Municipal Theatre, where serious
national plays had been almost unknown. One of the works included
was his own initial venture, *Como en la vida,* written three years
earlier. His later output, characterized by irony, keen observation,
and skill with dialog, include the realistic *Caída de flores,* a tragedy
of dementia and suicide, and *Lo que ella no pudo prever,* both of
1923, and *Miramar* (1932), about Emperor Maximilian. He revealed
his admiration for Franz Molnar in several farces that also had their
serious aspects: *Cándido Cordero, empleado público* (1925; published 1929), about a bureaucrat of thirty years' experience, and *La
silueta de humo* (1927), with characters like "Dama vestida de
negro," "Una joven rubia," etc.

The arrival of the Argentine actress Camila Quiroga in 1923 with
a repertory of South American plays, especially of those of Florencio Sánchez, was additional stimulus to Mexican dramatists searching for dramatic themes of their own country. Again Dr. Jiménez
Rueda provided impetus. From his position in the Ministry he established open-air theatres and arranged for money to engage the actress
María Tereza Montoya for four performances of national plays at
the Municipal Theatre during 1923. Her offerings consisted of his
own *Lo que ella no pudo prever;* Monterde's *La que volvió a la vida;*
two short plays by Parada León, *La agonía* and *La esclava;* and
Cosas de la vida by a Mexican woman, María Luisa Ocampo.

The tragedy *Cosas de la vida* (published 1926) was the first effort
of twenty-year-old María Luisa Ocampo (1907–   ). This emotional play launched Miss Ocampo on a career as dramatist, interspersed with fiction. Her next, the successful *La hoguera* (1924)
was followed by the high comedy *La jauría* (1925) and the folk-
loric *El corrido de Juan Saavedra* (1929; published 1934), for which
Diego Rivera painted scenery.

Most of Miss Ocampo's plays stress the problems of Mexican wom-
en of all classes and are told with a woman's vision. Many were performed by La Comedia Mexicana, which she helped found in 1929

and which continued to function till 1936. Another of her plays was the cynical *Castillo en el aire pero la casa en ruinas* (1931; published 1936). Later plays are *La virgen fuerte* (1942; published 1950) concerning mercy killing; a symbolic farce, *Las máscaras,* and *Al otro día* (1955), in which a harassed farmer, plagued by floods and unreliable hired help, is assured by the sixty-year-old Madre that these are the usual rural problems.

Miss Ocampo was one of a long line of Mexico's women dramatists. Perhaps they should be considered together, because their productions, either because of sentimentality or authentic treatment of feminine psychology, can usually be distinguished from the products of mere males. The line began with the popular writer of melodramas "Catalina D' Erzell" (Catalina Dulché Escalante, 1897–1950). She dealt with moral and social problems in a dozen plays, some of them receiving more than a hundred performances apiece. First came *Cumbres de nieve* (1923), then *¡Esos hombres!* (1923). *El pecado de las mujeres* (1925) blamed woman's sin on masculine temptation. Tears fell profusely in her *Lo que solo el hombre sufre,* the hit of the 1936 season, and *Maternidad* (published 1946) dampened handkerchiefs in 125 performances during 1937.

"Catalina D' Erzell" opened theatre doors to a great number of women writers at this period of Mexico's drama history. Amalia de Castillo Ledón (1898–   ) provided the important *Cuando las hojas caen* (1929), characterized by beautiful theme and careful composition, as well as the more realistic play of customs, *Cubos de noria* (1934). Concepción Sada Hermosilla (1899–   ) made her debut with one of the last plays performed by La Comedia Mexicana, *El tercer personaje* (1936), in which Destiny is the title character. *Como yo te soñaba* (1938) deals with the psychology of teen-agers; *Un mundo para mí* (1942) concerns women's rights. Sentimental plots characterize a half-dozen other comedies written by Miss Sada since she became head of the Childrens' Theatre of Instituto Nacional de Bellas Artes (INBA) in 1942.

Magdalena Mondragón (1913–   ) began with *Cuando Eva se vuelve Adán,* considered the best play of 1938. Then followed *No debemos morir* (1942); *La tarántula* (1945); *El mundo perdido* (published 1948); *La sirena que llevaba el mar* (1950), a poetic fantasy about a fisherman's wife, lured into the ocean by a siren song; and *Porque me da la gana,* a success of the 1953 season. Most recent is her *Torbellino,* about a husband who loves his wife only after he has gone insane. Among other women dramatists is Julia Guzmán, represented by such plays as *Divorciada* (1941) and *Quiero vivir mi vida* (1948). This last is about a widow who is unresponsive when her son-in-law shows an inclination to have an affair with her. *La casa sin ventanas* (1954) is a recent play by Miss Guzmán, as is *Buenos días, tristeza,* a commercialized distortion of the Françoise Sagan novel. María Luisa Algarra (1916–1957), born in Barcelona, married into Mexican nationality and has been active in Mexico's dramatic circles since the production of her *La primavera inútil* by Proa in 1942. Her *Casandra* (1953) gave Mexican significance to the Greek prophetess. *Los años de prueba* (1954), winner of the "Juan Ruiz de Alarcón" award, studies the concern of young people.

Less important is Margarita Urueta (1914–   ), but she has gifts for humor and conversation. *San Luis* (1941) and *Mansión para turistas* (1943), with its "Porfirista" Aunt and ridiculous Professor Fantasía, were better received than was her attempt to recreate Aztec times in *Ave de sacrificio.* One of the youngest women to invade the theatre is Margarita Villaseñor, who appeared briefly as dramatist in *Lazy Monday* and *Sunshine Trio* in 1941 for Fernando Wagner's Pan American Theatre. In Spanish she wrote *El corrido de Elena.* She also selected plays for The Palace of Fine Arts Theatre.

Another woman, Elena Garro, after having written a historical tragedy, *La muerte de Felipe Ángeles,* which dealt with some of the nonproductive members of Mexico's Revolution, turned out a series of one-act plays, published in one volume by the Universidad Veracruzana in 1958. *El hogar sólido* is a macabre play set in a family tomb where the dead of several generations, with a mingling of humor and irony, discuss their lives until the dawn. *Andarse por las ramas,* based on a proverb, is a disconnected presentation of people who somehow achieve integration. *Los pilares de doña Blanca,* with folklore elements, dramatizes a children's song about a girl in a tower, besought by mythical princes. This same unreality, showing Miss Garro's study of Ionesco, appears in *Ventura Allende,* about humans transformed into beasts. Myth and magic are also apparent in *El encanto, tendajón mixto* and *El rey mago;* the latter contains symbolism in its story of a captain who sees an innocent youngster through the bars of his cell, but cannot keep him in sight. Three of these short plays, performed on one program in 1960, drew attention to Miss Garro as a promising dramatist. A later *La señora en el balcón* was performed by a touring student group throughout Central America and appeared in a collection of Mexican one-act plays, testifying to her importance in Mexico's contemporary national theatre.

In the efforts of dramatists in 1923 to encourage and develop Mexico's theatre, another step was the founding of the Union of Dramatic Authors as a center for lectures about world drama and public readings of translations of foreign plays. This establishment led to renewed activity by another group, the Society of Authors, originally founded in 1902 but long moribund. Under its secretary Alberto Tinoco, a season of Mexican plays was scheduled in the old Virginia Fábregas Theatre, named for an actress who began her career in the previous century. Between July, 1925, and January, 1926, the public was offered a hundred showings of forty different plays by Mexican authors. Thirty-two had never been previously performed. Unfortunately the public did not respond, and with no government support the venture ended. But between then and 1934, in some way or other, 134 Mexican plays were performed.[5]

The attempt at a theatre for the masses was a failure. The trouble was that what most Mexicans preferred was not serious drama in regular theatres, but the kind of near-burlesque turns that had been entertaining them for years in barnlike tents in small towns and public fairs. They were called "carpas" because they were performed under canvas. This distant cousin of the Italian *commedia dell' arte* had been introduced late in the nineteenth century by the Orrin Circus in what it called "acuáticas." Instead of a black-out, each comic sketch ended with the ducking of the most obnoxious character. For instance, after violent altercations between a married couple and the bride's mother, the audience got a vicarious satisfaction out of seeing the mother-in-law thrown into a tub of water. These slapstick plays gradually evolved into satires on Mexican life, with political jibes providing much of the humor. One wonders how many potential revolutions were averted by this escape valve of political steam for actors and audience. Most performances lasted less than an hour and, admission was only a few centavos, but this rugged school of drama

[5] Armando de Maria y Campos, *Presencias del Teatro*, pp. 181–187; Alejandro Cervera y Andrade, *El teatro regional de Yucatán.*

graduated many later stars of the stage and screen. Medel, fat Roberto Soto, the late Don Catarino, and Cantinflas all got their first experience in *carpas*.[6]

This form of entertainment reached the capital in 1913 with the building of El Teatro Ideal, the "House of Laughter," which seated seven hundred spectators and provided slightly more artistic *carpas* shows than were known to the rural tents. These *carpas* did not concern themselves with the problems of the Revolution. That subject was left to another kind of drama, the *género chico*, a descendant of a type that began in Spain about 1868. Reaching Mexico in 1876, it called forth plays about socialism and labor troubles.[7] In the early years of the century it offered jibes in music at politicians and laborers, mostly in the form of zarzuelas or brief musical comedies. An unbelievable number of actors and authors shared in the output. The most fertile dramatists for it were Aurelio González Carrasco (for example *La sargenta* (1903) with music by Rafael Gascón), and Rafael Medina.[8] Even the mystic poet Amado Nervo (1870–1919) furnished the libretto for one, *Consuelo* (1901).

The most succesful producers of these musical comedies along a lighter vein was the poet and humorist José F. Elizondo (1880–1943), author of more than forty librettos, such as *El surco, La vendedora de besos, El tenorio maderista*, and the most popular of all Mexico's musical plays, *Chin-Chun-Chan* (1904), which he wrote in collaboration with Rafael Medina and which, according to González Peña, had more than ten thousand performances.[9] Its Chinese title is due to the plot, in which Columbo Pajarete, married to Hipolita (who should have been named Dinamita), falls in love with Encarnación. To escape his wife, he disguises himself as a Chinese and invents an appropriate name from the name of the Mexican town of Tzintzuntzán.

This was one of the better plays of its type, but the lovers of good

---

[6] See *Mexican Life* (Mexico) July, 1937, p. 12, and January, 1939, p. 21; Miguel Covarrubias, "Slapstick and Venom," *Theatre Arts Monthly* (August, 1938), pp. 587–597; Concha Villareal, "Desaparece el teatro del pueblo," *Orientación Musical*, IV, No. 37 (July, 1947).

[7] Armando de Maria y Campos, *El teatro del género chico en la revolución mexicana*.

[8] Carlos González Peña, *Historia de la literatura mexicana*. This book has been published in English as *History of Mexican Literatura*. The page reference here, p. 423, is to the English edition.

[9] *Ibid.*

drama in Mexico determined to fight against it and its many inartistic cousins that had been developing a public for more than a quarter century. In February, 1926, a "Group of Seven" issued a manifesto pointing to the low level of Mexico's plays and begging the public to get acquainted with some of the excellent foreign dramatists. The group included Monterde, J. J. Gamboa, Noriega Hope, Díez Barroso, Parada León, and the two Lozano García brothers. Monterde declared they were "opening the windows to let out the stale air,"[10]— but critics nicknamed them "Los Pirandellos," to imply they were seven authors in search of an actor, and accused them of being more Spanish than Mexican.

Oldest of the Seven, and the first of them to have ventured into playwriting was José Joaquín Gamboa (1878–1931). Beginning by reading and translating French plays, some of which were later used in the campaign of theatrical education, he wrote his first play, the zarzuela *Soledad* (1898) at the age of twenty. Two years later he completed his first drama, *La carne* (published 1903), originally *Teresa*, for its heroine, who was torn between mystic aspirations and carnal desires. *La muerte* (1902; published 1904) foreshadowed Gamboa's eventual symbolism. *El hogar* (1903) and a psychological drama, *El día del juicio* (1908), ended his first period as he left Mexico for a diplomatic post in Europe.

The stirrings of drama by the time he returned in 1923 caused him to write the local-color comedy *El diablo tiene frío*, about a contemporary prodigal son in a middle-class family. *Los Revillagigedo*, the first of three plays written and performed in 1925, presents a usually disregarded side of the Revolution. A wealthy landowner faces the loss of his estate, which is to be distributed among the Indians unless he gives his daughter in marriage to a crooked politician. In 1925, besides the farcical *Un cuento viejo*, there was a performance of the best of Gamboa's thoroughly realistic plays, *Vía crucis*, which covers three periods in the degeneration of a Mexican family.

Gamboa's greatest play, and the most powerful of its kind in the Mexican theatre, was the symbolic *El caballero, la muerte y el diablo*, staged in 1931 only twenty days before La Muerte took away El

---

[10] *Teatro mexicano del siglo XX*, I, ix–xxviii; Antonio Magaña Esquivel and Ruth S. Lamb, *Breve historia del teatro mexicano*, pp. 123–127, discuss the many experimental groups from 1928 to 1957.

Caballero who wrote it. In the play, Death and the Devil strive for the soul of El Caballero, who is trying to save his family and his country.

Following Gamboa among the Seven, in birth and production, came perhaps the most interesting member, Victor Manuel Díez Barroso (1890–1930). Turning to the theatre after travel in the United States and Europe, he began writing plays in 1910 and in 1914 published three realistic and never performed dramas. In 1925 his *Las pasiones mandan* was performed and his *Véncete a ti mismo* won an important newspaper competition. In the latter, Díez Barroso's ability to make the unreal real is evident, as is his knowledge of French drama and Pirandello. Here the subconscious makes its appearance in Mexican drama, as the doctor gives his wife, "Ella," a play to read. In the second act the play she is reading becomes reality. It is about a man whose father was a strangler. Has the son inherited these tendencies? When he embraces his wife in the moonlight he begins to strangle her. In Act III "Ella" tells her husband she does not like the play. When she then teases him about a flower he begins to strangle her. The curtain leaves the audience in doubt as to the outcome.

This prolific dramatist wrote twenty-six plays during his short lifetime, ten of them one-act plays, including the charming *Nocturno*, published posthumously with six others in 1935. His deepest probe into the subconscious is the vague and symbolic *El y su cuerpo*, which imagines the return of Mexico's aviator Carranza, killed in a plane accident. It was performed and published after the playwright's death. His wife, a concert pianist, composed music for his four-act "Meditation," *Estampas*, another posthumous production.

Francisco Monterde (1894–   ), university professor and historian of the theatre, wrote one play in 1913, never published, then translated French and English plays for the campaign of education inaugurated by his fellow members in the Group of Seven. His *La que volvió a la vida* (1921) formed part of the Jiménez Rueda season of 1923. It tells of a nonconformist widow, Angela, who refuses to end her own medical career just because her husband has died. *En el molino* (1923) is a one-act tragedy of the Revolution about a son who unwittingly kills his father during a cattle raid. *Viviré para ti* was part of the 1925 theatrical season. *Oro negro* (written 1926), a realistic study of the unpleasant oil man, Mr. Taylor, is set in 1911 and reveals the desire of peons to destroy the oil wells and go back to their happier farming. In the one-act *La careta de cristal* (1932), the flirt Josefina gets her just deserts. *Proteo* (1931), another of Monterde's score of plays, is a symbolistic fable chosen by Julio Bracho's Experimental Escolares del Teatro in 1934 for a performance, along with Strindberg's *Miss Julie* and Synge's *Riders to the Sea.* However Monterde's greatest contribution to his country's stage is his *Bibliografía del teatro en México* (1934).

The novelist Carlos Noriega Hope (1896–1934) started his brief dramatic career in 1932 when two acts of his *La señorita Voluntad* appeared in his newspaper *El Universal Ilustrado,* the same paper that recognized Díez Barroso's *Véncete a ti mismo* with a prize in 1925. Noriega Hope's own play of newspaper life got its final act, with a new character inserted, in time for the 1925 season. Carmen wants to provide Cordero with will power. Though he has deceived women and takes dope, she insists at the end that she can be his Señorita Voluntad.

Noriega Hope then set a love story against a rural Mexican background in *Una flapper* (1925). *El honor del ridículo* was finished in 1926. His employment in Hollywood resulted in *Che Ferrati* (1926). *Margarita de Arizona* (1929) is a comedy of international relationships, first performed in English in the Pan American Theatre. The death at the early age of 38 of this witty, ironical, kindly writer was a great loss to Mexican drama, especially because the columns of his newspaper were always open to encourage it.

Ricardo Parada León (1902–) made his biggest contribution not with his dramatic comedies, but with his insistence at the rehearsals of his *La agonía* and *La esclava* in 1923 that the director make the actors talk Mexican instead of Castilian. He was a realist with an interest in psychology, not only Mexican but universal. Three plays depict the tragedy of the middle class: *Los culpables* (1925); *El dolor de los demás* (1929), a triangle play about a lawyer, his wife, and his sister-in-law; and *El porvenir del doctor Gallardo* (1936). In *Hacia la meta,* completed about 1930 but not performed till 1956, Parada León anticipated automation in industry. The small number of Parada León's plays is explained by his greater interest in contributing to the movies. He did write *Camino real* (1949).

Youngest of the Group of Seven were Lazaro Lozano García (1899–) and Carlos Lozano García (1902–), strong advocates of the national theatre program. Inspired by a visit to the United States to write for the theatre, they collaborated in three plays which were performed in the same theatre in 1925: *Al fin mujer* (published 1927); *El chacho*, full of Mexican flavor; and *La incomprendida*. The first, suggested by a Tagore story, was elaborated with Mexican material about María who loses her sight because her husband-doctor tries by himself to cure her. When her cousin Margarita makes a play for the doctor, María's talk of their unborn son wins him back.

Of the six plays by these brothers, *Hembra* (1936) was the last. The demise of the Comedia Mexicana discouraged Carlos, who went into business.

Of course, the careers of these seven dramatists extended far beyond the year of 1926, and during their lifetimes other Mexicans joined them in their campaign for the theatre. Reports of new intellectual life in Russia and France led three writers, Novo, Villaurrutia, and Gilberto Owen, to found the literary review *Ulises* in 1927. Antonieta Rivas Mercado, just back from Europe, met the printers' bills. Out of this interest in modern literature came their establishment of the Ulises Theatre the next year; they were helped out by many young, enthusiastic amateurs like Celestino Gorostiza, Manuel Rodríguez Lozano, Roberto Montenegro, and Julio Castellano. Their first actresses were Clementina Otero and Isabela Corona. Critics called them "El grupo de los snobs," but their idea in offering French and North American plays in translation was to go beyond the local themes flavored with Benavente and to show the possibilities of universal themes appropriate to contemporary problems and people.[11]

Through the efforts of Miss Ocampo and others, La Comedia Mexicana came into being in 1929, designed to concentrate on Mexican authors. It survived till 1936, though in its final years, in an attempt to survive, it performed foreign works as well.

By this time the Teatro Orientación, organized in 1932, was in operation and could take its place. Celestino Gorostiza (1904–   ) was its moving spirit. He had worked in the Department of Education, and in his spare time had been a drama critic and collaborator, with Novo and the rest, in creating Teatro de Ulises in 1927–1928. Promoted to the head of the Department of Fine Arts, Gorostiza used his department to sponsor actors in plays to educate the Mexicans in

[11] Anna L. Oursler, "El drama mexicano desde la revolución de 1910 hasta el año 1940," *Congreso Internacional de Catedráticos de Literatura Iberoamericana.*

world drama. So came into being Teatro Orientación, the most important of all Mexico's amateur groups. Its purpose was to perform "works characteristic of the universal theatre of every period." Plays by Russian, German, French, Italian, and English dramatists were put into Spanish by Villaurrutia, Gorostiza, and Lazo. Bertolt Brecht (1898–1956), later to have such an influence in Mexico, Chile, and Cuba, became more than a name, and his "epic theatre," meant to appeal and teach through the intellect rather than the emotions, began to assume the position of prominence it has come to occupy.

Though some of Mexico's best actors participated, there was no star system; Orientación insisted on "the subordination of the individual to the work of art." For its first two seasons, only foreign plays occupied the boards, so there was no opportunity for Mexican dramatists. However this same year Magdaleno and Bustillo Oro had opened the small Teatro de Ahora, where Mexican social and political plays had their opportunity. For it Mariano Azuela (1873–1952) unsuccessfully dramatized his novel *Los de abajo* (1932). In 1934 a theatre with two thousand seats was made available in the Palace of Fine Arts. At the same time, the number of amateur and experienced groups in Mexico increased. Some were centered in schools and universities, like the Escolares del Teatro founded in 1931 by director Julio Bracho. He later organized the Teatro de la Universidad and directed plays in the Escuelas Nocturnas de Arte para Trabajadores.

Then came a lag. Teatro Orientación died, smothered by the movies. The Medianoche, created in 1940 by Usigli, was the victim of adverse criticism. But along came a second wave. In 1942 the powerful Proa, the creation of José de J. Aceves, profiting from the mistakes of earlier experimental groups, took over a corner of the Palace of Fine Arts and performed twenty-five plays. In 1943 Teatro de Mexico made a start, followed in 1946 by the Magic Lantern, an appropriate name for a venture by drama lovers in the Electricians' Union. It was directed by José Retes (1918–   ). In 1947 came Teatro de Arte Moderno and Xavier Rojas' Teatro Estudiantil Autónomo (TEA), presenting farces and Mexican *sainetes,* and followed by many other small playhouses that were to provide training for dramatists who would produce for the professional theatres of the next generation.[12]

[12] *Teatro mexicano del siglo XX,* II, xxxi–xxxii.

A third period of activity among the amateur actors was marked by the founding in 1949 of Teatro del Caracol, a successor of Proa. Teatro de las Máscaras and Círculo de Arte were others. The first theatre-in-the-round (1953) had to be set up for each performance in the Society of Architects' Building after office hours, by Xavier Rojas, who was back from study in the United States. Its first offering was John Patrick's *Hasty Heart.* Later the actor J. Humberto Robles Arenas (1915–) used the theatre-in-the-round technique for his *Los desarraigados* (1956), which is about conflict between Mexicans uprooted by a move to the United States, and their American-born children, who feel no true nationality. Earlier, Robles Arenas had written *Dos boletos para México,* for the 1954 IBNA Festival, and *Provincia* (1955).

However, perhaps the greatest expression of confidence in Mexico's theatrical future and best encouragement to drama came on April 30, 1953, with the opening of Teatro de los Insurgentes, five miles from the center of Mexico City. The banker and play patron José María Dávila had determined to build the most technically perfect experimental theatre in Latin America. The building represented two years of work and five million pesos. Architect Alejandro Prieto created a fifty-foot-square stage, to be used either behind a proscenium arch or surrounded by 1,200 comfortable chairs. Mosaics by Diego Rivera across the front of the building added $55,000 to the cost. The theatre opened with *Yo, Colón,* a musical with Mexico's comic, Cantinflas. However—one example of Mexico's theatrical difficulties—the government set a top price of twelve pesos on admissions. Even if the house were full every night it couldn't operate at a profit.

This was also the year that the Instituto Nacional de Bellas Artes (INBA) opened its plant in Chapultepec Park. There is an auditorium holding fifteen thousand, a theatre-in-the-round, Teatro del Granero, Teatro del Bosque and a new Teatro Orientacíon named for the earlier group. INBA also started a school for actors. Mexican drama was on the move. Seven theatres opened in 1953 and three more the following year, with eight to come in 1955. In both 1956 and 1957 four more were established, and in 1958 three. Then the pace slowed.

But where were the dramatists coming from, to fill all these stages?

When the Seven started, all sorts of "-isms" were in the air. Russians talked of drama of the masses. Shaw was building a social theatre on foundations by Ibsen. Lenormand was experimenting with psychology, and the Germans were investigating the abstract, while Pirandello worked with the mind. Mexican dramatists had a share in all these movements. Mystery and poetry and a universality beyond the family life of a peon or the quaintness of a Mexican in a big sombrero were characteristic of the many plays written before 1938.

The demand by Comedia Mexicana for local material for its 1929 season enticed Carlos Díaz Dufoo (1861–1941) back into drama. He had written two one-act *juguetes, De gracia* and *Entre vecinos,* when he got back to Mexico in 1885 after fourteen years of study in Spain, but for forty-five years he had been interested chiefly in poetry. He was one of the founders of the influencial *Revista Azul* (1894), the first modernist poetry magazine. Now, nearly seventy, he wrote *Padre Mercader,* a three-act comedy on the theme "shirtsleeves to shirtsleeves in three generations." Opening on August 24, 1929, it was the first serious Mexican play to run for a hundred performances.

To prove that this technically excellent play about a merchant and his stupid grandchildren was not just luck, this almost-blind journalist wrote *La fuente del Quijote* (1930), a Ramón de la Cruz parade of characters along the Chapultepec promenade. A later play *Un hombre solo* (published 1937) had only one performance before the censor stopped it. Miguel's outspoken criticisms of Mexico's social and economic conditions and an attack on the union in a knitting mill made it seem dangerous to the government. Discouraged, this master of flexible dialog, well-developed climaxes, and believable characters, gave up the struggle. His son, Carlos Díaz Dufoo Jr. (1888–1932) tried to enter the field with a farce, *El barco* (1931), set aboard a transatlantic liner, and *Temis municipal* (1931), ridiculing Mexican legal procedure, but he lacked his father's craftsmanship.

In 1932 two collaborators, the lawyer Juan Bustillo Oro (1904–   ) and Mauricio Magdaleno (1906–   ), a successful novelist, established the tiny Teatro de Ahora in the Hidalgo Theatre, to present thesis plays on social problems. In his violent attacks the poet Magdaleno was no dramatist. Bustillo, though more logical, was prosy. But though their technique differed, they were united in their demands for social reforms.[13] In *Tiburón* (1931) Bustillo made a Mexican adaptation of Ben Jonson's *Volpone.* Then he completed three origi-

[13] J. H. Crow, "Drama revolucionario mexicano," *Revista Hispánica Moderna,* V (1939), 20–31.

nal dramas, designed to "record the [political] temperature of the times." One bore the title *Los que vuelven*—ironic, since of the four members of José María's family who went to the United States looking for work, none returned. However it was voted one of the five best plays in a Latin American competition in Spain in 1933. *Masas,* in which the workers vainly fight dictatorship in an imaginary Latin American country, and *Justicia, S.A.* (written 1931), about a judge shaped by the pressure of money and power in spite of his efforts to be fair, were never performed, though Bustillo published them all together in 1933. He wrote a fine trilogy, *San Miguel en las Espinas* (1932), an idealized sociological demand that those who till the soil be allowed to own it. In its mingling of the races it is intensely patriotic, but its cast of thirty-two men and three women, besides crowds of soldiers, laborers, and women, presents staging problems.

Teatro revolucionario (1933) by Magdaleno, published within a week of the publication of his partner's collection, contains three plays which were performed in Teatro de Ahora. In *Trópico* (written 1931) white men try to raise bananas, find the land deceptively yielding. In *Pánuco 37* North American oil men acquire land from farm-loving peons through the help of unscrupulous judges, while overdressed and ill-mannered North American girls look on. In *Emiliano Zapata* Magdaleno tried to include in one ironic play everything about that revolutionary leader, to show that his reward for trying to provide land to the downtrodden Indians was betrayal and death.

After the closing of their theatre, Bustillo and Magdaleno collaborated in a happier vein on several nationalistic *sainetes* for the comedian Roberto Soto, among them *El Periquillo Sarniento* and *El Corrido de la Revolución* (1932).

Another of those who wrote for his own theatre was the director of Teatro Orientación, Celestino Gorostiza (1904–   ). With his brother José he had shared many duties in the older Teatro Ulises. His early plays were intellectual, tried out in Orientacíon. First came *El nuevo paraíso* (1930), intended as practice work and using Adam and Eve and a mirror to symbolize present conditions. *La escuela de amor* (1933) presents liars in a café. *Ser o no ser* (1934; published 1935) deals with Enrique and his dreams of wealth and success.

Having learned his craft and served as play director, after an interval of work for the movies Gorostiza went on with *Escombros del sueño* (1938), first tried out by amateurs in San Luis Potosí, and intended to demonstrate that only by idealizing reality can one realize a dream. The play that first brought him general attention, however, was his attack on racial discrimination, *El color de nuestra piel.* It won the Theatre Critics' Award for 1952.

Gorostiza's *Columna social* (1952) a "You Can't Take It with You" comedy about the newly rich, unadjusted Moncada family ran for seventy-three performances in the Puebla University Theatre in 1955 and inaugurated the Comedia Theatre in Mexico City that same year. He also provided the Mexican entry in the Pan American Theatre Festival of 1958. *La leña está verde* is a historical drama about Martín Cortés—a tough mixture of the silver of his conquistador father and the copper of his Indian mother Malinche.

But most important of Gorostiza's efforts are those in support of Mexico's developing theatre. As head of the theatre branch of INBA, he has encouraged scores of amateur groups throughout the republic.

Another playwright learning his craft with Gorostiza at Teatro Orientación was Xavier Villaurrutia (1903–1950), essentially a poet with an obsession about death.[14] After translating Chekhov, Pirandello, Lenormand, and others for Teatro Ulises and Orientación, he branched out on his own, took to heart the title of one of his own farces, *Sea Ud. breve* (1934), and wrote a number of short, intellectual plays characterized by well-made plots and excellent dialog, intended for the select audiences of Orientación. *Parece mentira* (1933), his first and one of his best plays, presents an unsolved mysterious situation. In the disorientation of his protagonists and their efforts to communicate beyond the level of the purely perfunctory, most of Villaurrutia's theatre might be labeled existentialist; for instance, *Invitación a la muerte* (1940; published 1947) has a Hamlet theme, except that the hero tries to escape life. *Ha llegado el momento* (1934) deals with a suicide plot. *¿En qué piensas?* (1934) is a triangle play.

In 1936 Villaurrutia, along with Usigli, received a scholarship to study drama at Yale University. He returned to Mexico with a sense of a wider panorama and a determination to be a universal rather than merely a national dramatist. His *La hiedra* (1941) was de-

---

[14] Antonio Moreno, "Xavier Villaurrutia: The Development of His Theatre," *Hispania*, XLIII (December, 1950), 508–514; also Vera L. Beck, "Xavier Villaurrutia, dramaturgo moderno," *Revista Iberoamericana*, XVIII, 25 (December, 1952), 27–29.

clared the best play of the year. He achieved one success after another with well-plotted and well-developed plays and characters
which were authentic in spite of their poetic and noble-sounding dialog. His chief flaw is his inability to create emotions. These qualities,
good and bad, appear in *La mujer légitima* (1943), a tragedy about
the mistress who replaces the dead wife, only to face the enmity of
her insane new daughter. *El yerro candente* (1944) is an *Electra* sort
of play describing family strife: Eduardo marries Isabel, knowing she
is to have a child by Román, and Román later lusts after his own
child. The humorous *El pobre Barba Azul* (published 1946; performed 1947) makes fun of sentimentality in following the fortunes
of Carmen and her two suitors. When Samuel declares he is a modern
Bluebeard, wanting all women, a psychoanalyst upsets him by showing that it is the woman who conquers the man; and so the other
suitor gets Carmen. Villaurrutia's final play was another balanced
and well-made tragedy, *Juego peligroso* (1949).

At almost the end of Orientación's activities, one of Latin America's
greatest dramatists joined the group as translator. Rodolfo Usigli
(1905–   ), on the stage at twelve and a theatre critic before he was
twenty, already had abundant experience. Often at odds with society,
nicknamed "Visconde" by teasing schoolmates, Usigli's combative
qualities stood him in good stead in early disappointments in getting
his plays produced. To get background, this self-taught dramatist
studied eight to ten well-known plays a day. Then he ventured to
write his first play, *El apóstol* (1928). Producers turned it down,
not because he was introducing psychiatry to the Mexican stage,
but because of the staging problem presented by an earthquake
in Act II. Only his translations for Orientación were staged. His
Noche de estío (1933) was refused and his *El niño y la niebla*
(1936) was turned down, though when finally produced in 1952,
after Usigli had acquired a reputation, it broke all Mexican records
with an eight months' run of 450 performances.

Such early theatrical experiences further embittered Usigli. However in 1936 he was given a scholarship to study drama in the United
States. *El gesticulador* (1937) was one result, a story of Professor
Rubio who died martyred and famous through taking on the identity
of a famous revolutionary general. But its implication that Mexicans
were *gesticuladores* offended his countrymen and delayed any performance till 1947. *Medio tono*, a three-act tragedy written in 1937, is

the first naturalistic play since Gamboa. In contrast, there is a happy ending to Usigli's later *La familia cena en casa* (1943). *Medio tono* was the first original play by Usigli to be staged, with a performance by María Tereza Montoya, but Usigli later disavowed any interest in this sort of drama.

Otra primavera (1938), introducing an old man considered insane by his family and saved only by his wife's pretense of being herself insane, ruffled no one's feelings and was another that got an immediate performance. It was turned into an excellent movie. However *La mujer no hace milagros* (1939) needled the critics so severely that when Usigli tried the following year to open his Teatro de Medianoche as a home for Mexican plays, they attacked his efforts and closed the Teatro within six weeks. Usigli continued his interest in abnormal psychology with *Aguas estancadas* (published 1939; performed 1952), a melodrama about a poor girl who prefers her poor suitor to a wealthy old lunatic who sees in her his dead wife.

Generally considered the masterpiece of Usigli, and the first in a proposed trilogy, was *Corona de sombra* (published 1943; performed 1947) an interpretation, rather than a historical account, of Maximilian and Carlota in Mexico. This tragedy, much admired by George Bernard Shaw in an English translation, embodies a favorite theme of Mexican dramatists. Miguel Lira (1905–   ) in *Carlota en México* (1943) and Agustín Lazo (1898–   ) in *Segundo imperio* (1946) were treating of it at almost the same time; but there is a nobility in the Usigli play that shows a masterly control of technique and heightens the emotions. The second of that trilogy, *Corona de fuego*, was finished in 1961. It concerns Cuauhtémoc.

An entirely different sort is the sentimental *Función de despedida* (1949; published 1953) about a farewell tour by an aging actress. The surrealistic device of the voice of thought helps to mingle reality and imagination. In a 1960 competition for translated Latin American dramas, this one received the first prize. Shortly after it came another by this master of creating enemies, *Jano es una muchacha* (1952), about an amateur prostitute and her righteous father, who really owns the establishment where she works. Its staging raised a storm of protests. Among Usigli's other works is *Mientras amemos* (published 1956), an intense psychological drama about a possessive nursemaid and her repressed "child" of thirty-eight years.

However, despite the many criticisms of this lone wolf of the Mexican stage, Usigli is probably the Mexican dramatist most likely to be remembered, because of his many contributions to the theatre along so many lines. As a dramatist he is a man of reason, where Villaurrutia was an imaginative intellectual. Usigli is interested in the psychology of his characters, and is the dramatist of Mexican reality, implied in his plays and stated in prefaces and epilogs. After his own success as a dramatist, he helped train actors for the Mexican stage, and in his classes in playwriting he gave formal training, such as his generation never had, to the next generation. Among his students were Carballido, Hector Mendoza, Sergio Magaña, Ignacio Retes, Jorge Ibargüengoitia, and Luisa Josefina Hernández, who took over Usigli's classes when he became a diplomat.

Other hands prepared Usigli's work for the movies. The scenario for *El niño y la niebla* was written by Edmundo Báez (1914–   ) himself a practicing dramatist. For it he won an Ariel, the Mexican equivalent of an Oscar. Lured from the medical profession after opening a clinic for mental diseases, Dr. Báez also wrote two rural tragedies about the problems of farmers: *Ausentes* (published 1940; performed 1942) and *El rencor de la tierra* (published 1942; performed 1943). Then he went on a scholarship to Hollywood and returned to supply scripts to the Mexican movie industry. Spain gave him a prize for his work on *Doña Diabla,* but he also continued with original plays. One was *Un alfiler en los ojos* (1952), about the domination of a dead mother over her family, and another was the more recent *Un macho* (1959), a plotless criticism of Mexican "machismo."

Two others of the dramatists originally connected with the early experimental theatres were Novo and Lazo. Salvador Novo (1904–   ) collaborated with Villaurrutia in founding Teatro de Ulises in 1928, and for it translated and adapted plays by O'Neill, Dunsany, Synge, and Italian and French dramatists. His own first attempts, the one-act *Divorcio* and the dialog, *La señorita Remington,* were both performed and published in Noriega Hope's paper, *El Universal Ilustrado* in 1924. He also wrote *El tercer Fausto,* never performed, though later published in French in 1937. But Novo's early days were devoted to the teaching of courses on the theatre and on acting. As head of the Theatre Department of INBA from 1947 to 1952, he wrote and directed a couple of children's plays: *Don Quijote* (1947) and *Astucia* (1948), which was based on Gonzaga Inclán's story. Then he turned to longer adult plays, like the satire on high society *La culta dama* (1951). *A ocho columnas* (1956) is an attack on corrupt journalism. *Yocasta o casi* won the critics' second prize in 1961. Between times, Novo founded Teatro de la Capilla, with ninety-eight seats, in his home town of Coyoacán in 1953, and many first plays by budding dramatists have been tried out there. Carballido and Magaña are some of those encouraged by Novo in their early playwriting days.

Another veteran of the Ulises, first as scene painter, was the artist Augustín Lazo (1898–), who went on to translate French and Italian dramas, then produced original plays about familiar people and moments of history. First written was *Segundo imperio* (1946) in which Carlota, realizing her husband's dangerous position in Mexico, begs him to trust Colonel López, who eventually betrays him. Because it was delayed in being staged, Lazo became first known through his play of the Revolution, *La huella* (1947), completely Mexican in atmosphere, about a young overseer in love with the daughter of his boss. It ends with the suicide of the couple. Lazo then introduced a mysterious, compelled murderer of colonial times in *El caso de D. José Manuel* (1948), which anachronistically employs psychiatry before its time.

Eventually, in a later era, a new generation began writing for the professional stage. Though they expressed the realities of Mexico, they also became more universal. Unfortunately, in their attempts to provide theatrical qualities they often sacrificed literary qualities.

One of the most successful, commercially, is Luis G. Basurto (1920–) a critic at the age of nineteen and in his earliest plays a disciple of Benavente. His *Diálogos de Suzette* (1940) opened Usigli's Teatro de Medianoche. After other brief plays he spent several years in Hollywood in preparation for a career in Mexican movies. Back in the theatre in 1945 with his own *La que se fue*, in 1959 he took Virginia Fábregas and a Mexican company on a tour to Spain, then returned to promote the first drama festival of the Unión Nacional de Autores, in 1961. One of its offerings was his own *Frente a la muerte*, a box-office success about a wife who shoots her husband's mistress when the lovers attempt to elope across the border with a cargo of dope.

This was followed by *Cada quien su vida* (1952; published 1958) based on a popular song. It describes New Year's Eve capers in a slum nightclub. Its performance in 1955 was made into Basurto's greatest financial success through its denunciation by the League of Decency. From then on, an eager public awaited his every play. *Toda una dama* (1954) about Rogelio through whom a million pesos was stolen from the bank and whose apparently heartless wife proved to be "quite a woman," was another smash hit, as were *Miércoles de ceniza*, the favorite of the 1957 season, and *Los reyes del mundo*, a success of 1959. *El escándalo de la verdad* was a 1960 hit. Another favorite is *La locura de los ángeles*, which pits an idealistic old woman against a usurer who seeks to exploit penniless residents of a tenement house. Basurto plays a many-sided role in the Mexican theatre as author, impresario, and promoter. His latest venture was a 1961–1962 jaunt to Buenos Aires with actors and six Mexican plays.

Another Usigli-trained dramatist is Sergio Magaña (1924–   ), a Jesuit-taught writer with great power and sense of the dramatic. He is especially concerned with life among the poor. Magaña began with *La noche transfigurada* (1947) and *El suplicante* (1950), a one-act dramatization of his novel of 1942. His power was first realized, however, at the première of his *Los signos del zodíaco* (1951; published 1953), influenced by Sartre. It somewhat resembles that much debated leftist play by José Revueltas, the cruel *El cuadrante de la soledad* (1950), for which Diego Rivera designed scenery. Salvador Novo directed Magaña's play in the Palace of Fine Arts. In spite of its depressing picture of life of student, anarchist, and prostitute in a Mexican boarding house in 1944, Magaña's bitter play enjoyed a run of a hundred performances when revived in the Teatro del Bosque. The crime and its dramatic resolution make a crashing final curtain. More than one critic has termed it among the greatest plays of the Mexican theatre.

It was followed by Magaña's *Montezuma II* (1953; published 1954), which some critics believe will also emerge as one of the great Mexican plays. The action takes place on November 7, 1519, the last day of Montezuma's power, when the fatalistic Aztec emperor feels himself a figure of destiny. He determines to overcome the white man's God by passive resistance. The curtain falls just before the arrival of Cortés and his army, and a chorus of old women gloomily chants the doom of a race. This play was one of the first published in the short-lived monthly *Panorama del teatro,* established July, 1954, to report on the state of Mexico's drama and to give permanence to national plays and foreign drama in translation.

Later Magaña offered a sort of detective play, *El pequeño caso de Jorge Lívido* (1958), which combines social criticism with a statement of the essential humanity of mankind. It was performed in Teatro de los Insurgentes. The villain, masquerading as a good man, is given skilful character revelation, and the action is interesting with convincing situations. The language, however, sometimes becomes rhetorical and unnatural, and the title is weak, as is that of his next *Meneando el bote* (1959), a flaw he shares with Hernández and Carballido; their imitators, like Torres Septién and Cecilia Guilarte, do even worse in selecting titles.

An important year in Mexican theatrical history was 1945, for then the capital witnessed a performance in Spanish of Tennessee William's *A Streetcar Named Desire*. Not only did it make the reputation of María Douglas, its leading lady, but it deeply impressed at least five dramatists of the modern school, who attribute their careers to its inspiration.[15]

Best known of the quintet, in prizes won and popular successes, was Federico Schroeder Inclán (1910–   ). Educated in the United States, and experimenter in a number of professions before finding his field in the drama, he won first prize in the 1950 Fiesta de Primavera with his first play, the dramatic *Luces de carburo*, about ten miners trapped underground. *Espaldas mojadas*, about a wetback accused of murder in Texas and cleared by a North American woman, gave him a repeat award the following year. *El duelo* (1951), a class struggle between a poor boy and the son of a millionaire in a military school, won the INBA competition. *Hoy invita la Güera* (1955), an anachronistic farce about the Pastry War, dealing with the famous "Güera Rodríguez," won the Critics' Award for that year.

Other plays by Inclán that did not receive awards include *Hidalgo* (1953), about the Mexican Independence, and *Una señorita decente*, about a young woman who marries a disgusting colonel to save her brother's life. In *Una mujer para los sábados* (published 1956; performed 1959) Graciela manages to remain a rich old man's darling while married to the poor young man she loves. The Teatro de los Compositores made its debut in 1956 with Inclán's *El deseo que llega al anochecer,* and Teatro de la Esfera was inaugurated with his *El seminarista de los ojos negros,* later renamed *Yo pecador me confieso,*

---

[15] Maria Luisa Mendoza, "New Directions for Mexican Theatre," *Américas,* No. 10 (April, 1958), 14.

in which a weak, immoral man, educated for the priesthood, blames his mother for all his troubles.

Inclán has written nearly a score of commercially successful, if not always artistic, plays. One of the best is *Una esfinge llamada Cordelia* (1958). It appeared in book form that year with four other current successes: Luis Moreno's *Los sueños encendidos*, Magaña's *El pequeño caso de Jorge Lívido*, Cantón's *Malditos*, and Gorostiza's *La leña está verde*, now rechristened *Malinche*.

The story of an attempt by a director to stage *Romeo and Juliet*, in *Cada noche muere Julieta*, won for Inclán the 1959 Ruiz de Alarcón prize. Less skilful, but saved by the acting of Montoya, was his *Deborah* (1960); however his *Cuartelazo* was the hit of the Lunes Popular de Teatro series that year.

Frederick Schroeder Inclán came to the theatre at the mature age of forty. Experience and critical ability have usually enabled him to avoid the uncontrolled exuberance that flaws the work of some of Mexico's younger dramatists. Simplicity, an ear for dialog, and skilful management of situation, along with dedication to the theatre have made Inclán a leading figure among Mexico's contemporary dramatists.

Competing with Inclán in the 1950 Spring Festival, and receiving the second prize for *La zona intermediata,* a modern *auto sacramental,* complete with its *loa, El auto de la triple porfía,* was Emilio Carballido (1925–   ), a close competitor in prizes won. In fact, practically every play by Carballido has received some sort of recognition. Salvador Novo first made him known through a performance in 1950 of Carballido's *Rosalba y los Llaveros*. Set amid the gaiety of a Veracruz festival and overlaid with Freud, it records satirically, yet tenderly, the attempts of the cosmopolitan heroine to solve the problems of her provincial family.

That year Carballido went to New York for two years of drama study. Returning in 1953 to the Veracruz School of the Theatre, he promptly won a prize for his opera *El Pozo.* In 1954 *El Nacional* prize went to him for *La danza que sueña la tortuga,* about a middle-class provincial lady who learns to put up with her griefs. It contains the same types as in his earlier *Rosalba,* but is without its psychiatry. The new play takes place in a refreshment shop run by two spinsters in Córdoba, Mexico, where the author was born. It combines the two currents that characterize Carballido's work: realism and fantasy. As a neo-realist, he brings the Mexican daily life to the stage with careful attention to Mexican psychology. As a writer of phantasy and imagination, he gave an example in his first work, with its account of dead souls on their way to their final abode, and again in *La hebra de oro,* the only prize winner in the National University Contest of 1955. In it two women preserve the illusion that the grandson who loved them will eventually return from a foreign land. *El relojero de Córdoba* (1955), produced successfully in 1960, combines fantasy with a realistic satire on the world's false liberty and false justice. *El día que se soltaron los leones* also has its poetic side, as does the retelling of an old myth in *Medusa.* The latter won a ten-thousand-peso Centro México unproduced-play prize in 1961. *Felicidad,* in contrast, has a down-to-earth treatment of a middle-class Mexican family and its lonely and unhappy women who have no interests. It earned first prize in the 1955 Dramatic Festival. *D.F.* is a collection of nine one-act plays permeated by a fatalistic indifference to life. The publication of four of Carballido's works in 1960 honors one of the most interesting of modern Mexican dramatists, a man who refuses to be classified.

Another dramatist urged toward the theatre by Tennessee Williams was the novelist, poet, bullfight authority Rafael Solana (1915–   ), who had been in newspaper work since the age of fourteen, and at thirty-seven started a drama career with the fantasy *Las islas de oro* (1952; published 1954), about an imaginary refuge for suicides. It was performed in Basurto's Union Nacional de Autores series. Encouraged by its reception, Solana issued a stream of gay, light plays, in some of which the satire was rather heavy. One of them, based on one of his short stories, was *Estrella que se apaga* (1953), about an aging movie star who commits suicide when make-up will no longer restore her allure. *Solo quedaban las plumas,* offered that same year, treats whimsy as if it were reality. In 1954 Solana completed his amusing *Debiera haber Obispas* and *La ilustre cuna.* In the first, the housekeeper for a priest uses for the good of the community what she claims were the old man's deathbed babbling of secrets of the confessional. Some of the religiously inclined critics found this play immoral when it was produced by an experimental group. Solana paid his respects to them in *La ilustre cuna,* about false standards used by the press to determine greatness.

Lázaro ha vuelto (1955) is also based on Solana's formula for his comedies: Supposing that something possibly fantastic should happen, what would be its logical results? This combination of realism with imagination provides opportunity for both satire and wit. In *Lázaro*, a famous tenor, long retired, tries to make a comeback. *El plan de Iguala* (1955), later called *La edad media*, considers the plight of the creator of a plan for absolute equality when the time has come for him to be killed for having outlived his productive period. It was not as well received as the later *A su imagen y semejanza* (1957), in which an orchestra director, in his scorn of critics, devises a puppet to take over his duties. It even takes over his wife. Performed in 1960 during Mexico's Month of the Theatre, it won the prize for the best revival. Translated into German, it was performed in Berlin in 1962. Then Solana was silent for three years till he dramatized his novel *La casa de La Santísima* and wrote *Espada en mano*, both excellent in dialog, movement, and character development. They prove again that if Solana were less ambitious to equal Lope de Vega's speed of composition, he might become one of Mexico's great dramatists.

One of those who studied under Usigli at the Mexican National University, continued her training in the United States, and eventually replaced Usigli as teacher was Luisa Josefina Hernández (1928–   ). Her debut as dramatist with *Aguardiente de caña* won first prize in the 1951 Spring Festival. *Los sordomudos* (1953), about a tyrannical father finally abandoned by all except a deaf-mute servant, was followed by *Botica modelo*. Though displeasing to critics, it won the 1954 prize of the newspaper *El Nacional*. *La corona del ángel* deals with poor Fernanda, a suicide because she can't decide between two sweethearts. One of Miss Hernández' best efforts is *Los frutos caídos* (1957), submitted as her M.A. thesis. *Arpas blancas, conejos dorados,* though somewhat inferior, was considered the best of the 1959 season. In it the completely selfish Celia sells her country home, though she makes destitute all her relatives dependent on it. *La paz ficticia* was Miss Hernández' important contribution to the stage in 1960, and in 1962 she published *La calle de la gran ocasión*, consisting of nineteen dialogs ranging from whimsy to depression. They offer excellent character delineation, especially one in which two people meet after twenty years, he the jeweler, and she needing to sell her family jewels. Apparently Miss Hernández is a pessimist at heart; certainly she uses her technical ability chiefly to show the futility of life. That is true of her best play *Los huéspedes reales* (1957) that, like other plays by her, shows her study of Bertolt Brecht.

Three other contemporary dramatists deserve mention. Jorge Ibargüengoitia (1928–   ), the only one of Usigli's students called "maestro" by the professor, turned from engineering to drama in 1949. He never published his first attempts, but his *Susana y los jóvenes* (1952) was performed by the Unión Nacional de Autores in its 1954 season. Set in university circles, it deals with the vain pursuit of Tacubaya, an opportunist, by middle-class Susana. This won Ibargüengoitia a Rockefeller scholarship for drama study in New York. During his absence from Mexico his three-act comedy *Clotilde en su casa* was performed in a commercial theatre under its new title, *Adulterio exquisito*. This triangle about Clotilde and her mild affair with the friend of her husband was selected as representative of this playwright's technique for inclusion in Volume III of *Teatro Mexicano del Siglo XX*. Other performed but unpublished plays by him include *Ante varias esfinges*, dealing with the interests of three generations: death, money, and love, and *La lucha con el ángel* (1954), about the marriage of Carmen and Alberto being nearly wrecked by her old flame and his intimate friend.

Juan Miguel de Mora is best known through his pacifist play, *Los héroes no van al frente*, which is involved with a wife and her eighteen-year-old brother-in-law during three periods of war. Mora also wrote *Una cruz para cada hombre*, a three-act tragedy set in 71 B.C., about Spartacus, master of slaves, who tries to remain humane; *Un hombre de otro mundo*, a three-act drama about Pedro's difficulties in the world of the theatre; and what Mora called a "philosophic drama," the symbolic *Primero es la luz*.

Youngest of the Mexican dramatists with a secure position is Hector Mendoza (1932–   ), a playwright at seventeen and a prize winner in the 1952 Spring Festival. His *Las cosas simples* won the 1953 Critics' Award. In Café La Concordia it held the boards for a year and a half and has had a total of a thousand performances all over Mexico. It is rightly named for it deals with simple things— penniless students, plans to cheat in a Latin examination, and light love affairs. Mendoza's comedy *Tobogán* (1959), named from a street in Guanajuato, presents a group of old and young and their acceptance of life's truths. Most recently his *Ahogados* (1960) tells what happens when the trustee of the estate dies in an airplane crash and the penniless family cannot claim the money due it.

There is so much activity on the Mexican stage that even to name the new writers would fill a paragraph. In the 1960 season, eighty plays were produced professionally in the capital, twenty-four by Mexican writers. The 1961 season was fair, but in 1962, only twelve new plays appeared, mostly unimportant. The professional theatre follows two lines: sure successes and experimental sampling of world drama. Betweentimes local authors get a chance. Fernando Sánchez Mayán's *Las alas del pez* was one of 1960's outstanding performances, along with Hugo Argüelles' macabre comedy *Los cuervos están de luto*. This author, now looming large in Mexico's theatre, first attracted attention with his prize-winning *Los prodigiosos* in 1957, about crooks who play on the religious beliefs of a country town. It won the Critics' Award for its 1961 production. He also wrote *El tejedor de milagros*.

As elsewhere in the Hemisphere, it is the activities of the amateur and experimental groups that offer greatest hope for drama. Only such groups would give a hearing to José Attolini (1916–), forerunner of existentialism, and his morbid and combative plays that demolish without offering solutions: *Suburbio* (1938), covering twenty-four hours in the life of a suburban public square; *Vecindad* (1940), showing life in a tenement; *Vertedero* (1943), about a prostitute and her unsuccessful painter-brother; and *Kupra* (1944), whose protagonist is a union leader who acquires power during a strike and goes crazy.

Mexico has many such groups; Teatro Estudiantil de la Universidad was founded by Hector Azar, author of vanguard plays like *El periquillo sarniento*, best experimental play of 1961. Lola Bravo directs plays for children in Teatro del Bosque and heads a group of the Drama School of INBA. There are, besides, the Theatre of UNAM, Teatro de Coapa, a Jewish theatre under Seki Sano, the Instituto Nacional de la Juventud, actors from the Architecture School of the University, and many others with ambitions to appear before audiences. Some of them took part in the Seventh Annual Drama Festival of INBA in September, 1960, where the prize went to *El juicio* by Alfredo Pacheco Buenrostro, a play originally seen when Teatro Rotunda opened in 1955. Second prize winner was *Columbus*

1916 by José María Camps, a novelist from Barcelona. The play commemorates the fiftieth anniversary of Pancho Villa's foray into Texas.

Of course, things do not always go smoothly. The government Department of Spectacles forbade a dramatization of Rojas' *Celestina* and Anouilh's *Jezebel* in 1960 and of Strindberg's *Sonata de los Espectadores* in 1961. Yet the professional stages show vigor, and the offerings of amateur groups are vital and frequently touch on human social problems. Two flaws are evident. First, good critics are scarce. Many who review drama are biased, prejudiced toward writers following European models or toward new types. Too often they belong to cultural or economic cliques and praise their friends while stressing the flaws of outsiders.

Second, too many dramatists take up pen before thoroughly analyzing their material. They may not realize it because there is little intelligent criticism even for the ambitious dramatists. But actors in Mexico are plentiful, opportunities to try out new plays are available, and good critics are bound to evolve. Though the Mexican theatre will continue to have its ups and downs, in comparison with its early periods, the increased activity and quality today are unquestioned.

APPENDIX

A Reading List of Spanish American Plays

Rushing, un-angel-like, into the shower of brickbats that always falls upon a compiler of "Best" lists, I am venturing to suggest plays for the consideration of that compiler of an eventual anthology of modern Spanish American plays, excluding the younger dramatists. Fourteen of them are represented in Carlos Solórzano's *El teatro hispanoamericano contemporáneo* (Mexico: Fondo de cultura Económica, 1964).

As an umbrella against the storm, it might be wise to explain my methods before I announce results. First I went through my card file, which lists all the plays in my library and others that I have seen or read, besides a few titles mentioned in "Best Play" compilations that I have not been able to track down. These latter, when cited below, are preceded by an asterisk. About them I know only what I have read in books.

From them all I selected those that made interesting reading, those important in the development of some country's theatre, and those written by dramatists representative of a nation or a movement. Only those written in the nineteenth and twentieth centuries are included.

Following these titles I have listed the plays included in a recent anthology which covers the four centuries of Latin American drama.

In a final grouping I have indicated my own selection of a small number of plays which would give students a good idea of the state of drama south of the Río Grande. I have screened my selections to the extent that if they were gathered into an anthology they would comprise a single volume.

Bolivia

Aguirre, Nataniel (1843–1888). *La represalia del héroe* (1869), a five-act patriotic play written in Cochabamba; *Condehuillo o La Calle del Pecado* (1870 ?), now being filmed.

*Aguirre Achá, José (1877–). *La capital disputada.*

Bustamante, Ricardo (1821–1886). *Más pudo el suelo que la sangre* (1845 ?, published 1869), poetic comedy of environment versus heredity.

Díaz Villamil, Antonio (1897–1948). *La Rosita* (1924), excellent costumbrismo; *La hoguera* (1924), poetic drama of the War of the Pacific; *La voz de la quena* (1922), Indian drama.

*Eduardo, Isaac G. (1868–1910). *Contra el destino* (1892), a "dead" soldier returns to his wife.

Flores, Mario (1901–). *Padre Liborio* (1928), with 2,000 performances in Buenos Aires; *La gringa Federica* (1935); *Veneno para ratones* (1950) Bolivian political satire.

Francovich, Guillermo (1901–). *Un puñal en la noche* (1956), historical drama with psychological conflict.

Gantier, Joaquín (1903–). *La ansiada paz* (1937), post-Chaco War problems.

Jofré, Hermógenes (1841–1890). *Los mártires* (1868), Civil War of 1861.

*Ortiz Pacheco, Nicolás (1893–1953). *Aniversario de boda* (1915), satire on manners of Europeanized Bolivians.

Pol Terrazas, J. *Athawalpa* (1869), romantic play with good minor characters.

Saavedra Pérez, Alberto (1895–). *Las cholitas del amigo Uria* (1922), costumbrista comedy by prolific dramatist.

Chile

Acevedo Hernández, Antonio (1886–1962). *Canción rota* (1921); *Caín* 1927); *Arbol viejo* (1930); *Almas perdidas* (1932), realism by one of Chile's best writers.

Aguirre, Isidora (1909–). *Las Pascualas* (1957), rationalization of a Chilean legend.

Caldera, Daniel (1852–1891). *Tribunal de honor* (1877), first play of serious Chilean theme.

Luco Cruchaga, Germán (1894–1936). *La viuda de Apablaza* (1928), matriarchal power in southern Chile.

Moock, Armando (1894–1942). *Pueblecito* (1917); *Mocosita* (1929), charming *costumbrismo* by one of Chile's best dramatists; *Rigoberto* (1935), the comedy of a meek man.

Moreno, Gloria (1909–). *Instituto de la felicidad* (1938), comedy; *Ultima victoria* (1942), about O'Higgins; *La breva pelá* (1945).

*Neves, Ana (1895–). *Más fuerte que la sangre* (1926), called by Villaespesa "one of the best ever written by a Spanish-speaking woman."

Orrego Vicuña, Eugenio (1901–1959). *Vírgenes modernas* (1929), drama of upper-class society.

Requena, María Asunción (1915–). *Pan caliente* (1962), problems of Chile's lower classes.

Silva, Victor Domingo (1882–1960). *Nuestras víctimas.*

Soto Aguilar, Matías (1882–1942). *El beso* (1912), one–act drama of Chilean feudalism.

Vodánovic, Sergio (1926–). *Deja que los perros ladren* (1960), a local-color, social drama.

Wolff, Egón (1926–). *Los invasores* (1960), a modern criticism by way of a nightmare.

Colombia

Acevedo Vallarino, Arturo (1876–   ). *Retazo de la vida* (1917), one-act comedy about a kindly priest.

Alvares Lleras, Antonio (1892–1956). *Víboras sociales* (1911), comedy; *El zarpazo* (1938), drama; *El virrey Solís* (1948), great historical drama.

Caicedo Rojas, José. *Castillo de Berkeley* (1853), early romanticism, set in England.

*Gómez Corena, Pedro (1882–   ) and Carlos Castello. *Hacia la vida* (1913), Sociedad de Autores prize comedy.

Lemos, Marino (1922?–   ). *Sangre verde* (1953), comedy.

Mesa Nicholls, Alejandro (1896–1920). *Juventud* (1920), comedy, one of Colombia's "three best plays."

Osorio, Luis Enrique (1896–   ). *El iluminado* (1929), four-act drama of revolutions; *El doctor Manzanillo* (1943), political tragedy with 50 performances the first year.

Restrepo J., José Luis. *La llama* (1925), Little Theatre Contest prize winner.

Reyes R., Germán. *Margot* (1924), drama of customs.

Samper Ortega, Daniel (1895–1943). *El escollo* (1925), drama about divorce.

Torres, Carlos Arturo (1867–1911). *Don Lope de Aguirre* (1891), a belated cape-and-sword drama.

*Valencia, Miguel Santiago. *Madame Adela* (1913), drama.

Zalamea, Jorge (1905–   ). *El rapto de las Sabinas* (1941), farce; *El hostel de Belén* (1939), poetic one–act Christmas play.

Costa Rica

Calsamiglia, Eduardo (–1918). *Bronces de antaño* (pub. 1919), poetic drama.

Escalante Durán, Manuel. *La bruma* (1948), metaphysical tragedy.

Garnier, José Fabio (1884–1956). *A la sombra del amor* (1921), tragedy.

Cuba

Baralt, Luis A. (1892–   ). *La luna en el pantano* (1936), drama of lower-class life.

*Foxá, Francisco Xavier (1816–1865). *Don Pedro de Castilla* (1836), first romantic play of the New World.

Galarraga Sánchez, Gustavo (1892–1934). *La vida falsa* (1913), two-act comedy; *La máscara de anoche* (pub. 1918), one-act matrimonial farce.

Ramos, José Antonio (1885–1946). *El traidor* (1915), one-act tragedy of Cuban revolution; *Tembladera* (1918), colonial versus modern Cuba.

Sánchez Varona, Ramón (1893–   ). *María* (1918), interpretation of war fever; *La sombra* (1938), tragedy of the influence of the dead.

Ecuador

Aguilera Malta, Demetrio (1905–   ). *Lázaro* (1941), tragedy of a school-teacher; *Dientes blancos* (1955), one–act social satire.

Avellán Ferrés, Enrique (1908–   ). *Como los árboles* (1927), anti-divorce tragedy.

Icaza, Jorge (1906–   ). *Como ellas quierren* (1932), feminine hysteria.

Moscoso Vega, Luis A. (1909–   ). *Conscripción* (1941), tragedy of Indian mistreatment.

El Salvador

Contreras, Raúl (1896–   ). *La princesa está triste* (1925), dramatization of a Rubén Darío poem.

Guatemala

Béneke, Walter (1928–   ). *Funeral Home* (1958), existentialism.

Galich, Manuel (1912–   ). *Papa Natas* (1938), modern satire of materialism versus idealism.

Mexico

Calderón, Fernando (1818–1845). *A ninguna de las tres* (1831), courtship comedy in verse; *Ana Bolena* (1843), romantic drama in verse about Henry VIII.

Díaz Dufoo, Carlos (1861–1941). *Padre Mercader* (1929), long-run, merchant-to-beggar-in-three-generations comedy.

Gamboa, José Joaquin (1879–1931). *El caballero, la muerte y el diablo* (1931), powerful symbolic mysticism.

Gorostiza, Celestino (1904–   ). *El color de nuestra piel* (1952), attack on racial discrimination.

Magaña, Sergio (1924–   ). *Los signos del zodíaco* (1951); *Montezuma II* (1953).

Navarro, Francisco (1902–   ). Trilogy: *La ciudad, El mar, La montaña*, one-act naturalistic plays.

Peón Contreras, José (1843–1907). *La hija del rey* (1876); *Gil González de Avila* (1876), examples of belated Mexican romanticism.

Saavedra, Rafael M. *La cruza* (1922), one–act Indian folk drama.

Usigli, Rodolfo (1905–   ). *El gesticulador* (pub. 1947), satire on boasting Mexicans; *Corona de sombra* (1947), the "why" of Maximilian and Carlota.

Villaurrutia, Xavier (1903–1950). *Ha llegado el momento* (1934), one-act near-tragedy of a married couple; *El ausente* (1937); *La hiedra* (1941).
*Villaseñor, Eduardo. *La grabiela* (1923), one act.

Nicaragua

Cuadra, Pablo Antonio (1912–   ). *Por los caminos van los campesinos,* (1958) customs comedy.
Robleto, Hernán (1893–   ). *El vendaval* (1925), C.A. contest winner.

Paraguay

Alsina, José Antonio (1897–   ). *La marca de fuego* (1926); *Intruso* (1934), evils of alcoholism,
*Casaccio Bibolini, Benigno (1907–   ). *El bandolero* (1932).
Halley Mora, Mario (1928–   ) *En traje para Jesús* (1958), a modern Christ visits Paraguay.
Pla, Josefina (1907–   ) and Roque Centurión Miranda (1900–1960). *Paterfamilias* (1939), life among peasants during Chaco War.
Rivarola Matto, José María (1917–   ). *El fin de Chipí González* (1954), the fate of a champion football player.

Peru

Aguila, Humberto del (1893–   ). *La dama blanca,* Peruvian jungle life.
Chioino, José (1898–   ). *El retorno* (1923), the rights of a genius in Lima society.
Salazar Bondy, Sebastián (1924–   ). *Rodil* (1952), existentialist historical tragedy. *El fabricante de deudas* (1962) social satire, following Brecht.
Segura, Manuel Ascencio (1805–1871). *Sargento Canuto* (1839), one-act farce in verse; *Ña Catita* (1858), comedy of a Lima Celestina.
Yerovi, Leónidas (1881–1917). *La casa de tantos* (1917), social drama.

Puerto Rico

Arriví, Francisco (1915–   ). *Bolero y plena* (1955), trilogy on Puerto Rican mulatto problems.
Belaval, Emilio S. (1903–   ). *La muerte* (1953), universal satire set in Europe.
Marqués, René (1919–   ). *La carreta* (1952), Puerto Rican love of the soil; *Los soles troncos* (1958), three old maids preserve ancient customs.

River Plate

Aldama, Orlando. *El diablo andaba en los choclos* (1941), 400 performances in two years.

Berruti, Alejandro (1888–1964). *Madre tierra* (1920), problems of drought.

Berrutti, José J. (1871–1951). *El señor maestro* (1929), education versus politics.

°Castellanos, Joaquín (1860–1932). *Carta blanca.*

Coronado, Martín (1850–1919). *Piedra de escándalo* (1902), the honor of a gaucho.

Cuzzani, Agustín (1917–   ). *El centro forward murió al amanecer* (1955), a millionaire buys a football player; influence of Brecht.

Darthés, J. F. C. (1889–   ), and C. S. Damel, (1890–1959). *Hermana Josefina* (1938), comedy of a country quack doctor; *Delirio* (1942).

Dragún, Osvaldo (1929–   ). *Túpac Amarú* (1957), historical drama.

Eichelbaum, Samuel (1894–   ). *Un guapo del 900* (1940), a loyal political hatchetman.

García Velloso, Enrique (1880–1938). *Jesús Nazareno* (1902); *Mamá Culpina* (1916), gaucho plays.

Gorostiza, Carlos (1920–   ). *El puente* (1949), a rich engineer and a humble laborer build a bridge.

Granada, Nicolás (1840–1915). *¡Al campo!* (1902), satire on social climbers.

Gutiérrez, Eduardo (1853–1890), and Jose Podestá (1858–1937). *Juan Moreira* (1886), a gaucho circus pantomime with words.

Herrera, Ernesto (1886–1917). *El león ciego* (1911), Uruguayan tragedy of an outmoded gaucho.

Laferrère, Gregorio (1867–1913). *Locos de verano* (1905); *Las de Barranco* (1908); social comedies.

°Landivar, G. M. and Arturo Cancela (1895–   ). *Día de la flor* (1915), comedy.

Leguizamón, Gregorio (1858–1935). *Calandria* (1896), comedy of a gaucho minstrel.

Lizárraga, Andrés (1919–   ). *Santa Juana de América,* revolution in Peru (1809–1825).

Martínez Cuitiño, Vicente (1887–   ). *El malón blanco* (1912), poetic tragedy of low life and a man who sells his daughter.

Maturana, José (1884–1917). *Canción de primavera,* charming play in verse.

Nalé Roxlo, Conrado (1898–   ). *Una viuda difícil* (1944), comedy of colonial Buenos Aires.

Pacheco, Carlos Mauricio (1881–1924). *Primera cana; Los disfrazados* (1906), *sainete*, life is a masque.

Payró, Roberto (1867–1928). *Sobre las ruinas* (1902), gringo versus Creole; *Triunfo de los otros* (1907); *Vivir quiero conmigo* (1923), by a master of gaucho plays.

Peña, David (1865–1930). *Facundo* (1906), biography of a gaucho governor.

Pico, Pedro E. (1882–1945). *Del mismo barro* (1918), one-act naturalism; *Luz de un fósforo* (1926), comedy of actresses.

Roldán, Belisario (1873–1923). *El bronce* (1920), comedy of Creole-gringo conflict.

*Roquenda, Miguel. *Los saguaipés.*

Sánchez, Florencio (1875–1910). *M'hijo el dotor* (1903), social climbers; *La gringa* (1904), foreigner versus Creole; *Barranca abajo* (1905), tragedy of a proud gaucho.

Sánchez Gardel, Julio (1879–1937). *Los mirasoles* (1911), a girl who wants to go to Buenos Aires.

Venezuela

*Antonio, José. *Redención.*

Ayala, Michelena, Leopoldo (1891–   ). *Bagazo* (1933), one-act "slice of life" in a big store; *Almas descarnadas* (1950), drama of a selfish son.

*Calcaño, Eduardo (1831–1904). *En pos de la gloria; Policarpa Salavarrieta*, historical play with revolutionary heroine.

Certad, Aquiles (1914–   ). *Lo que faltaba a Eva* (1943), high comedy; *Cuando quedamos trece* (1944), superstitions and a man who wants to have his fling.

*Hernández, Domingo Ramón (1828–1893). *Poncio Pilato en Viena.*

Padrón, Julián (1910–1954). *La vela del alma* (1940), one-act tragicomedy.

Peraza, Luis (1908–   ). *El hombre que se fue* (1938), amusing social comedy; *Mala sembra* (1940), comedy drama.

Planchart, Julio (1885–1948). *La república de Caín* (1936), powerful political satire.

Anthology

Antología del teatro hispanoamericano Mexico. Studium, 1958, covering the whole field of the Spanish American theatre, contains all or parts of the following plays: Sor Juana Inéz de la Cruz, *Sainete segundo* (c. 1670); Segura, *El sargento Canuto* (1839); Usigli, *Corona de Sombra* (1947); Acevedo Hernández, *Chañarcillo* (1936); Sánchez, *Barranca abajo* (1905); Eichelbaum, *Un guapo del 900* (1940); Aguilera Malta, *El tigre* (1955).

Here is my nomination for a representative, interesting anthology of Latin American plays, representative of types and countries, and not too bulky for a single volume.

DRAMA

Leguizamón (Argentina), *Calandria.*
Roldán (Argentina), *El bronce.*
Sánchez (Uruguay), *Barranca abajo.*
Reyes (Colombia), *Margot.*

ROMANTICISM

Peón Contreras (Mexico), *Gil González de Avila* (one act).

TRAGEDY

Soto Aguilar (Chile), *El beso* (one act).
Ramos (Cuba), *El traidor* (one act).
Navarro (Mexico), *La ciudad* (one act).

COMEDY

Nalé Roxlo (Argentina), *Una viuda difícil.*
Moock (Chile), *Mocosita.*
Darthés and Damel (Argentina), *Hermana Josefina.*
Certad (Venezuela), *Cuando quedamos trece.*

POETIC DRAMA

Zalamea (Colombia), *Hostel de Belén* (one act).

SATIRE

Usigli (Mexico), *El gesticulador.*

BIBLIOGRAPHY

This Bibliography includes materials useful for the study of the theatre of Spanish America. The alphabetization is by English standards. The word in capital letters at the right margin indicates the region studied in the volume.

Books

Abascal Brunet, M. *Apuntes para la historia del teatro en Chile.* 2 vols. Santiago de Chile: Universitaria, 1941. CHILE

———, and E. Pereira Salas. *Pepe Arias o la zarzuela chica en Chile.* Santiago de Chile: Universitaria, 1955. CHILE

Abreu Gómez, Ermilo. *Juan Ruiz de Alarcón, bibliografía crítica.* México: Botas, 1939. MEXICO

———. *Semblanza de Sor Juana.* México: Letras de México, 1938. MEXICO

———, *et al. Cuatro siglos de literatura mexicana.* México: Leyendas, 1946. One-act samples from 20 old and new plays, with dates. MEXICO

Acosta, José de. *Historia natural y moral de las Indias.* Seville, 1590; México: Fondo de Cultura Económica, 1940. MEXICO

Acuña de Figueroa, Francisco. *Diario histórico del sitio de Montevideo.* Vols. 1 and 2 of *Obras.* 12 vols. Montevideo: Vázquez, Cores, Donaleche y Reyes, 1890. URUGUAY

Aguirre, Juan Francisco de. *El discurso histórico que comprende el descubrimiento, conquista y nombre de Río de la Plata (1793).* Buenos Aires: Biblioteca Nacional, 1900, 1960. RIVER PLATE

Alpern, Hymen, and José Martel. *Teatro Hispanoamericano.* New York: Odyssey Press, 1956. GENERAL

Amunátegui, Domingo. *La alborada poética en Chile después del 18 de septiembre de 1810.* Santiago de Chile: El Nacional, 1892. CHILE

Amunátegui, Miguel Luis. *Las primeras representaciones dramáticas en Chile.* Santiago de Chile: Nacional, 1888. CHILE

Anderson-Imbert, Enrique. *Historia de la literatura hispano-americana.* 3d ed. 2 vols. México: Fondo de Cultura Económica, 1961. Translated by John V. Falconieri in *Spanish American Literature.* Detroit: Wayne University Press, 1963. GENERAL

Angulo Iñiguez, Diego. *Planos de monumentos arquitectónicos de América y Filipinas.* 4 vols. Panama, 1774; Seville: Laboratorio de Arte, 1933. PANAMA

Antología de la literatura dominicana. 3 vols. Santo Domingo, n.d. SANTO DOMINGO

Apstein, Theodore. "New Aspects of the Theatre in Latin America," *Conference of Latin American Fine Arts.* Latin American Studies, No. 13. Austin: University of Texas Press, 1952.   MEXICO; GENERAL

Arango Ferrer, Javier. *La literatura en Colombia.* Buenos Aires: Facultad de Filología, 1940.   COLOMBIA

———. "Medio siglo de literatura colombiana," Vol. I, *Panorama das literaturas das Américas,* Nova Lisboa: Município de Nova Lisboa, 1958.
                                                                   COLOMBIA

Arias-Larreta, Abraham. *Literaturas aborígenes.* Los Angeles: Sayuri Collection, 1951.   PERU; CENTRAL AMERICA

Arias Robalino, Augusto. *Panorama de la literatura ecuatoriana.* Quito: Tip. Nacional, 1936, 1948.   ECUADOR

Arrieta, Rafael A. (ed.). *Historia de la literatura argentina.* 6 vols. Buenos Aires: Peusser, 1958–1960.   ARGENTINA

Arriví, Francisco. *La generación del treinta: el teatro.* San Juan: Sociedad de Cultura Puertorriqueña, 1960.   PUERTO RICO

Arrom, José Juan. *Certidumbre de América.* Havana: Anuario Bibliográfico Cubano, 1959. 10 essays.   CUBA

———. *El teatro de Hispanoamérica en la época colonial.* Havana: Anuario Bibliográfico Cubano, 1956. With extensive bibliography.   GENERAL

———. "Entremeses criollos," *Estudios de literatura hispanoamericana,* pp. 71–91. Havana: Ucar, García, 1950.   CUBA

———. *Historia de la literatura dramática cubana.* New Haven: Yale University Press, 1944.   CUBA

———. "Raíces indígenas del teatro americano," *Proceedings of the Twentyninth International Congress of Americanists,* II. Edited by Sol Tax. 2 vols. Chicago: University of Chicago Press, 1952. Elaborated as Chap. 1 of *Teatro de Hispanoamérica en la época colonial.*   MEXICO

Artacho, Manuel. *Índice cronológico de datos de Bosch.* Buenos Aires: Instituto de la Literatura Argentina, 1940.   ARGENTINA

Ayala Michelena, Leopoldo. *Teatro seleccionado.* Caracas: El Creyón, 1950. Preface by Luis Peraza.   VENEZUELA

Baker, Henry Barton. The London Stage. 2 vols. London: W. H. Allen, 1889.   GENERAL

Balaguer, Joaquín. *Historia de la literatura dominicana.* Ciudad Trujillo, 1956.   DOMINICAN REPUBLIC

Ballesteros, Mercedes, *Vida de la Avellaneda.* Madrid: Colección Hombres y Ideas, 1949.   CUBA

Ballinger, Rex Edward. *Los orígenes del teatro español y las primeras manifestaciones en la Nueva España.* 3 vols. México: Universidad Nacional Autónoma de México, 1951. With preface to each play. MEXICO

Ballivián y Rojas, Vicente de. *Archivo boliviano. Colección de documentos relativos a la historia de Bolivia.* Paris: A. Franck, 1872.   BOLIVIA

Balmori, Clemente Hernando. *La conquista de los españoles y el teatro indígeno americano.* Tucumán, Argentina: Universidad Nacional, 1955.
ARGENTINA

Bareiro Saguier, Rubén. "Panorama de la literatura paraguaya, 1900–1959," Vol. III, *Panorama das Literaturas das Américas.* Nova Lisboa: Município de Nova Lisboa, 1959. PARAGUAY

Barrera, Isaac. *Historia de la literatura ecuatoriana.* Quito: Casa de Cultura Ecuatoriana, 1950. ECUADOR

Barrett, W. E. *Woman on Horseback.* New York: Stokes, 1938. PARAGUAY

Basadre, Jorge. *Literatura Inca.* Vol. I, *Biblioteca de cultura peruana.* Paris: Desclée de Brouwer, 1938. Introduction; *Ollantay*, pp. 198–253; *Usca*, pp. 334–402. PERU

Bastardi, Francisco. *Yo también con mis memorias; cincuenta años de teatro argentino.* Buenos Aires: Ancora, 1963. ARGENTINA

Batres Jáuregui, Antonio. *Memorias de antaño, con una historia del teatro en Guatemala.* Edited by Manuel Mejía Bárcenas. Oakland, California: Pacific Press, 1896. GUATEMALA

Bayona Posada, Nicolás. *Panorama de la literatura colombiana.* Bogotá: Samper Ortega, 1942. COLOMBIA

Bello, Andrés. *Obras completas.* 16 vols. Caracas: Ministerio de Educación, 1956. COLOMBIA; CHILE

Beltrán, Oscar. *Antología de poetas y prosistas americanos.* 4 vols. Buenos Aires: Anaconda, 1937. GENERAL

——. *Los orígenes del teatro argentino.* Buenos Aires: Luján, 1934; Sopena, 1941. ARGENTINA

Berenguer Carisomo, Antonio. *Las ideas estéticas en el teatro argentino.* Buenos Aires: Comisión Nacional de Cultura, 1947. ARGENTINA

Betancourt (or Vetancurt), Fray Agustín de. *El teatro mexicano.* México: María de Benavides, viuda de Juan Rivera, 1698. MEXICO

Bianchi, Alfredo A., *Veinticinco años del teatro nacional.* Buenos Aires: Nosotros, 1920, 1927. ARGENTINA

Bibliografía de las controvesias sobre la licitud del teatro en España. Edited by Cotarelo y Mori. Madrid: Revista de Archivos 1940. GENERAL

Bischoff, Efraín U. *Tres siglos de teatro en Córdoba, 1600–1900.* Córdoba, Argentina: Impta. de la Universidad, 1961. ARGENTINA

Blest Gana, Alberto. *Ideal de un Calavera.* Santiago de Chile: Zig-Zag, 1942. CHILE

Boettner, Juan Max. *Música y músicos del Paraguay.* Asunción: Autores Paraguayos Asociados, 1957. PARAGUAY

Boner, Carmelo M. *El teatro de Ernesto Herrera.* Buenos Aires: Instituto de Literatura Argentina, 1925. URUGUAY

Borges Pérez, Fernando. *La historia del teatro en Costa Rica.* San José: Imprenta Española, 1942. COSTA RICA

Bosch, Mariano G. *Historia de los orígenes del teatro nacional y la época de Pablo Podestá.* Buenos Aires: L. J. Rosso, 1929.   ARGENTINA
———. *Historia del teatro en Buenos Aires.* Buenos Aires: El Comercio, 1910.   ARGENTINA
———. *Manuel de Lavardén, poeta y filósofo.* Buenos Aires: Argentores, 1944.   RIVER PLATE
———. *Teatro antiguo de Buenos Aires.* Buenos Aires: El Comercio, 1904.   ARGENTINA
Buenaventura, Enrique. *Teatro.* Bogata, Ediciones Tercer Mundo, 1963. 261 p.   COLOMBIA
Bueno, Salvador. "Itinerario del teatro," *Medio siglo de literatura cubana.* Havana: UNESCO, 1953.   CUBA
———. "La literatura cubana en el siglo XX," Vol. II, *Panoramas das Literaturas das Américas.* Nova Lisboa: Município de Nova Lisboa, 1958.   CUBA
———. *Medio siglo de literatura cubana.* Havana: UNESCO, 1953. CUBA
Burga, Napoleón M. *La literatura en el Perú de los Incas.* Lima: Gil, 1940. Especially pp. 103–108 and 121–124.   PERU
Cabrera, Francisco Manrique. *Historia de la literatura puertorriqueña.* New York: Las Américas, 1956.   PUERTO RICO
Callcott, Maria Dundas Graham. *Journal of a Resident in Chile during the year 1822.* London: Longman, Hurst, 1824; New York: Carter, 1849; Spanish Version, Madrid: Editorial Americana, 1916.   CHILE
Campa, Arthur. *Spanish Religious Folk Theatre of the South West.* Albuquerque: University of New Mexico, 1934. 2 cycles. UNITED STATES
Campbell, Margaret V. *The Development of the National Theatre in Chile to 1842.* Gainesville: University of Florida Press, 1958.   CHILE
Cañete, Manuel. *Teatro español del siglo XVI.* Madrid: M. Tello, 1885.   MEXICO
Capdevila, Arturo. *La Trinidad Guevara y su tiempo.* Buenos Aires: Kraft, 1951.   RIVER PLATE
Carias Reyes, Marcos. *Hombres de pensamiento.* Tegucigalpa, Honduras: Calderón, 1947.   HONDURAS
Carrera Andrade, Jorge. "Medio siglo de literatura ecuatoriana," Vol. II, *Panoramas das Literaturas das Américas.* Nova Lisboa: Município de Nova Lisboa, 1958.   ECUADOR
Carvalho, Joaquim de, and João Cruz Costa (eds.). *Panorama das Literaturas das Américas.* 4 vols. Nova Lisboa, Angola: Município, 1958–1966. Separate studies by national authorities.   GENERAL
Casadevall, Domingo F. *El tema de la mala vida en el teatro nacional.* Buenos Aires: Kraft, 1957.   ARGENTINA
Castagnino, Raúl H. *Centurias del circo criollo.* Buenos Aires: Perrot, 1959.   ARGENTINA

————. *El circo criollo.* Buenos Aires: Lajouane, 1953. ARGENTINA

————. *El teatro de Roberto Arlt.* La Plata, Argentina. Universidad Nacional de La Plata, 1964. ARGENTINA

————. *El teatro en Buenos Aires durante la época de Rosas.* Buenos Aires: Comisión Nacional de Cultura, 1944. ARGENTINA

————. *Esquema de la literatura dramática argentina, 1717–1949.* Buenos Aires: Instituto de Historia del Teatro Americano, 1950. ARGENTINA

————. *Milicia literaria de mayo.* Buenos Aires: Nova, 1960. ARGENTINA

————. *Sociología del teatro Argentino.* Buenos Aires: Nova, 1963. ARGENTINA

Castro Leal, Antonio. *Ruiz de Alarcón, su vida y su obra.* México: Cuadros Americanos, 1943. MEXICO

Catálogo del teatro mexicano contemporáneo. México: Secretaría de Educación Pública, 1960. 500 plays listed, with summaries. MEXICO

Centurión, Carlos R. *Historia de las letras paraguayas.* 2 vols. Buenos Aires: Ayacucho, 1947–1951. 2d ed., Asunción: Biblioteca Ortiz Guerrero, 1961. PARAGUAY

Cerretani, Arturo. *Historia del teatro argentino.* Buenos Aires: Poseidón, 1955. ARGENTINA

Cervera y Andrade, Alejandro. *El teatro regional de Yucatán.* Yucatán: Guerra, 1947. MEXICO

Chambers, Edmund K. *The Medieval Stage.* 2 vols. Oxford, England: Oxford University Press, 1903. GENERAL

Chávez Franco, Modesto. *Crónicas del Ecuador antiguo.* Guayaquil: Universitaria, 1930. ECUADOR

Churión, Juan José. *El teatro en Caracas.* Caracas: Vargas, 1924. VENEZUELA

Cid Pérez, José. "El teatro en Cuba republicana," Preface to *Teatro Contemporáneo: Cuba.* Madrid: Aguilar, 1959. Chronological list of plays and dramatists, 1902–1958. CUBA

Colección de documentos inéditos del Archivo de Indias. 42 vols. Madrid: Rivadaneyra, 1864–1884. GENERAL

Collection de documents dans les langues indigènes. 5 vols. Paris: Arthus Bertrand, 1862. GENERAL

Cometta Manzoni, Aida. *David Peña, Noticias para la historia del teatro nacional.* Buenos Aires: Universidad, 1917. ARGENTINA

Coni, Emilio A. *El gaucho.* Buenos Aires: Academia Nacional de la Historia, 1945. RIVER PLATE

Cordero y León, Gregorio. *Tres tragedias rurales.* México: Rondador, 1954. MEXICO

Córdoba Ladrón de Guevara, Darío. *Salvador Brau, su vida, su obra, su época.* San Juan: Universidad, 1949. PUERTO RICO

Correa, Gustavo, *et al. The Native Theatre in Middle America*. New Orleans: Tulane University, Middle America Research Institute, 1961.
MIDDLE AMERICA

Cortazar, Augusto Raúl. *Nicolás Granada y su importancia en la revolución teatral*. Buenos Aires: Imprenta de la Universidad, 1937.
RIVER PLATE

Corti, Dora. *Abdón Arózteguy*. Buenos Aires: Instituto de Literatura Argentina, 1938.   RIVER PLATE

———. *Florencio Sánchez*. Buenos Aires: Instituto de Literatura Argentina, 1937. Tomo I, No. 9, with bibliography.   RIVER PLATE

Corvalán Mendilaharsu, Dardo. *Continuación de la historia del teatro en Buenos Aires*. Buenos Aires: Gleizer, 1913.   ARGENTINA

Cotarelo y Mori, Emilio. *Bibliografía de las controvercias sobre la licitud del teatro en España*. Madrid. Revista de Archivos, 1904.   GENERAL

———. *La Avellaneda y sus obras*. Madrid: Tipografía del Archivo, 1930.
CUBA

Cristóbal, Juan. *La vida romántica de Alejandro Flores*. Santiago de Chile: Zig-Zag, n.d.   CHILE

Cruz, Sor Juana Inés de la. *Obras completas*. 4 vols. México: Fondo de Cultura Económica, 1957. Prologs and notes by important Mexican scholars.   MEXICO

Cuadra, Pablo Antonio (ed.). *Tres obras de teatro nuevo*. Managua: Academia Nicaragüense de la Lengua, 1958. Review of Nicaraguan theatre, pp. 217–225.   NICARAGUA

Cúneo, Dardo (ed.). *Obras de Florencio Sánchez*. Buenos Aires: Claridad, 1941; 2d ed., 1952.   RIVER PLATE

Daireaux, Max. *Panorama de la littérature hispanoamericaine*. Paris: Kra, 1930.   GENERAL

Dauster, Frank N. *Teatro hispanoamericano: Tres piezas*. New York: Harcourt, Brace and World, 1965. Carballido, Arriví, and Solari in textbook form.   MEXICO, PUERTO RICO, PERU

Dávalos, Marcelino. "El teatro en México," in *Monografía del teatro*. 2 vols. México: Dirección de Educación Pública, 1917.   MEXICO

———. *Lectura escénica*. México: Mercantil, 1913.   MEXICO

Demaría, Bernabé. *Obras literarias*. Buenos Aires: Imprenta de la Universidad, 1906. Contains *América libre* (1860) about General Belgrano.
ARGENTINA

Díaz Vasconcelos, Luis Antonio. *Apuntes para la historia de la literatura guatemalteca*. Guatemala: Tipografía Nacional, 1942; 2d ed., 1950.
GUATEMALA

Díaz de Medina, Fernando. *La literatura boliviana*. La Paz: Tejerina, 1953.
BOLIVIA

Dibarboure, José Alberto. *Proceso del teatro uruguayo, 1808–1938.* Montevideo: García, 1940.   URUGUAY

Discépolo, Armando. *Tres grotescos de Armando Discépolo.* Buenos Aires: Losange, 1958.   ARGENTINA

Domínguez, Franklin. *El último instante.* Ciudad Trujillo: Silbo Vulnerado, 1958. Preface, pp. 7–36, contains study of theatre.   SANTO DOMINGO

———. *Marionetas.* Ciudad Trujillo: Ateneo Dominicano, 1959. Introduction, pp. 11–29.   SANTO DOMINGO

Doyle, Henry Grattan. *A Tentative Bibliography of the Belles-Lettres of the Republics of Central America.* Cambridge, Massachusetts: Harvard University Press, 1935.   MIDDLE AMERICA

Drama de los palanganas, Veterano y Bisoño. Edited by Luis Alberto Sánchez, in *Revista Chilena de Histora y Geografía,* Vols. 84–86 (1936–1937) and published separately in Santiago de Chile in 1938.   PERU

Dramatists Alliance. *Plays of the Southern Americas.* Stanford, California: Stanford University, 1943. Translations from Sánchez and others. Mimeographed.   GENERAL

———. *Short Plays of the Southern Americas.* Willis K. Jones (ed.). Stanford, California: Stanford University, 1964. Eight more translations from eight countries.   GENERAL

Durán, Diego. *Historia de las Indias de Nueva España.* 2 vols. México: Andrade y Escalante, 1867–1880.   MEXICO

Durán Cerda, Julio. *Panorama del teatro chileno, 1842–1959.* Santiago de Chile: Pacifico, 1959. Prolog and 6 plays.   CHILE

———. *Repertorio del teatro chileno, bibliografía, obras inéditas y estrenadas.* Santiago: Universidad de Chile, 1962.   CHILE

Durón y Gamero, Rómulo Ernesto. *Pastorelas del presbítero doctor José Trinidad Reyes.* Tegucigalpa: Tipografía Nacional, 1905.   HONDURAS

——— (ed.). *Honduras literaria.* 4 vols. Tegucigalpa: Ministerio de Educación, 1957. Tomo I, Escritores en verso, contains a *pastorela.*
                                                                        HONDURAS

Echagüe, Juan Pablo ("Jean Paul"). *Al margen de la escena.* Buenos Aires: Coni, 1922.   ARGENTINA

———. *Seis figuras del Plata.* Buenos Aires: Losada, 1938.   RIVER PLATE

———. *Teatro argentino.* Madrid: América, 1917.   ARGENTINA

———. *Una época del teatro argentino, 1904–1918.* Buenos Aires: América, 1926.   ARGENTINA

Echanove Trujillo, Carlos. "El periodismo . . . La literatura dramática," Vol. V, *Enciclopedia yucatanense.* México, 1944–1945.   MEXICO

Ediciones Populares del primer Festival del Libro Cuzqueño. Cuzco: Garcilaso, 1954.   PERU

Escudero y Perosso, Francisco. *Anales bibliográficos de la ciudad de*

Sevilla desde el establecimiento de la imprenta hasta fines del siglo XVIII. Madrid: Sucesores de Rivadeneyra, 1894.   GENERAL

Eslava, Fernán González de. *Coloquios espirituales y sacramentales,* edited by José Rojas Garciadueñas. Mexico: Porrúa, 1958. Two colloquies are reprinted in Rojas Garciadueñas, *El teatro de Nueva España en el siglo XVI,* México, 1935, and two others in *Autos y coloquios del siglo XVI,* Mexico, 1939.   MEXICO

Fernández, Francisco. *Obras dramáticas.* Buenos Aires: Librería de Mayo, 1881; and in *Publicaciones del Instituto de Literatura, Argentina,* Serie III, 5.   ARGENTINA

Fernández de Castro, Feliciano, *Elisio Peruano.* Lima: Librería de la del Palacio, 1725.   PERU

Fernández de Oviedo y Valdés, Gonzalo. *Historia general de las Indias.* Part I, Salamanca: Juan de Junta, 1547. Part II, Valladolid: Fernández de Cordona, 1557. Reprinted as *General y Natural Historia de las Indias,* Santiago de Chile: Colección de Historiadores, 1901. GENERAL

Fernández Navas, Luis. *Teatro visto a tontos y a locos.* Antofagasta, Chile: Taller de Liceo de Hombres, 1956.   CHILE

Ferretti, Aurelio. *Farsas.* Buenos Aires: Tinglado, 1953.   ARGENTINA

Finot, Enrique. *Historia de la literatura boliviana.* México: Porrúa, 1943: La Paz: Gisbert, 1955.   BOLIVIA

Foppa, Tito Livio. *Diccionario teatral del Río de la Plata.* Buenos Aires: Argentores, 1962.   RIVER PLATE

Freire, Tabaré J. *Florencio Sánchez, sainetero.* Montevideo: Universidad de la República, 1959.   RIVER PLATE

———. *Ubicación de Florencio Sánchez en la literatura dramática.* Montevideo: Universidad, 1961.   RIVER PLATE

Frézier, Amedée F. *Relation du voyage de la Mer du Sud aux côtes du Chile.* Paris, 1716; London: Bouwer, 1717; Santiago de Chile: Mejía, 1922.   CHILE

Furlong, Padre Guillermo. *Los jesuitos y la cultura rioplatense.* Montevideo: Urta y Curbelo, 1933.   RIVER PLATE

Furth, Jorge M. (ed.). *Colección de textos dramáticos.* 3 vols. Buenos Aires, n.d.   ARGENTINA

Gage, Thomas. *The English-American, His Travail by Sea and Land.* London: E. Coates, 1648. Reprinted in Broadway Travelers Series. New York: McBride, 1929.   MEXICO; GUATEMALA

Gagini, Carlos. *Obras dramáticas.* San Juan, C.R.: Tipografía nacional, 1905; 2d ed., 1963.   COSTA RICA

Galich, Manuel. *Obras de Teatro.* Guatemala: Comité Nacional de Alfabetización, 1946.   GUATEMALA

Galindo, Miguel. *Apuntes para la historia de la literatura mexicana.* Colima, El Dragón, 1925.   MEXICO

Gallegos Valdés, Luis. "Panorama de la literatura salvadoreña." Vol. II, *Panoramas das Literaturas das Américas.* Nova Lisboa: Município de Nova Lisboa, 1958.　　　　　　　　　　　　　　SALVADOR

Gallo, Blas Raúl. *Historia del sainete nacional.* Buenos Aires: Quetzal, 1958.　　　　　　　　　　　　　　　　RIVER PLATE

Gamir Aparicio, Manuel. *Compendio histórico del teatro.* Santiago de Chile: Nacional, 1902.　　　　　　　　　　　　CHILE

Gantier, Joaquín. *El teatro en Sucre.* Sucre: Charcas, 1918.　　BOLIVIA

García, José Gabriel. *Compendio de la historia de Santo Domingo.* Santo Domingo: García Hermanos, 1867.　　　　SANTO DOMINGO

García Esteban, Fernando. *Vida de Florencio Sánchez.* Santiago de Chile: Ercilla, 1939.　　　　　　　　　　　　RIVER PLATE

García Hernández, Manuel. *Literatura venezolana contemporánea.* Buenos Aires: S.I.A., 1945.　　　　　　　　　　VENEZUELA

García Icazbalceta, Joaquín. *Bibliografía mexicana del siglo XVI.* México: Francisco Díaz de León, 1886.　　　　　MEXICO

———. *El teatro de Nueva España en el siglo XVI.* México: Luis Álvarez, 1935.　　　　　　　　　　　　　　　MEXICO

———. *Obras.* México, 1891–1899.　　　　　　　　MEXICO

——— (ed.). *Colección de documentos para la historia de México.* 2 vols. México: Librería de Díaz de León, 1886; reprinted, 1941.　MEXICO

———. *Los coloquios espirituales de Eslava.* 2d ed. México: Antigua Librería de Díaz de León, 1887.　　　　　　MEXICO

García Velloso, Enrique. *El arte del comediante.* 3 vols. Buenos Aires: Angel Estrada, 1926.　　　　　　　　　ARGENTINA

———. *Memorias de un hombre de teatro.* Buenos Aires: Kraft, 1942.　　　　　　　　　　　　　　　　　　ARGENTINA

Garcilaso de la Vega, El Inca. *Comentarios reales que tratan del origen de los Incas (1609).* In Clásicos Castellanos. Madrid: La Lectura, 1911; Buenos Aires: Emece, 1943.　　　　　　　　　PERU

Garibay K., Padre Angel María. *Historia de la literatura Nahuatl.* 2 vols. México: Porrúa, 1953–1954. Especially I, 331–384; II, 121–159.　　　　　　　　　　　　　　　　　　MEXICO

———. *La poesía indígena de la altiplanicie.* México: Universidad Nacional, 1940.　　　　　　　　　　　　　　MEXICO

Garland, Antonio. *Por entre los caminos del teatro nacional.* Lima: ENAE, 1946.　　　　　　　　　　　　　　　PERU

Gascón de Guilarte, Cecilia. *Sor Juana de la Cruz, claro en la selva.* Buenos Aires: Amorrartu, 1958.　　　　　　MEXICO

Gilder, Rosamond. *Enter the Actress.* Boston: Houghton Mifflin, 1931.　　　　　　　　　　　　　　　　　GENERAL

Giménez Pastor, Arturo. *Historia de la literatura argentina.* 2 vols. Buenos Aires: Labor, 1948.　　　　　　　ARGENTINA

Giusti, Roberto. *El drama rural argentino.* Buenos Aires: Instituto Nacional de Estudios de Teatro, 1938.   ARGENTINA

——. *Florencio Sánchez.* Buenos Aires: Justicia, Agencia Sudamericana de Libro, 1920.   RIVER PLATE

——. "Las letras argentinas en el siglo actual y sus antecedentes en el XIX." Vol. III, *Panoramas das Literaturas das Américas.* Nova Lisboa: Município de Nova Lisboa, 1959.   ARGENTINA

Goetz, Delia, and Silvanus G. Morley (trans.). *Popol Vuh.* Norman: University of Oklahoma Press, 1950.   MIDDLE AMERICA

Golding Cooper, Alyce. *Teatro mexicano contemporáneo, 1940–1962.* México: Aguilar, 1962.   MEXICO

González, Juan Natalicio. *Proceso y formación de la cultura paraguaya.* Asunción: Guaranía, 1948.   PARAGUAY

——, and Pablo M. Ynsfrán. *El Paraguay contemporáneo.* Paris: Asunción, 1929.   PARAGUAY

González, Manuel Pedro. "Los dramas de Juan Montalvo," *Estudios sobre literaturas hispanoamericanas.* México: Porrúa, 1941.   ECUADOR

González, Otto-Raúl. "Panorama de la literatura guatemalteca." Vol. III, *Panorama das Literaturas das Américas.* Nova Lisboa: Município de Nova Lisboa, 1959.   GUATEMALA

González del Valle, Francisco. *La Habana en 1841.* Havana: Oficina del Historiador de la Ciudad, 1952.   CUBA

González Freire, Natividad (ed.). *Teatro cubano contemporáneo, 1928–1957.* Havana: Sociedad Colombista Panamericana, 1958.   CUBA

González Obregón, Luis, *México viejo.* Paris: Viuda de C. Bouret, 1900. "El primer teatro," pp. 331–341; "El antiguo Coliseo," pp. 347; "El nuevo Coliseo," pp. 349–357.   MEXICO

González Peña, Carlos. *Historia de la literatura mexicana.* México: Polis, 1929, 1940; Porrúa, 1945. In English, Dallas: Southern Methodist University Press, 1943.   MEXICO

Graham, Maria. See Callcott, Maria Dundas Graham.

Gramko, Ida. *Teatro.* Caracas: Ministerio de Educación, 1961. VENEZUELA

Grases, Pedro. *La singular historia de un drama y de Andrés Bello.* Caracas. Artes gráficas, 1943.   VENEZUELA, CHILE

Greg, Walter W. *Pastoral Poetry and Pastoral Drama.* London: Bullen, 1906.   GENERAL

Grez, Vicente. *La vida santiaguina.* Santiago de Chile: Gutenberg, 1879. Chapter V, "Nacimiento de la escena dramática."   CHILE

Grifone, Julia. *Leguizamón y su égloga.* Buenos Aires: Publicaciones del Instituto de Literatura.   ARGENTINA

Grismer, Raymond, *et al., Vida y obras de autores venezolanos.* Havana: Alfa, 1945. Other national literatures in this series.   VENEZUELA

Güell y Mercader, José. *Literatura venezolana.* 2 vols. Caracas: Opinión Nacional, 1883. VENEZUELA

Guerra y Sánchez, Ramiro (ed.). *Historia de la nación cubana.* 10 vols. Havana: Editorial Historia de la Nación, 1952. CUBA

Gutiérrez de Santa Clara Rodríguez, Pedro. *Historia de las guerras civiles del Perú, (1544–1548).* 6 vols. Madrid: Suárez, 1904–1929. PERU

Henríquez Ureña, Pedro. *La cultura y las letras coloniales en Santo Domingo.* Añejo II of Biblioteca de Dialectología Hispanoamericana. Buenos Aires: Instituto de Filosofía, 1936. Contains the text of Llerena's *Entremés.* SANTO DOMINGO

————. "Las letras en la República Dominicana." Vol. III, *Panorama das Literaturas das Américas.* Nova Lisboa: Município de Nova Lisboa, 1959. DOMINICAN REPUBLIC

————. *Literatura dominicana.* Paris: Revue Hispanique, 1917. SANTO DOMINGO

————. *Panorama histórico de la literatura dominicana.* Rio de Janeiro: Companhia Brasileira de Artes Gráficas, 1945. SANTO DOMINGO

————. *Seis ensayos en busca de nuestra expresión.* Buenos Aires: Biblioteca de Buenas Ediciones Literarias, 1928. MEXICO

Hernández, Roberto. *Los primeros teatros de Valparaíso.* Valparaíso, Chile: San Rafael, 1928. CHILE

Hernández Gwynne, B. *Francisco Fernández, notas biográficas.* Dolores, Argentina: Hernández, 1937. ARGENTINA

Herrera, Pablo. *Ensayo sobre la literatura ecuatoriana.* Quito: J. Campuzano, 1860, 1889. ECUADOR

Hills, E. C. *Hispanic Studies.* Stanford, California: Stanford University Press, 1929. PERU

Historia de la poesía hispanoamericana. 2 vols. Madrid, 1911. GENERAL

Historia general de las literaturas hispánicas. Barcelona: Barna, 1959. Vol. IV contains a study of the theatre by Agustín del Saz. GENERAL

Historia sintética de la literatura uruguaya. Edited by Carlos Reyles. 3 vols. Montevideo: Alfredo Vila, 1931. URUGUAY

Humboldt, Alejandro de. *Viaje a las regiones equinocciales.* Caracas: Escuela Técnica Industrial, 1941. VENEZUELA

Huneus Gana, Jorge. "Bosquejo histórico del teatro chileno," *Cuadro histórico de la producción intelectual de Chile.* Santiago: Universidad, 1910. CHILE

Imbert, Julio. *Florencio Sánchez, vida y creación.* Buenos Aires: Schapire, 1954. RIVER PLATE

Jiménez Rueda, Julio. *Historia de la literatura mexicana.* México: Cultura, 1928; Botas, 1934, 1946. MEXICO

————. *Juan Ruiz de Alarcón y su tiempo.* México: Porrúa, 1939. MEXICO

———. *Sor Juana en su época.* México: Fondo de Cultura Económica, 1951.
                                                              MEXICO
Johnson, Harvey L. (ed.). *An Edition of "Triunfo de los Santos," with a Consideration of Jesuit School Plays in Mexico before 1650.* Philadelphia: University of Pennsylvania Press, 1941.   MEXICO
Jones, Willis Knapp. *Antología del teatro hispanoamericano.* Mexico: Studium, 1958. Seven plays of different periods and countries GENERAL
———. *Breve historia del teatro latinoamericano.* México: Studium, 1956.
                                                              GENERAL
———. "The Caribbean Drama—A Literary Cocktail," *The Caribbean: Its Economy,* Series I, Vol. 4. Gainesville: University of Florida, 1954.
                                                       CARIBBEAN AREA
———. "Jose Martí, dramaturgo," *Memoria del Congreso de Escritores Martianos.* Havana: Ucar, García, 1953.   CUBA
———. *Short Plays of the Southern Americas.* Stanford, California: Stanford University, 1944. Mimeographed.   GENERAL
———. *Spanish American Literature in Translation.* New York: Frederick Ungar, 1963. Excerpts from various plays.   GENERAL
——— (trans.). *Representative Plays of Florencio Sánchez.* Washington, D.C.: Pan American Union, 1961. Ten translated plays. RIVER PLATE
Jones, Willis Knapp, and Josefina Pla. "The Guaraní Theatre of Paraguay," *Theatre Annual.* Cleveland, Ohio: Western Reserve University, 1960.
                                                            PARAGUAY
Juana Inés de la Cruz. *Obras completas.* Edited by A. Méndez Plancarte, F. Gutiérrez, and Alberto G. Salceda. 4 vols. México: Fondo de Cultura Económica, 1954–1957.   MEXICO
La Farge, Oliver. *The Year Bearer's People.* New Orleans: Tulane University Press, 1931.   GENERAL
Laferrère, Gregorio. *Obras escogidas.* Edited by Monner Sans. Buenos Aires: Estrada, 1943.   ARGENTINA
———. *Teatro completo.* Santa Fe, 1952; Buenos Aires: Argentores, 1959.
                                                           ARGENTINA
Lamb, Ruth S. *Bibliografía del teatro mexicano del siglo XX.* México: Studium, 1962.   MEXICO
Landa, Diego de. *Relación de las cosas de Yucatán.* Mexico: Robredo, 1938. English translation by A. F. Tozzer, Cambridge, Massachusetts: The Museum, 1941.   MEXICO
Landarech, Alfonso María. *Estudios literarios.* El Salvador: Ministerio de Cultura, 1959.   MIDDLE AMERICA
Lángara, Manuel F. *Los gauchos argentinos.* Edited with prolog by Ismael Moya. Buenos Aires: Instituto de Literatura Argentina, 1943.
                                                           ARGENTINA

Lara, Jesús. *La poesía quechua.* Cochabamba: Universidad de San Símón, 1947. BOLIVIA

Larra, Raúl. *Payró.* Buenos Aires: Claridad, 1938. Especially pp. 147–160. ARGENTINA

———. *Roberto Arlt el torturado.* Buenos Aires: Futuro, 1950. ARGENTINA

Laverde Amayo, Isidoro. *Un viaje . . . a Venezuela.* Bogotá, 1889. Vol. II contains bibliography of Venezuelan dramatists. VENEZUELA

Lazo, Raimundo. "La literatura cubana en el siglo XX," *Historia de la nación cubana.* Havana, 1952. CUBA

Leal, Luis. *Historia mexicana.* México, 1953. A one-volume edition, Boston: Houghton Mifflin, 1955. MEXICO

Leguizamón, Julio A. *Historia de la literatura hispanoamericana.* 2 vols. Buenos Aires: Editoriales Reunidas, 1945. GENERAL

Leonard, Irving A. *Pedro de Peralta y Barnuevo, obras dramáticas.* Santiago de Chile: Imprenta Universitaria, 1937. PERU

Lizarralde, Fernando. *El Ollantay argentino.* Buenos Aires: Término, 1953. ARGENTINA

Llamosas, Lorenzo de las. *Obras de Llamosas.* Edited by R. Vargas Ugarte. Lima: Compañía de Impresiones y Publicidad, 1950. PERU

Llorens Castillo, Vicente. *Liberales y románticos.* México: Colegio de México, 1954. MEXICO

Lohmann Villena, Guillermo. *El arte dramático en Lima durante el virreinato.* Madrid: Escuela de Estudios Hispanoamericanos de la Universidad de Sevilla, 1945. PERU

MacDonald, Mary B., and Dwight McLaughlin. *Vida y obras de autores de Costa Rica.* Havana: Alfa, 1941. COSTA RICA

Madariaga, Salvador de. *Rise of the Spanish American Empire.* New York: Macmillan, 1948. GENERAL

Magaña Esquivel, Antonio. *Imagen del teatro.* México: Letras de México, 1940. MEXICO

———. *Sueño y realidad del teatro.* México: I.N.B.A., 1949. MEXICO

———, and Ruth S. Lamb. *Breve historia del teatro mexicano.* México: Studium, 1958. MEXICO

Mantzius, Karl. *History of Theatrical Art.* 6 vols. London: Duckworth, 1903. GENERAL

Mañón, Manuel. *Historia del Teatro Principal de México.* México: Cultura, 1932. One chapter, "El teatro en la colonia," reprinted in *Máscara* (Buenos Aires) No. 93 (June, 1948), 11–14. MEXICO

Maria y Campos, Armando de. *Andanzas y picardías de Eusebio Vela.* México: Populares, 1944. MEXICO

———. *Archivos de teatro.* México: Populares, 1949. MEXICO

———. *Breve historia del teatro en Chile.* México: C.E.P.S.A., 1940. CHILE

————. *De la reforma al imperio*. México: Temas Teatrales, 1958. MEXICO

————. "El programa de cien años de teatro en México." Vol. 3, *Enciclopedia Mexicana de Arte*. México: Ed. Mexicanas, 1950.   MEXICO

————. *El teatro de género chico en la revolución mexicana*. México: Instituto Nacional de Estudios Históricos, 1956.   MEXICO

————. *El teatro de género dramático en la revolución mexicana*. México: Instituto Nacional de Estudios Históricos, 1957.   MEXICO

————. *El teatro guadalupano*. México: Populares, 1954.   MEXICO

————. *Entre cómicos de ayer*. México: Arriba el telón, 1949. GENERAL

————. *Informe sobre el teatro social (XIX–XX)*. México: Cuahtemoc, 1959.
                                                                      MEXICO

————. *La dramática mexicana durante el gobierno de Lerdo*. México: Populares, 1946.   MEXICO

————. *Las costumbres teatrales en México en el siglo XIX*. México: Sociedad Mexicana de Geografía, 1938.   MEXICO

————. *La Virgen frente a las candilejas o el teatro guadalupano*. México: Populares, 1954.   MEXICO

————. *Manuel Acuña y su teatro*. México: Populares, 1952.   MEXICO

————. *Manuel Eduardo Gorostiza y su tiempo*. México: Talleres Gráficos de la Nación, 1959.   MEXICO

————. *Presencias del teatro*. México: Botas, 1937.   MEXICO

————. *Representaciones teatrales en la Nueva España (siglos XVI al XVIII)*. México: La Escena, 1959.   MEXICO

————. *Teatro mexicano de muñecos*. México: El Nacional, 1941. MEXICO

Marial, José. *El teatro independiente*. Buenos Aires: Alpe, 1955.
                                                                   ARGENTINA

Mariátegui, José Carlos. *Rumbo literario del Perú*. Buenos Aires: Emece, 1947.   PERU

Marín, M. M. *El teatro en el Zulia*. Maracaibo, 1896.   VENEZUELA

Markham, Clement R. *Ollanta, an Ancient Inca Drama*. London: Smith, Elder, 1871; reprinted in *The Indians of Peru*, London: Smith, Elder, 1910.   PERU

————. *Ollanta, A new translation in verse*, in *The Incas of Peru*. London: Murray, 1912.   PERU

Marqués, René. *Teatro*. México: Arrecife, 1959.   PUERTO RICO

Marsili, Ernesto. *El verdadero origen del teatro argentino*. Buenos Aires: Lajouane, 1935.   ARGENTINA

Martínez, Elsa. *Casacuberta*. Buenos Aires: Argentores, 1945. One chapter reprinted in *Máscara*, Nos. 53–54 (February–May, 1945). RIVER PLATE

Martínez, José Luis. *Literaria mexicana, siglo XX*. 2 vols. México: Antigua Librería Robredo, 1949–1950.   MEXICO

Martínez Arzanz y Vela, Nicolás. *Historia de la villa imperial de Potosí*. Buenos Aires: Emece, 1943. Especially pp. 304–306.   BOLIVIA

Martínez Cuitiño, Vicente. *Obras de Florencio Sánchez.* Buenos Aires: Ateneo, 1951.   RIVER PLATE

Matto de Turner, Clorinda. *Don Juan de Espinosa.* Lima: Bacigalupi, 1887.
                                                                        PERU

McPharlin, Paul. *The Puppet Theatre in America, 1524–1949.* New York: Harper Brothers, 1949.   GENERAL

Medina, José Toribio. *Historia de la literatura colonial de Chile.* 3 vols. Santiago de Chile: Librería del Mercurio, 1878.   CHILE

Mejía de Fernández, Abigail. *Historia de la literatura dominicana.* 5th ed. Santiago, R. D.: El Diario, 1943.   SANTO DOMINGO

Melfi, Domingo. *El viaje literario.* Santiago de Chile: Nascimento, 1945.
                                                                       CHILE

Mencos Franco, Agustín. *Literatura guatemalteca en el período de la colonia.* Guatemala: Tipografía Nacional, 1937.   GUATEMALA

Méndez Pereira, Octavio. *Parnaso panameño.* Panama: Istmo, 1916.
                                                                      PANAMA

Méndez y Méndez, Eugenio. "Teatro nacional," *Primer libro venezolano de literatura, ciencia y bellas artes.* Caracas: Impta. Nacional, 1895. 336 pages of introduction and 216 pages of excerpts from authors.
                                                                   VENEZUELA

Menéndez y Pelayo, Marcelino. *Historia de la poesía hispanoamericana.* 2 vols. Madrid: Suárez, 1911–1913; 2d ed., Santander, 1948. GENERAL

Millán, José Agustín, *Biografía de don Francisco Covarrubias, primer actor de carácter jocoso en los teatros de la Habana.* Havana: Imprenta del Faro, 1851.   CUBA

Miró, Rodrigo. *La cultura colonial en Panamá.* México, 1950. pp. 60–69.
                                                                      PANAMA

———. "La literatura panameña de la república." Vol. III, *Panoramas das Literaturas das Américas.* Nova Lisboa: Município de Nova Lisboa, 1959.   PANAMA

Miró Quesada, [César] Aurelio. *Teatro peruano contemporáneo.* Lima: Huascarán, 1948.   PERU

Mitjans, Aurelio. *Historia de la literatura cubana.* Madrid: América, 1918.
                                                                       CUBA

Mogollón Araque, Luis F., *El teatro en Colombia.* Bogotá: Patria, 1914.
                                                                    COLOMBIA

Molina, Fray Antonio de. *Antigua Guatemala, 1677–1678.* Guatemala: Unión Tipográfica, 1943.   GUATEMALA

Moncloa y Covarrubias, Manuel. *De telón adentro.* Lima: Escuela de Ingenieros, 1891. Lima theatres from 1602 to 1891.   PERU

———. *Diccionario teatral del Perú.* Lima: Badiola y Berrio, 1905. PERU

———. *El teatro en Lima: apuntes históricos.* Lima: Gil, 1909.   PERU

Monner Sans, José María. *Introducción al teatro del siglo XX.* Buenos Aires: Columba, 1955. ARGENTINA

———. *Panorama del nuevo teatro.* Buenos Aires: Losada, 1942. ARGENTINA

Montalbán, Leonardo. *Historia de la literatura de la América Central.* San Salvador: Ministerio de Instrucción Pública, 1929–1931.
MIDDLE AMERICA

Monterde, Francisco. *Bibliografía del teatro en México.* México: Secretaría de Relaciones Exteriores, 1934. MEXICO

——— (ed.). *Teatro indígena prehispánico (Rabinal Achí).* México: Universidad Nacional Antónoma, 1955. MEXICO

Morales, Ernesto. *El sentimiento popular de la literatura argentina.* Buenos Aires: Ateneo, 1926. ARGENTINA

———. *Historia del teatro argentino.* Buenos Aires: Lautaro, 1944.
ARGENTINA

More, Federico. *Gregorio Reynolds y Leónidas Yerovi.* La Paz: González y Medina, 1918. PERU

Morgado, Benjamín. *Eclipse parcial del teatro chileno.* Santiago de Chile: Senda, 1943. CHILE

Moya, Ismael. *Costumbrismo en el teatro de Sánchez Gardel. Vol. I, Orígenes del teatro argentino.* Buenos Aires: Universidad, 1935.
ARGENTINA

———. *Ezequiel Soria, zarzuelista criollo.* Buenos Aires: Instituto de Literatura Argentina, 1938. Part reprinted in *Boletín de Estudios de teatro,* No. 16 (1947), 14–17. ARGENTINA

Nacci, Chris N. *Concepción del mundo en el teatro mexicano del siglo veinte.* México: Económica, 1951. Bibliography of 85 dramatists and 252 works. MEXICO

Navarro, Humberto. *Actividades dramáticas en el Ecuador.* Quito: Casa de Cultura Ecuatoriana, 1956. ECUADOR

Nicoll, Allardyce. *Development of the Theatre. A Study of Theatrical Art from the Beginnings to the Present Day.* 3d ed. London: G. G. Harrap, 1948. GENERAL

Nolasco, Flérida del. *Días de la colonia.* Ciudad Trujillo: Imprenta Dominicana, 1952. SANTO DOMINGO

Núñez y Domínguez, Roberto. *Cuarenta años de teatro en México.* Madrid: Rollán, 1956. MEXICO

Olavarría y Ferrari, Enrique de. *Reseña histórica del teatro en México.* 2d ed., 4 vols. México: La Europea, 1895; 3d ed., 5 vols., edited by Salvador Novo, México, 1961. MEXICO

O'Leary, Juan J. *Ildefonso A. Bermejo, falsario, impostor y plagario.* Asunción: Biblioteca FF. AA. de la Nación, 1953. PARAGUAY

Olivares, Adolfo F. *Poesía dramática de los Incas.* Buenos Aires, 1883.
PERU

Ordaz, Luis. *Breve historia del teatro argentino.* 4 vols. Buenos Aires: Universitaria, 1962. Prolog and 4 plays: (1) De la revolución a Caseros; (2) La organización nacional; (3) Afirmación de la escena criolla; (4) La época de oro. ARGENTINA

———. *El drama rural.* Buenos Aires: Hachette, 1959. ARGENTINA

———. *Siete sainetes porteños.* Buenos Aires: Losange, 1958. Plays by important River Plate dramatists. RIVER PLATE

———. *El teatro en el Río de la Plata.* Buenos Aires: Futuro, 1946; and Leviatan, 1957. RIVER PLATE

Orígenes del teatro nacional. Buenos Aires: Instituto de Literatura Argentina, Sección de Documentos, 1925–1938. 6 vols. of individual studies about plays and playwrights of the early period, many also appearing separately. Ricardo Rojas (ed.). ARGENTINA

Orrego Vicuña, Eugenio. *El nacionalismo en el teatro chileno.* Santiago de Chile: Universidad de Chile, 1927. CHILE

Ortega Ricaurte, José Vicente. *Historia crítica del teatro en Bogotá.* Bogotá: Colombia, 1927: Chromos, 1935. COLOMBIA

Ortíz de Montello, Bernardo. *El sombrerón.* México: Estampa mexicana, 1946. MEXICO

Ortiz Fernández, Fernando. *Los bailes y el teatro de los negros en el folklore de Cuba.* Havana: Dirección de Cultura, 1951. CUBA

Ory, Eduardo de. *Los mejores poetas de Costa Rica.* Madrid, n.d. COSTA RICA

Osorio, Luis Enrique. *Teatro,* Tomo I. Bogotá: Editorial La Idea, 1963. COLOMBIA

Oteiza, A. M. *Payró y la Argentina.* Buenos Aires: Olimpo, 1958. ARGENTINA

Oursler, Anna L. "El drama mexicano desde la revolución de 1910 hasta el año 1940," *Congreso Internacional de Catedráticos de Literatura Iberoamericana.* Berkeley, California, 1941. Published separately, México: Universidad Nacional, 1941. MEXICO

Oviedo y Valdés, Gonzalo Fernández de. See Fernández de Oviedo y Valdés.

Pabón, Luis Alberto. "Bosquejo para una historia del teatro paceño." Vol. III, *La Paz en su IV centenario, 1548–1948.* Buenos Aires: Comité pro IV Centenario, 1948. BOLIVIA

Pacheco, Armando Correia (ed.). *Diccionario de la literatura latinoamericano.* Washington: Pan American Union, 1957–. Separate volumes are appearing for each country. GENERAL

Panorama das Literaturas das Américas. 4 vols. Nova Lisboa, Angola: Município de Nova Lisboa, 1958–. First editor, Joaquim de Montezuma de Carvalho. Separate articles by authorities in all New World countries covering all phases of their literature in the last fifty years. GENERAL

Parker, Jack H. *Breve historia del teatro español.* México: Studium, 1957.
                                                                    SPAIN and MEXICO
Pasarell, Emilio J. *Orígenes y desarrollo de la afición teatral en Puerto Rico.*
San Juan: Universitaria, 1951.   PUERTO RICO
Pasquariello, Antonio M. *Bibliografía general de la literatura hispano-
americana.* Buenos Aires: Reunidas, 1954.   GENERAL
————. *El entremés, sainete, y loa en el teatro colonial de Hispanoamérica.*
Ann Arbor: University of Michigan, 1950. Microfilm No. 2426. Bib-
liography.   GENERAL
Pedemonte, Hugo. "Panorama de la actual literatura uruguaya." Vol. II,
Panoramas das Literaturas das Américas. Nova Lisboa: Município de
Nova Lisboa, 1958.   URUGUAY
Pendle, George. *Paraguay, A Riverside Nation.* London: Royal Institute of
International Affairs, 1954.   PARAGUAY
Peña, Nicolás. *Teatro dramático nacional.* Vol. IX, *Biblioteca de Escritores
de Chile.* Santiago: Barcelona, 1912 and 1923. Prolog and 7 early
Chilean plays, 1817–1877.   CHILE
Peñalosa, Juan. *Teatro Colón.* Bogotá: Ministerio de Educación, 1956.
                                                                    COLOMBIA
Peón Contreras, José. *Obras dramáticas en verso y prosa.* México: Comer-
cio, 1897. Prolog by F. Gómez Flores.   MEXICO
Peraza, Luis (ed.). *Teatro seleccionado de Leopoldo Ayala Michelena.*
Caracas: El Creyón, 1950. Prolog.   VENEZUELA
Pereira Salas, Eugenio. *El teatro en Santiago de Nuevo Extremo, 1709–
1809.* Santiago de Chile: Universitaria, 1941.   CHILE
Pereyra Olazábal, Renée. *Casacuberta, un actor bajo la tiranía.* Buenos
Aires: Kraft, 1956.   RIVER PLATE
Pérez Estrada, Francisco. *Teatro folklórico nicaragüense.* Managua:
Nuevos Horizontes, 1946.   NICARAGUA
Pérez Rosales, Vicente. *Recuerdos del pasado.* Santiago: Gutenberg, 1886;
Zig-Zag, 1955?. Translated by Silvanus Morley and Arturo Torres–
Rioseco, San Francisco: Book Club of California, 1947.   CHILE
Perrier, José Luis. *Bibliografía cubano, incluye a Puerto Rico y Santo
Domingo.* New York: Phos Pres, 1926.
                                                CUBA, PUERTO RICO, SANTO DOMINGO
Phillips, Ruby Hart. *Cuba, Island of Paradox.* New York: McDowell and
Oblenski, 1959.   CUBA
Picón Febres, Gonzalo. *La literatura venezolana en el siglo XIX.* Caracas:
El Cojo, 1906.   VENEZUELA
————. *Teatro crítico venezolano.* Curaçao: Bettencourt, 1912. VENEZUELA
Picón Salas, Mariano. *Formación y proceso de la literatura venezolana.*
Caracas: Acosta, 1940.   VENEZUELA

Pillado, José Antonio. *Buenos Aires Colonial, edificios y costumbres*. Buenos Aires: Compañía Sudamericana de Billetes de Banco, 1900. ARGENTINA

Piñera, Virgilio. *Teatro completo*. Havana: Ucar, García, 1960.   CUBA

Pirotto, A. D. *La literatura en América: el coloniaje*. Buenos Aires and Montevideo: Sociedad Amigos del Libro, n.d.   RIVER PLATE

Podestá, Blanca. *Algunos recuerdos de mi vida artística*. Buenos Aires: Chiesino, 1951.   RIVER PLATE

Podestá, José. *Medio siglo de farándula*. Río de la Plata: Imprenta Córdoba, 1930.   RIVER PLATE

Polo de Ondegardo, Juan. *Información acerca de la región y gobierno de los Incas*. Included in Padre José de Acosta, *Historia natural y moral de las Indias*. Madrid, 1589 and 1608; Sevilla, 1590; México: Fondo de Cultura Económica, 1940. Also separately, Lima: Sanmarti, 1916. PERU

Poma de Ayala, Felipe Huamán. *El primer nueva crónica y buen gobierno*. La Paz: Instituto Tiahuanaco, 1944.   BOLIVIA

Pons, Francisco de. *Viaje a la parte oriental de Tierra Firme*. Caracas: Americana, 1930. Translation of original edition, Paris: Colnet, 1806.   VENEZUELA

Popol Vuh. Translated by Delia Goetz and Silvanus G. Morley. Norman, Oklahoma: University of Oklahoma Press, 1950.   MIDDLE AMERICA

Portal y Espinosa, Ismael. *Del pasado limeño*. Lima: Gil, 1932.   PERU

Pozo, Antenor del. *El de Junient en el drama de los Palanganas*. Lima: Universidad de San Marcos, 1955.   PERU

Proceedings of the Twenty-ninth International Congress of Americanistas. Edited by Sol Tax. 2 vols. Chicago: University of Chicago Press, 1952.   MEXICO

Quesada, Vicente G. *La vida intelectual en la América española durante los siglos XVI–XVIII*. Buenos Aires: Noen, 1910; Cultura Argentina, 1917.   GENERAL

Rela, Walter. *Contribución a la bibliografía del teatro chileno, 1804–1960*. Montevideo: Universidad de la República, 1960.   CHILE

———. *Contribuciones a la bibliografía de la literatura uruguaya, 1835–1962*. Montevideo: Universidad de la República, 1963.   URUGUAY

———. *El mito Santos Vega en el teatro del Río de la Plata*. Montevideo: Universitaria, 1958.   RIVER PLATE

———. "Fundamentos para una historia del teatro paraguayo," *Jornadas de Cultura Paraguaya*. Montevideo: GOES, 1955.   PARAGUAY

———. *Literatura dramática suramericana contemporánea*. Montevideo: Instituto de Estudios Superiores, 1957.   GENERAL

Remos y Rubio, Juan J. *Historia de la literatura cubana*. 3 vols. Havana: Cuadernos, 1945. I, 69–73; II, 508–514; III, 326–340.   CUBA

———. "Letras y artes en los siglos XVI y XVII," *Historia de la nación*

542 Bibliography

cubana. Ramiro Guerra y Sánchez (ed.). 10 vols. Havana: Editorial Historia de la Nación, 1952. CUBA

René-Moreno, Gabriel. *Estudios de la literatura boliviana.* Potosí: Editorial Potosí, 1956. Especially Pt. II. BOLIVIA

Retes Bisetti, Rogel. *El último mutis: memorias de 58 años de teatro en Perú, Chile, Argentina, Uruguay y Bolivia.* Santiago de Chile: La Nación, 1961. GENERAL

Reyes, Alfonso. "Los autos sacramentales en España y América," *Capítulos de literatura española, Segunda Serie.* México: Colegio de México, 1945. Also in *Boletín de la Academia Argentina* (Buenos Aires), V (1937). GENERAL

Reyes de la Maza, Luis. *El teatro en la época de Juárez.* México: Universitaria, 1961. MEXICO

———. *El teatro en México con Lerdo y Díaz.* México: Universidad Autónoma de México, 1963. MEXICO

———. *El teatro en México entre la Reforma y el Imperio.* México: Universitaria, 1958. MEXICO

———. *El teatro en 1857 y sus antecedentes.* México: Instituto de Historia de la UNAM, 1956. MEXICO

Reyles, Carlos (ed.). *Historia sintética de la literatura uruguaya.* 3 vols. Montevideo: Alfredo Vila, 1931. Vol. II, No. 4, Carlos R. Princivalle, "Florencio Sánchez"; Vol. III, No. 3, Juan C. Sabat Pebet, "Teatro nacional." URUGUAY

Richardson, Ruth. *Florencio Sánchez and the Argentine Theatre.* New York: Instituto de las Españas, 1923. RIVER PLATE

Riva Agüero, José de la. *Por la verdad, la tradición y la patria.* 2 vols. Lima, 1938. Vol. II, "Lima Española," early theatres and arrival from Spain of cultural material. PERU

Rivera de Álvarez, Josefina. "Panorama literaria de Puerto Rico durante el siglo XX." Vol. II, *Panoramas das Literaturas das Américas.* Nova Lisboa; Município de Nova Lisboa, 1958. PUERTO RICO

———. *Diccionario de literatura puertorriqueña.* Río Piedras: Universidad de Puerto Rico, 1955. PUERTO RICO

Rivera Morilla, Humberto. "La literatura hondureña en el siglo XX." Vol. II, *Panoramas das Literaturas das Américas.* Nova Lisboa: Município de Nova Lisboa, 1958. HONDURAS

Rivera Muñiz, José. *Bibliografía del teatro cubano en la biblioteca de . . . Coronado.* Havana: Biblioteca Nacional, 1957. CUBA

Rivet, Paul, and Georges de Créqui-Montfort. *Bibliographie des langues aymara et kicua.* 4 vols. Paris: Université de Paris, 1951. PERU

Robles Segreda, Luis. *Indice bibliográfico de Costa Rica.* 6 vols. San José: Ministerio de Educación, 1927–1934. COSTA RICA

Rohde, Jorge Max. *Las ideas estéticas en la literatura argentina.* 4 vols. Buenos Aires: Coni, 1921.   ARGENTINA

Rojas, Arístides. "Orígenes del teatro en Caracas." Serie I, *Estudios Históricos.* Caracas: El Comercio, 1926.   VENEZUELA

Rojas, Ricardo. *Historia de la literatura argentina.* 8 vols. Buenos Aires: La Facultad, 1924–1925; Losada, 1948–1949.   ARGENTINA

———. *Obras.* 12 vols. Buenos Aires: Roldán, 1924.   RIVER PLATE

———. *Un dramaturgo olvidado, Don Francisco Fernández y sus obras dramáticas.* Buenos Aires: Coni, 1923.   ARGENTINA

———. *Un titán de los Andes.* Buenos Aires: Losada, 1939.
   PERU, ARGENTINA

Rojas, Ricardo (ed.). *Documentos del Instituto de Literatura Argentina.* The Section of Documents of the University of Buenos Aires began in 1925 under the editorship of Dr. Rojas the publication of early Argentine plays and criticisms of dramatists. Vols. 1, 2, and 4 included Teatro en verso; 3 and 6, Teatro en prosa; and 5, Teatro político. Up to a dozen pamphlets, also sold separately, made up each volume. There was also a volume of studies of dramatists. Some of the most interesting are listed in this bibliography.   RIVER PLATE

Rojas Garciadueñas, José. *El teatro de Nueva España en el siglo XVI.* México: Luis Alvarez, 1935.   MEXICO

——— (ed.). *Autos y coloquios del siglo XVI.* México: Universidad Nacional, 1939. Samples of early Mexican theatre.   MEXICO

———. *Coloquios espirituales y sacramentales de Fernán González de Eslava.* México: Porrúa, 1958.   MEXICO

Rolando, Carlos A. *Las bellas artes en el Ecuador.* Guayaquil: Talleres Municipales, 1944. Bibliography of printed books.   ECUADOR

Rosa-Nieves, Cesáreo. *La lámpara del faro.* San Juan: Club de la Prensa, 1957.   PUERTO RICO

Rosas Moreno, José. "Sor Juana Inés," *Calendario de la antigua casa de Murguía para 1880.* México: J. Rosas, 1882.   MEXICO

Rossi, Vicente. *El teatro nacional rioplatense.* Córdoba, Argentina: Imprenta Argentina, 1910.   RIVER PLATE

Roxlo, Carlos. *Historia crítica de la literatura uruguaya.* 7 vols. Montevideo: Barros y Ramos, 1911–1916.   URUGUAY

Rouanet, Leo. *Autos, farsas y coloquios del siglo XVI.* 4 vols. Madrid-Barcelona: Biblioteca Hispánica, 1901.   SPAIN

Ruiz Aldea, Pedro. *Tipos y costumbres en Chile.* Santiago de Chile: Zig-Zag, n.d.   CHILE

Rumazo González, Alfonso. *Historia de la literatura ecuatoriana.* 5 vols. Quito, 1935.   ECUADOR

Rusconi, Alberto. "Resumen de la literatura uruguaya en el siglo actual,"

Panoramas das Literaturas das Américas. Nova Lisboa: Município de Nova Lisboa, 1958.   URUGUAY

Sabat Pebet, Juan Carlos. *Juan Casacuberta.* Montevideo: Siglo Ilustrado, 1950. One chapter, "Sobre el origen y la carrera de Casacuberta," was printed in *Boletín de Estudios de Teatro,* No. 31 (October, 1950).
                                                                       RIVER PLATE

————. *Las bibliotecas de D. Manuel Cipriano de Melo y doña María Clara Zabala.* Montevideo, 1958. Separate reprint of magazine article.
                                                                       RIVER PLATE

————. "Teatro nacional." Vol. III, *Historia sintética de la literatura uruguaya.* Edited by Carlos Reyles. Montevideo: Vila, 1931.   URUGUAY

Sáez, Antonia. *El teatro en Puerto Rico.* San Juan: Universitaria, 1950. Revision of a 1930 doctoral thesis.   PUERTO RICO

Salamanca, Octavio. *Dramas y comedias.* Cochabamba: F. O. Cuenca, 1944.   BOLIVIA

Salas, Angel. "La Literatura dramática en Bolivia," *Bolivia en el primer centenario de su independencia.* New York: Sociedad Universitaria, 1925.   BOLIVIA

Salaverri, Vicente A. *Del picadero al proscenio.* Montevideo. M. García, 1913.   URUGUAY

————, (ed.). *El teatro del uruguayo Florencio Sánchez.* 2d ed. Valencia: Cervantes, 1919–1920.   RIVER PLATE

Salazar, Ramón A. *Historia del desenvolvimiento intelectual de Guatemala.* Guatemala: Tipografía Nacional, 1897. Covers up to 1821. Only Vol. I published.   GUATEMALA

Salazar y Roig, Salvador. "El teatro cubano," *Evolución de la cultura cubana.* Havana: Siglo XX, 1928.   CUBA

————. *Historia de la literatura cubana.* Havana, 1939.   CUBA

Samper Ortega, Daniel. *Selección Samper Ortega de Literatura Colombiana.* 100 vols. Bogotá: Minerva, n.d. A few plays included.   COLOMBIA

Sánchez, Luis Alberto. *Historia de la literatura americana desde sus orígenes hasta 1936.* Santiago de Chile: Ercilla, 1937; 3d ed., Buenos Aires: Americalee, 1944.   GENERAL

————. *La literatura peruana.* Lima, 1928; Santiago de Chile, 1936; Buenos Aires, 1939 and 1951, 6 vols. See Theatre: III, 62–67, 160–180; V, 117–143; VI, 378–383.   PERU

Sánchez Quell, Hipólito. *Estructura y función del Paraguay colonial.* Buenos Aires: Tupa, 1947; 3d ed., Kraft, 1955.   PARAGUAY

Sanín Cano, E. *Letras colombianas.* México: Fondo de Cultura Económica, 1944.   COLOMBIA

Santa Cruz Pachacuti, Juan. *Relación de antigüedades deste reyno de Perú.* Madrid: Biblioteca Nacional, 1867; Lima: Sanmarti, 1927. Trans.

in C. R. Markham, *Narratives of the Rites and Laws of the Yncas.*
London: Hakluyt Society, 1873. PERU
Saz, Agustín del. *El teatro del poeta nativista del Uruguay.* Montevideo:
Monteverde, 1956. URUGUAY
——. "El teatro hispanoamericano del siglo XIX." Vol. IV, *Historia general
de las literaturas hispánicas.* 4 vols. Barcelona: Barna, 1959. GENERAL
——. "Literatura Iberoamericana." Vol. VII, *Enciclopedia Labor.* 7 vols.
Barcelona: Labor, 1957. GENERAL
——. *Teatro hispanoamericano.* 2 vols. Barcelona: Vergara, 1964. Com-
plete study, too recent for citations in this volume. GENERAL
Schilling, Hildburg. *Teatro profano en la Nueva España, 1530–1750.*
México: Universitaria, 1958. MEXICO
Schyttneru, Eugene. *Vida y obras de autores ecutorianos.* Havana: Alfa,
1943. ECUADOR
Secretaría de Educación Pública. *Catálogo del teatro mexicano contem-
poráneo.* México: Talleres Gráfico de la Nación, 1960. MEXICO
Shoemaker, William H. *The Multiple Stage in Spain during the XVth and
XVIth Centuries.* Princeton University Press, 1935. GENERAL
Sienna, Pedro. *La vida pintoresca de Arturo Bührle.* Santiago de Chile:
Osiris, 1933. CHILE
Silva, Lafayette. *Historia de teatro brasileiro.* Rio de Janeiro: Ministério de
Educaçao, 1938. BRAZIL
Silva Cáceres, Raúl H. *Estructura y temática en la dramaturgia de Moock.*
Santiago: Universidad de Chile, 1960. CHILE
Silva Castro, Raúl. "El drama," *Panorama literario de Chile.* Santiago:
Universitaria, 1961. Summary of the whole field with brief appraisal of
each dramatist. CHILE
Solórzano, Carlos. *Historia a escena.* Guatemala: Ministerio de Educación,
1949. GUATEMALA
——. *El teatro hispanoamericano contemporáneo.* 2 vols. México: Fondo
de Cultura Económica, 1964. Fourteen plays of the last decade from
fourteen countries. GENERAL
——. *Teatro latinoamericano del siglo XX.* Buenos Aires: Nueva Visión,
1961. GENERAL
——. *Teatro latinoamericano en el siglo XX.* México: Pormaca, 1964. Aug-
ments but does not replace the previous volume. GENERAL
Sotela, Rogelio. *Escritores y poetas de Costa Rica.* San José: Imprenta
Lehmann, 1923. COSTA RICA
——. *Literatura costarricense.* 3d ed. San José: Ministerio de Cultura,
1938. COSTA RICA
——. *Valores literarios de Costa Rica.* San José: Alsina, 1920. COSTA RICA
Spell, Jefferson R., and Francisco Monterde. *Tres comedias de Eusebio
Vela.* México: Universitaria, 1948. MEXICO

Tapia y Rivera, Alejandro. *Biblioteca histórica*. San Juan: Imprenta de
Marquez, 1854.   PUERTO RICO
———. *Mis Memorias*. New York: DeLaisne and Rossbro, 1928.
                                                                  PUERTO RICO
Taullard, Alfredo. *Historia de nuestros viejos teatros*. Buenos Aires: López,
1932.   ARGENTINA
Tauro, Alberto. *Elementos de literatura peruana*. Lima: Huascarán, 1946.
                                                                  PERU
Tax, Sol (ed.). *Proceedings of the Twenty-ninth International Congress of
Americanistas*. 2 vols. Chicago: University of Chicago Press, 1952.
                                                                  MEXICO
Teatro contemporáneo. Madrid: Aguilar, 1959–. Series of volumes of 400
to 500 pages with 5 or 6 plays of the same country and introductions by
some local authority. They include: Argentina (Arturo Berenguer Cari-
somo); Cuba (José Cid Pérez); Guatemala (Carlos Solórzano); Mexico
(Antonio Espina); Peru (José Hesse Murga); Uruguay (Fernán Silva
Valdés). Chile and Puerto Rico in press.   GENERAL
Teatro mexicano del siglo XX. México: Fondo de Cultura Económica, 1956.
Three volumes with lengthy and excellent introductions by their editors:
I, 1920–1927, Francisco Monterde; II, 1928–1946, Antonio Magaña
Esquivel; III, 1947–1956, Celestino Gorostiza.   MEXICO
Teatro puertorriqueño. 5 vols. San Juan: Universidad de Puerto Rico,
1959–1963. Plays from Drama Festivals.   PUERTO RICO
Terrero, Blas José. *El Theatro de Venezuela y Caracas*. Caracas: Litografía
del Comercio, 1926. Chiefly Church matters.   VENEZUELA
Thomas, Cyrus, and John H. Swanton. *Indian Languages of Mexico and
Central America*. Washington: Government Printing Office, 1911.
                                                                  MIDDLE AMERICA
Tobar Garcia, Francisco. *Teatro*. 2 vols. Quito: Editorial Casa de la Cultura
Ecuatoriana.   ECUADOR
Torre Revello, José. *Crónicas del Buenos Aires colonial*. Buenos Aires:
Bajel, 1943. Chap. 12, "El teatro," reprinted in *Boletín*, No. 4 (Janu-
ary, 1944).   ARGENTINA
Torres-Rioseco, Arturo. *Ensayos sobre la literatura latinoamericana*. Méx-
ico: Gráfica Panamericana, 1953. Teatro indígena de México, pp. 7–23;
Tres dramaturgos: Eslava, Alarcón y Sor Juana, pp. 26–56.   MEXICO
———, and Raúl Silva Castro. *Ensayo de bibliografía chilena*. Harvard University, 1935.   CHILE
Toruño, Juan Felipe. "Sucinta reseña de las letras nicaragüenses en 50
años (1900–1950)." Vol. III, *Panoramas das Literaturas das Américas*.
Nova Lisboa: Município de Nova Lisboa, 1959.   NICARAGUA
Trenti Rocamora, J. Luis. *El repertoria de la dramática colonial hispanoamericana*. Buenos Aires: Alea, 1950.   ARGENTINA

———. *El teatro en la América colonial.* Buenos Aires: Huarpes, 1947.
GENERAL

Trueba Urbina, Alberto. *El teatro en la república.* México: Botas, 1954.
MEXICO

Turbyfill, Hubert. *My Panama Canal Theatre Adventure.* Philadelphia, 1849.
PANAMA

Ugarte Chamorro, Guillermo. *Bernardo O'Higgins, precursor del teatro chileno. Estudio de Teatro,* V, 9. Lima: Teatro Universitario, 1961.
CHILE

———. *El Perú y el teatro en la obra de fray Camilo Henríquez. Estudios de Teatro,* V, 10. Lima: Teatro Universitario, 1961. GENERAL

———. *Las primeras representaciones teatrales en el Alto Perú. Estudios de Teatro,* V, 13. Lima: Teatro Universitario, 1963. PERU

———. *Las primeras representaciones teatrales en la ciudad de Cali. Estudios de Teatro,* V, 12. Lima: Teatro Universitario, 1963. COLOMBIA

Ulloa Zamora, Alfonso. "Panorama literario costarricense (1900–1958)." Vol. III, *Panoramas das Literaturas das Américas.* Nova Lisboa: Município de Nova Lisboa, 1959. COSTA RICA

Urbina, Luis Gonzaga. *La literatura mexicana durante la Guerra de la Independencia.* Madrid: García y Sáez, 1917. MEXICO

———. *La vida literaria de México.* México: Porrúa, 1946. MEXICO

Urquidi G., José Macedonio. "Panorama de Bolivia." Vol. I, *Panoramas das Literaturas das Américas.* Nova Lisboa, Município de Nova Lisboa, 1958. BOLIVIA

Usigli, Rodolfo. *Caminos del teatro en México.* México: Secretaría de Relaciones Exteriores, 1933. MEXICO

———. *Itinerario del autor dramático.* México: Casa de España en México, 1941. MEXICO

———. *México en el teatro.* México: Mundial, 1932. MEXICO

———. *Teatro completo,* Vol. I. México: Botas, 1963. MEXICO

Utrera, Cipriano de. *La Universidad de Santiago de la Paz y de Santo Tomás de Aquino.* Santo Domingo: Editorial Franciscana, 1932.
SANTO DOMINGO

Vaca Guzmán, Santiago. *La literatura boliviana.* Buenos Aires: Coni, 1883.
BOLIVIA

Valle y Caviedes, Juan del. *El amor alcalde; El amor médico; Baile del amor tahur.* Edited by Luis Fabio Xammar in *Fenix* (Lima); reprinted in book form, Lima: Escuela Nacional de Arte Escénico, 1953. PERU

Vaquero Dávila, Jesús. *Síntesis histórico de la cultura intelectual y artística del Ecuador.* Quito: Editora Jodoço Ricke, 1947. ECUADOR

Varela, H. F. *Elisa Lynch.* Buenos Aires: Tor, 1933. PARAGUAY

Varey, J. E. *Historia de los títeres en Europa.* Madrid: Revista de Oriente, 1957. Includes "Representaciones de títeres, 1211–1760," from *Revista de Filología Española*, XXXVIII (1952), and "Títeres en Valencia," from *Revista Valenciana de Filología*, III (1953).   SPAIN

Vargas Ugarte, Rubén. *De nuestro antiguo teatro*. Lima: Compañía de Impresiones y Publicidad, 1943. Prolog and 8 comedies from sixteenth to eighteenth centuries.   PERU

——. *Vida y obras del venerable fray Francisco del Castillo Andraca y Tamayo*. Lima: E. R. Lulli, 1946–1948.   PERU

——. (ed.). *Obras de Llamosas*. Lima: Compañía de Impresiones y Publicidad, 1950.   PERU

Vega, Daniel de la. *Luz de candilejas: El teatro y sus miserias: 1920–1930*. Santiago de Chile: Nascimento, 1930.   CHILE

Vela, David. *Literatura guatemalteca*. 2 vols. Guatemala: Tipo. Nacional, 1943.   GUATEMALA

Vera, Pedro Jorge. *Teatro*. Quito: Casa de Cultura Ecuatoriana, 1957.

ECUADOR

Vergara y Vergara, José María. *Historia de la literatura en Nueva Granada, 1538–1820*. (1st ed., 1867) Bogotá: Restrepo, 1905.   COLOMBIA

Vetancurt, Fray Agustín de. See Betancourt.

Vial, Román. *Costumbres chilenas*. 2 vols. Valparaíso: Mercurio de Tornero, 1889–1892.   CHILE

——. *Obras completas*. 4 vols. Valparaíso: Mercurio de Tornero y Letelier, 1872.   CHILE

Vicuña Mackenna, Benjamín. *Historia de Santiago*. 2 vols. Santiago de Chile: Universidad, 1938.   CHILE

——. *Historia de Valparaíso*. Valparaíso: Cox, 1869.   CHILE

——. *Obras*. Santiago de Chile: Universidad, 1936.   CHILE

Vincenzi, M. *Los ídolos del teatro*. Costa Rica, 1957.   COSTA RICA

Wagner, Fernando (ed.). *Teatro Mexicano*, No. 98. México: Secretaría de Educación Pública, 1946. Contains: Eslava, *Coloquio Séptimo;* Peón Contreras, *Gil González de Ávila*.   MEXICO

Weisinger, Nina Lee. *Selections from South American Plays*. Dallas: Banks Upshaw, 1948.   GENERAL

Wenrich, Francis C. *Ollanta, an Ancient Peruvian Drama*. Boston: Badger, 1920.   PERU

Williams, Edwin B. *Life and Dramatic Works of Gertrudis de Avellaneda*. Philadelphia: University of Pennsylvania Press, 1924.   CUBA

Woodford, Archer. *Obras de Cueta y Mena*. Bogotá: Instituto Caro y Cuervo, 1952.   COLOMBIA

Xammar, Luis Fabio. *Valores humanos en la obra de Leónidas Yerovi*. Lima: Antena, 1938.   PERU

Yépez Miranda, A. *Pasado y presente de las letras peruanas*. Cuzco: Rozas, 1942.   PERU

——. *Peruanidad literaria y revolución*. Cuzco: Rozas. 1934.   PERU

——. *Proceso cultural del Perú.* Cuzco: Rozas. 1940.   PERU
Zapiola, José. *Recuerdos de treinta años (1810–1840).* Santiago de Chile:
Zig–Zag, 1945. Plays and actors, 1820–1840.   CHILE
Zum Felde, Alberto. *La literatura del Uruguay.* Buenos Aires: Universidad,
1939–1940. Montevideo: Colorado, 1941.   URUGUAY
——. *Proceso intelectual del Uruguay.* Montevideo: Colorado, 1930;
Buenos Aires, 1941.   URUGUAY

Periodicals

Abreu Gómez, Ermilo. "Sor Juana," *International Review of Bibliography,*
VIII, No. 3 (July, 1958), 272.   MEXICO
Acchiardi, Pablo. "Casacuberta y el arte del actor," *Cuaderno de Cultura
Teatral,* No. 14 (1940), 61–100.   RIVER PLATE
Acevedo Hernández, Antonio. "Consideraciones sobre el teatro chileno,"
Atenea (Concepción), No. 95 (March, 1933), 146–158, and No. 96
(April, 1933), 309–319.   CHILE
——. "Cuarenta años de teatro," *En viaje* (Santiago de Chile), XXX, No.
257 (March, 1955).   CHILE
Alarcón, Abel. "La literatura boliviana, 1545–1916," *Revue Hispanique,*
XLI, No. 100 (December, 1917), 563–663.   BOLIVIA
Alegría, Fernando. "Chile's Experimental Theatre," *Interamerican* (New
York), IV, No. 10 (October, 1945), 10.   CHILE
Aloisi, Enzo. "Tras de las candilejas," *Américas* (Washington, D. C.), IV,
No. 3, 21–23, 44–45.   ARGENTINA
Alonso, Amado. "Biografía de Fernán González de Eslava," *Revista de
Filología Hispánica,* II (1940), 213–319.   MEXICO
Amunátegui, M. L. "Establecimiento del teatro en Chile después de la
Independencia," *Revista de Santiago,* I (1888), 481. Reprinted, Santi-
ago: Imprenta Nacional, 1888.   CHILE
——. "Las primeras representaciones dramáticas en Chile," *Revista de
Chile,* I (1872), 433–447, 647–665. Also published separately, San-
tiago: Peña, 1888.   CHILE
Ángeles, Pedro de. "Curiosidades puertorriquenãs," *Revista Blanca*
(Managuez, P. R.), I, No. 26 (January 10, 1897), 339–340.
                PUERTO RICO
Anonymous. "Matilde Cuyas, primera dramaturga argentina," *Hogar*
(Buenos Aires), December 10, 1937.   ARGENTINA
Anrique Reyes, Nicolás. "Ensayo de una bibliografía dramática chilena,"
Anales de la Universidad de Chile (Santiago: Cervantes, 1899).
                CHILE
Antolínez, Gilberto. "El teatro, institución de los Muku y Jirajara," *Revista
de Cultura* (Caracas), No. 56 (May, 1946), 113–129.   VENEZUELA

Apstein, Theodore. "Samuel Eichelbaum, Argentine Playwright," *Books Abroad* (Norman, Oklahoma), 19 (1945), 237–241.   ARGENTINA

Arizaga, Domingo A. "La divisa punzó," *Nos*, LXV (July, 1929), 151–156.   ARGENTINA

Arriví, Francisco. "Perspectiva de una generación teatral puertorriqueña, 1938–1958," *Revista del Instituto de Cultura Puertorriqueña*, No. 1 (October, 1958), 41–47.   PUERTO RICO

Arrom, José Juan. "Actos del cabildo de Caracas, 1573–1600," *Universidad de la Habana*, XXI (1946), 6–24.   VENEZUELA

——. "Bibliografía dramática venezolana," *Anuario Bibliográfico Venezolano, 1946*, (Caracas, 1949), pp. 199–209.   VENEZUELA

——. "Documentos relativos al teatro colonial en Venezuela," *Universidad de la Habana*, XXI–XXII (January–December, 1946), 80–101; also in *Boletín de la Academia Nacional de la Historia* (Caracas), XXIX, No. 114 (April–June, 1946), 168–183; also in *Boletín de Estudios de Teatro*, No. 15 (December, 1946), 211–224; and also published separately.   VENEZUELA

——. "Drama of the Ancients," *Américas*, IV, No. 3 (March, 1952), 16–19.   GENERAL

——. "El teatro de José Antonio Ramos," *Revista Iberoamericana*, XII, No. 24 (June, 1947), 263–271; also in *Revista Cubana*, XXIII (1948); and in *Estudios de Literaturas Hispanoamericanas*. Havana: Ucar, García, 1950. 147–159.   CUBA

——. "En torno al teatro venezolano," *Revista Nacional de Cultura* (Caracas), No. 48 (January, 1945), 5 ff.   VENEZUELA

——. "Perfil del teatro contemporáneo," *Hispania*, XXXVI (February, 1953), 30–31.   GENERAL

——. "Primeras manifestaciones dramáticas en Cuba: 1512–1776," *Revista Bimestre Cubana* (Havana), XLVIII, No. 2 (September, 1941), 274–284.   CUBA

——. "Una desconocida comedia mexicana del siglo XVII," *Revista Iberoamericana*, XIX (1953), 79–103.   MEXICO

Ayala Duarte, Crispín. "Historia de la literatura en Honduras y San Salvador," *Anales de la Universidad Central de Venezuela* (March, 1931), 193–224.   HONDURAS: EL SALVADOR

——. "Historia de la literatura en Nicaragua," *Anales de la Universidad Central de Venezuela* (May–June, 1931), 259–291.   NICARAGUA

Babín, María Teresa. "Apuntes para *La carreta*," *Asomante*, X (1953), 380–383.   PUERTO RICO

Bach, Marcus. "Los pastores," *Theatre Artes*, No. 24 (April, 1940), 283–288.   MEXICO

Banner, J. Worth. "Ildefonso Bermejo, iniciador del teatro en el Paraguay," *Revista Iberoamericana*, XVIII (July, 1951), 79–107.   PARAGUAY

Barros Arana, Diego. "El teatro en Santiago," *El Correo del Domingo* (Santiago), No. 11 (June 29, 1862).   CHILE

Bayle, Constantino. "El teatro indígena en América," *Lectura* (Mexico), LII (June 15, 1946), 219.   MEXICO

Beck, Vera F. "Xavier Villaurrutia, dramaturgo moderno," *Revista Hispanoamericana*, XVIII, 25 (December, 1952), 27–29.   MEXICO

Bello, Andrés. "El teatro," *El Araucano* (Santiago), No. 173 (January 3, 1834); also in his *Obras completas,* 16 vols. Caracas: Ministerio de Educación, 1956, IX, 114–115.   CHILE

Bello, Enrique. "Isidora Aguirre define los móviles de su teatro," *Ultramar* (Santiago de Chile), No. 4 (April, 1960), 1–9.   CHILE

Benavente, Fray Toribio de. See Motolinía, Padre.

Berenguer Carisomo, Arturo. "Casacuberta," *Boletín de Estudios de Teatro,* No. 26 (July, 1949), 50–54.   RIVER PLATE

———. "Martín Coronado, su tiempo y su obra," *Cuaderno de Cultura Teatral,* No. 15 (1940), 9–40. Also in *Boletín,* Nos. 29–39 (1950).   RIVER PLATE

———. "Siripo," *Boletín de Estudios de Teatro,* No. 8 (January, 1945), 1–22. Reprinting of Act II of (perhaps) the Lavardén version.   ARGENTINA

Boletín de Estudios de Teatro. Nos. 1–31, January, 1943–1954.   RIVER PLATE

Boletín Teatral. August 15, 1953–October 25, 1955.   MEXICO

Bosch, Mariano G. "De quien es el Siripo," *Boletín de Estudios de Teatro,* No. 12 (March, 1946), 5–18.   ARGENTINA

———. "Lavardén y el teatro," *Boletín de Estudios de Teatro,* No. 1 (January, 1943), 15–20.   ARGENTINA

———. "1700–1810: Panorama del teatro," *Cuaderno de Cultura Teatral,* No. 13 (1940).   RIVER PLATE

———. "1830–1880, Panorama del teatro," *Cuaderno de Cultura Teatral,* No. 14 (1940), 13–32.   RIVER PLATE

———. "Orígenes del teatro nacional argentino," *Boletín de Estudios de Teatro,* Nos. 18–19 (September–December, 1947), 177–179; also published in *Instituto de Literatura Argentina,* IV, No. 2.   RIVER PLATE

Braschi, Wilfredo. "Treinta años de teatro en Puerto Rico," *Asomante,* XII (January–March, 1955), 95–101. From his University of Puerto Rico Ph.D. thesis.   PUERTO RICO

Brncic Juricic, Zlatko. "El teatro chileno a través de cincuenta años," *Anales de la Universidad de Chile* (Santiago), CXI (1952), 113–169; reprinted in *Desarrollo de Chile en la primera parte del siglo* (II, 358–416), Santiago: University of Chile Press, 1953.   CHILE

"Buenos Aires: Teatro del Pueblo," *Panorama* (Washington, D. C.), No. 17 (1941), 1.   ARGENTINA

Cabrera, Pablo. "Antecedentes de la representación teatral en Córdoba," *Revista de la Universidad Nacional de Córdoba*, XVIII, Nos. 1–2 (March–April, 1931), 3–20. ARGENTINA

Caillet Bois, Julio. "El teatro en la Asunción a mediados del siglo XVI," *Revista de Filología Hispánica*, IV (1942), 1. PARAGUAY

——. "Las primeras representaciones teatrales mexicanas," *Revista de Filología Hispánica*, I (1940), 377–378. MEXICO

Calcaño, Eduardo. "El teatro infantil y sus proyecciones en Hispano-América," *Educación* (Caracas), July, 1940, 12 ff. VENEZUELA

Cantes, Juan, "Bibliografía de 'Calandria'," *Boletín del Instituto de Investigaciones Históricas*, Año XX, Tomo XXVI (1941). ARGENTINA

——. "El teatro de la Ranchería o casa de comedias," *Revista Argentina de Ciencias Políticas*, XX (1920), 115–117; 145–153. ARGENTINA

Capdevila, Arturo. "Noticias del teatro argentino en los años gloriosos de Trinidad Guevara," *Cuaderno de Cultura Teatral*, No. 1 (1936), 19–29. RIVER PLATE

——. "Las varias muertes y la verdadera defunción de Trinidad Guevara," *Cuaderno de Cultura Teatral*, No. 19 (1944), 9–22. RIVER PLATE

Cárdenas y Chávez, Miguel de. "La literatura cubana," *La Prensa* (Havana), October 29, 1841. CUBA

Castagnino, Raúl H. "El romanticismo en el teatro porteño (1830–1853)," *Lyra* (Buenos Aires), Nos. 174–176; also published separately, no date, no pagination. RIVER PLATE

——. "El sentido de la universalidad en el teatro de Armando Moock," *Boletín de Estudios de Teatro*, No. 14 (September, 1945), 134–136. CHILE: ARGENTINA

——. "El teatro en la obra de Rojas," *Revista Iberoamericana*, No. 46 (July, 1958), 227–238. ARGENTINA

——. "La iniciación teatral de Martín Coronado," *Boletín de Estudios de Teatro*, Nos. 29–30 (April–September, 1950), 73–80. ARGENTINA

——. "Integración del repertorio de Coronado," *Boletín de Estudios de Teatro*, No. 20 (1948). ARGENTINA

——. "Teatro del Río de la Plata," *Boletín de Estudios de Teatro*, No. 1 (January, 1943), 6–12. RIVER PLATE

Chamberlain, Vernon A. "Dramatic treatment of the Conde Alarcos theme," in *Hispania*, XLII (December, 1959), 517–523. GENERAL

Cid Pérez, José. "Cincuenta años de teatro cubano," *Carteles* (Havana), XXXIII (May 18, 1952), 110–113, 188–189. CUBA

——. "El teatro en América de ayer y hoy: Guatemala," *Boletín de Estudios de Teatro*, No. 16 (March, 1947), 2–13. GUATEMALA

"Cinco años en Buenos Aires: 1820–1825," *Boletín de Estudios de Teatro*, No. 1 (January, 1943), 28–34. ARGENTINA

Cione, Otto Miguel. "Biografía," *Boletín de Estudios de Teatro*, No. 18 (October, 1947), 35–36. RIVER PLATE

Coe, Ada M. "Notes on Puppetry," in *Hispania*, XXVIII (1945), 197–207. With bibliography of puppet plays written by famous authors. GENERAL

Coll y Toste, Cayetano. "Relación verídica de lo acaecido en Puerto Rico a fines del año 46 y principios del 47 con el motivo de llorar la muerte de Felipe Quinto y celebrar la exaltación a la corona de N.S. don Fernando Sexto," *Boletín Histórico de Puerto Rico*, V, No. 3 (May, 1948), 148–192. PUERTO RICO

Corbató, Hermenegildo. "Misterios y autos del teatro misionero en México durante el siglo XVI y sus relaciones con los de Valencia," *Anales del Centro de Cultura Valenciana*, Anejo, No. 1, n.d. MEXICO

Cortazzo, Alberto P. "Don Gerónimo Podestá," *Cuaderno de Cultura Teatral*, No. 23 (1949), 41–97. RIVER PLATE

Cosentino, Orestes. "Pablo Podestá," *Máscara*, VII (November, 1947), 8. RIVER PLATE

Covarrubias, Miguel. "Slapstick and Venom," *Theatre Arts Monthly*, (August, 1938), pp. 587–597. MEXICO

Crow, J. H. "Drama revolucionario mexicano," *Revista Hispánica Moderna*, V (1939), 20–31. MEXICO

Cuaderno de Cultura Teatral. No. 1. 1936–No. 23, 1949. ARGENTINA

Curie Gallegos, Luis. "La primera representación de *Quijote*," *Escena* (Lima), I, No. 3 (1954), 14–15. PERU

Curotto, Ángel, "Carlos Brussa," *Boletín de Estudios de Teatro*, No. 12 (March, 1946), 55–62. RIVER PLATE

Custodio, Ángel. "José Antonio Ramos," *Hoy* (Mexico), March 7, 1943. CUBA

Dauster, Frank. "Contemporary Mexican Theatre," *Hispania*, XXXVIII (March, 1955), 31–34. MEXICO

———. "Francisco Arriví: The Mask and the Garden," *Hispania*, XLV (1962), 637–643. PUERTO RICO

Decoud, José Segundo. "La literatura en el Paraguay," *Revista del Ateneo Paraguayo*, November 28, 1884. Published separately, Buenos Aires: Peusser, 1889. PARAGUAY

D. M. S. "El teatro paraguayo," *Paraguay* (Asunción), 1 (September, 1957). PARAGUAY

"Documentos del teatro de la Ranchería," *Máscara*, No. 49 (October, 1944), 10–11. ARGENTINA

Dreidemie, Oscar J. "Los orígenes del teatro en las regiones del Río de la Plata," *Estudios* (Buenos Aires), LVII (1937), 61–80; also in *Congreso Internacional de Historia de América* (Buenos Aires), III (1938), 651–661. RIVER PLATE

Durón, Jorge F. "Sobre el teatro en Honduras," *Honduras Rotaria*, June, 1958, 12–13.   HONDURAS

Eichelbaum, Samuel. "Ernesto Herrera," *Cuaderno de Cultura Teatral*, No. 4 (1936), 31–48.   URUGUAY

Elliot, Marshall, "El baile de Güegüence," in *American Journal of Philosophy*, V (1884), pp. 50 ff. Other editions in Spanish paraphrase: *Cuadernos del Taller San Lucas*, I (Granada, Nicaragua, 1942), 73–122; and, edited by Francisco Pérez Estrada, in *Teatro folklórico nicaragüense* (Managua, 1946), pp. 19–49. For an English translation, by Daniel G. Brinton, see *Library of Aboriginal Literature*, III(Philadelphia, 1883).   NICARAGUA

Englekirk, John E. "El teatro folklórico hispanoamericano," *Folklore Americanas*, XVII (June, 1957), 1–36.   GENERAL

———. "The Source and Dating of New Mexican–Spanish Folk Plays," *Western Folklore* (Berkeley, California), XVI, No. 4 (October, 1957), 332–355.   UNITED STATES

Erskine, John. "The People's Theatre," *Tomorrow* (New York) (March, 1943), 17–19.   ARGENTINA

Escalada Yriondo, Jorge. "Alquiler de terreno con destino a teatro," *Revista del Notariado* (Buenos Aires), No. 516 (July, 1944).   ARGENTINA

———. "Orígenes del teatro porteño," *Boletín de Estudios de Teatro*, No. 8 (1943), 23–32.   ARGENTINA

Espinosa, Aurelio M., and J. Manuel. "*The Texans*: A New Mexican-Spanish Folk Play," *New Mexico Quarterly Review* (Autumn, 1943), 397–408.   UNITED STATES

Fabregat Cúneo, Roberto. "El teatro en el Uruguay," *América* (Havana), XLIII (1945), 1–6.   URUGUAY

Fernández Macgregor, Genaro. "La mexicanidad de Alarcón," *Letras de México*, II, No. 8 (August 8 and 15, 1939).   MEXICO

Franklin, Albert. "A Versatile Ecuadorean," *Inter-America*, I (November, 1942), 33–35.   ECUADOR

Gallegos Valdés, Luis. "Semblanzas de los dramaturgos salvadoreños," *Síntesis*, I, No. 6 (September, 1954), 25–30.   EL SALVADOR

Gallinal, Gustavo. "Documentos relativos al padre Martínez," *Revista del Instituto Histórico y Geográfico del Uruguay*, III (1924), 663–691.
                                                                RIVER PLATE

García, Lautaro. "Anotaciones sobre el teatro en Chile," *Zig-Zag* (Santiago de Chile), Número Especial (December, 1955), 248–253.   CHILE

García Calderón, Ventura. "La literatura peruana," *Revue Hispanique*, XLI, No. 80 (August, 1914), 305–391.   PERU

Garland, Antonio. "Miquita la Perricholi," *Estudios de Teatro Peruano*: Series VI, No. 20 (Lima, 1955).   PERU

Gavidia, Francisco E. "Discurso del poeta Gavidia en la coronación del

Hijo Predilecto de San Miguel," in *Boletín de la Academia Salvadoreña,* August, 1940, III.   EL SALVADOR

———. *Ursino de Orbaneja,* in *Revista del Ministerio de Cultura,* July, 1946, 67–109.   EL SALVADOR

Ghiraldo, Alberto. "Un precursor del teatro en América," *Atenea* (Concepción, Chile), No. 142 (April, 1937), 88–97.   ARGENTINA

Girard, Rafael. "Una obra maestra del teatro maya," *Cuadernos americanos,* VI (1947), 157–188.   MIDDLE AMERICA

Giusti, Roberto C. "Estudio histórico-literario del teatro venezolano en el siglo XIX y apreciación de su actualidad," *Revista del Liceo Andrés Bello* (Caracas), No. 2 (October–November, 1946), 34–64. Bibliography of nineteenth-century plays, pp. 50–57.   VENEZUELA

———. "Florencio Sánchez y el teatro rioplatense," *Inter-American Review of Bibliography* (Washington, D. C.), Nos. 17–18 (January, 1962), 73–88.   RIVER PLATE

Goico Castro, Manuel de Jesús. "Raíz y trayectoria del teatro en la literatura nacional," *Revista de la Universidad de Santo Domingo,* IX (1945), 71–90; X (1946), 155–202.   SANTO DOMINGO

Gómez Restrepo, Antonio. "Literatura colombiana," *Revue Hispanique,* XLIII, No. 103 (June, 1918), 79–204. With bibliography.   COLOMBIA

González, J. Natalicio. "La instrucción pública en el Paraguay de la colonia," *Revista de las Indias,* 2ª serie, II, No. 4 (October, 1957), 69–184.   CUBA

González Castillo, José. "El sainete criollo," *Cuaderno de Cultura Teatral,* No. 5 (1936), 40–52.   RIVER PLATE

González Curquejo, Antonio. "Breve ojeada sobre el teatro cubano al través de un siglo, 1820–1920," *Revista Bimestre Cubana* (Havana) July-August, 1923. Published separately, Havana: La Universal, 1928.   CUBA

Gorostiza, Celestino. "Apuntes para una historia del teatro experimental: 1900–1950," *México en el Arte* (Mexico), Nos. 10–11 (1950).   MEXICO

Guardia, Alfredo de la. "Raíz y espíritu de Eichelbaum," *Nosotros;* III (April 1, 1938), 2; reprinted in *Nos,* Series II, No. VI (1938), 385–400, and No. XIV (1941), 84–89.   ARGENTINA

Gutiérrez, H. C. "Antecedentes históricos del títere venezolano," *Revista Nacional de Cultura* (Caracas), XXV (May–August, 1963), 149–162.   VENEZUELA

Henríquez Ureña, Max. *Panorama de la literatura dominicana,* reviewed in *Panorama* (Pan American Union), No. 31 (1946), 27–39.   SANTO DOMINGO

Henríquez Ureña, Pedro. "El teatro en la América española en la época colonial," *Cuaderno de Cultura Teatral,* No. 3 (1936), 9–50, also in

Boletín de Estudios de Teatro, No. 27 (October, 1949), 161–183.
Lengthy bibliography. GENERAL

Hernández, José Alfredo. "Aspectos del teatro peruano," *Boletín de Estudios de Teatro*, Nos. 18–19 (June–December, 1947), 157; also in *Universidad Nacional de Colombia* (Bogotá), No. 9 (1947). PERU

Hill, E. C. "The Quechua drama 'Ollanta'," *Romanic Review*, V (1914), 127–176. PERU

Horcasitas Pimentel, Fernando. "Piezas teatrales en lengua náhuatl: bibliografía descriptiva," *Boletín Bibliográfico de Antropología Americana* (Mexico), XI (1949), 154–164. MEXICO

House, Roy Temple. "Eichelbaum," *Books Abroad* (Norman, Oklahoma), 18 (1944), 68. ARGENTINA

——. "Florencio Sánchez, A great Uruguayan Dramatist," *Poet Lore*, XXXIV (Summer, 1923). URUGUAY

Icaza, Francisco A. de. "Cristobal A. de Llerena y los orígenes del teatro en la América Española," *Revista de Filología Española*, VIII (April, 1921), 121–130. SANTO DOMINGO

——. "Origen del teatro en México," *Boletín de la Real Academia Española* (Madrid), II (1915), 57–66. MEXICO

Ichaso, Francisco. "Medio siglo de teatro en Cuba," *Diario de la Marina* (Havana), September 15, 1957. CUBA

Imbert, Julio. "El teatro rioplatense y Fernán Silva Valdés," *Revista Nacional* (Montevideo), No. 199 (1959), 1–15. URUGUAY

Irving, T. B. "Three Mayan Classics," *Universidad de San Carlos*, XLIV (January, 1958), 127–136. Also in *University of Toronto Quarterly*, October, 1950. MIDDLE AMERICA

Jiménez Pastor, Arturo. "Nicolás Granada," *Cuaderno de Cultura Teatral*, No. 14 (1940), 105–130. ARGENTINA

Jiménez Rueda, Julio. "Documentos para la historia del teatro en la Nueva España," *Boletín del Archivo General de la Nación* (Mexico), XV, No. 1 (January–March, 1944), 101–144. MEXICO

Johnson, Harvey L. "Compañías teatrales en Arequipa en 1621 y 1636," *Nueva Revista de Filología Hispánica* (Mexico), VII (1953), 449–460. PERU

——. "Disputa en la ciudad de México por el auto del año de 1819," *Revista Iberoamericana*, No. 19 (November, 1945), 131–168. Data on Mexican drama since 1600. MEXICO

——. "La historia de la comberción de San Pablo," *Nueva Revista de Filología Hispánica*, IV (1950), 115–160. GUATEMALA

——. "Loa representada en Ibagué (Colombia) para la jura del rey Fernando VI," *Revista Iberoamericana*, VII, No. 14 (February, 1945), 293–308. COLOMBIA

———. "Notas relativas a los corrales de la Ciudad de México, 1626–1641," *Revista Iberoamericana*, III, No. 5 (1941), 133–138.　　　MEXICO

———. "Noticias dadas por Tomas Gage a propósito del teatro en España, México, y Guatemala, 1624–1637," *Revista Iberoamericana*, VIII, No. 16 (November, 1944), 257–273.　　　MEXICO: GUATEMALA

———. Nuevos datos para el teatro mexicano de la primera mitad del siglo XVII," *Nueva Revista de Filología Hispánica* (Buenos Aires), IV, No. 3 (1942), 127–151.　　　MEXICO

———. Nuevos datos sobre el teatro en la ciudad de Guatemala: 1789–1820," *Revista Iberoamericana*, XVI, No. 32 (January, 1951), 345–386. Printed separately in Mexico, 1951.　　　GUATEMALA

———. "Primer siglo del teatro en Puebla de los Ángeles," *Revista Iberoamericana*, X, No. 20 (March, 1946). 296–339.　　　MEXICO

———. "The Staging of Eslava's Coloquios," *Hispanic Review*, VIII (1940), 343–346.　　　MEXICO

———. "Una compañía teatral en Bogotá en 1618," *Nueva Revista de Filología Hispánica* (Mexico), II, No. 4 (October–December, 1948), 377–380.　　　COLOMBIA

Jones, Willis Knapp. "Armando Moock, Forgotten Chilean Playwright," *Hispania*, XXII (February, 1939), 41–50; also in *Atenea* (Concepción, Chile), Año XVI, Tomo LVI, No. 168 (June, 1939), 436–460.　　　CHILE

———. "Bolivia Hails a Dramatist," *Poet Lore*, 49 (Autumn, 1943), 279–282.　　　BOLIVIA

———. "Chile's Dramatic Renaissance," *Hispania*, XLIV (March, 1961), 89–94.　　　CHILE

———. "El Drama en el Ecuador," *Anales de la Universidad de Guayaquil*, II, No. 2 (1950). Reprinted in *América* (Havana), XL, No. 1 (June, 1953), 15–22.　　　ECUADOR

———. "Latin American Drama, A Reading List," *Books Abroad*, 17 (1943), 27–31; 121–125.　　　GENERAL

———. "New Life in Chile's Theatre," *Modern Drama* (Lawrence, Kansas), May, 1959, pp. 57–62.　　　CHILE

———. "Paraguay's Theatre," *Books Abroad* (Norman, Oklahoma), 15 (1941), 40–42.　　　PARAGUAY

———. "The Chilean Huaso Everybody Knows," *Pan American Magazine* (New York), March, 1945, pp. 34–36.　　　CHILE

"José Antonio Saldías," *Boletín Argentores*, No. 50 (January, 1946), 3–7, and No. 56 (October, 1946), 13–14.　　　ARGENTINA

King, Charles A. "Apuntes para una bibliografía de la literatura de Panamá," *Inter-American Review of Bibliography* (Pan American Union, Washington, D.C.), XIV (1964), 262–303, 264–265, 300.　　　GENERAL

"La conquista de Santafé de Bogota," *Boletín de Historia y Antigüedades* (Colombia), March, 1925.　　　COLOMBIA

Latcham, Ricardo A. "Curtain Time in Chile," *Las Américas,* IV, No. 9 (September, 1952), 16–19.   CHILE

Latorre, Mariano. "Anotaciones sobre el teatro chileno en el siglo XIX," *Atenea* (Concepción), Nos. 291–292 (September-October, 1949), 239–277.   CHILE

——. "Apuntes sobre el teatro chileno contemporáneo," *Atenea* (Concepción), No. 278 (August, 1948), 254–272; No. 279 (September, 1948), 281–292; No. 281–282 (November–December, 1948), 92–104.

                                                                       CHILE

——. "El teatro chileno en la colonia," *Atenea* (Concepción), XCIII, No. 288 (June, 1949), 462–472; No. 289 (July, 1949), 138–151; No. 290 (August, 1949), 291–302.   CHILE

Leal, René R. "Actuales corrientes en el teatro cubano," *Nueva Revista Cubana,* I, No. 1 (April, 1959), 162–170.   CUBA

Lebrón Saviñón, Mariano. "Mirtha Primavera," *Cuadernos Domínicos* (March, 1949), 23–24.   SANTO DOMINGO

Lemos, Martín. "Tres figuras del viejo sainete criollo," *Boletín de Estudios de Teatro,* No. 28 (January, 1950), 13–24.   RIVER PLATE

Leonard, Irving A. "A Shipment of *comedias* to the Indies," *Revue Hispanique,* II (January, 1934), 39–50.   PERU

——. "El teatro de Pedro de Peralta y Barnuevo," *Letras* (Lima), 2° and 3° cuatrimestres, 1937; reprinted in *Pedro de Peralta y Barnuevo, obras dramáticas.* Santiago de Chile: Imprenta Universitaria, 1937.   PERU

——. "El teatro en Lima: 1790–1793," *Hispanic Review,* VIII, No. 2 (April, 1940), 93–112.   PERU

——. "More Conjectures concerning 'Amarilis Indiana'," *Hispania,* XX (1937), 113 ff.   PERU

——. "1790 Theatre Season in the Mexico City Coliseo," *Hispanic Review,* XIX (1951), 104–120.   MEXICO

——. "Temporada teatral de 1792 en el Nuevo Coliseo de México," *Nueva Revista de Filología Hispánica,* V (1951), 394–410.   MEXICO

——. "Theatre Season of 1791–1792 in Mexico City," *Hispanic American Historical Review, XXXI* (1951), 349–364.   MEXICO

Leonhardt, Carlos. "Datos históricos sobre el teatro nacional en la Compañía de Jesús de la Provincia del Paraguay," *Estudios* (Buenos Aires), XXVI (1924), 46–59.   PARAGUAY

Letras (Buenos Aires). January, 1931–September, 1933.   ARGENTINA

Lindo, Hugo. "Panorama de la literatura salvadoreña," *Atenea* (Concepción), No. 114 (1934), 366–401.   EL SALVADOR

"Loa que representó el colegio Mayor y Seminario de S. Luis de la ciudad de Quito celebrando la elección del obispo de Santa Marta, hecha en el Doctor D. Juan. nieto Poto de Aguila, natural de Popayán y colegial que fue de dicho colegio, y hoy obispo dignísimo de la Sta Iglesia de Quito,"

Museo Histórico (Quito), V, No. 17 (September, 1953), pp. 132–148.
ECUADOR

Lohmann Villena, Guillermo. "El teatro en Lima en el siglo XVI," *Cuadernos de Estudio del Instituto de Investigaciones Históricas* (Lima), I (1938), 45–75.
PERU

———, and Raúl Moglia. "Repertorio de las representaciones teatrales en Lima hasta el siglo XVIII," *Revista de Filología Hispánica* (Buenos Aires), V, No. 4 (1943), 313–343.
PERU

López Prieto, Antonio. "Apuntes para la historia del teatro en Cuba," *El Palenque Literario* (Havana), III (1882), 121–126, 145–150.
CUBA

López Rosas, José Rafael. "El teatro colonial en Santa Fe: Antecedentes históricos," *Boletín del Departamento de Estudios Etnográficos y Coloniales* (Santa Fe, Argentina, December, 1948), 67–85.
ARGENTINA

Lothrop, S. K. "Further Notes on Indian Ceremonies in Guatemala," *Indian Notes*, VI (1929), 2–5.
GUATEMALA

Luaces, Joaquín Lorenzo. *Aristodemo*, in *Alma Cubana*, Época II (May, 1929), 19–29.
CUBA

MacHale, Tomás P. "Notas sobre Luis Alberto Heiremans." *Mapocho* (Santiago de Chile), III, No. 1 de 1965, pp. 59–106, including Heiremans' play "Buenaventura."
CHILE

Magaña Esquivel, Antonio. "El pasado: Drama de Manuel Acuña," *Revista Mexicana de Cultura*, No. 127 (August 28, 1949).
MEXICO

Mañón, Manuel, "El teatro en la colonia," *Máscara*, No. 93 (June, 1948), 11–14.
ARGENTINA

Maria y Campos, Armando de. "El teatro en México antes de Eusebio Vela," *Boletín de Estudios de Teatro*, No. 16 (November, 1947), 40–48.
MEXICO

———. "El teatro nacional de Costa Rica," *Hemisferio* (June, 1944), pp. 25 ff.
COSTA RICA

Marqués, René. "Apuntes para una interpretación de *La Muerte*," *Asomante*, No. 4 (1953).
PUERTO RICO

Martin, John L. "El alferez real," *Hispania*, XXIV (1941), 195.
COLOMBIA

Martínez, Juan Francisco. "La lealtad más ascendrada y Buenos Aires vengada," *Parnaso Oriental* (Montevideo) 1937. See also Rojas, Ricardo (Ed.). *Documentos del Instituto de Literatura argentina*, Primera serie, No. 2. Buenos Aires: Facultad de Filosofía, 1924.
RIVER PLATE

Martínez Cuitiño, Vicente. "Elogio de Pablo Podestá," *Boletín de Estudios de Teatro*, No. 11 (April, 1944), 43–47.
RIVER PLATE

———. "Elogio de Sánchez Gardel," *La Nación* (Buenos Aires, August 17, 1941).
ARGENTINA

Mayorga Rivas, Rafael. "La literatura de San Salvador," *Nueva Revista de Buenos Aires*, VI (1882), 18–35.
EL SALVADOR

Mendoza, María Luisa. "New Directions for Mexican Theatre," *Américas* (Washington), No. 10 (April, 1958), 14. MEXICO

Meneses, Teodoro L. "El monólogo de Yauri Tito," *Sphinx* (Lima), Año 4, Nos. 10–12 (June–December, 1941), 119–123; translated by Meneses in *Documenta* (Lima), Año 2, No. 1 (1949–50), 22–161; published separately, Lima, 1951. PERU

Mertens, Federico. "Orfilia Rico," *Cuaderno de Cultura Teatral*, No. 21 (1945), 69–87. RIVER PLATE

Milanés, José Jacinto. "El conde Alarcos," in *Alma Cubana*, Época II (May, 1929), 31–64. CUBA

Moglia, Raúl. "Relación de la grandiosa fiesta y representación escénica en Potosí en 1663," *Revista de Filología Hispánica*, V, No. 2 (April–June, 1943), 166–167. BOLIVIA

Moncloa y Covarrubias, Manuel. "El teatro en Lima," *Boletín de Estudios de Teatro*, No. 17 (June, 1947), 113–114. Chapter from his 1909 book of the same title. PERU

Monterde, Francisco. "Autores del teatro mexicano: 1900–1950," *México en el Arte*, Nos, 10–11 (1950), 39–46. MEXICO

———. "Pastorals and Popular Performances: The Drama of Viceregal Mexico," *Theatre Arts Monthly*, No. 22 (1938), 597–602. MEXICO

Moreno, Antonio. "Xavier Villaurrutia: The Development of His Theatre," *Hispania*, XLIII (December, 1950), 508–514. MEXICO

Motolinía, Padre, "Adán y Eva," *Boletín de Estudios de Teatro*, No. 27 (October, 1949), 168. MEXICO

Nacarrati, Pacual. "El teatro de Roberto Arlt," *Trompo* (Buenos Aires), 2ª Época, No. 1 (September, 1946), 2. ARGENTINA

———. "Recuerdos de Arlt." *Trompo*. 2ª época, No. 1 (September, 1945). ARGENTINA

Obrea, Fernando de. "La conquista de Santafé de Bogotá (1718)," *Boletín de Historia y Antigüedades* (Bogotá, March, 1925). COLOMBIA

Ochoa Sandoval, Eglantina. "Sobre el humorismo en México," *El Libro y el Pueblo* (Mexico), No. 21 (1956), 5–59. MEXICO

Orozco, Manuel A. *"La divisa punzó* vista por un provinciano," *Nos*, L (June, 1925), 230–266. ARGENTINA

Pacheco, Carlos Mauricio. "Los defraudados," *Bambalinas*, No. 49 (March, 15, 1919). ARGENTINA

Panizza, Delio. "Martiniano Leguizamón," *Cuaderno de Cultura Teatral*, No. 15 (1940). ARGENTINA

Panorama. Published in thirty-one mimeographed issues by the Pan American Union, Washington, D.C., between October, 1935, and August, 1948. GENERAL

Panorama del Teatro en México. July, 1954–November, 1955. MEXICO

Pasquariello, Antonio M. "The *Entremés* in 16th-Century Spanish America," *Hispanic American Historical Review,* XXXII, No. 1 (February, 1952), 44–58.   GENERAL

———. "The 18th-Century Peruvian Interludes," *Symposium* (Syracuse, New York), VI, No. 2 (November, 1952), 385–390.   PERU

Pereira Salas, Eugenio. "El teatro en Santiago del Nuevo Extremo: 1709–1809," *Revista Chilena de Historia y Geografía* (Santiago), XC, No. 98 (January, 1941), 30–59; published separately, Santiago: University of Chile, 1941.   CHILE

Pérez Cadalso, Eliseo. "Panorama de la literatura hondureña," *Universidad de Honduras,* July–August, 1961.   HONDURAS

Pérez Petit, Victor. "¡Cobarde!" *Máscara,* No. 50 (November, 1944); and in *Revista de la Comisión de Teatro,* No. 5 (1959).   URUGUAY

Pérez Vila, Manuel. "Polémicas sobre representaciones dramáticas: 1775–1828," *Revista Nacional de Cultura* (Caracas), No. 127 (March, 1958), 95–104.   VENEZUELA

Petit, Magdalena. "The Little Theatres of Chile," *Bulletin of the Pan American Union* (Washington, D.C.), 82, No. 10 (1948), 560–565.   CHILE

Phillips, Ruby Hart. "Drama and Burlesque on the Cuban Stage," *Inter-America,* II (January, 1943), 24–25.   CUBA

Picone, J. C. "El teatro de Roberto Payró," *Claridad* (Buenos Aires), No. 18 (1929).   ARGENTINA

Pineda, Rafael. "Pasado y presente del teatro en Venezuela," *El Faro* (Caracas, March, 1954), 32–33.   VENEZUELA

Pla, Josefina. "300 años de teatro paraguayo." *Comunidades* ([Asunción], January–April, 1965). To be combined in book form later.   PARAGUAY

"Plácido" (Gabriel de la Concepción Valdés). "Soneto a Don Pedro," *Revista de la Habana,* 1953.   CUBA

Pompa Preda, Julio César. "Éxito del teatro paraguayo," *El País* (Asunción, August 15, 1958), 7–8.   PARAGUAY

Ponferrada, Juan Oscar. "La sugestión telúrica en el teatro de Sánchez Gardel," *Cuaderno de Cultura Teatral,* No. 22 (1947), 95–133.   ARGENTINA

Potenze, Jaime. "Breve historia crítica del teatro argentino," *Cuadernos Hispanoamericanos* (Madrid), No. 13 (1950), 99–111.   ARGENTINA

Ramírez, Antonio. "Un autor que ha estrenado 100 obras," *Carteles* (Havana), XXXII (August 28, 1936), 42–45.   CUBA

Ramos, José Antonio. *Tembladera,* in *Anales de la Academia Nacional de Artes y Letras* (Havana), III (January, 1918), 31–158.   CUBA

Ratto Valerga, T. O. "El teatro de la cultura incaria," *Máscara* (Buenos Aires), No. 90 (1948), 6–9.   PERU

Raynaud, George, and Luis Cardoza y Aragón. "El varón de Rabinal,"

Anales de la Sociedad de Geografía e Historia de Guatemala, VI (1929), 45–51, 197–201; VII (1930), 347–370, 481–491.   GUATEMALA

Real, Cristóbal. "Gran alboroto en Puerto Rico al establecer el primer teatro," *El Mundo* (San Juan, November 30, 1947).   PUERTO RICO

Rela, Walter. "Fundamentos para una historia del teatro paraguayo," in *Jornadas de Cultura* (Montevideo, November, 1955), 28.   PARAGUAY

———. Literatura dramática suramericana contemporánea," *Revista del Instituto de Estudios Superiores* (Montevideo), I (1957), 123.

                                                                GENERAL

Revista de la Comisión Teatros Municipales. (Montevideo, September, 1958–December, 1959. Five issues with out-of-print plays and articles.

                                                                URUGUAY

Reyes, Padre José de la Trinidad. *Olimpia,* in *Revista de Archivos* (Tegucigalpa), June 30, 1936, 707–766. A *pastorela.*   HONDURAS

———. *Pastorela,* in *Honduras Literaria,* No. 3. (Tegucigalpa: Ministerio de Educación, 1957). A different *pastorela* from *Olimpia,* cited above.

                                                                HONDURAS

Riva Aguero, José de. "Algunos datos sobre la biografía de don Pedro de Peralta y Barnuevo," *Revista de la Universidad Católica del Perú,* VI (1938), 241–285.   PERU

"Rodri-Mur, Enrique." Under this pen name, Enrique Rodríguez Murillo published a series of articles in *El Diario Nacional* of San José, C. R., beginning June 9, 1955.   COSTA RICA

Rojas Garcidueñas, José. "Piezas teatrales representadas en Nueva España en el siglo XVI," *Revista de Literatura Mexicana,* I, No. 1 (July, 1940).

                                                                MEXICO

Rosa-Nieves, Cesáreo. "Notas para el origen de las representaciones dramáticas en Puerto Rico," *Asomante,* VI (January, 1950), 63–75; reprinted in his *Lámpara del Faro,* San Juan: Club de la Prensa, 1957. Covers the period from 1844 to 1855.   PUERTO RICO

Rosenback, A. S. W. "The First Theatrical Company in America," *Proceedings of the American Antiquarian Society* (Worcester, Massachusetts), XLVIII (October, 1938), 300–310.   PERU

Sabat-Pebet, Juan Carlos. "Sobre los orígenes teatrales montevideanos," *Boletín de Estudios de Teatro,* No. 11 (1945), 232–243.   URUGUAY

Sacotto Arias, Augusto. "La furiosa manzanera," *Revista del Mar Pacífico* (Quito), June, 1943.   ECUADOR

Sánchez, José. "Círculos literarios de Iberoamérica," *Revista Iberoamericana,* No. 18 (May, 1945), 297–323.   GENERAL

Sánchez y Galarraga, Gustavo. "El arte teatral en Cuba," *Cuba Contemporánea* (Havana), X (1916).   CUBA

Saz, Agustín del. "La farsa dramática moderna en Hispanoamérica," *Cuadernos Hispanoamericanos* (Madrid), No. 89 (1957).   GENERAL

Schanzer, George O. "A Great National Drama of Uruguay," *Modern Language Journal*, XXXVIII (1954), 220–223. URUGUAY

Sierra, Francisco. "Reseña histórica del teatro en Buenos Aires," *Letras*, Número extraordinario (Buenos Aires, 1936). ARGENTINA

Silva, Victor Domingo. "Panorama del teatro chileno," *Máscaras* (Santiago), No. 1 (June, 1930), 3–4; No. 3 (August, 1930), 3–4; No. 4 (September, 1930), 3–4. CHILE

Silva Valdés, Fernán. "Los primitivos en el teatro uruguayo," *La Prensa* (Buenos Aires, December 21, 1958). URUGUAY

Simmonds, Adolfo S. "Dramaturgos del Ecuador," *Revista del Colegio Nacional Vicente Rocafuerte* (Guayaquil), II, No. 1 (January, 1941), 3–14. ECUADOR

Solórzano, Carlos: "El Teatro de la posguerra en México," *Hispania*, XLVII, No. 4 (December, 1964), 693–697. MEXICO

Sorenson, Thora. "Recent Developments in the Argentine Theatre," *Hispania*, XXXIX (December, 1956), 445–449. ARGENTINA

Spell, Jefferson R. "Some Little Known Plays of Gorostiza," *Romanic Review*, XXIII (1932), 131–141. MEXICO

Sumel, Humberto. "Teatro cubano," *Policía* (Havana, November, 1942), 30–33. CUBA

Tálice, Roberto A. "La comedia de Moock que rechazaron todas las actrices," *Argentores*, No. 56 (October, 1946), 29–30. ARGENTINA

Tamayo Vargas, Augusto. "La Perricholi fue limeña," *Turismo* (Lima), LX, 98 (1944); also in *Estudios de Teatro Peruano*, Series VI, No. 18 (Lima: University of San Marcos, 1954). PERU

———. "Peruvian Literature in 1961," *Books Abroad* (Norman, Oklahoma), 36 (1962), 269. PERU

———. "Tema, drama, y problema de *Ollantay*," *El Comercio* (Lima, July 13, 1953); reprinted in *Estudios del Teatro Peruano* (December, 1956). PERU

Teatro. (Mexico) (July, 1954–October, 1956). MEXICO

"Teatro nicaragüense," *Revista de América* (Mexico: *Instituto Panamericano de Geografía e Historia*), No. 23 (June, 1947). NICARAGUA

Temple, Ellen Dunbar. "Letras en la Lima a fines del siglo XVIII," *3* (Lima), No. 8 (March, 1941); reprinted in *Estudios de Teatro Peruano*, Series VI, No. 17 (1955). PERU

Theatre Arts Magazine. Vol. XXII, No. 8 (August, 1938), is entirely devoted to Mexico. MEXICO

Tiempo, César. "Mitre en el teatro," *Máscara*, No. 93 (June, 1948), 2–4. ARGENTINA

Torre, Guillermo de. "Nuevas direcciones del teatro," *Atenea*, No. 299 (May, 1950), 125–135. CHILE

Torre Revello, José. "El teatro en la colonia," *Humanidades* (La Plata), XXII (1933), 145–165. Also published as Chapter 12 of Torre Revello, *Crónicas del Buenos Aires colonial;* also reprinted in *Cuaderno de Cultura Teatral,* No. 1 (1936), 45–57; and in *Boletín de Estudios de Teatro,* No. 4 (January, 1944). RIVER PLATE

———. "Los teatros en el Buenos Aires del siglo XVIII," *Boletín de Estudios de Teatro,* No. 10 (September, 1945). ARGENTINA

———. "1700–1810: Panorama histórico, social y literario," *Cuaderno de Cultura Teatral,* No. 13 (1940), 33–60. ARGENTINA

———. "Montevideo del siglo XVIII; La casa de comedias," *Revista del Instituto Histórico y Geográfico del Uruguay,* VI (1929). URUGUAY

———. "Orígenes del teatro en Hispanoamérica," *Cuaderno de Cultura Teatral,* No. 7 (1937), 49. GENERAL

Torres-Rioseco, Arturo. "El primer dramaturgo americano," *Hispania,* XXIV (1941), 161–170. MEXICO

Trenti Rocamora, J. Luis. "Cristóbal de Aguilar," *Boletín de Estudios de Teatro,* No. 20 (March, 1948), 7–18. With a summary of *Venció el desprecio al desdén.* RIVER PLATE

———. "El primer teatro porteño," *Boletín de Estudios de Teatro,* No. 16 (March, 1947), 22–23. ARGENTINA

———. El repertorio de la dramática colonial hispanoamericana, con bibliografía," *Boletín de Estudios de Teatro,* No. 26 (July, 1949), 104–124. Published separately, Buenos Aires: Alea, 1950. ARGENTINA

———. "El teatro en la época colonial dentro de los límites del Virreynato de Río de la Plata," *Lyra* (Buenos Aires), IV (1946), 35. RIVER PLATE

———. "El teatro porteño durante el período hispánico," *Estudios* (Academia Literaria del Plata), LXXVIII, No. 425 (December, 1947), 408–434; also in *Cultura en Buenos Aires hasta 1810.* University of Buenos Aires, 1948. ARGENTINA

———. "Gente de teatro del Buenos Aires colonial," *Boletín de Estudios de Teatro.* No. 17 (June, 1947), 69–83. ARGENTINA

———. "La primera pieza teatral argentina," *Boletín de Estudios de Teatro,* IV, No. 15 (December, 1946), 224–234. ARGENTINA

———. "Un impreso de interés para la historia del teatro colonial porteño," *Universidad* (Santa Fe), XXI (1949), 289–297. ARGENTINA

Ugarte Chamorro, Guillermo. "Amezaga, autor teatral peruano," *Estudios de Teatro Peruano,* Serie VI, No. 35 (1957). PERU

———. "Piezas teatrales del Perú que procedieron a *Frutos de la educación,*" *Estudios de Teatro Peruano,* Serie VI, No. 38 (1958). PERU

Valdés-Rodríguez, J. M. "Tablas y Pantalla," *El Mundo* (Havana, February 26, 1953). CUBA

Valencia, Gerardo. "Reflexiones en torno al teatro colombiano," *Revista Universitaria de Colombia* (Bogotá), No. 2 (1945). COLOMBIA

Valle, Rafael Heliodoro. "Historia intelectual de Honduras," *Biblioteca Nacional de Honduras* (March–April, 1946), 385–411.　HONDURAS

———. "Las pastorelas de José Trinidad Reyes," *Universidad* (University of Nuevo León, Mexico, 1950), 23–48.　HONDURAS

Vicuña Mackenna, Benjamín. "Teatro en Chile," *Revista de Santiago*, V (1881), pp. 584–593.　CHILE

Villacorta, José Antonio. " 'Rabinal Achí,' tragedia danzada de los Quichés," *Anales de la Sociedad de Geografía e Historia*, XVII (1942), 353–371.　MIDDLE AMERICA

Villareal, Concha. "Desaparece el teatro del pueblo," *Orientación Musical*, IV, No. 37 (July, 1947); reprinted from *Excelsior*.　MEXICO

Warren, Virgil A. "Status of the Modern Cuban Theatre," *Hispania*, XXIV (May, 1941), 205–210.　CUBA

Weber, Delia. "Los bellos designios," *Cuadernos Domínicos de Cultura* (Ciudad Trujillo, April–May and June–July, 1951).　SANTO DOMINGO

———. "Los viajeros," *Cuadernos Domínicos de Cultura* (July–August, 1950).　SANTO DOMINGO

Xammar, Luis Fabio. "El teatro: el eco," *Boletín de Estudios de Teatro*, No. 11 (December, 1945), 196–201.　PERU

———. "El teatro: la voz," *Boletín de Estudios de Teatro*, No. 11 (December, 1945), 201–204.　PERU

———. "Juan de Arona," *Peruanidad, III*, No. 12 (January, 1943), 951 ff.　PERU

Yáñez Silva, Nataniel. "Panorama de 150 años de teatro nacional," *La Nación* (Santiago de Chile, September 18, 1960).　CHILE

———. "Veinte años de teatro chileno," *Atenea* (Concepción), No. 90 (August, 1932), 206–228.　CHILE

Yunque, Álvaro. "Roberto Arlt," *Nos*, Series II, XVIII (1942), 113–114.　ARGENTINA

Unpublished Material

Apstein, Theodore. "Contemporary Argentine Theatre, 1920–1942." Unpublished Ph.D. dissertation, The University of Texas, 1945.　RIVER PLATE

Avellán Ferrés, Enrique. "La evolución del teatro ecuatoriano." Read over Radio Quito, January 14, 1941.　ECUADOR

Elstun, Maurice. "The Origin of the National Theatre of Argentina, 1900–1920." Unpublished Ph.D. dissertation, University of North Carolina, 1930.　RIVER PLATE

Munro, Edwin C. "The Nativity Plays of Mexico." Unpublished Master's thesis, University of New Mexico, 1940.　MEXICO

Schanzer, George O. "Vida y obras de Ernesto Herrera." Unpublished Master's thesis, University of Iowa, 1950.　URUGUAY

INDEX

584

Index